Church of England Record Society

Volume 10

CONFERENCES AND COMBINATION LECTURES IN THE ELIZABETHAN CHURCH

DEDHAM AND BURY ST EDMUNDS 1582–1590

During the heart of Elizabeth I's reign, a secret conference of clergymen met in and around Dedham, Essex, on a monthly basis in order to discuss matters of local and national interest. Their collected papers, a unique survival from the clandestine world of early English nonconformity, are here printed in full for the first time, together with a hitherto unpublished narrative by the Suffolk minister, Thomas Rogers, which throws a flood of light on similar, if more public, clerical activity in and around Bury St Edmunds, Suffolk, during the same period. Taken together, the two texts provide an unrivalled insight into the minds and the methods of that network of 'godly' ministers whose professed aim was to modify the strict provisions of the Elizabethan settlement of religion, both by ceaseless lobbying and by practical example. The editors' introduction accordingly emphasizes the complex nature of the English protestant tradition between the Tudor mid-century and the accession of James I, as well as attempting to plot the politico-ecclesiastical developments of the 1580s in some detail. A comprehensive biographical register of the members of the Dedham conference, of the Bury St Edmunds lecturers, and of many other important names mentioned in the texts, completes the volume.

PATRICK COLLINSON is Regius Professor of Modern History in the University of Cambridge Emeritus, and a Fellow of Trinity College; JOHN CRAIG is Associate Professor of History at Simon Fraser University; BRETT USHER is currently a Visiting Research Fellow in the University of Reading.

Plate 1 Edmund Sherman's house, opposite Dedham church, looking west. From this angle the ancient structure is clearly visible behind the early eighteenth-century facade. An Extraordinary meeting of the Dedham conference was held here on 17 February 1585 (see below, p. 20 and plate 3). *Photograph by Carolynn Usher, 2002.*

CONFERENCES AND COMBINATION LECTURES IN THE ELIZABETHAN CHURCH

DEDHAM AND BURY ST EDMUNDS 1582–1590

EDITED BY

Patrick Collinson
John Craig
Brett Usher

THE BOYDELL PRESS

CHURCH OF ENGLAND RECORD SOCIETY

First published 2003

A Church of England Record Society publication
Published by The Boydell Press
an imprint of Boydell & Brewer Ltd
PO Box 9, Woodbridge, Suffolk IP12 3DF, UK
and of Boydell & Brewer Inc.
PO Box 41026, Rochester, NY 14604–4126, USA
website: www.boydell.co.uk

ISBN 0 85115 938 9

ISSN 1351–3087

Series information is listed at the back of this volume

A catalogue record for this book is available
from the British Library

This publication is printed on acid-free paper

Printed in Great Britain by
St Edmundsbury Press Ltd, Bury St Edmunds, Suffolk

Contents

Illustrations

Plates

Maps

Abbreviations

Alum. Cantab.	John and J. A. Venn, *Alumni Cantabrigienses. A biographical list of all known students, graduates and holders of office at the University of Cambridge, from the earliest times to the year 1900. Part I. From the earliest time to 1751* (4 vols., Cambridge, 1922–7)
Alum. Oxon.	Joseph Foster, *Alumni Oxonienses. The members of the University of Oxford 1500–1714* (4 vols., Oxford, 1891–2)
APC	*Acts of the privy council of England*, ed. J. R. Dasent (32 vols., London, 1890–1907)
Bancroft, *Daungerous positions*	Richard Bancroft, *Daungerous positions and proceedings, published and practised within this iland of Brytaine, under pretence of reformation and for the presbiteriall discipline* (London, 1593)
BL	British Library, London
Bodl.	Bodleian Library, Oxford
BR	*Biographical Register* of present volume
Bullen, 'Catalogue'	R. F. Bullen, 'Catalogue of the beneficed clergy of Suffolk, 1551–1631', *Proceedings of the Suffolk Institute of Archaeology and Natural History*, XXII (1936), 294–333
Byford, 'Birth of a protestant town'	Mark Byford, 'The birth of a protestant town: the process of reformation in Tudor Colchester, 1530–80', in *The Reformation in English Towns 1500–1640*, ed. Patrick Collinson and John Craig (Basingstoke, 1998), pp. 23–47
Byford, 'Price of protestantism'	Mark Byford, 'The price of protestantism: assessing the impact of religious change in Elizabethan Essex: the cases of Heydon and Colchester, 1558–1594', unpublished D.Phil. thesis, University of Oxford, 1988
CHUL	Chicago University Library
Collinson, *EPM*	Patrick Collinson, *The Elizabethan puritan movement* (London, 1967)
Collinson, *Godly people*	Patrick Collinson, *Godly people. Essays on English protestantism and puritanism* (London, 1983)
Collinson, *Grindal*	Patrick Collinson, *Archbishop Grindal, 1519–1583. The struggle for a reformed church* (London, 1979)
Collinson, 'John Field'	Patrick Collinson, 'John Field and Elizabethan puritanism', in *idem, Godly people*, pp. 334–70

Collinson, 'PCM'	Patrick Collinson, 'The puritan classical movement in the reign of Elizabeth I', unpublished Ph.D thesis, University of London, 1957
'The condition'	Rev. Dr Jessopp, C. H. E. White and F. Haslewood, 'The condition of the archdeaconries of Suffolk and Sudbury in the year 1603', *Proceedings of the Suffolk Institute of Archaeology and Natural History*, VI (1888), 361–400; XI (1903), 1–46
CPR	*Calendar of the patent rolls*
CSP Dom.	*Calendar of state papers, domestic*
CUL	Cambridge University Library
Davids, *Annals*	T. W. Davids, *Annals of evangelical nonconformity in the county of Essex* (London, 1863)
DL	Duchy of Lancaster [in PRO]
DWL	Dr Williams's Library, London
Emmison, *Essex gentry wills*	F. G. Emmison, *Essex life: wills of Essex gentry & merchants proved in the prerogative court of Canterbury* (Chelmsford, 1978)
ERO	Essex Record Office, Chelmsford
ERO (Colchester)	Essex Record Office, Colchester
Fasti	John Le Neve, *Fasti ecclesiae Anglicanae 1541–1857*, ed. Joyce M. Horn (London, 1969–)
Foxe, *A & M*	John Foxe, *Actes and Monuments* [followed by date of the edition quoted]
GL	Guildhall Library, London
Hasler, *House of commons*	P. W. Hasler, *The house of commons 1558–1603* (3 vols., London, 1981)
HMC	Historical Manuscripts Commission
JEH	*Journal of Ecclesiastical History*
Knappen, *Two puritan diaries*	*Two Elizabethan puritan diaries, by Richard Rogers and Samuel Ward*, ed. M. M. Knappen (Chicago, 1933)
LMA	London Metropolitan Archives [formerly Greater London Record Office]
LPL	Lambeth Palace Library, London
M, MM	Meeting, Meetings – references to the meetings of the Dedham conference
Morant, *Essex*	Philip Morant, *The history and antiquities of the county of Essex* (2 vols., London, 1768)

Muskett, *Suffolk manorial families*	J. J. Muskett, *Suffolk manorial families, being the county visitations and other pedigrees, ed. With extensive additions* (vol. 3 continued by F. Johnson) (3 vols., Exeter, 1900–14)
Newcourt, *Repertorium*	Richard Newcourt, *Repertorium ecclesiasticum parochiale Londinense* (2 vols., London, 1708–10)
NRO	Norfolk Record Office
Oxford DNB	*The Oxford dictionary of national biography*
Parker correspondence	*Correspondence of Matthew Parker*, ed. John Bruce and T. T. Perowne (Cambridge, 1853)
Parkhurst	*The letter book of John Parkhurst, bishop of Norwich, compiled during the years 1571–5*, ed. R. A. Houlbrooke (Norfolk Record Society, vol. XLIII, 1974–5)
PCC	Prerogative court of Canterbury [wills]
Peile, *Biographical register*	J. Peile, *Biographical register of Christ's College 1505–1905* (2 vols., Cambridge, 1910–13)
Petchey, *A prospect of Maldon*	W. J. Petchey, *A prospect of Maldon 1500–1689* (Chelmsford, 1991)
PRO	Public Record Office, London [Kew]
Redman's visitation	*Bishop Redman's visitation 1597*, ed. J. F. Williams (Norfolk Record Society, XVIII, 1946)
Reg. Bancroft	GL, MS 9531/14: the registers (in part) of Richard Bancroft, Richard Vaughan, Thomas Ravis, George Abbott, John King, George Montaigne and William Laud, bishops of London (1600–32)
Reg. Bonner	GL, MS 9531/12 (2 parts, foliated consecutively): the registers of Edmund Bonner, Nicholas Ridley and Edmund Bonner restored, bishops of London (1539–59)
Reg. Grindal	GL, MS 9531/13 (2 parts, foliated consecutively): the registers of Edmund Grindal, Edwin Sandys, John Aylmer, Richard Fletcher and (in part) Richard Bancroft, Richard Vaughan, Thomas Ravis, George Abbott, John King and George Montaigne, bishops of London (1559–1627)
Reg. Parker	*Registrum Matthei Parker diocesis Cantuarensis, AD 1559–1575*, ed. W. H. Frere (3 vols., Canterbury and York Society, London, 1928–33)
Registrum Vagum	*The Registrum Vagum of Anthony Harison*, parts 1 and 2, transcribed by Thomas F. Barton (Norfolk Record Society, vols. XXXII and XXXIII, 1963–4)
Seconde parte	*The seconde parte of a register*, ed. Albert Peel (2 vols., Cambridge, 1915)

SP	State papers
SRO	Suffolk Record Office
STC	*A Short-Title Catalogue of Books Printed in England, Scotland, and Ireland, and of English Books Printed Abroad, 1475–1640.* 2nd ed. Rev. and enlarged. Edited by W. A. Jackson, F. S. Ferguson, Katharine F. Pantzer and Philip E. Rider. 3 vols. London: Bibliographical Society, 1986–91.
Strype, *Annals*	John Strype, *Annals of the reformation . . . in the Church of England* (7 vols. in 4, 2nd edn., Oxford, 1820–40)
Usher, 1905	R. G. Usher, *The presbyterian movement in the reign of Queen Elizabeth as illustrated by the minute book of the Dedham classis* (Camden Society, 3rd series, vol. VIII, 1905)
VCH	*The Victoria history of the counties of England*
Venn, *Biographical history*	John Venn, *Biographical history of Gonville and Caius College, 1349–1897* (Cambridge, 1897), vol. I, 1349–1713
'A Viewe'	'A Viewe of the State of the Clargie within the Countie of Essex: The substance whereof is readie to be proved at the Kings Majesties pleasure wherein though many thinges be sett downe to be uppon report, yet the same are to be proved by wytnesses of good credit' (LPL, MS 2442)
Winthrop papers	*The Winthrop papers. Volume I: 1498–1628* (Massachusetts Historical Society, Boston, Mass., 1925)

In memory of Geoffrey Bill

Preface and Acknowledgments

This volume is the culmination of a number of preoccupations of its three editors, all of whose research has been intimately bound up with the chequered fortunes of Elizabeth I's 'but halfly reformed' church settlement. As a post-graduate student in the 1950s, Patrick Collinson early recognized the need to produce a complete and accurate edition of the text that lies at the heart of this book, now preserved in Manchester as Rylands English MS 874, but did nothing more about it.

The Church of England Record Society came into being many years later, in 1992, the fruit of the vision and creative way with finance of the late Geoffrey Bill, Librarian of Lambeth Palace from 1958 to 1991. With no less panache and after a relentless pursuit of his quarry, Dr Bill restored to Lambeth Palace Library the collection known, because of its archival wanderings, as the Laud-Selden-Fairhurst MSS. These remarkable papers contain much material relating to 'prophesying', that unofficial institution of the Elizabethan church which occasioned the downfall of Elizabeth's second archbishop of Canterbury, Edmund Grindal – not only Grindal's correspondence with his bishops on the subject, but also papers connected with his defiance of the queen, his sequestration and his subsequent trial. When Geoffrey Bill created the Church of England Record Society he hoped that this Grindal archive in the Laud-Selden-Fairhurst collection would constitute the first volume in the Society's projected series of publications, and that Collinson would be its editor. Although once again Collinson dragged his feet, the story which these documents have to tell formed the climax of Collinson's biography of Grindal, published in 1979.[1]

Thereafter another founder member of the Church of England Record Society, Brett Usher, suggested that a start be made with Rylands MS 874, the papers of the Dedham conference of ministers – a unique survival from that clandestine world of clerical self-regulation which came into existence in the 1580s, perhaps in equal and opposite reaction to the suppression of the prophesyings. There was support for the idea from the Reverend Gerard Moate, vicar and lecturer of Dedham and a council member of the Record Society. As a Cambridge undergraduate in the 1960s, Usher had been introduced to the complexities of Elizabethan churchmanship by Dr Harry Culverwell Porter, fellow of Selwyn College, Cambridge.[2] He first met Patrick Collinson in 1986 and was encouraged by him to continue his researches into the London diocesan records, strangely neglected by students of the Elizabethan church since the tragic early death of H. Gareth Owen, like Collinson a postgraduate pupil of Sir John Neale in London during the 1950s. As Associate Editors of the *Oxford DNB* since 1998, Collison and Usher have between them had responsibility for

---

1   Patrick Collinson, *Archbishop Grindal 1519–1583. The struggle for a reformed church* (London, 1979). There is still a firm intention that the Laud-Selden-Fairhurst MSS and other papers relating to the 'lectures by combination', the public successors of the prophesyings, will be published by the Society in a future volume.

2   Readers of this volume will discover that Dr Porter's second Christian name is of some significance.

overseeing (and in many cases writing) the entries for the Elizabethan clergy. It is hoped that these labours have helped to enrich and amplify the Introduction, footnotes and *Biographical Register* which follow.

The third member of the editorial troika, John Craig, was a research student of Patrick Collinson at Cambridge from 1988 to 1992 and the author of a thesis which led to the publication in 2001 of a kind of companion text to this volume, *Reformation, politics and polemics. The growth of protestantism in East Anglian market towns, 1500–1610*. In 1994 Craig located the Thomas Rogers manuscript relating to the Bury St Edmunds lectureship (MS Codex 109), in the Regenstein Library, Chicago, where it had lain largely forgotten since its purchase in 1925. It seemed to all three editors, and the Council of the Society, that it would be instructive to conjoin Bury with Dedham in what, strange to say, was originally envisaged as a comparatively slim volume. But as readers of this text will discover, that was far from the only reason for publishing it.

In the spring of 2000, as a visiting fellow at Selwyn College, Cambridge, Craig made a full transcription of Rylands English MS 874. Since then, Collinson and Usher have concentrated on producing an introduction and *apparatus criticus* for the Essex/Dedham material and Craig for the Suffolk/Bury material. Collinson and Craig were responsible for checking, and providing accurate footnotes for, the many biblical and patristic references scattered throughout both texts. The *Biographical Register* has been a joint enterprise. The whole was collated in Canada by John Craig before its dispatch to Stephen Taylor in Reading in the spring of 2002.

The nature of the Biographical Register perhaps calls for some comment, for there are some disparities in its arrangement and emphases. In the first place it is intended to take as full an account as possible not only of the careers of the members of the Dedham conference but also of its fellow-travellers – those local ministers who appear (to judge from references in the minutes and in the subsidiary material) to have been privy to its activities and, most particularly during the 'woeful year of subscription', 1584, to have backed its tactics and strategy. In the second place, the Register enshrines only brief accounts (John Knewstub being the exception) of those members and associates of the Bury exercise, so many of their careers being shadowy and incompletely documented. In the third place, full biographies have been provided for those Essex ministers who are known to have formed the nucleus of the conference which met in and around Braintree during the same period. The reason for this is twofold: apart from brief references in Bancroft's *Daungerous positions* (1593), we have no knowledge of the activities of the Braintree conference, and the only way of compensating for this imbalance in the material at our disposal has been to emphasize such aspects of its members' careers as are documented in the London diocesan records. From their biographical entries – those of Ezekiel Culverwell, George Gifford, Richard Rogers and Robert Wright in particular – it seems clear that, had the 'Braintree minutes' survived rather than those of Dedham, we would be in possession of considerably more vital information about the conference movement than is afforded by the Dedham records (in particular, one suspects, regular contact with John Field, its organizer-in-chief in London). It is an unfortunate irony that Dedham was a very minor affair in comparison with those conferences known to have been operating elsewhere, particularly in

Northamptonshire and Warwickshire, on whose activities a major star chamber trial was focussed in 1591.[3]

For students of puritanism and of its system of 'practical divinity', the major Essex names are ones to conjure with: Gifford of *The country divinity*, Rogers of the *Seven treatises*, Arthur Dent of *The plain man's pathway to heaven*. But here these legendary figures are presented in their working dress, a simple black gown, and, as was said of the workaday lives of the parishioners of George Herbert's country parson, 'wallowing in the midst of their affairs'.[4]

This is not the place to attempt yet another definition of 'puritanism' or of 'the puritan mentality'. Suffice it to say that the texts reproduced here provide invaluable (indeed, often unique) insights into the interconnexions of that 'godly' network of clergymen who wished, pressed (and in some cases forfeited their ministries) for a radical revision of the ecclesiastical settlement that had been agreed by Elizabeth's first parliament in 1559. They eloquently rebut the old high church historical tradition that the evolution of the Church of England between Elizabeth's accession and the civil war was a straightforward battle between convinced and loyal 'Anglicans' and recalcitrant, potentially subversive, 'puritans'. The keynote was (usually) an uneasy compromise between the demands of conformity to the Book of Common Prayer and the consciences of those whose reservations about 'the dregs of popery' led them in various ways to flout or disregard its most contentious provisions.

From 1820 until 1936, Rylands English MS 874 was owned by the Gurney family of Keswick Hall, Norfolk.[5] At some point during the early months of the twentieth century, Mr J. F. Gurney agreed to its transcription by the Harvard historian, Roland Green Usher,[6] whose main preoccupation throughout his distinguished career was the life and work of Archbishop Richard Bancroft . In 1905, under the auspices of the Royal Historical Society (Camden Series), Although Usher published a more-or-less accurate transcript of the 'Dedham minutes', together with a selection of what he considered the most significant items in the accompanying material, prefacing the whole with edited extracts from Bancroft's sensational piece of investigative journalism, *Daungerous positions and proceedings* (1593).[7] Although Usher's work was marked (one may say marred) by an obvious anti-puritan animus, the present volume would have been unnecessary had there been fewer errors, either of commission or omission, in his edition. At a time when historians were virtually unaware of the existence, let alone the significance, of the diocesan court books mouldering away in the damp muniment rooms of cathedral cities, many of Usher's sins of omission are understandable. Likewise, the constraints of the Camden Series

---

3   This is described in detail in Collinson, *EPM*, pp. 403–31.
4   George Herbert, *A priest to the temple* in *The Works of George Herbert*, ed. F. E. Hutchinson (Oxford, 1941), p. 247.
5   For the full provenance of the manuscript, see below: Introduction, viii, pp. cxiii–v.
6   Here it would perhaps be cruel not to satisfy the curious reader on one (equally curious) point. Brett Usher is not descended from nor, to the best of his knowledge and belief, collaterally related to Roland Green Usher.
7   *The presbyterian movement / in the / reign of queen Elizabeth/ as illustrated by the / minute book of the Dedham classis / 1582–89. /* Edited for the Royal Historical Society / from the MS. In the possession of J. F. Gurney, esquire / Keswick Hall, Norfolk / by / Roland G. Usher, Ph. D (Harvard). London / Offices of the Royal Historical Society / 3 Old Serjeants' Inn, Chancery lane, W. C. / 1905. [Camden 3rd series., vol. VIII].

may have made unavoidable the excision of much of the contents of MS 874 itself. And yet he was surely misguided in leaving out such precious evidence of the mental and institutional structures of Elizabethan puritanism as the angry letter from Dr Richard Crick to his brethren of the Dedham conference.[8] The reason for this may be that Usher had little interest in such matters, for his errors of commission flowed from the lofty 'Anglican' assumption that the careers of these earnest and committed clergymen were insignificant and ultimately irrelevant – mere irritating flea-bites on the otherwise healthy body of the emergent Anglican communion. That said, later historians owe Usher a real debt of gratitude as one of the first truly 'forensic' historians of modern times: his work in the field, together with that of Albert Peel and A. F. Scott Pearson, laid the foundations for all later studies of Elizabethan nonconformity.

The editors acknowledge many corporate and separate debts. Jointly, they are indebted to the Director and University Librarian of the John Rylands University Library of Manchester, and to Dr Peter Nockles, Methodist Church Librarian, for permission to reproduce Rylands English MS 874 in its entirety;[9] to the Special Collections Research Center at the University of Chicago Library and to its Associate Director, Daniel Meyer, for permission to reproduce Chicago MS Codex 109; to Gerard Moate, vicar and lecturer of Dedham, and the Dedham Lectureship Trust, for their enthusiastic support of the project and for a generous grant from the Trust and from Simon Fraser University's Publication Fund to defray some of the production costs; to Mr Reginald Piggott of Potter Heigham, Norfolk, for preparing the maps; and to Alan Pennie and Mark Byford for permission to quote freely from their unpublished Ph.D. dissertations. The editors have also benefited from the interest in the religion of the Stour valley developed by Frank Bremer of Millersville University, Pennsylvania, and present editor of the Winthrop Papers. David Crankshaw pointed out the existence amongst the Ellesmere MSS at the Huntington Library, San Marino, California, of a sermon by Edmund Chapman and especial thanks are due to Mary L. Robertson, Curator of Manuscripts, for her prompt response to the editors' further enquiries and for generously supplying a photocopy of the complete manuscript 'with the Library's compliments'. It is discussed in Appendix 3.

Delving back into things first noted almost fifty years ago, Patrick Collinson was reminded of what he has always owed to Edna Bibby (d. 1929), whose work on Elizabethan puritanism neatly bisected that of R. G. Usher and his own, for she died in the year that he was born. Patrick Collinson and John Craig wish to thank the staffs of the country record offices at Norwich, Ipswich and Bury St Edmunds and the staff of the Rare Books Room and Manuscript Room of the Cambridge University Library for their helpful assistance with many enquiries. In Norwich, Susan Maddock helped with the will of Laurence Whitaker. A grant from the Social Sciences and Humanities Research Council of Canada enabled John Craig to visit Chicago in order to consult MS Codex 109 and also financed a research trip to

---

[8] See below, pp. 147–9.
[9] In the event a late decision was taken not to reproduce the last two folios of the manuscript: see p. 149, n. 445 for the editors' reasons. They nevertheless remain indebted to David and Mary Alice Mirhady for undertaking a translation of the original Latin and offer apologies for the fact that these efforts have finally been omitted from the volume.

England. He received further support from the Dedham Lectureship Trust for a visit to Manchester as well as for some days of research in Norfolk and Suffolk.

Brett Usher wishes to acknowledge the always courteous and expert assistance offered by the staff of the Manuscripts Department at the Guildhall Library, London; by Harriet Jones, until March 2002 Senior Archivist of London Metropolitan Archives (formerly the Greater London Record Office); by Melanie Barber, until July 2002 Deputy Librarian of Lambeth Palace Library, whose unrivalled knowledge of the records in her care has over the years pointed him in the direction of several interesting discoveries; and by Dr Thomas Freeman for his unfailing generosity in supplying correct references to the four earliest editions of John Foxe's *Actes and Monuments*.

Stephen Taylor has always interpreted his responsibilities as General Editor of COERS very widely, and the editors are greatly in his debt for his careful attention to the project ever since it was accepted for publication. They are likewise grateful to Meg Davies, whose expertise as copy editor has eased the burden of proof-reading and final corrections, even though far too many revisions and corrections landed on her desk at a late stage in her work.

Despite all the generous help, encouragement and support they have received, the editors nevertheless take full responsibility for all errors and omissions.

INTRODUCTION

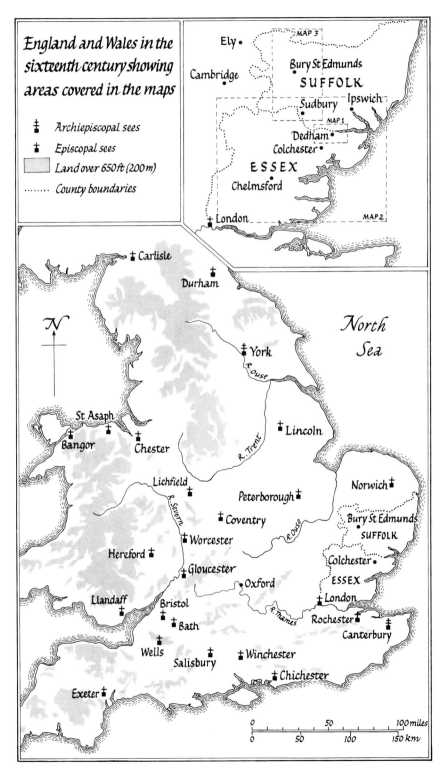

Map 1 England and Wales in the sixteenth century showing areas covered in the maps.

INTRODUCTION

i. The Elizabethan Church

The Church of England as redefined by the Elizabethan settlement of religion (1559–70) was a curious concoction, unique among the national churches of the reformation era. Traditionally described by Anglican historians as a compromise church of the *via media*, halfway between Rome and Geneva, something lauded as a piece of national pride (in George Herbert's words 'A fine aspect in fit array,/ Neither too mean, nor yet too gay'),[1] it was really nothing of the kind, unless the combination of strangely discrepant elements makes for a kind of compromise. The official doctrine of the thirty-nine articles, as glossed by leading Elizabethan churchmen and academics, aligned the English church not only with the churches of the reformation but with the 'best reformed churches' which followed the leads of Zürich, Geneva and Heidelberg, rather than with the Lutherans. In a conventional terminology which is a little too blunt an instrument, the Church of the Elizabethan settlement was 'Calvinist'.[2]

The most vocal of Elizabethan divines held Roman catholicism to be actually antichristian, and it was only by slow degrees that a more ecumenical vision made itself felt, through the writings of Richard Hooker and other theologians whom we can begin to call, cautiously, Anglicans.[3] Those who still defined themselves as catholics were exhorted by their *soi-disant* leaders, mainly members of the Society of Jesus, to distance themselves totally from a chimaera of a church. Many did, and became in the eyes of the Elizabethan state 'recusants', those who refused to go to church – and who paid the penalty under increasingly draconian penal laws, punitive fines in some cases, the most obscene of scaffold deaths in others. Many more looked for the best of both worlds, and in some respects conformed outwardly. In the eyes of the catholic hardliners these were 'schismatics', and protestants called them 'church papists'. We may regard them as 'closet catholics', and as long as they declined to come out, their indeterminate numbers aroused the fears and passions of totally committed protestants, who saw a papist under every bed.[4]

On the other hand, the church of the Elizabethan settlement worshipped according to a Book of Common Prayer which in form adhered more closely to traditional liturgies than any other reformed order of public prayer, and which retained ceremonial adjuncts, 'ornaments', including items of clerical attire, which even many of

---

[1] 'The British church', in *The works of George Herbert*, ed. F. E. Hutchinson (Oxford, 1941), p. 109.

[2] Sean F. Hughes, ' "The problem of 'Calvinism' ": English theologies of predestination c. 1580–1630', in *Belief and practice in reformation England. A tribute to Patrick Collinson from his students*, ed. Susan Wabuda and Caroline Litzenberger (Aldershot, 1998), pp. 229–49.

[3] Peter Lake, *Anglicans and puritans? Presbyterianism and English conformist thought from Whitgift to Hooker* (London, 1988); Anthony Milton, *Catholic and reformed. The Roman and protestant churches in English protestant thought 1600–1640* (Cambridge, 1995).

[4] Alexandra Walsham, *Church papists. Catholicism, conformity and confessional polemic in early modern England* (2nd edn., Woodbridge, 1999).

its own adherents considered to be 'popish dregs'. And while the monasteries great and small had been dissolved a generation earlier, England's great cathedrals survived, with their large ecclesiastical establishments and the quotidian *opus dei* of worship in the choir, together with some remnants of the musical tradition for which England had been famous. It was not clear what protestant cathedrals were for.[5] They were there because they were there (and no doubt because Queen Elizabeth wanted them to be there), and because, to be cynical, they provided relatively comfortable livings for their dignitaries. Together with the chapel royal, these were also 'nests' for closet catholics, such as the greatest English composer of the age and perhaps of any age, William Byrd.

Uniquely among reformed churches, the Church of England was still organized as a system of provinces and dioceses, governed, under the supreme authority of the crown, by archbishops and bishops, and by the considerable infrastructure of arch-deacons, commissaries and the rest of an apparatus of judicial and bureaucratic officialdom which the reformation had scarcely touched. Top-down government of an hierarchical character was reinforced, under the royal supremacy, by an ecclesiastical commission (or, later, a 'Court of High Commission') which, while it associated lay magistrates in the enforcement of church discipline, mostly had the effect of stiffening the episcopal sinews, with penalties such as imprisonment which the ecclesiastical courts proper were powerless to impose. This was hardly 'discipline' in the reformed sense, in which elements of church government, understood as a form of pastoral care, were devolved to rank-and-file ministers and even to lay representatives of congregations: a kind of ecclesiastical republicanism which we know as 'presbyterianism'.

Those who believed in properly reformed discipline, like our Dedham ministers, could believe that what masqueraded as such in the Elizabethan church was either false or non-existent, at least ill-defined, and this sense of a vacuum enabled them to experiment, exploring alternative methods of taking care of the common needs of their churches, which was what the Dedham conference was about. Perhaps these meetings were already the '*classes*', the lower, local rank of synod, of presbyterian ecclesiology at least in embryo. It appears from the records published here that the ministers were tempted to think in some such terms, although they never applied the technical term to their meetings, so that the time-honoured expression 'the Dedham *Classis*' is not really justified.

The first Elizabethan archbishop of Canterbury, Matthew Parker, wrote a scholarly history of what he called the 'British' church in the form of biographies of its seventy archbishops, he being its seventieth: continuity with the pre-reformation past rather than the radical discontinuity which many protestants believed to have occurred.[6] The canon law administered by the church courts (diocesan and archidiaconal), which was likely to affect at one time or another every inhabitant of the country, had been altered only piecemeal, and negatively, not by a programme of wholesale reform. This meant, for example, that only in England in all of western Christendom were the marriage laws retained unchanged.

5 Patrick Collinson, 'The protestant cathedral, 1541–1660', in *A history of Canterbury cathedral,* ed. Patrick Collinson, Nigel Ramsay and Margaret Sparks (Oxford, 1995), pp. 154–203.
6 Matthew Parker, *De antiquitate Britannicae ecclesiasticae* (London, 1572).

The Church of England remained a church composed of parishes, which had emerged from centuries-old processes of human settlement and organization. And now (and this was a change), with the disappearance of monks and friars and various kinds of 'mass priests', the majority of the clergy were parochial clergy possessed of 'benefices', which supported them from tithes, in principle a tenth of the gross local product. This made them freeholders, unlike the stipendiary and precarious ministers of other protestant churches. They were 'presented' to their livings, whether rectories or vicarages, by whoever held the 'advowson', that is to say, the patron, and, having been presented, were 'instituted' by the bishop. Legally, unless as in some rare cases, the patron was the parish itself, members of the parochial congregation had no say in who their minister should be. He was not, as in reformed practice, 'called' to his 'charge'. However in practice, as the Dedham papers make clearer than any other source, there often was an element of choice, nominally exercised by 'the people', although this may have meant the voice of some of the more weighty parishioners, or even of a single individual, like the wealthy clothier and merchant William Cardinal. He seems to have ruled the roost in East Bergholt, one of the parishes represented in the Dedham conference, although he was not its patron.

'Lecturers' were in a different position, legally, from incumbent, beneficed clergy. Their support was voluntary, sometimes in the form of an endowment, and while they required an episcopal licence in order to preach, they were appointed and sustained by their auditors, or, again, by a wealthy benefactor. Tradition asserts that Cardinal endowed the lectureship at Dedham which exists to this day.[7] The official standing of a prominent member of the conference, Henry Sandes of Boxford, was even less well-defined. But unbeneficed preachers like Sandes and the first lecturer of Dedham, Edmund Chapman, were considered to be 'doctors' in the presbyterian scheme of things, preachers and teachers without pastoral responsibilities.

Unlike catholic priests, and like almost all ministers in the reformed churches, the vast majority of English parish clergy were now married, their progenitive capacities resembling those of the gentry more than those of their humbler parishioners. One of our Dedham ministers, Richard Dowe of Stratford St Mary, fathered ten children in twenty years, and one has to wonder what became of them all.

As for its lay membership, the Elizabethan church was described by one radical critic as a constrained union of papists and protestants.[8] Another critic remarked, caustically, that with one blast of Queen Elizabeth's trumpet, a nation composed of all sorts of people had been transformed overnight into a godly protestant nation.[9] There can be little doubt that when religion was altered in 1559, only a minority of the nation, clergy and laity, would have considered themselves to be protestants, or would have known what that meant. All the rest, insofar as they conformed to the new order of things, were not unfairly described as 'cold statute protestants'. The credibility gap between what people were supposed to believe and practise and

---

[7] For the lectureship, see Appendix 2.
[8] Henry Ainsworth, *Counterpoyson. Considerations touching the points in difference between the Church of England and the seduced brethren of the separation* (Amsterdam, 1608), p. 228.
[9] *Writings of Henry Barrow, 1587–1590*, ed. Leland H. Carlson, Elizabethan Nonconformist Texts, III (London, 1962), 283.

where they actually found themselves, as religious persons, took years, in some parts of the country, decades, to bridge.

What was critically lacking in most places was preaching. The vast majority of the early Elizabethan clergy, who in truth were in many cases late Henrician or Marian clergy, so many vicars of Bray, were not preachers, not only for lack of the appropriate convictions but because they had not been exposed to a university education. In most places 'a godly, learned, preaching ministry' was still an impossible dream.

Protestants believed that preaching was 'the ordinary means of salvation', for which there was no substitute. But less dogmatically and more pragmatically, historians can agree that without their being preached, or imparted through a sustained process of catechizing, the essential protestant doctrines, and concomitant religious experience, were unlikely to take root. Not far short of the end of the century, a Kentish minister claimed that when he canvassed opinion in parishes where there had been no preaching, hardly anyone knew that they could never be saved by their own moral endeavours. Justification by faith alone was something of which they knew nothing.[10] In the opinion of the most recent historians of these processes, it was no earlier than the 1570s and 1580s that protestant indoctrination made much impact, and much later in the more remote, upland parts of the country to the north and west. Only towards 1600 could England be plausibly styled a protestant nation, and not even then, according to one authority, as a nation of protestants.[11] When most people became protestants (at least formally), protestants (in a more than formal sense) became puritans.

That is to say that the so-called puritans whom we meet in the documents published in this volume are not to be defined in themselves as a distinct religious species but only in the context of the imperfectly reformed church in which, as highly committed and fully informed protestants, they stood out as so many sore thumbs, a minority group, often obnoxious to the majority, and identifiable to themselves as 'the godly'.[12] They were not really of the same religion as many of their neighbours, although law and custom required that they take their places as part of the parochial congregation, and both administer and receive sacraments which did not mean the same thing to them as to others. When the first puritans made a stand against some of the ceremonies which Queen Elizabeth and her government and bishops attempted to enforce (and especially the white linen surplice as the garment of ministerial office), it was in part because they knew that these were concessions to the great majority of old-fashioned christians whom it was a necessary piece of public policy to embrace in an inclusive church, a church which still looked

---

[10] Josias Nicholls, *The plea of the innocent* (London, 1602), pp. 212–14.

[11] Patrick Collinson, *The birthpangs of protestant England. Religious and cultural change in the sixteenth and seventeenth centuries* (Basingstoke, 1988); Christopher Haigh, *English reformations, religion, politics, and society under the Tudors* (Oxford, 1993), especially p. 280; Patrick Collinson, 'The English reformation, 1945–1995', in *Companion to historiography,* ed. Michael Bentley (London and New York, 1997).

[12] Patrick Collinson, *English puritanism* (revised edn., London, 1987); Patrick Collinson, *The puritan character. Polemics and polarities in early seventeenth-century English culture* (Los Angeles, 1989); Peter Lake, 'Defining puritanism – again?', in *Puritanism: trans-atlantic perspectives on a seventeenth-century Anglo-American faith,* ed. Francis Bremer (Boston, 1993), pp. 3–29.

traditional, and in which no questions were asked, provided that clergy and people merely conformed.

The nonconformity of our puritan minority proved to be an insoluble problem for those, Queen Elizabeth above all, who aspired to the ideal of total uniformity. To be persuaded of that, one has only to trace the career trajectories of the ministers who belonged to, or were associated with, the Dedham conference. Elizabeth had appointed John Aylmer bishop of London in 1577 (and his jurisdiction embraced Essex, including the Dedham region) with strict instructions to deal with recalcitrants at both ends of the religious spectrum, papists and puritans, with equal severity.[13] Edmund Freke had gone to Norwich in 1575 with a similar mandate, and it was this new broom which had sent the core membership of the Dedham conference down from Norfolk to the outer fringes of Aylmer's diocese.[14] Aylmer, like Freke in Norwich, did his best to make life difficult for nonconformists. In 1583, John Whitgift was made archbishop of Canterbury, and Whitgift was a hammer of puritans who set out to deal with the problem once and for all. Yet, troubled as they were with demands to subscribe to Whitgift's code of conformity, the three articles (the royal supremacy, the articles of religion, the prayer book), and with frequent summonses to the courts, very few of our ministers can be said to have been martyrs to episcopal tyranny, and most remained more or less immune in their ministries. The loose and untidy textures of the Elizabethan church and society, of which so much evidence will be found in these records, saw to that.

However, episcopal harassment, together with a logical progression in the penetration of certain New Testament texts held to be normative for the constitution of a truly christian church, had already turned some puritans into rejectionists, radicals whose contention with the established religion went much deeper than scruples about ceremonies, most of which were allowed to be 'matters indifferent', obnoxious only insofar as they were enforced on consciences which in respect of such matters ought to be free, a matter of christian liberty.[15] In 1572, two young London preachers, John Field and Thomas Wilcox, critical of their elders, the original puritans, for concerning themselves only with 'shells and chippings' of residual popery,[16] launched an attack on the foundations of established religion, episcopacy and the prayer book. In his contribution to *An admonition to the Parliament* (1572),Wilcox proclaimed that 'we in England are so fare of, from having a church rightly reformed, according to the prescript of Gods worde, that as yet we are not come to the outwarde face of the same.' The 'marks' of a true church were pure doctrine, the sacraments 'sincerely' administered and ecclesiastical discipline. It was acknowledged that the Church of England professed sound doctrine. But the ministry required to teach it was lacking. Instead of ministers properly qualified, called and ordained, the church was served by 'tag and rag', 'learned and unlearned', 'popish masse mongers, men for all seasons, Kyng Henries priests, . . . Queene Maries priestes'. As for the sacraments, there was a great deal amiss. Preaching ought to accompany sacraments, but preaching was normally lacking.

[13] Bishop Aylmer to Sir Christopher Hatton, 28 May 1578, printed in Sir Harris Nicolas, *Memoirs of the life and times of Sir Christopher Hatton* (London, 1847), pp. 55–6.
[14] Collinson, *EPM*, pp. 202–5.
[15] John Coolidge, *The Pauline renaissance in England: puritanism and the Bible* (Oxford, 1970).
[16] Collinson, 'John Field', pp. 334–70.

'We borrowe from papistes, The body of our Lorde Jesus Chryst which was geven for thee.' And ecclesiastical discipline was almost entirely lacking. Instead of pastors, doctors, elders and deacons (the Calvinist, or presbyterian, model of ministry) 'the Lordship of one man over many churches, yea over sundrie Shieres'. 'Now then, if you wyl restore the church to his ancient officers, this you must doe. In stead of an Archbishop or Lord bishop, you must make equalitie of ministers.' In his contribution to this manifesto, *A view of popishe abuses yet remaining in the Englishe Church,* Field added the stiletto of satire: 'In all their order of service there is no edification . . . but confusion, they tosse the Psalmes in most places like tennice balles.' 'Fie upon these stinking abominations.'[17]

It is significant that in the second edition of the *Admonition*, Wilcox's 'not come to the outwarde face of the same' is altered to 'scarse', and the correction has been made by hand in three surviving copies of the first.[18] For 'not' suggests that its authors, and all who agreed with them, ought to leave a church which even in its outward constitution was not a true church, and find one which was: which indeed was the course taken by a succession of separatist groups and individuals, who were the founding fathers of sects and later denominations, outside the Church of England. But 'scarce', and even the small space between 'not' and 'scarce', allowed non-separatist puritans like Field and Wilcox to hang on in there, in the church if not entirely of it.

There were perhaps several notches between 'not' and 'scarce', and they were occupied, shiftingly rather than consistently, by our Dedham ministers, who included men of rigid and more elastic opinions. Were the church courts to be acknowledged as legitimate tribunals, that is, should ministers obey a summons to attend them? Was it possible to subscribe, with limitations, to the prayer book? Were the bishops to be considered as brethren? Above all, should the Dedham ministers put their names to the constitution for a presbyterian Church of England, the Book of Discipline? On this subject, caution, in the form of repeated adjournments of the question, seems to have prevailed. (Dedham was not to know, when these matters were later contested in star chamber, that clever lawyers would convince the bench that there was nothing actually illegal, or subversive, about such experiments.[19]) And yet in its pretensions to manage the affairs of the churches within its orbit, it appears that Dedham was already morally committed to a religious economy much like that enshrined in the Book of Discipline. This was 'presbytery in episcopacy', with as little deference to the episcopal element as possible.

ii. Prophesyings, Conferences and Combination Lectures

First, some definitions. A prophesying, or often 'exercise' (scil., an 'exercise of prophesying'), as practised in the Elizabethan church, especially in the 1570s,

---

[17] *Puritan manifestoes: a study of the origin of the puritan revolt*, ed. W. H. Frere and C. E. Douglas (London, 1954), pp. 9–16, 29, 32.

[18] *Ibid.*, p. 9; Collinson, 'John Field', p. 334.

[19] Collinson, *EPM*, Part 8, Ch. 3, 'The star chamber'.

consisted of two, three or four sermons preached in turn on the same text before a larger than ordinary, voluntary congregation drawn from the surrounding district, in the presence of the local clergy. Proceedings were presided over by a moderator, and were followed by private conference among the ministers, including 'censure' of the doctrine which had been publicly preached. When, in 1576–7, Queen Elizabeth ordered the suppression of the prophesyings, suspended Archbishop Grindal for his conscientious refusal to transmit her order, and then suppressed them (in the southern province) by her own peremptory command,[20] they were replaced by combination lectures, that is, monthly, fortnightly or weekly sermons preached according to a roster by a 'combination' of local preachers. The only difference was the single sermon on each occasion, taking the place of the public participation of two or three preachers, with its potential for debate. The entire combination would be present on each occasion, and would continue the public proceedings with private conference, often over dinner. Evidence has been found of no less than eighty-five combination lectures in twenty-two counties, and perhaps there were many more which have left no record so far uncovered.[21] 'Conference', in contemporary usage, always means ministerial conference which took place on such occasions, but also, as we learn from the Dedham papers, under more private and even secret conditions.

Now to the rationale. The greatest obstacle to realizing a genuinely reformed Church of England, reformed and informed about its doctrinal title deeds, was the lack of a preaching ministry. Addressing an audience of Norfolk gentlemen, justices of the peace gathered for the quarter sessions, John More, the 'Apostle of Norwich', harangued them: 'If ye will be saved, get you preachers into your parishes, . . . bestow your labour, cost and travell to get them. Ride for them, runne for them, stretch your purses to maintain them. We shall begin to be riche in the Lord Jesus.'[22] Like a modern prime minister announcing his programme as one of 'education, education, education', the Elizabethan MP Job Throkmorton told the house of commons that if he were to be asked what was the 'bane' of the Church and Commonwealth, he would answer 'the dombe ministerie, the dombe ministerye, yea, yf I were asked a thowsande times, I must say, the dombe ministerye'.[23]

If the creation of an eloquent preaching ministry were to depend upon natural wastage among Throkmorton's 'dumb' ministers and the recruitment from the universities of a new sort of clergy in whom the values of the reformation were to be thoroughly internalized, that would take time. And how were well-qualified graduates to be attracted to a profession which paid so poorly? Although the puritans rarely admitted it, much of the problem had to do with the thousands of parishes where the tithe income had been alienated ('impropriated', as lay owners took possession of what had been monastic property), leaving often pitiably small stipends for the curates put in by lay rectors to do the work. To reform that abuse would take for ever, since apart from a passing interest which James I took in the subject when he first arrived in England, nothing much would be done about

[20] Collinson, *Grindal*, pp. 233–65.
[21] Collinson, 'Lectures by combination: structures and characteristics of church life in 17th-century England', in *idem, Godly people*, pp. 467–98, 563.
[22] John More, *Three godly and fruitful sermons* (Cambridge, 1594), pp. 66–9.
[23] *Proceedings in the parliaments of Elizabeth I*, II, 1584–1589, ed. T. E. Hartley (London, 1995), 315.

impropriations for centuries to come. And historians know that it would take all the years between Elizabeth's accession and the death of James I for a graduate ministry (godliness could not be guaranteed) to become the norm in many if by no means all parts of the country.

But the likes of More and Throkmorton were not prepared to wait. They wanted a preaching ministry not tomorrow but now. The salvation of men and women and the security of the state depended on it. Throkmorton offered a syllogism: 'Ignorance of the holy word of God is the cause of treason . . . ; but the dombe ministery is the cause of such ignorance: ergo the dombe ministery is the cause of treasonn.'[24]

In the circumstances the only remedy was in-post training, a kind of open university created for the backlog of Henrician and Marian clergy, not to speak of the second- and third-rate material which the early Elizabethan bishops were still obliged to ordain. These were 'exercises', a system devised piecemeal by individual bishops but eventually codified for the whole of his province by Archbishop Whitgift. Exercises in this sense require little explanation. All clergy below the academic rank of master of arts were to undertake programs of study in biblical and other theological texts, recording their progress in what we may call exercise books, which were to be regularly inspected by the archdeacons or other well qualified clergy, sometimes styled 'commissioners for the exercise'.[25]

But a different if related kind of exercise went under the exotic name of 'prophesying'. The word was unfortunate, since it carried a whiff of chiliasm for those, including Queen Elizabeth, who did not like the sound of it. In fact the name, and the idea, derived from some things communicated by St Paul to the church at Corinth: 'let the prophets speak two or three, and let the other judge' (1 Corinthians xiv.29), and more succinctly in 1 Thessalonians v.20, 'despise not prophesying' (Geneva version), or 'despise not prophesyings' (Authorized Version of 1611), the plural interestingly making a noun out of the verb. Those who studied these texts derived from them something remote from what is now known in pentecostal church life as 'speaking with tongues', which St Paul had been anxious to discourage. They made of it a sober, exacting system of learned biblical exegesis.

The models were continental, with the origins to be found in the 1520s in Zürich, where *prophezei* was a daily exercise in the Grossmunster: two or three speakers gave an exegesis of the text from the original languages (presumably in Latin), followed by a vernacular sermon on the same scripture for the benefit of the laity. The reassembling in the Zürich Staats Bibliothek of Heinrich Bullinger's library suggests that it was intended for use by students and ministers in training. Seventy years later, in Bury St Edmunds, the combination lecture was similarly resourced from a town or parish library.[26]

The earliest prophesying in England seems to have been established in the diocese of Gloucester by the Edwardian bishop and Marian martyr John Hooper,

---

[24] *Ibid.*, p. 316.

[25] Collinson, *EPM,* pp. 170–1, 184–5. A much fuller account of exercises in this sense will be found in Collinson, 'PCM', pp. 244–60.

[26] We are grateful to Dr Leu of the Zürich Staats Bibliothek for showing Patrick Collinson the libraries of Bullinger, Huldreich Zwingli and Conrad Gesner. For the Bury parish library, see John Craig, *Reformation, politics and polemics: the growth of protestantism in East Anglian market towns, 1500–1610* (Aldershot, 2001), pp. 116–21, 205–19.

who would have seen the original model at first hand in Zürich. This was a closed, clerical exercise, in which care was taken that there should be no disputation 'before the unlearned'.[27] Similar experiments followed hard on the heels of Elizabeth's accession, for example at St Albans, where from 1560 the unlearned clergy were led through a series of theological commonplaces, 'according to Mr Cranmer and Peter Martyr bookes'. The examination of written, academic exercises was built into the proceedings. Only in 1572 did the St Albans meetings become public, with two or three speakers expounding, presumably in English, before a lay auditory.[28]

Perhaps it was the presence of 'the people' which became the distinctive essence of a prophesying. Describing a tradition of purely clerical exercises in London, the archdeacon reported: 'As for prophesying, there is none in the Archdeaconry of London.'[29] The popular element was always the Achilles heel of the Elizabethan prophesyings. For there was another continental model which had been brought into England by the protestant 'strangers' whose church was established in Edwardian London by John à Lasco. This was congregational prophesying, a weekly meeting in which any church member could discuss and even challenge the doctrine taught by the ministers.[30] Among the English exiles at Geneva it was lawful on such occasions 'for every man to speake, or enquire as God shall move his heart'.[31] But this looked risky, even to the Calvinist ministry of the stranger churches which were restored under Elizabeth.[32] When Archbishop Grindal tried to reform and save the prophesyings from the queen's demand that they be suppressed, he wrote: '*ante omnia,* that no lay person be suffered to speak publicly in those assemblies'.[33]

But Grindal stoutly defended the right of the laity to attend the prophesyings as hearers.[34] And here was an additional rationale for their existence. For as long as preaching was in short supply, the prophesyings provided sermons for an otherwise impoverished population. And the presence of large numbers of committed protestants, and above all, of the gentry and magistrates in the front seats, made for a show of strength which signalled the triumph of the protestant reformation in this or that locality. Hence the motivation of the tale-tellers whose reports led to the queen's demand that the prophesyings be suppressed.[35]

No reference can be found to prophesying in any official document of the Church of England before 1604, when the seventy-second of the new code of canons of that year ruled: 'Neither shall any minister, not licensed, as is aforesaid, presume to

---

[27] John Hooper, *Later writings* (Parker Society, Cambridge, 1852), p. 132.

[28] Archdeacon David Kemp of St Albans to Bishop Edwin Sandys, 6 July 1576; LPL, MS 2003, fos. 16–18.

[29] Archdeacon John Mullins of London to Bishop Edwin Sandys, July 1576; BL, Add. MS 29546, fo. 54v.

[30] Johannis à Lasco, *Opera,* ed. Abraham Kuyper (Amsterdam/The Hague, 1866), II, 101–2, 104–5.

[31] W. D. Maxwell, *John Knox's Genevan service book, 1556* (Edinburgh, 1931), p. 104.

[32] Patrick Collinson, 'Calvinism with an anglican face: the stranger churches in early Elizabethan London and their superintendent', in *idem, Godly people,* p. 224; Jeannine E. Olson, 'Nicolas des Gallars and the Genevan connection of the stranger churches', in *From strangers to citizens: the integration of immigrant communities in Britain, Ireland and colonial America, 1550–1750,* ed. Randolph Vigne and Charles Littleton (Brighton and Portland, Or., 2001), pp. 38–47.

[33] *The remains of Edmund Grindal,* ed. W. Nicholson (Parker Society, Cambridge, 1843), pp. 373–4.

[34] Grindal told Lord Burghley that he saw 'no reason why the people should be excluded . . . especially for the benefit that groweth thereby to the hearers' (*ibid.,* p. 391). This was the sticking point which determined that Grindal's career was effectively at an end.

[35] Collinson, *Grindal,* chs. 13 and 14.

appoint or hold any meetings for sermons, commonly termed by some prophecies or exercises, in market towns or other places.' That would appear to have been that. But the seventy-second canon is governed by its opening words: 'No minister shall, without the licence and direction of the bishop of the diocese first obtained and had under his hand and seal . . .'.[36] Although Queen Elizabeth made it clear, at the time of her suspension of Archbishop Grindal, that no mere bishop (or archbishop) had the power to issue such licences,[37] that was not the position adopted by the canon, and it is clear that both the prophesyings and the 'lectures by combination' which succeeded them, continuing far into the seventeenth century, were in many cases episcopally allowed and licensed.[38] The controversy at Bury St Edmunds which appears in the second document published in this volume arose when the bishop, Edmund Scambler, approved of the names in the combination presented to him by the local preaching ministers.

In the early 1570s, prophesyings flourished in market towns in most dioceses of the southern province, Ely, Salisbury and the Welsh dioceses, and perhaps Worcester, Bristol and Oxford only excepted.[39] In Kent, Archbishop Parker's home territory, they were held in Sandwich, Ashford, Faversham and Sittingbourne.[40] In Essex there were exercises at Rochford, Maldon, Horndon-on-the-Hill, Brentwood and Romford.[41]

Whose was the initiative? In some cases it may have belonged to the bishops, and a majority of the bishops responded to a circular from Grindal with support for the prophesyings. In Sussex, Bishop Richard Curteys, a vigorous new broom in the 1570s, claimed that he had introduced prophesying into all eight deaneries of his see, and in the western parts of the diocese had presided and moderated in person.[42] In the diocese of Exeter, Bishop William Alley was 'a furtherer therein, and took pains to travail in the work himself', while his successor, William Bradbridge, reported that he himself had acted as moderator if he happened to be near a centre of prophesying.[43] But in many cases the exercises arose from more local initiatives, the bishops merely giving their 'consent', or 'yielding' to arrangements already 'agreed unto by the ministers . . . touching the exercise of themselves', those being the words of the Buckinghamshire order sanctioned by Bishop Thomas Cooper of Lincoln.[44] Cooper wrote on a draft of the orders for Hertfordshire: 'These orders of exercise I think good and godly.'[45] Bishop John Parkhurst of Norwich merely gave

[36] *The Anglican canons 1529–1947*, ed. Gerald Bray (Church of England Record Society 6, 1998), pp. 362–4.
[37] Collinson, *Grindal*, pp. 262–3.
[38] Collinson, 'Lectures by combination', in *idem, Godly people*, pp. 467–98.
[39] Collinson, *Grindal*, ch. 13; Collinson, *EPM*, pp. 168–76.
[40] Kent Archives Office, Canterbury, MS Z.5.1, fos. 166v–7r, 169r, l7lr.
[41] Archdeacon John Walker to Bishop Edwin Sandys, July 1576, LPL, MS 2003, fo. 12; BL, Add. MS 29546, fos. 48r–50r; Collinson, 'PCM', pp. 184–5.
[42] Richard Curteys, bishop of Chichester to Grindal, 15 July 1576, LPL, MS 2003, fo. 4; BL, Add MS 29546, fos. 50v–1v.
[43] Bishop William Bradbridge to Grindal, 9 July 1576, LPL, MS 2003, fo. 8; BL, Add. MS 29546, fo. 40v.
[44] Copies in Cambridge University Library, MS Ff.v.14, fos. 85r–7r, Kent Archives Office, Canterbury, MS Z.5.1, fos. 164v–6r.
[45] LPL, MS 2007, fos. 106–8, where this note is in Cooper's own hand; other copies in BL, MS Cotton Vespasian C XIV (ii), fos. 248–50, and BL, Lansdowne MS 19, no. 24, whence printed, Strype, *Annals*, II, i, 473–4.

his blessing to arrangements made by the Norwich ministers 'both for their better exercise and also for the education of the people'; while the orders for Bury St Edmunds were solicited by 'sundrye godly and well learned persons, aswell of the clergie as otherwise, nere adjoinyng to the towne'.[46]

In all such circumstances the principle of hierarchy was preserved, with permanent moderators, the ranking preachers of the district, exercising delegated quasi-episcopal powers. At Bury they were to take 'chardge and order' of proceedings, with the power to convene the clergy at such times and places as they saw fit. But in 1575, with Parkhurst of Norwich and Archbishop Parker both dead, the Norwich ministers took advantage of the interregnum to restore a prophesying which had been put down on Parker's orders, and to establish it on a quite different, presbyterian basis. It was now 'judged meet by the brethren' that the exercise should be held every Monday in the cathedral, the table of speakers to consist of 'such as shall be judged by the brethren meet to speak', who were to submit to orders drawn up 'by the consent of the brethren only, and not by one man's authority'. All the participants were qualified preachers and there was no provision for the advancement of the unlearned. The office of moderator circulated throughout the membership, always falling on the first speaker from the previous week's exercise.[47]

The Norwich order cannot have long survived the arrival in the diocese of Bishop Freke, who proceeded to make life difficult for the Norwich preachers. Three of them, Edmund Chapman, Richard Crick and Richard Dowe, all members of the cathedral chapter, became exiles from the new conformist regime, finding new berths in the Dedham valley, Chapman in a lectureship created for him in Dedham itself by his brother-in-law William Cardinal, Crick in East Bergholt, and Dowe in Stratford St Mary. In October 1582, something like the Norwich order was revived: a conference of 'some of the godly brethren', who agreed to meet on a monthly basis to hear an exposition of scripture by one of the company, preaching and prayer to occupy the first hour, and 'the rest of the tyme to be employed in deciding some profitable questions, . . . or els in conference aboute other necessary matters'. This was the Dedham conference.

But this was quite unlike the prophesyings. Whereas even at Norwich in 1575 the exercise had been held in public, in the cathedral, and presumably for the edification of the people of Norwich, the Dedham ministers met in secret and preached only to each other. 'Silence also to be kepte aswell of the meetinge, as of the matters there dealte in.' Francis Bacon, in his *Advertisement touching the controversies of the Church of England* (about 1589) called for the restoration of prophesying in a modified form. 'I know prophesying was subject to great abuse, and would be more abused now, because heat of contentions is increased. But I say the only reason of the abuse was, because there was admitted to it a popular auditory, and it was not contained within a private conference of ministers.'[48] Bacon was a little naïve. Whereas combination lectures, already flourishing when he wrote, were conducted in the full light of day, with a 'popular auditory', and only rarely gave rise to

---

[46] Richard Gaston to Mr Holden, Master of Requests, *CSP Dom. Addenda 1547–65*, p. 552; *Parkhurst*, pp. 164–5.

[47] DWL, MS Morrice B 1, pp. 268–70; printed, John Browne, *History of congregationalism in Norfolk and Suffolk* (London, 1887), pp. 18–20.

[48] *Francis Bacon: a critical edition of the major works*, ed. Brian Vickers (Oxford, 1996), p. 13.

'abuse', the 'private conference' of the Dedham ministers was a secret and potentially subversive invention. It was also intrinsically sectarian, since the Dedham
ministers seem to have taken no interest in improving the quality of pastoral care in
neighbouring parishes without preaching ministers and not directly represented in
the conference. The Dedham orders constituted a church within the church.

iii. Elizabethan Religion in Essex and East Anglia

Religion in Essex

With just over four hundred parishes, the county of Essex was by far the largest
component of the vast diocese of London, which also encompassed the entire
county of Middlesex, scattered parishes in southern Hertfordshire, a handful in
Buckinghamshire, and the eighty-odd crowded ecclesiastical 'cells' – ancient
monastic 'liberties' as well as parishes – within the City of London itself.[49] Since
the mid-nineteenth century, urban and industrial sprawl has increasingly disfigured
its southern border, the Thames valley, and led in the more recent past to tasteless
jokes about 'Essex girls'. For those who have never visited its heartlands or its
far-flung outposts (of which the Stour valley is one, and the ancient borough and
port of Maldon another) the county of Essex is therefore widely perceived as stale,
flat and unprofitable.

It was not so when Elizabeth came to the throne. Essex was described by John
Norden as 'the English Goschen', a land flowing with milk and honey.[50] Its secret
lay in its diversity – rolling arable lands, good grazing for sheep and cattle, rich
fishing grounds in the windy estuaries of the Thames, Crouch and Blackwater.
There was still good hunting to be had in what remained of its ancient royal
forests.[51] Its cheeses were prized and Colchester oysters were famous throughout
Europe: barrels of them arrived in London when the Colchester authorities wished
to flatter, placate or seduce an influential patron at court. The saffron grounds which
clustered in and around the parish of Walden, not far south of Cambridge, were likewise renowned: hence the fact that this gracious country town, with its magnificent
fifteenth-century church, is officially known today as Saffron Walden. Weaving and
clothmaking had in the late middle ages added to Essex's industrial prosperity – in
Braintree, Bocking, Halsted and other townships, including the parish of Dedham.

If the precise nature of the protestant revolution of the sixteenth century remains,
and will forever remain, hotly debated, there is no denying that within a mere fifty
years – roughly, 1520 to 1570 – reformed churchmanship outside the Roman catholic church had been catapulted from the status of heresy into that of an alternative
world-view. How did this revolution occur? Was it imposed from above or was it a
spontaneous reaction to changing economic and social conditions? To put it another

---

[49] For the complex structure of the diocese see Brett Usher, 'The deanery of Bocking and the demise of
the vestiarian controversy', *JEH*, LII (July 2001), 434–55.

[50] See William Hunt, *The puritan moment* (Harvard, 1983), ch. 1, for an overview – geographical,
economic and social – of Elizabethan Essex.

[51] For which see Oliver Rackham, *The last forest: the story of Hatfield Forest* (London, 1989), in
particular the map of Essex on p. 42. The editors are grateful to Dr Margaret Aston for drawing their
attention to this study.

way, was it the religion of an emerging, entrepreneurial middle class determined to throw off the restraints imposed by a conservative 'establishment'? Tudor Essex provides fertile ground for this continuing debate. To the south, it fell under the awesome influence of the City of London and, to the north-east, under that of the Low Countries, with which, via the port of Harwich, the borough of Colchester was in constant communication. It is a truism that Lutheranism and smuggled English bibles proved congenial in a region where a strong Lollard tradition still lingered. Iconoclasm thus became a growing feature of the 1520s. On the very eve of Henry VIII's official break with Rome there was a 'minor epidemic', with the destruction of crosses and images at Coggeshall, Great Horkesley, Sudbury and Ipswich, and the celebrated burning of the rood of Dovercourt – the parish to which the port and chapelry of Harwich owed ecclesiastical allegiance.[52]

If in a very a real sense, therefore, the Henrician reformation was not an act of state imposed from above but rather one which made convenient use of anti-catholic sentiment in London and the home counties to further a political strategy, the bewildering tergiversations of Henry's 'reforms' between 1534 and his death in 1547 – now best perceived through the eyes of Archbishop Thomas Cranmer, as relayed to us in masterly fashion by Diarmaid MacCulloch[53] – have, however, forced historians of the early reformation to pause for thought. Can it be said that Essex had in any sense become a protestant county at Henry's death? How far did the advances made by Cranmer and his colleagues in the short reign of the 'godly imp', Edward VI, propel it into the 'spacious days' of Elizabeth I?

Although during Mary's reign Colchester became 'the city on a hill', a beacon of light for beleaguered protestants at home and abroad, the town's most distinguished modern historian urges caution in making easy assumptions. No more than ten per cent of its population of 4,000 can be accounted truly protestant by 1547. Its sixteen parishes (eight within and eight without the walls) were poorly endowed or else not endowed at all, most having been appropriate to the mitred abbey of St John or else to the priory of St Botolph. Thus, for strictly economic reasons, there was no evangelist of any stature resident there under Edward VI and it had to take what it could get from roving preachers and be thankful.[54] Ironically, this peripatetic tradition stood the protestant cause in good stead when it had to disappear into the undergrowth during Mary's reign.

By contrast, there is considerable evidence of systematic evangelization in the Thames valley from the mid-1540s. Thanks, it would seem, to the activities of 'Father' Richard Alvey – the only early reformer apart from Miles Coverdale to be accorded that honorific title – there had sprung up, no later than 1551, a fully protestant coterie amongst the local clergy which looked to Alvey, rector of Sandon, for inspiration and guidance. It was centred on the burgeoning township of Billericay – technically a hamlet within the parish of Great Burstead, whose

[52] Eamon Duffy, *The stripping of the altars. Traditional religion in England c.1400–1580* (Yale, New Haven, 1992), p. 381.

[53] Diarmaid MacCulloch, *Thomas Cranmer* (Yale, New Haven, 1996).

[54] Byford, 'Birth of a protestant town', pp. 26–9. The extent to which Edward VI's reformation was effected by means of a cohort of 'roving' preachers, authorized or otherwise, has yet to be fully explicated. In the meantime, see Diarmaid MacCulloch, *Tudor church militant* (London, 1999), for the best account of Edwardian evangelism.

inhabitants at this time included the future exile John Finch, the future martyrologist Thomas Brice and the future martyr Thomas Watts – and it owed not a little to the patronage of Richard 1st Lord Rich. Generally dismissed as a sinister time-server (did he not betray Sir Thomas More and supervise many of the Marian burnings?), Rich in fact appears to have been an active and convinced lay evangelist. As Lord Chancellor at the very heart of Edward's reign (October 1547–January 1552), he had the vast bulk of crown livings in his official gift and it would have been surprising indeed if the majority had not been bestowed on candidates acceptable to an increasingly militant protestant regime. He had, moreover, acquired a considerable amount of ex-monastic and other property in the Thames valley (including his secondary seat, Rochford Hall) and likewise promoted members of the Alvey circle to local livings in his personal gift. One of the most intriguing, William Aston, rector of Wickford and then of Leigh, was sent to the Tower in January 1555 for spreading abroad a 'slaunderouse bill' against Philip and Mary and thereafter disappears from the records.[55] As early as 1548 Rich bestowed his vicarage of Matching, near Chelmsford, on Robert Horne, later dean of Durham, who would return from exile under Mary to become Elizabeth's first bishop of Winchester.[56]

Evidence for the early evangelization of central Essex is more problematic. The best documented comes from the clothing towns of Braintree and Bocking, where in late 1550 a group of Kent 'freewillers' who included the master of Maidstone school, Thomas Cole, arrived to disseminate their views. Their activities came to the attention of the privy council and Cole was one of those who publicly recanted his 'heresy', dutifully preaching a sermon in defence of predestination before Archbishop Cranmer.[57]

Otherwise our knowledge of protestant advances before 1559 comes to us retrospectively from the pages of John Foxe's *Actes and Monuments*, for there is little, outside his instructive ordination book,[58] to be gleaned from the scanty records which survive from the brief episcopate of London's first protestant bishop, Nicholas Ridley (1550–3). During the long years of Foxe's researches, numerous correspondents kept him generously supplied with first-hand evidence of protestant activity in the county and he documents more 'humble' martyrs within its boundaries than are recorded for any other shire. (It is perhaps no accident that the most celebrated, William Hunter, hailed from Brentwood – an easy ride, and hardly more than a brisk walk, from Billericay.)

Edmund Grindal, 'Ridley's Achates', returned from exile under Mary to be consecrated bishop of London in December 1559, patiently fostering the evangelical energies of rural Essex for a decade before being dispatched northwards as archbishop of York in 1570. Grindal was a national, not merely a local, figure and his almost daily contact with Archbishop Matthew Parker, with the court and in

---

[55] *APC 1554–56* (London, 1892), p. 89. For a full account of early protestant advances in the Thames valley see Brett Usher, 'The Essex evangelists under Edward VI: Richard Lord Rich, Richard Alvey and their circle' in *John Foxe: at home and abroad*, ed. David Loades (papers delivered at the fourth John Foxe Colloquium, Boston, Lincs, 2000).

[56] Reg. Bonner, fo. 171r.

[57] D. Andrew Penny, *Freewill or predestination* (London, 1990), pp. 52–4, 68–73; Usher, 'The deanery of Bocking', pp. 438–9.

[58] This is printed *verbatim* in W. H. Frere, *The Marian reaction* (London, 1896), pp. 181–210.

particular with Sir William Cecil has left a body of correspondence and memoranda which allows of a detailed treatment of his episcopate.[59] What, unfortunately, is missing from the picture is a true appreciation of his role as chief pastor: he conscientiously visited his diocese on three occasions (1561, 1565 and 1568), but of the three call books (*libri cleri*) and three act books of office business which those visitations will have generated, only the call book of 1561 now survives.[60]

It is, however, abundantly clear that evangelization was his chief concern and Grindal rapidly turned London into an 'exile diocese', largely staffed by men who had been active in Frankfurt or Geneva. He appointed as his vicar general the able Welsh lawyer Thomas Huick and preferred (or arranged for the preferment of) many who would form the backbone of resistance to Archbishop Parker's drive towards ritual conformity during the vestiarian controversy of 1564–7.[61]

Essex was routinely governed by three archdeacons – those of Essex (the southern half of the county), Colchester (two divisions, to the north-east and north-west) and Middlesex, whose jurisdiction for some arcane reason snaked north beyond London into Hertfordshire and then into the Essex deaneries of Harlow, Dunmow and Hedingham. As archdeacon of Essex Grindal chose the reformed freewiller, Thomas Cole, who had signed the 'new discipline' in Frankfurt.[62] The archdeaconry of Colchester went to John Pullan (Pulleyne), another disciple of Richard Alvey, who had heroically sustained the protestant cause both in the City of London and in Colchester during Mary's reign before departing for Geneva. His appointment 'formalized the natural leadership which he had exerted among the godly' in the years before Elizabeth's accession.[63] By the time of Pullan's unexpected death in 1565 he had 'effectively taken Colchester for Protestantism. Speed and decisive action had enabled him to channel the anti-Catholic energies of the town into the creation of a specifically protestant identity.'[64] Pullan was succeeded by the Edinburgh-born James Calfhill, who established a strong working relationship with Colchester's common preacher, William Cole (possibly Thomas's brother), and with the town authorities, for the reformation of morals.[65] Calfhill's demise in 1570 at the age of only forty provides us with one of the most intriguing might-have-beens of Elizabethan churchmanship.[66] The first Elizabethan archdeacon of Middlesex was Alexander Nowell, swiftly elevated to the deanery of St Paul's after the death of William May, and his successor (January 1561) was the somewhat patrician figure of Thomas Watts (d. 1577), another Frankfurt exile who signed the 'new discipline' and one who also had Colchester connexions since his wife, Grace Cocke, was born there.[67]

[59] Collinson, *Grindal*, pp. 107–83.
[60] GL MS 9537/2.
[61] Collinson, *Grindal*, pp. 113–17.
[62] Cole's activities as archdeacon and as Parker's roving commissary in Essex and Suffolk are fully set out in Usher, 'The deanery of Bocking'.
[63] Collinson, *Grindal*, p. 115. For Pullan's short tenure in Colchester, see Byford, 'Birth of a protestant town', pp. 36–42.
[64] *Ibid.*, p. 42.
[65] Byford, 'Price of protestantism', pp. 164–9.
[66] See the entry by Brett Usher in *Oxford DNB*; and Usher, 'The deanery of Bocking', pp. 444, 447–9, 453–4.
[67] See the entry by Brett Usher in *Oxford DNB*.

Under this cohort of convinced radical leaders the protestant ethos rapidly began to spread through the county. Very early in the reign clerical exercises were introduced for the instruction of the 'weaker sort' of clergy, and by the eve of the vestiarian controversy these had in many places 'come to assume the shape of conferences organized for prophesying'.[68] In the archdeaconry of Essex they took place regularly in Rochford, Maldon, Chelmsford, Horndon-on-the-Hill and Brentwood.[69] The vestiarian controversy itself did little or nothing to deflect the progress of evangelization, in part because Bishop Grindal dissociated himself from Parker's methods as far as he dared and in part because the archbishop's recipe for ritual conformity, his 'Advertisements', virtually withered on the bough, being stoutly resisted by committed protestants both clerical and lay.[70] By 1570, moreover, Oxford and (more particularly) Cambridge had turned out a generation of young divinity students ideologically committed to the protestant cause. These had started to seek comfortable livings in which to deploy their energies and Essex proved a happy hunting ground. By the beginning of James's reign the average rectory theoretically yielded nearly £65 per annum from tithes and the average vicarage well over £43, figures which compare very favourably with, for example, neighbouring Suffolk and with Lincolnshire.[71] During a period of gradual inflation it may be hazarded that the rich diversity of Essex's titheable assets allowed the majority of incumbents to maintain a realistic income.

Grindal was succeeded as bishop of London in 1570 by Edwin Sandys, bishop of Worcester, who had been in exile at Strasburg and Zürich.[72] He had little hesitation in picking up where Grindal had left off. One of his earliest acts was to collate George Withers as archdeacon of Colchester in succession to James Calfhill on 11 October that year.[73] Withers had carried the vestiarian controversy from Oxford into Cambridge, much to the annoyance of Archbishop Parker,[74] and in 1567 crossed the channel to plead the nonconformist cause before Bullinger in Zurich and Beza in Geneva. He ended up in Heidelberg and, apparently with the full approval of the Elector Palatine Friedrich III ('the Pious'), delivered a doctoral dissertation in which he denied the right even of godly magistrates to interfere in ecclesiastical affairs. This diatribe incurred the wrath of Heidelberg's professor of medicine, Thomas Erastus, whose ringing response gave us the word 'Erastian'. If it is obvious that Withers must have moderated his views with some rapidity on his return to England, he was to preside at Colchester for twenty-five years (he resigned in 1595) as an *oculus episcopi* considerably more sympathetic to the aspirations of the 'moderate puritans' than his future diocesan, John Aylmer. Chapman and the Dedham members clearly felt that they could rely on his good offices as far as the

---

[68] Collinson, *EPM*, p. 171.

[69] LPL, MS 2003, fo. 12r.

[70] Collinson, *EPM*, p. 93.

[71] Christopher Hill, *Economic problems of the church from Archbishop Whitgift to the Long Parliament* (Oxford, 1956), p. 111.

[72] Sandys has never been accorded a full-scale biography, but see the entry by Patrick Collinson in *Oxford DNB*.

[73] Reg. Grindal, fo. 157r.

[74] *Parker Correspondence*, pp. 234, 236.

law allowed, although how much he actually knew about their meetings must remain a matter of conjecture.[75]

Although Sandys was thoroughly alarmed (and was made increasingly irascible) by the activities of Thomas Cartwright and his followers, he remained a fully-fledged evangelist. As archdeacon of Essex in succession to Thomas Cole he collated, on 10 July 1571, John Walker, one of those who, along with Edmund Chapman, had in 1570 destroyed the organ in Norwich cathedral.[76] Sandys and Walker were both firm that the prophesyings should be further encouraged and when Elizabeth first expressed her distrust of them in 1574 Sandys earnestly petitioned the privy council for their continuance. His diocese 'being at this time in good order and quiet' (a perhaps debatable claim), he feared that the 'chaunge of such profitable exercise . . . will breed further unquietnes than I shall be well able to staie'.[77] When in 1576 Elizabeth finally put her foot down, demanding that Grindal, newly elevated to Canterbury, convince her of their utility or else order their suppression, Sandys hastily solicited his archdeacons for their views. Replies from Watts and Withers unfortunately do not survive but Walker sent in an incredibly detailed set of answers to Sandys's anxious enquiries, thereby providing the most composite picture of clerical life in the rural parishes to survive from this period. He was able to reel off an impressive list of those who acted as moderators, all masters of art or else bachelors and doctors of divinity, including George Withers and his brother Fabian, vicar of All Saints and St Peter Maldon, John Freke, son of the bishop of Norwich, and, at Brentwood, William Fulke, now rector of neighbouring Great Warley.[78] This evidence gives the lie to the cynical assumption that the high-flyers of the Elizabethan regime were usually pluralist absentees who enjoyed the income from their benefices without doing anything in return for their emoluments. Rather, it points to a coterie of committed evangelists who, at least during the summer months, came together conscientiously to monitor the doings of, and further instruct, their less able brethren, in the process setting a pattern of local self-regulation which gives us some inkling as to how the conferences of Braintree and Dedham finally came into being.

Not the least of Walker's reasons for his passionate defence of prophesying was that many gentlemen, JPs 'and others as they may for the[ir] other necessarie business frequent the exercise & friendlie use the ministers whom they see do well'.[79] In other words, it was partly a question of social cohesion and Walker's portrait of his archdeaconry at this highly critical juncture shows us a society in the throes of transition. It appears to answer one of the questions already proposed: that the protestant ethic was not imposed from above but was rather, after 1559, a process of – what? Spontaneous combustion? Peer-group pressure? Increasingly widespread conviction? But it is true that there was a dramatic upturn in the quality of the Essex clergy during the 1570s – much more dramatic, in fact, than has been

[75] See 'Certain requests to be moved to D. Withers . . .', below, p. 82. For Withers see the entry in *Oxford DNB* by John Craig and Brett Usher.
[76] *Fasti*, I, 9.
[77] LPL, MS 2003, fo. 27r; 13 July 1574.
[78] *Ibid.*, fo. 12r; see also the almost equally informative report of David Kemp, archdeacon of St Albans, where exercises had been held once a month for the last sixteen years: *ibid.*, fos. 16r–18r.
[79] *Ibid.*, fo. 12r.

generally admitted – and that graduate clergy began settling into the rectories and vicarages of Essex in increasingly large numbers during the episcopate of Sandys. The biographical register printed below partially indicates the extent to which they had done so by 1582.

To what extent were the efforts of Grindal and Sandys helped by the lay patrons who had the primary responsibility for bringing likely candidates to the bishops' attention? After the death of John 16th earl of Oxford in 1562, the influence of the de Veres, emanating from their ancient seat of Castle Hedingham in the north of the county, was entirely eclipsed.[80] Thereafter there was no peer of the realm or landed magnate in Essex to rival the influence of Lord Rich. We have seen that under Edward VI he appeared in the guise of protestant evangelist in the Thames valley, but he had other livings to bestow in central Essex, clustered around his primary residence, (Little) Leighs Priory. At the beginning of the reign (November 1559) he gave the valuable living of High Ongar to Thomas Cole, newly appointed arch-deacon of Essex,[81] but by and large his few Elizabethan appointees were undistin-guished and/or short-lived. His son and heir Robert 2nd Lord Rich, head of the family for only fourteen years (1567–81), seems to have been converted to radical courses by his bastard brother Richard, the only one of the first lord's illegitimate children to be recognized in his will. In 1569 he appointed Edmund Barker to Thames-side Prittlewell, and Barker remained a staunch ritual nonconformist until his death in 1593.[82] In 1570 he preferred to Leigh John Bowden (d. 1584/5), who never fell foul of authority but clearly represented the early ideal of a conscientious reformed pastor: his bequests included a Geneva bible, 'my bible used daily in the house', Calvin's *Institutes*, Peter Martyr on Paul's epistles to the Romans and 'my great book of Acts and Monuments of the Church'.[83] In 1572 High Ongar went to William Tabor, STB, a future archdeacon of Essex Laurence Newman received Coggeshall in 1576 and Arthur Dent South Shoebury in 1580.[84]

The Riches developed a network of client gentry such as the Lawsons, the Butlers of Thoby, the Harrises and, most notably, the Barringtons of Hatfield Broad Oak,[85] but Sir Walter Mildmay, who had a modest estate at Danbury (to which parish he preferred George Withers in 1572),[86] never seems to have been part of it. Nor did the family exercise much influence within the county town, Chelmsford, despite the fact that its first Elizabethan incumbent, William Ireland (1561–71), was a returned Marian exile. It was the much more conservative figure of Sir Thomas Mildmay of

[80] His son Edward, the seventeenth earl, was a minor who after coming of age in 1571 systematically squandered his patrimony. See B. M. Ward, *The seventeenth earl of Oxford, 1550–1604* (London, 1928).
[81] Reg. Grindal, fo. 483v.
[82] *Ibid.*, fos. 151v, 274r.
[83] *Ibid.*, fo. 153v; LMA DL/C/358, fos. 328v–9r.
[84] Reg. Grindal, fos. 105v, 186r, 200r.
[85] For whom see *Barrington family letters 1628–1632*, ed. Arthur Searle (Camden Society, 4th series, vol. 28, 1983), introduction.
[86] Reg. Grindal, fo. 168v.

Moulsham (brother of Sir Walter) who dominated affairs: the crown had granted him the manor and advowson of the rectory at the beginning of the reign.[87]

Nor did the Rich interest penetrate into the north-west of the county, around Thaxted and Saffron Walden, close as they were to the university of Cambridge: the residual heirs of Lord Audley of Walden, the Howard family, held this corner for what would later be called a 'court' (pro-establishment) party against Rich's 'country' party: it was not the third Lord Rich but Thomas Howard, earl of Suffolk from 1603 and the builder of Audley End, to whom James I was to look to manage the affairs of the county.[88]

Elsewhere patterns of patronage are considerably more difficult to establish since where livings were not vested in the crown or at the collation of the bishop they were as likely as not to have remained in the hands of small local families whose reasons for presenting often had less to do with ideology than with obligations to friends and relatives. To that extent Essex was evangelized against some quite heavy odds.

Ardent protestant convictions did not necessarily lead to strident nonconformity but historians of the period have found it increasingly difficult to locate the elision. Were the strict provisions of the Book of Common Prayer the only yardstick of 'conformity' to the Elizabethan settlement or were there accommodations to be made?[89] It was a disaster for the Essex evangelists of the 1570s that the decision was for more than thirty years taken out of their hands by the cataclysmic events of 1576–7. Grindal, backed by the likes of Bishop Sandys and Archdeacon Walker, begged the queen not to order the suppression of the prophesyings. She remained adamant. Grindal refused to obey her and in April 1577 he was suspended from his metropolitical functions. Meanwhile Sandys had been confirmed as Grindal's successor at York (a nice irony, considering his known views) and the same palace revolution which had assuredly prompted Elizabeth's stand over the prophesyings – the spectacular rise of Sir Christopher Hatton – ensured that his successor in London was a man who had no doubts on the subject of 'conformity'. It was no more and no less than strict adherence to the terms of the 1559 settlement and the provisions of the prayer book.

John Aylmer had been passed over for a bishopric in 1559 upon his return from exile and since 1562, lacking an influential patron at court, had languished as arch-deacon of Lincoln. Now facing his seventh decade, he was catapulted into Fulham in March 1577 and within days woke up to find himself (if not, like Lord Byron, famous) certainly *de facto* primate of All England, for as dean of the southern province the bishop of London exercised metropolitical rights in the absence (or in this case suspension) of an archbishop of Canterbury. So matters continued until, following Grindal's death on 6 July 1583 (poignantly, perhaps, for the likes of

---

[87] In 1587 Richard Rogers described Chelmsford, his native town, as 'that doungehil of abhominacion': Knappen, *Two puritan diaries*, p. 61.

[88] Hunt, *Puritan moment*, p. 163.

[89] The debate was initiated by Lake in *Anglicans and puritans?* The most recent contribution is Kenneth Fincham, 'Clerical conformity from Whitgift to Laud' in *Conformity and orthodoxy in the English church, c.1560–1660* , ed. Peter Lake and Michael Questier (Woodbridge, 2000), pp. 125–58. See also Usher, 'The deanery of Bocking', pp. 453–5.

Leicester and Burghley, the thirtieth anniversary of that of Edward VI), John Whitgift was swiftly appointed to succeed him.

Aylmer was a man of considerable administrative ability who never learnt the real art of administration – that of sympathetic engagement with his subordinates.[90] He lost little time in imposing himself on the diocese – Dedham, as we shall see, was immediately put on notice of where his priorities lay – and by 1579 he was in full cry. He brought the hitherto self-regulating archdeaconry of St Albans, Hertfordshire, under much stricter episcopal control and kept a beady eye on the underfunded parishes of Colchester as well upon ecclesiastical developments in Maldon.[91] More damaging for the future of good relations between the bishop and his heterogeneous flock was the Rochford Hall affair of 1579–82. With the full approval of Robert 2nd Lord Rich and his bastard brother Richard, the unordained Robert Wright began conducting quasi-congregational meetings at the Hall in which he did not scruple to criticize the activities of the local clergy (who included Arthur Dent). Aylmer was forced to bide his time, observing that he was hardly in a position to send in a posse to extract Wright from a nobleman's household. The unexpected death of Lord Rich in February 1581 temporarily broke up the ménage. Wright went abroad, to be ordained by a presbyterian rite in Antwerp, but was back in Rochford by the summer of 1581. His new character as an ordained minister seems to have excited 'Dick' Rich to new heights of enthusiasm. In September he and his nephew Robert, the twenty-one-year-old 3rd Lord Rich, appeared at Fulham to solicit a preaching licence for Wright, and when Aylmer refused to grant one without further knowledge of his orders, 'Dick' Rich physically assaulted the bishop in his own study. This extraordinary incident led to a High Commission hearing which resulted in the imprisonment of both Dick Rich and Robert Wright.[92] Thereafter Aylmer was to conduct an increasingly bitter feud with Lord Rich but in the last analysis found himself outgunned by the unnegotiable circumstance that only weeks after the Fulham incident the young peer (financially, the most eligible bachelor in England) married Penelope Devereux, sister of Robert 2nd earl of Essex, and thus could count on the unassailable interest at court of Essex's step-father, the earl of Leicester.[93]

Was it for that reason that there follows a surprisingly strange lull in Aylmer's drive towards the eradication of nonconformity? His third episcopal visitation in 1583 was full of sound and fury but in the event signified very little. It was largely concerned with an investigation into preaching licences – in itself solid proof that the evangelization of the diocese was proceeding apace – but is otherwise remarkably uninstructive,[94] and that in the wake of the founding of the two Essex conferences.

Hard on its heels followed the elevation of Whitgift to Canterbury in September 1583 and the 'subscription crisis' of 1583–4, which, insofar as it directly concerned

[90] Like Sandys, Aylmer awaits a modern biographer. Meanwhile, see Brett Usher's entry in *Oxford DNB*, on which the following paragraphs are based, and Collinson, *EPM, passim*.
[91] For events in Maldon, see *BR*, pp. 209–14.
[92] For full details, see *BR*, pp. 269–72; also Collinson, *EPM*, pp. 343–4.
[93] See Brett Usher's entry on Robert 3rd Lord Rich in *Oxford DNB*.
[94] GL MS 9537/5; LMA DL/C/300 and 301.

the Dedham membership, is discussed in detail below.[95] Its first casualty was
Colchester's common preacher, George Northey, about whose plight the Dedham
members seem to have been little concerned, and its sacrificial victim within
London diocese was George Gifford, deprived of the vicarage of All Saints with
St Peter, Maldon, in the summer of 1584. Although Whitgift, Aylmer and their
episcopal allies had been harried into retreat by September 1584 the effect of the
subscription crisis had been to separate the sheep from the goats. Henceforth
Aylmer knew exactly in which of several directions to level his pistols.

But in truth, even at the height of the ideological warfare which marked the late
1580s, there were never more than sixty Essex clergymen who drew Aylmer's fire.
An act book of office was kept in being from 1584–6 (that is, *after* the official
closure of that created for the visitation of 1583) – it is thus a unique document
amongst the diocesan records – but, surprisingly, it contains only eight Essex cases
concerning subscription or ritual nonconformity.[96] It was closed on 1 July 1586, on
the eve of Aylmer's fourth visitation of the diocese.

It is a calamity for the present study that the office book for 1586 does not
survive, but we do know from John Field's papers that twenty-eight men were
suspended in the aftermath of the visitation for refusing the surplice and no fewer
than twenty of them are to be found in the *Biographical Register* printed below. The
list which is preserved probably emanated from the Braintree conference, since it is
headed by the names of its original members and their associates. Of the names
which follow, six were currently members of the Dedham meeting, whilst William
Negus had recently departed.[97]

At the same time, we enter a world of topsy-turvydom, for the prophesyings
which had toppled Archbishop Grindal had in 1585 been re-introduced in a modified form throughout the southern province by Archbishop Whitgift. In the convocation of 1586–7, detailed orders were enacted 'for the better increase of learning in
the inferior ministers' by the appointment of 'certain grave and learned preachers
who shall privately examine the diligence and view the notes of the said ministers,
assigning six or seven ministers as occasion shall require to every such preacher that
shall be next adjoining to him'.[98] Aylmer anticipated these orders during the 1586
visitation, its call book preserving lists of commissioners for each rural deanery. In
every case they are headed by the incumbent archdeacon, but many include leading
'nonconformists'. For the deaneries of Colchester and Tendring, one of the six
appointees was Robert Lewis, just carpeted for refusal of the surplice. Similarly,
two of the five for Lexden deanery were Edmund Chapman and Lawrence Newman.
If, for Rochford deanery, George Gifford seems to have been rather pointedly
omitted, Arthur Dent was not. In all, 188 Essex clergy were 'tied to the exercise' in
1586 but at least fifty-three of these were stipendiary curates, who appear to have

---

[95] See pp. xc–xcii.

[96] LMA DL/C/301 [paginated]: Thomas Tyrrell (pp. 113–14), Samuel Cottesford (pp. 138–9), Richard
Allison (pp. 185–6), Robert Wright (p. 272), William Ban(n)ar (pp. 308, 394–5), Laurence Newman
(p. 397), William Tunstall (pp. 456, 459, 463) and Thomas Carew (pp. 487–8).

[97] *Seconde parte*, II, 260–1. The twenty men who have entries in the *Biographical Register* appear in
this order: Gifford, Whiting, Hawden, Carr, Tunstall, Huckle, Negus, Rogers, Northey, Newman, Tey,
Parker, Farrar, Searle, Lewis, Cock(e), Beamont, Culverwell, Chapman, Knevett.

[98] Collinson, *EPM*, p. 171, quoting LPL, Register of Whitgift, I, fo. 131r; see also *EPM*, pp. 183–6.

been 'tied' whether they were competent or not.[99] During the 1589 visitation only forty-four men were specifically mentioned as undergoing exercises, ten of them stipendiary curates. Even more encouraging was the circumstance that no fewer than thirty-four men were ordered to seek certification from their archdeacon that they were competent to receive a diocesan preaching licence.[100]

Meanwhile the conferences were coming increasingly under threat. The somewhat mysterious deprivation in May 1587 of two members of the Braintree conference, William Tunstall of Great Totham and Giles Whiting of Panfield, may indicate that the authorities knew considerably more about it than they ever discovered about Dedham. In March 1588, however, Chapman came into serious collision with Aylmer at Fulham. John Field died the same month and the earl of Leicester in September, whilst Aylmer's fifth episcopal visitation in July 1589 may perhaps be construed as an exercise in nailing the lid on the coffin of the conference movement – Ezekiel Culverwell came under particular pressure – and may in part have paved the way for the star chamber trials of 1590/1 which marked the death of 'political puritanism' in England for the rest of Elizabeth's reign.

It is virtually impossible to follow the Essex evangelists into that final Elizabethan decade since, with the exception of the ordination and vicar general's books, most of the diocesan records have perished.[101] Yet our final glimpse of Aylmer's episcopate, as advanced protestantism 'returned to the parishes', presents an encouraging picture. He conducted his last visitation in the summer of 1592 and thirty-seven of the listed preachers are described as *concionator notus*. These included not only members of the hierarchy like Richard Bancroft and Archdeacon Theophilus Aylmer of London, the bishop's son, but also several of the nonconformists so regularly pursued during the 1580s: Stephen Beamont, Richard Rogers, George Northey and William Tey. Altogether, throughout the whole diocese (excluding the City) only 146 incumbents (including all fifty-six absentees) were not listed as holding a preaching licence and only twenty-nine seem to have been tied to the exercises.[102] The radicals had lost the battle for further reformation of the Church of England but they had perhaps gained a more subtle victory.

East Anglia: the diocese of Norwich under Bishops Parkhurst and Freke

According to a generalization repeated in many a textbook, the protestant reformation took precocious hold in East Anglia. Factors often mentioned include the traffic between East Anglian ports and the Netherlands and north-west Germany, especially in cloth, the immigration into Norwich and other places of Dutch protestants, and the close vicinity of Cambridge University, which sent so many of its clerical products into East Anglian livings. But this broad-brush approach is of limited use in understanding the complex and varied religious scene in the early Elizabethan diocese of Norwich.

In Suffolk, the ecological differences between the cornfields of the western division of the county, around Bury St Edmunds, the heavy loams of 'High Suffolk'

---

99   GL MS 9537/6, fos 175r–81v.
100   GL MS 9537/7, fos 14v–91r, *passim*.
101   For an overview of the decade, see Collinson, *EPM*, pp. 432–47.
102   GL MS 9537/8, *passim*.

in the centre, famous for its hard cheese, and towards the east coast the lighter soils, the 'Sandlings', were pronounced, and they were reflected in the ecclesiastical situation.[103] An unusually large number of the eastern parishes were impropriate and worth very little. In the 1560s, there was in the whole of those eastern margins only one active preacher, an itinerant layman called John Laurence whom the clergy were ordered by the bishop to admit to their pulpits, *faute de mieux*. Laurence was a kind of proto-John Wesley in these coastal parishes for much of a long life, and became a folk memory.[104] The isolated coastal half-hundred of Lothingland, the hinterland of Lowestoft to the north-east, was a notorious catholic enclave, more like parts of Lancashire than East Anglia, to the considerable concern of the government.[105] Ipswich, of course, was another matter, and although its parishes too were chronically under-endowed, the town was hiring its own preachers from the beginning of the reign.[106] In the west, Bury contained a prominent godly protestant element, but it seems to have been outnumbered and outweighed by conservative conformists and church papists, some of whom were attracted to the neighbouring parish of Hawstead, where the musical tradition of the lost world of English catholicism was still kept alive.[107] The conversion of some of the leading gentry of West Suffolk to a distinctively progressive protestantism meant that, from the early 1570s, many parishes where they enjoyed the patronage were taken over by preaching ministers from Cambridge.[108] Of sixty-four Suffolk ministers who resisted subscription to Whitgift's articles in 1584, twenty-nine of the beneficed clergy in the group were based in the parishes around Bury, as against only seventeen in the remainder of the county.[109]

Norfolk, as always, was another place. With not far short of a thousand parishes, forty of them in Norwich, it was by no means a protestant stronghold; on the whole, the reverse, with many of its leading gentry favourable to the old ways. When catholics began to be formally listed as 'recusants', the diocese of Norwich was found to contain the largest number in the whole province of Canterbury outside London, with no less than 143 recusant households, mostly gentry, detected in Norfolk alone.[110] Pockets of protestantism tending to puritanism confronted clusters of catholics. There were few regions of Elizabethan England with such an acute awareness of religious polarization. As one recusant put it, with Bishop Freke vainly trying to establish some kind of even-handed Anglicanism, 'the state could not longe stand thus; it wold ether to Papistry or to Puritanisme'. Chief Justice Christopher Wray, who rode the East Anglian assize circuit in Freke's time, commented on the

103 Diarmaid MacCulloch, *Suffolk and the Tudors: politics and religion in an English county 1500–1600* (Oxford, 1986), ch. 1, 'Alternative communities'.
104 *Ibid.*, pp. 189–90; *Parkhurst,* p. 260.
105 MacCulloch, *Suffolk and the Tudors,* pp. 212–15.
106 Diarmaid MacCulloch and John Blatchly, 'Pastoral provision in the parishes of Tudor Ipswich', *Sixteenth Century Journal,* 22 (1991), 457–74; Patrick Collinson, *The religion of protestants. The church in English society 1559–1625* (Oxford, 1982), pp. 170–7.
107 Craig, *Reformation, politics and polemics,* pp. 98–9.
108 Collinson, *EPM,* p. 128; Collinson, *Religion of protestants,* pp. 153–64; Collinson, 'PCM', ch. 9, 'Puritanism and the gentry in Suffolk, 1575–1585: a case-study'.
109 *Seconde parte,* I, 243–4; MacCulloch, *Suffolk and the Tudors,* pp. 38–9.
110 A. Hassell Smith, *County and court. Government and politics in Norfolk 1558–1603* (Oxford, 1974), pp. 201–2.

multitude of suits and great disorder for religion. 'There is no county in England so far out of order as these two.'[111]

One reason for persistent religious conservatism in the region was the long shadow cast by the last vigorous catholic bishop of Norwich, Richard Nix (1501–35), and the political shadow of Thomas Howard, duke of Norfolk, who until his fall from grace and execution (1570–2) regarded East Anglia as practically his personal fief. Norfolk was not formally a catholic (John Foxe the martyrologist lived in his household), but many of his gentry clients were, especially in Suffolk, including, conspicuously, his chief agent, Sir Thomas Cornwallis, an energetic and attractive individual, not least to the queen herself. As for the church, throughout the 1560s its machinery remained in the hands of catholic or crypto-catholic survivors of the world of Bishop Nix and John Reve, the last abbot of Bury St Edmunds.[112] These included Dr Miles Spencer, Nix's chancellor and archdeacon of Sudbury (who enjoyed virtual independence from the see of Norwich), 'a monstrous pre-Reformation anachronism' and an obstacle in the path of reform down to his death in 1570.[113] Bishop Parkhurst complained that all his archdeacons were 'popish lawyers or unlearned papists'.[114]

But when Andrew Perne, the notoriously Janus-faced master of Peterhouse and leading figure in Elizabethan Cambridge, referred to Norwich as 'that great disordered diocess', he spoke as a crypto-catholic native of Norfolk, and it was not catholicism he was complaining of.[115] William Cecil, a staunch protestant, had earlier referred to the diocese in similar terms, perhaps prompted by the queen's sense of outrage when she went on progress in East Anglia in August 1561. 'The bishop of Norwich is blamed even of the best sort for his remissness in ordering his clergy. He winketh at schismatics and anabaptists, as I am informed.'[116] It was symptomatic of the religiously polarized condition of the region that there were pockets of very hot protestantism, some of them along the Stour valley, including the village of Bures, the scene of particularly drastic acts of iconoclasm in 1559; and it was from hard by Bures that Cecil expressed his concern to Matthew Parker, who had only recently left that very area to become archbishop. But the hottest of protestant hot spots was created in his own cathedral by the bishop of whom Cecil was so critical, the most evangelical of all Elizabethan bishops, the veteran of Swiss exile, John Parkhurst.

Parkhurst was a man of letters, a good humanist, and tutor to John Jewel in Oxford. But he was no politician and a weak administrator who found it hard to confront the conservative Howard ascendancy full frontally, so that even when invited by the privy council to provide his own critique of the Norfolk and Suffolk justices, he failed to make use of the opportunity and was clearly anxious not to rock the local political boat.[117] On repeated occasions he was criticized by the privy

---

[111] *Ibid.*, pp. 201, 204.

[112] MacCulloch, *Suffolk and the Tudors,* chs. 2, 4 and 5, *passim.*

[113] *Ibid.*, p. 164.

[114] *Parkhurst*, p. 27.

[115] Patrick Collinson, 'Perne the turncoat: an Elizabethan reputation', in *idem, Elizabethan essays* (London and Rio Grande, Ohio, 1994), p. 181.

[116] *Parker Correspondence*, pp. 148–9.

[117] Mary Bateson, ed., 'A collection of original letters from the bishops to the privy council, 1564', *Camden Miscellany,* IX, Camden Society n.s. 53 (1893), 48, 58–9; Smith, *County and court,* pp. 34–5; MacCulloch, *Suffolk and the Tudors,* pp. 85–6.

council for failing to deal more effectively, judicially and administratively, with the problem of catholicism. Instead, towards 1570, Parkhurst seems to have decided to make Norwich cathedral, hitherto 'a cosy nest for neuters',[118] a powerhouse of protestant evangelism, compensating for the dismal fact that only ten per cent of his diocesan clergy were preachers, which is not to say that even they were all 'forward' protestants.[119] Hence his stacking of the cathedral chapter with preaching prebendaries and other clergy: George Gardiner, Thomas Roberts, John Walker, Robert Johnson – and our future Dedham trio, Edmund Chapman, Richard Crick and Richard Dowe, strongly supported from outside the close by John More of St Andrew's parish, the celebrated 'apostle of Norwich'.

The Apostle More deserves separate attention. He was a northerner from Westmorland, like John Knewstub of Suffolk, which may be significant – perhaps a blunt voice and style not mortgaged to local political interests. More was otherwise a product of Christ's College, Cambridge, where he was a contemporary of his Norwich colleague Thomas Roberts (who was Welsh) and of Edward Dering, the exemplar of the pastoral strain of Elizabethan puritanism.[120] Such was More's standing among the committed protestants of Norfolk that in their perception he was of more significance than any bishop. This is strongly implicit in the sermon preached to the Norfolk bench, which Nicholas Bound, the Suffolk preacher who later married More's widow and inherited his pulpit of St Andrew's, included in a posthumously published collection of sermons, dateable from internal evidence to 1572–3, and from which we have already heard.[121]

> I can not preach to the whole land, but for the discharge of my conscience I desire you, good brethren, so many of you as have any voyces in place and parliament where these things may be reformed, consecrate your tongues to the Lord in the behalfe of your poor brethren. . . .

According to Bound, these were but three of the 'many hundred sermons, or rather certaine thousandes' which More had delivered in Norfolk over a period of twenty years, preaching every day of the week and three or four times on Sundays.[122]

We catch occasional glimpses of More preaching and catechizing in gentry households, particularly up at Stiffkey on the coast, where Nathaniel Bacon, one of the sons of the Lord Keeper, Sir Nicholas Bacon, was busily creating a small godly commonwealth,[123] and negotiating with gentry patrons in the placing of preachers in their parishes. This stretegy went badly wrong when More, having persuaded the wife of Sir Thomas Knyvett to appoint to the living of Westhall his offsider in the ministry of St Andrew's, Samuel Greenaway, Greenaway proved too radical, which

---

[118] *Parkhurst,* p. 44.
[119] MacCulloch, *Suffolk and the Tudors,* p. 189.
[120] Collinson, *Godly people,* pp. 294–8.
[121] See above, p. xxvii.
[122] John More, *Three godly and fruitful sermons* (Cambridge, 1594), Epistle and pp. 66–9.
[123] Collinson, 'PCM', pp. 316, 688. See *The papers of Nathaniel Bacon of Stiffkey,* I, *1556–1577,* ed. A. Hassell Smith, G. M. Baker and R. W. Kenny (Norfolk Record Society, XLVI, 1979); II, *1578–1585,* and III, *1586–1595,* ed. A. Hassell Smith and G. M. Baker (Norfolk Record Society, XLIX and LIII, 1983 and 1988); IV, *1596–1602,* ed. V. Morgan, J. Key and B. Taylor (Norfolk Record Society, LXIV, 2000).

sent the Knyvetts in search of a more conformable minister, who proved difficult to find.[124] On another occasion, More sent a minister to be vetted by Bacon. 'He is a very godlie mann and therefore I lyke hym better.'[125] One of the most popular of catechisms, *A briefe and necessary instruction*, intended primarily for household use, which went through at least fifteen editions between 1572 and 1614, was often ascribed to Edward Dering but was primarily the work of More and known in Norfolk as 'Mr More's Catechism'.[126]

William Burton, a Norwich minister who migrated to Bristol, has left on record a memorable description of civic religious life in Norwich, perhaps towards the end of the Parkhurst years and before the advent of the unsympathetic Bishop Freke. 'Oh the heavenly harmony and sweet amitie that then was amongst you from the highest to the lowest! The Magistrates and Ministers imbracing and seconding one to another, and the common people affording due reverence and obedience to them both.' According to Burton, addressing the mayor and aldermen in a dedicatory epistle, 'no matters of weight were usually concluded in your common assemblies for the good of your citie, before you had first consulted with your grave and godlie Preachers', to whose sermons the magistrates resorted daily. Burton's account includes a description of More and Roberts as 'presidents, or leaders of an armie'.[127] More's St Andrew's was virtually a civic church, as became clear in 1607, when official attempts were made to remove certain stately seats, recently erected, 'in which seates', the parishioners explained, 'the ministers of the city were placed in one roumthe, and in another, next them, the aldermen.' The early morning sermons at St Andrew's earned for their devotees the name of 'Saint Andrewes birds'.[128]

The result of Parkhurst's attempt to turn his cathedral into a citadel of godliness was polarization, even in the cathedral close itself: an act of remarkable iconoclasm in the destruction of the organ and 'other outrages', perpetrated by Thomas Fowle, George Gardiner, John Walker (later archdeacon of Essex) and Edmund Chapman, which earned stinging rebukes from the queen and the earl of Leicester,[129] and much disorderly preaching, which brought Perne to the cathedral to deliver a sermon against John More.[130] Meanwhile Gardiner and Roberts fell out over who had the right to be archdeacon of Norwich. Parkhurst sided with Roberts, 'my deare friend' and his not particularly competent steward, while the queen, through Leicester, ordered him to respect her mandate in favour of Gardiner, an old protégé of Leicester who, following the onslaught on the organ, which Gardiner had led, now leant towards the side of order and conformity.[131] Before the end of this eventful year of 1573 the queen and Leicester had made Gardiner dean of Norwich, and when

[124] *Ibid.*, pp. 658–9.
[125] *Ibid.*, p. 881.
[126] Collinson, *Godly people*, p. 298.
[127] Desiderius Erasmus, tr. William Burton, *Seven dialogues* (1606), Epistle.
[128] Collinson, *Religion of protestants*, pp. 141–5.
[129] Ralph Houlbrooke, *Church courts and the people during the English reformation 1520–1570* (Oxford, 1979), p. 252; PRO SP 12/73/68; Magdalene College, Cambridge, Pepysian Library, MS 'Papers of State', II, 633–40.
[130] Collinson, *Elizabethan essays*, p. 181n.
[131] *Parkhurst*, pp. 37–42, 193, 197–200, 202–9.

Chapman and others 'inveighed against the mannor of the singing' in the cathedral, he 'verey pithelye confuted' their arguments.[132]

And then came the affair of the prophesyings, a dry run for the queen's confrontation with Archbishop Grindal in 1576–7. Parkhurst had given his blessing to the exercises in Norwich, Bury and other parts of his diocese. But in 1574 he (and presumably the other bishops) received a royal command, via Archbishop Parker, 'to suppresse those vayne prophecienges'. His disingenuous response was to ask whether only 'vain' exercises were to be put down. Scarcely had Parker told him not to be so pedantic ('it is pitye we shold showe any vanitye in our obedience') than a letter arrived from Bishop Sandys of London and three privy councillors (Sir Thomas Smith, Sir Walter Mildmay, Sir Francis Knollys) advising him to restore the exercises 'generally', assuming that they had been threatened by 'some not well mynded towardes true religion and the knowledge of God'.[133] In this dispensation, the right hand not only did not know what the left hand was doing but often chose to be ignorant.

And then Parkhurst (and Parker) died, allowing the Norwich preachers to reinvent the cathedral prophesying on a presbyterian basis. The powers that were knew that something had to be done about Norwich. Parker had favoured the dean of Westminster, Gabriel Goodman, who was as far to the religious right as a conforming Elizabethan churchman could get. He was 'too severe' for London, but well equipped for Norwich, given his 'sad and sure governance in conformity'. Parker's short list had also included John Piers and John Whitgift, two future archbishops. Goodman, with Bishop John Jewel, had been charged with persuading Cornwallis to conform, and with partial success.[134] But in the event the choice proved to be either inspired or maverick. The lot fell on the bishop of Rochester, Edmund Freke, hitherto a moderate who had supported the prophesyings, but who had conservative East Anglian connexions. He was not given a free hand, but (as with John Aylmer in London at about the same time) rather a mandate to suppress both kinds of nonconformity, especially that of the puritans. The result was the most disturbed ten years in the religious history of East Anglia, and a kind of precondition for the existence of the Dedham conference.

Freke was not as tough as he needed to be. The gossip in Norfolk was that he was a Proudie of a bishop, totally ruled by his domineering wife.[135] In order to deliver what the queen expected of him he had to find a political affinity, which, since 'Anglicanism' had no real existence, could only consist of catholics and crypto-papists such as Cornwallis. In Freke's primary visitation of 1576 there was a wholesale suspension of the Norwich preachers, including More and Roberts. According to a puritan source, the effect was to silence nineteen or twenty exercises of preaching and catechizing in the city. This was the beginning of a *cause célèbre* which lasted for four years, with the privy council in London pursuing a pro-preachers, anti-Freke line diametrically opposed to the ecclesiastical policy of the queen. Things came to a head in the summer of 1578, when a hastily arranged and

---

[132] *Ibid.*, pp. 254–5.

[133] *Ibid.*, pp. 235, 236, 241, 242–3, 245. See Collinson, *Grindal,* pp. 235–6; Collinson, *EPM,* pp. 191–2.

[134] *Parker Correspondence,* pp. 360, 473, 476, 477; MacCulloch, *Suffolk and the Tudors,* pp. 97–8; Julia Merritt, 'Westminster Abbey, 1558–1630', *JEH,* LII (2001), 627–8.

[135] PRO SP 15/25.

circuitous royal progress through East Anglia led to the suspension and even imprisonment of many catholic and crypto-catholic justices, and the knighting of Suffolk's five leading protestant gentlemen, including Sir Robert Jermyn and Sir John Higham, strong supporters of the Bury preachers and, in the 1580s, of the Dedham conference, ardent protestants who had inherited their estates and dignities from catholic fathers. This event, in which Elizabeth was manipulated, to say no more, proved a watershed in East Anglian political history, for the puritan ascendancy established in 1578 would endure far into the seventeenth century.[136]

This political reversal was also intended as a snub for Freke, whom Sir Thomas Heneage, no puritan, called 'the foolish bishop' for picking a feud with 'divers most zealous and loyal gentlemen of Suffolk and Norfolk'. While in Norwich, the privy council forced Freke to accept a promise of limited conformity from the suspended ministers, which it was hoped would provide a model for other places. Two years later, Freke tried to slip out of this deal, and earned a sharp reminder from the council that he ought to handle the preachers 'as charitably as becometh a man of his profession'. More and Roberts undertook to tread the line of the 'somewhat conformable'. But it must have been at this point that our Dedham trio, Chapman, Crick and Dowe, shook the dust of Norwich off their feet and headed for the Stour valley.[137]

They left behind a precociously advanced presbyterian movement in Norwich. In 1583, 175 citizens 'with infinite more in this shire of Norfolke', were to petition the queen for the establishment of presbyterian church government, a request which is unique among all the many petitions subscribed by laymen in the puritan cause. By 'removing the doctrine of Antichrist and planting the doctrine of Christ', Elizabeth had done half the job required of her.

> So it might seem good to your highnes to fulfill up your happie work, by removing the government of Antichrist allso, with all his archprelates, and all his Court keepers, which keepe not the lordes Courts, by planting that holie Eldership, the verie senew of Christ's Church . . . ; and by removing the dumbe ministerie, that horrible evill, which filleth hell paunch with the soules of the people.[138]

The signatories are all named and would repay analysis. How many were members of the ruling élite? Or did they, as with similar petitioners from Bury St Edmunds, represent the broad middle of Norwich society?[139] How many were parishioners of St Andrew's?

Towards 1580 the battleground shifted to Bury St Edmunds, the scene of notorious 'stirs' which lasted for years.[140] Bury had hitherto contrived to remain at peace with itself, the four hundred or so card-carrying protestants, those 'which

---

[136] MacCulloch, *Suffolk and the Tudors,* pp. 195–6; Zillah Dovey, *An Elizabethan progress* (Stroud, 1996); Collinson, *Religion of protestants,* pp. 153–64.

[137] Collinson, *EPM,* pp. 203–4. A fuller account will be found in Collinson, 'PCM', pp. 313–19.

[138] *Seconde parte,* I, 157–60.

[139] Craig, *Reformation, politics and polemics,* pp. 91–5.

[140] Accounts of the Bury stirs include Collinson, 'PCM', pp. 860–930; MacCulloch, *Suffolk and the Tudors,* pp. 198–209, and, more fully, in MacCulloch's article, 'Catholic and puritan in Elizabethan Suffolk: a county community polarises', *Archiv fur Reformationsgeschichte,* 72 (1981), 232–89. The latest account, which brings the townsmen of various persuasions fully into focus, is in Craig, *Reformation, politics and polemics,* ch. 4.

have allwaies stood with the gospell', perhaps ten per cent of the population, co-operating in the management of affairs with the more conservatively inclined.[141] That was now to change. The disputes were kaleidoscopic in their variety. They had to do with control of the Bury parishes and preachers: a conflict of religious and moral jurisdiction between the bishop's commissary and the local puritan gentry who in the absence of a corporation aspired to run the town; factional infighting among the most prominent townsmen along ideological lines, above all between the two magistrates resident in the town, the conformist Thomas Andrews, who shared the outlook of the conservative oligarchy who controlled the guildhall feoffment, a corporation in embryo, and the puritan Thomas Badby, an intruder who lived ostentatiously in the grounds of the abbey, where he entertained the queen in 1578; and a struggle of some complexity involving the bishop, the puritan justices, the privy council which arbitrated rather one-sidedly in favour of the justices, and the judges riding the East Anglian circuit, Edmund Anderson and Christopher Wray, who proved to be aggressively anti-puritan. Several of the West Suffolk preachers were hauled before the assizes along with common criminals, and in some cases imprisoned. When a delegation of gentlemen, including seven knights and headed by the lord lieutenant, Lord North, waited on the judges, asking them to 'handell trifling matters the more kindly' for their sakes, they were humiliated, and the preachers were allegedly prosecuted even more severely. A vivid edge was given to the stirs by the presence in and around Bury, and in some strength, of radical separatist puritans, 'Brownists', their activities including the scandalous inscription of words from the Book of Revelation, intended as criticism of the queen's lukewarm religious policy, around the royal arms in St Mary's church. At the summer assizes of 1583, two of the separatists were executed. Loose words were uttered here and there in the county that it would be a good thing if the preachers too were hanged.

But the headline story in all this was the credit of the puritan JPs and their preachers, the very future of that alliance of 'ministry and magistracy' which would be so famous a feature of public life in seventeenth-century Suffolk. The victory of 1578 had to be secured, and for a time it looked as if it might be reversed. Jermyn and Higham were removed from the commission of the peace, and Jermyn suffered the added indignity of being made to serve on a common jury. Their suspension lasted for years and it was a nonsense, since in those same years the pair served as knights of the shire in parliament, and both were appointed deputy lieutenants and muster masters. As for Bishop Freke, he was worn down and worn out by the Bury battle royal and towards the end of 1584 successfully petitioned his transfer to the quieter see of Worcester. He was succeeded by Edmund Scambler, a veteran of the Marian exile and the secret protestant congregation in Marian London. Scambler was by now elderly, complacent, and content to leave the hotbed of the archdeaconry of Sudbury to John Still, the future bishop of Bath and Wells, a fellow-traveller with the puritans.

Such was the background to an extraordinary conference held at John Knewstub's parish of Cockfield, eight or nine miles to the south-east of Bury, which we know about from one of the letters written to John Field which came into the hands of Richard Bancroft, to be exploited in his *exposé* of 1593, *Daungerous positions*. The

[141] Craig, *Reformation, politics and polemics*, pp. 88–114; 92.

letter was written on 16 May by Oliver Pigge, who was serving the parish of Rougham on behalf of William Tey. Pigge's own part in the Bury stirs (a quarrel with the lord of the manor, Robert Drury) was a prominent one, and he would spend time in Bury gaol in 1583. Pigge reported an assembly of sixty ministers 'appointed out of Essex, Cambridgeshire and Norfolk' which had met on 8 May, 'there to confer of the Common Book what might be tolerated, and what necessarily to be refused in every point of it; apparel, matter, form, days, fasting, injunctions etc.' 'Our meeting was appointed to be kept very secretly', Pigge went on (but how could the presence of so many ministers in a small village be kept secret, and where did they all stay?), 'and to be made known to none.' He added: 'Concerning the meeting, I hope all things were so proceeded in as you your self would like of, as well for reverence to other brethren, as for other matters. I suppose before this time some of the company have told you by word, for that was permitted unto you.'[142]

Five months later it was decided to set up what we know as the Dedham conference. It is reasonably safe to assume that the prime impetus came from Dr Edmund Chapman, who was in Dedham no later than November 1577.

iv. The Town of Dedham[143]

Dedham, which lies on the river Stour, marking the frontier between Essex and Suffolk, is the last point where the river can be safely forded, a mile downstream from Strat-ford (the ford of the street), where the road from Colchester to Ipswich crosses, and a couple of miles upstream from already tidal Flat-ford, indelibly associated with chocolate-box images of *The Haywain* and Willie Lot's Cottage. Today Dedham is a picturesque tourist destination, the heart of 'Constable Country', and a dormitory for Colchester and the University of Essex, just outside its walls. But Dedham's bucolic serenity is deceptive. In the sixteenth century this was a busy industrial as well as market town of some 200 to 250 households (which suggests a population of 1,200 or so), in which two thirds of the inhabitants who were in employment worked in some capacity or other in the production of cloth. The High Street is, as estate agents tend to say, no less deceptive. The Georgian and Victorian façades of many of the houses disguise the fact that these were the small mansions of the richer Dedham clothiers four hundred years ago.

If in the sixteenth century you were coming down into Dedham and its vale from the high ground to the south, the road called the Kings Way would take you across Dedham Heath, with woods to your right, both essential elements in the local economy, and you would notice that many poor and flimsy cottages had recently been erected on the heath. In the seventeenth century it would be noted that 'we maie builde our houses, and let them fall, at our willes', but that was to assume that

---

[142] Bancroft, *Daungerous positions*, p. 68.
[143] It would not have been possible to provide this account of Elizabethan Dedham without recourse to A. R. Pennie, 'The evolution of puritan mentality in an Essex cloth town: Dedham and the Stour valley 1560–1640' (unpublished Ph.D thesis, University of Sheffield, 1990). But see also Gerald H. Rendall, *Dedham in history: feudal, industrial and ecclesiastical* (Colchester, 1937), which is written with the advantage of grass-roots local knowledge, but somewhat patchy in its coverage. See also C. C. Thornton, 'Dedham', in *VCH Essex*, X, 154–86.

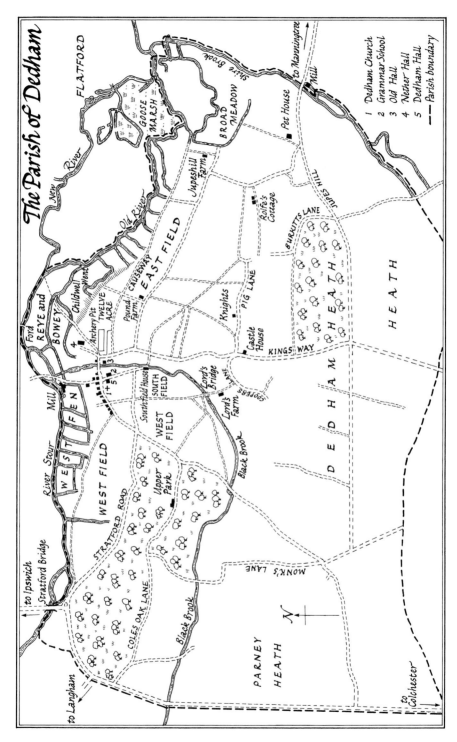

Map 2 The parish of Dedham.

no bricks were involved in the construction.[144] Soon lanes would lead off to right and left, one, populated by cottagers, called Pig Lane (compare Hog Lane in neighbouring East Bergholt), but dominated by one of the more imposing clothiers' houses, Castle House. A quarter of a mile on, you would encounter, to the other side of the Kings Way, Southfields, the grandest house in Dedham, a small version of a gentry manor house with courtyard and entrance gatehouse. If you had arrived in the 1580s you might have chosen to put up there, for Southfields was briefly an inn before being sold to the clothier Simon Fenn in 1594. You would now be surrounded by the three open fields of the town, two consisting of meadowland, the third, East Field, divided into cultivated strips. Soon you would come to the High Street, running at right angles, and, if you arrived on a Tuesday, crammed with all the bustle of a market: cloth, animals, and God knows what else. You might be disappointed to find only two inns, but three more licences were granted in 1589, 1592 and 1600. By 1608 there were five inns, a disorderly house having been closed down in 1604.[145] Ahead of you, vestiges of the strong monastic connexions of the town before the reformation (the priories of Butley (male) and Campsey (female), both in Suffolk), two fish ponds and, on the river, a mill, a flour mill which had doubled up since the thirteenth century for the fulling of cloth; to the right, the Archery Pit where Elizabethan schoolboys were still encouraged to shoot, as volunteers did, with different weapons, in the 1914–18 War.

But by this time your attention would be commanded, to your left, by the magnificence of Dedham church, a monument to this day to the exuberant and ostentatious piety of the last generations before the reformation.[146] The rebuilding of the church had begun in 1492 and much was complete by 1500, although it was only in 1519 that Dedham acquired the ultimate status symbol of any ambitious early Tudor town: a lordly and crenellated tower. And it was as late as the 1530s that the north porch, a little theatre for weddings, was constructed. Here were what Marxists used to call internal contradictions. Dedham rectory, which had been appropriated to Butley priory, became annexed to the duchy of Lancaster in the mid-sixteenth century and the vicarage was so poorly endowed that in the early years of Elizabeth it stood vacant for years. When ministers arrived to staff it, they preached a protestant gospel which cried out against the purposes for which the church had been designed; or shall we say that the stones cried out against them?

But there were internal contradictions in the Stour valley long before the Elizabethan preachers turned up in Dedham. If Dedham managed to complete its steeple, East Bergholt did not, perhaps a failure of conviction, and to this day the East Bergholt bells, in their ground-level bell cage, are an object of curiosity for tourists. Although thinly documented, there was clearly a pre-reformation tradition of heretical, Lollard, dissent in the valley. In 1532 there was a notable act of illegal iconoclasm, when three men of Dedham and a man from East Bergholt walked on a moonlit night all the way to Dovercourt, a distance of ten miles, where they burned a famous cross and object of pilgrimage, the rood of Dovercourt, making their way home by the light of the flames. Three of the four were hanged. It is thought that this

---

[144] Rendall, *Dedham in history*, p. 33.
[145] Pennie, 'The evolution of puritan mentality', p. 63.
[146] Duffy, *Stripping of the altars, passim*.

may have been intended as an act of revenge for the burning in Norwich of a celebrated if not yet quite protestant heretic, Thomas Bilney, who though a learned Cambridge scholar had his links with the Lollards.[147] In Mary's reign there was a sizeable cell of heretical dissent in Dedham, conventicles and 'schismatic sermons and preachings', involving a husbandman, a clothier, a tailor and twenty others.[148] This was on the interface of old Lollardy and new protestantism. However, it is probably a mistaken perspective to see Elizabethan puritanism in the Vale of Dedham as the lineal descendant of pre-reformation Lollardy. The protestant clothiers and other worthies who turned Dedham and other churches against all architectural logic into lecture rooms were the sons and grandsons of the devout catholics who had erected and adorned those very churches.

Legally, Dedham consisted of three manors, Dedham Hall, Netherhall (the property of Campsey priory before the dissolution) and Faites-and-Wades. But by the sixteenth century there was no longer a resident lord of any of the manors. Dedham Hall, hard by the church, belonged to the duchy of Lancaster, and the duke of Lancaster in the late sixteenth century, Queen Elizabeth, did not choose to live there. Indeed, the house lay in ruins. This manor was farmed by Thomas Seckford, another absentee, for Seckford was a man of some consequence (he was a Master of Requests), who had built for himself a magnificent house in Ipswich called Great Place, besides another house in his native Woodbridge.[149] So Dedham conformed to the model of the wood-pasture settlement, which was not effectively manorial, or feudal, but was looked after by its own inhabitants, whose places in the local pecking order were determined by their wealth and 'credit', in contemporary parlance, the 'ancients' of the town.

But this is not say that the institution of the manor was extinct. On the contrary, the courts leet to which the tenants paid suit attended to many matters of common concern which would later become the responsibility of parish councils. The byelaws and customs of Dedham, as codified in the seventeenth century, and enforceable only in the leet court of Dedham manor, include the following provisions: no-one was to make hay before Midsummer Day (a fine of £1); pigs were to be controlled in public places (a fine of 4d); contamination of the common water supply carried a fine of £2; exceeding the allowed numbers of cows on the commons, £1; keeping ferrets for any purpose other than for hunting rabbits on one's own property, half a mark.[150] It is a good question how these byelaws related to the puritanically motivated 'orders' for the town of Dedham, drawn up and agreed to in the days of the Dedham conference.[151] What can perhaps be said is

---

[147] Foxe, *A & M* [1563], pp. 1030–1. The story in Foxe is illustrated with artistic licence by showing the three suspended from one scaffold, whereas they were in fact hanged in three different places. And in the bottom left-hand corner the Dovercourt image of Christ is shown engulfed in flames. It appears to be somewhat larger than life-size, with the label above the head with the crown of thorns reading not INRI but IHS: rare evidence of what countless images of Christ on the 'rood' would have looked like.

[148] ERO, QSR 2/15, 25 July, 3 and 4 Philip and Mary.

[149] John Blatchly, 'Thomas Seckford's Great Place: a lost Ipswich Tudor town house', in Carole Rawcliffe *et al.* (ed.), *Counties and communities. Essays on East Anglian history presented to Hassell Smith* (Norwich, 1996), pp. 203–12.

[150] Rendall, *Dedham in history*, pp. 33–6.

[151] See pp. 124–30 below.

that the court leet and its jurisdiction were not held to be adequate in providing a
sufficiently 'godly' regime.

There were no large land holdings in Dedham and, unlike some other towns and
villages in the region (for example, the Essex village of Terling),[152] no tendency
towards larger, concentrated holdings. The land was exploited for purposes of
stockrearing, dairying, wool production, and the growing of rye and wheat; and
what enabled the small- to medium-sized tenement to provide a living were
different kinds of what in more modem times has been called diversification. The
Elizabethans survived by stitching together a variety of bye-employments, in a
diverse economy. Even fishing was a not insignificant source of income, and of
protein. Among the Dedham byelaws was a rule imposing a fine of half a mark for
keeping 'any castinge nettes to caste into other mens waters without leave or
license': no playing about with rod and line.

But the production of cloth was on such a scale as to make Dedham almost a
one-industry town, along with many other communities running up into south
Suffolk and north Essex from the estuary of the Stour and up the little rivers of the
Box and the Brett: neighbouring East Bergholt, Hadleigh, Bildeston, Sudbury,
Coggeshall, Lavenham, and many more. Dedham manufactured 'cloth' in the strict
and traditional sense, often called Suffolk broadcloths, or true blues, 'dyed in the
wool', and those active in this industry and trade were called 'blue men'. The cloth
travelled to Antwerp and beyond into the Baltic 'Eastland' region, even as far as
Russia, and these north-eastern markets were holding up well in the years of the
conference, whereas they were in recession by the 1620s. Other towns, particularly
Colchester and, increasingly, Bildeston[153] specialized in the lighter 'stuffs' called bays
and says, the so-called 'new draperies', which sold in the Mediterranean and Levant.

According to evidence supplied to the privy council in 1627–8, Dedham was a
small model of a stage of economic development much debated by economic
historians: proto-industrialization, which had already given rise to a two-tier if not
two-class society of employers and employed. The work was done in the cottages of
the spinners and weavers and with distaffs, looms and other equipment which they
owned, but it was financed by clothiers who supplied the raw materials and, in
effect, bought the labour of the weavers and other trades (such as the 'shearmen',
whose expertise was in 'finishing' the cloth) at rates which were set by the clothiers
(or the market). At Bildeston the various tradesmen (but they included women, who
did the combing and spinning of the wool, and children, who were essential for the
manning of the loom) were called the 'workfolks' of the clothiers.[154] The council

---

[152] Keith Wrightson and David Levine, *Poverty and piety in an English village: Terling, 1525–1700*
(2nd edn., Oxford, 1995).

[153] Patrick Collinson, 'Christian socialism in Elizabethan Suffolk: Thomas Carew and his *Caveat for
Clothiers'*, in *Counties and communities*, ed. C. Rawcliffe, R. Virgoe and R. Wilson (Norwich,
Centre of East Anglian Studies, 1996), pp. 161–78. For the Suffolk cloth industry more generally
(with much applicable to Dedham), see George Unwin, 'Industries', in *VCH Suffolk*, II (London,
1907), 254–66; George Unwin, 'The history of the cloth industry in Suffolk', in R.H. Tawney, ed.,
Studies in economic history: the collected papers of George Unwin (London, 1927), pp. 262–301; N.
Heard, *Wool, East Anglia's golden fleece* (Lavenham, 1970); *An historical atlas of Suffolk*, ed. D.
Dymond and E. Martin (Ipswich, 1988–9); E. Kerridge, *Textile manufactures in early modern
England* (Manchester, 1985).

[154] Collinson, 'Christian socialism', pp. 167–9.

was told that Dedham 'consisteth only of a small nomber of clotheyeres, and a great company of poore people which are by them sett on worke'.[155] But there is little or no evidence of 'class' antagonism between the clothiers and their employees: rather both groups were aware of a common interest in preserving and promoting the export trade in their product, and the poor seem to have found a target for their discontents in the corn merchants or 'badgers', who were blamed for forcing up the price of bread.

Contemporaries had a tendency to exaggerate the size of the units of production and of the work force employed by clothiers. Many were very small-scale entrepreneurs and it has been calculated that the typical early seventeenth-century Dedham clothier provided work for between six and eight households.[156] From wills and inventories made in Bildeston, it appears that the distinction between 'weaver' and 'clothier' was not always clear-cut. The Bildeston evidence confirms George Unwin's judgment that clothiers were 'a class of the most varied status', and whereas some testators who so styled themselves died in debt and poverty, we can find examples of weavers in relatively comfortable circumstances.[157]

But big fish there undoubtedly were, and none bigger than William Cardinal of Great Bromley, Essex, a native of Dedham with interests and property in East Bergholt, who in 1577 founded the Dedham lectureship and put into it his brother-in-law, Dr Edmund Chapman. Cardinal dealt on such a scale in the Antwerp market that the cloths exported from the Stour valley to the Netherlands came to be called 'cardinals'.[158] The Cardinals, like the more celebrated Springs of Lavenham, had made the transition from clothier to gentleman. Cardinal's father served in several mid-Tudor parliaments as MP for Colchester, and our William Cardinal was for a time recorder of Colchester and represented Dartmouth (which indicates a connexion with the earl of Bedford) in the parliament of 1572. He also transferred his considerable legal skills (acquired at Grays Inn) to Nottinghamshire, and served as a member of the council in the north from 1582.[159]

One institution made a greater difference to sixteenth-century Dedham than any other: the Free Grammar School.[160] In the 1540s Dame Joan Clarke donated a building near the church to serve as a schoolhouse, and the beginnings of grammar-school education were established in 1548 with the opportunistic sale of church plate by the churchwardens. In 1568 Thomas Seckford provided a house for the schoolmaster. But the principal benefactor was William Littlebury, a native of Dedham who had purchased the manor of Netherhall in the nearby parish of Bradfield. In 1571 he assigned a piece of land in Bradfield called Ragmarsh to a group of trustees, mostly Dedham men, who were to use the endowment to pay a stipend to a schoolmaster who would teach twenty children of the poorer inhabitants of Dedham free of charge. It was probably Seckford who in 1575 obtained letters patent from the crown which converted the trustees into governors of 'the Free and

---

[155] PRO SP 16/529/117.
[156] Pennie, 'The evolution of puritan mentality', pp. 26–7.
[157] Collinson, 'Christian socialism', pp. 167–8.
[158] Pennie, 'The evolution of puritan mentality', pp. 32–3.
[159] Hasler, *House of commons*, I, 536–7.
[160] Pennie, 'The evolution of puritan mentality', ch. 7, 'Education and literacy in Dedham and the Stour valley: 1560–1640'.

Perpetuall Grammar School of Queen Elizabeth in Dedham'. 'Perpetual' it was for more than three centuries, closing its doors only in 1889. These were precocious developments, in which Dedham was ahead of Colchester, and Ragmarsh would yield a salary of £20 as against the £16 later paid to the schoolmaster at Colchester. The statutes of Dedham School allowed the master to instruct an additional ten fee-paying children. It is rather impressive that as many as thirty boys out of perhaps no more than two hundred households found it worth their while (or their fathers did) to learn Latin and Greek, and if necessary to pay for the privilege. The master was expected to have the degree of MA, and it was soon found desirable to assist him with one or two ushers, or under-masters. When one of the early masters, William Bentley MA (never, for some reason, a member of the conference), solved his personal problems by applying for a sideways move to Colchester, he collected impressive references from the great and good of Cambridge, as well as more locally. One referee reported that his pupils had been exposed to Virgil, Horace, Cicero and Julius Caesar in Latin, and Homer and Socrates in Greek.[161]

Further developments resembled the history of 'free' grammar schools in many other towns. The free places were progressively monopolized by the sons of the *élite*, and when further funds were found (by William Cardinal) to provide Cambridge exhibitions for the cleverer boys coming out of the school, most of the university places over the next fifty years were taken up by the better-off: nothing actually scandalous about that, since the intention was not so much to create upward social mobility as to recruit the next generation of godly preaching ministers. And as for the displacement of the 'poor', for whom the free places in the grammar school were ostensibly intended, it may have been a realistic judgment that their needs were better served by the English, or elementary, school also founded at about this time, and provided with an endowment in 1601 by Edmund Sherman, in whose house, 'Shermans', it continued to flourish into the 1870s.[162] The Dedham orders required that all young children of the town be taught to read English and that no apprentices were to be taken on who were not literate in English.

The coping-stone on the edifice of Dedham's self-definition as a godly, well-ordered little commonwealth was provided by the 'Orders agreed upon the ixth of August [1585] by mr doctor Chapman, mr parker and the Auncientes of the Congregation of dedham to be diligently observed and kepte of all persons whatsoever dwellinge within the said Towne'.[163] An earlier version, or draft, of these orders is linked in the manuscript with business transacted at the twenty-ninth meeting, held on 5 April 1585 – 'a profession freely made and approved by the voyces and handes of us whose names are underwritten' is subscribed by nine of the 'ancients', which indicates social rank rather than age, since one of them, Richard Upcher, was no more than twenty years of age.[164]

These Dedham papers may be compared with other orders providing for a kind of self-government made in some other parishes in the late sixteenth century, and most

---

[161] References for Bentley in ERO (Colchester), Morant MSS D/Y 2/4, pp. 97, 113, 131, 135, 143, 149–50, 173, 193, discussed in Collinson, 'PCM', pp. 598–606. See also Appendix 1 below.

[162] Pennie, 'The evolution of puritan mentality', pp. 142–6.

[163] See pp. 128–30 below.

[164] See pp. 124–8 below. It seems improbable that Upcher should have been only twenty in 1585, but he gave his age as twenty-five when he gave evidence in court in May 1590 (LMA DL/C 213).

instructively with the 'articles' drawn up in the Wiltshire parish of Swallowfield (by an administrative anomaly embedded in Berkshire) in 1596.[165] Such documents are evidence of communal self-consciousness on the part of 'the better sort', 'ancients', or (in the case of Swallowfield) 'chief inhabitants', in itself constitutive of a kind of self-governing micro-commonwealth; and of concern with various abuses requiring correction at a time of unusual social stress. But there are interesting differences between the two documents. The Swallowfield articles provide for the regular holding of town meetings and, in some detail, for the orderly conduct of business in the meetings. The Dedham orders represent a kind of godly constitution, or covenant, by which the town, defined as a church or congregation above all, is to be governed, with the agreement of its ministers and ancients, who were evidently seen as 'elders' in the presbyterian scheme of things. They provide for monthly meetings on the Tuesday (market day) following the celebration of the Lord's Supper, of the ministers and ancients 'concerninge the good government of the towne' but the note of élite democracy or oligarchy sounded in the Swallowfield articles is absent. This was not so much a town meeting, or even a vestry, as a 'consistory' on the presbyterian model.

The Swallowfield concerns are relatively secular and are suffused throughout by the values of parity and neighbourhood among the parish élite. They include measures to ensure due deference on the parts of 'suche as be poore and will malapertlye compare with their betters and sett them at nought', and to minimize vexatious litigation. Other problems addressed included the arrival in the parish of unwanted 'inmates', the birth of bastard children, and the marriage of young persons without the ways and means to keep house, all matters affecting the pockets of rate-payers. It seems unlikely that the local clergyman had much or even anything to do with the articles.

The Dedham orders were also concerned to avoid 'all discord, or revenging by wordes, actions or suites', and to limit unwelcome immigration into the town. But, in contrast to Swallowfield, they are otherwise imprinted with the earnest godliness of their authors, whom we may assume to have been the ministers, perhaps the vicar, Richard Parker, who had the pastoral charge, and in whose handwriting the orders appear in the Dedham papers; but surely not without much help from the dominant partner in this team, Dr Edmund Chapman. The majority of the orders concern the strict observance of the Sabbath, church attendance, the monthly communions, and Dr Chapman's twice-weekly lectures on Tuesdays and Thursdays. (The Tuesday lecture, symbiotic with the market, was to continue until 1907.) In the case of Dedham, the restrictions on illegitimacy are expressed in more 'religious' terms, 'the filthie profaninge of mariage'. It is unlikely that the town of Dedham would have submitted itself to such orders if it had not experienced a religious 'moment', with the creation of the Dedham lectureship and the formation of the conference. The fact that one of the architects of this programme, the vicar Richard Parker, would soon be up to his neck in moral scandal, something we shall soon notice,[166] is, in a sense, neither here nor there. Was this ambitious programme

---

[165] Steve Hindle, 'Hierarchy and community in the Elizabethan parish: the Swallowfield articles of 1596', *Historical Journal*, XLIV (1999), 835–51.

[166] See pp. lxxii–iv below.

of reformation otherwise a success? When have 'thorough' drives for the reformation of manners ever wholly succeeded?

The religious concerns of the orders intersect with the social in what is said, and
done, about the poor. As at Swallowfield, the authors distance themselves from the
poor as a distinct and even alien social group, but the Dedham orders lack the
fear-inspired negativity of the Swallowfield articles. Those 'of habilitie' were to
invite to their tables 'one couple of such of their poore neighbors as have submitted
themselves to the good orders of the Churche, and walke christianly and honestlie in
their callinges'. The Jacobean writer John Downame would suggest that if the poor
were visited in their own homes, 'they would not so often have occasion to visit us
at ours'. But this was kindly meant, for the visitors would see for themselves the
condition of the poor, 'their provision, hungrie fare, thinne cloathes and hard
lodging: the children crying for hunger, and the parents out crying them because
they have no food to give them; some lying in straw for want of beddes, others
drinking water in stead of drinke.'[167] House-to-house visitation, in such localities as
Pig Lane, was a practice built into the Dedham orders. Once every quarter,
Chapman and/or Parker, with two or three of the ancients, 'alwaies accompanied
with one of the Constables', were to visit 'the poore, and chiefly the suspected
places, that understandinge the miserable estate of those that wante and the naughtie
disposition of disordered persons [the earlier draft had specified 'whordome,
dronkennes, robbery and such like'] they may provide for them accordinglie'.

In the spirit of this order, one of the ancients, William Butter, the first to sign the
orders, required his executors 'to take view of the poorest, to go into their houses to
see what lodging [that is, bedding] they have'; and if it proved 'too bare for any
Christian', they were to distribute blankets and sheets, as far as the money would
go. Other signatories, Pearce Butter and Edmund Sherman, the benefactor of the
English school, left substantial sums to the poor in their wills.[168]

It is not easy to compare the quality of charity in different communities, since in
some (such as Hadleigh) the provision of poor relief depended heavily, and satisfac-
torily, upon the legally enforceable poor rates, whereas in other places, voluntary
giving still counted. Dedham seems to have been a place where voluntarism, related
to 'godliness', was still a significant component in social policy, which gives the
town a relatively and perhaps deceptively generous appearance. And the Dedham
clothiers were, on the evidence of their wills, less likely to forget their 'workfolks'
when they came to write their wills than the clothiers of, for example Bildeston,
whose 'unconscionable' conduct and appalling reputation as employers was lam-
basted from the pulpit by their minister, Thomas Carew, in a sermon printed under
the title *A caveat for clothiers*.[169] But it may be going too far to credit Dedham and
places like it with what John Bossy has called 'the social miracle'.[170] A few years

---

[167] John Downame, *The plea of the poore* (London, 1616), pp. 59–60.
[168] Collinson, *Religion of protestants*, p. 219n.
[169] Patrick Collinson, 'Puritanism and the poor', in *Pragmatic utopias: ideals and communities,
1200–1630* , ed. Rosemary Horrox and Sarah Rees Jones (Cambridge, 2001), pp. 242–58; Marjorie
McIntosh, 'Networks of care in Elizabethan English towns: the example of Hadleigh, Suffolk', in
The locus of care: families, institutions, and the provision of welfare since antiquity, ed. Peregrine
Horden and R. M. Smith (London, 1998); Collinson, 'Christian socialism', *passim*.
[170] John Bossy, *Christianity in the West 1400–1700* (Oxford, 1985); and see his more recent *Peace in
the post-reformation* (Cambridge, 1998).

after the end of the Dedham conference the preacher Bezaleel Carter, another whistle-blower like Carew, would tell a congregation in Clare that 'some even of our greatest professors' were 'gripers, grinders of the poor, extortioners, usurers, merciless'. Carter thought that there were 'but few charitable professors'. 'I have read of Cannibals, men-eaters. I think that there are some in our times little better.'[171]

v. Ecclesiastical Dedham

'Greater Dedham'

Mention has already been made of Dedham's Lollard past and its early links with protestantism. What follows is an attempt to map out the parish's stormy ecclesiastical history in the seventy-five years following the dissolution of the monasteries. And yet by way of introduction, it would be salutary to keep in mind that to focus exclusively on Dedham itself would be to distort, or at least narrow, a much broader picture. If Edmund Chapman was the acknowledged leader of the conference, his influence only just outranked that of Richard Crick and Richard Dowe, neither of whom ever ventured south of the Stour in the exercise of their ministries. We do not know where the inaugural assembly of 22 October 1582 was actually held, while the first official meeting took place, presumably with Crick as host, in East Bergholt (**1M**). It was swiftly decided that Dowe should 'accepte of his callinge at Stratforde' (**2M**).

Indeed, Dedham had long been linked to Stratford St Mary by more than just a bridge and a ford, and the Morse household there may well have been accorded some kind of honorary primacy amongst the godly of the Stour valley. If so, it would go some way to explaining the prominence in the minute book of the obscure figure of Anthony Morse, for he came from a branch of the extensive Morse clan which was clearly influential, wealthy and pious.

In 1526 Edward Morse of 'Stratforth iuxta Dedham' mentioned in his will the chapel built there by his father, leaving money to his executors to 'make up' the north aisle of Stratford church 'in forme and manner as the other yle is on the sowthe syde'. He divided his considerable property between his sons John and Edward.[172] This younger Edward appears to have been deeply affected by the religious developments of the 1530s. When one of Suffolk's earliest evangelists, Thomas Rose, found himself barred from nearby Hadleigh in 1534, he spent the next three years preaching in Stratford before the bishop of Norwich and the Bury justices pounced and forced him to flee, while in 1538, according to Wriothesley's *Chronicle*, the mass was conducted in English 'divers tymes' both there and in Hadleigh.[173] It may plausibly be assumed that Edward Morse, like so many others, frequently journeyed to Hadleigh during the following years to hear the preaching of Nicholas Shaxton, Rowland Taylor and their associates, since when he made a will, as clothier of Stratford, on 13 November 1557 – the very height of the Marian

---

[171] Bezaleel Carter, *Christ his last will, and John his legacy, in a sermon preached at Clare in Suffolk* (London, 1621), pp. 56–86.

[172] PRO PCC PROB11/22 (14 Porche), fo. 106v: proved 4 December 1526.

[173] Craig, *Reformation, Politics and polemics*, pp. 158, 171.

Plate 2 The chancel of St Mary, Dedham, showing the memorial tablet to Edmund Chapman at the far end of the north wall. The monument to 'roaring' John Rogers, lecturer of Dedham from 1605 to 1636, is on the left. *Photograph by Carolynn Usher, 2002.*

Reaction – he began it with an unabashed protestant preamble, eschewing all reference to the Blessed Virgin and the holy company of heaven.

The will divides his assets between his wife, Julian, and his seven children – Edward, William, Nathaniel,[174] Anthony, Alice, 'Lidi' and Elizabeth, all still minors. His 'brother' William Forth esquire was named as his executor, along with young Edward, and his 'brother' Henry Brown as overseer.[175] The third Edward inherited the family home and was living there with his mother and brother Anthony during the life of the Dedham conference (**27M** and **Extra M**, 17 February 1585). Julian Morse – not impossibly, to judge from her late husband's will, a sister of William Forth of Butley – had in the interim, however, remarried and been widowed a second time. As Julian Jeffrey, she received a legacy from John Roger, a yeoman of Fobbing, Essex, in 1584.[176] This raises the intriguing possibility that Julian Morse had married the son of John Jeffrey of West Mersea, Essex, who was apparently the chief organizer of that cell of 'heretical dissent' under Mary alluded to in the preceding section. On 25 July 1556 he had been indicted at Colchester quarter

---

[174] As clothier of Dedham, Nathaniel made his will on 18 December 1590, his goods to be divided equally between his wife Joan and four children. Joan and his brother-in-law John Jeffrye were appointed executors: Emmison, *Essex gentry wills*, p. 299.

[175] PRO PCC PROB11/39 (51 Wrastley), fo. 389v: proved 24 November 1557.

[176] She was also forgiven the jointure that Roger should have had on his marriage to her late daughter, Lydia: F. G. Emmison, *Essex wills: the archdeaconry courts 1583–92* (Chelmsford, 1989), no. 1. For Roger's bequests to his Morse brothers-in-law and their families, see *BR*, pp. 229–31.

Plate 3 The memorial tablet to Edmund Chapman in the chancel of St Mary, Dedham. *Photograph by Carolynn Usher, 2002.*

sessions (dying before he could be tried) for gathering conventicles of twenty or more persons in West Mersea and Dedham to hear the itinerant preacher and future martyr George Eagles. He is surely to be identified with the John Jeffrey who was brother-in-law of John Laurence, an Essex 'freewiller' and disciple of Rowland Taylor: both were denounced by an informant as active protestants in London during the Marian years.[177]

If all or any of that scenario is true, the Morse household, which could count the Forths of Butley among its relatives or close allies, will surely have been respected along the Stour valley, not only for its pious benefactions to the parish of Stratford St Mary, but also for its wider godly connexions, which stretched back way beyond George Eagles's martyrdom.

'Greater Dedham', then: except for the archival accident that the 'Dedham' papers were transmitted by Richard Parker, it would be just as appropriate to refer to the documents printed below as the 'Stratford', or even 'Bergholt' papers. Where the real centre of gravity lay we shall never know.[178]

Dedham after Butley

Few late Tudor parishes are as well documented in the diocesan and exchequer records as Dedham. Few exhibit such a peculiar history of mismanagement, neglect and acrimony. Its vicissitudes during the reigns of Mary and Elizabeth, both economic and religious, have profound implications since, to reduce matters to a naked truth, if Dedham had been better endowed there would have been no pressing need for a privately financed 'godly' lectureship, and Chapman might never have set foot there.

Dedham's slender tithes demonstrably proved a major obstacle to its stability during the mid-century. Assessed in the *Valor Ecclesiasticus* at only £10 0s 2½d, the benefice remained in the crown's hands following the dissolution of Butley priory and on 29 October 1541 Edmund Bonner, bishop of London, instituted John Worth at Henry VIII's presentation.[179]

Worth, one of the few Essex incumbents who escaped detection and deprivation in the spring of 1554 following Mary's order for the removal of married clergy, was still listed as vicar at Bonner's visitation that October. Only at this point, apparently, did the visitors discover that he was married. More significantly, they also added the

---

[177] ERO QSR 2/15; Foxe, *A & M* (1563), p. 1605. The editors are grateful to Dr Thomas Freeman for supplying the latter reference.

[178] Analysis shows that the conference met most frequently at East Bergholt (seventeen occasions, eight of them specifically stated to be at Crick's house – though once 'for Mr Gale' – and the remainder apparently in Hog Lane). Of the thirteen meetings in Dedham, seven were held at Chapman's, five at Parker's, and the emergency meeting of February 1585 at Edmund Sherman's house opposite the church. The ten meetings at Stratford were hosted more or less alternately by Dowe and the Morse household, the nine at Boxford by Sandes or (twice) Birde. Thus three of the four major venues were in Suffolk, accounting for thirty-six out of forty-nine meetings. Dedham apart, the conference convened in Essex comparatively seldom. Farrar of Langham was host on seven occasions; Tey of Peldon and Layer Hall on six; Lewis of Colchester and Newman of Coggeshall on five; 'Morse' of Boxted and Lowe of Colchester only once each. The remaining handful of meetings took place in Suffolk – three times each at Wenham and Erwarton and once at 'Chatsam'. Altogether, therefore, the 'Dedham' conference met north of the Stour on forty-three out of eighty-one occasions.

[179] Reg. Bonner, fo. 145v.

note '*effugit*'.[180] Two attempts to fill the benefice failed the following year, from which it appears that Worth was never formally deprived after his flight.[181] It remained vacant at Edmund Grindal's primary visitation of the diocese in 1561 when it was being served only by a *lector* (lay reader), John Clerke.[182]

During the months following Worth's self-removal, Dedham was apparently left to its own devices. Thus it was that John Jeffrey and George Eagles could impose themselves on the township until detected some time in the spring of 1556. It was only at this juncture, if John Foxe's dates are to be believed, that the authorities clamped down in the region, for in the same year Matthew Parker's brother-in-law, Simon Harlestone, was driven out of Mendlesham, Suffolk (eighteen miles north of East Bergholt) with his wife and five children, whilst Harlestone's friend, Elizabeth Lawson of Bedfield (nine miles east of Mendlesham), was arrested for refusing to attend mass.[183] 'Out of Dedham', Foxe also tersely reported, 'were driven William Bets and William Birde, with their wifes'.[184]

Not that the local godly were deterred. We have seen that Edward Morse defied all recognized authority by penning a fully protestant will in 1557. Drummed out of Mendlesham, Simon Harlestone gravitated southwards for what was left of Mary's reign: it was reported to Bonner that he was active in Colchester and that 'his abyding is alwaye at a place in Essex called Dedam . . . at one Harries house, a Tucker, and he is a greate perswader of the people, and they do mightely buylde upon his doctrine'.[185]

Having surveyed the state of his diocese in 1561, Grindal took immediate steps to have the benefice filled – not, perhaps, without judicious advice from Simon Harlestone, whose brother-in-law was now Primate of All England. On 23 April 1562, at Grindal's personal petition, letters patent were issued by the Lord Keeper, Sir Nicholas Bacon, to one Richard Reynoldes.[186] They were never enrolled, presumably because Reynoldes had the foresight to make enquiries about his likely income and promptly renounced his claims. That would certainly explain why, only one month later, the exchequer issued a commission to seven local notables to investigate the impoverished state of Dedham's revenues.[187] They convened at

---

[180] GL MS 9537/1, fo. 28v.

[181] Thomas Norley received letters patent on 24 September 1555: *CPR 1555–57*, p. 216. Henry Slythurst was collated by Bonner *per lapsum* on 11 October *per cessionem et dimissionem John Worthe, presbyteri coniugati*: Reg. Bonner, fo. 464r.

[182] GL MS 9537/2, fo. 65v.

[183] Foxe, *A & M* (1563), pp. 1522, 1677: according to Dr Thomas Freeman, Harlestone himself was probably Foxe's source for the latter account.

[184] *Ibid.*, p. 1678. This statement heads a checklist of 'the persecuted in Essex' which was never reprinted in later editions and thus relegated to an appendix by Foxe's Victorian editors: thanks are due to Dr Freeman for providing a transcript. Betts (d. 1572) was probably the man of these names who went into exile with his wife at Aarau (C. H. Garrett, *The Marian exiles* (Cambridge, 1938), no. 49), returning to be ordained by Grindal in 1560 and instituted rector of Wivenhoe, contiguous to Colchester, in March 1564: GL MSS 9535/1, fo. 88v; 9531/13, fo. 133r. Birde is possibly the man who became a member of the Dedham conference: see *BR*, pp. 189–90.

[185] Foxe, *A & M* (1563), p.1606. Harlestone returned to his old stamping grounds at the beginning of Elizabeth's reign: Robert Blomefield, bailiff of Little Stonham, Suffolk (contiguous to Mendlesham), threatened him with arrest because he would not wear the surplice when saying service: *ibid.*, p. 1677. Thanks are again due to Dr Freeman for this reference.

[186] BL, Lansdowne MS 443, fo. 117r.

[187] William Cardinal, George Christmas, Edmund Bocking, Henry Golding and Edward Waldegrave, *armigeri*; Benjamin Clere and John Best, *generosi*. In the event Golding and Clere took no part in the proceedings: PRO E337/4, no. 44, m.1.

Colchester on 22 May 1562, requiring answers to five interrogatories from thirteen jurors, none of whom was actually a Dedham parishioner.[188] To the first they replied that the queen was patron but that the benefice had been 'voyde synce the second of yere . . . of the late quene Mary for lack of sufficient living'; to the second, that it had 'a greate mansion or dwellinge house with a gardeyne contyninge one roode of grounde wherin the vicars there for the tyme being have most comonly dwelt.' This, however, was now 'in greate ruyn & decay and therefore of smale yerely value'.

The third interrogatory concerned the benefice's income. The vicar had been entitled 'tyme out of mynde to have tythe of woll, lambe, mylke, keen, calves, gese, piggs, and all manner of frute except grayne remayninge and growing yerely within the said parishe'. Profits, however, were slim.[189] The answers to the fourth interrogatory explained that they had been decayed 'by the space of theis ix or tenne yeres and more' because there was 'muche lesse occupyeng in clothmakyng then heretofore' and also because no privy tithes were paid 'as heretofore hath bene'. Finally, the jury explained the outgoings of the vicarage, amounting to £2 10s 10d;[190] calculated its current profits at only £8 17s 10d; and asserted that its clear yearly value to the incumbent was therefore only £6 7s 0d.

Whilst this calculation may have been entirely accurate it may also have been intended as an astute manoeuvre. The Act for the Restitution of First Fruits and Tenths (1559), by which the exchequer continued to regard clerical incomes as assessed in the *Valor* as its yardstick for clerical taxation, had decreed that vicarages worth less than £10 and rectories worth less than ten marks (£6 13s 4d) were henceforth exempt from first fruits. Clearly any downward revision of Dedham's revenues would technically exempt it from first fruits as a vicarage, but were the jurors guarding also against the possibility that the exchequer might, for some arcane reason, classify it for tax purposes as a rectory?

That seems the only logical construction to be placed on what happened next. The immediate result of the Colchester enquiry was that on 18 January 1564 the barons relieved future incumbents from the necessity of paying annual tenths to the crown as income tax.[191] It was something, certainly, but it would have been more realistic to have relieved them of first fruits by a simple downward revision of the *Valor* assessment. By discharging Dedham from 36s 10d in annual tenths they were in fact deftly revising its estimated income back up to £8 3s 10d, a figure just above the threshold for the exemption of *rectories*. In the event, all later Elizabethan vicars are recorded as compounding for first fruits.

---

[188] Richard Horsepitt and John Smyth of Great Horkesley; John Warner and John Mannyng of Lawford; Robert Yonge and Anthony Robson of Alresford; Gyles Aleyn, William Heckford, John Smarte and Richard Yeman of Ardleigh; Richard Wollock, John Warner and John Reynold of Langham: *ibid.*

[189] Tithe wool was estimated at 6s 8d a year; tithe lambs (at 1d a lamb) 3s 4d; tithe geese (at 2d a goose) 2s 6d; tithe pigs (at 3d a pig) 3s 0d; tithe fruit 3s 4d; tithe 'mylche keen' (at 4d a cow) £3; tithe calves (at 1d a calf) 15s 0d; tithe of sixteen acres of meadow 15s 0d. The profits of the four offering days 'moost comonly amountynge to the number of XX xx/iiij [280] persones' were, at 2d per person, assessed at £4.

[190] Annual tenths, 36s 10d; fees to the archdeacon, 9s 4d; fees to the bishop, 4s 6d, amounting in all to 50s 10d (sic).

[191] PRO E337/4, no. 44, m. 2.

John Worth *redivivus*

Dedham did at least finally manage to attract an incumbent: on 17 November 1564 John 'Wrothe' was granted letters patent by Lord Keeper Bacon upon his own petition for them.[192] Was this in fact John Worth, stated to have fled by October 1554, returning to his old haunts? Although unlisted amongst the identified Marian exiles, there must be a presumption that Worth had gone abroad in the entourage of his own family, since on 13 October 1559 one John Worth compounded for the first fruits of Clopton, Suffolk, producing as one of his sureties no less a personage than Edward Isaac – friend of Hugh Latimer, patron of Edwin Sandys and, during the troubles in Frankfurt, the vanquisher of John Knox. Since Isaac's wife was probably the daughter of another prominent exile, Sir Thomas Wroth, kinship (of the 'country cousin' variety, at least) seems highly possible.[193] It was presumably the same John Worth who was further preferred to Burgh, Suffolk, in 1560.[194] Thus circumstantial evidence suggests that the fugitive vicar of 1554 and the man appointed in 1564 were one and the same but that on his re-emergence in 1559 he was not initially interested in returning to Dedham. Indeed, despite his letters patent he was not instituted by Grindal until 13 October 1565.[195]

He had evidently married Alice, daughter of Thomas Webbe of Dedham, since in February 1566 Webbe appointed one John Worth as his executor, although describing him neither as vicar nor even 'cleric'. Webbe's house 'in the Row with the appurtenances' was left to Alice for life, Worth to have the right of letting it in order to pay debts and legacies.[196] The parish register records that 'Mr Worth his wife' was buried on 21 May 1568 and that on 25 October 'Mr Worth' married Joan Hutton.[197]

In June 1575 Michael Upcher bequeathed Worth twenty shillings to preach a funeral sermon.[198] Otherwise he scarcely surfaces in his parishioners' wills, never appearing as writer of, or witness to, any proved in the Colchester archdeaconry court and only three times in those proved by the commissary *in partibus*.[199] There can, however, be little doubt that he fostered, or at least condoned, Dedham's radicalizing tendencies. The parish records reveal a steady trickle of names which, a generation later, would be regarded as hallmarks of a 'puritan' tradition. In July 1561 a daughter of Lewis Sparhawke was baptized Patience. During the 1560s and

---

[192] BL, Lansdowne MS 443, fo. 139v; not found in *CPR 1563–66*.

[193] PRO E334/7, fo. 25r; Garrett, *Marian exiles*, pp. 195–6.

[194] He compounded on 10 November 1560, one of his sureties being Robert Cole of East Bergholt, Suffolk, clothier: PRO E334/7, fo. 94r.

[195] As 'Woorth', *per mortem ultimi vicarii*: Reg. Grindal, fo. 137v. By whose death was the benefice deemed to be vacant? Despite the jurors' assertion in 1562 that Dedham had remained vacant for 'lack of living' since Worth's departure, Henry Slythurst's institution in 1555 was perhaps regarded as valid. Otherwise the phrase may be no more than a convenient fiction. Worth compounded in November (at the original *Valor* valuation) with sureties William Starling of Dedham, clothier, and William Stracye of Colchester, merchant: PRO E334/8, fo. 65v. For the wills of *Robert* Starling of Dedham (d. 1581/2), clothier, and of William *Stratchie* of the New Hythe, Colchester, merchant (d. 1569), see Emmison, *Essex gentry wills*, pp. 310–11.

[196] F. G. Emmison, *Essex wills (England) Volume 2: 1565–1571* (Boston, Mass., 1983), no. 568.

[197] ERO D/P 26/1. William, son of John Worth, was buried on 28 May 1572.

[198] Emmison, *Essex gentry wills*, pp. 314–15.

[199] F. G. Emmison, *Essex wills: the commissary court 1569–1578* (Chelmsford, 1994), nos. 44, 696, 1000.

1570s there occurs a sprinkling of female names like Grace, Prudence, Constance, Faith and Charity (never 'Hope'!) as well as a handful of biblical ones: Sara and Judith (both daughters of Michael Upcher), Rebecca and Miriam. Amongst the boys there are several Nathaniels, a Josias, a Daniel, and by 1583 even a Moses. Japheth, Ezechiell, Joseph, Ephraim and twins called Abraham and Isaac all crop up during the 1580s. Dedham families nevertheless drew the line: a boy called Godsgift was buried in 1586 but no other outlandish names, targets of Ben Jonson's City comedies of the early 1600s, are to be found.

Towards the end of Worth's incumbency there occurred the most important social change in Dedham since the decline of clothmaking a generation earlier. On 14 May 1575 letters patent were granted and subsequently enrolled for the foundation of a free grammar school there, and Worth was named as one of the first governors.[200] The following month, in response to an exchequer enquiry concerning clerical subsidy, 'Leonard'[201] Sparhawke provided a convenient thumbnail sketch of his ministry: Worth had been vicar for the past eleven years, 'resydent all the time and hathe paid all his subsidies duly as he thinketh'.[202]

Worth soon resigned and on 8 November 1575, at the presentation of William Cardinal, was instituted rector of Cardinal's home parish of Great Bromley. The following day he and William Butter, clothier, were granted letters of sequestration for Dedham.[203]

John Keltridge, 1577–8

With Worth's departure Dedham's affairs were plunged into further legal confusion. Whilst there is no hint of it in earlier records, the parish was now apparently deemed, following the dissolution of Butley priory, to have come to the crown not *pleno iure* but in its legal capacity as duke of Lancaster. Amongst the papers of the incumbent chancellor of the duchy, Sir Ralph Sadler (1568–87), there exists a letter of presentation, dated 29 April 1577, from Elizabeth to John Aylmer, bishop of London since 24 March, to institute Samuel Cottesford to Dedham following the resignation of Giles Wigginton.[204]

There is not a scintilla of evidence elsewhere to link either Cottesford or Wigginton, both clerics of a decidedly radical stamp, to the internal affairs of Dedham,[205] and whatever politico-ecclesiastical game Sadler may have been playing he appears to have lost it. The letters of sequestration granted to Worth and Butter evidently remained valid until 18 June 1577, when sequestration was granted instead to John Keltridge. On 10 July Keltridge was duly listed present as

---

[200] See Appendix 1 below.
[201] Undoubtedly an error for Lewis (Ludovic) Sparhawke.
[202] Sparhawke also confirms the impression gained from the patchy evidence of the earlier records: before Worth's incumbency 'the Cure was somtymes served by Curates and somtymes by none': PRO E178/3268, m. 30 (15 June 1575). The editors' thanks are due to Dr Kenneth Fincham for drawing their attention to this valuable, and hitherto neglected, source.
[203] Reg. Grindal, fo. 184v; LMA DL/C/333, fo. 26v. Worth died as rector of Great Bromley, making a modest will (his wife Joan to be executrix) on 8 August 1581. It was proved on 26 August: F. G. Emmison, *Essex wills: the archdeaconry courts 1577–1584* (Chelmsford, 1987), no. 703.
[204] PRO DL 42/100, fo. 7r: as duke of Lancaster, the crown did not present to livings in its gift by means of letters patent, as it did to livings held *pleno iure*.
[205] For Wigginton, who ended his life in a state of semi-separatism, see the entry in *Oxford DNB* by William Sheils.

sequestrator during Aylmer's primary visitation and on 20 July was instituted at his hands to the vicarage on the crown's presentation, without any reference to its rights regarding the duchy of Lancaster.[206]

However it had been engineered, Keltridge's appointment ushered in twelve months of unexampled acrimony which appears to have been provoked in about equal measure by Aylmer's arrival at Fulham in the guise of stern authoritarian, Keltridge's sincere but divisive theological stance and the foundation in the autumn of 1577 (necessarily with Aylmer's official approval) of the Dedham lectureship.[207]

Keltridge, son of a London merchant, was baptized in the parish of St Michael Cornhill on 22 May 1553 and graduated BA from Trinity College, Cambridge, in early 1572, shortly before his nineteenth birthday.[208] A protégé of Aylmer, then archdeacon of Lincoln, he was ordained deacon and priest there in 1576.[209] Within months, Aylmer selected Keltridge – who had no clerical status within the diocese until his institution to Dedham and was not appointed a personal chaplain to the bishop until 19 January 1579[210] – to preach before him at Fulham on Ascension Day (16 May) 1577 on the occasion of his first ordination ceremony as bishop of London. To the hierarchy who had served Sandys, the intrusion of this twenty-four-year-old upstart must have seemed a provocative, even insulting, action.

Keltridge's sermon was provocative in quite another sense: he gratuitously departed from the edifying commonplaces usually considered appropriate on such occasions, attacking ministers of the church who, like Eli, were only interested in using their livings to advance their 'jolly' sons. 'There is some in Englande that have good and large stipends for serving the Lord, and they spende it as liberally on their sonnes to make them Courtiers. Well, Aaron did not so.'[211] In the circumstances this could only have been construed as a direct attack upon the nepotism of Sandys, now promoted archbishop of York.[212]

---

[206] LMA DL/C/333, fo. 80r; GL MS 9537/4, fo. 32r; Reg. Grindal, fo. 191r: the benefice was merely stated to be *de iure legitime vacantem*; no letters patent were subsequently enrolled. Keltridge compounded on 3 August 1577, bringing in as sureties his father, William, of St Michael Cornhill, and Lawrence Gough (Goffe) of St Peter Cornhill, both 'drapers' – that is, members of the Drapers' Company: PRO E334/9, fo. 118v. In 1560 Gough had stood surety for John Pullan, archdeacon of Colchester, when Grindal secured him the rectory of Copford: PRO E334/7, fo. 78r.

[207] The following paragraphs could not have been written if Keltridge had not elected to go into print: thus does 'the truth' hang by a slender thread. In 1578 he published *The Exposition, and Readynges of Iohn Keltridge: Mayster of the Artes: Student of late in Trinitie College in Cambridge, Minister, Preacher and Pastor of the church of Dedham, that is in Essex. Upon the wordes our Saviour Christe, that bee written in the. xi. of Luke.* This title page does not reveal that Keltridge appended (from p. 219 onwards) *A Sermon, made before the reverend father in God, John, Bishop of London, (by J. Keltridge, Preacher) at his Mannor at Fulham, before them of the clergie, at the making of Ministers: in the yeare of the Lorde God, 1577, and nowe set out in print.* For ease of reference this volume is referred to below as both *Exposition* and *Ordination sermon*.

[208] For a summary of Keltridge's career, see the entry by Stephen Wright in *Oxford DNB*.

[209] He dedicated his *Exposition* to Aylmer 'for that, by good right, you chalenge the first frutes of my youthe: Whom it pleased in younge dayes, and this my infancie, to ingrafte & plant in, as one thought worthie of some place in the vineyarde of the Lorde' (preface, sig. Aii r).

[210] LMA DL/C/333, fo. 132v.

[211] *Ordination sermon*, pp. 236–7.

[212] Sandys had refused Burghley's request to cede London's revenues to Aylmer from Michaelmas 1576 (to which Sandys was legally entitled) as a *quid pro quo* for the grant of those of York from the same date. Aylmer's tactlessness in pressing for such restitution sent Sandys into a paroxysm of rage, provoking a vitriolic attack on Aylmer's probity. Aylmer retaliated by launching what was to prove

When eschewing the politics of the moment, Keltridge reveals himself as a committed, evangelical Calvinist. Aylmer's first ordinands were exhorted: 'Scatter your selves thorowe every angle and quarter of the Realme, in severall Congregations, that all countries may heare your voice, and everie part thereof glorifie the Lord.'[213] Among them was one who needed little prompting on the subject: Arthur Dent. Others whose future careers would have a more decisive influence on the course of events within the upper echelons of the Church of England were Richard Montague and William Cotton.[214] Thus were the doctrinal winds blowing as Aylmer embarked upon his stormy episcopate.

Keltridge's brief ministry began at the very moment when his patron was authorizing the establishment of the Dedham lectureship. Whilst the exact circumstances of its foundation are obscure, it was created by William Cardinal as a means of promoting his brother-in-law, Dr Edmund Chapman – evidently a wandering maverick since his departure from the chapter of Norwich some months earlier – to a strategic preaching post. Not mentioned during Aylmer's primary visitation in July, Chapman subsequently received licence to preach throughout London diocese on 2 November 1577, as of Dedham.[215] No evidence survives of the negotiations and/or private interviews between Aylmer, Cardinal and Chapman which must surely have taken place before Chapman was formally admitted and licensed.

For his part, Keltridge could be forgiven for suspecting that a public lectureship would prove prejudicial to his own ministry. He must also immediately have crossed swords with two of Dedham's leading parishioners, William Butter and Lewis Sparhawke. On 23 April 1578 the office of the judge, promoted by Keltridge, sued Sparhawke at instance. Similar proceedings begun against Butter went no further. The action against Sparhawke was listed again on 29 April, 12 May and in late June but thereafter disappears from the record. It was probably a dispute over tithes, like so many instance cases inaugurated by the clergy.[216]

Although, according to his canonical duty, the new vicar general, Edward Stanhope,[217] apparently reconciled the parties out of court in both these cases, Keltridge was otherwise comprehensively worsted, resigning within the year. On 21 June 1578 he completed the dedicatory preface to his *Exposition*, the importance of which, for understanding the interactive and reactive religious culture of 'greater Dedham', would be hard to exaggerate. Keltridge's dedication to Aylmer, his 'verie good Lorde', is disingenuous to say the least, declining to notice the possibility that there could be any fundamental divisions between the bishop and his heterogeneous flock. Keltridge was sure that 'that rule and government wherewith god hath blessed

the most scandalous suit for episcopal dilapidations of Elizabeth's reign: Felicity Heal, *Of prelates and princes* (Cambridge, 1980), pp. 300–3.
213 *Ordination sermon*, pp. 249–50.
214 GL MS 9535/1, fos. 152v–4r.
215 LMA DL/C/333, fo. 90r. This despite the fact that, earlier in 1577, Aylmer had been complaining that he, William Charke, Field and Wilcox were now preaching 'God knows what' in private houses. Although he had 'hopes' of Chapman and Charke, Aylmer suggested that Field and Wilcox be sent north to expend their radical energies on the unconverted: Collinson, *EPM*, p. 202.
216 LMA DL/C/10, pp. 319, 349, 430. Keltridge's dispute with Butter may, however, have had its origin in the accounts which Butter would have been obliged to submit as sequestrator between John Worth's departure and Keltridge's grant of the temporalities.
217 Aylmer replaced John Hammond with Edward Stanhope on 15 May 1578: Reg. Grindal, fo. 105r.

you in the Common welth of England, shall have as glorious an ende, in the
suppressing & rooting out of sinne, as it hath had a blessed entraunce, and continued
untill this day, in supporting and mainteining of the truth . . .'.[218]

According to his own lights, Keltridge was a godly, devoted, unimpeachably
Calvinist pastor of the first water.[219] And yet, he took the trouble to add, if anything
in the *Exposition* should 'appeare to be lesse studied, and more craggedly handled,
then commonly the stoorehouses of young Occupiers, as I am, ought to be', the
reason was to be sought in the months of absolute hell which he had endured in
Dedham where:

> a more troublesome and perelous time, never happened, by the space of this one
> whole yeare, then hath done unto me: either els lesse fruit, and smaller com-
> moditie gleaned up by the hands of any one labourer: or greater sorrowe, or
> lingering hope: or sore attempts, or the like flames, and such contentions (as your
> Honour verie well knoweth) that I have thought him much disquieted, that hath
> not sought quietnesse, in so unquiet a life. And yet in these tossings and
> tumblings, wherein I am sweltered in manner, and overcome, without any hope of
> recovery, I may not be altogether dismayed: neither will I stay the course I have
> begonne: but faire and saftely step by step drayle forwarde, till that time the Lorde
> God shall release us.[220]

Given Keltridge's anti-catholic, pro-Calvinist stance, what precisely had been the
problem? Surely not just a tithe dispute or a quarrel about William Butter's accounts
as sequestrator.

What we appear to be dealing with is a complete mental block on Keltridge's side
and, therefore, in equal and opposite reaction, a sense of continuous and continuing
outrage on the part of the local godly. The *Exposition*, not least in its marginal notes,
is a sustained polemic against unnamed and unidentified schismatics and precisians,
'such as presume to appoincte the elect of the lord at their severall judgements'. He
speaks also of 'precise men oftentimes unwise men', of 'upstart and fond heresies
budding up in our churches', of 'vain glorious men', of 'sectes and divisions about
orders in the Church', of 'much severinge, litle inclininge to the worde, brought in
by Scismatickes'. In a more sustained consideration of his own predicament he
articulates what is surely Aylmer's eye-view of the true character of radical communities like Dedham:

> yet will it never be brought to good passe, that any one shoulde sever the
> congregation, plucke the Lorde Christ in peeses, devide his church, bring in
> brawls, contentions, strife, debate, grudging, without greate perill and joperdie to
> the flock and houshoulde of God . . . [for] there is little consideration of the
> kingdome of God, when the apparell & attyre that is worne in the church shall

---

[218] *Exposition*, sig. Aii v.

[219] For example, the 'ordinarie means to come to God is by hering [the word preached]'; free will men
'that give salvation to their deedes' are roundly condemned, as is the Family of Love; 'The abuse of
England in feastinge and banquetting is a byworde to all the nations of the earth': *Exposition*, pp. 124
(margin), 129, 135, 165 (margin). In his *Two godlie and learned sermons appointed and preached
before the Jesuites, Seminaries, and other adversaries to the Gospell of Christ in the Tower of
London* (1581), in which he repeatedly denounces his opponents as 'heretics', his virulent
anti-catholicism was hardly parallelled in his generation.

[220] *Exposition*, sig. Aii v.

drive the[m] from it: And it is not a sufficient cause for any of you all, to crie out reformation and reformation . . . The people is as the priest, the priest must give place to the people, & that man that commeth not to please them, is thought unworthy to speak among them.

He returns to that theme in a later marginal note: 'I marveile how they can excuse them selves, that put so great religio[n] in a surples, and a cap, or in orders . . . Magistracie, is the ordinance & gifte of God . . .' Elsewhere he remarks that amongst those that 'thinke them selves purest, are greatest heresies'. Such are 'aptly' named puritans.[221]

Thus Keltridge has worked out for himself a model of 'preciseness': scruples about such 'trifles' as the surplice, the ring in marriage and even baptizing in fonts. He regards such scruples as hypocritical concomitants of actual wickedness of life. What remains tantalizingly unclear is whether he was drawing attention to full-scale, principled separatism or only to the pragmatic 'separatism' of 'gadding' to the sermons of preachers whose views were more congenial to the gadders than those of their own incumbents, such as himself.

Probably only the latter: his phraseology is constantly reminiscent of the manuscripts edited by Dr Albert Peel as *Tracts ascribed to Richard Bancroft* (Cambridge, 1953). Yet at the same time we are forewarned that the Dedham leaders were not, in the altercations which were to follow, to have it all their own way. We cannot speak of the Stour valley as 'godly' simply because Chapman held sway in Dedham, Crick in East Bergholt and Dowe in Stratford: the minute book reveals with monotonous regularity how often the brethren clashed with their flocks to the point of alienating them completely; and, as Keltridge's subtext demonstrates, there was an 'alternative congregation' ever lurking in the background. Not everyone wanted to hear about hellfire, damnation and double predestination.

Particularly intriguing is Keltridge's insinuation that the phenomenon he attacks is too close to 'anabaptism' to call. He continually asserts the necessity of unity within the christian congregation and attacks 'precisians' for destroying it. Yet he remained sanguine – or else astonishingly naïve – until the end. Despite its constant jibes at those in a position to harass him, the preface to his treatise has a dying fall, sounding a note of sorrow rather than of anger. His final thoughts, reaching us through the medium of a long-outdated prose style which nevertheless suddenly achieves the dignity of simplicity, invite immediate sympathy. He had evidently written the *Exposition* during his beleaguered months in Dedham in order to justify himself in the eyes of his recalcitrant congregation. Was it a distillation of the three dozen sermons he must have preached there?

In this my short Treatise, if I have done any good, I am glad thereof . . . Onely at this time take my present farewell, as a grayne or two left behinde, to till up your measure: for I would have no man suspect me for my waight. And let not my doctrine be an offence to any: this was only the true meaning that I had, to teach one Lorde and Jesus Christ.[222]
Ave atque vale.

---

[221] *Exposition*, pp. 16–17, 22 (margin), 25 (margin), 27, 28, 31, 118–19, 184 (margin), 130, 175.
[222] *Ibid.*, p. 217.

There was, however, a sting in the tail. He referred Aylmer to 'the causes' of his troubles and 'my judgment of the same: please it you to turne over but a fewe leafes, they will showe what manner a ones they be'.[223] In the circumstances it was fortunate for Keltridge and for the Dedham godly that all were saved from further internecine strife by the Suffolk gentleman John Tyler, on whose presentation Keltridge was instituted on 2 September 1578 to the rectory of Capel St Andrew.[224] It must be supposed that Keltridge spurred his horse across Stratford bridge with some degree of alacrity.

Timothy Fitzallen, 1578–82

The career of Timothy Fitzallen is in almost every respect mysterious. He was instituted to Dedham by Aylmer on 20 December 1578, apparently without reference to the chancellor of the duchy of Lancaster.[225] Unknown to the English university records and instituted only as *clericus*, he was nevertheless demonstrably a graduate and in some sense must, like Keltridge, have been Aylmer's protégé. He appears out of the blue on the eve of his short incumbency and, also like Keltridge, disappears into Suffolk at the end of it.[226]

Although not ordained there, he was certainly in London by early 1578, for on 13 February he had licence from Aylmer's vicar general to marry Ann Luke, widow, of St Stephen Coleman Street.[227] Upon Keltridge's resignation he was dispatched to Dedham, for on 10 October, as MA and curate, he was granted licence to preach throughout the diocese, especially in Dedham. On 1 June 1579, again as MA, he further received a teaching licence.[228] He duly presented himself at Aylmer's episcopal visitation in 1580, along with William Derby, schoolmaster.[229] Whilst no act book of office survives, there can be little doubt that Fitzallen appeared prominently in it: within months Aylmer had summarily suspended him from all his functions. His reasons were rehearsed in a letter, couched in somewhat obscure Latin, to the rest of his diocesan clergy. From this it appears that Fitzallen had openly scoffed at numerous monitions after apparently attempting to set up some kind of court for the correction of morals: this was against the law, no proper legal instruments having been drawn up.[230]

Aylmer perhaps suspected that Chapman was behind this illegal attempt at local self-regulation, so strikingly reminiscent of the efforts of James Calfhill, archdeacon of Colchester from 1565 to 1570, to enter into cahoots with Colchester's ruling *élite*

[223] *Ibid.,* preface, sig. Aii v.

[224] NRO, Reg/14/20, fo. 29v.

[225] Reg. Grindal, fo. 194v. The benefice was stated to be vacant only *per cessionem.* He did not compound for the living until 19 November 1579, which may suggest that he applied for exemption from his first fruits but had finally been turned down. In the event his sureties were William Lewes and Richard Starling of Dedham, both *generosi*: PRO E334/9, fo. 183v.

[226] He compounded for 'Capeles' [Capel St Andrew?], Suffolk, on 16 February 1585: PRO E334/10, fo. 86.

[227] In Dedham, Ann gave birth to a daughter, Abigail, baptized on 1 September 1579, and to a son, Timothy, baptized on 21 January and buried on 21 April 1582: ERO D/P 26/1.

[228] LMA DL/C/333, fos. 98r, 124r, 163v.

[229] GL MS 9537/4, fo. 95v.

[230] LMA DL/C/333, fo. 242r.

in a concerted attempt to effect a reformation of morals there.[231] It may account for his canny letter, dated 12 January 1581, in which he informed Chapman that 'uppon some occasion me specially movinge' he had suspended Fitzallen

> and bycause I would not have the parishe there voyde of common prayer during the tyme of his Inhibicion, I have thoughte good by these presents to appoint you upon the Sabothe dayes and other dayes by her Maj[es]ties booke appointed to reed the common prayer appoincted in the same according to the booke and other wise to occupye yorself in preachinge and catechising to yor good discretion, wishing you to deliver me present Answere by yor letter whether you will perform it or not, or otherwise, yf you shall refuse so to doe till you shall heare further of Mr Fitzallen's restitucion to surceas in like manner yor preaching there till you shall have made yor personall appearaunce before me. Soe fare you well in the lord, whose peace I hartelye wish in your whole parish. From my howse in London this xiith of January 1580.[232]

This was a perfect example of Aylmer's ability to insert the iron fist into the velvet glove. Since there is no further reference to the matter in the vicar general's book, Chapman presumably complied. Fitzallen, however, had resigned by 30 June 1582, when Richard Parker took his place. Do we take it that it was his semi-public efforts – far too bold in the face of Aylmer's relentless scrutiny – which determined the nature of the much more clandestine activities of the conference which was to be founded within weeks of his departure?

Richard Parker, 1582–90

By the time of Fitzallen's departure, Sir Ralph Sadler had finally asserted his right to present to Dedham on behalf of the duchy of Lancaster. Richard Parker, a young Cambridge graduate, received letters of presentation dated 27 June 1582, by reason of Fitzallen's resignation, and was instituted three days later.[233]

Parker's incumbency was to prove virtually coterminous with the life of the Dedham conference, in which he played a very minor part. Although his steady refusal of the surplice brought him into conflict with the ecclesiastical authorities at regular intervals, it was not his ritual nonconformity which was to furnish the next chapter in Dedham's turbulent history, but rather what appears to have been a brand-new ingredient in its affairs: clerical incontinency.

Altogether Parker's dealings with his female parishioners appear to have lacked subtlety. During 1587 and 1588 the High Commission took cognizance, at her petition, of his refusal to accept Marion (Mrs Thomas) Barker to communion.[234] Nothing further is heard of the matter after the early weeks of 1588 but during 1589 Parker was engulfed in a sexual scandal of major proportions which must have played its sorry part in the final dissolution of the Dedham conference.[235]

This tragi-comic episode is never alluded to in the minute book, nor does Parker himself mention it in his surviving papers. The sad and silly details would finally

[231] Byford, 'Price of protestantism', pp. 165–9.
[232] LMA DL/C/333, fo. 242r.
[233] PRO DL 42/99, fo. 19v; /100, fo. 10v; Reg. Grindal, fo. 205v.
[234] See *BR*, pp. 242–44.
[235] See below, pp. lxxiii–iv; ci–ii.

emerge during court hearings which took place in 1590, and Edward Stanhope appears to have taken up the case for the first time only on 5 November 1589, fully five months after the conference last met. On that day Parker was called into consistory to purge himself under the hands of four beneficed clerics, while Elizabeth, wife of John Martin, a tailor of Dedham, was ordered to 'deliver in writinge what she had to chardge Mr Parker withall'. Parker produced as compurgators the faithful William Tey; Stephen Beamont of Easthorpe, a staunch ritual nonconformist who had undoubtedly been privy to many, if not all, of the conference's activities;[236] and two local 'fellow travellers', Lionel Foster, rector of Little Tey (1588–97), and Laurence Lyde, vicar of Ardleigh (1569–1602), a friend of Thomas Farrar.[237] For technical reasons (a similar charge was pending against him), the court would not accept Foster as a compurgator and the case was therefore adjourned until Monday 24 November.[238] Two days later Parker pointed out that it would be difficult to produce compurgators on a Monday, 'being the morrow after the sabbath' and the case was therefore further adjourned until 28 November.[239]

Parker had still not got his act together. This time he brought in with him Lyde of Ardleigh, William Kirby, rector of East Donyland (1572–91), and Richard Cayzer, now rector of All Hallows Honey Lane, London, but formerly (1570–83) vicar of Elmstead, near Colchester. Parker alleged that Tey could not appear because of a 'sudden sickness'; that John Bound of Great Horkesley (another of the Dedham meeting's outer circle) had promised to come when the two of them had lately met in Colchester; and that Richard Forth, rector of Frinton (1585–1616), 'beinge in the citie at this present' had also agreed to appear. Evidently Bound and Forth were in the event conspicuous by their absence. Lyde, Kirby and Cayzer were therefore accepted as sufficient compurgators – a ruling that argues considerable leniency on Stanhope's part[240] – but at that crucial point, it seems, John Martin appeared and petitioned for the promotion of his wife's cause at instance. This was allowed, Martin thereupon submitting articles which Parker, predictably, repudiated ('*non credit*'). The case was therefore scheduled for its first full hearing on St Valentine's day 1590, Parker to the last dissenting from the court's ruling.[241]

Behind these formalities lay a hotbed of allegation and counter-allegation which would only come fully to light when sworn depositions were submitted to the court in the early summer of 1590.[242] Rumours had apparently been rife in Dedham for some time that Parker (still a bachelor) had made attempts on the chastity of the wife of Robert Thorne, then serving as a sidesman. Her maidservant had overheard Parker's 'filthie speeches' with her mistress and the matter had been presented

---

[236] See *BR*, pp. 185–7.

[237] See *BR*, pp. 205–7.

[238] LMA DL/C/616, pp. 119, 126. It is unclear whether Elizabeth Martin actually appeared at this hearing.

[239] *Ibid.*, p. 119.

[240] Since 1583 Kirby had frequently appeared in consistory for 'unruliness' and irregularities in his capacity of curate of St Botolph Colchester, which he served from the early 1570s until 1585: LMA DL/C/300, pp. 181, 451–2; /301, pp. 200, 376–7, 399, 411–12, 428, 437. And how could Cayzer, who had left the Stour valley within months of Parker's arrival in Dedham, be expected to prove a reliable witness concerning allegations which had not been brought until five years afterwards?

[241] LMA DL/C/616, p. 205.

[242] What follows relies on the depositions dated 10 May, 14 May and 4 July 1590 preserved in LMA DL/C/213.

before the archdeaconry court. A further allegation concerning the wife of the miller of Stratford St Mary had been heard before the bishop of London's commissary (whose court books for this period do not survive). But it was assuredly John Martin's incursion into court on 28 November 1589 which administered the *coup de grâce* to Parker's credibility.

Parker and the Martins lived under one roof in a property which, since John's tailor's shop was its principal frontage, was presumably owned or leased by him, Parker being his tenant. (Was the vicarage house still decayed and ruinous after all these years, or had Parker chosen to lease it out advantageously, husbanding his slender resources by living in rented accommodation on the proceeds?) It was alleged that Parker had made several indecent advances to Elizabeth, who had recently given birth. Once, when the baby cried and Martin came downstairs to investigate, he found Parker and his wife together in his shop, even though he had previously warned the vicar not to enter it. Martin sighed: 'Yf Mr Parker be of that sorte, what shall one saye to ytt?' – and returned to bed.

The Dedham ancients had tried to get to the truth of the matter long before it came to court. At first Parker denied everything, calling Elizabeth Martin a whore. Her response was robust: she was 'no bodyes whore but a whore of his makinge'. Subsequently Parker admitted to Richard Upcher, who had at first believed his strenuous denials, 'that for the attempte he woulde not deny but for the facte he never did, and that the Lord did knowe how sorrowefull he had bynn for that his greate oversighte'. Oversight indeed. Parker begged Upcher to 'stande his frende and consider his estate, being a yonge man, and that his creditt once taken away he was utterly undone, showinge himselfe verye much greved, with wepinge eyes'. Stephen Ellinot, clothier and Upcher's fellow churchwarden, confirmed that Parker had confessed that he had indeed propositioned Mrs Martin 'but, quod he, I proteste before god that I never did the deede with her'.

Yet Parker could scarcely have remained in Dedham after all that. Although the case appears simply to have petered out – Parker was ordered to do penance in church for attempting to seduce Mrs Robert Thorne but not for his overtures to Mrs Martin[243] – he had relinquished the benefice before 14 September 1590.

The aftermath of the conference, 1590–1615

Upon Parker's enforced departure, Dedham was bestowed on Henry Wilcock, four times mentioned in the Dedham papers. The chancellorship of the duchy of Lancaster had passed on Sadler's death in 1587 to Sir Francis Walsingham and upon Walsingham's to Sir Thomas Heneage in the summer of 1590. Thus it was as Heneage's protégé that Wilcock was presented on 14 September 1590 and duly instituted by Aylmer on 15 October[244] – but not before he had been subjected to merciless scrutiny by Aylmer and Stanhope. It may be hazarded that, after all his recent efforts, Aylmer was furious that Heneage had masterminded such a presentation.

---

243 ERO D/ACA 19, fos 101r, 117r. Dr Alan Pennie, in private correspondence with the editors, suggests that Parker may have forestalled his deprivation for sexual misconduct by agreeing to co-operate with Bancroft's investigations into the conference movement.

244 PRO DL 42/99, fo. 25r; /100, fo. 16r; Reg. Grindal, fo. 251r.

Wilcock's connexion with the Dedham leaders is obscure. If he was an old and valued friend of one of them it does not emerge from the scanty evidence. He had studied at Trinity College, Cambridge, between 1567 and 1575, was ordained at Norwich at the end of the decade and is thereafter lost to sight for four years.[245] He applied to the conference for financial help around Christmas 1583, and by April 1584, when he was to be 'admonished' for failing to acknowledge receipt, had been sent a total of £6 15s 0d, pledged by ten of its members (**14, 17MM**). It was not until 10 July that they received a formal letter of thanks, written from Erwarton, where he was presumably ministering before the arrival there of Edmund Salmon, and from which it appears that he had sunk into a state of severe depression about his debts.[246] In August 1585, following another letter from him to Chapman and Crick (not extant), the conference considered giving him further aid but nothing seems to have been done (**34, 35MM**).

On 13 October 1590, two days before his institution to Dedham, Wilcock was interviewed by Aylmer in his 'great chamber' at Fulham and is officially recorded as renouncing nonconformity and all its works. He stated that he now positively desired to use the surplice (*vult imposterum uti superpellicio*) at all times, 'excepte when by occasion of the washinge thereof yt happen to be kepte from him'. One perhaps hears Aylmer's hollow laughter between the lines. Wilcock also promised to use the ring in marriage and the cross in baptism and to minister communion only to those who knelt. He was prepared to use the Book of Common Prayer in all things 'excepte through brevetie of tyme or some speciall occasion he be letted'. To this submission he duly signed his name.[247]

Over to Stanhope. On 15 October, the day of his institution, Wilcock was summoned to his rooms in the College of Advocates. The surroundings were presumably intended to make this an awe-inspiring experience. Stanhope demanded to know 'whether he was ever Called before any ministers eyther in Essexe or Suffolke concerninge any Triall or approbacion to be made of him before he weare receaved to the Vicaredge of Dedham'; and whether 'he weare ever presente at any tyme after his preachinge at Dedham, which was abowte a Monthe before Michaelmas last past, concerninge eany election to be made by the sayd parishioners of Dedham of him to the same Vicaredge or whether he have harde that they made any suche election of him'. Wilcock denied that he had heard of 'any suche election . . . nor anye suche thing tendinge to that eande, save onelye their wrightinge to one of Sir Thomas Hennageis gentlemen for the furtheringe of him in this his Sewte'. He assured Stanhope that he meant to take 'no other callinge to the sayde benefice then this he hathe, which is by takinge of Institucion and Induction'.[248]

Between them, Aylmer and Stanhope could hardly have pushed matters further in order to extract a promise of ritual conformity and complete subservence to the processes of ecclesiastical law. It was obviously a forensic exercise designed to bang the final nails into the coffin of the conference movement in and around

---

[245] Matriculated sizar from Trinity at Michaelmas 1567; scholar 1571; BA early 1572; MA 1575. Ordained deacon and priest at Norwich on 13 December 1579 and 17 January 1580; 'vicar of Runham, Norfolk' (no dates given); 'perhaps' vicar of Dedham 1590: *Alum. Cantab.*, IV, 395.

[246] See below, p. 88.

[247] LMA DL/C/335, fo. 3v.

[248] *Ibid.*

Colchester. By 8 September 1592, however, when Wilcock was absent through illness from Aylmer's final episcopal visitation, it was clear that the fervent protestations of October 1590 had amounted to very little. The churchwardens admitted that Wilcock had been absent on some holy days but not presented for it. Although he had worn the surplice 'but once', they had likewise never presented him. They were duly ordered to lay it out every Sunday and to certify that they had done so when further called.[249]

Six years later, on 22 September 1598, when Richard Bancroft's visitors examined the clergy of Lexden deanery in Colchester, things had not greatly changed. Wilcock was again absent, having been excused by letter. The churchwardens, Roger Vaughan and Simon Fenn (later Edmund Chapman's executor), were ordered into consistory for not presenting him for the surplice. Wilcock himself is noted as appearing on 18 October, when he was absolved from the routine penalties automatically incurred by his absence.[250] He resigned within a year but there is no evidence as to whether he did so voluntarily or under pressure.

Following Bancroft's second visitation in 1601 (no call book survives) the fifth vicar of Dedham inside a generation faced his diocesan on disciplinary charges. On 19 October 1598, upon Wilcock's resignation, Meredith Powell had received letters of presentation from Heneage's successor as chancellor of the duchy, Sir Robert Cecil.[251] On 29 March 1602 he and his curate, David Waine, appeared in consistory because Powell had been absent from the visitation and because Waine sometimes failed to conduct weekday services, did not always use the surplice and confessed to baptismal irregularities: he did not 'cross them upon the forehead but doth saie he laie the signe of the Crosse uppon them'. Waine's excuse for omitting weekday services was that Chapman (evidently still vigorous) preached regularly on Tuesdays and Fridays.[252]

Powell proved yet another unmitigated disaster. On 18 April 1603 he appeared before Stanhope with his proctor, exhibiting letters of resignation from Dedham dated 10 January, which he prayed might be accepted. Stanhope countered with the allegation that it was common fame that Powell had 'sought by divers unlawfull simoniacall contracts to putt away his sayd vicaredge of Dedham as namely by asking fortie or fiftie pounds or som other like sum to give over or resign the same'. Powell offered to purge himself, asserting that he did 'simply and absolutely' resign his benefice into the hands of his Ordinary without ever having had 'any speeche or conference with any of paying giveing or receyving any som of money whatsoever for the resigning of the same'. Nor had he, directly or indirectly 'covenanted or made promis with any partie whatsoever for anything to be given unto him either before or after the resignation of the same . . . or in respect of his relinquishing of his sayd benefice by any meanes whatsoever, neither doethe expect any thing for the same of any man'. He added that the report as to his asking forty or fifty pounds to resign probably arose from the circumstance that 'som of the townesmen of Dedham when he was at Dedham about Allhallowtide last did aske him if he would

---

[249] GL MS 9537/8, fo. 55r.
[250] GL MS 9537/9, fo. 100v. Dedham's new schoolmaster, Richard Ravens, was present but described as licensed *sine subscriptione*; he duly subscribed the next day.
[251] PRO DL 42/100, fo. 23v.
[252] LMA DL/C/303, p. 550: undated note that both Waine and Powell were later absolved.

take 30 or 40 ^{li} for his chardges and leave the same benefice and suffer them to have
the naminge of a minister for it'. Since he was aware that his successor would have
to make oath that he had not come in by simony he 'therefore . . . would not aske or
take any thing of them for his sayd Resignation'. Stanhope – with a deep sigh,
perhaps? – accepted these disclaimers, declaring Dedham vacant and setting in
motion the necessary legal processes. Letters of sequestration were duly drawn up
that day and issued on 7 May to the churchwardens. [253]

On the basis of Powell's original letters of resignation, the new chancellor of the
duchy, Sir John Fortescue (1601–7), had already, on 10 February 1603, issued
letters of presentation, under one of Elizabeth's last signatures, for the institution of
Thomas Folx, MA.[254] Folx's claim failed, perhaps because of the death of the
queen.[255] On 21 May Fortescue issued a presentation deed in King James's name to
Samuel Wright, STB,[256] but early in 1604 it was stated that Bancroft would not
institute him because 'he refuseth to subscribe, thoughe he offereth to subscribe soe
farre as the lawe in that case requireth, there are above 800 communycants in that
Cure'.[257] Wright's efforts to secure the benefice did not survive Bancroft's implaca-
bility. Instead, Thomas Ledsam, MA, was presented by Fortescue on 8 May 1604
and instituted five days later by Powell's resignation.[258] This incumbency also
quickly failed. The benefice returned to the duchy of Lancaster on 20 March 1605,
letters of sequestration having been issued on 20 January to Dedham's churchwardens by Richard Vaughan, the new bishop of London, because the barons of the
exchequer had instructed him that Ledsam had not compounded for his first
fruits.[259]

Henry Sage received letters of presentation from Fortescue on 25 June and was
instituted on 29 June 1605 by Ledsam's resignation.[260] Sage, born in Toddington,
Bedfordshire, in December 1573, was a Cambridge graduate who had been vicar of
Little Brickhill, Buckinghamshire (1598–1602) before gravitating to London diocese
and gaining a preaching licence from Stanhope in January 1603.[261] Like most
nonconformists he was spared Vaughan's attentions during 1605–6 but his activities
were grist to the mill of Vaughan's authoritarian successor, Thomas Ravis, who
conducted his primary episcopal visitation in the late summer of 1607.

Dedham proved to be in its usual state of disarray – at least, as far as the diocesan

[253] LMA DL/C/338, fos. 105r, 107r.
[254] PRO DL 42/100, fo. 28r.
[255] Between 12 and 15 May, two *caveats* were submitted to the diocesan registrar, one on Folx's behalf,
the other anonymously: LMA DL/C/338, fo. 108r.
[256] PRO DL 42/100, fo. 29r.
[257] 'A Viewe', p. 3. Of two contemporary Samuel Wrights, the elder (by a decade) matriculated at
Corpus Christi College, Cambridge, in 1577, graduating from Magdalene in early 1580; MA 1583;
STB 1593; STP 1604; rector of Doddington, Cambridgeshire, c.1597–1639 (d.). The candidate for
Dedham in 1603–4 is more likely to have been the younger man, admitted pensioner at Emmanuel
College, Cambridge, on 22 June 1587; BA early in 1591; MA 1594. Appointed one of the original
fellows of Sidney Sussex in 1599, he will have been well-known to Thomas Gataker, Richard Stock
and William Bradshaw, also foundationer-fellows and stalwarts of the Jacobean Calvinist tradition in
London during the following two decades. He died about 1612, having published various sermons:
Alum. Cantab., IV, 477.
[258] PRO DL 42/100, fo. 30r; Reg. Bancroft, fo. 63v.
[259] LMA DL/C/338, fo. 195r.
[260] PRO DL 42/100, fo. 31v; Reg. Bancroft, fo. 79v.
[261] *Alum. Cantab.*, IV, 4; GL MS 9537/10, fo. 44v.

authorities were concerned. On 18 September, before Stanhope and three commissioners appointed by Ravis – Thomas Corbett, Richard Crackenthorpe and Robert
Ram – Sage frankly admitted that 'there is no surplice'. Even more frankly, he
admitted that 'he hathe not demanded it' and administered communion to parishioners 'somm standing and som sitting'. The visitors went through the weary business all over again: the churchwardens were ordered to provide a surplice and Sage
to wear it. He was to administer only to those that knelt and to preach the following
Sunday on 'the true use' of kneeling at communion. Yet despite Ravis's determined
drive for conformity it seems that the godly were still capable of resisting pressure
from Fulham and from Lambeth. Dedham's schoolmaster, Nicholas Humfrey, certified to be ill, was excused until 24 November. John Rogers, Edmund Chapman's
successor as Lecturer, had for reasons unspecified been suspended but that suspension was now 'stayed' by letters to Corbett from Stanhope.[262]

Although Sage was not deprived in 1609, like William Negus and Ezekiel
Culverwell, it may have been a close-run thing. On 3 December 1607 he had been
further ordered to certify that he wore the surplice and administered communion
only to those who knelt,[263] and in the summer of 1608 was again summoned for the
surplice, for failing to carry out perambulations and for leaving the vicarage house
in decay.[264]

On Sage's resignation in 1614/15 yet another presentation failed. The duchy
of Lancaster records preserve the presentation deed of Edmund Marcelyn on
11 February 1615 but nothing further is heard of him.[265] They do not, by contrast,
preserve that of Thomas Cottesford, MA, but it was Cottesford who on 18 October
1615 was instituted at the king's presentation, in right of the duchy of Lancaster *ut
asseritur, per cessionem* Henry Sage.[266]

Cottesford survived until 1641. It remains for an expert in seventeenth-century
ecclesiastical politics to elucidate how, after more than sixty years of regular dis-
location, Dedham managed to retain a godly pastor for a full twenty-five.

vi. The Dedham Conference

Origins and beginnings

We have already heard about the extraordinary and supposedly secret conference of
sixty East Anglian and Essex ministers held at John Knewstub's parish of
Cockfield, not far from Bury St Edmunds, in May 1582.[267] The future archbishop,
Richard Bancroft, was preaching in Bury in favour of conformity and against the
puritan preachers soon after this, and he would write a deliciously satirical account
of the famous alliance of ministry and magistracy.[268] But sleuth though he was, even

---

[262] GL MS 9537/10, fo. 44v.
[263] LMA DL/C/306, fo. 59r.
[264] LMA DL/C/307, pp. 462, 488.
[265] DL 42/100, fo. 38r.
[266] Reg. Bancroft, fo. 208r.
[267] See above pp. xlix–l.
[268] 'The plattforme of a precisians Sermon, and the acceptacion thereof', in *Tracts ascribed to Richard
Bancroft,* ed. A. Peel (Cambridge, 1953), pp. 71–3.

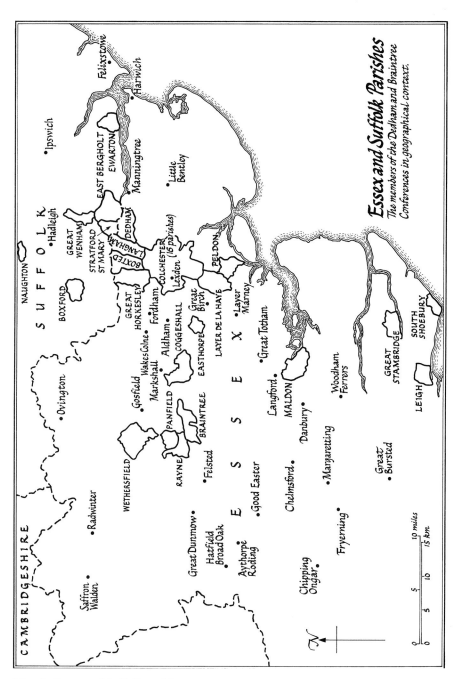

Map 3 Essex and Suffolk parishes.

Bancroft seems to have known nothing about the Cockfield meeting until John Field's correspondence fell into his hands, which was after Field's death in 1588, and in the series of raids on ministers' studies conducted in the aftermath of the affair of the Marprelate Tracts in 1589. This uncovered incriminating evidence which led to the prosecution of a number of the ministers, headed by Thomas Cartwright, first before the court of High Commission and then in star chamber, trials intended to prove the seditious nature and purpose of such meetings.[269] It was then that the vicar of Dedham, Richard Parker, from the midst of his personal troubles, went up to the high commission and sang like a canary, naming the leading members of the Dedham conference, although neither he nor they were prosecuted.[270]

But even then Bancroft and his fellow sleuths knew very little about conferences before 1582, and nor are we much the wiser. It is important to appreciate that with the exception of the Dedham minutes and papers, which are a unique archival survival, never seen by Bancroft, and which we owe in the first instance to Parker, who seems to have acted as secretary to the conference throughout its history, almost all our knowledge of the conference, or so-called 'classical' movement, is of a forensic nature, much of it relating to the conferences in Northamptonshire and Warwickshire, which had involved the majority of the ministers prosecuted in 1590–1.[271] But for the existence of Parker's little archive, now Rylands English MS 874, all that would be known about the meetings in and around Dedham would be a brief reference to his testimony to the High Commission included in Bancroft's *Daungerous positions*.

Only the London minister Thomas Edmundes, parson of All Saints Bread Street, who had turned his coat, had anything to tell the star chamber about what organization there may have been in the 1570s, describing how, from about 1571, 'the mynisters of the brotherhood' in London, led and organized by the Admonitioners, John Field and Thomas Wilcox, had met together 'att their owne howses by course', at first on Mondays and later on Thursdays. 'And when they mett they used to interprete some booke of scripture, none beinge presente but themselves, excepte by consent some stranger mynister ... was admytted into their Company.' In the course of the decade the 'brotherhood' grew in size, as preachers like William Charke, Walter Travers, Thomas Crook and Stephen Egerton swelled their ranks. 'And shortly after thinges beganne to growe to greater Rypenes, and then the name of discyplyne beganne to be in the mouthes of manye.' According to Edmundes, it was now agreed that since years of petitioning queen, parliament and privy council, not to speak of the writing of many books, had failed to make progress, 'every man should labor by all the meanes he could to bringe in the said reformacion themselfes.' Motions were made and conclusions set down: that the prescribed apparel was unlawful; that the prayer book was to be used only according to the discretion of the ministers; that all ecclesiastical titles, from archbishops and bishops down to their functionaries, were 'utterly unlawfull', to be abolished and replaced by 'thonly discyplyne and governement of Jesus Christe', pastors, doctors,

---

[269] Collinson, *EPM*, Part 8, 'Discovery, prosecution and dissolution'.
[270] Bancroft, *Daungerous positions*, p. 84.
[271] *Ibid.*, pp. 77–8; and Collinson, *EPM*, pp. 403–31.

elders and deacons, which was to be put into covert practice, only concealing the names of presbytery, elders or deacons.[272]

Edmundes was a hostile witness and his testimony must be treated with caution, particularly when he alleges that the London conference was all about the secret practice of the presbyterian 'discipline', possibly a back-projection. However, we can recognize a model for the Dedham conference in the kinds of meeting which he describes: regular gatherings of ministers in their own homes and in secret, devoted to expositions of set passages of scripture, but also making a forum for discussion of other matters, and especially what was to be done in the face of episcopal harassment and the continued frustration of the puritan aspiration for 'further reformation'.

On surviving evidence, it is not possible to say how far developments in Suffolk and Essex were self-generating within those counties, or dictated from London, although Oliver Pigge's letter to Field is suggestive of London's leadership. As well as reporting the Cockfield meeting, Pigge looked forward to the annual Commence-ment (or graduation ceremonies) in Cambridge, approving of Field's 'motion', presumably for another conference, 'as generall as might be', which could easily be done 'if you at London shall so thinke well of it and we here may understand your minde'.[273] Pigge had been in London only weeks before,[274] and no doubt had been one of the 'stranger ministers' admitted to Field's conference. On the other hand, the matters discussed at Cockfield, questions of conformity and nonconformity, were the pressing issues of the day in East Anglia and Essex, needing no prompting from London to form the agenda. Bishops Freke and Aylmer were in full repressive flood, and Pigge himself was in very hot water.

The momentum was kept up as summer turned to the autumn of 1582. In September there was another rally at Wethersfield, a village near Braintree in Essex, where a conference closely resembling the Dedham conference was about to be established. At Wethersfield Edmund Chapman's opposite number, well known to historians as a puritan diarist, was Richard Rogers, the first of a long line, even a dynasty, of powerful preachers, including Richard's nephew John Rogers, who would succeed Chapman as the most charismatic of Dedham's lecturers.[275] Chapman came across in September 1582 to preach, 'and sundry other godly preachers and other persons were then and there assembled to hear him'. A local farmer exploded: 'What make all these knaves here todaye, what will they make a god of Rogers? There were fortye of the knaves lyke rebelles indicted at the last assizes, and more had bene yf they had not made friendes.' The local magnate, Lord Rich, one of those friends, had ears to hear this provocative outburst, which is how we know

[272] PRO, Star Chamber 5 A 49/34.
[273] Bancroft, *Daungerous positions*, pp. 44–5.
[274] Pigge dated his *Comfortable treatise upon the latter part of the fourth chapter of saint Peter* (1582) from London, 6 April 1582.
[275] Knappen, *Two puritan diaries*. For the stirring ministry in Dedham of John Rogers, and the Rogers clan more generally, see Tom Webster, *Godly clergy in early Stuart England. The Caroline puritan movement c.1620–1643* (Cambridge, 1997), almost *passim*; Pennie, 'The evolution of puritan mentality', chs. 4 and 5; Sarah Bendall, Christopher Brooke, Patrick Collinson, *A History of Emmanuel College, Cambridge* (Woodbridge, 1999), pp. 189–91.

about it, since it was the unfortunate farmer who now found himself indicted, at the quarter sessions.[276]

Only a month later, ministers met, perhaps in Dedham itself, 'as a preparation to a meeting purposed by them',[277] and the first regular meeting of the conference was held before the year was out, on 3 December 1582. Insofar as this was a conspiracy, of which it bears some marks, it is unlikely to have been planned from London. The arrival of Chapman, Crick and Dowe on the banks of the Stour was a cunning move, mostly it would seem on William Cardinal's part. His native heath, the Vale of Dedham, was as far away as it was possible to get from the centres of diocesan administration and ecclesiastical justice in Norwich and London (and Norwich had never taken much interest in these Suffolk parishes in the far south of the diocese). Two of the local archdeacons, George Withers of Colchester and John Still of Sudbury, were sympathetic to the godly preachers, if themselves not, or no longer, nonconformists, and Withers had a radical past. As for the form of the conference and its protocols, the Norwich exiles, as we have seen, brought with them their own model for a conference of preaching ministers enjoying formal parity, the Norwich prophesying of 1575.[278] Nevertheless, Chapman, while more moderate than Oliver Pigge, might well have told Field in London, with whom he had corresponded, but not recently, that he hoped things had been 'so proceeded in as he would have liked of'.

It was agreed on 22 October 1582 that meetings would take place on the first Monday after the first Sunday in every month, proceedings to begin at 8 o'clock and end at 11. The speaker on each occasion would occupy the first hour in handling some portion of scripture, starting with the second letter of St Paul to the Thessalonians, a somewhat apocalyptic text, perhaps chosen because of its opening references to the love, faith and perseverance of persecuted Christians:

Wee ought to thanke God alwayes for you, brethren, as it is meete, because that your faith groweth exceedingly, and the love of every one of you toward another aboundeth. So that wee our selves rejoyce of you in the Churches of God, because of your patience, and faith in all your persecutions and tribulations that ye suffer. (2 Thess. i. 3 and 4, Geneva version)

Later choices included the first and second letters of St Paul to Timothy, the concentration in 2 Timothy to be on its relation to 'some controversy betweene the Papists and us'. St Paul had warned Timothy that 'the time will come, when they will not suffer wholesome doctrine: but having their eares itching, shall after their owne lusts get them an heape of teachers' (2 Timothy iv.3, Geneva version) (**15, 56MM**). Parker kept no record of this part of the business.

On each occasion the speaker and moderator for the next meeting would be appointed, by general consent. After his exposition (and following the tradition established in the prophesyings), the speaker would withdraw 'and every man's judgment to be asked of his handling of the said scripture, and the moderator to declare unto him, what the brethren judge of yt', the procedure known to Calvinists

[276] ERO QSR 84/33, 43.
[277] See pp. 3–5 below.
[278] See above p. xxxi.

as 'censure'. But this was not always done in the presence of the speaker, for in May 1589 (and the troubles into which he was falling headlong may have been relevant), Parker of Dedham wished that the judgment on the sermon should be delivered 'to the partie himself, bicause he thought it an injury that all shuld know his fault and not he himself', leading to 'an ill conceite of the speaker in the mindes of the rest'. He was told that not everyone would wish to be 'shamed or rebuked' before the whole body (**79M**). The first part of the meeting having ended with prayer uttered by the moderator, the two remaining hours were to be spent 'in decidinge some profitable questions', these to be propounded by the brethren a month in advance, 'or els aboute other necessary matters, for the furtheringe of the gospell, and preventinge of evill, as farre as we mighte deale in by our callinges', and of these Parker made minutes.[279]

Some days of meeting were to be devoted to a fast, which would provide occasion to admonish any of the brethren 'tutchinge their mynistery, doctryne, or liffe', if anything had been 'espied' which warranted it. Now the fast, universally observed in the Calvinist churches, was another development out of the prophesyings tradition. It usually consisted of a whole day of prayer and preaching, perhaps shared by a number of preachers, on an empty stomach, often ending with a communion and a shared meal, and almost always including a collection for some godly cause, perhaps related to the occasion of the fast.[280] The Dedham orders provided that on these days there would be interpretation of the Word by 'some' of the brethren, at first four, later three. This happened on twelve occasions, out of eighty meetings (**5, 10, 15, 23, 25, 27, 34, 44, 49, 54, 62, 76MM**). Usually no reason for holding a fast was given, although the three fasts in quick succession between October 1584 and February 1585 must have been related to the subscription crisis at that time. In August 1586, when it was decided not to have a fast, Henry Sandes explained 'the reasons that moved them unto it in Suffolk'. '1 the scarsity of all thinges 2 the little good it had wrought in men 3 the state of the Frenche Churche, and the matters of the lowe cuntreis and generallie the contempte of the gosple' (**46M**).

Thirteen ministers, headed by Edmund Chapman, Richard Crick and Richard Dowe, were 'chosen for the Assembly', some of them apparently not present but nominated at the inaugurating meeting as 'fitte persons', and the orders are endorsed by the signatures of twenty ministers, Chapman and Crick signing first, but including six who joined later in the life of the conference.[281] There was presumably an obligation to attend all meetings, although Parker did not record attendance and 'apologies for absence'; there are only occasional references to members being absent, once and once only Parker himself (**63M**). The first meeting was held at East Bergholt, with Crick the speaker and Chapman the moderator, the second at Dedham, in Chapman's house, Chapman the speaker, Crick the moderator, the third at Stratford St Mary, when Dowe was the speaker (**1, 2, 3 MM**). That this was a displaced Norwich initiative cannot be in doubt. The core of the conference consisted of the triangle formed by Dedham and the neighbouring Suffolk parishes of Stratford and East Bergholt ('Barfold'), Cardinal's town, which was home to two

[279] See pp. 5–46 below.
[280] Collinson, *EPM*, pp. 214–18; Collinson, 'PCM', pp. 323–46.
[281] See pp. 4–5 below.

members, Crick and John Tilney, neither of them beneficed in the parish. But the wider membership came from as far afield as Colchester, Peldon and Coggeshall to the south (Robert Lewis, William Tey and Laurence Newman), and Ipswich to the north (William Negus), with two members from Boxford (Henry Sandes and his father-in-law William Birde), who divided their loyalties between Dedham and a conference in Suffolk. Suffolk was also represented by Bartimaeus Andrewes and, after him, Ranulph Catelyn, rectors in turn of Great Wenham.[282]

The conference was to meet in secret: 'silence also to be kepte as well of the meetinge, as of the matters there dealte in'. However, in August 1583 it was reported that 'our meetinges were known and thretned', and it was decided to take advice from 'some godlie lawier' in order to establish how the conference could stay within the law (9M).

At a time when graduate clergy were still a minority of the clergy, all but two of the twenty-two members in the seven-year history of the conference were university men, seventeen of them graduates, including two Doctors of Divinity (Chapman and Crick) and ten MAs. Yet only half of the members were beneficed clergy, and two of those (Andrewes and Lewis) left their pastoral charges to become salaried town preachers in the lifetime of the conference. To that extent, the conference and many of its members were marginal to the structures of the established church, from which they were alienated, although in their own perception they were the true church. With historical detachment, we may consider that Dedham demonstrated the pathology of the Elizabethan church, as it emerged from the catastrophe of Grindal, the failure of liberalism, into the uncomfortable embrace of Aylmer and Whitgift.

There is no evidence in the Dedham record that the conference, unlike the earlier prophesyings, took any interest in the improvement of any of the unlearned and non-preaching clergy in its vicinity. For a closed society sworn to secrecy, that would not have been easy. But it seems that the Dedham brotherhood was sufficiently sectarian to have lost any such ambition, although it shared a typical puritan concern with scandalous or 'evil' ministers. On one occasion it was agreed 'that a wicked man being a mynister served at Higham' should be dealt with, two of the brethren to 'get articles against him' (11M). As the parliament of 1584 approached, it was decided to make a count of 'mynisters nere unto us which are both insufficient in lerninge and notoriously offensyve in liffe', and two members were deputed to deal with 'the gentlemen in Suffolke' about this problem (20, 21MM). This was part of an almost nationwide 'survey of the ministry' which fuelled the agitation in the house of commons about the dumb and insufficient ministry.[283]

More positively, the conference, on the motion of Henry Sandes, thought it a

---

[282] See the biographies of Andrewes and Catelyn, pp. 184–5; 191–2 below.

[283] *Seconde parte,* II, 88–184; survey of 'the unpreaching ministers in Essex with their conditions', 'a surveie of the double beneficed men in Essex', 'preachers of a scandalous life in Essex', *ibid.,* 156–65. There are no equivalent surveys extant for Suffolk, although Bancroft reported that 'as hee hath heard' surveys were made in Norfolk, Suffolk and Essex *(Daungerous positions,* p. 81). The surveys are placed securely in context, as documents, the context of other more official 'states' of the clergy, by D. J. Crankshaw, 'Elizabethan and early Jacobean surveys of the ministry of the Church of England' (unpublished Cambridge Ph.D. thesis, 2000). For the parliamentary campaign of 1584–5, see J. E. Neale, *Elizabeth I and her parliaments, 1584–1601* (London, 1957), pp. 58–83; Collinson, *EPM,* pp. 277–88; Hartley, *Proceedings in the parliaments,* II, 9–193, but especially 44.

good thing that 'men of fitt giftes and good liff' should be 'found out' to supply the church's want, although it was thought important to maintain the principle of residence, not 'a ranging ministery' (**20M**). Dedham was party to an agreement that ministers able to afford it were to accommodate students of divinity in their house-holds and to provide them with pastoral training. But these were to be 'well grounded in other knowledge of Artes and tongues',[284] and Thomas Stoughton, who seems to have been in training at East Bergholt, was the only conference member known to have been in this situation, and he had been fellow of a Cambridge college.

We should now analyse and categorize the 'profitable questions' and 'other necessary matters' which occupied the conference for two thirds of its allotted time, distinguishing between seven areas of concern, debate and activity: (1) learned conference on a contested matter of divinity; (2) all kinds of pastoral problems, some of them one-off, but many suggestive of a more general pastoral concern, even malaise; (3) other more public concerns in which the conference took an interest or assumed it had some responsibility; (4) the problem of conformity and subscription, and relations more generally with the bishops, archdeacons and ecclesiastical courts, in many ways the principal rationale for the conference; (5) the quasi-presbyterian conduct of church affairs in the catchment area of the conference, including the parochial placement of conference members, and liaison between ministers and their congregations; (6) promotion of reform, especially reform of the ministry, and adoption of the 'discipline', which is to say, the pursuit of a proactively presbyterian agenda; (7) the uncomfortable exploration of what the discipline might actually mean, in the internal relations of the conference members with their churches, and they and their churches with the conference, a prolepsis of what would happen to puritan ecclesiology in the 1640s. On all of these 'profitable questions' there was usually disagreement, even deadlock, with the consequence that the conference, embodying as it did the principle of formal parity, had some difficulty in deciding anything conclusively. And like those of any other competent secretary, Parker's minutes probably edited out the extent of the acrimony and heated words when there was failure to agree. One is reminded of Churchill's famous anatomy of democracy: the worst of systems, except for all the rest.

The debate on the Sabbath

The conference only once attempted to have a full-scale debate, resembling a formal university disputation, on a problematical question in divinity. This was the nature and use of the Sabbath, which of course was by no means a merely academic issue.[285] It was the first item of business to be raised at the very first meeting, and remained on the agenda throughout 1583 and the first half of 1584, resurfacing in

---

[284] See p. 86 below.

[285] Patrick Collinson, 'The beginnings of English sabbatarianism', in Collinson, *Godly people*, pp. 429–43; Kenneth Parker, *The English sabbath: a study of doctrine and discipline from the reformation to the civil war* (Cambridge, 1988). A health warning needs to be attached to Parker's study, since it elides the considerable difference between the low-grade sabbatarianism (if it is right to call it that at all) of the kind professed by Crick, and the more totalitarian sabbatarianism represented in this debate by Sandes. See also John H. Primus, *Holy time: moderate puritanism and the sabbath* (Macon, Georgia, 1989), especially ch. 2, 'The Dedham sabbath debate'.

March 1585, when Parker asked that the question might be 'determined'. But it was again deferred and not heard of again. (**1, 2, 3, 8, 9, 11, 12, 14, 17, 19, 28MM**). The original initiative lay with Richard Crick, who was not a sabbatarian, in the stricter sense, and who proposed that there is a Sabbath, but that it is not 'a whole naturall daie', and that christians are not bound to the same divine-moral and ceremonial observance as the Jews. He was opposed by Henry Sandes of Boxford, whose robust sabbatarianism anticipated the arguments of his fellow Suffolk minister Nicholas Bound (with whom he was probably in conference in Suffolk) who in 1595 would publish the first full-length treatise on the subject in English, *The doctrine of the sabbath.*

The conference sought advice from brethren in other places, especially Cambridge, but it was primarily Crick and Sandes who slugged it out over many months, and according to the rules of syllogistic disputation, generating more paper in Parker's files than any other single matter.[286] Sandes argued that the church had no liberty to alter the christian Sabbath, which derived from the creation and was built into the moral law, the Decalogue; that it was a whole day of twenty-four hours in which 'the busynes of the Sabboth' would occupy all the time available; and that breaches of the Sabbath merited the same punishment as blasphemy (presumably death), anticipating the insistence of John Dod and Robert Cleaver in their exposition of the Commandments that those who broke the Sabbath would suffer 'all curses and wretchedness', while those who observed it would 'thrive', both spiritually and materially. Sandes insisted: 'Further when it hath his name the lordes day I thinke it is of his authority in commaunding yt and severing it from the rest, which if it be soe . . . I see not how any man may alter yt.' 'That the Jewes Sabboth was a natural day I do like very well, but that ours shuld not be methinkes I yet do not see.'[287]

Crick stood in an older English protestant tradition going back to William Tyndale when he asserted that 'to thinke one tyme more holie then another is to observe tymes', that the Sabbath was not part of the moral law but an ecclesiastical rule or convention, for 'the churches receyved this daie at their owne choise, and not havinge any expresse commaundement' (the nub of the debate); and that 'if any writer affirmeth yt necessarie to have the resurrection of our Savyour only remembered by a daie, it is more then I knowe.'[288] The debate is remarkable for the extensive knowledge shown, especially on the part of Crick, of the Greek Fathers (Irenaeus, Chrysostom, Theophylact) and of the continental theologians who had written on the matter, including Bullinger, Peter Martyr, Beza, Danaeus, and the Heidelberg theologians and Hebraists whose scholarship undergirded the learned Tremellius Bible, printed in London in 1580. In 1581 the gentlewoman Frances Jermyn bequeathed copies of the Tremellius Bible to a number of Suffolk ministers, and within two years Sandes was relying on his copy to score points in this debate.[289]

Although their differences were not resolved, the Crick–Sandes disputation more than anything else in the Dedham papers helps us to understand how important it

[286] See pp. 46–70 below.
[287] See pp. 53–7 below.
[288] See pp. 57–70 below.
[289] Collinson, 'The beginnings of English sabbatarianism', pp. 434–5.

was for relatively learned ministers to enjoy a 'critical mass' of godly learning, and not to be isolated spiritually and intellectually. Some years later Ralph Cudworth, who under the college statutes had been obliged to leave his fellowship at Emmanuel for a country living, wrote from the relatively barren soil of Aller in Somerset to Archbishop Ussher: 'I should desire noe greater earthly blessing, then to live in that or such like societie, where I might have the continuall companie of learned men, to conferre together about Controversies and Antiquitie: and if I might have their good company either there or elsewhere, I should think myselfe happy.'[290] However, Dedham, for whatever reason, never repeated the experiment of a full-scale debate about 'Controversies', although in December 1585 Richard Dowe suggested that 'when we had no speciall causes to deale in, some Question of divinity might be propounded to the rest' (**38M**).

Pastoral problems

But 'speciall causes', bread and butter pastoral issues, predominated. Was the second marriage of a man who had divorced his wife for a just cause valid? The conference concluded that by the word of God it was (**3, 4MM**). Was it proper to baptize children who were conceived before marriage? (deferred). And should the child of a 'strumpet', abandoned in the church, be baptized? (deferred) (**4, 21MM**). Was it 'convenient' that a woman should pray, 'having a better gift then her husband'? (deferred to the next meeting, when it was thought 'not necessary to be handled') (**18, 19MM**). The marriage of cousins was deemed to be lawful (**20M**). John Tilney of East Bergholt needed to know whether he could marry a young man of twenty-four to a woman over fifty, and he got some helpful advice (**26M**).

Several members shared their local pastoral difficulties with the brethren. Crick of East Bergholt sought advice, not for the first time, on what to do with 'some kind of people that disturbe him in his mynistery (**24, 28MM**), and that encouraged Dowe of Stratford St Mary to complain against 'such as wold not come to heare him nor receyve the Sacramentes from him' (deferred 'for want of tyme') (**28M**). But Crick's problem was taken more seriously, and would not go away, since matters in 'Barfold' were building up to a crisis. Some thought Crick should excommunicate these 'disordered persons', while others preferred that he should 'rather desire the chieff and forwardest in the Congregation' to deal with them, and, if that failed, to bring them before a magistrate (**29, 30, 32, 42MM**). When Crick went over to Hadleigh in March 1587, perhaps to see his father, there was an 'outrage' committed in his absence: a case of husband-beating which had provoked a 'skimmington', a carnivalesque demonstration involving a man in woman's clothing and a woman dressed as a man. 'His credytt was gretlie tutched in yt' (**54M**). When Chapman asked how to deal with 'some careles persons that had no regard of the word or Sacramentes', it was noted that this problem was always coming up, and that the line now agreed upon was to complain to the magistrates (**40M**). But that did not deter Ranulf Catelyn of Wenham, an inexperienced minister, from asking how to deal with a feud involving defamatory words. Could he admit the parties to the communion? And what to do with 'some froward poore men that were every way disordered'? (**72M**).

---

[290] Quoted, Collinson, *Religion of protestants*, pp. 135–6.

Robert Lewis of Colchester had a rather different problem. He could not compete against the popular town preacher, George Northey, and was losing his congregation to Northey's sermons. This was a delicate matter but the conference thought that it might help if Lewis tried not to preach on the same texts as Northey (**8, 29, 54, 55MM**). This was another running sore, healed only when Lewis left Colchester to become a preacher in Bury St Edmunds (**65, 75MM**).

Some questions raised, especially by the more junior members, were just silly. Edmund Salmon should not have had to ask what to do with the sum of one pound, collected at a fast for the French church in London (**58M**). Nine meetings later, Salmon wanted to know how to detect a witch, and whether boys of sixteen might wear hats in church. Both questions found opinion divided. Some members were all for searching the woman's body for the devil's mark, while others more sceptical thought witchcraft a popular fantasy and dangerous delusion (**67M**). Later Salmon asked whether he could baptize the child of an Irish woman, a vagrant. He was told that he could not, since she was unable to give an account of her faith, and it was not known whether the baby was legitimate (**80M**).

The commonest pastoral problems raised in the conference concerned access to the sacraments: which children should be and which ought not to be, baptized, who should receive communion, making concrete the tension between the public ministry of the members towards all and sundry, and their own more sectarian vision of what constituted the true church and its sacraments. Reviewing the record of the minutes, and the *Biographical Register* included in this volume, it is apparent that many, perhaps most, of the Dedham brethren were not very successful pastorally. Some indeed were pastoral disasters. Why was this, and how typical or untypical were these particular Elizabethan clergy? Is it just that we happen to know a lot about them? Or was strenuously aspirant godliness in itself a recipe for failure?

It may be by no means a *non sequitur* to follow these comments on the pastoral competence, or incompetence, of the Dedham ministers with some observations on their material state. The more distinguished and popular of the ministers, such as Henry Sandes of Boxford, appear to have done very well out of their more committed followers, and none better than Dr Edmund Chapman of Dedham itself. Of the 'ancients' who signed the Dedham orders, Henry Sherman left £6 to Chapman in his will of 1590 (and £2 to Richard Parker); in his will written in August 1599, Pearce Butter made arrangements for Chapman to receive £5 a year over six years; while in a codicil to his will dated 20 December 1600, Edmund Sherman left a further £5 to Chapman for six years, for as long as he remained in Dedham, to be paid in quarterly instalments of 25s.[291] Even if, as Alan Pennie has suggested,[292] such 'legacies' may reflect the testators' obligations with regard to the arrangements which underlay the foundation and financing of the Dedham lectureship, the sums involved argue that Chapman was receiving a handsome stipend, far in excess of the tithe income of many humbler clergy. And when we add, as many other cases suggest we should, such extra perks as fees for funeral sermons, it is clear that Chapman's prosperity was more than spiritual. It would be surprising if

[291] See p. 127 nn. 363–65 below.
[292] See Appendix 2.

this relative affluence had not been resented by some run-of-the-mill clergy, and perhaps more widely.

Wider concerns

The conference dealt with a great variety of more public matters, external to itself and its parochial concerns. In March 1583 it was proposed that Thomas Cartwright be written to, to encourage him in the writing of his *Confutation* of the catholic version of the New Testament, published in Rheims, the so-called 'Rhemish Testament', a project of considerable public interest, which Cartwright's old opponent, Archbishop Whitgift, would try to block (**4M**).[293] Although the minutes say that the matter was deferred, eight members of the conference wrote to Cartwright on 19 April, and Cartwright replied, from Middelburg in the Netherlands, on 5 May.[294] The matter was revived in November 1586 (**50M**). In May 1583, the conference intervened in an effort to put a stop to the seasonal plays still being performed in the down-river parish of Manningtree (**6M**). But the conference found that it had no public competence to deal with the problem of tramps, 'the multitude of roges wherewith the cuntrey was charged at their dores', this being a matter for the magistrate (**13M**). Complaints brought to the conference about Dedham clothiers dyeing their cloth on the Sabbath were a more legitimate concern, to be handled by dealing with 'the godliest of that trade' (**34M**). Perhaps in response to a privy council brief (or licence to collect), the brethren put their hands in their pockets and found the considerable sum of £6 15s for the relief of Henry Wilcock, a bankrupt minister who would later succeed Parker as vicar of Dedham, although this was a loan and not a gift, and Wilcock came back a year later for more (**14, 15, 17, 21, 34, 35MM**). Henry Sandes, who seems to have come from Lancastrian stock, twice raised problems which had arisen in his native county, but Lancashire was thought by the conference to be a far away country of which they knew little (**34, 59MM**).

A landmark in the life of the conference came in January 1585 when the ministers were commissioned by the privy council (implying recognition and approval in that quarter at least, although it was apparently Cartwright's brother-in-law, the redoubtable John Stubbs, who had fixed it up) to debate with a prominent catholic lawyer, Andrew Oxenbridge, who was given his own house in Dedham, with arrangements for his meals, linen and bedding (**26, 27MM**). This too left plenty of paper in Parker's files. Crick, as probably the most learned of the brethren, had the first go at Oxenbridge, followed by his protégé Thomas Stoughton and Richard Dowe, and then there was another bout with Crick.[295]

Error on the right hand, error on the left, to quote the titles of two books published in 1608.[296] The conference was also concerned with radical puritan separatism, and with heresies of the kind often labelled 'anabaptist', Chapman complaining in June 1585 of 'some that make a Schisme and rent from our Churche' (**31M**). By the end of the year, the threat of sheep-stealing came close to home with

---

[293] A. F. Scott Pearson, *Thomas Cartwright and Elizabethan puritanism* (Cambridge, 1925), pp. 198–210.

[294] See pp. 72–4 below.

[295] See pp. 97–106 below.

[296] Henoch Clapham, *Errour on the right hand, through a preposterous zeale* (London, 1608); *Errour on the left hand. Through a frozen securitie* (London, 1608).

the arrival in Suffolk of Edward Glover, who as 'E.G.' had just published A *present preservative against the pleasant, but yet most pestilent poyson, of the privie libertines, or carnall gospellers,* about to be confuted in Stephen Bredwell's *A detection of Ed. Glovers hereticall confection, lately proffered to the church of England.* Here too the conference seems to have played an almost official role, keeping track of transactions which involved 'the Bishopp' (Aylmer), 'the magistrate', and perhaps themselves (**38, 39MM**). Presently it was necessary to make decisions about Glover's followers. Should they not be brought to Dedham to be confronted with the doctrine of justification by faith, which Glover's polemic against 'carnal' gospellers was undermining? No, better that their own ministers should deal with them 'mildly' and, if that had no effect, to convent them before 'some of the Congregation', and failing that, to bring them 'before the whole churche' (**40, 41MM**): presbyterian discipline in action. Glover had been in prison, but in April 1586 was again at large, to the consternation of the ministers (**45M**). But this was probably a flash in the pan. History knows of 'Brownists' and even of 'Barrowists', but not of 'Gloverites'.[297]

Conformity, nonconformity and subscription

The entire life of the conference was lived in the shadow of the episcopal campaign against nonconformity, begun in the Essex parishes by Bishop Aylmer of London, and made more comprehensive throughout his province by Archbishop Whitgift, and by his drive to secure submission to the three articles – the royal supremacy, the prayer book, and the thirty-nine articles – which he launched soon after his arrival at Lambeth in November 1583.[298] Indeed, without the provocation of this emergency there would probably have been no conferences, in Dedham or elsewhere. Already, in January 1583, the question had been raised how far the Book of Common Prayer could be used in worship (**2M**). In May, William Tey wanted to know whether he should respond to a citation to attend the archdeaconry court, perhaps implying that he was not inclined to do so, and in August the question was put 'whether we might goe to the B[ishop] or noe: it was thought good not to goe', and again the question arose 'how far a pastor might goe in reading the book of common praier' (**6, 9MM**). These were like distant rumbles of thunder before the storm. By October 1583, it was known that Whitgift was on his way, and the conference agreed to write to the new archbishop 'to be favourable to our Church and to discipline' – not '*the* Church', as in Usher's 1905 edition – and to write to other brethren, Chapman to London and Norwich, Sandes to Cambridge and Suffolk, and that a letter should also be sent to Archdeacon Withers (**11M**).

As soon as the demand for subscription was made, Dedham busied itself with getting into its hands responses and forms of limited subscription from other areas,[299] and Chapman now wrote to Field, the first letter he had written to him for

---

[297] Champlin Burrage, *The early English dissenters in the light of recent research (1550–1641)* (2 vols., Cambridge, 1912); Michael R. Watts, *The dissenters from the reformation to the French Revolution* (Oxford, 1978).

[298] Collinson, *EPM*, Part 5, 'Whitgift'.

[299] See pp. 87; 108–24 below. Many of these papers, some of them duplicated in the Dedham file, are calendared in the first volume of *Seconde parte*. See Collinson, *EPM*, pp. 243–72, with references to copies of some of these items in other MS collections; more fully in Collinson, 'PCM', pp. 407–78,

some time, conveying a typically eirenical and rather vague proposal for 'a more generall conference . . . a holy meeting . . .', so that a united front could be formed, but hinting strongly his desire that it should be of a moderate, non-confrontational nature. This brought a more robust and hard-line response from Field, referring to the Grindalian years as an 'unhappy tyme of loosenes and liberty' which had made him less zealous and diligent in God's cause than he ought to have been. There should be no shilly-shallying with Whitgift. 'The peace of the Church is at an end if he be not curbed.'[300] The difference between Field's intransigence and Chapman's desire for a peaceful, uniting solution to the crisis would now be dramatized in the Dedham conference itself.

In April 1584 Chapman moved that 'the B[isho]ps' proceedings indicated that there should be a general meeting to confer on a common policy, and in May it was agreed that there was need for 'a generall meetinge of lerned brethren' 'to advise and consent about the cause of subscriptions' (**17, 18MM**). By now ministers had been suspended in some numbers, and the conference was disposed both to organize petitions for their relief, and to make pastoral provision for the parishes affected. Parker's papers include a long petition to the privy council from six of the Essex members of the conference, which probably dated from this time.[301] Laurence Newman of Coggeshall was deputed to go up to London to find out what the brethren there intended about a general meeting, and arrangements were made to find a temporary replacement for him in his absence (**19M**). But for once, and at this time of all times, Field's organizing capacity seems to have been deficient. So far as we know, there was no general meeting in 1584, only encounters with Field as the county delegations came up to London, and the circulation of various forms of limited subscription from different counties (very many of them collected at Dedham and filed by Parker while the subscription crisis played itself out at the highest political level); together with Field's ironically intransigent advice that it would be as appropriate to subscribe to Aesop's fables as to Whitgift's articles.[302] But probably there was no deficiency on Field's cunning part. He knew that a general conference would probably, like Chapman, head for the middle ground, which he had no intention of occupying. Among many other relevant papers filed by Parker, there were arguments from 'a lerned man' (no reason to suppose that he was a conference member) that it was not lawful to cease from preaching when inhibited by a bishop. The interest of this document lies in the copious historical citations from John Foxe's *Actes and monuments*.[303]

In August Chapman showed his moderate hand: 'mr Chapman moved whether it were thought good that a reconciliation shuld be offered to the B[ishop]s, that since we professe one god and preache one doctrine we may joigne together with better consent to build up the Churche.' It was not thought good, 'lest we shuld seeme to yeld in our cause, and sought to be of their company' (**21M**). So much for

---

annotations. There is another cache of documents of this kind, 'matters touching the Archbishop of Caunterburye and the Ministers' in Sir Walter Mildmay's papers, Northamptonshire Record Office, Fitzwilliam of Milton Papers, F. (M). P. 5. 60, 148, 162.

[300] See pp. 89–90 below.
[301] See pp. 91–2 below.
[302] 'Mr Feilde and Mr Egerton their tolleration', *Seconde parte*, I, 284–6.
[303] See pp. 94–5 below.

moderation. In November, Chapman wrote privately to Cartwright, still overseas in the Netherlands, about 'that miserable distraction that is betwene the preachers and professors of our English church for matters of ecclesiasticall governmente', confessing his dislike of both parties 'for their hotte and violent manner of proceedinge, ether seeking by all meanes to conquere and deface thother, not dulie regarding the holie communion they have in their head Christ Jesus . . .'. He went on that he knew that truth was precious and must be stood for, but could it not be combined with 'a more mild and brotherlie course'?[304] But the conference as a body was not ready for compromise. Newman wanted to know whether he could make a limited subscription, and was told he could not. On the other hand, Newman and John Tilney were advised not to 'presse soe farre' as to continue to preach while suspended, a ruling with which they and William Negus of Ipswich were not happy (**22, 23MM**).

The real firebrand of the conference, as militant as Field if not more so, was William Tey of Peldon, a man of means and status; his contempt for the bishops perhaps reflected his social self-esteem. When he occupied the role of speaker, in one of the later meetings of the conference (held at his own house, Layer Hall, which he had recently inherited) in March 1588, he used his discourse to ask whether the bishops were 'anie longer to be tolerated or noe'. The conference was perhaps embarrassed: 'Not delt in'. But Sandes of Boxford was perhaps emboldened by Tey to use even more provocative words three months later, when he moved 'whether the course of the B[ishop]s were such and of such moment, that they were not to be thought of as of brethren, and soe to be delt withall in our publike and in our private speeches and praiers'. At the next meeting the motion was referred to Crick, Newman and Tey, but after that it seems to have been quietly buried (**66, 68, 69, 70MM**). Tey's extreme views had earlier been expressed in justification of his insistence that ministers, even when inhibited by lay magistrates, should continue to preach (**19M**). Asked for his 'reasons', Tey chose to understand the issue to be whether to obey the bishop's jurisdiction, and asserted, with brutal finality, 'the B[ishops]s authority is Antichristian, ergo not to be obeyed.'[305] In an almost hysterical letter, Tey wrote of 'Antichrist tyrannizing the Church by our B[ishop]s magnified and exalted above measure'. 'Are these thinges yet to be tolerated?' 'The truth of these points being serched and found out, the Lord give us courage and fortitude to stand in the truth and to quitte our selves like valiant men in the Lorde his cause.'[306]

But the conference would have to go on living with a problem which had to be negotiated rather than fought on a battlefield. In January 1587 a *cri de coeur* from Newman of Coggeshall, facing suspension, was answered by deciding that Chapman and Crick should go to Sir Robert Jermyn and Lord Rich to get letters written to the privy council, the result of the *démarche* being that Jermyn would write to Rich 'to deale throughlie and effectually in that matter' (**52, 53MM**).

---

[304] See p. 75 below.
[305] See p. 94 below.
[306] See pp. 80–1 below.

The Conference as Classis

It should already be clear that the Dedham conference was more than a debating society. There was an assumption built into almost all of its proceedings that it had some authority to make and impose decisions: in other words, although it never so styled itself, it operated in practice as a kind of *classis* (or, in Scottish parlance, presbytery) within the reformed, or presbyterian, polity; and there was an assumption that the churches within its remit were congregations which also enjoyed the liberty and the powers allowed to them within that vision of the nature of the church, particularly to 'call' their ministers. The minutes know nothing of the legal processes of patronage and episcopal institution. From a conformist, Bancroftian, point of view, here was a Trojan horse, consciously committed to the infiltration and subversion of the Church of England as duly and legally constituted. There was something in that. But much of what Dedham undertook was less conspiratorial and deliberate. The conference merely took advantage of the latitude which loosely constituted ecclesiastical institutions allowed within the tiresome and in many ways irrelevant encasement of bishops, archdeacons and church courts. It would have been nice to have seen the pie in the sky of 'the discipline' inaugurated, in all its glory. But the ramshackle structure of the Elizabethan church already permitted much of the writ of discipline to run, much as a derelict mansion may tolerate any number of squatters within its shaky walls.

At its first meeting, the conference considered the 'placing' of Richard Dowe, whether at East Bergholt or Stratford, at the second decided 'for diverse reasons' that he should 'accepte of his callinge at Stratford', and at the sixth thought it 'inconvenient' ('verie' deleted) that Dowe should continue to read a lecture at Higham (**1, 2, 6MM**). When Bartimaeus Andrewes announced his intention of leaving his pastoral cure of Wenham and began to negotiate with Yarmouth for the better-paid and higher-profile post of town preacher, the conference assumed that it had a role to play, if not quite a jurisdiction to exercise. Two of its members were deputed to discuss Andrewes's stipend with the people of Wenham. That was in September 1584. By February 1585, Andrewes had either already left for Yarmouth or was moonlighting, and the conference 'admonished' him for his absence and moved the question 'whether a Pastor called to a place may leave the people they being unwilling of his departure'. Andrewes told his side of the story. It was then decided to hold an Extraordinary meeting on the matter, staged in the house of a leading Dedham clothier, Edmund Sherman, and attended by one of the Yarmouth bailliffs, who had indeed requested the meeting, acknowledging the competence in the matter of the conference. Parker's minutes of this meeting are more copious than for any other in the history of the conference. The debate went against Andrewes and the move to Yarmouth, the grounds including the conviction that the bond between pastor and people was inseparable, like a marriage, and that it was not right to move from the higher calling of pastor to the inferior position of doctor. Negus of Ipswich hit the nail on the head when he said that 'every man that professetn himself desirous of discipline shuld exercise it himselfe in his own causes soe farre as he coulde'. But in such a matter the conference was in practice toothless and impotent. By the next regular meeting in early March, Andrewes had already left Wenham and merely sent a message to the conference, which reconciled itself to a *fait accompli* (**22, 27MM, Extra M, 28M**).

In spite of his ringing affirmation about self-imposed discipline, Negus had chosen the occasion of the Extraordinary meeting to propose that he himself should leave his present post, where relations with his congregation had broken down, in order to accept a 'good callinge' from 'the congregation of Lee' in south Essex, Lord Rich territory. Chapman and Crick were deputed to confer with 'the people of Ipswich'. At the next regular meeting, Negus again went through the motions of asking advice, and the advice he got was that he should stay in Ipswich. But of course Negus accepted the job at Leigh, and at the next meeting desired the brethren 'to allow of him, if not to admonish him, thanking god for the benefite of the meeting, acknowledging he had failed in many thinges, and craved their praiers to god for him.' Another story concluded (**Extra M, 28, 29MM**).

The conference continued to be active in what was no doubt understood to be an advisory role when it came to 'callings'. When Thomas Stoughton announced the likelihood of his appointment to a living in his native Kent, the conference gave him its blessing and continued to be supportive in what proved to be an abortive negotiation. Stoughton was then presented (by the godly Ipswich merchant John More) to the living of Naughton, only eight miles to the north of East Bergholt where he had been living with Crick, and the conference no doubt congratulated itself on another problem solved. But Stoughton got off on the wrong foot with his parishioners, and soon Crick was suggesting to the conference that it might be best for him to move on. As usual, the conference was not happy about this and in this case Stoughton seems to have listened to their advice, remaining at Naughton in spite of continuing difficulties (**35, 36, 45, 55, 65, 78MM**).

There was an aspiration towards uniformity in the affairs of the churches represented in the conference. Having approved the publication of Edmund Chapman's *Catechism* 'for the use of the people of Dedham especially', the conference looked for a uniform, or at least 'certayne', form of catechizing in all the churches (**3, 13MM**). This led to a full-scale debate on the practice of catechizing, and on what basis, revealing a surprising hostility to written catechisms among some members. Dowe supported the proposition that 'it is not lawfull to expound Catechismes in the Church' with this syllogism: 'No mans writings are to be expounded in the Church, but written Catechismes are such. ergo.'[307] It was Dowe who proposed that all the ministers should use the same form and order in their prayers before and after the sermon, and when he further suggested that all the churches should minister the sacrament on the same day, Chapman agreed, desiring that the churches communicate with one another about such arrangements, 'that there might be asmuch conformity as might be outwardlie' (**29M**).

Agitation for Reform and the Reception of the Discipline

The Dedham papers and minutes contain some of the most valuable information we have about the concerted, even organized, activity of puritan ministers in the 1580s, designed to promote 'further reformation' and even to build a properly reformed

---

[307] See pp. 83–5 below. Chapman's catechism (his only publication) was printed in 1583 as *A catechisme with a prayer annexed meete for all christian families.* In view of the Dedham debate on the subject, the distinction between a catechism designed for household use and one to be expounded in church is no doubt of significance.

church, with 'the discipline' replacing hierarchy.[308] They tell us about the liaison with other conferences, and especially with 'the brethren in London'; about more general conferences, which, if local conferences on the Dedham model were *classes* in embryo, were aspiring to be 'synods'; and about dealings with sympathetic gentry, both in the locality and at Westminster, in the parliaments of 1584 and 1586. There were three prongs to this fork: resistance to subscription and the response to suspensions and other impediments to the ministry of the godly ministers; the wider cause of reforming the ministry more generally, especially through dramatizing, in parliament, its allegedly woeful condition; and the moves made towards the formal adoption of a Book of Discipline, which would entail the construction of a pres- byterian 'church within the Church', without, as the separatist Robert Browne famously put it, 'tarrying for the magistrate'.[309]

As we have seen, in October 1583 the conference responded with alacrity to the news of Whitgift's elevation to Canterbury, writing letters in all directions (**11M**). In April 1584, Chapman moved that the bishops' proceedings required the ministers to have 'a generall meeting to conferre what might be done', and in May such a meeting was approved, 'for better advise and consent about the cause of subscrip- tions' (**17, 18MM**). In June William Tey, ever the activist, moved that the churches should energize their congregations in petitioning, it 'being a duty in them to sue for their pastors being faithfull and they deprived of them' (**19M**).[310] As the 1584 parliament, in which the state of the ministry was to loom very large, approached, Dowe and Stoughton were deputed to deal with 'the gentlemen of Suffolk' (and this would have meant Sir Robert Jermyn and Sir John Higham especially) 'about the number of ill mynisters' (**21M**). Three weeks before parliament actually met, it was agreed that a fast should be held 'against parliament that was at hand'; and 'at this tyme, that in every cuntrey some shuld be chosen so farre as we could procure it that some of best creditt and most forward for the gosple shuld goe up to London to solicite the cause of the Churche' (**24M**).[311] In December, Henry Sandes reminded the conference that everyone acquainted with 'any gentlemen of worth and godli- ness shuld stirre them up to be zealous for reformation' (**25M**). In January 1585, it was thought necessary to hold another fast, and if possible to synchronize with arrangements in London 'that we might joigne with them, and that some shuld contynue to solicite the cause of the Church there' (**26M**).

In June 1585 Chapman announced that there was to be a meeting in Cambridge 'of diverse godlie men' (no doubt timed to coincide with the annual Commence- ment), who would be asked for their judgment about how far the prayer book could be used, how to prevent the mischief of separatism, and 'whether we may use the Bishops and come to their Courtes'. A month later it was decided that Laurence Newman and Henry Sandes would represent Dedham at this meeting (**31, 32MM**).

---

[308] Collinson, *EPM,* Part 6, 'The grand design' and Part 7, 'Presbytery in episcopacy'.

[309] *The writings of Robert Harrison and Robert Browne,* ed. Albert Peel and Leland H. Carlson (Elizabethan Nonconformist Texts, II, 1953), 153, and more generally in this tract, 'A treatise of reformation without tarying for anie', pp. 150–70.

[310] For examples of 'popular' petitions from other parts of Essex to the privy council and parliament, see *Seconde parte,* II, 187–92. The 1586 'Supplication of Dunmow . . . to the L. Rich, appointed to the Parliament' bears 236 names, which would repay analysis.

[311] For the implications of this, see Neale, *Elizabeth I and her parliaments, 1584–1601,* pp. 60, 146–7.

Newman reported in August that the questions proposed had not been dealt with at Cambridge, but that it was intended to meet again (at Stourbridge Fair time, in September?), and that it would be best for John Knewstub 'to deale with the brethren that shuld be there assembled' (**33M**).

In October 1586 a new parliament gathered at Westminster. Its main business was to deal once and for all with Mary Queen of Scots, but it provided an opportunity to renew the agitation for church reform. And now the ministers, in the country and in London, were better prepared for concerted action. Chapman, and this was surely superfluous advice, wrote to Field warning him not to 'let slip this notable opportunitie' by

> notinge out all the places of Governement in the lande, for which Burgessis for the Parliament are to bee chosen; and using all the best meanes you canne possibly for the procuring the best gentlemen of those places, by whose wisdome and zeale, Gods causes may be preferred: conferre amongst your selves, howe it maye best bee compassed. You are placed in the highest place of the Churche and lande, to that end.[312]

So far, the word 'discipline' had occurred only twice in the minutes, and tangentially at that. In March 1585, Tey had moved that letters be sent to the masters of colleges, 'to have a care of the Church discipline' (which could have meant anything) (**28M**), and in June 1585, when no parliament was in immediate prospect, Sandes moved 'that some thinges might be considered of for the helpinge forward of discipline the next parliament', which was 'liked of' but deferred (**31M**). From the Dedham minutes one would not suspect that the 1584 parliament, beyond discussing problems of the ministry, had been presented by one of its members, Dr Peter Turner, with a 'Bill and Book' which, in the utterly unlikely event of its gaining parliamentary approval and the queen's assent, would have replaced the prayer book with the Genevan liturgy, or Book of Common Order, and the rule of bishops by a presbyterian constitution for the church, an initiative which would be renewed with rather more determination, arousing more interest in the house of commons, in the 1586 parliament.[313]

With some exceptions, notably William Tey, the Dedham ministers seem to have been less confident about these radical and bold initiatives than some other conferences, certainly in Northamptonshire, but possibly also in Suffolk, where Sandes, for one, enjoyed cross-membership. There was more than a hint of this in November 1586, when, with the new parliament already in session, Chapman proposed writing to 'the godlie brethren in London', who 'though they were forward in furthering the discipline, yet a letter wold encourage them to be more zealous'. This did not mean quite what it might have been taken to mean. Chapman went on: 'We shuld be moved the rather to write bicause some of them are of mynd to ask a full reformation and to accept of none if they had not all', whereas Chapman thought that Dedham's position was that it would prefer half a loaf to no bread, attributing to his

---

[312] Richard Bancroft, *A survay of the pretended holy discipline* (1593), p. 369. The extent and significance of this precocious electioneering in an ideological cause is underestimated in Derek Hirst, *The representative of the people? Voters and voting in England under the early Stuarts* (Cambridge, 1975).

[313] Collinson, *EPM*, pp. 286–8, 303–16.

brethren the judgment 'that some reformation might be accepted of, if it were graunted' (**50M**). And this in spite of the fact that the conference had (earlier?) responded positively to a proposal from London that 'a generall supplication' should be presented to the queen 'with a full draughte of the discipline we desire'.[314] But Chapman's extreme moderation was in fact untypical. When six members of the conference, including Chapman, Crick, Dowe and Parker, duly wrote to the London ministers, they exhorted them to work vigorously with their parliamentary allies to promote 'the cause of the Church', but nothing was said about accepting 'some' rather than all-or-nothing reformation.[315]

By now (1586) the preparation of a constitution for a fully reformed Church of England, a 'Book of Discipline', was well advanced, although we cannot be sure whether the principal author was Thomas Cartwright or Walter Travers.[316] It was a complex operation, for account had to be taken of thirty years of creative improvization in a dozen other national churches, and of marked differences of opinion among the English puritans themselves. Probably there was more than one discarded draft before the version was perfected which in 1587 was referred to the conferences in the country. It was accompanied by 'the testimony of the brethren tutching a draught of discipline'. That at least is the heading of the copy filed by Parker at Dedham.[317] The 'testimony' entailed a form of subscription: 'We acknowledge and confesse the same agreable to godes most holy worde soe far forth as we are able to judge and discerne of yt.' This was the order which the subscribers desired to see established by humble suit to queen, privy council and parliament and by all other lawful means; also (and here was the crunch), 'soe farre as the lawes of the land and the peace of our present state of our Church may suffer and not enforce to the contrary we promise to guide ourselves and to be guided by it and according to yt.' So far as meetings and assemblies were concerned, the testimony contained a promise to meet every six weeks 'in Classicall conferences', and every half-year in 'provinciall meetinges'. The Dedham version of the document seems to have arrived from an Essex direction, for it nominates 'about Essex' seven ministers, including George Northey of Colchester, George Gifford, farther south at Maldon, and Arthur Dent from the Thames estuary, but, of the Dedham ministers, only Laurence Newman of Coggeshall was named. London was to be the location of the next provincial conference, 'about the midst of Michaeltide terme' (1587)?

But Dedham was careful to have nothing to do with this, which calls into particular question the description of its meetings as 'the Dedham *classis*'. It appears that only Tey and Sandes would have been willing to sign the 'testimony' and to the Book of Discipline itself. On 6 March 1587, Tey 'moved that the booke of discipline set downe by the brethren might be viewed and, their judgments given of yt: yt was deferred' (**54M**). On 3 April, the Book of Discipline, referred to as 'Mr

---

[314] See p. 91 below.

[315] See p. 90 below.

[316] Collinson, *EPM*, pp. 238, 294–6.

[317] See pp. 85–7 below. Other copies include one appended to the LPL text of the Book of Discipline (MS 113, fo. 186), a copy seized by the authorities in Warwickshire, bearing the names of twelve subscribers (the only copy to carry signatures) (BL, MS Harley. 6849, fo. 222), and another in the first printed edition of the Book of Discipline, *A directory of church-government* (London, 1645). See the depositions of two ministers in star chamber (PRO, Star Chamber 5 A/49/34). These all agree in substance but vary in detail.

Taies Question', was deferred 'till some other tyme' (**55M**). On 8 May Tey was absent and the question was again left on one side (**56M**). But in another ruling at this meeting it was made clear that Dedham would never subscribe to the Discipline. In February, Sandes had asked how he would stand if the same question were to be moved in both conferences of which he was a member and contrary rulings given. It is clear enough what question he had in mind. He was now told that he was free to state his own opinion, verbally, in either meeting, but he was urged to subscribe to nothing, for 'to geve our handes or judgment in matters was not thought saffe in any respecte' (**53, 56MM**). Tey was back again on 12 June, moving that 'the booke of discipline might be vewed and judgement given of it'. But, once again, it was 'deferred'. Sandes now brought a message from his Suffolk brethren, asking for help from Dedham in concluding the matter of discipline, requesting specifically the expertise of Crick and Chapman. This too was deferred to the next meeting (**57M**). But it was not until 8 August that Crick told the conference of his unwillingness to go to the Suffolk conference, which was due to meet at 'mr fowles'. The Book of Discipline was yet again deferred, since Tey was again absent (**59M**). And that is interesting, since Mr Fowle was Thomas Fowle, rector of Hinderclay and Redgrave, an old associate of Chapman and Crick when all three had held office in Norwich cathedral, Fowle having been one of the four who had attacked the organ.[318] On 4 September 'the former matters', which presumably included the Book of Discipline, were again deferred (**60M**). And that, it seems, was that. Dedham was reluctant to incriminate itself by subscription, while a more radical meeting like the Suffolk conference felt incompetent to decide on large and controversial matters without learned help from outside.

As preparations were made for a general conference in Cambridge at Stourbridge Fair time, September 1587, with Newman and Lewis chosen to represent Dedham, Chapman's only declared interest in the meeting was that it should offer guidance to ministers forced to choose between conformity and the loss of their livings: 'how farre they might goe with peace of conscience and the good of the Church' (**59M**). The *Acta* formally passed at this Cambridge conference indicate that it clearly considered itself to have the powers of a kind of synod. While something like Chapman's question was certainly discussed, much more time was spent on the Book of Discipline, especially in elaborating the provision for meetings which the subscribers had promised to put into immediate practice, and in measures to extend the conference movement and to persuade more ministers to join up. The implications are clear. Those who carried the day at Cambridge (and there may have been dissenters, since decisions were referred to further debate and the advice of other churches) clearly considered that they and their churches derived their validity from the practice of true discipline, and that their *Acta* were the deliberations of a provincial assembly of a nascent English presbyterian church.[319]

Sherlock Holmes alerted us to the significance of the dog that didn't bark. It is noticeable that apart from the 'testimony', which was not generated from within the Dedham conference itself, Parker's papers contain nothing about the Book of Discipline. Rather, the Dedham ministers may have taken more interest in a scheme

---

[318] *Parkhurst*, pp. 41n, 60n, 129.
[319] Collinson, *EPM*, pp. 321–3.

to interest the by no means unsympathetic archdeacon of Colchester, George Withers, in modifying the machinery of the archdeaconry in a reformed, synodical direction. Rather surprisingly, it seems to have been Tey the hothead who thought of this relatively eirenical notion, although this was back in September 1584, when the Book of Discipline was still no more than a pipe dream. Saying that he had forgotten to raise the matter in conference, Tey wrote to his especial friend Richard Parker, suggesting that Withers be persuaded to convert his visitations into primitive synods, with himself as moderator. This might mean that instead of cooling their heels in formal attendance at his court (where, of course, they were more likely to be dealt with not by Withers but by his officials), with all the waste of time and money that that entailed, the ministers, under Withers's benign presidency, could 'conferre of such points as concerned the Churche'. Arguments were attached, drawing on ancient practice and proving knowledgeable about relevant points of canon law. Chapman was persuaded to write to Withers about this, presuming on his 'zeale and courage in the lordes cause', and twelve ministers wrote asking to be free from the vexatious constraints of the courts, and that the archdeacon should convert his visitations into synods as they were 'in thold tyme', where they could meet with him as 'fellow labourers and brethren'.[320] This resembled various projects for 'reduced episcopacy', or 'presbytery in episcopacy', of which much would be heard for a hundred years to come. Withers's response is unknown.

Problems with 'the Discipline'

There were perhaps other reasons why Dedham was reluctant to sign up to the Book of Discipline, and these were, in embryo, some of the same issues which would divide the English puritans into various kinds and degrees of 'presbyterians' and 'independents' in the civil war years of the 1640s, inside and outside the Westminster Assembly. Presbyterianism was anti-hierarchical and its very taproot was the principle of ministerial parity, symbolized by the circulation in its various meetings of the office of moderator. But in its most robust form, as it developed, for example, in Scotland, the higher bodies and assemblies had an advisory role in respect of the lower, which effectively constituted an alternative, non-episcopal model of top-down management. Congregations could in principle 'call' their pastors, but in practice these appointments were made by the ministers who ordained them, 'placed' them, and instituted them. 'Presbyteries' in Scotland, '*classes*' in England, were all-powerful. We have already found plenty of evidence that the Dedham conference assumed that it had real powers in respect of 'placing', even if they could not always be enforced. 'Elders', in origin leading lay members of congregations, became, with the passage of time, non-preaching presbyters, a different kind of clergy. By the same token, higher assemblies, or synods, exercised authority over local conferences and *classes*. The democratic forces within the reformed church polity were effectively restrained.

What the record suggests is that as a conference, and as a kind of federation of ministers and their congregations, Dedham leant, as it were instinctively, in the direction of a devolved independency. When push came to shove, ministers would resist the high-handedness of the conference in their affairs and those of their

---

[320] See pp. 81–2 below.

congregations, although perhaps sweetening the pill of their resistance with affirmations of respect for advice which they were not going to take; while the conference, equally, would reckon to know better than general meetings, in principle higher bodies, and especially 'London', what was good for it. The fact that no kind of 'discipline' was established, and that the situation was ill-defined and unstable, seems to have favoured devolution.

The cases of Andrewes, on his way from Wenham to Yarmouth, and Negus, on the move from Ipswich to Leigh, have already been noticed.[321] But the most revealing episode concerned the church of East Bergholt, which seems to have enjoyed the ministrations of no less than three ministers, none of them beneficed in the parish: Richard Crick, John Tilney and Thomas Stoughton. Initially, Tilney was the pastor, Crick the 'doctor', while Stoughton was a minister in training.[322] Something went very badly wrong at 'Barfold': Tilney was thrown out and Crick chosen as pastor in his stead, by a perhaps dominant faction in the congregation. It is clear from the minutes that the conference was unhappy about what had happened to Tilney, and in particular objected to 'the peoples course in rejecting and receyving their Pastors without counsell of others', although, perhaps reluctantly, most members thought Crick 'fitt' to undertake the charge. But it was only when Crick, who could no longer face his brethren, wrote them a letter of bitter recrimination that it was agreed to appoint Chapman to preach 'at his election to the pastorall charge' **(51, 59, 61, 65, 66MM)**.

Crick's letter would undoubtedly have been much quoted by students of presbyterian and independent policies had R. G. Usher not omitted it from his edition in 1905.[323] Crick first complained that one of the brethren had said that if the duty of preaching at his entrance to the pastoral charge were laid on him he would not do it, 'seinge the Church dealt as shee did, . . . forasmuch as she caried herselfe as having all *in scrinio pectoris sui*, he would give her no counsel if she sought it.' There had been 'boysterous woordes', and Crick was afraid that he might not be able to control his own tongue, 'being now become at length as jealous for the Honor of the Church as any of you are for your owne'. A particular cause of sadness was that it had been said that he and Chapman had 'fallen out', two men who had been 'coupled in so strong a bond of amitie'. The congregation which had thrown out Tilney would fetch counsel from as far beyond London as London was from them 'rather then from you, though you would begg to be of Counsel with them'.

As it was between conference and congregation, so it was with the dealings between Dedham and other conferences, and with the high command in London. The debate in 1587 about the Book of Discipline had picked up the anomaly that some conferences were stronger in numbers than others, and some rationalization was now thought desirable. In January 1587, Laurence Newman of Coggeshall warned the conference that there were moves afoot to transfer his membership to the conference meeting around Braintree, which was effectively led by Richard Rogers of Wethersfield and George Gifford of Maldon, and in July Chapman shared with the conference a letter from Braintree wanting Newman 'wholy'. Dedham was

[321] See above, pp. xciii–iv.
[322] See *BR*, pp. 196–9; 251–5; 260–2 below.
[323] See pp. 147–9 below.

reluctant to let him go, hoping that he could belong to both meetings, but said that if
he decided to leave they would have to put up with it. But at the next meeting,
Newman said that since he could not belong to two conferences he would prefer to
stay with Dedham, 'he more enclyned to be of us', and letters were sent to Rogers
and the rest at Braintree to that effect (**52, 58, 59MM**). The Braintree letter bears
five signatures, headed by Rogers and Ezekiel Culverwell, and refers to a decision
taken at the time of the recent parliament 'by many of our godlie brethren and
fellow labourers assembled at London', that the ministers desiring reformation
should 'sorte themselves together' in their meetings, and that none should exceed
the number of ten. Braintree was now well under this limit while Dedham was way
over. Dedham's response was robust:

> We reverence our faithfull brethren at London with their gratyous advises, and
> hartelie praise god for that good which the Church receyveth from them. Yet
> being best privy in our conference, what inconvenience we see likely to ensue by a
> separation, we praie and besech you lovinglie to respecte us, although in our
> consultacion we find not motives sufficient to persuade us to remove mr Newman.
> There hath bene some like motion made for others on Suffolke side, but we cannot
> be induced to departe with any, who having joigned themselves are willing still to
> cleave unto us.[324]

Everyone in this ideological carousel, even on this occasion John Field, was obliged
to accept *faits accomplis*.

The end of the Conference
Writing all this up in Norfolk, many years later, Parker put the best gloss he could
on the abrupt demise of the Dedham conference, after its eightieth and final
meeting, held on 2 June 1589. It was not intended that things should be wound up so
suddenly. The eighty-first meeting had been arranged to take place at William Tey's
Layer Hall, Newman to speak, Tey to moderate. But it never happened. Parker
wrote: 'Thus longe contynued through gods mercie this blessed meetinge and now
yt ended by the malice of satan.' He reported that one reason was complaints
preferred to Bishop Aylmer 'for which cause I was called up to London and
examyned of it'. But he claimed that the 'chiefest cause' was the death of some of
the brethren and their departure from Dedham to other places (**80M**). This last
explanation is implausible. Crick died in 1591 but Chapman, Dowe and Sandes
were still in place for years to come. So were William Birde, Ranulph Catelyn,
Arthur Gale, Edmund Salmon (at whose rectory of Erwarton the last meeting was
held), Thomas Stoughton and the irrepressible William Tey: nine members, and
others could well have been recruited.

No doubt Parker's grilling by the High Commission, in which he named names,
put the fear of death into him and everyone else and this may be sufficient explanation for the termination of the conference. When the prosecuted ministers emerged
from star chamber in 1591, they were forced to sign an undertaking not to hold their
meetings in the future.[325] But the cloud of scandal which enveloped Parker in those

[324] See p. 108 below.
[325] Collinson, *EPM*, pp. 428–31.

last months, and of which he makes no mention, must have been a relevant factor.[326] In any case, he soon abandoned Dedham.

One of the minor mysteries surrounding Richard Parker's little archive is why it should include a number of papers from a much later period, when the accession of James I in 1603 saw a revival of agitation for further reformation, and, in the aftermath of the Hampton Court Conference in 1604, a new subscription crisis.[327] It must mean that Parker, from his new base at Ketteringham in Norfolk, was at the very least still on the mailing list. But the most poignant of the later papers in the file makes a fitting epitaph to the Dedham story. It is a letter from Edmund Chapman to his 'verie deare frinde and right faithfull brother in the Lorde Mr Thomas Cartewright'.[328] Parker cross-referenced the letter to the fourth meeting of the conference, in March 1583, when it was certainly resolved to write to Cartwright, on the subject of the Rhemish Testament (**4M**); but Chapman's letter cannot have been written earlier than 1589, given its reference to 'that marre matter martin' and to 'what small pleasure you ever tooke in such inventions'. For the reference is to the Marprelate Tracts and Chapman's letter will have been written as Cartwright was caught up in the sequel to this affair, at about the time of the last meeting of the Dedham conference.

Chapman thought that this was a time for some *post-mortem* reflexions on the so-called classical movement.

> And what though now after a second vew of your proceedinges in this great cause of Church goverment, yow find that some thinges are not unjustly found fault withall, yet oughte not that much afflicte yow, seeing yow are not the first man of fame, lerninge and piety, that have confessed and retracted some error, if the substantiall and mayne pointes of your worke stande . . . If the worke were to begynne againe yow could mend some peece of the matter or manner of yt.

And then came this remarkable piece of prescience: 'And what know yow or we, whether all the fruites of your labors be yet risen and sprunge up, or lie still closse and hidden under the grounde, bicause of the stormy and sharpe seasons and winterlike wether . . . Yow have noe cause to repente that ever you tooke yt in hande.' Chapman wrote 'almost with teares'. Some of these 'fruits', a second crop, were to appear in the Stour valley and north Essex in the 1620s,[329] while the 1640s, towards which Chapman unconsciously looked, would bring a bumper harvest: presbyterianism, temporarily, in the saddle.

vii. Thomas Rogers and the Combination Lecture in Bury St Edmunds

The combination lecture in Bury St Edmunds

About the time that Edmund Chapman penned that poignant and prescient letter to Thomas Cartwright and Satan was doing his best to bring an end to the Dedham conference, decisions were being made and work was undertaken with respect to the

---

[326] See above, pp. lxxii–iv.
[327] See pp. 130–33 below.
[328] See pp. 70–72 below.
[329] Webster, *Godly clergy in early Stuart England.*

Map 4 Parishes surrounding Bury St Edmunds.

exercise, or combination lecture, in the town of Bury St Edmunds, some thirty miles north-west of the Stour valley, the consequences of which broke out with some force in December 1589 and formed the subject of the second manuscript edited in this volume. To move from Rylands English MS 874 to Chicago Codex MS 109 is to move from the veritable hodge-podge of letters, minutes, meetings and appeals collected by Richard Parker to a much shorter and cleaner text penned by one man, Thomas Rogers, yet the two texts are tied together in a number of ways. As we have already seen, the links between Dedham and Bury St Edmunds were well established by this time and the members of the Dedham conference were well aware of the parts played by John Knewstub in Cockfield and the wholly sympathetic stance of the godly magistracy of Sir Robert Jermyn, Sir John Higham, Robert Ashfield and others. And when Robert Lewis packed his belongings to move from Colchester to Bury in the spring of 1589, he must have gone as someone who knew well the situation to which he was 'called'.

By 1589, Bury, like Banbury a generation later, was on its way to becoming in certain circles a byword for godliness and puritanism, with Thomas Nashe mocking the 'preaching brothers of Bury'.[330] Much of this reputation was due to the religious controversies that had taken place in and around Bury in the early 1580s, to which we have already had occasion to refer. Several years on, the heat generated by the confrontation between the bishop of Norwich and the preachers and puritan gentry of the region had been largely dissipated. Bishop Freke had left the diocese in 1585, the challenge from a group of radical Brownists had been dealt a harsh blow with the exemplary punishments of two of their number in 1583 and the success of the godly townsmen in gaining control of the guildhall feoffment (a kind of corporation in embryo), hiring new preachers and drawing up new statutes for the grammar school meant that when Lewis arrived in Bury the godly preachers, gentry and townsmen had some cause for satisfaction at the extent to which events had gone their way.[331]

Situated as close as it was to Cambridge, along with the civility of its own amenities, the town of Bury and its immediate vicinity was an attractive prospect for aspiring clergy, and by 1589 few parishioners within west Suffolk can have lived far from a learned minister, many of whom possessed Cambridge connexions. Monday, market day in Bury, was a little fiesta of activity both worldly and spiritual as traders and consumers flocked there to buy and sell and their protestant ministers rode into the town clad in their distinctive black gowns to meet with their fellow brethren in spiritual conference. Conference on Mondays in Bury came in the form of a combination lecture, an institution which can be dated back to the 'godlye exercise of expounding the scriptures by the way of prophecie' allowed by Bishop John Parkhurst in 1573.[332] With the exception of a period of time in the late 1570s when all prophesyings were officially suppressed, the tradition of a Monday lecture in Bury was well established, and by the mid-1580s this had evolved into a popular occasion at which perhaps as many as thirty clergymen assembled together with an

330 Thomas Nashe, 'An almond for a parrat' (1590), ed. R. B. McKerrow, *The works of Thomas Nashe* (5 vols., Oxford, 1958), III, 373.
331 Craig, *Reformation, politics and polemics*, pp. 88–114.
332 Collinson, 'Lectures by combination', *Godly people*, p. 477.

unknown number of townsfolk and neighbouring gentry. And it was in this setting that scores of sermons by noted clerics – John Knewstub, Nicholas Bound, Miles Mosse and others – were delivered, many of which were put into print.

Episcopal control over the combination seems to have been largely delegated to some of the more senior named clergy involved, although the ordering of the Monday exercise was ultimately at the behest of the bishop of Norwich, as the Chicago MS makes clear. Thomas Rogers speaks of the exercise having 'begunne' at the direction of Bishop Scambler 'at his first comming unto the Bishoprick', whereas the letter sent by John Knewstub and his colleagues speaks of having had by the bishop's direction 'an exercise continued upon the <*Mon*>daie at Burie ever since your L[ord's]. comming to the diocesse'.[333] The difference between 'begun' and 'continued' was not insignificant but both views acknowledged the importance of the bishop's oversight. Before we go too far with an account of the exercise, something needs to be said about the author of Chicago Codex MS 109.

Thomas Rogers

Thomas Rogers was born in London about 1550 and matriculated at Christ Church, Oxford, in 1571.[334] He graduated BA on 7 July 1573 and commenced MA on 6 July 1576. He was ordained priest by John Aylmer, bishop of London, on 25 March 1578, giving his age as about 25.[335] Instituted no fewer than three times (23 November 1581, 10 December 1581 and 13 May 1582) to the living of Horringer, Suffolk, a parish two miles from Bury St Edmunds, the confusion perhaps stemmed from doubt about who was the true patron. He was presented in November 1581 by Thomas Sackville by grant from Thomas Lord Paget, and in December 1581 by the queen.[336] On 28 August 1588, he married Bridget Wincol, the daughter of John Wincol of Netherhall in Little Waldingfield, Suffolk, a wealthy clothier, and their only child, a son Robert, born in October 1589, probably died in infancy. He served as rector of Horringer until his death in 1616 when he was succeeded by William Bedell, town preacher of Bury St Edmunds and future bishop of Kilmore. He became chaplain to Sir Christopher Hatton and Richard Bancroft, although the details of these appointments are not known.[337] Such are the known facts of an unremarkable Elizabethan clerical career.

Yet there was more to this man than at first meets the eye. Rogers was pre-eminently a writer, who owned a remarkable collection of books.[338] Much of his literary work, especially until the appearance of *The English creede* in 1585, involved translating various texts and making them acceptable to godly opinion. Between 1577 and 1592, Rogers produced no fewer than twelve separate translations of works by Niels Hemmingsen, Johann Habermann, Philippus Caesar, Joannes Rivius, Diego de Estella, Thomas à Kempis and meditative texts attributed

333 CHUL 109, fo. 1r.
334 *Alum. Oxon.*, III, 1276.
335 GL MS 9535/2, fo. 1v.
336 And possibly again in 1584? See NRO DN/REG/14, fo. 72v. Lord Paget was in prison in 1580, fled overseas in 1583, and was attainted in 1587, which may explain Rogers's multiple institutions.
337 He dedicated the second part of *The English creede* (1587) to Hatton so perhaps had become his chaplain by this time.
338 There are scores of titles cited by Rogers in his copy of *Miles Christianus*. See BL C. 124.c.7 and n. 363 below.

to Augustine; ten of these appeared between 1577 and 1581. This was translation with a twist, as the titles invariably read 'corrected, translated and adorned' (STC 938), 'translated, purified and adorned' (STC 944) or 'purged from divers super-stitious points' (STC 950). Two works were best-sellers. The first was his trans-lation of the mystical and rabbinical study by the Emden civil lawyer, Sheltco à Geveren, entitled *Of the ende of this worlde and second comyng of Christ* (London, 1577), subsequent editions of which were revised and amended. He may well have visited à Geveren in Emden (possibly in 1577, as is implied by a letter he included in the 1578 edition). The second was his protestant translation of *The Imitation of Christ* by Thomas à Kempis, which first appeared in 1580 and in which Rogers claimed he had left nothing out 'but what might be offensive to the godlie' but which, he hastened to add, was 'neither for quantitie much, nor for number above foure sentences'. Although a stout protestant, his tastes were catholic in the true sense of that word, and he argued that 'were other bookes that I could name, excel-lent for manie good pointes, yet for some thinges superstitious, purged and corrected, sure I am, both God would greatly like thereof, and many men would read them, who nowe reject them'.[339]

When Rogers first came to Horringer, he appears to have entertained godly convictions which recommended him, despite his Oxford credentials, to men like John Knewstub and Walter Allen. In the prefatory epistle of *A pretious Booke of Heavenlie Meditations* (1581) dedicated to Sir Thomas Wilson, Rogers inveighed against stage plays. He called on Wilson not only to reform the abuse of corrupt books but also to

> remember another abuse that hurteth more than both those which I have alreadie mentioned, namelie prophane Plaies, publikelie used, set foorth as banners of open defiance to the Gospel and godliness and that upon Holi daies, yea and in those places to[o] (I meane the Universities for learning, and London for resort) which ought to be the Lanternes of godliness unto al the land beside.

And although he would later write dismissively of the crisis of conscience that afflicted many godly ministers as a result of Whitgift's insistence on subscription, calling such men 'factious spirits and malcontented ministers',[340] there is evidence that in 1583–4, Rogers sided with the Suffolk ministers 'not resolved to subscribe' and may also have been suspended himself for failing to do so.[341]

His nonconformity was short-lived. By 1585, when he came to write his exposi-tion of the thirty-nine articles under the title *The English creede*, Rogers had aligned himself firmly with those who believed that Whitgift's policies had 'made not a little unto the glorie of God, and comfort of his servants', yet was careful to proffer the olive branch to his nonconformist colleagues. He noted that 'some are of the opinion that much hurt therby hath redounded to the church of God' and argued, no doubt with his godly colleagues in mind, that no one challenged the queen's

[339] Rogers, *Of the imitation of Christ* (London, 1602), Preface.
[340] Thomas Rogers, *The faith, doctrine and religion, professed and protected in the Realme of England and dominions of the same* (Cambridge, 1607), p. 37.
[341] *Seconde parte*, I, 242.

supremacy or condemned the Book of Common Prayer and that he believed that all clergy would subscribe if

> that which is offensive, reformed and that which is crooked, made streight; and that which is doubtfull, made evident and plaine. Which things also are for number but verie fewe, and therefore maie the more easilie be removed; and remaine for the most part, in the directions and rubricks, and therefore with lesse offence maie be taken awaie.[342]

This was the opening gambit in a heartfelt plea for 'holy unitie' in which Rogers deplored contentiousness and the importance given to 'petie and trifling things of no waight' that were an obstacle to Christian love.[343] Yet there was a touch of frustration in his eirenical tone when he spoke of the sin of fellow ministers keeping 'out of the Lord his vine-yard, such as both for abilitie could and for their zeale would, either implant this Faith in the ignorant, or confirme it in the learned'.[344] This well-read preacher and author from Oxford was clearly beginning to chafe at the restrictions he faced in the vicinity of Bury St Edmunds where so much of the clerical running was in the hands of the Cambridge godly, led by John Knewstub.

The Bury exercise in 1589–90

Rogers, as a learned cleric, was almost certainly a member of the combination lecture from the time of his coming to Suffolk. He later wrote of 'having taken great pains among you [referring to the company of preachers] not a yeere or two but almost the tyme of a prenteship',[345] which would place his entry into the combination lecture to 1583 or 1584. Prior to 1587, there appears to have been an extremely informal arrangement of who might preach and when. John Knewstub,[346] the long-serving rector of Cockfield and 'principall Senior praesent at the boorde', clearly dominated the proceedings and, together with 'his table of consultacion', determined who preached. There was no rota, just an informal process of being nominated and approved 'with moste voices'. Rogers complained that before the lecture was reorganized, that 'some preached often, yee knowe, some sildome, some not at all'. Worst of all, 'no man ever knewe his turne, nor anie (whatsoever his businesse were, and the matter he had to handle never so waightie) had more than 7 daies at the moste, and sometime not 4 to provide for the place.' This situation was rectified in 1587 when a 'set and certaine number of Preachers with free voices and choise were appointed, successivelie and in theire knowen courses to preach',[347] a division which included Thomas Rogers in its company. This appears to have been a local initiative carried out by Knewstub and his colleagues and ratified in turn by the bishop of Norwich. The lecture itself was an exercise in biblical exegesis and expository preaching. Rogers mentions that 'the two epistles of S. Paull unto the Thessalonians . . . have fully and wholie bine expounded' since Scambler's arrival

---

[342] Rogers, *Faith, doctrine and religion*, Preface.
[343] *Ibid.*, Preface.
[344] *Ibid.*, Preface.
[345] CHUL fo. 2v.
[346] See *BR*, pp. 220–23.
[347] CHUL 109, fos. 1r–2v.

in 1585 and that the preachers were currently working their way through the Paul's letter to the Romans. Following the sermon, there was a short time for questions and discussion before the preachers retired for dinner at Michels 'according to the custome'.[348]

Comparing the letter sent by the ten members of the exercise to the bishop of Norwich and Rogers's response to the same tells the following story. In the weeks before Christmas 1589, the Monday exercise was working its way through the book of Romans, when it came to the sixth, seventh and eighth verses of the twelfth chapter, a particularly controversial passage, the controversy heightened by the anonymously published but avowedly presbyterian work from the press of Robert Waldegrave, entitled *A fruitful sermon* and attributed to Laurence Chaderton, Master of Emmanuel College, Cambridge.[349] The passage in question concerns the differing gifts given within the church, which Chaderton had interpreted to refer to a prescribed form of church government consisting of pastors, doctors, elders, deacons and widows. Some of the senior men in the exercise, John Knewstub and Walter Allen, decided that this passage needed to be handled 'responsibly' and although the passage fell by course to 'some of oure younger men (men of good giftes, but not the fittest, as we thought to handle that matter)', it was decided that 'the handling of those verses should be committed to the auncientest and discreetest of our companie.' (Rogers denied this, claiming that the passage 'fell orderlie unto them which did handle that Scripture.')[350] In the event, the responsibility was shared between Walter Allen, John Knewstub, Robert Holt and Reginald Whitfield, each of whom preached a sermon on the passage, and in such a way 'as that no question <arose> among the people concerning discipline: a speciall part of <their> speech tending to this issue, viz to beate doune those which <do> wante of the discipline that theie desired, did condemne <the> Church of England, and would separate themselves from <us>'. Rogers claimed not to have been at the sermons preached by Allen or Knewstub and to have registered his dissent from some of the interpretations put forth by Holt and Whitfield, and that so plainly that Knewstub rebuked him for being in error. Rogers's turn came next. Instead of continuing with verse 9 ('Let love be without dissention . . .') as all expected, he pulled out of his pocket a copy of the *Fruitful sermon* (he claimed later not to have known the author) and launched into a comprehensive attack upon the same, 'cleane leaving his texte and so spending his time contrarie to all good order'. What appears to have irritated his fellow ministers most of all is that Rogers 'reproached the author of that Sermon comparing <him>the penner thereof firste to H.N. the familist,[351] and afterward to Campion and Reignoldes, two traiterous Papistes . . . as that the mislike of th'auditorie did openlie appeare therein, judging by his manner of dealing that he came rather to make an invective than a Sermon'.[352] The audience was shocked and

[348] CUL 109, fos. 3r, 5v, 13v.
[349] [Laurence Chaderton], *A fruitful sermon upon the 3, 4, 5, 6, 7, and 8 verse of the 12 chapter of the epistle of St Paule to the Romanes* (London, 1584). See also Collinson, *EPM*, p. 274; Peter Lake, *Moderate puritans and the Elizabethan church* (Cambridge, 1982), pp. 26–35.
[350] CHUL 109, fo. 3v.
[351] Bancroft levels the same charge against Cartwright in *A survay of the pretended holy discipline* (London, 1593), sigs. A-Ai.
[352] CHUL 109, fo. 9r.

a group of ministers later claimed to have 'lovinglie and gentlie admonished' Rogers 'for his strange and unusual manner of dealing' although they noted that 'since which time he hath wholie absented himselfe from our companie, as if we had done him injurie.'[353] Rumours started to circulate that when Rogers preached again, there would be a fiercer invective and, fearing another such sermon, the senior ministers of the combination artfully 'secluded' Rogers under the guise of reorganizing the exercise by presenting Bishop Scambler with a new list of names which he then authorized as constituting the Bury exercise, the name of Thomas Rogers being carefully omitted.[354]

Stung by his removal, Rogers was deeply angered. His exclusion from the exercise was a blow to his pride and seems to have followed hard upon the death of his first and only child. He wrote complaining of this unfair treatment to Scambler, who in turn wrote to the Bury ministers seeking an explanation, which prompted their letter of 1 April 1590. The date coincided with the first day of the general Assizes in Bury, which produced a scornful comparison from Rogers:

> The firste of Aprill, it seemeth, the honourable Judges with the rest of the Gentlemen and Commons of the contrie were not so occupied at Burie St Edmunds in one kind, for the go<od of some?> but at the same verie time and toune yee were as much busied in another kinde for the hurt of some. Theie met openlie, yee secretlie and classically. The fructes of theire assembling is notable knowen to the greate good of the contrie: and this letre (brought to my sight by Gods providence, contrarie to your expectation) testifieth in part th'end of your meeting at Burie St Edmundes 1 Aprilis.[355]

Whether or not Rogers intended to publish an account of his seclusion from the combination or whether he was preparing a detailed refutation of the case made against him in the letter sent to the bishop is not known. The manuscript is carefully written with a number of emendations but not so many that it could not stand as a fair copy. His detailed defence concluded with a satirical set of 'articles drawen (according to the verie thoughte of the classical Brethren, (the Informers above mentioned) for the wel managing of theire Moondaie exercise at Burie, and such like els-where in Marcate townes, on Mercate daies', in which Rogers caricatured his opponents as men that would 'pull the raines of government from the nowe and alwais receaved eclesiastical; and put them into the handes of certaine newelie devised consistorial and laical Elders and States-men in everie parish.' The proceedings against Rogers were to be an example to 'those of his minde, following his steps, what theie maie expect at our handes; and to our successors, with what endlesse and perfect hatred theie are to be pursued, that shal dare to thwart, and crosse us, or our Brethren wheresoever in our political courses and discourses about Discipline'.[356]

Although the name of John Knewstub appears at the head of the list of signatories, Rogers believed that the real villain behind his 'shameful secluding' was Miles Mosse, the preacher of the parish of St James in Bury St Edmunds. Mosse

---

[353] *Ibid.*, fo. 11v.
[354] *Ibid.*, fos. 14r, 16v.
[355] *Ibid.*, fo. 19v.
[356] *Ibid.*, fos. 21r–v.

was an insider, Suffolk born, undoubtedly a protégé of Knewstub and Chaderton, the son of a yeoman from Chevington, who proceeded from the grammar school in Bury to Caius College, Cambridge, and eventually via a charge in Norwich back in 1586 to Bury, where he served as the preacher of the parish of St James from 1586 to 1598, possessing a handsome stipend from 1589 of £40 per annum. It initially puzzled Rogers that Mosse's name was nowhere to be found among the names of the ten ministers who complained of his 'strange and unusuall manner of dealing': 'I see John Knewstub, Reginald Whitfield, Gualter Alen, Thomas Seffray etc., I looke for Miles Mosse and I cannot spie his name neither firste nor laste. Wil not he justifie the truth hereof, as yee will, because his hand is not heere? Will he that was the firste and foremost in this action against Thomas Rogers, be neither the firste nor last nor at all in this writing?'[357] But it eventually dawned on Rogers that 'we have his hande for this (the letter) was his handie worke'.[358] One can sense Rogers's deep dislike for Mosse in his sarcastic denunciation of the way in which he was admonished for his sermon:

> Neither lovinglie nor gentlie did yee admonish him. M. Mosses grinning at him in moste disdainful manner before moste of you, and objecting so often unto him the Cambridg boies,[359] maie tell you howe lovinglie and gentlie he was admonished. Successe Marten and all yoe Martinistes[360] from charging our Bishops with hard using of the ministers: Bend yourselves henceforward against the Brotherhood. Yee cannot from all the Bishops proceedings their 32 yeeres, all circumstances waied, produce an example of so injurious dealing against theire infereiors, as this the Bretheren against a fellow minister. Theire roughnes is mildnes in comparison of theis mens gentle dealing.

This was but the beginning of the quarrell between Rogers and Mosse which took a strange turn. Shortly after Rogers had been excluded from the exercise and had put his sermon confuting Chaderton's into print,[361] Mosse published, or rather re-published, the extremely popular catechism by John More and Edward Dering with a short preface dedicated to the bishop of Norwich in which he complained that 'men will speak before they have learned' and that 'manie ministers of the word write much but preach little', statements which the suspicious and sensitive Rogers interpreted as an attack upon his own efforts as a writer.[362] Rogers responded at

---

[357] *Ibid.*, fo. 20r.

[358] *Ibid.*, fo. 20r. Rogers's first attempt at this was 'Though we have not his hande, yet we have his hed saith another. The cause is secret, saith a third, he was our secretarie and his hart is with us, and this sufficeth.'

[359] A term of disdain. Robert Beale spoke of Whitgift's 'common and wonted place of boying' the ministers. See Collinson, *EPM*, pp. 254–5. And see also Bancroft's comment about those that run 'uppe and downe after every young start up, hether and thether, to seeke new platforms of church government in this place or that place . . .': Bancroft, *A survay of the pretended holy discipline*, 'to the reader.

[360] A reference to the Marprelate controversy. See W. Pierce, ed., *The Marprelate Tracts 1588, 1589* (London, 1911), p. 238. See also W. Pierce, *An historical introduction to the Marprelate Tracts* (London, 1908).

[361] T. Rogers, *A sermon made upon the 6. 7. and 8. verses of the 12 chapter of S. Paules Epistle unto the Romanes . . . made to the confutation of so much of another sermon* (1590).

[362] The More-Dering catechism was variously entitled *A briefe and necessary instruction, A briefe and necessary catechisme* and *A short catechisme for householders*. See Ian Green, '"For Children in Yeeres and Children in Understanding": the emergence of the English catechism under Elizabeth and the early Stuarts', *JEH* (1986), XXXVII, 399.

length and once again, paragraph by paragraph, line by line, in a bitter attack upon Mosse's preface under the title *Miles Christianus or a just apologie of all necessarie writings and writers specialie of them which by their labored writings take paines to build up the Church of Christ,* the opening lines of which wished Mosse 'more soundnes of judgement, more substance of learning with more wisdome and discretion in all his actions'.[363] The polemics continued for another thirty-six pages in a similar vein. The last that is heard of this particular affair is found in a letter written by Rogers in the summer of 1591 to John Still, archdeacon of Sudbury, in which Rogers wrote that

> I finde that M. Mosse is much grieved at me for two thinges, viz 1. for my sermon wch I made last at Burie (and since through bad dealing offend me for the same, I have bine urged to imprinte) and for an answer unto his epistle prefixed to that catechisme by him published. What he wil object against either or bothe of these bookes I know not: and though unto whatsoever he can object, or might answere, I have donn nothing which is not sufficientlie approved by thauctoritie of our Church . . .

Mosse's grinning response to Rogers's attack upon Chaderton was remembered with bitterness as Rogers complained to Still that Mosse had attacked his sermon 'with most reprochful speiches . . . and in the hearing of divers both godlie and learned ministers of the Word depraved the same exceedinglie'. 'Hence that shameful (as themselves call it) secluding me from the Burie exercise; Hence the conspering of no lesse than tenn of the chiefest ministers of the faction in Suffolk in a lettre against me and my sermon unto my Lord of Norwich', which Rogers deemed 'a prasident of greater audacitie I verilie think since your worships coming into Suffolk you never knewe' and promised to tell the full story 'with thanswere thereunto at large'.[364] It is not clear why Rogers made his appeal to Dr Still. Perhaps he thought that Still would be more sympathetic to his stance[365] than Scambler's officials, as it was clear that some kind of investigation by the diocese had been initiated. 'Midsomer is at hande, before which time our matters muste be heard and ended or els Mr Chancelour himself will resume into his owne handes and set such order as in justice he shall think most meete.'

The aftermath
As is so often the case with historical research, the evidence peters out and we are left with unanswered questions. How did Scambler respond to Rogers's complaint of unjust dealing? Was Rogers's public attack on *A fruitful sermon* part of an orchestrated response masterminded perhaps by Richard Bancroft? Was Rogers ever

---

[363] Thomas Rogers, *Miles Christianus. or a just Apologie of all necessarie writings and writers speciallie of them which by their labored writings take pains to build up the Church of Christ in this age And in a publique and diffamatorie Epistle lately set forth in Print are unjustly depraved* (London, 1590). The copy in the British Library (C 124.c.7) belonged to Thomas Rogers and is interleaved with many notes in Rogers's hand.

[364] All of the above can be found in 'The true copie of a certen leter unto the right Worshipfull D. Stil in defense of Miles Christianus' penned into the British Library copy of Thomas Rogers, *Miles Christianus.* Although the letter is dated 'from Horringer the 8 of June', and the year is missing, the most likely date is 1591.

[365] It is notable that Still's sermon to the parliament that met in February 1589 appears to have been along the lines of Christopher Hatton's attack on both 'papists and puritans'. Collinson, *EPM,* p. 397.

reconciled with his colleagues and what happened to the Bury combination lecture in the 1590s? Most of these matters remain obscure. It is possible that Rogers was reinstated to his position as one of the preachers of the exercise, but the most that can be said with any certainty is that there is no evidence of his preaching in the exercise until 1599, which was two years after Miles Mosse left Bury for the rich living of Combes.[366] It is clear from the way in which Rogers stewed over his marginal notes in the British Library's copy of *Miles Christianus*, adding and amplifying references, that the quarrel with Mosse had struck a raw nerve with him,[367] and there is no doubt that after December 1589, Thomas Rogers had come completely out of the closet and now championed the cause of conformity and his 'detestation and renunciation of old adversaries and errors'. He publicly opposed Thomas Seffray's resistance to kneeling for communion,[368] and most famously attacked Nicholas Bound's *Doctrine of the Sabbath*, in the pulpit and in print.[369]

In the final analysis, it is the power, influence, reputation and danger of the sermon preached rather than printed that strikes home. Whether in the scrambling of Mosse and his colleagues to rid themselves of a loose cannon, or in the evident desire on the part of Rogers to take his part in the combination exercise, access to the pulpit was a coveted and controversial matter in late Elizabethan England and nowhere more so than in Bury St Edmunds, where sermons preached might become the stuff of conversations thirty miles away in Bungay. A cryptic, yet revealing, letter from Thomas Daynes[370] in Bungay to Lady Anne Drury on 20 August 1604 expressed concern about the news of a sermon preached in Bury by the godly town preacher, William Bedell, who 'set down his judgment' on the 'point of these indifferent thinges'. 'I hope he used warie caveates and all little enough in a matter of this difficultie', wrote Daynes, who felt Bedell would have been better advised to have 'drowned those thoughtes in a sea of silence'. The report of Bedell's sermon had reached Daynes third-hand and 'they sounde harsh in the eares of the best'. The specific issue is never identified, but Daynes confessed 'it had bene fit for a clerum in Camebridge or Synate in the countrie, but how fitt for a pulpitt or Bury pulpitt I knowe not', and beseeched Lady Drury to communicate with Bedell 'that we may be certified of his wordes and meaning. Least an unfitt tyme or place of uttering, or not soe advised hearing, turne unhappiely our joynt consultations for comon good into distracted expositions of mens persons and speaches'.[371] Such handwringing in 1604 seems to corroborate the fretting on the part of John Knewstub and Miles Mosse in 1590 that another salvo from Rogers would undo all, which may have been nothing more than special pleading, but perhaps owed most to an awareness that the ascendancy of godly magistracy and ministry in Suffolk was a delicate business that demanded constant vigilance and discretion.

---

[366] BL, Add MS 38492, fo. 104.

[367] BL C. 124. c. 7.

[368] Thomas Rogers, *Two dialogues or conference . . . concerning kneeling in the very act of receiving the sacramental bread . . .* (London, 1608).

[369] BL Add MS 38492, fo. 104; Thomas Rogers, *Faith, doctrine and religion*, preface.

[370] Daynes may have been a minister in Bungay. He is probably the same man who served for a time as the minister in the Suffolk parish of Flixton. NRO DN DEP 24, fos. 8v–14r.

[371] CHUL, Bacon 4178.

viii. The Sources

Rylands English MS 874

What became English MS 874 was purchased by the John Rylands Library on 31 March 1936 for £42 at an auction at Sotheby's which sold off the Gurney papers. The volume in question was part of a block of manuscripts bought in 1820 by Mr Hudson Gurney of Keswick Hall (1775–1864) from the collections of the antiquary Dr Cox Macro who died in 1767. Fifty-two years later, Macro's manuscripts had come into the possession of John Patteson, MP for Norwich, who sold them (for a trifling sum apparently) to a bookseller. The following year they were put up for auction (February 1820) and sold at a large profit. Forty-one lots were bought by Mr Dawson Turner; the rest were purchased by Mr Hudson Gurney. Many of the Macro manuscripts acquired by Gurney came originally from the collection of the Norfolk antiquary and historian, Sir Henry Spelman (?1564–1641).

The volume consists of fifty-eight leaves of various sizes, most of it copied out by Richard Parker in the summer of 1604 in the Norfolk parish of Ketteringham. On fo. 39r, Parker states that 'this booke I fynished in Kettringham being the work of one moneth space beside myne ordenary exercises, ended I say the 10th of July. 1604.' Examining the original foliation demonstrates that 'this booke' was a more modest affair than the present volume in the Rylands library, only twenty-six folios in length and corresponding to the following three sections: the eighty meetings of the conference (fos. 1–12; original foliation 1–13); letters (fos. 26–30; original foliation 14–18) and further letters, forms of subscription and related writings (fos. 32–9; original foliation 19–26). Parker explained again on fo. 39r that 'the letters which I have here written from one godlie mynister to another, these subscriptions, and the rest of the writinges following I inserted them together in this booke because they were conferred of in our meetinges, as I have noted on their heades the meetinges wherin these things were moved, and the page wher yow shall fynd them.' This was the original backbone of the present volume which at some point was enlarged with the addition of the material on the Sabbath (fos. 13–25), the holograph letter from Henry Wilcock (fo. 31r) and the remaining material (fos. 40r–58v). It is noteworthy that Parker appears not to have copied any of the Sabbath material which he presumably received directly from Tey, Sandes and Crick. The remaining documents (fos. 40r–58v) are written in a variety of hands albeit with various notes, references and endorsements made by Parker. A detailed list of the contents and present foliation is provided below:

Contents and foliation

fos. 1r–12r	Details of conference meetings 1–80
fo. 12v	blank
fos. 13r–14v	'A few notes gathered by Mr Tay of the Sabb[ath] and use of it.'
fos. 15r–19r	Mr Sandes on the Sabbath
fo. 19v	blank
fos. 20r–5v	Richard Crick on the Sabbath
fos. 26r–8v	Copies of various letters to and from Thomas Cartwright, Edmund Chapman, Richard Parker, William Tey

	enjoigned to observe the booke of common praier . . . Ends: 'The Lorde kepe me and all good men out of their handes and delyver us from their Tyranny. Amen Amen.'
fo. 51r	'What course is the best for a good mynister in thenglishe Churche . . .'
fos. 52r–3v	'That private men joigning with their neighbours may deale for order ecclesiasticall in admonishinge and barringe from the Sacramentes . . .'
fo. 54r	blank
fo. 54v	Endorsement: 'A lerned mans judgement what course a mynister shuld take with disordered persons and whether Auncientes in a Congregation may not use discipline in the defect of others that shuld doe it.'
fo. 55r	Holograph letter from Richard Crick to the brethren
fos. 55v–6r	blank
fo. 56v	Endorsed: 'To my most Reverend brethren Mr Doctor Chapman, Mr Farrour, Mr Newman and the rest at Mr Teyes geeve these'
fo. 57r	*'Propositiones ministrorum Scotiae Serenissimo Regi oblatae'*
fos. 57v–8r	*'Scriptum Archiepiscopi Sanctae Andrae in Scotis responsorum quorundam pastorum ad scriptum in Ecclesia Scotiae'*
fo. 58v	Endorsed: *'Propositiones ministrorum Scotiae'*

Chicago Codex MS 109

Like Rylands English MS 874, Chicago Codex MS 109 was a volume originally owned by Sir Henry Spelman. This volume appears to have been owned by Francis Palgrave in 1842 but by 1859 it had come into the possession of Mr Dawson Turner who sold it on 7 June 1859 for £1 2s. Owned for a time by the Suffolk antiquary Charles Golding, the volume was purchased by the University of Chicago in 1925, where it remains in the Department of Special Collections and is now known as Chicago University Library Codex MS 109.[372]

The following transcription has been made from what are the first two texts in a small bound volume measuring 5¾ inches wide by 7¹¹⁄₁₆ inches long and containing in all six separate items described by Francis Palgrave in a covering note dated 1842. He described the items written by Thomas Rogers as

> A Narrative of an Exercise or Disputation apparently amongst certain ministers assembled at Bury St Edmunds, 1 April 1590, between Mr John Knewstub, Reginald Whitfield, Gualter Alen, Thomas Seffray, John Ward, Nicholas Bownde, Richard Grundridge [sic], Robert Lewis, Leonard Greaves and Lawrence Whitaker: Mr Rogers being their opponent. Followed by "Articles drawen according to the verie thoughts of the classical Brethren (the informers above mentioned) for the wel managing of theire Mondaie exercise at Burie and such like elsewhere in Marcate townes on Mercate daies."

On the inside of the volume is a book plate of the Suffolk antiquary, Charles Golding, and a smaller plate from the University of Chicago.

---

[372] For a full description of MS 109, see *A census of medieval and renaissance MS in the United States and Canada*, ed. S. De Ricci, I (Chicago, 1935), 565.

There is no doubt that Thomas Rogers was the author of the two texts in question, and the hand and substance can be fruitfully compared with the British Library's copy of Thomas Rogers's tract attacking Miles Mosse, *Miles Christianus* (1590), which is replete with copious marginal annotations (BL C. 124.c.7). In the early eighteenth century, Anthony à Wood noted the existence of this text in his thumb-nail sketch of Rogers. Touching on Rogers's embattled relations with his godly colleagues, he wrote that Rogers's views had enraged his clerical neighbours and caused them 'maliciously to asperse and blemish him. Whereupon he wrote a Vindi-cation of himself in MS now in the hands of a near relation of his.'[373] Apart from the notice taken by a number of historians of the details of the volume of 'Ecclesiastical Miscellanies' in the 1859 sale by Messrs Puttick and Simpson of Dawson Turner's manuscripts,[374] the volume, albeit safely stored away in Chicago from 1925, appeared to have disappeared from sight. In 1958, Mary Klein, a graduate student at the University of Chicago, produced a reasonably accurate transcript of Rogers's treatise as part of her MA thesis, 'The godly conspirators: Elizabethan puritanism and the classis at Bury St Edmunds', but this work, like Rogers's text, achieved no wider circulation. The present transcript was made from a photocopy of the manu-script taken in 1994, and in September 1996 this transcript was carefully checked against the original in the Department of Special Collections in the University of Chicago. The manuscript has been cropped with a very slight loss of text on the margins of the recto side of the folios. Three-quarters of the way down the page, the page itself has sustained damage from damp and usage and the first number of folios are partially damaged with some loss of text.

---

[373] Anthony à Wood, *Athenae Oxoniensis* (2 vols. in 1, London, 1721), I, 401.

[374] John Craig, 'The "Cambridge Boies": Thomas Rogers and the "Brethren" in Bury St Edmunds', in *Belief and practice in reformation England,* ed. Susan Wabuda and Caroline Litzenberger (Aldershot, 1998), p. 154.

THE TEXTS

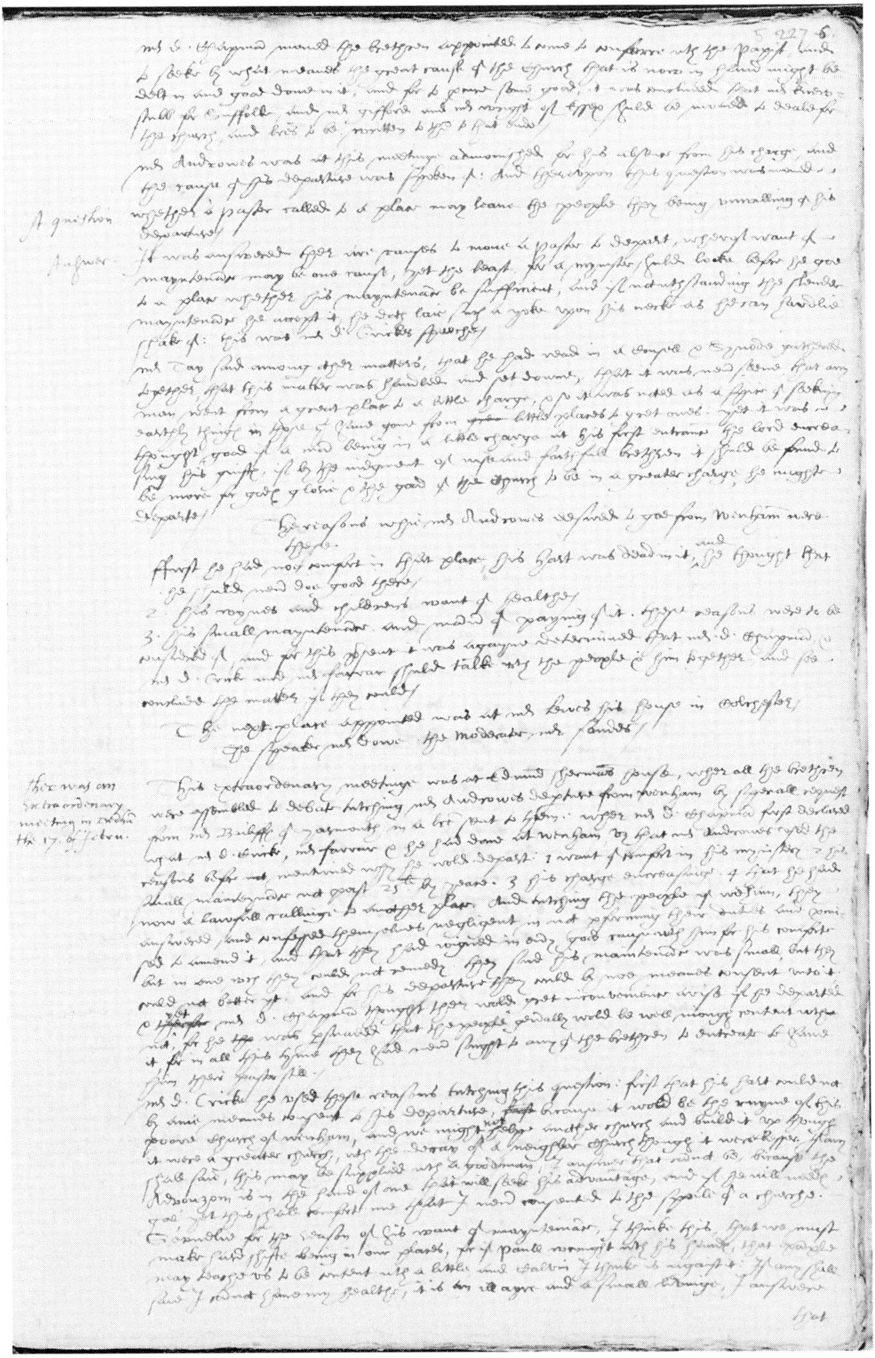

Plate 4 Folio 5 *recto* from Rylands MS 874. The penultimate paragraphs begin the record of the Extraordinary meeting of the Dedham conference which took place at Edmund Sherman's house, opposite the church (see frontispiece), on 17 February 1585 (see p. 20). *Photograph by kind permission of the John Rylands University Library, Manchester.*

The Dedham Conference
(John Rylands English MS 874)

Editorial conventions

1.   This transcript retains the original spelling, punctuation and capitalization, although all standard abbreviations have been silently extended and modern usage – j for i, u for v, v for u and th for the thorn – has been used. Other abbreviations have been expanded between square brackets.

2.   Emendations made by Parker have been placed in < > and with a line through the text where that text is legible.

3.   Marginal notes have been enclosed with curly brackets { } thus.

4.   In the first few folios of the manuscript, Parker used two different inks. A black ink and a more formal secretary hand have been indicated through the use of bold type.

[fo. 1r]

A note of such thinges as are agreed upon to be observed in our meetinge

There was a conference had by some of the godly brethren the xxijth of October 1582 as a preparation to a meetinge purposed by them, and to be concluded and agreed upon by the rest who shuld after be chosen, as fitte persons for such an Assembly.

The order wherof was this:

First yt was agreed on in that first conference that there shuld be a day of meetinge wherin some portion of scripture shuld be handled briefly by the speaker, that shuld be appointed by consente of the reste: the place of scripture then chosen to be contynued in, is the second Epistle of St. P[aul] to the Thessal[onians]: the tyme to be spente therin, and in prayer to be one howre: the rest of the tyme to be employed in decidinge some profitable questions, if any were propounded by the brethren, or els in conference aboute other necessary matters, for the furtheringe of the gospell, and preventinge of evill, as farre as we mighte deale in by our callinges.

The persons chosen for the Assembly are these.

   Mr Doctor Chapman.
   Mr Doctor Cricke.
   Mr dowe.
   Mr Farrar.

Mr Lewes.
Mr Androwes.
Mr Sandes.
Mr Taye.
Mr Lowe
Mr Tye.
Mr Antony morse.
Mr Stocton.
Mr Parker.

Moreover that at every meetinge there be some one of the brethren chosen to be enterpretor of that scripture appointed to be handled, and another to be Moderator of the whole action, and he to begynne and end with prayer.

That none be broughte in as one of this company, without the generall consente of the whole. silence also to be kepte aswell of the meetinge, as of the matter<s> there dealte in, withoute yt be first signified to the reste. the certayne day of the meetinge to be the first Monday after the first sunday of every moneth: and the tyme appointed <to come> to be at eighte of the clocke in the morninge and so to contynue till eleven or thereaboute.

And that some of these daies appointed to meete in be spente in prayer and fastinge, and that then admonition be geven to any of the brethren, ether tutchinge their mynistery, doctryne, or liffe, if any thinge have bene observed or be espied by the brethren necessarely requiringe the same. And that there be upon the dayes of prayer and fastinge exercise <of> and enterpretation of the worde by some of the brethren, that shallbe chosen and thoughte meetest for the same.

[fo. 1v]

That the enterpretor of the place of scripture, after the action done, departe oute from the rest of the brethren, and every man's judgmente to be asked of his handlinge, of the said scripture, and the moderator to declare unto him, what the brethren judge of yt.

That any of the brethren may propounde any profitable questions to the rest, to be considered of, at that presente (if tyme permitte) or at the nexte meetinge followinge.

[the following names are all signatures]

Edm[u]nd Chapman
Richard Crick
Thomas Farrur.
Willi[a]m Teye.
Rychard dowe
Bartimeus andrewes.
Roberte Lewis.
Thomas Stoughton
Thomas Lowe

           Antony Morsse
           Thomas Tye
           Richard Parker
           Hen[ry] Sands
           Laur[ence] Newman
           John Tylney
           Wyll[ia]m Negus
           Wyll[ia]m byrde
           Ranulphe Catelyn
           Edmund Salmon
           Arthur Gale

[fo. 2r]

The matters concluded of in our meetinges as followeth

{December 3 . 1582, was our first meeting at Barfold.[1] Mr Doctor Cricke Speaker: and Mr Doctor Chapman moderator.}

The Question tutchinge the right use of the lordes daie then propounded.[2]
1 left to be considered of till the next meetinge after save one: 2 was for the placing of mr dowe, whether at Barfold or Stratford, deferred till the next meetinge. 3. mr stocton moved whether fornication make affinity: not thought convenient to be decided. <of> doctor chapman was chosen to be the next speaker, doctor Crick moderator, and the place at doctor Chapman's house.

{Second meeting. 7: January: at Dedham: at Doctor Chapmans house: Doctor Chapman speaker, and Doctor Crick moderator.}

It was thoughte best to the brethren for diverse reasons that mr dowe shuld accepte of his callinge at Stratforde.
The 2 question propounded was tutching the Sabboth as before. This also was spoken of that the booke of common praier shuld be considered of how farre a Pastor might read therein: mr dow speaker at his own house, mr Lewes moderator.

{Thirde meeting 4 February: at Stratforde. Mr Dow Speaker Mr Lewis moderator.}

mr Lewis propounded whether the people ought to leave their pastor when he teacheth to goe to heare others ordenarely.[3]

---

1   East Bergholt, Suffolk, on the river Stour. West Bergholt is in Essex, south of the Stour but not bordered by it, and contiguous to Lexden.
2   For the Dedham debate on the Sabbath, mainly conducted between Henry Sandes of Boxford, a strict sabbatarian, and Richard Crick of East Bergholt, whose more moderate views corresponded to an earlier stage in the evolution of this question in the post-reformation Church of England, see pp. lxxxv–vii above and pp. 46–70 below.
3   The first of several references to Lewis's running battle with George Northey, common preacher of Colchester, whose sermons attracted the parishioners of St Peter away from Lewis's regular parish services.

It was thought meete that the people of every congregation shuld joigne with their owne pastors in the use of the word and Sacramentes.

It was also concluded of by the brethren havinge perused and allowed the doctrine conteyned in mr Chapman's little Catechisme, that yt was not inconveniente to be published for the use of the people of Dedham especially: for mr. doctor Chapman craved at this tyme the brethrens advise tutching the publishing of his Catechisme.[4] The Question of the use of the Sabboth was then debated of but left undetermined till further conference of brethren in other places might be required. Another question was propounded by mr dowe whether a man divorced from his first wief justly and marying a second shuld retaine the second as his wieff, to be determined the next meetinge.

{Fourth meetinge 4 . march at Boxted[5] Mr morse, Speaker: Mr Dowe moderator.}

It was concluded that <a man> the worde of god alloweth that a man justlie divorced from his first wieff might mary a second, so his proceedinge to the second mariage be orderly and in the lorde.[6] This question was propounded how a pastor might deale in the baptising of the children of those which have committed filthines before mariage, the handlinge of it was deferred ether till we shall come unto it in the booke of common prayer, or some occasion necessarely require the handling of it. A motion also was now made for to write to mr Carthwright to undertake the answeringe of the Rhemish Testament, but it was deferred.[7] It was also agreed on that the next meetinge shuld be spent in praier and fasting and handling of the word from 8 to three in the afternoone. the speakers chosen, mr Androwes, mr farrar, mr Sands, mr Lewis. The place of scriptures left to their discretions to consider of: the place Barfold at mr stoctons. The Moderator Mr morse.

---

4 See *BR*, pp. 192–6 below. On the division of views among members of the conference as to the propriety of employing a man-made catechism in church, see pp. 83–5 below.
5 Boxted, Essex, lies three miles west of Dedham and is separated from it only by the parish of Langham. This is the only time the conference met at Boxted, and for the possibility that in this case 'Mr Morse' was not Anthony but Thomas, vicar there 1573–9, see *BR*, p. 232. Boxted, Suffolk, is about eighteen miles north-west of Stratford St Mary, well outside the orbit of the Dedham members.
6 An important decision at a time when divorce *a mensa et thoro* was the only kind condoned under canon law. Such divorce was no more than what is now known as judicial separation, neither party being permitted to remarry during the lifetime of the other. The conference's judgment was not unique: in 1599 Matthew Hutton, archbishop of York, accepted that the divorce and remarriage of his dean, John Thornborough, bishop of Limerick and later bishop of Worcester, was legal on precisely the same grounds 'although much disliked by the clergy of this realm' (PRO SP 12/270/75).
7 At a time when the puritan ideologue Thomas Cartwright was negotiating his return to England after many years of absence/exile, latterly in Antwerp and Middelburg, Sir Francis Walsingham proposed that he improve his profile, not least with the queen, by undertaking a confutation of the catholic version of the New Testament, recently published at Rheims. But his old enemy Archbishop John Whitgift placed obstacles in the way, and understandably so since Cartwright's *Confutation* was at many points a new vehicle for his unreconstructed presbyterian convictions. It was published only after his death, in 1618 (at Leyden). See A. F. Scott Pearson, *Thomas Cartwright and Elizabethan puritanism* (Cambridge, 1925), pp. 198–211. See the correspondence between Dedham and Cartwright, pp. 70–75 below.

{Fifth meeting 8 . April: 1583. Barfold.}

where the time was spent in extraordenary praier with fastinge as was appointed before and performed by the fornamed brethren.

{Sixt meeting. 6 may. Colchester.}

A couple of the brethren viz mr lewis and mr dowe **were appointed to deale with mr Joanes**[8] **to staie the playes of Manitree which they did but could not prevayle.**[9] It was moved whether a day of praier and fasting shuld be appointed at this tyme, it was thought meete the certeyne day shuld be deferred till some occasion were offred. It was alsoe thoughte <~~verie~~> **inconvenient that mr dowe shuld reade an ordenary Lecture at Higham <~~for diverse causes~~> any longe tyme.**[10]

It was propounded by mr Tay whether a man may goe into the Courts of the Official[11] being cited by the Somner, yt was agreed to be spoken of the next meetinge and mr Tay was required to geve in his reasons to some of the brethren to be answered and soe to be decided.[12] mr Parker craved the brethrens counsell for preventinge of the meetinges of some in Dedham and namely of Pariman.[13] yt was thought meete that their dealings shuld be <espee> espied and then to be talked with all and if they leave not, then the Magistrate to be acquainted with it to reforme yt.

---

8   Richard Jones, BD, rector of Mistley-cum-Manningtree, Essex, 1581–5 (d.). Not otherwise mentioned in the minutes but probably well known to all the conference members since he had graduated from Christ's College, Cambridge, in 1569 and become a fellow of Magdalene (*Alum. Cantab.*, II, 487). Mistley-cum-Manningtree is bordered by the Stour and separated from Dedham only by the parish of Lawford.

9   The plays performed at Manningtree, significantly in the month of May, may be regarded as a relic of the old tradition of parish and town plays on biblical and hagiographical subjects, for many places a significant element in fund-raising, since their success depended upon drawing an audience from neighbouring parishes, which in this case would have included Dedham. The tradition was already in steep decline in Essex, and it was opposed by all 'godly' ministers. For the last days of the old drama, and the case of Manningtree specifically, see the Essex volume in *Records of early English drama* (Toronto, forthcoming).

10   It is not clear why it should have been thought (very) inconvenient that Richard Dowe should 'for diverse causes' cease to preach at Higham, a Suffolk parish to the north of the Stour valley, in spite (or because?) of the fact (**11M**) that the incumbent was held to be 'a wicked man'.

11   Bishops and archdeacons traditionally appointed a civil lawyer trained in canon law to preside over their courts. Here Tey is probably anticipating the forthcoming episcopal visitation of London diocese, scheduled for July 1583.

12   Tey's frequent challenging of the jurisdiction of the church courts is in contrast to the caution of most of his fellow members. It is one of the elements in the Dedham papers that led to the erroneous assumption that the conferences were subversive attempts to overthrow episcopal jurisdiction.

13   Presumably William Perryman of Greenstead Juxta Colchester who, with his wife, was in 1584 before the archdeaconry court at St Peter Colchester for refusing to pay towards the making of a surplice. He alleged that in that regard he was 'over-taxed': W. J. Pressey, 'The surplice in Essex', *Essex Review*, XLV (1936), 43. Although nothing more is known of 'Periman', the reference to 'the meetinges of some in Dedham' and his elusiveness (**7M**) may indicate that he was some sort of separatist, 'gathering' a small following out of the parish. Cf. the activities of Edward Glover a little later. See p. 29 below.

[fo. 2v]

{Seventh meeting. 3 . June. Langham.}

~~<It was thoughte good that <for the handlinge of the scriptures> <tutching the manner of enterpreting of the scriptures> <to be observed emongst ourselves in this exercise that> every man shuld be lefte to the measure of his giftes geven him of God, and not to be tied to any precise order therin>~~

mr Lewis had spoken to the magistrate to enquire for Periman by faithfull men but he could not be founde. **It was thought good that tutching the manner of enterpretinge of the Scriptures to be observed emongst our selves in this exercise that every man shuld be lefte to the measure of his giftes, and not to be tyed to any certayne and precise order true doctryne being reverently and discretely delyvered.**

{8 meeting 24 . June . at Boxford.}

Tutchinge the baptisinge of <the> children base borne it was concluded that they shuld be baptised, some approved christians of the congregation undertakinge for their religyous education.[14] moved by mr. dowe. mr farrur desired the brethren to advise him what to do with a wicked man that was come into his parish[15] and saieth he hath the B[ishop]'s authority for all will not be conformable, it was thought meet to get witnesses of his wordes and their handwriting to prove it and call him before a magistrate.

It was thoughte good mr Lewes shuld cease his readinge upon Genesis and choose some other place of Scripture, the same texte beinge publikely at the same tyme enterpreted by mr Northie.[16]

It was agreed on that the Question of the Sabboth before propounded shuld carefully be considered of and every man give in his reasons to doctor Cricke and he to answer them at our next meetinge, and that mr doctor Chapman, mr Stocton and mr morse crave the judgmentes of some godly men in Cambridge tutching the question of the Sabboth. The state of the question is this. first that ther is a Sabboth. 2 that it is not a whole naturall daie. 3 that we be not bound to the same rest that was with the Jewes.

---

[14] This touched on a small dilemma for the puritan ministry. Puritans often condemned the institution of godparenthood, insisting that the natural parents should answer for the child. The policy proposed here, that 'some approved christians of the congregation' should undertake the religious education of bastards, was consistent with this position.

[15] It is not clear whether Farrar refers to a clergyman who had obtained Bishop Aylmer's licence to serve the cure, but no curate is listed in the call book of visitation in July 1583.

[16] George Northey, common preacher of Colchester. See *BR*, pp. 240–42 below. The entry suggests that his fellow members were not particularly sympathetic to Lewis's feud with Northey in their battle for an auditory.

{9 Meeting 5 . August.[17] at Peldon. Mr. Tay speaker. Mr stocton moderator}

Here some tyme was spente aboute the use of the Sabboth. some reasons were gathered by doctor Cricke, it was ordered doctor Chapman shuld have the oversight of them, and doctor Cricke shuld answer any reason brought in by doctor Chapman against his judgment set downe, and then the brethren to have the fruit of his labors. It was propounded whether we might goe to the B[ishop] or noe:[18] it was thought good not to goe, if the message mr Tuke[19] brought were true, that we shuld not need come till he sent for us. It was propounded how far a pastor might goe in reading the book of common praier, but nothing was said to yt.

It was said our meetinges were knowen and thretned,[20] yet it was thought good not to be left but that some godlie lawier[21] shuld be talked with how we may meet by law and mr Tay and mr Lewis thought fitt men.

{10 meeting. 2 September at Barfold at hoglane.}

Where the time was spente in prayer joigned with fastinge wher mr doctor Cricke, mr dowe, mr stocton and mr Lowe were speakers and mr Tay moderator.

{11 meeting 7. October at Wenham. Mr Dow speaker. Mr Androwes moderator.}

More tyme was spente about the cause of the Sabboth in examyninge of mr doctor Crickes travayles about that Question to whom that charge was chiefly committed by consente. The thinges moved were these: first that it were good the Archb[ishop][22] shuld be written unto to be favourable to our Church and to discipline. the answer was, that lettres shuld be sent to other brethren about it, and that doctor Chapman shuld write to London and Norwich, and mr Sandes to Cambridge about it, and to the brethren in Suffolk, and that mr doctor withers[23] shuld be written unto.

---

[17] The comparatively long gap between meetings 8 and 9 is accounted for by Aylmer's episcopal visitation in July. The visitors sat in the church of St Botolph Colchester on 11 July to examine the clergy of Colchester, Lexden and Tendring deaneries: GL MS 9537/5, fo. 58r.

[18] Aylmer took up residence at his manor of Much Hadham, Hertfordshire, during the course of the visitation. Many clergy whose preaching licences and liturgical practices had been scrutinized by his visitors were ordered to 'attend' him there and receive further directives. Tuke's message suggests that Aylmer was using cat-and-mouse tactics, picking off the nonconformists as and when it suited him.

[19] See *BR*, pp. 262–3 below.

[20] This sounds like the timid voice of Thomas Lowe, who dropped out of the conference within weeks.

[21] Probably James Morice, for whom see Hasler, *House of commons,* and *BR*, pp. 228–9.

[22] John Whitgift, bishop of Worcester, had been confirmed as archbishop of Canterbury on 23 September 1583. It is instructive that the brethren do not seem to have regarded his elevation as a watershed in their affairs – perhaps because they had already been coping with Aylmer for five and a half years and did not yet see the wood for the trees. But note that these were early days, that Whitgift had conveyed some contrary signals in the months leading up to his preferment, reassuring the earls of Leicester and Warwick that there would be nothing to fear, and saying that he regretted his earlier controversy with Thomas Cartwright; this may explain why John Field in 'this 11th month' of 1583 (November, or February 1584?) told Edmund Chapman that 'our new Archbishopp, now he is in, sheweth himself as he was wonte to be' (Collinson, *EPM,* pp. 243–4, and pp. 89–90 below).

[23] See above pp. xcviii–ic.

It was said an ungodlie sermon was made by mr Beaman of hadleigh,[24] defacing the man of Antwerpe,[25] it was thought good doctor Cricke shuld get some notes of the sermon and so mr. doctor still[26] to be dealt with about it.

It was also signified to the brethren that a wicked man being a mynister served at Higham, it was agreed that mr dowe and mr morse shuld deale with it and get articles against him.

{12 meeting 4. November at Stratford at Mr Morses: Mr Tye speaker, Mr Doctor Crick moderator.}

It was thoughte most convenient that <a~~ Pastor Catechisinge~~> untoward persons shulde <~~seeke to wynne those that will not come to~~ > be trayned to the use of the word <~~of~~> and Sacramentes by all lovinge and gentle admonityons.
At this tyme it was agreed that every man shuld bring in his reasons for the right use of the Sabaoth. 2 that every one yeld his opinion whether a Catechisme shuld be followed and be enterpreted.

[fo. 3r]

{13 meeting 1º. December at Colchester at Mr Lowes house. Mr Low speaker Mr Lewis moderator.}

<~~As tutchinge the order to be used by the Pastor in Catechisinge of the youthe~~> It was agreed that some certayne forme of Catechisinge might be followed by the mynisters in the Churche especially for the use of the yonger sorte, as a preparatyve to the publike and ordenary exercises of the worde and prayer.
This was here moved, what course was to be taken to redresse the multitude of roges wherwith the contrey was charged at their dores notwithstanding they paid money besides,[27] it was not thought convenient for us to deale in yt, except the creditt of any were such as to deale with some Magistrate for it, and then to deale as a private man in it.

---

[24] John Bemond compounded for the benefice of Aldham, Suffolk, on the outskirts of Hadleigh, on 4 November 1583: PRO E334/10, fo. 52v.

[25] Possibly a reference to Robert Wright, who had been ordained in Antwerp according to his own admission and never subsequently took English orders. See *BR*, pp. 269–72 below. It remains possible that 'man' is a slip of the pen, and that 'men' was meant. That would suggest that Bemond was attacking the whole congregation of English merchants at Antwerp (with its connexions with the Stour valley clothing towns), whose church under the guidance of Walter Travers and Thomas Cartwright was effectively a congregation living under 'the discipline', rather than the laws of the Church of England. The problem here is that the merchants, their staple and their church had moved from Antwerp to Middelburg in Zealand a year earlier, in October 1582.

[26] For Still's activities as a sympathetic *oculus episcopi* see Diarmaid MacCulloch, *Suffolk and the Tudors* (Oxford, 1986), p. 51; Collinson, *EPM*, p. 338.

[27] The meaning of 'paid money besides' is that many communities in this region were already rated for poor relief, as they would be by statute law, after 1597. The godly ministers were second to none in their denunciations of begging vagrants, 'ulcers, scabs and vermin'. And note that when the (Dedham) practice of visiting the poor in their own homes was advocated by the London preacher John Downame, he suggested that if this were done, 'they would not so often have occasion to visit us at ours.' See Patrick Collinson, 'Puritanism and the poor', in *Pragmatic utopias. Ideals and communities, 1200–1630*, ed. Rosemary Horrox and Sarah Rees Jones (Cambridge, 2001), pp. 242–58.

{14 meeting. 13 January: at Dedham at Mr Parker's. Mr. Sands speaker   Mr Androwes moderator.}

mr. wilcockes lettres of request for helpinge of him in his present necessitye were then read and considered of.[28]

mr. Sandes alledged some reasons against mr doctor Crickes labors about the Sabboth, which were to be brought in writing the next meeting.

It was moved what course the ministers might take for going before the Bishop, but nothing done in it.[29] mr. Tie[30] was desired to lay out the money for mr wilcock and it shuld be repaid him the next meetinge.

Tutching the book of common praier it was thought good that mr. Sandes and mr Tay shuld vew it over and note out the thinges might be used with a good conscience and what not.

It was moved that a day of fasting might be kept, which was concluded to be the next meetinge and in the meane tyme to have some extraordenary praiers used in our families to that ende.

{15 meeting. 3 February. at Barf[old] at hoglane. The persons that spake at this fast were Mr Doctor Chapman, Mr Sands: Mr Tay: Mr farrar[31] and Mr Doctor Crick, Moderator.}

The time was spente in praier with fastinge: At this time also the firste Epistle to Timothie was chosen to be enterpreted.

mr farrar was then moved by the brethren to renewe his exercise of prechinge in his owne congregation.[32]

mr. Tie signified to the brethren that the money was paid to mr wilcocke he being released before out of prison, it was agreed that a letter shuld be made to him to repay it or to promise payment of yt.

{16 meeting 2 . march at Dedham at Doctor Chapmans. Mr Androwes speaker mr farrar moderator}

It was thoughte good if anie of the brethren were called to subscribe to require tyme to deliberate.[33]

---

28 Although assumed in Usher 1905 to be Thomas Wilcox, co-author with John Field of *An admonition to the Parliament*, this was in fact *Henry* Wilcock(e), Parker's successor as vicar of Dedham: see above, pp. lxxiv–vi and below, p. 88 [for his letter].

29 Further evidence that Aylmer continued to conduct enquiries into nonconformist activities for many months after the episcopal visitation of 1583. But the act book for 1583–6 suggests that he achieved little. See above, p. xli.

30 For the possibility that Thomas Tie was Thomas Tey, brother of William Tey, see *BR*, pp. 264–5.

31 See *BR*, pp. 205–07.

32 Farrar appears to have been of a nervous disposition. See *BR*, pp. 205–06.

33 In March 1584 a climax was approaching in Archbishop Whitgift's campaign to obtain subscription from all the clergy of his province to three articles, validating the royal supremacy, the Book of Common Prayer as containing nothing contrary to the word of God, and the articles of religion. The second article, in particular, was a conscientious sticking point for many hundreds of ministers. Delegations of ministers, suspended or facing suspension and ultimately deprivation for failure to subscribe, went up to London, county by county, even, as in the case of Kent, descending on the archbishop without warning. When they found Whitgift obdurate, they transferred their appeals for indulgence to the privy council and Lord Burghley. Eventually, many qualified forms of subscription

{17 meeting. 6 April at Colch[ester]: 1584 at Mr Lewes house. Mr Doctor Crick, speaker. Mr Sands moderator.

Mr. Doctor chapman	20 s.
mr. Doctor Crick	20 s.
Mr. Tay	20 s.
mr. Sands	20 s.
mr. farrar	10 s.
mr. morse	10 s.
mr. Tilney	10 s.
mr. Lewis	10 s.
mr. Tye	10 s.
mr. Parker	5 s.}

<mr Wilcock requiring help from the brethren being in prison was relieved by them every one <giving som> lending hym a porcion to the summe of vi li xv s>

It was then determyned that a certeyne somme of money shuld be raised by the brethren, which is noted in the margent for mr wilcocke. which was done and paid to mr Tye that laid it out, and it was concluded that a letter shuld be sent to admonish mr wilcock of his fault for not signifying the receipt of the money by some note of his hande. mr Sandes brought in his reasons against mr doctor Cricke labors about the Sabboth: it was thought good mr doctor Cricke shuld have them and answer them the nexte meetinge.

mr. Tay brought in his judgment and reasons for the book of common praier. mr Chapman moved that the B[ishop]'s proceeding[34] did admonish the ministers to have a generall meeting to conferre what might be done. it was thought good every one shuld stirre up his frind to consider of it.

{18 Meeting 4. May. at Langham.[35] Mr Lewis speaker, Mr Tay moderator.}

It was thought good mr morse shuld accepte of a callinge in Sir drew drurie's house with certayne condicions.[36]

were offered, and accepted, leaving Whitgift and the High Commission to pick off known extremists with examinations under the *ex officio mero* oath (Collinson, *EPM*, pp. 249–72). For copies of some of the relevant documents, preserved by Richard Parker, see pp. 87; 91–3 below.

[34] It is not clear to which 'proceeding' Chapman here refers. Aylmer was still refusing to restore George Northey unless he subscribed, whilst on 5 and 10 March he had personally summoned several prominent nonconformists in southern Essex, including George Gifford and Arthur Dent, and threatened them with suspension if they had not subscribed within a fortnight: LMA DL/C/334, fos. 18r–19r. Alternatively the reference is to Bishop Edmund Freke of Norwich. But if there has been a small scribal error with the apostrophe the reference may have been to the bishops' proceedings in general, as subscription to the three articles was pressed. If so, that would have strengthened the need for 'a generall meeting' to co-ordinate strategies of non-compliance.

[35] At Thomas Farrar's house.

[36] Dru Drurie, a member of an extensive East Anglian gentry family which included several catholics or crypto-catholics (including Robert Drurie[y], the preacher Oliver Pigge's *bête noire* at Rougham, Suffolk), was himself staunchly protestant. He was *custos rotulorum* in Norfolk in 1583, a deputy lieutenant in 1588, a gentleman usher in the queen's privy chamber, and would serve as Lieutenant of the Tower. As a commissioner appointed to enquire into the dispute between Bishop Edmund Freke and his chancellor, Thomas Becon, in 1578, he shared in inflicting public humiliation on Freke. See

It was thought good a generall meetinge of lerned brethren shuld be procured for better advise and consent about the cause of subscriptions.

It was also thought expedient that congregations beinge depryved of the use of their owne mynisters shuld be provided for by some other preachers to be procured for a tyme.

mr Dow moved this, whether it were convenient a woman shuld pray having a better gift then her husband, reserved to the next meeting to be considered of.

mr Tilney whether the minister and thelements in the Sacrament be of the essence of the sacrament, it is reserved till the next meetinge.

mr. Sandes moved the brethren for a fast, it was thought meete every man shuld stirre up himself to it.

[fo. 3v]

{19 meeting 1. June. at Chatsam.[37] Mr Tilney speaker. Mr Tye moderator.}

Advise was geven by the brethren to mr. Negus tutchinge his estate and dealinge with his people.[38]

mr Sandes brought not his replie against doctor Crickes reasons bicause he was absente.

For the generall meeting moved before, it was thought good that mr newman shuld goe to london and understand the brethrens mynd and certify us of it.

The question for the womens praier is omitted as not necessary to be handled. The question of the mynister and elements in the Sacraments is deferred till some other tyme. mr newman moved whether he might get a standing supply for his place. it was thought fitt, so it be a scholer in the university, lest the B[ishop] shuld send a hirelinge, but it was feared the B[ishop] wold suspend him, if he were a good man.

mr. Tay moved whether the Churches shuld not joigne in supplication with others, being a duty in them to sue for their pastors being faithfull and they deprived of them, as it is to sue if they had noe pastors, it was thought necessary the congregations shuld make a supplication. he moved also whether a minister might cease preching being forbidden by the magistrate it was answered that they that doubted shuld bring in their reasons. 2 Chronicles amasia staied his speech. looke 26 Jeremiah.[39]

A. Hassell Smith, *County and court. Government and politics in Norfolk 1558–1603* (Oxford, 1974), pp. 69, 220.

[37] Chattisham, a tiny Suffolk parish immediately east of Hadleigh, is nowhere mentioned in the minutes, nor is it known which, if any, of the Dedham members was living there.

[38] William Negus was at this time preacher at Ipswich. See *BR*, pp. 234–8.

[39] The biblical reference is obscure. 2 Kings xiv (rather than 2 Chronicles, which the Elizabethans often referred to as '4 Kings') tells how Amaziah, king of Judah, refused to hear the threatening messages which had come from King Jehoash of Israel, in response to Amaziah's message 'come, let us look one another in the face', with the result that Jehoash defeated Judah and took Amaziah captive, before wasting Jerusalem. The point, if any, would seem to be that the ministers would be wise to remain in communication with the bishops. The relevance of Jeremiah xxvi is more obvious, and appears to be on the other side of the argument. Jeremiah had prophesied the fall of Jerusalem, which aroused extreme anger among his hearers. His response was to say: 'The Lord sent me to prophesy against this house and against this city', and he refused to be silenced. These verses were printed as a kind of validating motto on the title-page of *A second admonition to the parliament* (1573). See *Puritan manifestoes*, ed. W. H. Frere and C. E. Douglas (London, 1954), p. 80.

{20: meeting 1. July at Boxford at Mr Sands. Mr farrar speaker   mr Doctor Chapman moderator}

It was thought good that enquiry should be made of the number of mynisters nere unto us which are both insufficient in lerninge and notoriously offensyve in liffe.[40] moved by doctor Cricke. It was thought good that men of fitt giftes and good liff shuld be found out to supply the churches want if they can come in with favor: so that it might not mainteyne a ranging ministery:[41] mr Sandes moved it.

Tutchinge mariage of Cosins Children, moved by mr Negus, it was determyned to be lawfull; and the conveniency of it to be waighed by circumstances of the place and people there wher such questions shall come in use. mr Dow moved this, what course he shuld take for stratford one having gott the presentacion, he was advised to ask counsell and to gett his parish to joigne with him.[42] mr Tilney moved whether he shuld goe to the Court, he was at his 3 admonition, it was thought good he shuld not goe. mr Negus, was advised to tarry with his parish if the godlie desired it and wold mainteyne him. mr Tay moved whether we might not stand in the truth of the doctrine of christs office as we doe in the truth of his natures it was thought good to be better weighed and so was deferred.

{21 meeting 3. August at Peldon. Mr Negus speaker[43] mr Parker moderator}

It was thought good mr Lowe shuld be earnestly delt withall by some of the brethren and persuaded to joigne with us in our meetinges ordenarely with diligence and cherfulnes[44]
mr Lewis told us that the ArchB[ishop] offred Articles to some, and an othe: and therfore moved the brethren to shew what course shuld be taken, it was answered we shuld heare something by the brethren to whom the othe was offred.[45] mr farrar moved, what course shuld be taken with the child of a strumpett brought into his church secretly and left there: whether it shuld be baptised, it was thought that by the next meeting he shuld heare of some order taken for it, and soe not now fitt to be

[40] The result is to be found in the Essex survey of the ministry in *Seconde parte*, II, 163–5.
[41] In the first days of the Church, the Apostles had exercised what is here called a ranging ministry. We read in some Elizabethan puritan texts of 'roving apostles'. The practice of itinerancy by preachers was late medieval (the friars) and was continued in the early Elizabethan days of scarce preaching by the likes of John Laurence in Suffolk (see above, p. xliii). But the orthodox presbyterian line was that the days of the Apostles were no more, and that it was absolutely necessary for a preacher, whether pastor or doctor, to have received a valid calling to minister in one place.
[42] One Blase White received letters of presentation from the queen, in right of the duchy of Lancaster, dated 22 April, 26 Elizabeth, because of the attainder of John Christian *de felonia*. This was overturned. Dowe eventually received letters of presentation dated 18 January, 30 Elizabeth, because of the death of John Christian. PRO DL 42/100, fos. 12r, 14v.
[43] It was probably this heading which led W. A. Shaw in the *DNB* (unaware of Negus's activities in Ipswich and misled by Newcourt's typographical error for William Tey at Peldon) to propose that Negus was perhaps beneficed in Peldon. There is in fact no evidence whatsoever to connect Negus with the parish.
[44] For Lowe's faint-heartedness, see *BR*, pp. 225–7.
[45] Lewis signals to the conference the shift in Whitgift's policy. Offering twenty-four articles 'to some' and an oath (the *ex officio* oath) represented the more selective strategy adopted against 'ringleaders' by the archbishop and the High Commission in response to pressure from the privy council, Burghley in particular. This led to some deprivations, including that of George Gifford of Maldon. See Collinson, *EPM*, pp. 266–9.

delt in but deferred. mr Chapman moved whether it were thought good that <to> a reconciliation shuld be offred to the B[ishop]s, that since we professe one god and preache one doctrine we may joigne together with better consent to build up the Churche. this was not thought convenient of the most lest we shuld seeme to yeld in our cause, and sought to be of their company. mr Tay was moved to deale with mr Lowe to know the cause of his absence and his reasons, and if he prevailed not to joigne mr farrar with him, and afterward mr doctor Chapman and mr Parker were willed to conferre with him about his absence from us. mr dow and mr stocton delt with the gentlemen in Suffolke about the number of ill mynisters as it was before appointed and are enjoyned to goe agayne before the next meeting to knowe more fully of them. The judgment of the lawyers is that the othe offred by the Bishops is not to be allowed.[46] It was concluded that a letter shuld be written to mr wilcocke signifying the brethrens mynd in their benevolence to be this, not to geve him but to lend him the money. mr Androwes shewed some causes to move his departure from wenham which was deferred. mr Parker moved a day of fast which was deferred to the next meeting save one.

[fo. 4r]

{The 7 September the 22 meeting at Coxall[47] at Mr Newmans house Mr morse speaker Mr stocton moderator}

At this tyme mr Androwes asked the brethrens advise tutching his departure from wenham: it was appointed that mr doctor Chapman and mr farrar shuld deale with the people to see what they would pay him, for the tyme past and for the tyme to come. mr Tilney and mr Newman moved this, whether they might preach and exercise their ministery being suspended, it was not thought good to presse soe farre considering the state of the tyme. mr Newman moved whether he might goe to the Archbishopp and yeld to that subscription is offred to the xxxvij article, and to the article tutching faith and the Sacraments, it was thought not to yeld to that subscription.[48] It is agreed that the next daie of meeting shuld be spent in praier and fastinge the speakers to be mr Sandes, mr stocton and mr Negus. mr stocton moved whether he might safelie in conscience preach being requested thereunto he being yet no minister, it was not delt in. The next place at Dedham, mr doctor Chapman Moderator.

---

[46] A number of prominent lawyers, including the clerk of the privy council, Robert Beale, and, significantly, James Morice, closely connected as he was with Colchester, were active in agitation against the *ex officio* oath. In the parliament of 1593, Morice mounted an attack on the legality of the proceedings in the court of High Commission which led to an inquest before the privy council and house arrest. These events marked the opening of what has sometimes been called the second, and more authoritarian, reign of Elizabeth I. See J. E. Neale, *Elizabeth I and her parliaments 1584–1601* (London, 1957), pp. 267–79; T. E. Hartley, ed., *Proceedings in the parliaments of Elizabeth I*, III, *1593–1601* (London, 1995), esp. 30–49.

[47] Coggeshall, south-west of Dedham, where Laurence Newman was vicar.

[48] In the event Newman did yield in some sense, on 28 November handing in a 'note in writing' to Aylmer's registry by which the bishop accepted Newman's subscription and so released him from suspension: LMA DL/C/301, p. 397. But was this *full* subscription to Whitgift's articles or yet another judicious compromise? See *BR*, pp. 238–40 below.

{The 5 of October was the 23. meeting at Mr chap[man's] house.}

This daie was spent in praier and fasting as before was appointed. The questions moved and delt in were these. mr Sandes moved whether it were best for him to take his journey at this tyme[49] to prevent some mischieff might come by the Commissary, at whose hand he feared some ill measure: the most of the brethren were of this mynd that he shuld goe, if he had determyned it, having regard that his going might be noe disgrace to his cause. mr Lewis moved whether one having secretly committed filthines being now tutched with it in conscience and promising publike confession of it, he shuld secretly or openly confesse his fault, it was not thought fitt to be delt in. mr Tilney desired to heare some reasons why he shuld not preach though the B[ishop] shuld restreigne him, it was thought best to be deferred and to be talked of afterward.   yet the brethren willed mr Tilney and mr Negus to bring in reasons why they shuld preach being forbidden.[50] mr Negus alledged the B[ishop] had proceeded with him against law, and therfore he thought he might preach agayne, it was said unto him, that he might aske advise of some wise and discreet lawyers tutching that point and if it be not against law then to proceed. mr Androwes moved how he might deale with an offensyve person that hath his child to be baptised, it is thought good he shuld baptise the child if some of the frindes or of the church that be godlie be procured answer for it, and to bringe the partie to repentaunce if it may be. mr Newman moved whether he and his people might not goe to the B[ishop] for his liberty the Archb[ishop] being willinge he shuld be restored if the Bishopp wold. it was not delt in. mr Tuke was sent for to the B[ishop] and required ether to read the praiers as they be set downe in the book of common praier, and to mynister the Sacramentes as is appointed or els to cease preching: he is willing to do it if he may be confirmed in it by the advise of the brethren.[51] this nothing was said of it. The next place <is> appointed is mr dowes house in Stratford. mr newman speaker. mr farrar moderator.

{The 2. of November was our 24 meeting at Stratford.}

Wher these thinges were moved to be considered of. First whether it were not convenient that a fast shuld be against Parliament[52] that was at hand: it was thought necessary that ther shuld be one, and every man to stirre up his people to earnest prayer for the good of the Churche. mr Tay put the brethren in mynd that some of Malden were cast into prison[53] and did crave helpe of the brethren. mr doctor Cricke

[49] Possibly referring to a journey into Sandes's native county of Lancashire, with which he seems to have kept closely in touch.

[50] Here is further good evidence that the conference members did not think they were justified in defying the episcopal and archidiaconal courts as a matter of course.

[51] This confirms the impression gained from the earlier reference to Tuke (9M) that other godly clergy were allowed on occasion to 'sit in' on the meetings.

[52] The parliament of 1584–5 was summoned to meet on 23 November 1584, three weeks after this meeting.

[53] This is unlikely to be a reference to George Gifford, deprived by the High Commission of the vicarage of All Saints with St Peter in the summer of 1584 but (by yet another compromise) restored as town preacher of Maldon shortly afterwards. There is no evidence that Gifford was ever imprisoned, nor are the Dedham brethren likely to have referred to him under the umbrella title of 'some'. Who these 'some' were, however, remains mysterious.

moved how he shuld deale with some obstynate contemners and raylers of his doctryne, it was deferred till some more fitt tyme. It was agreed upon at this tyme that in every cuntrey some shuld be chosen so farre as we could procure it that some of best creditt and most forward for the gosple shuld goe up to London to solicite the cause of the Churche. The daie for the next fast is appointed to be on the 2 december being wednesday for some considerations. The place to be at Langham at mr farrars house. The speakers in the fast to be mr doctor Cricke, mr Tay. mr Negus. mr Newman moderator.

[fo. 4v]

{The 2 of December was our 25 meetinge at Langham.}

At this tyme praier and fastinge was used as it was before decreed. The speakers were the persons before mentioned.
There was nothing moved at this meetinge, but mr Sandes wished that every one as he was acquainted with any gentlemen of worth and of godlines shuld stirre them up to be zealous for reformation.

The next place appointed was at Barfold at mr doctor Crickes house. mr doctor Cricke speaker. mr morse moderator.

{The 4 January was our 26 meeting at Barfold:}

At this tyme, these thinges were moved to the brethren as followeth:
First mr doctor Chapman craved the brethrens advise, what order might be taken for a Papist remayning in dedham, one Doctor Uxenbridge:[54] yt was agreed, that these persons shuld conferre with him, mr doctor Chapman, mr doctor Cricke, mr farrar, mr Lewis, mr dowe, mr stocton.
mr dow moved this, whether it were not needfull that ther shuld [be] praier and fastinge agayne bycause of the assembly of Parliament: yt was thought necessary, and that the brethren of London should be written unto, to know when they appoint to have theirs, that we might joigne with them, and that some shuld contynue to solicite the cause of the Church there.
mr Farrar craved the brethrens advise in this, whether being chosen by some persons

---

[54] Andrew Oxenbridge, a prominent catholic lawyer from Essex, was one of the few lay prisoners at Wisbech Castle, which is some indication of how, as a recusant, he was rated by the authorities. In May 1583, Oxenbridge signed a statement of allegiance which squared the circle of his loyalty to the queen and spiritual allegiance to Rome. He acknowledged Elizabeth as 'most rightful and lawful Queene [of England] *de jure*' and that he owed her 'all my loyalty, service, and whole duty of subjection under God', and would continue so to do, in defiance of any papal Bull, believing that to hold that the pope could depose a sovereign was 'a traitorous article'. 'As touching matter of religion', Oxenbridge promised that if in conference he was persuaded of any error on scriptural authority, he would change his mind. Hence his delivery into the hands of the Dedham ministers. See W. R. Trimble, *The catholic laity in Elizabethan England 1558–1603* (Cambridge, Mass, 1964), pp. 117–18.

unknowing to him to be a Commissioner[55] for examyninge of witnesses for matters depending betwene a bad mynister and his people he might deale in it: It was thought good he shuld further this present occasion for the good of the people, but els to certify the people that they shuld choose fitter men another tyme, that might better deale in such causes then any mynister.

mr Tilney craved the advise of the brethren, what he might doe for marying <a couple> a couple of unequall ages, a young man but of 24 yeares and the woman fifty and more. he had by request published the contract once: It was thought meete he shuld deale with the chieff of the parish to dissuade the parties from mariage, and to see how farre the parties had gone <at> in it, and to consider the lawfulnes of the contract, and to proceed accordinglie.

mr Sandes asked how he shuld deale with some persons that carelesly refuse the Sacraments for two or 3 <sp> yeares space, whether he shuld spare them, since by that meanes other negligent persons looked to be spared in like case. it was deferred to be considered of.

mr Tay moved that some thing might be done for that our Clarkes chosen for the Convocation house were refused at the Bishops handes.[56]

The next meeting is appointed to be this day moneth viz. the first of February and to be spent in praier and fasting according to the motion made by mr dowe. The speakers were these 3 mr Newman: mr Lewis and mr Parker. The Moderator mr dowe. the place was at mr morses of Stratforde.

{The first of February was our 27 meeting at Stratforde.}

wher praier and fasted [sic] was used by the persons before named.

It was now moved whether mr Edward morse[57] (being a good man and we assembled in his house) might be admitted amongst us for that tyme, it was thought well of, so it might not be made an example hereafter for others to doe the like.

mr Negus moved the brethren that in this publike exercise they wold pray to god for him, and commend his state unto the highest, being about to take his journey to london for his restoring to liberty in his callinge.[58] It is to be remembred, that he was at that tyme restored to his publike mynistery agayne before he came back to us.

mr Sandes moved the same question tutching such as for light causes refuse the Sacramentes but it is still deferred.

---

[55] Although not necessarily styled 'commissioners' (but note the expression 'commissioners for the exercise', see above, p. xxviii), it was the regular practice of the Essex archdeaconry courts, and in all probability more widely, to refer problems relating to 'bad', ignorant or misguided ministers to some of the better qualified clergy of the locality. See Collinson, 'PCM', p. 260n.

[56] Little enough is known about the process by which members of the inferior clergy were 'elected' as 'proctors' to the Lower House of Convocation. In principle, it should have been synodical. But evidence such as this is suggestive of a kind of 'guided democracy', especially, perhaps, in the circumstances of 1584–5. There is no reference to Aylmer's refusal of delegates in his extant correspondence or in the diocesan records.

[57] Eldest brother of Anthony Morse. See p. lx above and BR, pp. 229–31 below. From internal evidence of bequests, he was evidently not related to the Edward Morse of Taddington, Suffolk, whose will was granted probate on 30 January 1584: PRO PCC PROB 11/66 (23 Butts).

[58] It is not clear to whom he was applying. During his stay in London, however, he was offered the benefice of Leigh, Essex, by Robert 3rd Lord Rich. See BR, pp. 234–8 below.

mr morse craved the brethrens advise, whether hit were best for him to goe to a private place wher mr pigge[59] now is: but it was deferred to be considered of.

This was also moved, whether a fact committed by a minister not knowen generally in the <pl> parish wher he is but knowen of diverse in other places may be satisfied for by a private reconcliation [sic], it was deferred.

[fo. 5r]

mr doctor Chapman moved the brethren appointed to come to conferre with the Papist,[60] and to seeke by what meanes the great cause of the Church that is now in hand might be delt in and good done in it, and for to procure some good, it was concluded that mr knewstubb[61] for Suffolke, and mr gifford[62] and mr wright of Essex[63] shuld be moved to deale for the church and lettres to be written to them to that ende.

mr Androwes was at this meetinge admonished for his absence from his charge, and the cause of his departure was spoken of: And thereupon this question was moved

{A question}

whether a Pastor called to a place may leave the people they being unwilling of his departure.

{Answer}

It was answered ther are causes to move a Pastor to depart, wherof want of mayntenance may be one cause, yet the least, for a mynister shuld looke before he goe to a place whether his mayntenance be sufficient, and if notwithstanding the slender mayntenance he accept it, he doth laie such a yoke upon his necke as he can hardlie shake of: this was mr doctor Crickes speeche.

mr Tay said among other matters, that he had read in a Counsell and Synode gathered together, that this matter was handled and set downe, that it was never seene, that any man went from a great place to a little charge, and so it was noted as a spice of seeking earthly thinges in those that have gone from <grea> little places to gret ones: yet it was thought good if a man being in a little charge at his first entrance the lord encreasing his guiftes, if by the judgment of wise and faithfull brethren it shuld be found to be more for godes glorie and the good of the Church to be in a greater charge, he mighte departe.

The reasons whie mr Androwes desired to goe from Wenham were these.

First he had noe comfort in that place, his hart was dead in it, and he thought that he shuld never doe good there.

2. his wyves and childrens want of healthe.

3. his small mayntenance and manner of paying of it. these reasons were to be considered of, and for this present it was agayne determined that mr doctor

---

[59] For an attempt to elucidate the roving ministry of Oliver Pigge, see Brett Usher in *Oxford DNB*. He was probably ministering in a godly household in Suffolk at this time but it is not clear whose.

[60] Dr Andrew Oxenbridge. See above n. 54.

[61] See *BR*, pp. 220–23 below.

[62] See *BR*, pp. 209–14 below.

[63] See *BR*, pp. 269–72 below.

Chapman, and mr doctor Cricke and mr farrar shuld talke with the people and him together, and soe conclude the matter if they could.

The next place appointed was at mr Lewes his house in Colchester. The speaker mr dowe the Moderator mr sandes.

{Ther was an Extraordenary meeting in Dedham the 17 of february.}

This extraordenary meetinge was at Edmund sherman's house,[64] wher all the brethren were assembled to debate tutchinge mr Androwes departure from wenham by speciall request from mr Bailiffes of yarmouth in a lettre sent to them: wher mr doctor Chapman first declared what mr doctor Crick, mr farrar and he had done at wenham, viz that mr Androwes used the reasons before <not> mentioned why he wold depart: 1 want of comfort in his mynistry. 2 his small mainteynance not past 25 li by yeare. 3 his charge encreasinge. 4 that he had now a lawfull callinge to another place. And tutching the people of wenham, they answered, and confessed themselves negligent in not performing their duties and promised to amend it, and that they had joigned in every good cause with him for his comforte but in one, which they could not remedy. they said his maintenance was small, but they could not better yt. and for his departure they could by noe meanes consent unto it and <therfor> yet mr doctor Chapman thought ther wold gret inconvenience arise if he departed not, for he <tho> was persuaded that the people generally wold be well inough content with it, for in all this tyme they had never sought to any of the brethren to entreate to have him their pastor still.

mr doctor Cricke he used these reasons tutching this question: first that his hart could not by anie meanes consent to his departure, <first> bicause it wold be the ruyne of this poore Church of wenham, and we might not helpe another church and build it up though it were a greater church, with the decay of a neighbor Church though it were lesser. If any shall saie, this may be supplied with a good man, I answer that cannot be, bicause the Advouzom[65] is in the hand of one that will seeke his advantage, and if he will needes goe, yet this shall comforte me that I never consented to the spoile of a churche.

Secondlie for the reason of his want of mayntenance, I thinke this, that we must make hard shifte being in our places, for if Paull wrought with his handes, that example may teache us to be content with a little, and Calvin I thinke is against it: If any shall saie I cannot have my healthe, it is an ill ayre and a small livinge, I answere [fo. 5v] that it is the place god hath appointed thee and the ayre he seeth best, and therfore to be content and tutching his comfort the fault is in himself bicause of his straungnes to them and though I shuld yeld to his departure from wenham yet can I in noe sorte yeld to his going to yarmouthe, for if I have any skill at all, as his giftes may be to great for wenham soe it is not fytt for yarmouthe, his guifte being rather in exhortation then in doctryne.

[64] Sherman's house was opposite the church. See above p. ii, plate 1.
[65] I.e. 'advowson', the legal right to present to a benefice, either as 'true patron' by inheritance or purchase, or 'for this turn' by grant from the true patron. Laymen frequently acquired (usually by purchase) the right to present to a benefice for the next turn in order to provide for a relation or protégé.

mr Tay tutching this point said: that ther was a neere conjunction betwene the Pastor and the people that thone shuld not forsake thother no more then man and wieff shuld. And if the people were untoward he shuld looke what the cause was, whether the fault were in him, if it were then to humble himself, if it were in the people to apply it unto them, and the rather to tary with them to reforme them, for Ezechiell was <told> told he shuld doe noe good with the people yet god sent him to them.

mr dowe said the same in effecte, and added this moreover that the mayntenance must be smaller before he could depart with a good conscience and hope of blessinge.

mr Lewes he thought there were causes might move a Pastor to departe, and that we are not soe streitly tied to his flocke in these confused daies wherin we have noe discipline, nor good order, And wheras mr doctor Crick said he could not consent for his going to yarmouth bycause his gifte was not for a Teacher in that great place, he said tutching that pointe that he was to applie himself as soundly in wenham as in yarmouth, and if he could not delyver doctryne in wenham, he was not fitt for it in yarmouthe.

mr Negus thought that he might not departe being of mr Tay his judgment and he added this that he thought every man that professeth himself desirous of discipline shuld exercise it himself in his owne causes soe farre as he coulde.[66]

mr Stocton also was against his departure <also> and said further, that he might not goe from being a Pastor which was the higher callinge to be a Teacher which was the inferior. but to this reason, some of the brethren answered, that in these disordered tymes they thought it might be, wherin every teacher doth for the peoples good exhorte.

The brethren having thus yelded their severall judgments, the messenger one mr Mayham that came with lettres from the Bailliffes of yarmouth to the brethren was called in, and it was signified to him, what was adjudged of <his> mr Androwes departure from wenham. and mr doctor Cricke said unto mr Mayham, blame not the people for being lothe to part with their pastor, for if I were one of that church, I had as lieve thou shuldest plucke out myne eie as take from me my Pastor, to whom mr Mayham answered, but Sir, if you cast out your eie yow will geve me leave to take it up: And soe the brethren ended debating about this matter and mr mayham departed unsatisfied.

At this extraordenary meetinge mr Negus propounded whether he might depart from Ipswiche, the most of his parish standing against him, and having covenanted with him to be there one yeare yet brake their covenant and did <eve> even thrust him out, since he had now a good callinge offred him to the congregation of lee: It was thought good that the people of Ipswich shuld be conferd with all by mr doctor Chapman and mr doctor Cricke.[67]

Tutching the motion which mr morse propounded before for going to a private place it was at this tyme adjudged by the most of the brethren that he shuld rather tary at

[66] Since Negus was shortly to abandon Ipswich for Leigh, one must suspect him of a generous share of self-righteousness. See *BR*, p. 235 below.

[67] This did not deter Negus from accepting Leigh. See *BR*, p. 236 below.

home with his mother, bicause the place he shuld goe to was but private as his mothers house was.[68]

{The 8 of march was our 28 meeting ordenary as before at Colchester at mr Lewis his house.}
At this tyme a little was spoken of mr Androwes departure, for he had desired mr Lewis and mr newman to signify to the brethren his desire to have bene there with them but he could not, but bicause he was alreadie departed from wenham, they thought it not good to deale in the matter of his going to any other place, but as he had gone from wenham without <his> their consent, soe they wold let him goe to any other place.
The questions moved at this tyme were these: mr doctor Cricke moved, as before he had done, what course was to be taken with some kind of people that disturbed him in his mynistery, it is deferred to be further considered of.

[fo. 6r]

mr Parker moved that the Question of the Sabboth might be determined, it was also deferred.
mr dowe <mig> moved the same question in effect which mr doctor Crick did, but he compleyned of such as wold not come to heare him nor receyve the Sacramentes from him, this was also deferred for want of tyme.
mr Negus craved the brethrens advise whether he might accept of the callinge of the Church in Ipswich, or of the Church in Lee,[69] it was thought meete if he might have convenient tymes to execite [sic] his ministery, and a good calling to them, not conditionall nor subjecte to soe much reading of service, that then he shuld rather tary in Ipswich bicause of the want of Pastors, and for feare, lest if he went noe noe [sic] Pastors shuld be gotten afterwarde.
mr Tay moved the brethren that the maisters of Colledges might be written unto to have a care of the Churche discipline.[70]
The next meeting is appointed to be at Barfold at hoglane at mr Cockrels.[71] the speaker mr doctor Chapman. mr Tilney moderator.

---

[68] For the importance of the family of Morse of Stratford St Mary, see above pp. lix–lxii.

[69] It is instructive that the minutes never once allude to the fact that Negus had been officially instituted to Leigh by Aylmer at Rich's presentation.

[70] That is to say, the Cambridge heads were expected to lobby officially on behalf of 'discipline' by using their influence in government circles. For example, in February 1592 Roger Goad, William Whitaker, Edmund Barwell and Laurence Chaderton wrote an unsolicited letter to Burghley in order to 'stirr up your sincere mynde to go on, speciallie in god's cause, against all impediments': BL, Lansdowne MS 69, fo. 123r.

[71] Perhaps a reference to Thomas Cockerell of Fordham, yeoman, who with Richard Aburford of Colchester, gentleman, stood surety for William Tey when on 7 May 1569 he compounded for Peldon: PRO E 334/8, fo. 172v. One Thomas Cockerell witnessed the will of William Abell of West Bergholt on 16 April, 1591: F. G. Emmison, *Elizabethan life: wills of Essex gentry & yeomen preserved in the Essex Record Office* (Chelmsford, 1980), p. 20.

{The 5 of Aprill was our 29 meeting 1585 at Barfolde:}

At this meetinge the Question moved before by mr doctor Cricke for those that wold <not> not heare nor come to the Communion was concluded upon thus, that he shuld use all lenity with them, and persuade them if he could by gentle means, and it was thoughte meete that mr doctor Chapman and mr doctor Cricke shuld use some conference with them to the same ende.

As tutching mr Sandes his question, being the same almost with the former, but differing in this point, that the persons he compleyned of wold come to the worde diligently but tooke every light occasions of brawles to hinder their comming to the Communion: It was answered that the auncientes in the towne shuld deale with them and professe an earnest dislike of their course, and if they wold not be reformed by that meanes, then to discountenance them, to this end that they might see their follye.

Another question moved by mr dowe was this, that mr Bird scholemaster of Cockfield[72] might be written unto to accept of wenham. It was thought good he shuld be hearde preach, and soe be allowed of by the brethren.

Also he moved that we the mynisters might use one forme and order in our praiers before our sermons, some praying for the church before some after, some making noe praier in thende, which was yelded unto by the brethren, all geving consent unto yt.

Againe he moved, that we might minister the Sacramentes if not so often in our Churches here aboute, yet all upon one daie, which the brethren yelded unto to be done all upon one daie, but it could not be agreed on to be done once a moneth, as it is in some Churches.

mr doctor Chapman liked well of the former motions and desired that the orders of our Churches for government might be imparted one to another, and the best to be taken and used, that there might be asmuch conformity as might be outwardlie.

Also he moved the brethrens advise in this: what course might be taken with one, that had committed an offence secretlie, and denied it before some persons of the same place wher he did the offence, and yet afterward unto some of those persons did confesse that he did lye, whether he were to confesse his fault onlie to those fewe, or to be urged to the publike confession of it, the suspicion that he is faulty being publike but not his confession: it was differred till the next meetinge.

He also moved whether the Auncients of a Church having once consented unto an order to have a Communion once a moneth, it be not a matter of conscience for them to withdraw themselves at anie communion without urgent business. differred till the next meeting.

mr Lewis required advise what course he shuld take with some, that refused to heare him on the lordes daie when mr [sic] did preache, and told of one woman that professed a desire to come to the Communion with him, and yet thought she shuld not overcome herself to be present at the Sacrament bicause she shuld lose thexercise of the worde, the consideration of it was deferred.[73]

---

[72] Perhaps a reference to Samuel Bird, sometime fellow of Corpus Christi College, Cambridge, and later of St Peter Ipswich, who was granted a licence to teach grammar throughout the diocese of London on 10 October 1578: LMA DL/C/333, fol. 124r.

[73] The omission of Northey's name from this sentence is in the nature of a Freudian slip. Whether a

He also signified that mr Tay of peldon desired the brethren to praie for godes blessing upon his busyness now left unto him by reason of his brothers deathe and that they wold helpe him with a contynuall supplie in his place and service[74] [fo. 6v] of his church for one moneth on the lordes daie, which was laid upon mr stocton and he yelded unto it and promised to goe every lordes daie.[75]

mr newman asked counsell what shuld be done with such men as trouble their ministers being altogether disordered against whom if the ministers compleyne, they may feare by their complaints agayne the overthrow of their ministery, differred till some other tyme.

The next place to be at dedham at mr Parkers house, the speaker mr Sandes, the moderator mr Newman.

{The 3 of May was our 30 meeting at Dedham.}

At this meeting, the question that mr doctor Chapman moved the last meeting was determyned thus, that the attempt of the facte being secrett, and the lie that he made in denying the attempte being but to one also, that if that one man to whom he disclosed his lie doe see fruites of repentance in him, he is not to be urged to a more publike confession of his faulte. For thother question that he moved tutching the coming to every communion, the brethren left it to his owne observation of the causes that might hinder them from cominge, and soe to deale with them accordinglie.

mr doctor Cricke desired againe some advise, how he shuld deale with some disordered persons in his Churche. mr doctor Chapman was entreated to talk with them.

mr Negus desired the brethren to take knowledge of his course taken in entringe the benefice of lee, if they liked it, to allow of him, if not to admonish him, thanking god for the benefite of the meeting, acknowledging he had failed in many thinges, and craved their praiers to god for him.[76]

{harleston}

mr dowe moved that mr Harleston might be talked withall for keping an extraordenary assemblie, for which he was like to be indited, and soe good men might come into trouble by it: It was answered the assemblie was dissolved, and that it was not to be delt in by us, but if any going that waie could talk with mr harleston about it, yt were well.[77]

minister should 'have his own people', or whether godly people should be free to cross parish boundaries in search of the sermons they found most 'edifying', behaviour known in the Elizabethan period as 'gadding to sermons', and, in later generations, as 'sermon tasting', was a controversial matter, especially in London. It was addressed in 1598 in a London context in *Sophronistes A dialogue perswading the people to reverence and attend to the ordinance of God in the ministerie of their owne pastores.*

74 William Tey's elder brother, Thomas, owner of Layer Hall in the parish of Layer-de-la-Haye, had died since the last meeting. William had received letters of administration for his brother's estate three days before, on 2 April. See *BR*, pp. 255–60 below.

75 This is the earliest evidence we have that Stoughton was now ordained.

76 Negus had been instituted to Leigh by Aylmer on 31 March. See *BR*, p. 236 below.

77 In his will dated 1 February 1580, Thomas Morris, a godly shearman of Dedham, left 20s to Edmund Chapman, 10s to 'Mr Rice minister' and the same amount to 'Simon Hurleston of Cavendish, Suffolk, preacher'; 'James Anderson, minister' received 6s 8d: F. G. Emmison, *Essex wills: the archdeaconry courts 1577–1584* (Chelmsford, 1987), no. 728. Cavendish is only about seventeen miles north-west of Stratford St Mary and thus it seems likely that this is the same man. But if so, is he the same Simon Harlestone who was driven out of Mendlesham in 1556 and active in Dedham and Colchester for the

mr Newman renewed his former matter, and desired further to knowe, how farre a Pastor might safelie reade in the Common praier booke and hazard his liberty in the mynisterie for the same. this had bene handled before, and was referred to further consideration.

The next place appointed was at mr Sandes house in Boxforde. The speaker mr <farrar> Lewis and mr <Newman> Farrar Moderator.

{The 7 of June was our 31 meeting at Boxforde.}

At this tyme mr doctor Chapman signified, that there wold be a meeting at Cambridge of diverse godlie men, wher it were expedient that Questions shuld be moved to them to have their judgment how farre we may reade in the booke of common prayer. 2 <for> to crave their advise how to prevent the mischieff that is like to ensue by some that make a Schisme and rent from our Churche. And lastlie whether we may use the Bishops and come to their Courtes. the motion was liked well of and the persons to be chosen for this busynes were to be thought upon against the next meeting.

mr Sandes moved that some thinges might be considered of for the helpinge forward of discipline the next Parliament, it was liked of, but deferred.

The next place appointed was at Barfold at mr Tilneys house the speaker mr stocton. the Moderator mr Parker: the daie of meeting to be this daie three weekes upon some speciall considerations.

{The 28 of June was our 32 meetinge.}

where it was agreed upon for the Questions before propounded that mr Newman and mr Sandes shuld deale with the brethren at Cambridge, to knew their judgments in the same.

Tutching mr doctor Crickes question for disordered persons, it was said, that he shuld use all meanes to draw them forwarde and to wynne them, and if not to excommunicate them after longe patience according to our saviors rule, but some thought that first he shuld rather desire the chieff and forwardest in the Congregation to deale <and> with them, and if they prevailed not, to convent them before some [fo. 7r] magistrate as raylors, and soe to punishe them.

The next place was appointed to be at Coxall at mr Newmans house the speaker mr Taye, mr <do> doctor Chapman moderator.

rest of Mary's reign? See above, p. lxiii. If Harlestone, whoever he was, had been gradually moving towards a form of semi-separatism under Elizabeth, this entry makes it clear that he had now been brought to heel. The accepted annals of separatism propose a kind of apostolic succession, from Robert Browne, through Henry Barrow, and onwards (B. R. White, *The English separatist tradition* (Oxford, 1971)), but perhaps miss out on various, almost unrecorded, episodes such as this.

{The 2 August was our 33 meeting at Coxall.}

For the questions <shu> that shuld have bene moved to the brethren at Cambridge, mr Newman did signifie, that ther was nothing done in them there, but that the brethren purposed to meete againe, and at the same meeting mr knewstubb was thought fittest to deale with the brethren that shuld be there assembled, having the questions delyvered unto him.

For mr Lewis his matter before propounded, mr doctor Chapman and mr doctor Cricke and mr Taie are appointed to deale with mr Northie and the Bailiffes about it.[78]

mr stocton asked this question, whether the contents before the Chapters might be read, many of them being collected wronge: some debate was of it emong the brethren, some liked them bicause they had used them, and saw noe cause yet to move them to the contrarie, some disliked them, but nothing was done in it but referred it to further consideration.[79]

mr doctor Cricke wold know some sounde reason whie faith and hope shuld be earthlie benefites, and shuld not last in godes kingdome being said by thapostle Paull 1 Cor[inthians]. 13. to be <oppose> permanent, and be opposed against thother temporall giftes. it was not debated of.[80]

mr Tay moved the brethren to consider what course he might take to obteyne one for to read a Lecture at Layer on the Sabboth daie, it was deferred.[81]

mr doctor Chapman desired the brethren to enquire and consider of some fitt man for the Pastors place in Bedforde[82] and to name him to him: he also moved the brethren that there might be a faste used considering the judgment present upon us, which was yelded unto, and the daie appointed for it to be this daie forthe night at dedham at mr doctor Chapmans house.

The speakers were these mr doctor Chapman. mr doctor Cricke. mr sandes and the Moderator mr Taye. And tutching our usuall meeting the place at Peldon at mr Taies, the speaker mr Parker, mr Lewis the Moderator.

{Our Extraordenary meeting being the 34 was the 16 of August at Dedham.}

which <by> daie was spent in praier and fastinge as was before prescribed, being the xvi of August. bicause we wold have it before our usuall meetinge.

---

[78] That the Bailiffs (Colchester's 'joint mayors') were now to be embroiled in the Lewis/Northey feud argues that things had reached crisis point. But there is little later evidence, either from the minute book or from the borough records, to suggest what transpired.

[79] The bibles in current use in church, including not only the Bishops' Bible prescribed for lectionary use but the Geneva Bible (preferred by 'godly' ministers), provided a summary of the contents before each chapter. It was perhaps the puritan equivalent of the question how many angels can dance on the head of a pin scrupulously to enquire whether these words of human invention could be read as if they were part of holy writ. As usual, such knotty problems were not resolved.

[80] It is impossible to know what was bothering Richard Crick. 1 Corinthians xiii consists for the most part of St Paul's rhapsody on the subject of 'love' (Geneva Bible), or 'charity' (Authorized Version). In a sense love will outlast all other gifts and faculties, but not at the expense of faith and hope, although 'the chiefest of these is love'.

[81] Layer-de-la-Haye was a donative curacy which was not in the gift of the lord of the manor of Layer Hall, of which he was now in possession as his brother's designated heir. Hence Tey's concern to have a lecture read there. See *BR*, p. 257 below.

[82] For Chapman's continuing influence in his former stamping ground, see *BR*, p. 195, n. 12 below.

The thinges moved were these. First mr Taie moved to have a lecture read at Layer as before.[83] 2 mr dowe moved for mr Wilcockes gathering.[84] 3. mr Sandes craved that some advise might be geven to the brethren in lankishire tutching the keping of that Commission they had to punish synne and to sue for more power, rather then to lose it:[85] these were deferred till the next meetinge.

{The 6 of September was our 35 meeting at Peldon}

Where mr Taie moved the brethren to have a Lecture at laier, it was granted unto him by the brethren, that they wold helpe him and come thether in course as they shuld be requested to preache.[86]
mr farrar desired the brethrens counsell whether he might baptise the child of a good christian, that was come with his wieff from another towne wher an ill minister was bicause he wold not have it baptised of him, and it was borne in mr farrars parishe, the most thought there was daunger in it and wished him to refuse it.
mr doctor Chapman desired the brethren earnestlie for supplie to mr wilcocke more liberallie, laying out his state by a lettre of his sent to him and to mr doctor Cricke and the rest of the brethren, wherin every man promised to doe what he coulde.
mr stocton moved the brethren to advise him what he might doe in a matter wherunto he was entreated and called by common consent, viz to accept of a livinge: the brethren thought it very convenient he shuld accept the calling, if his affection stood unto the people and that he might have a lawfull callinge to them, and quietly passe through the B[ishop]'s handes.[87]
Tutching mr Sandes his question moved at our former fast the 16 of August bicause he was not present at this meeting, nothing was said to yt.
The next place at Boxford at mr birdes house. mr bird speaker. mr morse moderator.

[fo. 7v]

{The 4 of October was our 36 meeting at Boxforde.}

At this tyme mr Sandes tooke mr Birdes place excusing his father by sundrie busines that he had, soe as he could not performe it.
The Questions moved were these. First mr Tay sent a lettre by mr Lewis wherin he desired the brethren to helpe him this terme for the supplie of his place, and desired

[83] See n. 81 above.
[84] Clearly the result of another application by Henry Wilcock for further financial aid. See above pp. lxxiv–vi.
[85] For the relative ineffectuality of the ecclesiastical commission in Lancashire to deal with both 'popery' and various manifestations of irreligion, see Christopher Haigh, *Reformation and resistance in Tudor Lancashire* (Cambridge, 1975), pp. 133–5, 252, 286–7; and for the particular problems of the most prominent and powerful of protestant preachers in the county, Richard Midgley of Rochdale, which concerned Sandes especially (**59M**), ibid., pp. 221–2, 244, 305–6.
[86] Tey's importunity had won the day but there is no hard evidence of a regular lecture at Layer thereafter in the diocesan records.
[87] This proves to have been an unidentified living in Kent. See **36M**. This presentation came to nothing.

that mr morse might be delt withall for it, the brethren laid it upon mr morse and he accepted it.[88]

mr Stocton desired the brethren advise whether he might not send lettres againe to Kent about his livinge, his lettres being perished by the way, it was answered that he mighte.

mr doctor Cricke asked how he might deale with some untoward persons in his Church, it was answered ether he might convent them before some Justice, or present them at their leete[89] for absence from the Churche, or compleyne of them to the B[ishop] for redresse.

The place appointed was at Barfold at mr doctor Crickes house. the speaker mr Tilney, the moderator mr dowe.

{The 8 of November was our 37 meeting at Barfold}

Where mr Sandes propounded this for his father, whether he might not geve over his place to a third man, being aged himself it was spoken of but nothing concluded.

mr doctor Chapman spake of the Clothiers setting their woadfats on the Sabboth daie:[90] for this order was taken, that every one shuld deale with the godliest of that trade, <to> and to seeke out the best waie that might be taken for that matter.

mr Newman craved the brethrens allowaunce for a Catechisme that he had made for his people, ther was nothing concluded for it.[91]

mr Tilney moved this, whether he might allow <of> and admitt the children of those to baptisme that did refuse the lordes <sup> supper. it was not debated bicause the same in effect had bene handled before.

The next place appointed was at Langham at mr farrars house, mr Birde speaker, mr Tay moderator.

{The 6 of December was our 38 meeting at Langham:}

Where mr dowe was speaker, supplying mr Birdes place bicause he came late: At this tyme, mr doctor Cricke desired the brethrens advise in this: For one that had maried his wyves sister, and was desirous to have counsell for it, if it were thought a synne he wold leave her: It was answered that the mariage was unlawfull and that he lived in Adulterie, but the brethren knew not whether his motion came of conscience or of a carnall desire to have another, and therfore wold not geve counsell in it.[92]

---

[88] Morse, that is to say, agreed to act as Tey's *locum* in Peldon.

[89] A surprising example of how the godly were prepared to explore all possible avenues of legal discipline.

[90] This refers to dyeing, one process in the finishing of the cloth made in Dedham. The interesting implication is that this part of the productive chain, unlike weaving, was under the direct rather than indirect control of the clothiers, although for the ambiguity of the word 'clothier' (which could mean not so much entrepreneurial employer as cloth worker) see above, pp. liv–v.

[91] There is certainly no catechism (or any other published work) by Newman listed in the STC but a great many such catechisms were not published as we understand the term. See Ian Green, *The Christian's ABC* (Oxford, 1996), pp. 45–92.

[92] Marriage to a deceased wife's sister was technically forbidden but like full-scale divorce (rather than *divortium a mensa et thoro*, the equivalent of a modern judicial separation) now inhabited a twilight zone in the moral scheme of things. The dilemma is most fully set out for the modern reader in Shakespeare's *Hamlet*, where Hamlet and his father's ghost (but nobody else) regard his mother's

mr morse moved the brethren that he might [have?] some better assurance then the brethrens charge <to> for his preching in mr Taies place, lest he come into some trouble. which was deferred till the next meetinge.[93]

mr Sandes said they were troubled with Glover who laboured to hurt the people with his errors, it was reserved for further consultation.

mr dowe moved, that when we had no speciall causes to deale in, some Question of divinity might be propounded to the rest.

The place appointed to be at stratford at mr morses house, the speaker mr Birde, the moderator mr farrar.

{The 3 of January was our 39 meeting at Stratforde}

where it was agreed upon, that ther shuld be procured for mr morse as good Assurance as might be for his place.

And as tutching Glover, wheras he was bounde by the Magistrate to appeare before the Bishopp, he is now released upon conference to be had with him, and if he be not reformed by it, it is thought good by the brethren, that the magistrate shuld be delte with for the conventing of him agayne before the Bishoppe.[94]

Tutching the woad setting it is referred to further <conf> conference.

mr doctor Chapman moved this, that wheras mr morse had bene now a long tyme tried for his hability to teache, that he wold accept of a place to teach godes people now offred: the brethren thought very well of the motion and allowed it but mr morse desired a tyme to consider of it.

mr newman desired counsell how far a minister might goe to the hazarding of his ministery for the surplice, and other ceremonies, bicause of some good brethren that be in trouble for it, this was deferred till we might heare the advise of other lerned brethren.

[fo. 8r]

The next place appointed to be at Barfold <at> in Hoglane at mr Cockrels house,[95] the speaker mr morse. mr doctor Cricke moderator.

{The 7 of february was our 40 meeting at Barfolde.}

Where these thinges were propounded: First mr doctor Chapman desired the brethren to give him their advise how to deale with some that were seduced by

remarriage with his uncle as incest. The issue was not fully resolved in civil law until the passing of The Deceased Wife's Sister's Marriage Act (1907), which declared such marriages legal.

[93] Presumably a discreet hint that Morse should have Archdeacon Withers's authority at the least to continue his *locum* ministry at Peldon.

[94] Edward Glover was the author of A *present preservative against the pleasant, but yet most pestilent poyson, of the privie libertines, or carnall gospellers* (1585) (two copies only survive, both in LPL), to which Stephen Bredwell responded in 1586 in A *detection of Ed. Glovers hereticall confection, lately profferred to the church of England, under the name of A present preservative,* of which no perfect copy survives. Little is known of Glover, whose views seem to have placed him in the anti-antinomian tradition of the so-called Free Will Men. This is the only evidence we have that he was active as a proselytizer in south Suffolk.

[95] See above p. 22, n. 71.

Glover whether it were not necessary that some of them shuld come to dedham to confirme the doctrine of Righteousnes by faith: It was answered that they thought it meete that they shuld be first mildly delt withall by their ministers. 2 if that wold not serve to convent them before some of the Congregation, and if that prevailed not, then after our saviors rule to convent them before the whole churche and to lay open their errors, that the rest might not be hurte.[96]

mr doctor Chapman also moved, how he might deale with some careles persons that had no regard of the word or Sacramentes, it was said, the same question had bene handled before, but their advise now was to compleine to the Magistrates.

mr Lewis craved the brethrens advise, what course he might take to prevent the practise of mrs Awdley for his removinge <of> out his place, the gift of the benefice being in her hand, it was answered, that he shuld signifie to the people of his parish his mynd, and stirre them up to labor with my lorde Chauncelor for the <pr> preventing of it, and to procure unto them a good minister.[97]

It was agreed upon at this meeting also, that mr morse shuld consider of his livinge at Belsted and of the people there, and to geve an answere of his determination.[98]

It was at this tyme concluded upon that mr Catlyn of wenham shuld be allowed as one of our companie, if it could be perceyved by mr Tilney that he did desire the same and will promise contynuance in it, and submitt himself to the Lawes that be prescribed to be done in our meetinge.

The next place at mr Lewis his house in Colchester. The speaker mr Newman, mr Lewis moderator.

{The 7 of March was our 41 meeting at Colchester.}

At this tyme mr Catlin was admitted one of our companye.

mr Tilney desired advise how he might deale to kepe one out that went secretlie about to supplant him:[99] he was counseyled to stirre up the chieff of his parishe to use all meanes to prevent it,

mr doctor Cricke, desired to know whether he might not publikelie pray for those that did single themselves from the Church,[100] to commend them to the praiers of the Churche as men diseased and greatly needing it: some thought the Accion wold be straunge, and that they shuld be proceeded against till it shuld come to

---

[96] This was to follow the procedure laid down by Christ in Matthew xviii. 15–17, where, if earlier steps to correct an erring brother were to prove unavailing, 'tell it unto the Church', the biblical basis of all church discipline.

[97] Mrs Katherine Audley, a recusant, was true patron of the living of St Peter. The Lord Chancellor was Sir Thomas Bromley. It is unclear how the Chancellor's intervention could have settled a dispute at ecclesiastical law between the archbishop of Canterbury and a laywoman claiming *ius patronatus,* unless Lewis was prepared to take on the formidable burden of a chancery suit with all its attendant costs and inconveniences. Moreover, what is said here seems to anticipate Lewis's failure to retain the living, since attention shifts to how to 'procure unto them a good minister'.

[98] He seems never to have done so.

[99] This presumably refers to the moves about to take effect to replace Tilney as pastor of East Bergholt with Richard Crick. If so, and as recorded by Richard Parker, this is a slanderous accusation, although Crick will later, in effect, confirm its truth. See below, pp. 147–9.

[100] Here, as in some other references to the troubled state of the parish of East Bergholt, it is not easy to distinguish (among 'those') between religiously motivated separatists and the merely irreligious or religiously careless, Crick's 'disordered persons'.

excommunication and then be praied for: but most yelded, that he might pray for them not naminge them.

mr dowe asked counsell what he might doe for one James anderson[101] that goeth about as he feared with lettres from Glover or such as he is: he was advised to suppresse him if it might be and to be brought before the Magistrate.

mr doctor Chapman moved the brethren for some order to be taken with disordered persons, but it was deferred.

The next place is at mr Taies house in Layer: the speaker mr doctor Cricke: the moderator mr Stocton. the tyme to be the weeke after Easter weeke.

{The 11th of April was our 42 meeting at layer: 1586}

The Questions moved were these.

mr doctor Cricke did still compleyne of some disordered persons in their Church, but <nothing> nothing was said to it:

mr Sandes put the brethren in mynd that the tyme present thretned much misery to come; and thought it necessary for a fast to be appointed, it was deferred till the next meetinge.

The next place appointed was at <Barfold at mr Tilneys house> Boxford at mr Sandes his house the speaker mr farrar. the moderator mr dowe. and the tyme and day to be the second of May next.

[fo. 8v]

{The 2 of May was our 43 meeting at Boxforde.}

At this tyme it was agreed that the next meeting daie shuld be spent in prayer and fastinge, and the daie to be the last of May a moneth hence.

The next place to be at Barfold at mr Tilneys house.

The speakers at the fast to be these. mr Tay, mr Stocton, mr morse. The Moderator mr Newman.

{The 30 of May was the 44 meeting at Barfolde:}

mr Tay moved this, what good course might be taken for the Bishops comminge for the preventing of the Churchwardens othes: yt was said, they might sweare with protestacion, viz that they wold doe any thinge might stand with godes <glo> glory and the good of the Church: and the lawyers have said that the law did bynd to sweare to none other thinges then tutched <pet> piety and charitie,[102]

mr Sandes requested that mr Salmon pastor of Arwerton might be admitted as one of our company, yt was generally liked of, so that he might consider the gretnes of the journeies that he must take, and of his purpose to contynue, and that he shuld yet be staied from comminge, to harken whether mr Wright do labor to procure such a like meeting about him, or noe.[103]

---

[101] Glover's agent is unknown to history unless he was the 'James Anderson, minister' bequeathed 6s 8d in the will of Thomas Morris of Dedham. See n. 77 above.

[102] Tey here anticipates Aylmer's fourth episcopal visitation of summer 1586.

[103] For Edmund Salmon, of Erwarton, Suffolk, see *BR*, pp. 246–7 below. There is no evidence that

The next place appointed is mr dowes house at Stratford, the speaker mr doctor Chapman, the Moderator mr Birde, and the daie to be within one moneth viz the 27: of June.

{The 27 June was the 45 meeting at Stratforde.}

Where mr doctor Chapman shewed a lettre that came from the French churche requiring aide and relieff, to which every one professed themselues willing to helpe toward it so much as they could.[104]

Secondlie mr doctor Chapman desired to have their testimony that it was agreed upon emongst them, that if Glover could be taken he shuld be offred to the magistrate.

{mr Gale}

At this meetinge mr gale[105] was admitted to be one of our companye.

mr Tay moved the brethren to consider of the B[ishop]'s coming on visitacion, what we shuld doe if he shuld move subscription: it was answered nothing could be said of it, till they knew how he wold deale.[106]

mr doctor Cricke required the brethrens advise for mr Stocton accepting of Nowton livinge,[107] which they all agreed unto.

The next place appointed to be at mr Parkers house in Dedham. The speaker mr Catlin: the moderator mr Tilney.

{The 8 of August[108] was our 46 meeting at Dedham.}

where the matter moved before for the relieff of the French Church was considered of, and it was thoughte meete not to be done publikelie bicause the people were soe much charged, but to deale privately with the best affected.

mr Taie required, that there might [be] another fast as other brethren had done, wherto it was answered of most, that those that thought good of such an exercise and had reasons to move them to it might doe it, but yet none to undertake it without shewing their reasons to the brethren, that they might advise them in it.

mr Sandes at this tyme shewed the reasons that moved them unto it in Suffolk 1 the scarsity of all thinges 2 the little good it had wrought in men 3 the state of the Frenche Churche, and the matters of the lowe cuntreis and generallie the contempte of the gosple, howbeit, it was not thought meete that any fast shuld be used as yett.

{Salmon}

Robert Wright, now town preacher of Ipswich, ever organized a local conference of ministers on the lines of Dedham or Braintree.

[104] This almost certainly refers to the church of the French 'strangers' which met in Threadneedle Street in London, and was in regular need of charitable donations. A year later Edmund Salmon was to ask his rather silly question about what he was to do with £1 for the French church which he had collected at a fast (58M).

[105] See BR, pp. 207–8 below.

[106] In the event Aylmer did not press for subscription to Whitgift's articles.

[107] Naughton, Suffolk. See BR, p. 252 below.

[108] The long gap between meetings 45 and 46 was the result of Aylmer's episcopal visitation. The visitors sat in Colchester on 22 July to examine the clergy of Colchester, Lexden and Tendring deaneries: GL MS 9537/6, fo. 139v. Note that no reference is made to the fact in subsequent minutes.

At this meeting was mr Salmon admitted, and the orders of the meeting read unto him, and unto mr Gale whereunto they readelie consented.
The next place appointed at mr Newmans house of Coxall: the Speaker mr Parker: mr Tay moderator.

{The 5 September was our 47 meeting at Coxall.}

Where Questions were moved tutching supplications to be made to the Counsell, it was thought good that one shuld be made for many Townes, and Maulden to have one by itself.[109]

[fo. 9r]

The place for the next meeting to be at Boxford at mr Birdes. The speaker mr Salmon: and mr Catlin moderator.

{The 2 of October was our 48 meeting: at Boxforde.}

where a daie for thexercise of praier and fastinge was appointed to be the next meetinge: The speakers mr stocton, mr Lewis and mr Sandes: and the moderator mr farrar. the place to be dedham at mr doctor Chapmans house.

{The 10 of October was our 49 meeting at Dedham}

wher praiers and fastinge were used as before was concluded:
Ther was nothing now moved. The next place is at mr farrars of <lan> Langham. mr Dow speaker, mr Lewis moderator.

{The 7 of November was our 50 meeting at Langham.}

mr doctor Chapman moved the brethren, that a letter might be written to the godlie brethren in London who though they were forward in furthering the discipline, yet <by> a letter <to> wold encourage them to be more zealous, and we shuld be moved the rather to write bicause some of them are of mynd to aske a full reformation and to accept of <no> none if they had not all, but the judgment of the brethren was, that some reformation might be accepted of, if it were graunted.
Secondlie he required that in the letter they shuld put them in mynd of mr Carthwrights booke of the Confutation of the Rhemish Testament, to further yt unto the presse.
mr Sandes moved whether he might not have a Thankes givinge on the Queens daie[110] as before they had a faste; it was deferred.
mr Tilney moved the brethren to consider for a faste, it was answered that we expecte direction from the brethren at london, and soe doe deferre it a tyme.
The next place appointed to be at Hoglane for mr stocton:
The speaker mr Newman. mr Morse moderator.

---

[109] See *Seconde parte*, II, 187–8.
[110] 17 November, the anniversary of Elizabeth's accession in 1558.

{The 5 of December was our 51 meeting at Barfolde.}

where mr dowe was speaker in mr Newmans steede.

The matters propounded were these.

First mr Chapman desired the brethrens handes to that lettre he sent to mr doctor Cricke in his owne name, which was graunted him.

mr stocton moved that we shuld commend this our state of dearthe unto god in our publike praiers.

mr farrar signified that he was come to the 3. admonition, it was said, that the matter was handled at mr Birdes house and concluded that the Surplice shuld not be yelded unto, bicause they sought to have us yeld unto all the ceremonies.[111]

mr Tilney desired advise what he might doe to one, who having ever resisted his mynistery, and countes him noe minister nor their church noe Churche, whether he might mary him except he wold confesse his faulte: It was answered, that it was daungerous for him to denie him mariage, and better to let the Congregation forbid yt, and soe stoppe the askinge of it, or to drawe him by this meanes into the Church, and to signify before the sermon to him, that he wold not mary him except he did confesse his faulte, and soe to let him consider of it till the sermon were done.

mr dow moved whether the Churchwardens shuld not doe their duties to prevent such as offend (as not comminge to Church or Communion, for feare of hazarding his mynistery by their compleints against him, it was thought meete that they shuld kepe their oathes.

mr farrar moved that his brother of Holbrocke[112] mighte be admitted one of our company, which was yelded unto by the brethren:

mr doctor Cricke moved that there might be a disputation, it is deferred.

The next place at Stratford at mr Morses house: The speaker mr Newman. The Moderator mr Salmon.

[fo. 9v]

{The 2 of January was our 52 meeting at Stratforde.}

At this tyme, mr Newman moved whether he mighte not joigne in another conference[113] with some good brethren that did request yt of him, and that he wold be altogether with them: he professed he wold not doe yt without the brethrens likinge, desiringe to contynue still with us: the motion was liked of soe he wold contynue with us: Secondlie he moved what course the ministers suspended for the Surplice,

---

[111] This is the first reference to the aftermath of the 1586 visitation. If by 'Bird's house' the forty-eighth meeting is meant, the minutes do not refer to it. It was more probably an unofficial gathering at which Parker was not present or else for which he did not keep minutes.

[112] George Farrar, rector of Holbrook. Matriculated sizar from Queens' College, Cambridge, Easter 1576 ('Farrer'), as of Suffolk, graduating in early 1580: *Alum. Cantab.*, II, 123. He was considerably younger therefore than his brother. He compounded for the rectory of Holbrook, Suffolk, on 4 May 1586: PRO E334/10, fo. 122r. Thus Thomas Farrar's later assertion that he would not be 'tied to a place' reads oddly (**54M**), particularly since he appears to have remained at Holbrook for the rest of his life and survived to be remembered in Thomas's will (see *BR*, pp. 205–07 below). Meanwhile in 1597 he was reported ('[ ] Farcor, R.') for several ritual offences and 'woore the surplis not this xii month'. *Redman's visitation*, p. 153.

[113] The Braintree meeting: see below, pp. 106–08.

and like to be suspended shuld take: yt was thought best that some gentlemen be moved to solicite the cause to the Counsell, and yt was decreed that mr doctor Chapman and mr doctor Cricke shuld goe to my Lord Riche, and to Sir Roberte Jermin with lettres from the brethren to that end.[114]

mr morse moved whether he might not preach at mr fordes of Butley a tyme, being requested to exercise his guifte: It was granted <so> him, soe he did after proceed further, to accepte of a callinge there or els where.[115]

The next place at mr doctor Crickes house in Barfold: mr Tilney speaker. mr stocton moderator.

{The 6 of february was our 53 meetinge at Barfolde.}

Where mr doctor Chapman signified to the brethren what they did with Sir Roberte Jermin viz that he wold write to my Lord Riche to deale throughlie and effectually in that matter:[116]

mr doctor Cricke told the brethren that he shuld be moved to be of another meeting: yt was deferred till he shuld be moved.[117]

mr Sandes moved, that if the same Questions should be propounded in other meetinges that be with us in ours and the brethrens judgments shuld vary from us, how a man might kepe himself upright, it was deferred:

Thirdlie mr doctor Chapman moved there might be a fast, if the tyme were such, as he feared yt was, and the state of the Church noe better then he heard, it was yelded unto by the brethren.

mr Parker moved what course a mynister shuld take when disorders be risen up in a Church, and be publikelie reproved, and the chiefe of the parish, and the officers delt withall whom it specially concernes to reforme them, and yet nothinge is done, what then the minister shuld doe whether he shuld there cease, as having done his full duty. deferred.

mr morse moved whether he shuld not desire the B[ishop]'s allowance for his peace in that place he is in, it was thought best he shuld.

The next place of our meeting to be at Colchester at mr Lewis his house. The speakers appointed for the fast to be mr Parker: mr Catlin and mr Salmon and mr doctor Chapman moderator.

---

[114] No record of this proposed *démarche* survives, but there is evidence of petitions to the privy council from the gentlemen of Kent, seven Cambridgeshire gentlemen and five leading Norfolk justices. See Collinson, *EPM*, pp. 256–9.

[115] Mr Ford (Forth) of Butley Priory. For the last days of Butley Priory, which before the dissolution held property in Dedham, see 'The Register or Chronicle of Butley Priory, Suffolk, 1510–1535', in A. G. Dickens, *Late monasticism and the reformation* (London, 1994), pp. ix–xviii, 1–84. By 1604 Forth's sixth son, John, was established at Great Stambridge, Essex, with an only daughter, Mary. On 5 November 1604 William Forth and Adam Winthrop of Groton set out from Suffolk with Winthrop's seventeen-year-old son John, on a visit to Great Stambridge. After a solemn contract of marriage, John Winthrop and Mary Forth were married there by the rector, Ezekiel Culverwell, on 16 April 1605: *Winthrop papers*, I, 88–9. John Winthrop, first Governor of Massachusetts, admitted that it was Culverwell who had converted him to 'True Religion'. So Forth's house at Butley Priory links the last days of old England with the first of New England.

[116] See n. 114 above.

[117] It is possible that 'another meeting' was the Suffolk conference of which Henry Sandes was a leading light. However, the centre of gravity of this meeting was well to the west of East Bergholt, and even of Hadleigh, to which Crick naturally gravitated.

{The 6 of March was our 54 meeting at Colchester:}

where praier and fastinge was used as before was appointed.

mr Salmon moved whether mr Farrar of Holbrocke shuld know any more of our meetinge, not havinge accepted of yt hetherto: his brother answered that he found noe readines in him bicause he wold not be tied to a place, the brethren required him to charge his brother to be silent.

mr Lewis moved the brethren to have their handes set to a writinge for confirmation of that which they had alreadie set downe, that a Pastor shuld have his owne people: much debating was of yt: some said yt was better to have some or two delyver yt in doctrine to the people, that course was thought daungerous of some. Some thought yt might be set downe generally that a Pastor shuld have his people, that if another did at the same time preach, yet he shuld enjoy his people. Others thought to geve handes except the people required yt, was to doe a thing very likelie daungerous: But it was said that if two or three of the brethren did againe talke with mr Northie and the people of it, and could not <pre> prevaile, that then they shuld [give?] him their judgment in writinge under their handes and so yt was concluded.

mr doctor Chapman and mr doctor Cricke and mr Tay were appointed to talk with mr Northie.

mr morse signified that the B[ishop]. wold give noe libertie to any to preache without presentacion to a place, and soe he could not goe to Butley.[118]

mr Tilney asked the brethrens advise how to deale with a fellow in his parish, who being denied the solempnisation of his mariage for his vile speeches against our Church, hath since gott himself maried by one Greenewood[119] in a private house. yt was deferred.

mr doctor Cricke moved what he might doe for an outrage committed in his absence being at Hadleigh,[120] a mans wieff beatinge her husband: there was hereupon a man in womans [fo. 10r] <mans> attire and a woman in mans were caried on a cowle staff with a drumme and Calyver and morise pikes on mens shulders, he had vehemently inveighed against yt, and told them his credytt was gretlie tutched in yt, but he wold know what he shuld further do in yt.[121] yt was deferred.

---

[118] The reference is to Edmund Scambler, confirmed as Freke's successor at Norwich on 15 January 1585.

[119] It is just possible that this was John Greenwood, the separatist, who shared imprisonment with Henry Barrow and, in 1593, the gallows, and whose origins were certainly East Anglian. See *The writings of John Greenwood 1587–1590* and *The writings of John Greenwood and Henry Barrow, 1591–1593*, ed. Leland H. Carlson, Elizabethan Nonconformist Texts, IV and VI (London, 1962, 1970).

[120] Hadleigh, Suffolk, where the archbishop of Canterbury's commissary for his peculiars in Essex and Suffolk, known as the dean of Bocking, usually held court. Possibly therefore Crick was giving evidence in a case, but no contemporary court books survive to elucidate the matter. For the deanery of Bocking during Elizabeth's early years, see Brett Usher, 'The deanery of Bocking and the demise of the vestiarian controversy', *JEH*, LII (July 2001), 434–55. It is also possible that Crick's visit to Hadleigh was private. His father lived there, and as a tailor made Crick's clothes.

[121] For the best account of the shaming ritual of the 'skimmington' or 'rough riding' (the English equivalent of the French 'charivari'), famously depicted in Samuel Butler's *Hudibras* and later illustrated by Hogarth, see Martin Ingram, 'Ridings, rough music and the "reform of popular culture" in early modern England', *Past & Present,* no. 105 (November, 1984), 79–113. Hogarth is reproduced at p. 83.

mr. Tay moved that the booke of discipline set downe by the brethren might be vewed and their judgments given of yt: yt was deferred.[122]
The nexte place is appointed to be at Peldon at mr Tayes house. mr Taie speaker. mr Sandes moderator.

{The 3 of Aprill was our 55 meeting at Peldon. 1587.}

Where the matter that mr Parker moved in the 53 meetinge before was in part handled, but not concluded but deferred till our next meetinge to be better considered of and yt was appointed that mr doctor Chapman and mr Tay bring in their reasons for yt.
mr doctor Chapman and mr doctor Cricke moved mr Northie for mr Lewis his people, and he said he wold not deale in yt.[123]
mr Tilneys matter, mr doctor Cricke, mr Sandes, and mr Taies Question for vewing of the booke of discipline were deferred till some other tyme.
mr doctor Cricke moved the brethren to geve their advise, whether mr stocton shuld leave Nawton having, bene at soe great charge and like to be at more, and none wold beare any part with him, and yet having tried his right, yt was feared he shuld not be at quiet. yt was thought good he shuld move some to talk with mr more,[124] and if he wold not defend his righte and <defend> beare his charge, then to leave yt: Some thought it hard to leave the people, and make mr more to begynne suite afresh agayne. mr farrar moved the brethren to geve him advise tutching his appearinge before the B[ishop]: yt was said he shuld have lettres of Commendacion, and soe goe to the meeting of the brethren in London and have their advise:
mr Lewis craved that since mr Northie had bene dealt withall, the people that left his ministerie might likewise be conferred withall: this was not consulted of.[125]
The next place at mr Sandes his house in Boxforde. The speaker mr Tilney. the moderator mr doctor Cricke.

{The 8 of May was our 56 meeting.}

Where my Question was left undecided till the next meetinge bicause of mr doctor Chapmans and mr Tayes absence:
mr Sandes his question was delt in: viz that he might kepe himself upright in both meetinges, being free to yeld his judgment as he had done before, but if he had

[122] It is a remarkable fact that the conference seems to have regarded the Book of Discipline as the personal enthusiasm, or at least business, of William Tey, not discussing the matter in his absence, and ultimately doing nothing about it at all. See above, pp. xcvii–viii.
[123] Northey's final refusal to negotiate with Lewis in 'brotherly' fashion.
[124] John More, merchant of Ipswich and patron of the living of Naughton, had lifted himself into the ranks of the lesser gentry, owned two country houses and parcels of land scattered throughout east Suffolk and was an MP in 1571. He was also the principal promoter of godly religion in Ipswich, and in his will of 1588 left legacies to six Ipswich preachers, including William Negus and Robert Wright. Two of his daughters married wealthy London puritans, Richard Walter and Roger Ofield, both active patrons of the puritan enterprise, and Walter's widow, Elizabeth, made the most generous (to the puritan ministry) of all puritan wills. More's brother-in-law Robert Barker of Ipswich was in partnership with William Cardinal, Edmund Chapman's brother-in-law and patron. See Collinson, 'PCM', pp. 864–5, and BR, pp. 252–3 below.
[125] No more is heard of the Lewis–Northey dispute in the minutes, but see n. 136 below.

yelded his hand to one thinge in one meetinge, if the same were propounded not to be urged to geve his hand againe, but to geve our handes tutchinge or judgment in matters was not thought saffe in any respecte.

mr Farrar moved, what he might doe, being ether presentlie to be suspended, or if he went not to be excommunicate, yt was thought best to tarie at home, and abide thexcommunication for soe he shuld gaine some longer tyme, and he might be absolved by a Proctor: but some doubted whether by the worde he might be absolved by a Proctor.[126]

The second <Eple> Epistle of St Paul to Timothy[127] was chosen at this meetinge to be enterpreted and order given to runne spedely over yt, delyvering the doctrine brieflie, and passing over thexhortation, and onlie <to> stand upon some controversy betwene the Papistes and us, and to handle them throughlie.

The next place appointed to be <in> at mr Tilneys of Barfold. The speaker mr stocton. The Moderator mr dowe.

{The 12. of June was our 57 meeting at Barfolde.}

Where my Question was deferred till the booke of discipline were vewed.

mr Tay moved that the booke of discipline might be vewed and judgement given of it. deferred.

mr morse moved whether he shuld any longer contynue at Butley without authority, yt was said, yt was not saffe, nor convenient except he ment to take yt as his charge. and one said, though the livinge were small, yet he might doe well to serve the Lorde in that place, supplying the want of that church himself.[128]

mr Lewis craved the brethrens advise what to doe for his Excommunication; he said his meaning was if he could not be released to crave a daie, and soe to make short not to be troubled to goe up every terme: he was advised to procure his libertie soe longe as he could thoughe it were painfull to him.

mr Sandes delyvered a message from the brethren of another company, who desired that some thinges might be communicated from these meetinges one to another, and that for the concludinge [fo. 10v] of the matter of discipline some helpe might be had from us. and that they had concluded of mr doctor Cricke and desired mr doctor Chapman to deale in yt. deferred till the next meetinge.

mr doctor Chapman [moved?] what might be done with thexcommunications that were sent out: some said they might answere by a proctor: others declared their practise in their places to be this, that if thexcommunication were against a notorious offendor being obstinate they did it upon some holiday, but being some light fault they kept it in their handes and persuaded the partie to goe and end it. Some

---

[126] No more is known of Farrar's case from the consistory court records, the 1586 act book of office being lost. But probably by now it had in any case been transferred to the High Commission.

[127] The same epistle was currently being used for clerical exercises throughout the archdeaconry of Colchester: ERO D/ AEV 1, fo. 5r. The choice of this epistle, with its considerable potential for anti-catholic polemic, and the decision to concentrate on just those elements, may suggest that the conference was adopting the course, more generally associated with moderate puritanism, of seeking to occupy common and central ground with all other protestants in the stand against 'popery' in all its manifestations. See Peter Lake, *Moderate puritans and the Elizabethan church* (Cambridge, 1982).

[128] Evidence that Morse was a man of independent means. See *BR*, pp. 229–31 below.

thought they might saie thus much The Commissary hath sent out an Excommunication. Others thought bicause we wer subjecte to their government in other thinges, they saw noe cause why they shuld not yeld in this except they shuld renounce the whole. Some thought it not safe to answer by a Proctor, to let that be done by another which he wold not doe himself, so that in thend it was concluded, that the advise of some Lawyer shuld be asked how farre law did bind us to it.[129]

The next place appointed to be at Erwerton at mr Salmons house. the speaker mr morse the moderator mr Parker.

{The 10 of July was our 68 [sic] meeting at Erwerton.}

Wher the matters depending before were left undecided, only mr doctor Chapman shewed a lettre sent from the brethren about Braintree,[130] desiring mr Newman wholy: all said they were lothe to part with him, but if he thought he could be of bothe meetinges, and <hold out> hold oute, they wold be glad in it, but <he> if he wold goe they must be content.

mr Salmon moved what he might doe wth xx s that was gathered at a fast for the French church whether he shuld send it to them, or distribute it in his parish: yt was answered since it was soe published in the fast to be gathered for that use, it shuld be employed to that use, except he could understand that the necessity of the <Chur> French Churche were provided for, and then he might geve to the poore of his owne <par> parishe.

The next place Wenham at mr Catlins the speaker mr Lewis:
the moderator mr Newman.

{The 8 of August was our 59 meeting at Wenham.}

where first mr doctor Cricke wold knowe who shuld goe to the conference at mr fowles[131] 22 August. he was unwilling to doe, yet at length it was laid upon him:

The dealing with the booke of discipline was deferred till the next meetinge bicause mr Tay was now absent.

mr Newman and mr Lewis chosen and sent to deale in that generall meeting at Cambridge, and the matters wherin they shuld deale to be considered of.

mr doctor Chapman moved that bicause many ministers were troubled for ceremonies and more like to be, there were great use of that Question to be moved at that meeting, how farre they might goe with peace of conscience and the good of the Church.

mr Tilney moved his matter of departure from Barfold: It was not thought good it shuld be openlie debated, nor the matters betwene mr doctor Crick and him, or the Towne and him to be publikely delt in, but the cause to be deferred to mr doctor

---

[129] The precise course of Aylmer's proceedings against the Essex nonconformists since the 1586 visitation would have been found in the lost act book of office, but is conveniently summarized in *Seconde parte*, II, 163–5. Note that two of the men mentioned in this survey had already been deprived by the High Commission: William Tunstall of Great Totham on 5 May and Giles Whiting of Panfield on 12 May 1587: LMA DL/C/334, fos. 152v, 153v.

[130] See below, pp. 106–07.

[131] Thomas Fowle, former chaplain to Sir Nicholas Bacon and rector of Redgrave in Suffolk. For his earlier presence in Norwich and relationship with Chapman, Crick and Dowe, see above, p. xlvi.

Chapman, mr Newman and mr Lewis, to mr dowe, mr farrar and mr Sandes, and by them to be determined if it could be.

mr <Chapm> Farrar and mr Parker moved the same that doctor Chapman <did> had done <at> before them.

mr Catlin desired their praiers for his Church and people.

mr Sandes craved the helpe of the brethren to mr Justice Clenche[132] to move him, that if in his circuite the cause of a yong man that had gretlie abused one mr Miggeley <in> a Preacher in Lankishire (by making libels against him) did come before him, he wold deale severelie in it. It was thought unmeete to deale in it the persons being soe far of.   And some said that the Justices might take it ill to be told what to doe in their Offices, and soe they thought it good to deale in it, except one could speak with Judge clenche personally of yt.

mr Newman did freelie yeld his consent to be of our meetinge, bicause he could not be of both he more enclyned to be of ours, and soe it was concluded that lettres shuld be sent to mr Rogers[133] and the rest.

The next place at Coxall at mr Newmans. the speaker mr Gale. The moderator mr Taye.

{The 4 of September was our 60 meeting at Coxall.}

Where mr Parkers motion before made and the former matters were deferred.

mr Tilney moved the brethren to geve him advise tutching his departure whether he might warne the people of yt. some thought it meet and some thought otherwise.

The next place appointed at mr doctor Crickes house for mr Gale: The speaker mr farrar, the moderator mr Sandes.

[fo. 11r]

{The 2 of October was our 61 meeting at Barfold.}

Wher mr Tilneys matter for his departure was debated of, but nothing done, bycause the brethren were not possessed with the matter: the Townesmen offred reasons by mr doctor Cricke and mr stocton against mr Tilney, it was not thought good to deale in it, except they wold rest in their determination.

mr morse moved to goe to Butley a tyme, till mr ford might get him a preacher, it was graunted him.[134]

The next meetinge it is appointed to be at Dedham at mr Parkers house and the tyme to be spent in praier and fastinge. The speakers mr doctor Chapman. mr Lewis, and mr Sandes, and mr doctor Cricke Moderator.

---

[132] John Clench (or Clinch), who was presumably riding the Lancashire assize circuit in the summer of 1587, was a Suffolk man, a good friend to the godly ministers, and patron of the Suffolk livings of Holbrook (where George Farrar was beneficed) and Little Creeting. (Robert Cottesford of Creeting St Mary and Richard King of Creeting St Peter were both puritans.) His wife was a Brownist. See Collinson, 'PCM', pp. 657, 814. For Richard Midgley see n. 85 above.

[133] Richard Rogers, lecturer of Wethersfield, Essex. See above, pp. c–ci and *BR*, pp. 244–46 below.

[134] Evidence that Morse had not accepted Butley as urged on him (**57M**).

{The 6 of November was our 62 meeting at Dedham.}

Where the whole tyme was spent in praier and fastinge. the tyme wold not geve leave to debate of any matters.

The next place of meeting appointed to be at Langham at mr Farrars house. mr doctor Chapman speaker. mr Catlin moderator.

{The 4 of December was our 63 meeting at Langham.}

At which meetinge I was absent; and knowe not what was propounded.

The next place was appointed to be at mr doctor Chapmans house in Dedham and the tyme to be spent in praier and fastinge. The speakers mr doctor Cricke. mr Tay and mr Sandes. The Moderator mr doctor Chapman.

{The 8 of January was our 64 meetinge at Dedham.}

Where praier and fastinge was used.

A publike fast was agreed upon to be very necessary, and first to conferre with the Auncients of our parishes about yt, and they to intimate it to the rest. and the manner how was talked of whether many Churches together joigning in one or every church severallie, yt was answered it was not necessary, that every church shuld have a fast, the litle Churches might joigne with the greater. And for the daie yt was thought to be on the Lecture daies in every Church which some liked best; others said that a care must be had of the poore, that they in this hard tyme might not be kept from their worke, It was answered there shuld be a contribution geven them to helpe them.[135]

The next place at mr Morses of Stratford. mr Salmon speaker. mr morse moderator.

{The 5 of February was our 65 meeting at Stratforde.}

At which tyme mr stocton asked the brethrens counsell what he might doe with a froward person of his parish being the Churchwarden, he purposed to mynister the Communion, and if he should refuse him yt wold hazard his peace, it was deferred till the next tyme.

mr doctor Cricke moved the brethrens counsell tutching his calling to be Pastor of Barfold. Some thinges were spoken by some in dislike of the peoples course in rejecting and receyving their Pastors without counsell of others, but the most thought it fitt for him to undertake that Charge.

mr Lewis moved, what he might doe for his matter soe often propounded to them whether he might not receive another calling being offred him.[136] deferred.

mr Parker moved, what he might doe for supplie of his place being suspended by the B[ishop]. of London.[137]

---

[135] This is rare and perhaps unique evidence that the difficulty faced by working people in taking a whole day off to participate in a fast was acknowledged, and that fasts were sometimes subsidized, perhaps from the money invariably collected at a fast from those 'of ability'.

[136] Evidently Northey's ministry in Colchester had forced Lewis into considering resignation.

[137] This is almost certainly a reference to the High Commission suit brought against him in late 1587 by Marion Barker. See above, pp. lxxii–iii.

mr Newman desired to know whether he might not retayne another under him that wold accept of the surplice and read service. deferred till they heard from other brethren.[138]

The next place appointed to be at layer at mr Taies house.[139] mr Tay speaker. mr Farrar moderator.

{The last of March was our 66 meeting at layer hall. 1588.}

Where mr Tay moved in his exercise that the brethren wold consider whether the B[ishop]s were anie longer to be tolerated or noe: not delt in:[140]

At this tyme mr doctor Cricke sent his letter by mr gale requiring the brethren to consider of his suite, to have one to preach at his election to the pastorall charge at Barfolde. this was laid by consent on mr doctor Chapman, and he undertooke yt.

The next place to be at Barfold at mr doctor Crickes house. the speaker mr dowe, mr Salmon moderator.

[fo. 11v]

{The 6 of May was our 67 meeting at Barfolde.}

Where mr Catlin propounded, what course to take with one, who being forbid to sweare in a matter that he was ignorant of, yet did yt: whether he might admitt him to the Communion   It was answered, that he was to serche whether the man sware to the facte, or for the person that is for the creditt of the man with whom he sware being persuaded that the man wold take a true othe: if he did yt rashlie he was to be admonished, if of purpose he was perjured and the law wold convicte him he might be Indited.

mr Salmon moved how he might know a witche, it was thought fittest to geve it over to some Justice to examyne it, and that there must be some usuall experience of evell effectes to ensue of their displeasure, and some presumption of the death of man or beast: some said she might be found out by serche in her bodie, some thought that to be fancy in the people easelie conceiving such a thinge and to be reproved in them. he moved also whether he shuld kepe his fast, it was deferred. He moved also whether boyes of xvj yeares of age might put on their hattes in the Church, it was thought that the custome of the Church where they were was to be regarded. some said it was to be considered of whether it were unlawfull: some did saie, it was in such inconvenient and to be reproved in them.

The next place at mr dowes house in Stratforde. mr Newman speaker. mr Catlin moderator.

---

[138] This was a common tactic in the 1560s and 1570s and a compromise occasionally permitted by Aylmer himself. The distinction persisted, as seen in the letter written by William Bedell to Samuel Ward c. 1605 asking if someone willing to wear the surplice might be found for John Knewstub: Bodl. Library, Tanner MS 75, fo. 180. See also *BR*, pp. 220–3 below.

[139] Layer Hall, inherited from his brother Thomas. See above, p. 24, n. 74.

[140] This was probably the direct result of Aylmer's suspension of Edmund Chapman during his visit to Fulham on 9 March. See *BR*, p. 194 below.

{The . 2 : of June was our 68 meeting at Stratforde.}

Where mr Lewis enterpreted the word for mr Newman.

mr Lewis propounded whether he might weare the Surplice, rather then forsake his mynistery, the answer was made generally that he shuld not yeld, A more full answer to be deferred till we heard from our brethren.

mr Sandes moved whether the course of the B[ishop]s were such and of such moment, that they were not to be thought of as of brethren, and soe to be delt withall in our publike and in our private speeches and praiers, it was <not> debated of but not concluded.

The next place appointed to be at mr Sandes house in Boxforde the 24 June. the speaker mr Newman,   the moderator mr Lewis.

{The 24 of June was our 69 meetinge at Boxford.}

The question propounded the meeting before by mr Sandes is committed to mr doctor Cricke. mr Newman and mr Tay to determyne of against the next meetinge.

The next place appointed to be at Erwerton at mr Salmons house, The speaker mr Catlin, the moderator, mr Parker.

{The 5 of August was our 70 meeting at Erwerton.}

Where nothing was handled, but doctor Cricke acquainted the brethren with a confession of faith made by a woman of his parish, who desired to know whether he might admitt her to the Communion upon her confession or noe? it was referred to himself.

The next place at Coxall at mr Newmans house, the speaker mr morse, the Moderator, mr Newman.

{The 2 of September was our 71 meeting.}

Where mr dowe enterpreted the worde for mr morse. ther was nothing propounded.

The next place at wenham at mr Catlins. the speaker mr morse the Moderator mr Tay.

{The 7 of october was our 72 meeting at wenham.}

Where mr Lewis was moderator for mr Tay.

mr Catlin desired to know how he might deale with a couple of persons that were in hatred one against thother for wordes defamatory, viz saying that he had killed a sheepe; whether he might admitt them to the communion, it was answered if they wold professe love one to another he might, bicause he cannot worke love but onlie admonish them of the daunger of it, but if they be in open hatred the booke warrantes him not to receive them.[141] Secondlie he moved what he shuld doe with

---

[141] Defamation, often leading to litigation in the secular courts if the matter alleged, as here, was a felony, in the spiritual courts if it concerned sexual morality, was an outward manifestation of being 'out of charity', the commonest reason, supported by the Book of Common Prayer, for abstaining from the communion (typically, at Easter) or having it withheld. ('The same order shall the curate use with those betwixt whom he shall perceive malice and hatred to reign, not suffering them to be

some froward poore men that were every way disordered: It was answered he must admonish them, and if they wold not accept of it to accompt them as none of his flocke, but yet still to tell them of the daunger and misery wherin they stoode. Thirdlic he said he had warned a Communion and willed the people to resorte to be examyned and they wold not, what he shuld doe in it, it was answered he should let it alone, and still persuade them to it, denouncing godes judgments if they wold not accept of that mercy but deprive themselves of it.

mr dow moved, what shuld be done with a wicked man that did beate his wieff and yt was commonly knowen, whether he shuld be receyved to the Communion without publike confession, it was deferred for this tyme.

The next place of meeting at Barfold at mr doctor Crickes house for mr gale. The speaker mr stocton, the Moderator mr Sandes.

[fo. 12r]

{The 4 of November was our 73 meeting at Barfolde.}

where nothing of any weight was delt in.

The next place appointed to be at dedham at mr Parkers house. mr doctor Cricke speaker. mr Sandes moderator.

{The 2 of December was our 74 meeting at Dedham.}

mr stocton at this tyme propounded how he shuld deale with a yong man that had gott into the house of an honest man, he and his wieff being abroade, and bene with his maide in her bed chamber till he was <espe> espied at a window, it was answered that the mr of the house had good matter against him, and he might suspend him from the Communion till he saw fruites of repentaunce.

mr Sandes moved whether we shuld not make solempne profession of our thankes to god for the late great delyveraunce of us from the Spaniarde, as we did make solempne praiers, the most thought noe, bicause they had done it alreadie in their Churches publikely.[142]

The next place at Langham, at mr farrars house: the speaker mr farrar. The Moderator mr doctor Cricke.

---

partakers of the Lord's Table until he know them to be reconciled.') See Jim Sharpe, *Defamation and sexual slander in early modern England: the church courts at York,* Borthwick papers 58 (York, 1980), and his "'Such disagreement betwyxt neighbours": litigation and human relations in early modern England', in John Bossy, ed., *Disputes and settlements: law and relations in the West* (Cambridge, 1983), pp. 167–87. See also Martin Ingram, *Church courts, sex and marriage in England, 1570–1640* (Cambridge, 1987). On the role of the clergy in settling intra-communal disputes, see John Bossy, *Christianity in the West 1400–1700* (Oxford, 1985), and his *Peace in the post-reformation* (Cambridge, 1998), where this case is cited at pp. 76–7.

[142] England's deliverance from the Armada had been celebrated in London in mid-November, with an appropriate sermon at Paul's Cross on 17 November, Accession Day, a public holiday on the following Tuesday, with sermons, psalm-singing and bonfires, and a special service at St Paul's on 24 November. The suggestion that Sandes had, so to say, missed the boat, refers to these public celebrations, which were evidently replicated in the country.

{The 13. of January was our 75 meeting at Langham.}

mr Parker desired the brethrens judgments in these two points, whether a Pastor were bounde by vertue of his office to visite every particuler family in his charge nothwithstanding his publike teachinge, so that if he do it not he omittes a duty: some desired this might be practised and not made a question whether it shuld be done or noe. others said our publike calling of the people and admonishing of them, discharged us from such a <bur> burden. Others were of this mind that beside our publike teaching, we shuld take all occasions to admonish privately <whether> whersoever we mett them that had need of that helpe, though we went not to every house.[143]

The seconde thinge he moved, was this, what we might accompt to be a competent knowledge for a Communicant, which was deferred.

mr doctor Cricke moved a question tutching Churchwardens whether they and their offices were lawfull, it was not concluded.

mr Lewis toke his leave of the brethren at this tyme being called to St Edmondes burye.[144] There was a fast concluded on, to be holden the next meetinge

The place appointed for it to be at dedham at mr doctor Chapmans house.

The speakers, mr doctor Chapman. mr Sandes and mr morse. the moderator mr dowe.

{The third of February was our 76 meeting at Dedham}

The tyme was spent in praier and fastinge, and noe other causes handled.

The next place at Stratford at mr Morses. the speaker mr Tay The moderator mr Newman.

{The . 3. March was our 77 meeting at Stratforde}

Where mr doctor Crickes question was debated of, and he required to set downe his reasons, and he shuld heare the judgment of the brethren further.

At this tyme mr Gale entred the Schole of dedham and craved the brethrens prayers for him.[145]

The next place at Barfold at mr doctor Crickes. the speaker mr Catlin, the Moderator mr Parker.

{The 7 of Aprill was our 78 meeting at Barfolde 1589.}

Where mr stoctons motion tutching his benefice was handled and nothing els.[146]

---

[143] The classic account of house-to-house visitation by a minister is in George Herbert's *A priest to the temple, or, the countrey parson* (1632, but published 1652): 'The Countrey Parson upon the afternoons in the weekdays, takes occasion sometimes to visite in person, now one quarter of his Parish, now another. For there he shall find his flock most naturally as they are, wallowing in the midst of their affairs' (*The works of George Herbert*, ed. F. E. Hutchinson (Oxford, 1941), p. 247). Parker was perhaps wallowing too deep in his own affairs to feel entirely comfortable in performing this duty in respect of 'every particular family'. See above, pp. lxxii–iv and *BR*, pp. 242–44 below.

[144] See *BR*, p. 224 below.

[145] For Arthur Gale and his predecessor William Bentley as schoolmasters of Dedham, see above, pp. lv–vi.

[146] See *BR*, p. 252 below.

The next place at Boxford at mr Sandes house, the speaker mr Catlin, the Moderator mr Birde.

{The . 5 . of May was our 79 . meeting at Boxforde.}

Where mr Parker desired of the brethren, that when they censured any brother that did enterprete the scriptures before them, they wold delyver their judgments of his labors to the partie himself, bicause <I thinke> he thought it an injury that all shuld know his fault and not he himself, which leaveth an ill conceite of the speaker in the mindes of the rest it may be without cause, he being able to resolve the doubt if any were, or to answere for himself to their contentation. It was answered, that all were not of <my> his mynd, to be shamed or rebuked before all, and therfore they thought it best that some one of the brethren shuld tell the speaker of his fault if any were, but it was concluded it shuld be better considered of, when the next occasion was offred. The next place at Erwerton at mr Salmons house. mr Parker speaker and mr Salmon moderator.

{The . 2 . of June was our 80 . meeting at Erwerton.}

Wher mr Salmon moved whether he might baptise the child of a straunger an Irish woman who was there delyvered of Child, it was said noe bicause she could not delyver to him an accompt of her faith and he could not tell whether it were begott in lawfull mariage.
we now agreed of a fast to be holden the Sabboth sevennight after this our meetinge to be holden at every one of our Churches, soe many as were then present.
The next place was appointed at layer at mr Tayes.
The speaker mr Newman and the moderator mr Tay.

Thus longe contynued through godes mercie this blessed meetinge and now yt ended by the malice of satan, some cause of it was compleints against us preferred to the B[ishop] of london for which cause I was called up to london and examyned of it;[147] but the chiefest cause was the death of some of our brethren and their departure from us to <oth> other places.
Praised be <god> god for ever.

[fo. 13r]

Quest[io] 1a	Ther is a Sab[bath] etc.[148]		
Ra[tio]. 1 a	either ther is etc.		
2a	either the y.	1 meeting and 9 meeting, 12 meeting 3 foll.	
parva maioris	If God etc	17 meeting	4 foll

---

147 Richard Bancroft reported in *Daungerous position* (1593), p. 84: 'I might adde the depositions of one maister *Parker*, Vicar of *Dedham* in *Essex*, for the proofe of the *Classes* in that shire: as of one about *Brayntree side,* consisting of these ministers, maister *Culverwell*, maister *Rogers*, maister *Gifford etc.* another about *Colchester*, consisting of these Ministers, Doctor *Chapman*, Doctor *Chricke*, maister *Dowe.*, maister *Farrar*, maister *Newman*, master *Tey etc.*'
148 William Tey's cryptic and scribbled notes (fos. 13r–14v), of a debate conducted partly syllogistically, partly by reliance on numerous biblical and patristic citations, are hard for a modern reader to make much sense of.

3a   If adam
4   Thapostles etc
Actes 20. 7.[149] 1 Cor[inthians] 16. 2.[150] apoc[alypse] 1[151]
5   The cases etc

parva ante[cedens] The causes efficient is god himself. materiall that the worship of god by all sortes as well bond as free with the declaration of the providence of god towardes mankynd and publike thanksgiving for his benefites. formall that these thinges might be done of all decently and orderly. finall the glory of god, the edifying of his church and Salvation of mankinde but all these are perpetuall ergo the Antecendent is true.

6a   The practise of the churche in all ages <~~under~~> before the lawe in the time of the Lawe and synce Christ doth sufficiently prove the necessity of retayning the Sabbath. *vide Ireneum adversus haereses lib. 4 cap* 19. 20.[152]

Ra[tio] 2a   That the church:
If *religio* etc.
The proposition true as I think though these reasons to weake to prove it. first with one consent the Church affirmeth it, and example of some Churches prove the same.
<~~consequens maioris propos[itionis] falsum ut signa sacramentaria docent~~>
Danaeus Ethic. christ[153] *lib.* 2. *cap.* 10 fol. 160 *at vero precise octava dies ab omnibus ecclesiis pro solenni* συνάξετ *facienda observata est, sed ab aliis ecclesiis tertia dies, id est, martis: ab aliis quarta, id est, mercurii, vel alia, ut tradit Socrates Scholast. in histo. li. 5. c. 22 et est in tripartita historia. Dies autem Dominica quae et Solis dicitur, postea communi omnium ecclesiarum consensu sub imperatoribus Christianis statuta est.*[154] Cent. 4. *cap.* 6 *de ritibus, cae* 477. *Romae conventus ecclesiasticos non fuisse in sabbatho quemadmodum in aliarum terrarum ecclesiis Sozomenus indicasse videtur lib. 7 cap. 19.*[155]

Beza apoc. 1. 10 *die dominico. Diem autem dominicum vocat qui a paulo dicitur* μια σαββάτων *quo diem apparet iam tum solitos fuisse frequentiores coetus haberi a Christianis, sicut a Sabbatho Iudaei in synagogam conveniebant, ut appareat quartum praeceptum de septimo quoque die sanctificando, quod ad sabbathi quidem diem et ritus legales, fuisse ceremoniale, quod ad cultum autem dei attinet*

---

[149] 'And the first day of the weeke, the disciples beeing come together to breake bread' (Geneva version, as in all subsequent biblical quotations).

[150] 'Every first day of the weeke, let every one of you put aside by himselfe, and lay up as God hath prospered him, that then there be no gatheringe when I come.'

[151] Revelation i. 10: 'And I was ravished in spirite on the Lords day'.

[152] It is not known which edition of Irenaeus Tey was using. The 1570 edition published in Paris (*Divi Irenaei Graeci Scriptoris erdutitissimi*) has the following chapter headings: 19 '*Christum filiis Abrahae benefecisse sabbato et alias et de beneficentiae causis*', 20 '*Quomodo non contra legem faciebant discipuli Domini sabbatis spicas legentes, et quoniam Levitae omnes discipuli Domini.*'

[153] The reference is to the influential *Ethices christianae, libri tres* (Geneva, 1577) by Lambert Daneau (1530?-95), a French Calvinist, who taught in the Geneva Academy alongside Theodore Beza. As these excerpts accurately indicate, Danaeus was anything but a sabbatarian, interpreting the fourth commandment figuratively.

[154] '*at vero precise octava . . . Christianis statuta est*'. Tey is quoting accurately from Danaeus, *Ethices christianae, libri tres*. In the edition published at Geneva in 1588, this passage occurs in book 2, chapter 10, fo. 153.

[155] M. I. Flacius, *Quarta centuria ecclesiasticae historiae* (Basel, 1562) col. 477. This is clearly the edition used by Tey.

*esse legis moralis immote et in hac vita perpetuae praeceptum: et stetisse quidem
illum sabbathi diem a creatione mundi ad domini resurrectionem,*[156]

Consequens maiori propos[itioni] falsum ut signa sacramentaria docent
If it be a matter etc.
*falsum est maior. tota eccclesiastica de scripta est ordo politicus gubernande
ecclesiae, attamen est certa et perpetua*

[fo. 13v]

Ob[jection] 1a
a 1 Cor[inthians] 11. 2.[157]
b. Act 20. 7.
1 Cor[inthians] 16. 7.[158]   Apoca[lypse] 1. 10.   Beza *Dominicae diei coetus
apostolicae ac vere divinae sunt traditionis*[159]
The propos. etc.
these instances will not serve for those circumstances observed maketh to be
perpetuall in such places as Ro[mans] 14, 1. cor[inthians] 8
1 Cor[inthians] 11. v. 2.   the place is a generall commendacion for retayning
the decres of thapostles

ob[jection] 2a   delyverance at the last wordes
Chrysost[om] *to.* 3. 859 *de Resur[rectione] ab ipsa est dies quem fert dominus dies
dominicus alii diem panis. vide Tom.* 4. 667.[160] in 1 Cor[inthians] 16. *In una Sabb.
alii dicunt diem lucis* etc. 1. *die dominicae* etc.

ob[jection] 3a
1 Cor[inthians] 11. 20[161]   apoc[alypse] 1. 10
The policy is affirmed of all lerned to be perpetuall and the circumstances only
changeable.
Math[ew] 28. 18. 19. 20.[162]

---

[156] Tey is using an edition of Beza's *Annotationes maiores in novum . . . testamentum.* In the 1594
edition, this quotation from Beza's commentary on Revelation i.10 can be found on pp. 634–5. The
views of Theodore Beza (1516–1605), Calvin's successor as *antistes* of Geneva and an enormously
influential Calvinist theologian of the second generation, were most familiar to English readers
through his New Testament annotations, which were incorporated in Laurence Tomson's translation
of his New Testament, and soon in later editions of the Geneva Bible.

[157] 'Now, brethren, I commend you, that ye remember all my things, and keepe the ordinances, as I
delivered them to you.'

[158] 'For I will not see you now in my passage: but I trust to abide a while with you, if the Lord permit.'

[159] '*Dominicae igitur diei coetus (quos etiam Iustinus in Apolog. 2. diferte commemorat) Apostolicae ac
vere divinae sunt traditionis*', Beza, *Annotationes maiores in novum . . . testamentum* (London,
1594), p. 634.

[160] *Opera D. Ioannis Chrysostomi* (Basel, 1539). Although this edition was not the one used by Tey, the
reference is to '*De resurrectione, Homiliae 9*', found in book 3, and to '*ex epistola 1 Corinthians xvi
de elemosyna et collatione in sanctos*', found in book 4.

[161] 'When ye come together therefore into one place, this is not to eate the Lordes supper.'

[162] 'And Jesus came, and spake unto them, saying, All power is given unto me in heaven and earth. Go
therefore, and teache all nacions, baptizing them in the Name of the Father, and the Sonne, and the
holie Gost. Teaching them to observe all things, whatsoever I have commanded you, and lo, I am
with you alway, until the end of the worlde. Amen.'

act 1. 3.[163]
1 Cor[in]th[ians] 3. 15. 6. 13. 14.[164]
Heb[rews] 1. 3. 2. 3.[165]

our Sabb[ath] is not a natural etc.
If the Sabb[ath] of a naturall day were ceremoniall etc. this ys denyed except you
will say the 6. dayes also were ceremoniall
sonne of god. your last wordes
*Institutio Sabbathi, diei dominicae vel festorum non impedit ea quae ordinantur ad
hominum salutem corporalem vel spiritualem* Danaeus *lib* 2. *ca.* 10. fol. 158[166]

But the Sabboth of a natural day was ceremoniall
this will not prove the assumption
Deus ipse quievit ab omni opere creandi sed non providendi Job 5. 17[167]
one of 24 houres etc our savyor disproveth this whole reason math[ew] 12. 11.
12.[168] mar[k] 2. 27. 28.[169] and the fact of Josua 6. 18.[170]
Trem[ellius] John 7. 22. *A circumcisione qua die festo peragebatur, docet non
quoduis opus in Sabb[atho] esse prohibitum: sed tantum quod cum sacra quiete
pugnaret.*[171]
math[ew] 12. 1. 7.[172] *quera misericordia non prohibetur fieri Sabbatho*
breaking of it last wordes. Tertull. 4 *to* in mar. *quam dicat lex die opus tamen*

[163] 'To whome also he presented himself alive after that he had suffred, by manie infallible tokens, being
sene of them by the space of fourtie dayes, and speaking of those things which apperteine to the
kingdome of God.'
[164] 1 Corinthians iii.15: 'If anie mans work burne, he shal lose, but he shalbe safe him self: nevertheless
yet as it were by the fyre.' vi. 13–14: 'Meates are ordeined for the bellie, and the bellie for the
meates: but God shal destroie both it, and them. Now the bodie is not for fornicacion, but for the
Lord, and the Lord for the bodie. And God hathe also raised up the Lord, and shal raise us up by his
power.'
[165] Hebrews i. 3: 'Who being the brightnes of the glorie, and the ingreved forme of his persone, and
bearing up all things by his mightie worde, hathe by him self purged our sinnes, and sitteth at the
right hand of the majestie in the highest places.' ii. 3: 'How shal we escape, if we neglect so great
salvation, which at the first began to be preached by the Lord, and afterwarde was confirmed unto us
by them that heard him.'
[166] Danaeus, *Ethices christianae*. The passage may be found in Danaeus, *Opuscula omnia theologica*
(Geneva, 1583), book 2, chapter 10, fo. 117.
[167] 'Beholde, blessed is the man whom God correcteth: therefore refuse not thou the chastising of the
Almightie.'
[168] 'And hee sayd unto them, What man shall there bee among you, that shall have a sheepe, and if it fall
on the Sabbath day into a pit, will hee not take it and lift it out?'
[169] 'And he said to them, the Sabbath was made for man, and not man for the Sabbath. Wherefore the
Sonne of man is Lord, even of the Sabbath.'
[170] Tey appears to refer to the account of the destruction of Jericho in Joshua vi. 1–18 in which the
command to rest was superseded by the instructions for the taking of Jericho.
[171] 'Moses therefore gave unto you circumcision, (not because it is of Moses, but of the fathers) and ye
on the Sabbath day circumcise a man.' A common resource in this debate is the state-of-the-art
scholarly bible of the Italian scholar John Immanuel Tremellius (1510–80) (with input from
Franciscus Junius (Francois du Jon) (1545–1602)), with an edition published in London in 1580. The
critical notes in Tremellius' translation of the Old Testament from the Hebrew and of the New
Testament from the Syriac encouraged a serious interest in the Sabbath. Tremellius was a convert
from Judaism. See *Jesu Christi D. N. novum testamentum e lingua Syriaca latino sermone redditum
interprete Immanuele Tremellio* (London, 1580), p. 73.
[172] Matthew xii. 1–7: 'At that time Jesus went on a Sabbath day through the corne, and his disciples
were an hungered, and began to plucke the eares of corne to eat.'

non facies, de homino tantum opere prohibitio intelligenda est, quod quisque ex
artificio vel egetio suo exequitur non de divino[173]
for the rest therof being all one   ther is gret difference betwene the ordenary and
extraordenary exercises

[fo. 14r]

We be above etc   In diverse places mention is made of morning and evening
exercise then used but for some other respect   note their unity or concord, as we say
the fast and not fastes, although diverse sermons be on one day, and one parliament
etc
The sanctifying etc.
9o *multu magis*
dies naturalis
Ex[odus] 12. 16[174]   Levit[icus] 23. 7. 8. 21. [2] 7. 35. 36.[175]   this was not
the Sab[bath] day and the grant more liberty to be given other feastes then on the
Sabb[ath]. Exod[us] 12 cont.
Neh[emiah] 8. 4. this assembly retayned 7 daies and yet is called one convocation
vide Annotat[ionem] Tremel[lii] vers. 8. populo manente et 9 etsi non fecerant[176]
Act. 20. 7   this answereth to the objection out of the actes 13 *postea*
Neh[emiah] 9. 1. 2. 3.
Geneva transla[tion]   4 times a day
2 Chron[icles] 20. 23[177]   now concerning our selves etc. *ergo* a whole naturall day
wilbe short enough for us
Act 2. 6.[178]   and therfore stronger and more able to hold out a naturall day then the
Jewes
Lev[iticus] 23. 3.[179]   the ceremoniall part was the precise rest etc.
Ex[odus] 34. 21 16. 23. 35. 3.[180] matt[hew] 15. 32[181]

[173] Tey is making reference to Tertullian's treatment of the Sabbath in his work '*adversus Marcionem*', book 4, cap. 12. See *Patrologia Latina*, ed. J. P. Migne (Turnhout, 1844), II, cols. 383–6.
[174] 'And in the first day shalbe an holy assembly: also in the seventh day shall bee an holy assembly unto you: no worke shall bee done in them.'
[175] These verses repeat, in greater detail, the prescription in Exodus xii. 16, employing what for Crick is a crucial word, 'convocation', not, or so he claims, the Sabbath as such.
[176] Nehemiah viii tells of Ezra the Priest reading the law to the Jews returned from exile. Its relevance is that the reading appears to have gone on for days. ix.1 speaks of an assembly on 'the foure & twentieth day of this moneth', and verse 3 of a reading 'foure times on the day'. See Tremellius, *Biblia Sacra* (London, 1580), p. 283.
[177] 2 Chronicles xx concerns the fast proclaimed by Jehoshaphat and the resultant mixture of slaughter and worship which occupied the Israelites for a number of days in their fight with the Moabites and Ammonites. Chapter xxiii relates the death of Athaliah on the Sabbath day.
[178] Acts ii. 1–6. The coming of the Holy Spirit at Pentecost.
[179] 'Six daies shal worke be done, but in the seventh day shalbe the Sabbath of rest, an holy convocation: ye shal do no worke therein, it is the Sabbath of the Lord, in all your dwellings.'
[180] Exodus xxxiv. 21 repeats the command to rest from work. xxxv. 3: 'Ye shal kindle no fire throughout all your habitations upon the Sabboth day.' xvi. 23: 'Tomorrow is the rest of the holy Sabbath unto the Lord: bake that todaie which ye wil bake, and sethe that which ye wil sethe, and all that remaineth lay it up to be kept til the morning for you.'
[181] Matthew xv. 30–4 concerns the miraculous feeding of the multitude with seven loaves and a few fishes.

And we need not imagyne etc. the text noteth it playne and therfor we need not imagynation vers. 30. 31. 34.

rigoros proves it is true and equall justice

maketh it lawfull to do common thinges. It is called common in *proprie*

this is no right collection of the place

forbydden on the Sab[bath] the last wordes. the argument is a more *ad maioris* as thus it is no breach of the Sab[bath] to do such workes of lesse importance ergo a breach to do greater viz the workes of mercy

then the workes of mercy. this consequence is false

I will have mercy not sacrifice. our savyor compareth not the sacrifices with the rest but the duty of sacrificinge with workes of mercy.

If it be law free to use the Sabboth etc.

it is a ceremony consequent false

petition principii herupon I conclude etc

shuld leave us in this yoke equally etc. Our liberty is to serve god and therfore not to be reckoned with the Jewes ceremonies

agayne whatsoever man is lord of etc this is spoken aswell of the Jewes as of the Christians

[fo. 14v]

ob[jection] 5 the same liberty etc. *id est* the same morall commandment is to the Jew and Christians

your self have reckoned before the streight observations as ceremonies but this assertion is of the substance

act 1. 12. they might by the law go more then 2 or ten miles on the Sab[bath] but they stretned it by tradition. *Rabakiba, Simeon et Hille tradiderunt, ut bis mille pedes in Sabb[atho] ambulemus. Cent. 4. cap. 15. pag. 1465. 1467. de traditionibus In Sab. ultra bis mille pedes non ambulabant. Hier. ad Algasiam*[182] beza act. 1. 12. *distans itinere Sabbathi. Josephus et Marcus, quinque tantum stadiis ab urbe diffitum fuisse testatur; supputatione prorsus congruente cum Thalmudistarum sententia, qui non 2 miliaria sed 2. cubitorum millia, tradunt iter fuisse Sabb[ati]., ea ratione si Origeni, credimus quem Theophil. testem citat quod olim tot cubitis tabernaculum in deserto a castris Israelitarum distaret quod stadium singulis Sabbathis emetiri consuevissent ad sacrum coetum convenientes* etc.[183]

Tremel[lius] act. 1. v. 12 *locus observatione dignus ex quo manifeste colligitur, quae sit apud Hebraeos ratio itineris quod sabbatho emetiri ex veterum traditione concessum erat.* etc.[184]

The same liberty concerning the substance of the day is to the Jewes and Christians

Ra[tio] 1a Both Jewes and christians are alike to the morall commandment

---

[182] 'Rabakiba, Simeon et Hille . . . ad Algasiam'. Tey is quoting verbatim from M. I. Flacius, *Quarta centuria ecclesiasticae historiae*, book 4, chapter 15, cols. 1465, 1467.

[183] 'distans itinere Sabbati, Josephus . . . ad sacram coetum convenientes'. Tey is quoting from Beza's *Annotationes maiores* on Acts i. 10.

[184] Tremellius on Acts i. 12: *Jesu Christi D. N. novum testamentum*, p. 87.

bound but the substance of the day is the morall commandment ergo both Jew and Christian are alike bound to the substance of the day.

2a   the partition wall is broken downe betwene Jew and gentilc and of twayne are made one Eph[esians] 2. but only the ceremoniall law was the partition wall ergo only the ceremoniall law is broken downe for *per consequens substantiam manet.*

3a   this is not to be of righteosnes in all the commandements but Jew and Christian are alike bound to this rule in all thother command: ergo in this 4. command.

Irenaeus *lib.* 4 *contra hereses cap.* 31 *quoniam haec est vita tua, et longitudo dierum tuorum. In quam vitam praestruens hominem, decalogi quidem verba ipse per semetipsum omnibus similiter Dominus locutus est. Et ideo similiter permanent apud nos, extensionem et augmentum, sed non dissolutionem accipientia per carnalem eius adventum. Servitutis autem praecepta separatim per Moysem parecepit populo, apta illorum eruditioni sive catigationi. Quemadmodum ipse Moyses ait, et mihi praecepit Dominus in tempore illo dicere vobis justificationes et judicia. Haec ergo quae in servitutem et in signum data sunt illis, circumcinxit novo libertatis testamento. Quae autem naturalia et liberalia et communia omnium, auxit et dilatavit, sine invidia largitur, donans hominibus per adoptionem, patrem scire Deum, et diligere eum ex toto corde:*[185]

Calv[in] Har. luc. 4. vers. 16.   *Quanquam autem inter legis umbras Sabbathum numerat Paulus: hac tamen in parte communis nobis est feriandi ratio cum Judaeis, ut populus ad audiendum verbum, ad publicas preces, et reliqua pietatis exercitia conveniat. In quem usum Judaico Sabbatho succesit dies Dominicus.*[186]

The stretnes of this morall law which the Jewes held was by tradition and not by the vertue of the lawe. and further I say that many of their ceremonies they kept streyter then by the law they shold have done.

Ra[tio] 1a   our savyor kept the law most stretly according to the nature of the lawe, but he kept it not so streightly as the Jewes *ergo* ther keeping was by tradition not by the law.

2a   our savyor reproveth often their streite keeping of it but he <del>did reproveth the</del> never reproveth the stretnes of the law, ergo it was by tradition

3a   the property of hipocrites is to stretten the outward observation of ceremonies and to geve liberty to the inward truth, but those were hipocrites, ergo ther doynges were such.

A few notes gathered by Mr Tay of the Sabb[ath] and use of it.

---

[185] '*Quoniam haec est vita tua . . . ex toto corde*'. See *Divi Irenaei Graeci Scriptoris erdutitissimi* (Paris, 1570), book 4, chapter 31, p. 258.

[186] '*Quanquam autem inter Legis umbras . . . succesit dies Dominicus*'. Tey is quoting from *Harmonia ex evangelistis tribus composita, Matthaeo, Marco et Luca, commentariis Iohannis Calvini exposita* (Geneva, 1572), pp. 62–3.

[fo. 15r]

Mr Sandes[187]

That ther is a Sabboth I do alsoe frely confesse:

That the churche is at libertie to chaunge the day, although I professe my self ready to be informed yet me thinkes that which is said doth not satisfy me.

1. For as farre as I can conceyve this first reason cannot be stronge, for the persons in the worshipp of god may not be chaunged and the like may be said of diverse other thinges, yet is not religion tyed to them.

Propos[ition]   Methinkes this also doth not alwaies hold, for many thinges in the pollicy of the Church ther be which it is not in mans power to alter, as the generall matter of the government etc. and by this, except I be deceyved, we throw our selves downe before the adversaries of the Church government.[188]

Assump[tion]   Nether as I thinke is this to observe tymes nor geve religious worshipp to them more then to the matter of the Sacrament and persons in the government:

2.   For the second reason though it were granted that ther were some ceremony in it yet except it be proved that ther was no perpetuall pollicy in it, (as I thinke) that which is concluded of it cannot followe.

Propo[sition]   The thinge brought here to confirme the proposition serveth not except all pollicie be shutt out for though it be graunted that ther was some ceremony in it, yet doth it not followe that nothing concerning a setled 7 day was commanded.

[fo. 15v]

Assump.   That which is said here doth not satisfy for yf it were ceremoniall at all yet was it not only, agayne methinkes the practise of thapostles is proff sufficient to establish this day as the lords facte to establish thother

Obi 1a   As the objection doth not hold that every apostolicall institution is perpetuall, soe methinkes the answer is not sufficient except it were shewed that this

[187] In this first paper, Henry Sandes is responding to Richard Crick's 'labors about the Sabbath' (**17M**). What needs to be kept in mind is the question whether the Christian Sabbath is part of the moral and therefore perpetual law (which its place in the Decalogue, and even in the Creation story itself, would seem to indicate), or whether it was ceremonial, which would make it no longer absolutely binding in the christian dispensation. Henry Sandes leant to the first opinion, Richard Crick to the second. Most reformation writers on the subject began from the premise that the Sabbath was both moral and ceremonial. (See, for example, William Perkins's *A golden chaine*, in *Workes* (1603), p. 45.) However, Nicholas Bound observed in his *The doctrine of the sabbath* (1595), the first major printed treatise on the subject in English, that 'this argument of the Sabbath is full of controversie, above many other points of divinitie, wherein many learned and godly men dissent one from another' (Preface).

[188] 'Methinkes this also . . . Church government'. Sandes's argument at this point suggests a tight connexion between his brand of sabbatarianism and presbyterianism. If it is held to be in man's power to alter the Sabbath (the day, the use, etc.) then the same could be true of church government; 'and by this . . . we throw our selves downe before the adversaries of the Church government'. This may suggest that it was with some good reason that Thomas Rogers and, later, Peter Heylyn, admittedly polemically, linked sabbatarianism and presbyterianism. See John H. Primus, *Holy time: moderate puritanism and the Sabbath* (Macon, Georgia, 1989), pp. 24, 51, commenting critically on the thrust of Kenneth L. Parker, *The English Sabbath: a study of doctrine and discipline from the reformation to the civil war* (Cambridge, 1988).

is one of them that were not perpetuall. But for that which is added of doing without conference it maketh for the authority of the thinge that it was not a Church conclusion but came from heaven and therefore is more weighty

Ob. 2a   For the second Ob[jection] if Adam in his innocency had need of anie to helpe him in the remembraunce of the creation, we have much more need having now greater matters then the creation describing the justice and mercy of God much more lively and we being also soe farre inferyer to him in all thinges

a   Againe that this his resurrection is more specially to be remembered (although all the rest as his birth passion etc are included in this and must be remembered with it) is playne, for this was the especiall accomplishment of our recreation:

b   Further this doth not revive the Jewes daie but addeth a more glorious thing unto the former for if the creation was to be remembered in that day of Adam and the Jewes, yea and their redemption Deuteronomy 5[189] added to this, and joigned to be remembred by this though it was not [fo. 16r] accomplished that daie for them. then this thinge being more glorious may have the daie referred to it and the memory of thother brought unto yt:

c   Besides when this daie which we now hold hath his especiall name thapostles themselves putting it upon it and is called the lordes day, and as this daie the Resurrection of christ is said to be accomplished I thinke this maketh something to the strength herof.

d   And this also is somethinge, that all writers of accompte have also spoken of this.

e   I do not thinke that this is as necessary as prechinge but the lord hath also left other thinges which are not to be compared to this and yet are not therfore idle and without use and therfore this is nothing hindred by that inferred from the Galathians But I should reason thus:

1.   That which is expresly commanded, not for offence nor for toleration in the Church that must be observed, But this is such, and therfore 1 Corinthians 16. 1. he saieth not the first day of the weeke or the daie which is your seventh day if you thinke good to chaunge it or wordes importing this much but in playne wordes the first day of the weeke leaving them no liberty herin.[190]

2.   Againe that which no Church hath ever bene bold to breake, no not even the papistes which have transposed all thinges, that may not nowe by anie particuler church be chaunged, but this is such ergo

[fo. 16v]

3. Further when it hath his name the lordes day I thinke it is of his authority in commaunding yt and severing it from the rest, which if it be soe (as the speech in the scriptures is usual in this sense) I see not how any man may alter yt.

That the Jewes Sabboth was a natural day I do like very well, but that ours shuld not be methinkes I yet do not see.

For firste though it were graunted that ther have bene some signification and type

---

[189] Deuteronomy v contains the Ten Commandments (Decalogue), together with the promise (v. 33): 'But walke in all the wayes which the Lord your God hath commanded you, that ye may live, and that it may goe well with you: and that yee may prolong your dayes in the land which ye shall possesse.'

[190] The reference should be to verse 2: 'Every first day of the weeke. . .'.

put upon it[191] yet that the length was yt, I see it not yet proved as I thinke, for if ther had bene nothing but a figurative rest, then ther is something said here but I thinke the busynes of the Sabboth as it is described in the scripture will take up all the tyme.

Againe when it was thus longe afore the ceremonies for the rudenes of the Church and that burden of moses was instituted I <soe> see not how the length of it shuld be shutt up in a ceremony

moreover ther is nether expresse speech nor necessarie collection to enforce this abridgement of the tyme that I remember.

1.   Thassumption hath not the force which in this cause is requisite (as I thinke) for we see the lord hath dispensed with other of the morall law as murder in private persons etc

{*Prohibitiones*}

2.   The confirmation also methinketh may be objected against for labor is not simply forbidden, but such labor as on other daies [fo. 17r] are exercised that is to say professing common labor no more then in the rest of the Commandments the thinges are not in all their kindes forbidden but such ill use of them.

3.   Besides if this were thus then were ther no morall thing in it for necessity may dispense with us in the time of the period which you thinke to be the morall part of this commaundement.

4.   That other collection of the fact of paule for soe much as it is extraordenary giveth little direction but that men shuld be painfull in season and out of season.[192]

5.   As for the inconveniences I do not thinke any such daunger in them as for talke I doe not thinke ther is such libertie as may be on other daies as Esay speaketh 58.[193]

And as for abridging of the rest of that course used in the expiacion I do not thinke to be the usuall forme of the Sabboth no more then their lying in sackclothe, but rather peculier to that generall and streit faste.

But that our Sabboth is a naturall daie methinkes something may be said:

1.   That order is to be kept which was afore any ceremony (as we do speake of them) was, or the rudenes of the Church required any such thinge.

Agayne if we waigh the busynes of the Sabboth the meditation of the creation, redemption, mercy, justice, wisdome etc of god with the weeke past and to come, the meetinges with praying, thankes giving for them etc [fo. 17v] I thinke these busynes will take up all the time

---

[191] An anti-sabbatarian argument was that the Sabbath, like other ceremonies of the Old Testament, was for Christians no more than a 'type' or symbolic precursor of the new dispensation. See, for example, Wolfgang Musculus, *Common places* (English edn., London, 1563), sig Jiiii: 'The legale Sabbath was not of his nature suche, that it should be everlastyng. For it was not a trewe, but shadoyng: not perfect, but set for yonglynges, and to teach, very unperfect and meete to be geven to an untaught people. Therefore at the time of the newe Testament it did worthely cease, to give place to the libertie of the spirite. Christe is the body, at whose comming shadowes by good reason dyd cease.' And see sigs. Jv–vi, 'Of the abrogation of the lawishe Sabbath', which is critical of what Musculus' translator calls 'the Sabbatharies', a linguistic precursor of 'sabbatarians'.

[192] 2 Timothy iv. 2: 'Preach the word: be instant in season and out of season. . .'.

[193] Isaiah lviii denounces those who fast 'for a day' (verse 5). But the chapter ends with the promise (verses 13–14) that the reward of keeping the Sabbath as it should be kept will be richly rewarded.

3.   Besides if Adam had need of soe much time he being in farre better state
then we are, for meditation of the creation we have need rather of more then of
lesse.[194]

4.   Moreover this doth the commaundement charge us with without any
mitigacion that I remember

That we be not bound to the streit order of rest that they were, for the substantiall
part I do like of that is said for publike meetinge, but I do not yet thinke that this is
all the worke of the Sabbothe

For the ceremoniall part I do rather thinke that those thinges that are <were> named
were ceremoniall appendices as other Commaundements had in their kynd for the
pure worshipp of god in the 2 Comm[andment] that it might be the better regarded
and for cleanes in the 7. so in this also that the regard the lord had to have his
Saboths observed might be considered he added these ceremonies to yt, some as I
thinke, speciall to the wildernes, som contynuing till Christ but I do not see why
these shuld make this commaund: ceremoniall more then absteyning from bloud,
not killing the damme upon the yong ones[195] the 6 com[mandment]

1.   For the first reason why it shuld be ceremoniall, I see not how the assumption can follow of this place, for by being a signe I cannot see how any other thing
can be ment but a common token that the lord by this [fo. 18r] calling them from
their common busynes to heare his word and to be exercised specially this way doth
betoken to them that it is he that must worke their sanctification, as by forbidding
murder it is a signe that the liff of man is deare unto him and therfore the word here
doth not signify ane type but a common signe as Tremelius also speaketh of it
Exodus 31.[196]

If the principall end why it was commaunded were that as a type yt might figure
their sanctification then this had some force but I see not yet that it was
commaunded for this at all but the signe was nothing els but a common document,
the end why it was commaunded is that his word might be heard and his spirite
more effectually worke in them and this it doth note out to them.

and so for that which is said for servauntes rest and cattell, it is no wher said that it
was for a figure or type of this, nether dothe the word signify any such thinge, and
as for hearing the word and weighing it, though it be not all the busines yet is it
more especially enjoined that day then any other and must have more speciall tyme
allotted to it. And that which is spoken of other feastes as farre as I can see doth
helpe this that the daie was not ceremoniall, for when they being ceremoniall in
deed yet do differ from this it is a token that this had other matter in yt, for they
being all to one end must have had the like observaunce, but the streit [fo. 18v]
absteyning from some thinges was it that was the ceremony leading to regard the
religious observacion of thend of it. The straunger is forbidden worke as the Cattle

---

[194] Sabbatarians like Sandes pushed the obligation to rest on the seventh day beyond the Decalogue to
the Creation itself. Even before the Fall, Adam needed time 'for meditation of the creation'.

[195] Leviticus xvii. 12: 'None of you shal eat blood . . .'; Deuteronomy xxii. 6: 'If thou finde a birdes nest
in the way, in anie tre, or on the ground, whether they be yong or egges, and the dam sitting upon the
yong, or upon the egges, thou shalt not take the dam with the yong.'

[196] Exodus xxxi. 12–18 contains God's specific commands to Moses in respect of the Sabbath, which
was to be 'a signe betweene me and you in your generations', 'a signe betweene me and the children
of Israel for ever'.

is and therfor is not set emongst his household but after the Cattle so that no vauntage can be taken from him.

3   For the <2> 3 reason I do not see whie the breaking of the Sabboth may not have this punishment inflicted upon it as blaspheming of godes name, which breaking is not in any servile worke doing, no more then every manner of killinge or hurting is a breach of the 6 command:

4   Unto the 4 I have answered before that nothing doth beare us out in doing that daie as we do thother sixe daies, but this doth not with hold worke of necessity, no more then forbidding of adultery doth forbydd the lawfull use of mariage.

5. 6. 7.   For thother reasons taken out of Math[ew] 12: although they seeme to be of most moment, yet I thinke that in that place our lord Jesus doth reason (*ex hypothesi Phariseorum*) for they made the rest a part of the service of god which was but a constitution of their owne for the rest is commaunded not for it self but for another end as we have said, and therfor I thinke the arguyng of christ [fo. 19r] is not of equals but of the greater that if those constitutions which god himself had erected were subject to mitigacion much more were theirs.

But further I think that the debate here betwene Christ and the Pharises is not of that Sabboth that I speake of, but of thother Sabboths <weh> which I confesse are ceased, and were rudimentes given to that people, which we being under the banner of Christ are freed from, and this doth Luke plainly shewe saying that it was *Sabbatho secundo primo* which <being> being true doth make nothing for this argument as I thinke.

8.   for the making of the Sabboth for man I take it to be that which is said that his servant might have some rest and therfore if god had an end to mans liff in concluding this acte, ther is no cause why it shuld be so stretned[197]

So that methinketh (wherein I professe no resolucion but an hart I hope willinge to be enstructed) yet the Sabboth of the 7 day given in Paradise when the pure state of the Church needed not these ceremonies and rudimentes and renewed with the rest of the 10 wordes in Horeb afore the ceremonies were ordeyned, is cleared from ceremony.

[fo. 19v]
Blank

[fo. 20r]

{Prop.1}   1.   That which is alledged against the confirmation of my proposition, is not of force against my proposition. That a matter of meere pollicy and order might be altered: which maie appeare by adding the Assumption and conclusion unto the proposition, The generall matter of government cannot be altered, but the

---

[197] Matthew xii. 1–8 is the story of Jesus' hungry disciples plucking ears of corn on the Sabbath, provoking the criticism of the Pharisees, which occurs in all three synoptic gospels. In Mark ii. 27 Jesus pronounces: 'The Sabbath was made for man, and not man for the Sabbath', the ultimate anti-sabbatarian proof text. However, in Luke's version (Luke i. 1), this was supposed to have happened 'on the second Sabbath', which enables Sandes to claim that what was in question was not the Sabbath itself, any breach of which Jesus himself would not have condoned, but one of the lesser sabbaths.

generall matter of government is a matter of meere pollicy and order, ergo a matter of meere pollicy and order may not be altered. In which Sillogisme the Assumption is false, and doth in very deed throw us downe before the adversaries of Church government against whom we maynteyne the generall matter of government is an essentiall part of a reformed Church, and not a matter of meere pollicy and order

{Ass[umption]} To thinke one tyme more holie then another is to observe tymes, although ther be no religious worshipp given unto them. for this was never done of the godly, which as yet thother was given them in commaundement now whereas you say no more then to the matter of the Sacramentes and the persons in the government, you signify (as also before you have set downe) that ther is no holines in them. which I do not consent unto for concerning the Sacrament if they be most holie as they are, no lesse then the Sacramentes of thold church, then the matter whereof they consist, is also holie. If ther be anie holines in Baptisme, ther is some also in the water of baptisme and if ther be anie holines in the lordes supper, then is ther holines in the bread and wine of the supper. As for the persons in the government, I see not why they shuld not now be accompted holie and have holines graunted unto them, aswell as the priestes and levites and prophetes and apostles are called holie, not after the same manner that other Christians are but after a more excellent sorte wher also is answered that which is set downe in the begynning that although religion be not tyed unto them (for so yow speake otherwise then I did) yet they may not be chaunged, wherto I answer further, that if they were no more holie then other, yet the observation of them is a parte of the worshipp of god bycause they be enjoigned by him, which also may stand in the matter of the Sacramentes and so they be no instances against me who joigned both those together.[198]

{Prop[osition] 2}   That which is brought against the proposition is beside the purpose for I have not set downe that nothing concerning a setled 7 day was commaunded but the evident testimony of the scripture, what I and so that for the oppugninge herof it shuld have bene shewed I the Church is necessarily tyed unto that wherof she hath noe commaundement from the Lord

{Ass[umption]}   If it were not ceremoniall only, then must it be morall alsoe for Judiciall it was not. If it had bene morall then the day could not have bene chaunged unto another. for that of the law which was once morall contynueth soe for evermore and is not subject unto any chaunge. wher you say the practise of the apostles is prooff sufficient to establish this day, as the lordes facte to establish thother, concluding as I think heron that this day is commaunded, I say that it was not the lordes resting on that day that did establish the daie unto them but the commaundement, wherto he addeth strength by an argument taken from his owne facte, now if this day had a commaundement then the fact of thapostles shuld do as much to persuade unto the kepinge of it as the lordes did[199]

---

[198] Here Sandes is arguing that a negative attitude to the observing of times, such as we find especially in William Tyndale, is not justified, since days in themselves can just as well be holy as the matter of the sacraments and the persons of ministers. Tyndale had written: 'And as for the Saboth, a great matter, we be lords over the Saboth . . . Neither needed we any holy day at all, if the people might be taught without it.' *An answer to Sir Thomas More's Dialogue*, ed. H. Walter (Cambridge, Parker Society, 1850), p. 97.

[199] Crick is making a telling point. If the Sabbath is part of the perpetual moral rather than the merely ceremonial law (he insists that it cannot be regarded as part of the judicial law), then it could not have been shifted from the seventh to the first day. This proves that the Christian Sabbath was no more and

[fo. 20v]

Ob. 1   My answer is so sufficient unto the Objection, as it hath in such sort turned the edge of yt, that except it be set agayne, I need not feare the wound it can make for that except it were shewed that this is one of thise Apostolicall institutions that were not perpetuall hath no grounde, for why shuld I shew that here which was not avowched by the objection, And it is all one as if you had said that my answer is insufficient, except it shuld graunt that which I deny, for if I shew that this is one of the Apost: institutions which is not perpetuall, I grant it to be an Institution of theirs, which being the Assumption in the Argument was denied of me. Nether doth it suffise for the provinge of it to be one, that it was used in some places, no more then the Assemblinge together of the Church at Jerusalem every day in the <weeke> weeke, doth prove it to be an Apost: institution that we shuld assemble every day in the weeke, <nay> nay not soe much, seing this was done by all the apostles. If yt <obte> obteyneth any thing, it is this, that we ought to assemble upon some first daies and may meete upon all the first daies, but not that we are bound herunto. For if bicause the disciples at Troas, and the Corinthians mett at other tyme, it shalbe gathered necessary for us to meete every first day, then let me knowe why it is not a necessary institution of thapostles, that upon every lordes day the lordes supper shuld be celebrated as at Troas[200] and a collection made for the poore as at Corinth. But <Bes> Beza saieth that the assemblies of the Lordes day, are of an Aposticall and truly divine tradition,[201] but his meaning seemeth to be that they have their warrant from them and not from man, so that we may mainteine the holding of our meetinges by their example, as one may say, It is an apost: institution to celebrate the lordes supper, or to make a Collection for the poore every lordes day: not that every Church is bound therunto, but bycause if every Church like to use it, she hath here warrant from their example that she may do it. Wherefore that which Socrates[202] saith concerning the order of celebrating the Passeover hath place here. and bicause no man can shewe a commaundement tutching that matter committed to writinge, it is cleere that thapostles gave freedome unto every man to do that which was good, for that ther is no precept hereafter shall appeare
{Socrat lib 5 Ecclesiast cap 21}[203]
ob. 2. a. That which is spoken of Adam shalbe looked on afterward: that which is spoken, that the Resur[rection]: is more specially to <be> be remembered as the speciall <of> accomplishment of our recreation, is not the question betwene <us> us, but whether it be necessarely to be remembered by a weekly day. And if it be more specially to be remembered by one then also his birth, death etc specially by <one> one. And if that <were> more specially bicause it is the accomplishment of

---

no less than an apostolic institution, subject to the same variability as any other piece of apostolic practice.
[200] Acts xx. 6–7: 'and came unto them to Troas in five dayes, where we abode seven dayes. And the first day of the weeke, the disciples beeing come together to breake bread, Paul preached unto them'.
[201] See William Tey's note above, p. 48, n. 159.
[202] Not the Greek philosopher but Socrates 'Scholasticus' (c. 380–450), the ecclesiastical historian who continued the *Ecclesiastical History* of Eusebius.
[203] Socrates 'Scholasticus', book 5, cap. 21. See *Patrologia Graeca*, ed. J.P. Migne (Paris, 1859), LXVII, cols. 622–26.

our recreation, then those specially bycause they be the begynninges and proceedinges even almost unto perfection of our restoring. and I wold gladly know why
there must be one day every weeke for this, and not one or two at the least in the
quarter for thother. If it be, bycause this comprehendeth the former, I say that his
Ascension doth aswell comprehend his Resur[rection]: as his Resur[rection]: doth
his birth and passion. then let this [fo. 21r] daie also be swallowed up of another
appointed for the remembraunce of his ascending into heaven: yea I say that the
sending of the holy ghost upon his disciples doth comprehend his ascension aswell
as this doth his Resur[rection]: let this therfore devoure all the rest, and as those
leane kyne of Egipt were never a whitt the greater or better likinge when they had
eate up the fatt ones,[204] let this appeare <still> still in a common rate. nay I wold
know why ther shuld not be a day set a part for the remembraunce of the Creation,
seying it must be had in speciall memory, though not in more speciall
remembraunce. That which you say of the memory therof to be brought unto the
lordes daie, as the memorie of the peoples delyveraunce was referred unto the
Sabboth, is not sufficient, for I <rep> <reply> reply, that although it might be soe,
yet as the day of their deliveraunce, might not be eaten up of the Sabbath, but
though the benefite were then to be thought upon, yet the sett daie was to be
observed for evermore throughout all their generations, so although the creation
shuld be remembered then, yet the daie must not be devoured therof but must stand.
He that will cleare this matter of all doubtes must shewe not that this is more
specially to be remembered, but that it is by a daie only to be remembered in such
sorte. that which followeth I will answer anone. If any writer affirmeth yt necessarie
to have the Resur[rection]: of our savyor only remembered by a daie, it is more then
I knowe, If they doe let me knowe their reasons.[205] If they saie that the Church tooke
it up in the honor therof, it is nothing against me, who have not spoken a word
against yt. Towching the place to the Gal[atians]:[206] if we have sufficient meanes
without yt, which I have proved from thence, then is it not necessary for where
enough is alreadie, what need is ther of any more? wher you say other thinges
beside preaching of the word are lefte to this end, which yet are not idle: if yow
speake of the government and Sacramentes I grant it, but they are with the
preaching of the word comprehended in that place of thapostle. If yow meane any
other thinge I confesse I am ignorant of it.

1. Now here I answer unto your reasons. The proposition in the first argument is not
so warelie <set> sett downe, but exception may be taken against it, except you
meane if it were commaunded for ever and everywher, which must be your
meaninge. for what if the thing commaunded were but temporall, as was the

---

[204] Pharoah's dream, deciphered by Joseph: Genesis xli. 1–4, 17–31.

[205] Crick is grappling with Sandes's argument that the Christian Sabbath was commanded for
remembrance of the Resurrection, as the Jewish Sabbath was for the remembrance of the Creation;
which, as affirming the Resurrection as recreation, is a significant theological point. But Crick says
that other events, such as the Ascension, are equally as fit to be remembered as the Resurrection, and
he is unaware of any commandment (rather than an apostolic practice and institution) that the
Resurrection should, uniquely, be remembered by a divinely commanded weekly day.

[206] The whole of St Paul's Epistle to the Galatians is concerned with the problem of a church with its
roots in Judaism which has reverted to reliance on the old Law for salvation. See especially iv. 10:
'Yee observe dayes, and monethes, and times, and yeeres.'

anoynting with oile? or what if it being a ceremony matter grewe after unto most horrible abuse, as the brasen serpent?[207] lastlie, what if it were commaunded in respect of some place, as certayne thinges to the Corynthians? Now if yow make that your Proposition, then your Assumption is denied, which is so farre from being confirmed to be commaunded for ever and every wher by that place of P. that it is not confirmed from thence to be commaunded, for whie is this in the first daie of the weeke a commaundement then that in the Actes, in the first daie of the weeke, or that [fo. 21v] in the Apoc[alypse] in the lordes daie I <was> was in the spirite:[208] that is not the commaundement, but that which followeth tutching the collection, as if one knowing me to be ordenarely upon thexchange in London betwene eleven and twelve of the clocke shuld write unto me that upon thexchaung time I shuld deale in his busynes, he doth not enjoigne that I shuld be ther, but seyng I am there, that I shuld be a factor for him. And that this is no commaundement concerning the daie, it may appeare by Mr Bullinger, who having alledged this very place for prooffe of the custome of assembling this daie to the holie exercises of godes service, saieth that the churches receyved this daie at their owne choise, and not havinge any expresse commaundement: for ther is nether historie nor writer <may> wher this may be found. unto whom may be added Mr Martyr upon these wordes writinge, that it is stuble and firne [fern] to have one certeyne daie in the weeke geven up unto the worshipp of god but whether this or that daie be appointed it is temporall or chaungeable which nether of them could have said, if they had thought it commaunded there[209]

{Bulling in Apo. cap 1, v. 10[210] P. M. in 1 Cor[inthians] 16. 2.}[211]

2.   What necessitie is in this, that if no Church hath ever bene boulde to chaunge it, then no particuler Church maie do yt. What Church (till within these very few yeares if at all) hath bene bold to take away the feastes of Easter and Pentecost. Now if it be good reason that no Church maie chaunge this day now, bicause no Church hertofore hath changed yt, then this also holdeth that no Church now may utterly take away Easter or Pentecoste bycause none heretofore have done yt. the same might have bene said of the Lenten faste about 40 yeares paste, being never <til of>

---

[207] When the children of Israel were in the wilderness, Moses was commanded to set up a serpent of brass, which had the power miraculously to cure snake-bite (Numbers xxi. 8–9). In the New Testament (John iii. 14–15) this was a type for the crucifixion and its saving power. But the original brazen serpent later became a mere idol, an image in the Temple, and godly King Hezekiah broke it in pieces (2 Kings xviii. 4). Puritans connected this idolatrous image with the crosses in churches, and demanded that Queen Elizabeth play the part of Hezekiah in destroying them. Crick is arguing that the Sabbath, originally salvific, could be made into an idol.

[208] Revelation i. 10.

[209] Crick may be citing Heinrich Bullinger (1504–75) and Peter Martyr Vermigli (1499–1562) selectively and to his own advantage. Certainly Bullinger taught in his *Decades,* required reading for Elizabethan clergy, that the Sabbath was natural, universal and moral, a doctrine followed by the Anglo-Züricher John Hooper (Bullinger, *Decades* (Cambridge, Parker Society, 1849), I, 253–67; *Hooper, Early writings* (Cambridge, Parker Society, 1843), pp. 337–51). For essentially the same position in Martyr, see his *The common places,* tr. Anthony Marten (London, 1583), Part 2, pp. 374–7, and *In primum librum Mosis . . . commentarii* (Zurich, 1569), fos. 8v–9.

[210] H. Bullinger, *In Apocalypsim Jesu Christi* (Basel, 1559), pp. 13–14.

[211] Peter Martyr Vermigli, *In selectissimam D. Pauli priorem ad Corinthos epistolam* (Zürich, 1572), fos. 253r–v. '*In una sabbatorum quisque vestrum apud se deponat, recondens quicquid commodum fuerit: ne quum venero, tunc fiant collationes.*'

till of late daies utterly abrogated any where, for ought that I can lerne and soe within this 40 yeares this had bene no good argument. But what proffe is ther that it hath not bene chaunged at any tyme, but that everye Church hath reteyned it and held yt. I will shew some reason, why I think that it hath bene chaunged. Constantine the great made a law for the celebrating of that day and the sixt of the weeke, as it is manifest out of Sozomenus, { Sozom lib 1 Eccles. hist. cap 8}[212] which statute of his being made unto the Churches, is most likely to have had ground from their usinge of another day, which I do the rather gather bycause of Mr Bullinger his wordes, who makinge mention of this acte of the Emperor saieth: But this we have to understand that he renewed the custome of the Apostles and of the Catholike Church, rather then instituted any new thinge, for doth not that word, renewed the custome shew that it was almost worne out. for if it had bene commonly used, how might it well be said to be renewed? if it were fresh in use what need ther any renovation[213] Adde unto him Mr Beza and Danaeus. Now wheras you adde, no not the papistes, it is all one as though you sayde no Church hath bene bold to use her liberty in a ceremony, no not [fo. 22r] that malignant Church, which ever hath bene to servilely addicted unto ceremonies. And it seemeth unto me by your wordes that the universall Church may chaunge yt, for if you meane not soe, why did you not rather say the Church, then limite yt by adding the word particuler: which if you graunt me I gayne my question, which is not whether it maie be chaunged by this or that Church but whether it may be chaunged at all: yea that being aforded me, yt will followe first that it is no commaundement of thapostle which you sett downe seying the Church hath no more power to chaunge any precept then to turne the daie into nighte. Secondlie that a particuler Church may chaunge it for herself: which I prove by this argument: That which the universall Church may do for her self generally in a <~~counsell~~> councell oecumenical, the same may a particuler church national or provincial do for her self particulerly in a nationall or provinciall <~~counsell~~> councell for a particuler Church hath asmuch authority to take a particuler order for her owne private, as the whole hath to take a common order for the whole. If therfore that be graunted which I gather by your wordes, it falleth out that even a Church of a nation or Province might chaunge it if occasion served.

The name of the Lordes daie, dothe not shew it to be of his authoritie in commaundinge that the Church might take up that name bycause she tooke up that daye for the service of god. That thapostles put this name upon yt cannot be proved for it is one thing to call yt by a name and another to geve yt a name, for a thinge is called by a name, which it hath had geven of others, but it hath a name geven when it was not soe called before. And if they did put that name upon, yet it followeth not

---

[212] Hermias Sozomen, *Historia ecclesiastica*, book 1, cap 8. See *Patrologia Graeca*, ed. J. P. Migne (Paris, 1859), LXVII, col. 882.

[213] Henry Bullinger, *A hundred sermons upon the apocalipse of Jesu Christ* (London, 1573), fo. 14: 'it is to be understood that he rather renewed the custome of the Apostles and Catholicke Church than newly instituted the same.'

that it is not chaungeable if you inferre this, therfore the daie that is taken up by the Church shuld be soe called I will easely yeld.[214]

Towching the length of the day

I did not assume that which is confuted, but made yt a reason of yt which I assumed: which still I hold denying that ever the lord dispensed with other morall prohibitions. I have graunted that the lord upon necessity beareth with the leavinge of some thinges commaunded undone, soe ther be a mynd to doe yt, but I cannot aford yow, that he doth upon necessity allowe of the doing of that which is forbidden. for the lord shutting a man from all oportunity of doing that which is enjoined, he is free from blame when he doth it not, but in doing that which is forbidden, howsoever it be ther is a wickednes committed <which may answer to that which is said in the 3 place> No synne is dispensed with by God, whatsoever is prohibited in the morall law is synne ergo nothing prohibited in the morall law is dispensed with by God: which maie answer to that which is said in the 3 place. That which for prooffe is alledged of murder dispensed with in private persons, I do utterly deny. for when as our Savyor saieth whosoever is angry with his brother unadvisedly shalbe in daunger of judgment, but he that saieth to his brother Racha, shalbe in daunger of a counsell, but [fo. 22v] but he that saieth foole shalbe in daunger unto hell fier and when as every man is flatlie forbidden hatred, doth the lord dispense with private persons in murder, which is greater by manie degrees then the highest of these trespasses? Nay so farre is the lord from bearing with murder in a private man, that he could never abide it in any magistrate. for if he hath not winked at the putting of a malefactor to death with a corrupt eie (which appeareth by thexample of Jehu at whose handes he saieth he will require the bloud that was shedd,[215] although they were men of the lordes curse and by expresse commaundement appointed to the sword) hath he at any time borne with unjust violence in any of them.

The wordes of the commaundement are playne and lightsome forbidding not only the professing of common labor but the doing of any manner of worke even unto the gathering of a fewe stickes or kindling of a fire, or dressinge of a peece of meate. now to that, no more then in the rest of the commaundementes the thinges are not in all their kindes forbidden, but such ill use of them etc. I answer first nothing is forbidden in any of the commaundementes whereof all the kindes are not forbidden for if the generall, then also all the specials conteyned under it. and if anie of the specials comprehended underneath the speciall be excepted, then the generall is not prohibited: As if dishonoring of parentes and adultery be unlawfull generally, then can ther not be found one kynd of them allowable. Secondly in saying (But such ill

---

[214] From this it is clear that it would be incorrect to call Crick more 'moderate' than Sandes, who is shown to be inherently conservative in his attitude to the Sabbath. Crick comes close to equating Sandes's position with that of the papists. He argues that the fact that the Church Universal and particular churches have never abolished the feasts of Easter and Pentecost is no proof that those feasts could not be abolished, if an Ecumenical Council or even a particular church, such as the Church of England, were to decide to do so. Crick would presumably have applauded the abolition of the feast of Christmas by the English parliament in the 1640s.

[215] Jehu king of Israel carried out an almost genocidal slaughter of the house of King Ahab, and of all the followers of Baal. He had been anointed by God to do this, and although he himself subsequently failed to walk in the law of the Lord it is not clear from 2 Kings x or 2 Chronicles xxii that God required the blood that had been shed at his hands.

use of them) you insinuate some good use of the thinges forbidden, now when as nothing is forbidden but synne, it followeth that ther is some good use of synne.

4.   Howsoever Pawles example tutching his preaching in the night be extraordinary,[216] yet it maketh fitly to that purpose for which I alledged yt, which was to prove that our day shuld be holden rather from the risinge to the risinge, then from the sytting to the sitting of the sunne. Now when you say you do not thinke ther is in the inconveniences any such danger, tutching the first let the judgment be with others, but for the second I thinke I shall make it appeare a great inconvenience that the servauntes which cannot be occupied in stronge labor shuld not have sufficient rest to make them stronge therunto when Moses commaundeth that the mouth of the Oxe which treadeth out of the corne shuld not be musled,[217] meaning that sufficient provander shuld be allowed him, under that one kynd he comprehendethe all that is needfull for to make him lustie to endure labor and to goe through with his toylinge worke and therfore all sufficient rest and the beast were but poorely provided for, if he had his belly full of meate and wanted soe much rest as was needfull. Now if it be a great inconvenience and daungerous that the brute beastes being to labor in [fo. 23r] the morninge shuld be stunted of their needfull reste the nighte before, is it not a greater to have the servauntes pinched of it? If yt be iniquity toward a beast, is it equity toward a man? the rest on that day is to be streigthned, for if we be put altogether from the same speeches which are used at other tymes which those wordes of Esay shewe taken in that sence yow alledge them in:[218] and if we be abridged of all the same workes which are permitted us in the rest of the weeke, shall it be lawfull to take soe much rest as on another daye? then seying a man might somtyme rest from the syttinge unto the risinge of the sonne in the dead of winter perhaps 16. howres it may be permitted unto him also upon that Sabbothe: Now if it be cutt shorte and differ from the rest on other daies from whence shall we take the rule of the diversitye if not from this day of expiation, which was for all other thinges more like the Sabboth then anie of the feastes surely in my judgment ether from hence it is to be taken, or els no direction is geven at all. Sackcloth I remember none to have bene used upon that daie. Now unto these which seeme light I add further, that the Sabboth beinge from sunne rising to sunne rising the night before being no part of yt may be spent as other nightes so that we need not to prepare our selves to the Sabboths exercises before the sunne be up, that is to saye in some times of the yeare untill eight of the Clocke, when it is high time for us to resorte unto the Assemblies especially the supper being to be celebrated. But if this also seeme nothinge, yet how can this be avoyded as a great inconvenience? that it is as expreslie commaunded that the Sabb[oth] shuld be from Evening to Eveninge, as it is that ther shuld be a Sabboth and is confirmed by the first of your reasons, which by that I sette downe is manifestly encountred the lordes order being utterly inverted.

If you meane by the ceremonies those which moses instituted as you seeme to

---

[216] In Acts xx St Paul preaches at Troas 'unto midnight', causing the young man Eutychus to fall asleep and tumble out of the window.

[217] Deuteronomy xxv. 4: 'Thou shalt not mosel the oxe that treadeth out the corne.'

[218] Isaiah lviii. 13: 'If thou turne away thy fote from the Sabbath, from doing thy wil on mine holy day, and call the Sabbath a delite, to consecrat it, as glorious to the Lord, and shalt honour him, not doing thine owne waies, nor seking thine owne wil, nor speaking a vaine worde. . .'.

speake somwhat before and plainly sett downe in thende[219] nothing letteth the callinge backe of the orders of the Church in Abrahams tyme for it cannot be said that the rudenes of the Church then required or stood in need of any such ceremonies as he gave unto his people. As it cannot be said that the Church under him stood in need of the ceremonies that the Church hath now no more than it may be saide that the infant or suckling child hath need of stronge meate for if they had needed any such, it shuld not have stoode with the lordes beneficence to have witholden it. If you meane simplie whatsoever yow speake for a naturall day, I will from hence speake for the very <7 proh> 7 day for if the beinge of the order before etc. shalbe the <order> cause of kepinge the order still, then the being of the 7th day before etc shalbe cause of kepinge [fo. 23v] the 7. day for what color of reason is ther whie the beinge of the order before that time shuld not have strength inough for the retayninge of yt. If you say bycause the 7. day was ceremoniall but the order was not, besides that you take the question for graunted your Assumption which must be added will not be fitte, for the order of kepinge the Sabb[oth] a naturall daie was not before the Sabb[oth] but after yt as the order of dressinge the garden of Paradise was after the garden planted and man placed in yt. Now the truth is that at the begynning the Church needed ceremonies for what were the tree of liffe and the tree of knowledge of good and evill but ceremonies and what was that 7. day but a ceremony. If Adam did not need them wherfore did the lord appoint them being superfluous? And soe I come to answer your reason, which is that if Adam needed 24. howres we need then much more, for by the same reason it may be said that if adam needed those ceremonies we need them much more. But the truth is that we can no more say, If he had need of that then we much more then we can say, If Abraham had need of Circumcision then we have more need of Circumcision or if the Jewes had need of many feast daies then we have much more, the reason wherof is for that it was a ceremony appointed for him in that tyme. Now although in the Thesis the reason be good, If Adam needed a ceremony to helpe him we much more, yet it holdeth not in the Hypothesis that if he needed this therfore we need the same, seying the lord hath provided us of more excellent and more significant. and therfore if it shuld be graunted that we have more need, it followeth not therof that we must hold that rate of tyme, for if bicause we have more need of 24. howres then he therfore we be bounde to hold 24. howres, then bycause we have more need of fowrescore howres then he had of 24 we be bounde to hold 4. score and bycause we have more need of 10 Sacramentes then he had of two (our faith being weaker and we having tenne tymes greater matters to be put in mynd of) therfore we be bounde to have tenne. But I do deny that we have more need beinge otherwise provided for and by this which is said, I thinke that is answered which was illedged of Adam for the Resur[rection] day.

For the seconde a man may make himself busynes enough for six daies if he will, but I thinke they were not precisely tyed to all that which is set downe by yow. for the last let it be judged by that said on both sydes.[220]

---

[219] See above (fo. 19r), pp. 56–7.

[220] In exposing the fallacy that because the Jews had need of feast days and ceremonies Christians have all the more need, Crick is anticipating the polemic of future anti-sabbatarians that strict sabbatarianism was 'judaical' and most logically expressed in the seventh-day sabbatarianism which made its appearance in the seventeenth century.

Towching the rest of the Sabboth:

The thinges that I rehersed are in deed ceremoniall, as that commaundement for not labouring ys. but ceremoniall appendices they can no more fitly be called, then those preceptes of not [fo. 24r] uncovering the shame of ones mother, or sister, or daughter, or Aunt, can be called morall appendices of that commaundement thou shalt not committ adultry which be in deed species *illius generis*. If any of those thinges were for the wildernes, it skilleth not except the grounde of the commaunding of them was taken from the subject of the place for if the grounde of the commaunding of them was taken from the subjecte of the day, they will hold as longe as that holdeth, if either the same or the like occasion shuld fall out in the land of Canaan. As for example: The <cond> commaundement of not going forth to gather man[221] upon the Sabb[oth] being grounded upon this bicause it is the Sabboth wold bynd them from gathering any thing upon the Sabb[oth] even in their cuntrey. Howbeit this I say that if they had in ether place more libertie then in other I thinke they had it in the wildernes even in this matter of rest which I gather bicause in other thinges as precisely enjoigned as the rest, they had more freedome ther than at home. for although the Passeover were commaunded to be holded once every yeare yet during their abode in the desert it was celebrated but once in 40 yeares. Now to have spoken accordingly yow shuld have said That those do no more make this commaundement ceremoniall, then these and the like of not eating the swyne, nor the cony, nor the hare, nor the strangled, nor bloude maketh the forbidding of uncleane meates ceremoniall or then these of not killinge upon the yong this fowle or that fowle maketh the commaundement of not killinge the damme upon them of that sorte besides I brought not those thinges to make the commaundement ceremoniall, but to make playne what speciall thinges were forbidden in that generall precept (thou shalt doe no manner of worke upon the Sabboth)
I persuade myself the Sabb[oth] was such a signe unto them, as other so called were 1. a seale of blessinges and good thinges promised as the Rainbow that sealed up to Noah that the world shuld no more be drowned with water.[222] And as Circumcision which sealed unto Abraham that god was his god and he with his seed his people[223] and as the lamb which sealed up the delyveraunce from Pharao, and as the bloud upon the dore cheekes which sealed up the Aungels passing by them when he wold smite the Egiptians[224] for paule to the Coll[ossians] saieth let no man judge you in meates or drinkes or in respect of a feast or of a new <moone> moone or of a Sabboth (for soe τη σαββάτων is often used, and here must be soe taken) which are a shadow of thinges to come wherof Christ is the body:[225] wherby it appeareth that it is not called a signe bycause it is a common document as yow speake but bicause it caried a lively representacion of some good thing to come by Christ Jesus which was sanctification, as it is said in that place and els wher. And therfore the

---

[221] I.e. manna ('MAN' in the Geneva Bible). The children of Israel gathered enough manna on the sixth day to last over the Sabbath (Exodus xvi. 15, 22–4).

[222] Genesis ix. 15.

[223] Genesis xvii.

[224] Exodus xii. 22–3.

[225] Colossians ii. 16–17: 'Let no man therefore condemne you in meate and drinke, or in respect of an holy day, or of the new moone, or of the Sabbath dayes. Which are but a shadow of thinges to come'.

comparison yow make is not even, but thus had it bene fitte: It is a signe assuring you that I do sanctify yow, as the absteyninge from bloud and the not killinge of the damme upon her yonge is a signe that I will have you free from all cruelty. Nether doth Tremelis call yt *commune documentum*[226] bycause it hath no sacramentall signification, but [fo. 24v] but bicause it is a signe not proper ether to god or to the people but common to them both as moses saieth a signe betwene me and betwene yow on my part that I do sanctify you; on your part that yow ar not only to looke for sanctification from me, but also that you are to walke holily and purely with me as moses and Ezechiell speake of it.[227] and soe is answered that which followeth, wher also is τὸ χρινόμενον and that which is added of the servauntes for although it be not spoken in expresse wordes touching them yet the wordes appertayne unto them, for they being directed unto all the Church, ether the servauntes are none of the Church or els they are comprehended and aswell may yt be thought not to be spoken of the maisters, seying they be no more named then thother. But tutching them and the Cattell my reasons be not answered and therefore I say no more. now wheras you say that the difference of other feastes from this doth shew this to be more then ceremoniall, If you had said doth shew this to be more ceremoniall, you had said righte, but in saying it appeareth herby to be more then ceremoniall, i: morall what hindreth but that the day of expiation[228] which for the rest was holden as streitly (if not more) as the Sabboth and so differeth from thother feastes shalbe made by this meanes more then ceremoniall id est morall also for yt is not needfull that bicause they all served to one end, therefore they must have all the same observances, when as our fastes serve to the same end with the Jewes fastes that is to humble us as theirs to humble them, and our Sacramentes serve to the same end with theirs to helpe our faith as theirs to helpe their faith and yet nether thone nor thother are to be tyed to the same observacion.

3. If upon that already alledged and hereafter to be spoken it appeareth that the precise rest of the day was ceremoniall, the punishment cannot be brought into the common welth, but the ceremony must be revived in the Church which our savyor hath buryed longe synce. If it were morall you said true, but that I do not graunt yow. The Sabb[oth] is broken not only in doing servile worke apperteyninge to this present liffe but in makinge the holie garmentes and you in speaking of the breach of it shuld for the matching of thone member of your sentence with thother have sayde, the breaking is not in any servile worke, no more then the breaking of the sixt is in any manner of murdering (not in every manner of killinge) both which are false.

4. To this I say no more then hath bene save this, If the forbiddinge of worke be a morall precepte, working of necessity is not to be matched with the lawfull use of mariage but with whordome of necessity, which if it had bene lawfull Josephe might

[226] Tremellius, *Biblia Sacra* (London, 1580) in commenting on '*signum*' found in Exodus xxxi. 13, calls this '*documentum commune inter nos, mei ut creatoris et sanctificantis, vestri autem, ut qui creati estis et sanctificati: ideo subjungit, ad cognoscendum, q. d. quod observari jubeo, ut eius observatione haec cognoscatis.*'
[227] Exodus xxxi. 13–17; Ezekiel xx. 20.
[228] The annual day of atonement, Yom Kippur, as still observed by Jews.

have quitte himself of much trouble that he fell into[229] and for not doing of it is worthy of blame rather then any commendation.

5.6.7   What was their Hypothesis against which our savyor christ disputeth? that their constitutions shuld not be broken? nothing lesse, for they do not aske why the disciples did transgresse the traditions of the elders, which they wold have done if that had bene their quarrell, as they were wont to doe [fo. 25r] at other tymes, but they aske why they did that which they might not doe upon the Sabboth. and our Savyor wold not patiently have borne them inforcing their owne constitution, but have rated them as he was wont to doe upon that occasion. Besides if the question had bene concerning the breaking not of a Sabb[oth] but of a Pharisaicall custome our lord Jesus might have spared all that labor which he bestoweth in the defence of his disciples facte, this one answer being sufficient to have put them to silence that like hipocrites they were over eger in maynteyninge the devises of their owne head. Lastly not one of the three Evangelistes directing us unto this opynion by the light of soe much as one little sillable but with one mouth setting downe the state of that question that of their constitution is to be refused. The reason whie you thinke this to have bene their Hypothesis bycause they made the rest a part of the service of god of their owne head, if yt were true doth not enforce that which is set downe. But in deed it is not true for the lord himself did appoint the rest as a part of his service, as the absteyninge from meates, the washinges and purifyinges, the offringes of sacrifices were partes of his ceremoniall service and aswell in that as in these were they bounde to serve him. they were in that as in all other autward thinges more precise than the lawgiver: but he did assuredly make yt a part of his service for that presente. your reason to prove yt to have bene made a part of godes service by them holdeth not. for as the rest was not soe nether were the clensinges and washinges and sacrifices and solemnities commaunded for themselves but for another ende, which yet were from heaven and not from men. Therefore Christ doth not argue from the greater, If godes institutions may be mitigated, yors may much more: but from equals, if necessity might beare out david in that he dyd, necessity may beare out my disciples in this fact of theirs.[230]

That you add, viz the debate to have bene concerninge another Sabb[oth] may be denied with verie good reason, for if they had reproved the disciples for doing that as unlawfull upon any such Sabb[oth], our savyor had not needed to use those argumentes in their defence, but might with one word have ended all that quarrell, by saying, though it be not permitted unto men upon the principall Sabb[oth] to dresse any meate, yet upon these Sabb[oths] the law geveth liberty to make their provision. {Exo[dus] 12}   for the lord saieth upon the first and last of the Passeover thou shalt do no worke save about that which thou shalt eate and if this might be done before men did feele the bytinges of hunger, may not my disciples

---

[229] Potiphar's wife attempted to seduce Joseph, a Hebrew servant in her husband's house, and, when he rejected her advances, accused him of indecent assault, which led to his imprisonment. The argument is that if Joseph had taken the easy way out and slept with Potiphar's wife, he would have saved himself a lot of bother but that 'necessity' is no let-out from the operation of the moral law, in this case the law against adultery (Genesis xxxix).

[230] The story of the disciples plucking corn. See above, n. 197. At this point occurs the most sophisticated and learned passage in the debate, involving comparison of the three synoptic accounts, and the meaning of a number of Greek terms. See Primus, *Holy time*, pp. 49–50.

rubb in their handes a few eares of corne in their hunger. Nether is your prooff sufficient, bycause luke calleth yt δευτεροπρῶτον for first it is not gayned that it was
such a Sabb[oth] as yow speake of, the second after the firste. for not to speake of
the harshnes of this phrase, seconde after the first, it cannot be shewed in all the new
Testament that any of those feast daies are called by the name of Sabboth. I deny not
but they may be called soe in the lawe, but in the new Testa[ment] they are never so
termed but generally a feast and the first or last daie of the feast. wherupon (if in a
doubtfull matter I may shew my conjecture) I gather that by Sabb[oth] δευτ is
ment such a principall Sabb[oth] as had a second sabboth or feast day falling
upon it. such a one as St John calleth {John 19. 31} μεγάλην των ἡμέραν ἐκείνου
τόυ σαββάτου which I gesse bycause that St Luke saieth ἐν σαββατω δευτερ:
mat[thew] and mar[k] say ἔν τοις σαββασιν now although I deny not but
sometyme ther is a *Synecdoctre numeri* yet these being compared together, I see no
cause why we shuld flee unto that here. In which sentence I am yet more confirmed
by Mr Beza who interpreting δευτεροπ: in luke the last of the feast of unleavened
bread, upon mat[t]h[ew]. against Erasmus [fo. 25v] taking τοῖς σαββάσι for the
weeke saieth ther is no cause to understand yt of the weeke for that here the question
is of the 7th day and that a solempne one Luke sheweth nether could this murmure
of the Jewes have risen upon another day bycause the disciples had broken no lawe.
and if this will not serve looke Theophilact in 20 Joh,[231]

οἱ Ἰουδαῖοι πᾶσαν ἑορτὴν σάββατον, ὠνόμαζον ἀνάπαυσις γὰρ τὸ σάββατον
πολλάκις οὖν ἀπήντα ἡ ἑορτὴ ἐν τή παρασκευῆ και ἐκάλουν τὴν παρασκευὴν
σάββατον διὰ τὴν ἑορτὴν εἶτα τὸ κυρίως σάββατον ὠνόμαζον δευτερόπρωτον,
ὡς δεύτερον ὄν προηγησαμένης ἄλλης ἑορτῆς καὶ σαββάτου.

Secondly if it were granted that by δευτ: is ment such a Sabb[oth] as you would yet
this is no necessary conclusion, the fact was done upon that day, ergo the debate
betwene them was about that day or no other, seying we know that upon one facte of
our savyors upon one Sabb[oth] the pharises fall into a generall dispute tutching
every sabboth and the wordes are why do thy disciples that which is not lawfull to
doe upon the Sabb[oth] and not upon this Sabb[oth] and the answer of our savyor is
also generall and you in answering unto my 8th argument, taking the Sabb[oth]
properly, shew that it is so to be taken in all the dispute, except yow can give a
reason to the contrary. now if yt be said, that then they both must needes take that
day for a Sabb[oth] and our lord might have answered as in the lawe: I answer
perhaps they thought soe: but that notwithstanding our lord knowing their question
to be proposed by them generally, not meddlinge with their opinion whatsoever it
was, but leaving it unto themselves bycause they did not utter yt answereth
according as the question is proposed unto him.

8.   Last of all, your interpretation of making the Sabb[oth] for man to be that
which is said that his servaunt mighte have some rest is not warrantable. for why
shuld man signify the servaunt rather then the Master and not both, yea all, one and
other. If it signify him only, seying that which is added of the sonne of man being
lord of the sabboth also being a conclusion inferred theron must be understood of

---

[231] Crick is in error. The Greek passage is from Theophylact's commentary on Luke chapter 6. See
Patrologia Graeca, ed. J. P. Migne (Paris, 1859), CXXIII, col. 768.

him of whom that which went before is spoken and no other, it followeth that he only is lord of the Sabb[oth]: Againe if by being made for him, he ment appointed for his reste, it is nothing to the question which is in hande, it not being whether the disciples might rest or noe but whether they might doe any kynd of worke, for how followeth this, the Sabb[oth] was made for man to rest in, therfore it is lawfull for my disciples to do some worke on it as to plucke eares of corne, for further answere, see that which I have written before <that is> which is not answered.

[fo. 26r]

{This with the rest of the lettres following I here insert bicause they were spoken of in our metinges}[232]

To his verie deare frinde and right faithfull brother in the Lorde Mr Thomas Cartewrighte[233] delyver these

{4 meeting. 3 foll}

Grace and peace: My right deare brother, I have in some measure mourned for your afflictions, and not alwaies forgott to entreate the Almightie for a speedy and happie issue therout of, with a desire to have seene your face before this, if in respecte of my late weakened bodie with longe sicknes, and the sharpenes of the wether, I mighte safelie have traveyled soe farre:[234] which I mention not bicause I feare any faintinge in your love (which I freelie acknowledge to have alwaies in wonderfull strength, sweetnes and plentie flowed unto very many, and me especially, though unworthy) but rather to minister some matter as armor to your mynd with more ease to repell all cogitations of any unkindnes that mighte invade the same by meanes of anie longe absence or silence, a shewe I confesse of unworthie forgetfulnes. thus much by way of excuse, more than inough as yow will take yt, according to your old and constante curtesy. Now to minister comforte, I find my self much more readie in mynd, then able to performe, as in sondry respects so in this especiallie, that I am soe farre behind yow in experience of trouble, the best and happiest doctrix how to apply fitte medicines to such patients, for if I bringe any thinge that mighte ease some common patient, yt wilbe too weake or unseasonable, that and much more having bene found out by your selfe before: And if you sawe not, nor felte all (for who doeth) yet now all the wante happely is supplied by other Phisitions of greater valewe, which have prevented me in this care. yet one thinge encourageth me, a

[232] Richard Parker's cross-references to the meetings to which these letters allegedly related are not always to be relied upon. In particular, the first letter which follows, from Edmund Chapman to Thomas Cartwright, postdates the fourth meeting of the conference by six years, and has nothing to do with Cartwright's *Confutation of the Rhemists* Translation.

[233] From the internal evidence of this letter, Chapman was writing to Cartwright in 1589, or even 1590 (but 1589 is more likely, in that the letter remained in Parker's hands). When Chapman wrote, Richard Bancroft was closing in on a number of ministers, most of them from Northamptonshire and Warwickshire, whose involvement in the conference movement would be put on trial, first before the high commission and then in star chamber. Cartwright (who was Master of the earl of Leicester's hospital in Warwick) was dealt with last, being sent for in May 1590, but only examined in October, when he joined the other ministers in prison (the Fleet in his case) for his refusal to take the *ex officio* oath. See Collinson, *EPM,* pp. 408–11; Scott Pearson, *Thomas Cartwright*, pp. 315–20.

[234] Evidently Cartwright was still at Warwick when Chapman wrote.

persuasion that you longe to receive some thinge at my hande, as one that loveth yow well, soe as all defecte of skill on my parte may possibly be helped by the intention of your appetite. And where may I better begynne then at the cause of your smarte, which was not any affinity you ever had with that marre matter marten,[235] for I am a witnes (beside a thowsand other) what small pleasure you ever tooke in such inventions: but your earnest and open profession of grieff for the wante of perfecte comlines and bewty in this english spouse of your maister, which you desired and laboured according to the best of your skill and power to have made more pure and amiable in his eie. Now that this your zealous endevoure is noe better taken, nor of some of your fellow friendes of this bridegroome, yt may well adde unto your grief, but yt may not take away all your comforte, seeing the bride-groome will not soe much waighe, what you have done for him as what you mente to doe, nor how your endevors were taken by his other servauntes, as how they were to be taken. And that the more rebuke you susteyne for his sake, the more honor he will geve you one day, if you still contynue faithfull to him, loving to his spowse, and seeke also soe much as lieth in yow to be at peace with the rest of his houshold servauntes, howsoever they be displeased with yow for a tyme as mistakinge that which by yow was gratiously entended. And what though now after a second vew of your proceedinges in this great cause of Church goverment, yow find that some thinges are not unjustly found fault withall, yet oughte not that much afflicte yow, seeing yow are not the first man of fame, lerninge and piety, that have confessed and retracted some error, if the substantiall and mayne pointes of your worke stande. Regard not soe much the disgrace that may happen in matter, forme or proportion. Eleazar, Joshua and the rest of those chieff fathers of Israell missed in their division of Canaan to the 12 tribes, laying out to some to little and to other to much. The Apostles, and sometymes in some pointes the auncyent fathers left not their workes perfecte to posterity and the famous Instrumentes of restoring the purity of Christianisme in our age and in our english Church sawe not all ether in doctryne or discipline as is confessed of all partes. Therefore let yt not seeme any great matter in your eies, if you see now more then yow did at the first. If you have profited all this while (if the worke were to begynne againe yow could mend some peece of the matter or manner of yt) compte yt rather a large consolation and joy to your harte, that by yow as an instrument some good thinges haue bene put forwarde, some evell is discovered and begonn to be reformed. And what know yow or we, whether all the fruites of your labors, be yet risen and sprunge up, or lie still closse and hidden

---

[235] The clandestine publication of the pamphlets ostensibly written by 'Martin Marprelate' between October 1588 and July 1589, high quality satire against the bishops but according to the values of the time seditious libels, was a last desperate throw by some agitators for presbyterianism (including the MP Job Throkmorton, their most likely author), but a tactic which has been compared to the use of poison gas in warfare, which can blow back in the faces of those discharging it. It led to raids on many of the studies of godly ministers, especially in the Midlands, and the uncovering of the evidence used in the High Commission and star chamber trials. However, Cartwright was only one of many puritan ministers who distanced himself from 'Martin', assuring Burghley that 'from the first beginning of martin unto this day, I have continually upon any occasion testified both my mislike and sorrow for such kind of disordered proceeding' (Collinson, *EPM*, p. 393). But 'marre matter marten' (a construction unique to this letter) suggests that even grave ministers joined in the flurry of word-play which Martin provoked. The extraordinarily thorough Scott Pearson appears to have overlooked this letter, although he made use of Rylands English MS 874 when it was still the 'Gurney MS'.

under the grounde, bicause of the stormy and sharpe seasons and winterlike wether. A man may well take pleasure in a peece of worke, that many fare the better for, though it cost him deere. Wherfore if these tedious and manifold molestacions yeld some good fruicte to your selfe, that you might not be to high lifted up in the world, in the church or in your self, (as yt was with that noble Apostle by the most gratious providence of his god) if satan have lost by them, and Christ have gayned, if his spowse with us be growing in any respecte to some more comlynes and fruictfulnes if many be moved to mourne for your estate, and to pray for good issues, if your brethren happelie enjoy some more peace by your paynes, if such as speake roughly against yow acknowledge yet in their hartes, that they have lerned and gotten some good by that, which as yet they cannot soe well brooke: doe yow not see, that albeit your threde have not runne soe easely and evenly without knottes nor your webbe fallen out in such length and sise as yow looked for, nor soe farre and free from slaunder, yet yow have noe [fo. 26v] cause to repente that ever you <put>tooke yt in hande. What remayneth then but this that you advaunce yourselfe above all discomfortes, bringing forth your best presentes and fattest sacrifices of thankes-giving and praier, that your oversightes in matter or manner (If any such yow knowe) bene covered the good thinges you have bene fitted for and enabled unto may receive in due tyme such a blessinge upon them from his good hande, that is the Author therof, as may most redound to the joy of many, the good of all, and his owne everlasting praise: To whom be all thankes for his great mercy towardes yow, and us all in our Lord Jesus. Amen Amen. Thus praying yow (my good brother) almost with teares, to accepte in good parte, that I have written, and to pray for me and myne still, I take my leave for this tyme, hoping to see yow shortlie if god will. Salute good Mrs Cartwrighte, trustinge verelie that she is able even to mynister comforte to others if need be. my sicklie wieff[236] saluteth yow both hartelie.
Yours in Christ Jesus ever by his grace,
Edmunde Chapman

To our most reverend brother and fellow minister Mr Thomas Cartwrighte Pastor to the Church of the english merchauntes at Middleboroughe.[237]

In wrestling with brethren, who have set themselves with all their power to uphold those Romishe windshaken and ruynous walles, wherwith the goodly Orchard of the lord amongst us is compassed, not to the keping out, but to the letting in of all savage beastes that seeke to roote up and make havocke of the pleasaunte plantes that growe there, and to deface all that bewty which yt hath, what strength is in your armes and legges if the favourers of the same cause with yow shuld not with all thankfulnes to god acknowledge: yet the adversaries silence (of whom though now and then one (to shew that he wold bite if he could,) barketh and bawleth in some

---

[236] Susan Chapman nevertheless survived her husband: See *BR*, pp. 194–5 below.

[237] This letter does relate to the motion made on 8 April 1583 (**4M**) to write to Cartwright to encourage him 'to undertake the answeringe of the Rhemish Testament'. Cartwright had moved, with the Merchant Adventurers, from Antwerp to Middelburg in October 1582. He would return to England in April 1585. See Scott Pearson, *Thomas Cartwright*, pp. 187–8, 228–9.

corners, yet none is found willinge as afore, to undertake the shoringe, and proppinge up of that rotten buildinge, which the good hand of god by yow, have made to bend almost to the grounde) doth sufficientlie proclayme. Now Sir, yt remayneth that accordinglie, you shuld cause the enemies of us all to feele the deadlie stroke of your hand, in smiting of the head of that ill favoured and mishapen birth, (the Jesuits Translation) which after soe many yeares travell, they have at lengthe broughte forth unto us: wherin also, though a monster, they and theirs doe noe lesse delighte then if yt were a bewtifull child, or rather some mighty man, whom none is able to looke in the face, much lesse to throwe to the grounde. which enterprise, that yow would take in hand although consideringe how yow are worne with labors and cares continually, we cannot well open our mouthes once to aske, yet seeing <god> how god hath all manner waies furnished you with power, above any of his servauntes amongst us, for his Churches sake to serve her to the vanquishinge even of an hoste of proude Goliathes that shall put themselves in armes against hir we doe most earnestlie with all our hartes besech yow (and if <yo> we your brethren which are moe then yow, can doe any more than besech, we doe yt) that you will undertake cherfullie and with good courage, all excuses set apparte, and spedelie out of hand without delay, this great affaire: dispatch this monster that is come out of the Campe of these uncircumcised, to chalenge (as yt were), and we thinke that they which have set him forth being discouraged, will forsake the field, and turne their backes upon us. but whether they will or noe, the lordes army, as well the chieff Capteyns as the souldiers, being greatlie comforted by the foyle of the adversary shalbe forced to singe, He and he have slayne their thowsands, but this man of God hath slayne his tenne Thowsandes. And besides that, the performance of this enterprise may be a good meane to insynuate yow into the hartes of the highest magistrates to the restoring of yow unto us, and unto the service of the Church in some more highe and open place. Assure your selfe that yow shall doe a worthie peece of service unto God, which wilbe a cause of much peace unto your soule: therfore if yow have receyved all that yow have, to the relieff of the Church being any waies assalted, if you care for the discouragemente of the desperate enemy and the comforte of all your brethren, if you like to be brought into favoure to the greater and more publike use of those noble graces wherwith yow be endued: To conclude, if yow take any pleasure in doing that service which is acceptable to him, who hath called you and will bringe quietnes to your owne conscience, gird your sword unto your thighe, go forward in this strength of yours, make naked your arme, fighte manfully this battle and prevaile. we for our partes, soe long as yow are in the skirmishe, will hold up unto our god (as our weake handes will geve us leave) that staffe wherby he worketh all his miracles, and geveth all his victories unto his servauntes. Thus with our [fo. 27r] humble praiers unto our good god, for your good successe in your mynistery, and for the stirringe of yow up to this holie busynes, and the blessinge of yow in yt, we take our leave, desiringe yow to remember us with our Charges. From dedham. 19 Aprill. 1583.
your lovynge and faithfull brethren.

Edmund Chapman:	Richard Crick.
Thomas Farrur.	William Teye
Richard Dowe:	Thomas Stoughton.
Thomas Morse:	Richard Parker.

To his most loving and reverend brethren the mynisters of Suffolke and Essex to be directed unto them by the handes of mr doctor Chapman and mr Knewstub.[238]

To tell you the truth, my reverend and loving brethren, havinge bene diversly and earnestlie delte with in the same suite that yow write me of, I yelded my weake shulders unto soe heavy a burden, wherfore although I knowe, what interest yow have even to command me in the thinges which I can conveniently doe, yet having geven my promise before your request, I wante some parte of the comforte which I shuld have receyved, if your demaund had prevented my promise, for I shuld by soe much more have undertaken the worke with greater assurance, as by a fuller consent of the godlie lerned brethren, I mighte have heard the lord more plainly and more distinctly speaking unto me: howbeit your godlie carefull letters (I hope) shall not want their fruite in this matter, for although they cannot prevaile to cause me to undertake this labor, yet they shall (I hope in the lord, serve to stirre me up to a further diligence, wherby I may the rather overcome some of those imperfections which through myne infirmities and insufficiencies are like to cleame [i.e. stick to] myne answer. And although they could not (coming somewhat late) move me to enter this way, yet shall they serve me through the comfort of them to contynue the waie already entred upon. But well you know wherin the comfort of them standeth not verelie therein, that you promise yourselves soe much furniture in me which I esteeme much more in diverse of the brethren, whereof I know some amongst yow and in your partes, but in the only sufficiency of the Lorde. A good parte of the provision wherof I looke for from your godlie and faithfull praiers. and therfore I humblie desire yow by all those thinges which you adjure me by, and especially by the glorie of our god, and of his sonne Jesus christ our onlie lorde that yow wold strive with me day and nighte, for a mercifull and contynuall supply of all wisdome and strengthe for that victorie, wherby our david as the Prophet calleth him) may in the renowne of his noble actes not only contynue his kingdome over the faithfull in our londe as it were over two tribes therof, but that all the Israell of god which he hath amongst us forsaking the wicked house of Saull may come as yt were one man to annoynt our saviour Christ over them to be their kinge, and the kinge of their posterity for evermore. So shall yow also bynd me, which unrequired have yow in contynuall remembraunce, to a more neere care for yow in my praiers that yow may fulfill your mynisterie, so that having rejoiced many through the peace of your embassage, your selves may have a rich harvest of everlasting comforte, according to the comforte wherwith yow have comforted others. From Middleborough the 5. of May the morow after the receipt of your loving <la> letters.
your bounden and lovinge brother.
Thomas Cartwrighte

---

[238] Cartwright replied by return of post to the letters he had received from Dedham, and from John Knewstub, presumably in the names of members of the Suffolk conference of which he was the leading light. This letter may be not unkindly described as consisting of pious flannel.

To my most lovinge frind and christian brother mr Thomas Cartwright [be these] d[elivere]d[239]

Sir, I acknowledge with my brethren how excellent a benefite yt were to enjoy your conference at home in our owne Churche, but seeing that is still denied us for our unthankfulnes we are forced to require your counsell by writinge. and although I fully purposed not to have interrupted your studie before the perfectinge of that worthie worke the lord hath set yow aboute, yet presuminge of your patience, and desiring earnestly to be confirmed, or reformed in a cause of some weighte (as I take yt) I could spare yow noe longer. The cause is that miserable distraction that is betwene the preachers and professors of our english church for matters of ecclesiasticall governmente, which bicause yt waxeth stronger daily, and yeldeth forth manifold and fearfull offences, with small evidence or hope of good to springe there out, I confesse to yow, my most entier brother, that I feele in myself some dislike of both partes for their hotte and violent manner of proceedinge, ether seeking by all meanes to conquere and deface thother, not dulie regarding the holie communion they have in their head Christ Jesus, and among themselves being fellow members of him. I know the truth is pretious and must be maynteyned and stood for, and put forward as far as any waie is made open for yt: But I most humblie and earnestlie desire yow in whom I have long observed a speciall grace of sober and uprighte judgmente, to imparte with me some of your holy meditations in this behalf, as whether a more mild and brotherlie course were not to be taken up of <us> us for the framinge aswell of their affections as of their judgments to some better acceptation of us, and our cause, which being [fo. 27v] better approved and blessed of the Lorde, that huge blocke of our to open and bitter dissention mighte be taken out of their way that are yet to enter into the Church, the comfortes of all the professors might more abound, and a great deale of synne now committed in harte, gestures, speeches, practises and hard dealinges on both sides beaten back and prevented: which if it have come into your mynd with any allowaunce, I wold most gladlie be made partaker of it, with your best direction, if not now during the Parliament (a fytt tyme to deale for peace) yet afterward at your best leysure, what way might best be taken for the execution of any such good course, as might most stand with the rule of the holy word of God. Thus desiring yow unfeignedly to lay out your judgment freelie of this motion, I rest in this mynd not to imparte with any other brother what I thinke of it till I shall heare from yow. Thus not forgetting to entreate the lord of liff for your good estate and for yours to whom I pray yow make my very hartie commendacions, I cease for this tyme.

Dedham 4. November 1584.

To you greatlie beholden.

Edmunde Chapman.

---

[239] This is remarkable evidence of Edmund Chapman's extreme moderation. Not even those ministers who offered qualified subscriptions to Whitgift's articles are on record as expressing 'dislike of both partes for their hotte and violent manner of proceeding', or to have regarded the parliament of 1584 as an opportunity 'to deale for peace'.

{This letter was an answer of my letter following though it be set before it}

To his loving brother in Christ and fellow labourer in the worke of the Lorde, Mr
Parker Pastor to the Church at dedham, be these d[elivere]d.

Grace mercy and peace be multiplied upon yow etc I receyved your christian lettres
gratulatory, ministring partlie joy but most cause of sorow, in respecte of the obstinate ambitious tiranny of that Prelate in suspending your mynistery, and staying the
free course of the Gosple in your Church notwithstanding these daungerous daies,
when most need is of the Chariots and horses of Israell, and the Trumpets with
loude voices sounded to the battle that Joshua fighting the Lordes battle against the
Amalekites, Moses, Aaron and Hur shuld hold up their handes to the Lorde. the
Prelates profaninge of that holie ordynance of fasting[240] encreaseth this sorow
conceaved of a manifest prognostication of the Lordes wrath against this land in
hardening their hartes and stopping their eies and eares from seeing or hearing the
lamentable compleyninges of the estate of the Churches, but the Lord wilbe
revenged on them, and howsoever yow according to the measure of grace given
you, do apply their cruelty to your synnes, yet they respecte the contrary, even the
punishing of the gratious giftes of god in yow and would by subtelty or tiranny
quench the spirite of god in you. but stand fast, kepe a good conscience and yeld not
a hooffe, imitatinge the faithfull courage and constancy of moses in removing all
out of Egipt: Concerninge the fast appointed I pray yow certify me forthwith what
order doctor Chapman with other the godly brethren doe take, that we about Peldon
may joigne with one uniforme consent, or whether they deferre yt untill the next
meetinge, which I thinke wold be best for some considerations, if other Churches do
not begynn before, therfore in my judgment other faithfull brethren wold be
consulted with that with one harte, mynd and order, the Churches mighte deale with
the Lorde by fervent prayer, and make a manifest and open contradiction to the
B[ishop]'s superstitious or profane fastinge and mumbling of their mattens, so as
the common ignorant people may plainely see the difference betwene the glorious
ordinaunce of the Lord, and the imagined shadow of the B[ishop]'s traditions.
Salute doctor Chapman and other the saincts of god withall your wives: The lord
blesse you and encourage yow in this triall of your faith, beseching him to restore
yow to the worke of your mynistery. farewell. From Laierdelehay. 22. decembris.
yours in the lord to use.
W. Teye

---

[240] Partly because the date of this letter is uncertain, it is not possible to identify the officially
promulgated fast to which Tey evidently refers. There was a kind of antiphone in the Elizabethan
Church between such publicly authorized fasts and the very different arrangements (whole days of
preaching) associated with puritanism. In 1581 Archbishop Edwin Sandys had warned Bishop
William Chaderton of Chester that he was 'noted to yelde to muche to general Fastings, all the Daie
Preachinge and Prayinge. Verilie a good Exercise in Time and upon just Occasion, when yt cometh
from good Auchthoritye. But (when there is none Occasion, nether the Thing commaunded by the
Prince or Synod) the wisest and best learned cannot like of yt, nether will her Majestie permitt it'
(Francis Peck, *Desiderata Curiosa,* Lib. III (London, 1732), p. 29).

To my faithfull brother in the Lord Mr Tay
Pastor to the Church of God in Peldon.

The grace of the lord Jesus Christ be multiplied upon us. The care yow have over other Churches beside your owne moveth me to write, geving god thankes in your behalf and praying him that your zeale may abound more and more. Let the state of my people move you the oftener to solicite god for me and them. I see a miserable desolation like to come upon us, for as halfe the bewty of our Church, and half the food of our soules is quite taken away, soe I feare the losse of thother parte, if god be not mercifull unto us, soe as I am distracted what to doe for the people, not that I stand in doubte or wavering whether I shuld yeld or noe, for therein I am resolute, as I protested publikely in the Courte, but I am often solicited to preach not-withstanding my suspension, and therefore do desire some reasons to stay my conscience with comforte in this action, which I thought to have moved the brethren in the last tyme, but upon your lettres sent to that end and effecte, I staied, hoping the next tyme you will per [28r] sonally move the same who can follow yt with some force and weighte of argumentes out of the worde: for myself I professe, <I> that as yet I see little to hold me from preaching, yet these reasons I have thought of: first the practise of some lerned pastors that cease, and of the Teachers generally,[241] which example of the Teachers doth not weigh soe much with me being not so nerelie tied to their people:

Secondlie the peace and profitt of the Church, for by law I am irregular, and soe made unfitt to doe good to the Church in tyme to come. And againe I have thought of this; they doe not forbid us to preach in Christs name, but for our disobedience to politike lawes doe inhibit us for a tyme. Now let me heare your reasons, and let vs joigne for god and his cause joyntly and soundly with good advise out of the word of god, and if we see and find that god requireth it, let us with praier addresse our selves to yt whatsoever come of yt: I am the least of all the brethren, yet I hope I wold not be last to subscribe to such a course sufficiently warranted by the lordes worde: I thanke yow for your lettres sent me since mie troubles, which did confirme me, in that I was resolved in before, and hope shalbe alwaies to my comforte. Pray for me with lowde crie to god, for my synnes deserve that my voice shuld never be heard agayne in his Church.   Pray for this people I besech yow, that god would fill their harts full of love to his ma[jes]ty, and then shall follow love to his Church and zeale against synne. I heard of your cominge to our Church, if you were purposed hold on or els write to mr doctor Chapman moving him to sue for my release, and for the punishing of this lewd woman that is the ground of my trouble. I know he is forward inough and the people also, nether would I have any such thing intymated to him, yet your lettres wold not hinder but further this cause. Thus thanking yow for all the testimonies of your unfeigned love to me, and to my brother with yow, who was this night past in our Towne, and ridd hastelie away, with salutations in Christ to your wieff and your sonne, I commend yow to him [who?] is able to kepe

---

[241] Parker is referring to preachers and lecturers like his colleague Edmund Chapman in Dedham. Classified as 'doctors' within the presbyterian polity, they had no pastoral responsibilities and so were readier to cease preaching when silenced, 'being not so nerelie tied to their people'. See the issues raised in the debate about Bartimaeus Andrewes and the proposed move from Wenham to Yarmouth (pp. 19–22 above).

you safe, and blameles till the coming of his sonne Jesus Christ. pray. pray. Dedham this xviith February 1587.

your loving brother in Christ,

Richard Parker

Mr Tay sent not onlie the former lettre to answer myne but these reasons to confirme me.

{Objection} Thexample of other Pastors and Teachers

{Answer} That is no certeine rule, although to be regarded yet not sufficient to ground our obedyence.

Rom[ans] 14. 23. he that doubted is condemned bicause it is not of faith.

Also they did for a tyme beare in regard of the peace of the Church, which falling out rather hurtfull then to edifying is noe more tolerable.

{Objection} It maketh a man Irregular:

{Answer} That is by the popish Canon lawe but not by the worde of god.

{Objection} They inhibite for Disobedience to Positive Law and doe not forbid to preach in christs name.

{Answer} The divell can chaunge himselfe into an Aungell of light, if they shuld forbid plainly to preach Christ, then every one seeing their grosnes wold crie shame, therfore they undermyne the preaching of Christ. Paull is not simply forbidden to preach Christ but forbidden to preach Christ to the gentles [sic]. The Papists do not inhibite the preaching of Christ but the manner and false interpretation, as they saie, but in truth they forbid Christ.

{Objection} The Consistory or Eldership hath authority to inhibite as they have authority to ordeyne.

{Answer} Their authority both in Election, ordination, as also in deposing is lymited by certayne rules and precepts, which being not observed their Election <and> nor deposicion is available, but it is lawfull for the oppressed to appeale from the Eldership to a Synode, from a Synode to a provinciall Counsaile, from a provinciall to a nationall, from a nationall to a generall Counsell, after thexample of Athanasius and others who preached notwithstanding they were inhibited by their Bishops.

To his fellow labourer in the worke of the lord Mr Parker

Pastor to the Church at dedham.

Tutching the yong man yow write of, I pray you cause him to come over to Peldon, assoone as you can, who (assure your self) shalbe enterteyned to your good contentation being soe qualified as yow note, howbeit for better satisfying of my people, if it wold please doctor Chapman to write a few wordes or subscribe to that yow shall write, he shuld be better thought of. The Lord blesse yow: pray pray the daies are evell. At our meetinge I forgott to move the brethren concerning the Arch-deacons visitacions: in my mynd if doctor Withers wold thereunto consent, the auncient forme of Synodes might easely be restored: *scilicet* that doctor withers as Moderator of the Accion, wold cause all the godlie brethren to meete together and soe to conferre of such points as concerned the Churche, [fo. 28v] where as now we are called thether, and do nothing but lose our tyme and spend our money. I pray you therfore, (if yow and other brethren thinke convenient) conferre with doctor

Chapman desiringe him to write to doctor withers about it, that some begynninge may be at this visitacion, and more at the next synodes. I hope by this conference we shuld helpe our church wardens and free them of their oathe: or at least have their Articles made in such sorte that lawfully they might sweare. Salute all our good brethren. farewell. 8 September.

Yours in the Lord.

W. Teye

The Auncient Synodes were holden *bis in Anno*

Soe are ours

Then they began with praier and the word: soe they do now after a sorte and upon conference mighte be used more reverentlie.

Then the προὲςος [sic] ruler of the Action was chosen by voices of the brethren, here yt differeth: for ours is perpetually one and the same appointed by the Byshop, which difference being but in the circumstance and not in the substance, though it abridgeth our libertie may for a tyme be tolerated.

Then their conferences were about matters of the Churche: soe ours ought to be: For wheras now the Proctors intermeddle other thinges in wisdome doctor withers with the advise and consent of the brethren might leave those matters to his officiall and proctor and reserve the Church affaires to himself and to the conferences of the godlie lerned brethren and soe free the godlie ministers from the courts and Officials Jurisdicion. Consider of it and accordinglie deale in yt.

{6 meeting. 3 foll:} Certaine Observations deducted out of sondrie statutes for such as are suspended or Excommunicated by B[ishop]'s Chancelors, Archdeacons, Commissaries or Officials to defend themselves against their usurped Tiranny.

Noe excommunicated persons may exercise Jurisdiccion ecclesiasticall, but whatsoever such shall doe is meerely voyde.

But the B[ishop]s Chancelors Archd[eacons] etc. are persons excommunicate *ipso facto per Canones*, therfore they ought not to exercise Jurisdiction ecclesiasticall but whatsoever they doe is voyde.

All Canons repugnante to the holy worde of god and statutes of this lande are disanull and of noe force. But such Canons as wherby the B[ishop]s Chancelors, Archdeacons and Officials by their sole authority doe suspend or excommunicate are repugnant to godes worde and statutes of this lande, ergo such are voyde and so *per consequens* their suspensions and Excommunications of noe force.

All sentences Judiciall not done by a lawfull competente Judge are voyde:

But the Commissary and Official of Colchester is no lawfull nor competent Judge therfore such sentences as he adjudgeth are voyde. The reason of the Minor proposition is for that he is noe doctor of lawe. The statute Henry 8. 37. Cap. 17[242]

---

[242] The correct reference for the statute to which Tey refers is 25 Henry VIII cap. 19 (1534), 'An act for the submission of the clergy', which provided for a commission of thirty-two persons to review the ecclesiastical law ('constitutions and canons'), retaining only those deemed to be 'worthy to be continued, kept and obeyed', with the king's royal assent. (G. R. Elton, *The Tudor constitution* (2nd edn., Cambridge, 1982), pp. 348–9.) This procedure was never implemented, the ecclesiastical law remaining in a kind of limbo, although in principle governed by the common and statute law of England. This enabled a casuistical lawyer like Robert Beale to argue that the puritans were in order

{Henry 8. *Anno* 25 Cap 19}
Noe Canons or Injunctions shalbe of authority made by the Convocation house or
other Authority eccesiasticall except the kinges hand be to the same to authorise
them. But these Canons, Articles and Injunctions wherunto the Officials require
presentments were never subscribed nor authorized by her majesty therfore they are
of noe force but meerely voyde

Lindwood libro 5to de sententia Excommunicationis[243]

By the authority of God the father Almightie etc we excommunicate all such as
presume to deprave the Church or ecclesiasticall persons of their righte, or that ether
by malice or against justice do contend to infring or trouble the liberties of the same
Also we excommunicate all those which presume injuriously to trouble the peace
and quiet of the kinge and his kingdome and which do contend to deteyne or barre
the subjectes unjustly of the lawes of the Kinge.
Also we excommunicate all such as for lucre or gayne hatred or favoure or for any
other cause maliciously shall raise and impose any crime upon any wherby he is
defamed among good and grave men, that at least hereby he is put to his purgation
otherwise grieved or vexed
These Excommunications are inferred upon a perpetuall statute

[fo. 29r]

Weighing the profite of the Ecclesiasticall order and honor we decree that noe
Archdeacon or their Officials shalbe bold to publish their sentences of Excommunications suspencions or Interdictions except the fault be manifest, and except
Canonicall admonition have gone before
Also the Archbishops and Bishops of England doe excommunicate all those which
do against the great Charter of England.
The B[ishop]s Chauncelors Archdeacons Comissaries and officials are all gilty of
all these crymes therfore they are excommunicate persons ipso facto and therfor
ought not to execute any ecclesiasticall Jurisdiction.

To the reverend brethren and faithfull mynisters of the most holy worde Mr doctor
Chapman, doctor Cricke with others be these d[elivere]d
Grace mercy and peace be multiplied upon yow etc. my deere brethren, whom I reverence in the Lorde, with grieff of mynd and a troubled spirite, I am witholden from
your holie and blessed fellowshipp and mutuall conference, soe that which by word of
mouth, I was purposed to have moved, rudelie by pen I am to signify and lay before
your wisedoms to consider of: briefly the points be these: the glory of god dishonored,
the kingedome of Christ Jesus subverted, the ministration of the spirite abolished, the
freedome and authority of the ministery captivated and contemned, and Antichrist

when they proposed such a radical reform as the Book of Discipline, since the question of the canon
law was still wide open. 'There is as yet no certain ecclesiastical law for the government of the
Church of this realm,' (Collinson, *EPM,* p. 421).
[243] Tey refers to W. Lyndwood, *Constitutiones Angliae provinciales* (London, 1557), a digest of English
canon law completed by William Lyndwood (c. 1375–1446) in 1430. 'De sententia excommunicationis' is found on pp. 268–82.

tyrannizing the Church by our B[ishop]s magnified and exalted above measure: are these thinges yet to be tolerated What meaneth the holie Apostle to reproche the Corinthians for suffringe fooles gladly,[244] they being wise for <suf> suffring even a man to bring them unto bondage, to devoure them, to take away their goodes, to exalt himself, to smite them on the face. The lord give us understanding hartes to compare times persons and actions wisely. I pray yow resolve this question whether the synne of Diotrephes,[245] or the synne of our Bishops is the greater and more tolerable. And whether our B[ishop]s are not such as the Apostle Jude speaketh of .8: verse that despise government[246] *scil*: ecclesiasticall, and speake evell of them that are in authority scil. the presbitery preferring their politicall, carnall humane Jurisdiction and Hierarchie before the spirituall and heavenly ordynaunce of the Lorde for the government of his Church. The truth of these points being serched and found out, the Lord give us courage and fortitude to stand in the truth and to quitte our selves like valiant men in the lorde his cause. valete: pray, pray, pray for me: February 2.
yours in the Lord: W. Teye

{11 meeting. 3. foll.} To his very reverent and faithfull frind mr doctor withers, preacher of the glorious Gosple of Christ Jesus at danbury.

Grace and peace: whereas our faithfull brethren and fellow preachers of the gosple in these partes have preferred certeine requestes unto yow, verie much tending in my judgment to the comforte of many consciences: These are in most earnest manner to besech yow to tender and promote the same. wordly [sic] pollicy may minister many pretenses of rejectinge them, but the good persuasion I still retayne of your zeale and courage in the lordes causes greatly assureth me, that soe necessary and fruictfull motions, shall even thankfully be accepted of: and that you will cherfully employ your wisedome and aucthority to the good and speedy accomplishment of them: how the zeale of many decaieth, and the spirituall <slum> slumber invadeth, and possesseth many, you behold and lament with us. What will then become of the Church and of God his glory, if some steppe not forwarde to stoppe the course of these retirers, and to beare up the scepter of his holy truth: little yt is, that some of us can doe to the reforminge of any thing that is amisse in the Church with the peace of yt: and therfore the greater care oughte to be used to performe anything that lieth in our power. If I were not drawen into Northfolke at this presente, I wold have thoughte my journey righte well bestowed about further conference and larger debatinge with yow of this matter. but seeing opportunity for the performinge of this duty faileth, I pray yow most hartely in the lorde, to waigh all thinges according to that reverente and holie trust that we hold of yow in this and

[244] 2 Corinthians xi. 19: 'For yee suffer fooles gladly, because that ye are wise.'
[245] 3 John 9: 'I wrote unto the Church: but Diotrephes which loveth to have the preeminence among them, receiveth us not.' Tey may have been prompted by the tract published in 1588 by John Udall: *The state of the Church of England laid open in a Conference between Diotrephes a Bishop, Tertullus a Papist, Demetrius an Usurer, Pandochus an Inne-keeper, and Paule a Preacher of the worde of God*, always referred to simply as *Diotrephes*, an extreme pamphlet which helped to catch Udall in the net cast for Martin Marprelate.
[246] Jude 8: 'Likewise notwithstanding these dreamers also defile the flesh, and despise government, and speake evill of them that are in authoritie.' Tey's inversion of Jude's most likely meaning is typical of his radicalism.

such like causes. The same God of grace and power enable us alwaies to stand for his glory with zeale and knowledge: Dedham. 17. September 1584.

yours still in the Lorde.

Edmunde Chapman

[fo. 29v]

Certaine requests to be moved to doctor withers Archdeacon of Colchester for the libertie of those Churches in his Jurisdiction which have faithfull ministers set over them.

1.   Imprimis that he wold free the godly lerned mynisters from his Courts, inasmuch as by the word of god they oughte to be free from such bondages, and by the law of this land visitacion shuld be onlie where there was need.

2.   Secondlie that he would not exacte an othe of the Churchwardens and Sidemen seeing his office is not to require an othe, nether the Articles offred them deserve an othe, nether being sworne are they able to kepe their othe, excepte they shuld dishonor God, and breake the band of Charity.

3.   Thirdlie that he wold not receive any bill of presentment against any person except the mynister with the godlie Parishioners had first used all good meanes to bring the partye offending to repentaunce, which being refused and his obstinacy apparant, he mighte then proceed against him in his lawe, and this doth the law of god and of this land require.

4.   Fourthlie that he wold noe more abuse that sacred ecclesiasticall censure of Excommunication but to suffer those, whom god hath appointed by his Ordynaunce to use yt.

5.   Fiftlie that he wold not suffer any bare readers.[247]

6.   Sixthly that he wold not inducte any insufficient minister, but by the law of god and law of the land to withstand such.

7.   Seventhlie that he wold in some wise pollicy helpe to erecte some like exercise as was the prophecy for the triall and increasing of mynisters giftes, and for the acquayntinge of them together in love.

8.   Eightlie if he will not graunte us our freedome yet at least to chalenge his visitacions to be as Synodes were in thold tyme, where we may use our freedome in conference and determyning of ecclesiasticall matters with him as fellow labourers and brethren.

By your fellow mynisters and loving brethren.[248]

Mr Monke	Mr Cocke.
Mr farrur.	Mr upcher.
Mr Teye.	Mr Newman.
Mr Parker.	Mr Hawden:
Mr Lewis.	Mr Beamonde.
Mr Searle.	Mr Tunstall

---

[247] For lay readers, see Brett Usher, 'Expedient and experiment: the Elizabethan lay reader' in R. N. Swanson, ed., *Continuity and change in Christian worship* (Studies in Church History, XXXV, Woodbridge, 1999), 185–98.

[248] See *BR* for all signatories.

{13. meeting. 4 foll}

In the 13 meeting fol. 4. we find a question moved emong the brethren what forme of Catechisinge shuld be used, whether we mighte [use?] the formes set downe in a booke, or use only the written worde of god. The judgments of the brethren in this point follow:

{Mr farrar}   First bicause the word of God and man are confounded therfore we ought not to use a booke. 2. Although the Jewes had in their families formes of instructions yet for publike use in the church they had nothing but godes worde, and were commanded to use nothing els there.

Objection: what say ye then to the Creed: Answer. bicause it is soe universally receyved and so neere the wordes of scripture, and being not any private mans judgment, yt may be used: but for using a Catechisme I thinke it unlawfull, and see no cause why we shuld not receyve into the Church the labors of <other> men sound and godlie as a Catechisme, and why may not homilies be allowed in the Church aswell as they.

{Mr Sandes}   In the 6. Hebr[ews] we find certeine generall heades set downe wherin the yong ones were examyned. This is confirmed by the Apostles practise, that they took noe places of scripture, but some generall heades as of Justification and Resurrection etc. and so they teach. Againe the Lordes practise in setting out the 10. commandementes: and in that forme of praiers are receyved into the Church these shew that a Catechisme that is a forme of teaching the yonger may be used. And the forme of the Creed may be followed, and the history of all times, and writinges of all men speaking of the 6 hebr[ews] do confirme this that I have said.[249]

{Mr Chapman}   Some certeyne forme may be used for trayning the people in the Church: as for example, though there be good praiers in the scriptures set downe yet it is lawfull to use a larger forme of praier to edify: And bicause outward thinges and the ordring of ceremonies be left to the Church if they tend to edifying: and bicause also the people be simple and the [fo. 30r] yong ones cannot be els trayned up, I thinke yt lawfull to use a Catechisme.

{Mr Lewis} I thinke it lawfull to use a Catechisme. 1 It is the easiest and best way to trayne up yong ones and the ruder sorte.

2. we be enjoigned to it, and as we may doe it lawfully soe we shuld doe yt.

3. we have law to enforce them to come to be Instructed by a booke.

4. the practise of all reformed Churches and I shuld not without great examynation by my practise disprove the judgment of soe many godlie Churches who use a Catechisme.

{Mr. Dowe.} It is not lawfull to expound Catechismes in the Church.

No mans writinges are to be expounded in the Church, but written Catechismes are such. ergo

{Ratio 1a} The proposition is proved by an Argument from the office of the Mynister, who is the minister of godes worde, a dispenser of his misteries

---

[249] This is not how everyone would understand Hebrews vi, although it begins: 'Therefore leaving the doctrine of the beginning of Christ, let us bee led forward unto perfection'.

1 Cor[inthians] 4. 1.[250] a divider of the word of truth 2 Tim[othy] 2.[251] by the adjuncte of trueth is alwaies ment the meere word of god Colossians 1. 5.[252] Ephes[ians] 1. 13.[253] and bicause thapostlc Peter saieth he must speake the wordes of god. 1. Pet[er] 4. 11.[254] that is the pure word of god, I thinke that noe Catechisme compiled or made by man is to be expounded or enterpreted in the Church: for although Catechismes be good, necessary and according to godes worde yet this were to divide mans wordes and to utter the voyce of man and not of god, bicause noe Catechisme is soe purely or sincerely made that may be called the word of truth or the meere word of God. And yt is to be doubted whether all compilers of Catechismes have purely expounded every Article of faith and therfore soe much the lesse to be esteemed as the pure word of god.

The Assumption is manifest.

{Objection}   If yt be objected by this reason noe wordes oughte to be uttered in our sermons but meere scripture wordes that followeth not for yt is one thing to expound the scriptures and to lay out the meaning of the holy ghost in other wordes and another thing to expound mens writinges for that is godes ordynaunce, this is not: and that Catechismes be mens writinges it is manifest:

If yt be objected that all the scriptures were written by men and therefore the rejecting of these must follow the receiving of the others. yt is easely answered that the Apostles, prophets and Evangelists were speciall instruments appointed of God by whom one booke of sacred scripture is compiled for the publike use of the Church for ever to remayne but all other bookes have noe such authority for as much as the writers of them are noe such men.

{Ratio 2a}   They which are to be Catechised are before rude and ignorant of the principles and groundes of salvation but yt is the word onlie that maketh wise unto salvation, therfore the onlie scripture is to be expounded in the Church.

The Proposition is manifest. The Assumption. 2 Tim[othy] 3. 15.[255] I thinke rather that their myndes are to be embued with that milke of the pure worde then in the writinges of men, for when they shalbe taughte the use of the Sacraments and touching the Resurrection or Judgment to come, these thinges are to be laid out by the pure worde and not to be explicated in the writinges of men, that they may have their senses exercised more and more in the worde, there not being such power in the writinges of men to frame their myndes as in the word it selfe.

{3a}   If yt be said that in expounding of Catechismes they are referred to the textes of the scriptures and that is made the chieff grounde. Answ[er]. So it is in expounding of an homily, yet the thing expounded is the homilie and not the scripture, for the scripture is not expounded by the homilie but the homilie by the scripture: so yt is in expounding of a Catechisme the matter subject is the Catechisme written.

---

[250] 'The ministers of Christ, and dispensers of the secrets of God'.
[251] 2 Timothy ii. 15, 'Studie to showe thy self approved unto God, a workeman that nedeth not to be ashamed, dividing the worde of trueth aright.'
[252] 'For the hopes sake which is laid up for you in heaven, whereof ye have heard before by the word of trueth, which is the Gospel.'
[253] 'In whom also ye have trusted after that ye heard of the word of trueth, even the Gospel of your salvation, wherein also after that yee beleeved, ye were sealed with the holy Spirit of promise.'
[254] 'If any man speake, let him talke as the words of God'.
[255] 'And that thou hast knowen the holy Scriptures of a childe'.

{4}   If it be objected that by this reason I make all written Catechismes needles if they may not be taught in the Churches. Answ[er]. yt followeth as much that I make all bookes needles that are beside the holy bible, bicause they may not be read in the Churches, for there be many bookes needfull to be used in private houses of private persons that are not to be used in the publike ministery: and yt is one thing for a private person to instructe his family or a scholemaster his scholers and another for the mynisters to instructe in the Church for they may instructe owt of bookes written by men but these onlie out of the booke of God.

{3a}   Our begynnyng growing and nourishment is by the pure worde James 1 18.[256] 1 Pet[er] 2. 2.[257] and 1 Cor[inthians] 3. 1:[258] therfore the pure word is to be expounded not mens written Catechismes. And though it be said Catechismes hinder not the growing nor nourishmente yet bicause the ministers are fathers to begett 1 Cor[inthians] 4. 15.[259] and nurses to feed . 1 Thess[alonians] 2. 7[260] and the vertue of nourishing and begetting is inscribed only to the meere worde and not to mens writinges, I thinke they are not to be expounded in the Church but privately as accessary and helping to that is already begonne and wroughte by the worde, that the meere word may have the onlie praise of begettinge and nourishing, thother as a secondary meane that helpeth to nourishment and begettinge.

{Ratio 4}   The practise of the Apostles and Evangelists is to be followed in the laying of the principles of faith and religion. 2 Tim[othy] 1. 13[261] but they affirmed all thinges out of the booke of holy scripture. Acts 8. 39 and 17. 2. 3. and 18. 26.[262] If yt be said there were then noe Catechismes written and [fo. 30v] therfore they could expound none but the meere scriptures: yf that be true as yt is like enough yt proveth this poynte the more, for if an ordenary Catechisme had bene necessary to be expounded in the Church, they would suerlie have compiled one for the use of all Churches planted by the Apostles.

The testimony of the brethren tutching a draught of discipline[263]

The brethren assembled together in the name of god, having heard and examyned by the worde of god according to their best hability and judgmente in yt a draughte of discipline essentiall and necessary for all tymes <and> and Synodicall gathered out of the Synodes and use of the Churches have thoughte good to testify concerning yt as followeth.

---

[256] 'Of his owne will begate he us with the word of trueth'.

[257] 'As new borne babes desire the sincere milke of the worde, that yee may grow thereby.'

[258] 'And I could not speake unto you, brethren, as unto spirituall men, but as unto carnall, even as unto babes in Christ.'

[259] 'For though yee have ten thousand instructers in Christ, yet have ye not many fathers: for in Christ Jesus I have begotten you through the Gospel.'

[260] 'Wee were gentle among you, even as a nource cherisheth her children.'

[261] 'Keepe the true paterne of the wholesome words, which thou hast heard of me in faith and love which is in Christ Jesus.'

[262] Acts viii. 39 would appear to be an error for Acts viii. 35: 'Then Philippe opened his mouth, and began at the same Scripture, and preached unto him Jesus.' Acts xvii. 2–3 has St Paul coming to Thessalonica and disputing in the synagogue 'by the Scriptures'. Acts xviii. 26 tells of Apollos speaking boldly in the synagogue at Ephesus.

[263] For the relation of this draft to other versions of the same document, see above, pp. xcvii–ic.

1.   We acknowledge and confesse the same agreable to godes most holy worde soe far forth as we are able to judge and discerne of yt. we affirme yt to be the same which we desire to be established in this Church by daily praier to god and which we promise as god shall offer oportunities, and geve us to discerne it soe expedient by humble suite to her majestie, her honorable Counsell, and the Parliament and by all other lawfull and convenient meanes to further and advance.

2.   Soe farre as the lawes of the land and the peace of our present state of our Church may suffer and not enforce to the contrary we promise to guide ourselves and to be guided by it and according to yt.

3.   For more speciall declaration of some pointes more importune and necessary we promise uniformly to follow such order when we preach the word of god as in the booke allowed by us is set downe in the Chapters of the office of mynisters of the worde of preaching or sermons, of Sacraments of Baptisme and of the Lordes supper concerning the tyme.

4.   Further also to follow the order set downe in the Chapter of the meetinges as farre as yt concerneth the ministers of the worde, for which purpose we promise to meete every six weekes together in Classicall conferences with such of the brethren here assembled as for their neighborhood may fytt us best and such other as by their advise we shallbe desired to joigne with us.

5.   The like we promise for provinciall meetinges every half yeare from our conferences to send unto them as is set downe in the Chapter concerning the Provinces and conferences belonging to them being devided according to such order as is set downe in that behalfe.

6.   About Essex are nominated Mr Northie, Mr Teye, Mr Newman, Mr Gifford, Mr hawden, Mr Tunstall, Mr dente[264] and whomsoever els the brethren there shall thinke well of.

7.   The conferences of the brethren present to belong all to one province till yt be further ordered.

8.   For the booke of Lyturgie in use, yt is agreed to leave men for Questions concerning yt to the advise of their conferences seeing they already have had cause to discover the wantes thereof and forbeare them in many partes as they doe.

9.   The Geneva lyturgie[265] as yt hath bene corrected is to be communicated with the conferences and the booke to be preferred here at the Parliament and used in the partes abroade if the brethren there shall thinke good.

10.   It is agreed that the mynisters which are able to beare the Charges of yt, shall entertayne a student of divinity being well grounded in other knowledge of Artes and tongues, whom by directing in those studies by his owne example and all good meanes he may make fytte to serve the Church in the mynistery of the gosple and that such as are not able shuld yet, (the charges being otherwise borne performe the like duty and care that there may be alwaies sufficient and able men in the Church for that Callinge.

---

[264] See *BR* for all seven names.
[265] For an account of the various recensions of the Geneva liturgy, *The forme of prayers*, and especially the editions published in England by Robert Waldegrave and in Middelburg by Richard Schilders, and intended for use as schedules to the presbyterian bills offered to parliament by Peter Turner in 1584 and by Anthony Cope and others in 1586 ('bill and book'), see Collinson, *EPM,* pp. 286–8, 296–7, 303–16.

11. London the next place for the next provinciall conference about the midst of Michaeltide terme.

12. The oppressions of the B[ishop]s their courtes and officers are to be registered and gathered towardes the people, but especially towardes the mynisters.

13. The French Churches povertie is to be solicited according to their lettres in that behalf delyvered.

A note of the Articles wherunto some mynisters in Essex subscribed, whose names follow.[266]

1. To the first article concerninge her majesties soveraigne authority under god: we deny all foreigne authority and power, and according to the 37. article in the booke of Articles which is of civill magistrates teacheth us that is that all such prerogatyve is to be geven unto her majesty over all persons which we see to have bene geven to all godlie princes in holy scriptures by god himself we willingly subscribe and shall by the grace of Almightie god be ready to the uttermost with our goodes and lyves to maynteyne the same.

2. Concerninge the booke of common praier and of consecration of B[ishop]s as we have bene carefull and still wilbe for the peace of the Church both in ourselves and our people, soe we humbly crave we may be tendred herein, not daring for conscience sake subscribe thereto.[267]

3. To the 3 of the booke of Articles as farre as by Parliament they have bene thought meete shuld be required that is such only as concerne doctrine of faith and Sacramentes taking them in the best sense as is most meete for us soe to doe, we most willinglie subscribe.[268]

			Richard Parker
Lawrence Newman	John Bounde	Ralf hawden	Tho[mas] Knyvet
Thomas farrur	Robert Monke	Stephen Beamond	Tho[mas] Morris
Robert Lewis	Tho[mas] Lowe	John Walthar	Tho[mas] Upcher
Will[iam] Cocke			
Rob[ert] Searle			

---

[266] This is one of a number of forms of limited or qualified subscription, or of 'doubts', or proposed compromises, offered by ministers in various counties and apparently widely circulated among them. See pp. 108–14 below. Some of these, in effect the files of John Field, will be found in the first volume of *Seconde parte*, together with reasons against subscription and petitions from suspended or threatened ministers. See Collinson, *EPM*, pp. 249–72, and the references on pp. 487–9 to copies in other collections. The papers of Sir Walter Mildmay in the Fitzwilliam of Milton MSS in the Northamptonshire Record Office include a 15–folio 'book', endorsed by Mildmay as 'Matters touchinge the Archbishop of Caunterburye and the Ministers' (F.(M).P.63). In the same collection there is an account of exchanges about subscription between Whitgift and 'the Ministers of Essex' (F.(M).P.193).

[267] Cf. the subscription to the second article by 'the ministers of London' (fifteen in number, including none of the London hardliners), dated 13 February 1584(new style): 'For the booke of common prayer, we are content to use yt, for the peace of the church, or if we be founde offendinge in any parte thereof to submitt ourselves to the penalty of yt' *(Seconde parte,* I, 221).

[268] John Bounde, John Walthar, Tho Knyvet, Tho Morris: see *BR* for all four signatories.

[fo. 31r]

{17 meeting. 4. foll.}

Grace and peace in our lord Jesu be multiplyed etc

Seing that your christian and ready benevolence towardes me (my loving brethren) hath in meesure so far exceeded the common coorse of frendly good turns used in these our dayes: I cannot but hold myselfe bownden with lyke thankfulnes to answere the same agayne. But wheras I have much fayled and comme far behynde in that dutie wich the benefit receyved doth Justly chalenge at my hand partly as a fawti and partly as an Insufficient dettor I humbly crave your godly patience in this behalfe: For in deed the multitude of my cares and the greatnes of my trowbles are such and come upon me so fast, as that I doe verie ofte forgett myselfe in great affayeres: yea and those thinges which doe offer them selves (as it were) verie necessarily to be discharged I do some tymes omitt as one out of hart and corage; by reson of those pinching greefes of mynd which I susteyne. For as my late extremiti befell me, for taking to far upon me, for a brother of myne (as yee know so the same man being both unable and unwilling to ease me therin any whitt doth himselfe and an other of my brethren leave me unto far greater danger then that first was. Into which thei at the first (being men thought veri well able to lyve) brought me being their yonger brother partly by their great Intretie faythfully promysing myne Indempniti and partly by their large promyses of their help towardes my preferment in lyke case when soever I shold call for it. Wherupon havyng had good experience alredy of their frendship towardes me in thuniversitie and knowing their abiliti in welth to be verie sufficient at that tyme I did never refuse <I did never refuse> to be bownd with them when soever thei cawled me, and although thei discharged many thinges (which did also much incorage me) yet now of late <I> and to late I lerne (to my grete smart) that diverse of those dettes to the some of more then 200 li are lyke to be layd upon me, and havyng lent them diverse sommes of monei from tyme to tyme which I loked to receyve ageyne and cannot gett it I fynde my selfe <verie> so gretly Impoveryshed by them alredy as that I hardly have had wheron to lyve much lesse to answere so great dettes, and yet except I do pay them Imprisonment must be my lott whyle I lyve, so hard are those creditores in whose bandes I am. Now the fearfull syght of those so grete and verie Imminent dangeres doth so benumme my senses (as it were) and trowble my whole mynde as that I feel no gret Joy in any thing I goe abought. Wherefore (my good brethren in Jesu Christe) I besech yee pardon that want of duti which Justly yee may note in me, who have not all this whyle so much as remembered it in writinge to yee, that I receyved your christian contribution, which to my gret comfort I did in verie frutefull mesure, the lord our god be praysed for it who bless your store with much and moste happy increase to his glori and your comfortes for his Christes sake. Thus ende praying yee (my brethren) to help me with your godly cownseles in so dowbtfull cases, and hartie prayer unto our loving god for my ease comfort and reliefe as may be moste to his glorie and the benefit of his church unto the which and to every member herof the lord in merci grante trew peace and deliver it from all thraldom under the wicked. Erwton the 10th of Julie 1584

Your loving brother in all Christian dutie to commande Henri Wilcok[269]

---

[269] For the dealings of the conference with the bankrupt minister Henry Wilcock, see above, pp. lxxiv–v. Only from this holograph letter do we learn of the scale of Wilcock's indebtedness.

[fo. 31v]

Blank

[fo 32r]

To my verie good brother in Christ, Mr field preacher of godes worde.[270]
By the meanes of to much straungnes (as yt seemeth to me) we are distracted into a
miserable variety of Answers to these Articles; which I feare one day wilbe cast as
dunge upon our faces. Remove the cause, persuade to love and kindnes, correcte the
inordinate zeale of some, who thinke yt a greate peece of religion to judge and
exclude others whom they love not and let us growe to a more generall conference
for unity both in affection and judgment if yt may be, that we may see and feele
more comforte in ourselves and in our brethren. Such a holy meetinge is longed for
of many, write what you thinke good herin: Salute our good brethren and pray,
Yours in Christ
Ed[mund] Chapman.

To my reverent brother in Christ doctor Chapman Teacher of godes word at
Dedham.
Faith and assurance in Christ unto thend Amen. Sir, though our entercourse of
writinge hath faynted of late, yet methinkes there is good occasion given now that yt
shuld be agayne renewed for the trials being many that are laid upon us it shuld
provoke us to stirre up one another that we might stand fast and yeld a good witnes
unto that truth wherof he hath with comforte made us messengers unto many. And
surelie herof I feele my self to have great need, who am privy to myne owne
weaknes, having bene strongly drawen of late not to be soe carefull diligent and
zealous in godes causes as I was wonte, this unhappy tyme of loosenes and liberty[271]
gayning upon me, and choking those good thinges which I thanke good I was wonte
to feele in greater measure. I besech yow therfore helpe me with your praiers, with
your good counsell, and with those giftes, which God in mercy hath richly bestowed
on yow. Let not his mercies be in vayne, who hath of late visited yow that you
mighte remember to lyve to the praise of his name. Our new Archbishopp, now he is
in: sheweth himself as he was wonte to be. what good their ambitious pompe, and
Papall authority will bring to the gosple hath partly appeared already, and will
appeare more hereafter, if god break not his hornes: for certeinly he is egerly set to
overthrowe and wast his poore Church. use what meanes yow can by writinge,

---

[270] Once again, we are victims of Richard Parker's somewhat haphazard filing methods. Field's letter
can hardly be an answer to Chapman's, for it appears to initiate (or at least renew) their
correspondence, and, whether 'this xi moneth' be taken as November 1583 (most likely) or (old
style) February 1584, it clearly relates to an early stage in the crisis occasioned by Whitgift's
preferment ('Our new Archbishopp, now he is in . . .'), whereas Chapman's letter must have been
written some months into the crisis. For Field's role in 1584, and more generally, see Patrick
Collinson, 'John Field', pp. 334–70.
[271] Field refers to the (for him and many) relaxed years of Archbishop Grindal's archiepiscopate. In
1579, the earl of Leicester had obtained a preaching licence for him from Oxford University, and
Field duly thanked him 'as the instrument both of my peace and liberty and of the poor blessing [the
whole Church] enjoyeth by my preaching'. *Ibid.*, p. 351.

consulting and speakinge with those whom yt concerneth, and who may doe good. It wilbe to late to deale afterwarde. The peace of the Church is at an end, if he be not curbed.   you are wise to consider by advise and by joigning together how to strengthen your handes in this worke. The Lord directe both yow and us, that we may fighte a good fighte and fynish with joy. Amen.

Fare you well, the 19 of this xi moneth 1583.

yours assured in Christ

Joh[annes] Feilde

To our lovinge brethren the mynisters of the word of god in London[272] [be these] d[elivere]d

Grace and peace etc. As we are persuaded of your godlie care (our verie good brethren to put forward by all meanes the good estate of the Church, striving together with you by our hartie praiers and contynuall cries unto our most mercifull father for his gratious blessing therein: so we in absence from yow (as duty byndeth us being in some measure myndfull of yow and the good cause for the which yow are there to our comfortes emploied) have thought that whereas by the favoure of God, the Courte of Parliament is alreadie possessed with our peticion for Reformation, and standeth now in need of all helpes to further the same, this mighte be one good way emongst others, that by some of yow a very earnest supplication be drawen instantlie beseching them of the Parliament house by all meanes to promote the cause of the Church commended already unto them. and that all forceable reasons may be set downe in the best and most effectuall manner to persuade them thereunto, and the same to be delyvered by some faithfull gentlemen to the Speaker; requesting him openly to reade the same unto the whole house. Thus signifying unto yow what we thinke herein, and commending the same unto your godly considerations, we committ yow and all your labors to the blessing of our most <mers> mercifull father.

your loving brethren in Christ.

Ed[mund] Chapman	Richard Crick
Tho[mas] farrur	Richard Dowe
Laurence Newman	Richard Parker

{18 meeting. fol. 4}

A generall conference Agreed on:

Pridie Calendas September 1584.

It is thoughte good that a generall conference be procured from Suffolke, Norfolk, Kent, London, Essex, and for Essex these to begyne.[273]

Mr D. Chapman	Mr Newman	Mr huckle
Mr Gifforde	Mr Northy	Mr Tuke
Mr Wrighte	Mr Rogers	Mr Hawden
Mr Teye		

---

[272] See above, p. 33 (**50M**).

[273] See *BR* for all ten nominees.

[fo. 32v]

The matters to be considered of against the first day of the Terme with their opinion and advise of the same what way were best for the present grieff of the Churche: whether yt were not fytt that a generall supplication were presented to her majesty with a full draughte of the discipline we desire, and of the reasons for which Subscription is refused ether by all the mynistery favouring this cause, or such as already suffer. whether a fast were not to be holden upon the same day in as many places as may conveniently and whether publike or private.[274]

Our opinion of London. To the first affirmatively: So likewise to the second, soe to the third, but the fast private and by mynisters.

Last of all this was moved: If the proceeding begonn contynue and goe forward in putting the preachers to silence and laying wast the Churches what the duty of the mynisters is in this behalf, what charge they have from god of the Church, how far they may yeld to cease their preachinge, and what duty is to be done by them in such a case, whether after advise taken yt were not good that two or three mighte be appointed to signify the place and tyme agreed on.

{The supplication of the mynisters of Essex to the Lords of the Counsell. 19 meeting. 4. foll. concluded of 47. meeting foll. 9}

To the righte honorable the Lordes and others of her majesties most honorable privy Counsell certeyne mynisters in the County of Essex wish encrease of honor with all spirituall blessinges through Christ.

Our weak estate (right honorable) in the eie and estimation of the world together with dyverse other circumstances in our owne persons, cannot but minister some matter of discouragement unto us in this our attempte, yet the same is utterly wiped away and we do boldly and cherfully offer this our humble suite unto your honors being our only Sanctuary next unto her majesty which we have here upon earth to repaire unto in our present necessity, and most of all we are encouraged when we consider how richly god hath adorned your Honors with knowledge wisdome and zeale of the gosple with godlie care and tender love unto those which professe the same in simplicity: Most humbly therfore we do beseech your honors with your accustomed favoure in all godly and just causes to heare and to Judge of our matters. we have receyved the charge of her majesties loyall and faithfull subjectes to instructe and teach them in the way of life, and hearing this sounded out from the god of heaven upon every one of us which have receyved this callinge, woe unto me if I preach not the Gosple, according to the measure of godes graces geven unto us we have endeavoured ourselves to discharge our duties, and to approve ourselves both to god and men. Notwithstanding we are in great heavines some of us being already put to silence and the rest living in feare not that we have bene charged or can be (as we hope) ether with false doctrine or slanderous life but for that we refuse to subscribe that there is nothing conteyned in the booke of Common prayer and of

---

[274] These are evidently proposals sent out from London to conferences in the country, this being Dedham's copy, with its response. The 'generall supplication made to the Parliament in Anno 1586. November' a massive document, is in *Seconde parte,* II, 70–87.

ordeyning B[ishop]s priestes and deacons contrary to the word of god we doe
protest in the sighte of the livinge god, who sercheth all hartes that we do not refuse
in desire to dissent or other synister affection but in the feare of god and love of
sincerity. for if those reasons which lead us hereunto mighte soe be answered by the
doctrine of the sacred Bible that we mighte have a sure and setled persuasion we
wold not deny. Now thapostle teacheth that he which doth doubte if he eate is
condemned,[275] then if a man be condemned for doing a lawfull action bycause he is
in doubte whether yt be lawfull and yet doth it, how much more should we incurre the
displeasure of the lord and procure his just wrath to our destruction, if we shuld
subscribe, being certeinly persuaded that there be some thinges in the said bookes
contrary to his worde. Moreover by subscribing in manner aforsaid, we shuld not
only dissent from the written worde but also from other Churches which at this daie
professe the gosple by allowing some thinges which they disallowe and in some
points from the publike doctrine of our owne Church established and mainteyned in
the Apology and defence therof. Finally from the most excellent instrumentes of
god in these daies whose writinges are put into our handes by publike allowance. In
these and other respectes we humbly crave, that your honorable and sacred protection may be extended upon us, as those which from the <harte> harte doe entirelie
love, honor and obey her excellent Majesty and your Ho[nors] in the Lorde, geving
most hartie thankes to him for all the blessinges which we have received of his rich
mercy by your happy governmente, instantly praying both nighte and day, that he
will blesse and preserve her majesty and your honors unto eternall salvation.
your honors poore and humble suppliauntes

Laurence Newman	Will[iam] Teye
Robert Lewis	Richard Parker
Tho[mas] farrur	Tho[mas] Knyvett

[fo. 33r]

The Supplication of the inhabitantes of Malden and others[276]

To the right honorable the Lordes and others of her ma[jes]ties most honorable
privy counsell
In most humble and lamentable wise complayne unto your honors, her ma[jes]ties
faithfull and obedient subjectes the Inhabitantes of the towne of Malden, and other
places neere adjoigninge in Essex, beseching your honors, that wheras through the

---

[275] The reference is to St Paul's casuistry on the problem of eating meat offered to idols, in 1 Corinthians viii. Paul advised that idols were meaningless objects, so that eating meat offered to them (and sold cheap in the market) was an indifferent matter. But if the consciences of weak Christians should be offended, it was better not to eat it. All things are lawful, but all things are not expedient. This was the topos which guided puritans in the matter of conformity to things indifferent, such as, especially, the surplice.

[276] Another copy of this petition, with some variation in wording, is calendared in *Seconde parte*, II, 187–8. The full text is in DWL, MS Morrice B.1, 177–8. George Gifford had been deprived of the living of All Saints with St Peter, Maldon (where he continued to preach). Robert Palmer, vicar from 1587, allegedly spent his days in the bowling alley and his nights in the New Inn. See *BR* pp. 211–14 below, and Collinson, *EPM*, p. 377.

goodnes of Almightie god under her highnes most gracious and happy government, we have enjoyed to the great comforte and salvation of our soules the most rich and inestimable benefite of the Gosple, through such godlie teachers as the lord hath raised up unto us, who through the holie doctrine and unblameable conversation that they have bene and are endued with, have builded us up to obedience both towardes god, her soveraigne <hig> highnes and towardes all the mynisters of Justice under her: nether being seditious nor disobedient, as they have bene most unjustly charged: which said mynisters and Teachers being of late in parte removed from us, and in parte suspended from their functions for matters urged by the lord Arch-bishop's Grace, fewe are left unto us, but such as we can prove unto your honors are for the most parte utterlie unfytt for that calling, being altogether ignorant, and having bene ether popish priestes, or such persons as have thrust in upon the mynistery (when they knew not els where to lyve, men of occupation, serving men and the basest of all sortes, and (which is most lamentable) as they are men of noe giftes, soe many of them are of noe common honesty but raylers, dicers quarrellers, dronkerdes adulterers and offensyve lyvers committing the most grosse vices that are emongst men. These are the men that are supported whose supportes and suggestions especially against thother are already received and admitted. By meanes wherof the multitude of Papistes heretikes and other enemies of god and her most roiall ma[jes]tie are soe encreased and encouraged that as they sticke not openly to fill our bosoms with all contemptuous and bitter speeches mocking and tauntinge us with our profession, soe they give us great cause to feare some violence at their handes, if this encouragement (which is the suppressing of our godly preachers) be contynued. wherfore we most humbly besech your honors, even in the bowels of our lord Jesus Christ to be a meane for us, that our faithfull and godlie preachers may be restored and contynued that we may serve the Lord our god according to his blessed and everlastinge worde: So shall we and many thousandes of her highnes subjectes with cherfull hartes with our lyves and goodes in her highnes service contynue our faithfull supplications to the Almightie for her ma[jes]ties preservation that her yeares being multiplied with many happie daies with encrease of prosperity and victorie in the midst of her and our adversaries the gracious gosple of Christ may have a free passage amonge us all till yt have wroughte in us assurance of that ever-lasting kingdome and inheritaunce that he hath purchased for us which god for his holie names sake graunt: Amen.

The judgment of a lerned man that it is not lawfull to cease preaching, at the inhibi-tion of a Bishop and an answer to yt
{19. meeting. foll. 4.}

Not lawfull to cease preching at the B[ishop]s inhibition: which I prove thus.

1.   The true mynister is sent of god and approved of the Church to preach: ergo man alone ought not to inhibite but if man presume to inhibite the mynister is to stand in the callinge of god.
2.   If it be lawfull to kepe silence at the B[ishop]s inhibition, the strength and stability of the Church shuld depend upon a man, but that is intolerable, ergo, not lawfull to be silent.

3.   All authority over the Church ether in placinge or displacinge mynisters is given to Christ Math[ew] 28. 27;[277] Apocal[ypse] 1. 13: 16. 20. 3. 1. 7;[278] ergo where Christ doth place man ought not to displace.

4.   The B[ishop]s authority is Antichristian ergo not to be obeyed.

5.   The Prince cannot give that Authoritie which apertayneth not to that roiall estate or office of Magistracy, but to make or <diss> dismisse mynisters to or from the office of ministery apperteyneth not to the office of magistracy. ergo the Prince cannot give yt to others that is to Bishops or Commissioners.

6.   It is not lawfull to leave any dutie undone which god commandeth at the commandement of man for the mynister to preach is a duty commanded by god, ergo not to be left undone at the commandement of man.

7.   In matters of liffe landes or goodes no subjecte [ought?] to yeld his righte contrary to law to a tyrante but is bound in conscience to use all lawfull meanes to the uttermost of his [fo. 33v] power to defend his righte much more in matters concerning the glorie of god, the salvation of mens soules and the righte of the Churche as is the libertie of the mynistery and <freed> freedome of the people.

8.   The godlie mynister must avoyde all suspition of being esteemed as an hireling who seeing the wolfe comminge flieth but he ought in conscience to stand in defence of his sheep and not suffer the wolfe devoure them.

9   Whosoever is silent and useth not his talents of giftes to the edifying of the Church, must have good warrant out of the worde for his soe doing: but the scriptures aforde no such warrante, but rather accurseth such as doe not preach 1 Cor[inthians] 9. 16.[279] math[ew] 25. 26. 27.[280]

10   It is a note of wante of faith for a minister to be silente for feare of prosecution. 2 Cor[inthians] 4. 13.[281]

11.   The Apostles being forbidden preached. Actes 3. 4. 5.[282]

12.   Timothie Silvanus and others called by the Church and not immediatly from god as theapostles being forbidden preached still. 1 Thess[alonians] 2. 16[283] notwithstanding their inhibition.

13.   So did Chrysostome Athanasius, Basill, Gregory and others preached being inhibited and excommunicated. Read in the booke of martirs.[284] Wickliff Article 14 page 435 that yt ys lawfull for any man ether deacon or priest to preach without

---

[277] Matthew xxviii has only 20 verses. Perhaps the reference intended is to verse 18: 'And Jesus came, & spake unto them, saying, All power is given unto me in heaven, and in earth.'

[278] Revelation i. 13–16 and 20 concerns John's vision and identification of (verse 13) 'one like unto the Sonne of man'; Revelation iii. 1: 'These things saith he that hathe the seven Spirits of God and the seven starres'; verse 7: 'These things saith he that is Holie and True, whiche hathe the keye of David, which openeth and no man shutteth, and shutteth and no man openeth.'

[279] 'Woe is unto mee, if I preach not the Gospel.'

[280] The parable of the talents, and the fault of the servant who was given but one talent and went and hid it in the earth.

[281] 'I beleeve, and therefore have I spoken, we also beleeve, and therefore speake.'

[282] Chapters 3–5 of the book of Acts concern the preaching ministry of the apostles in spite of the prohibition issued by the high priest and Peter's subsequent arrest.

[283] The wrath of God is threatened against those who 'forbid us to preach unto the Gentiles, that they might be saved'.

[284] William Tey is making reference to the 1583 edition of John Foxe's *Actes and monuments*. This is some of the best evidence we have of in-depth knowledge and use of *Actes and monuments*, a quasi-biblical text.

lycence of the Apostolike see or any his Catholikes, and this he practised, for being forbidden by the Archb[ishop] of Canterbury he preached.[285]

14.   John hus defendeth the truth of this, 13 Article page 451 that all such as doe leave of preaching or hearing the worde of God for feare of excommunication are alreadie excommunicated and judged as Traytors to god.[286]

15.   The Bohemians. 3 Article. 655. the word of god oughte to be free for every man appoincted and ordeyned thereunto to preach and read in all places without resistaunce of any man or without inhibition ether of spirituall or earthly power openly or manifestlye[287]

William Thorpe page 532 avoucheth and defendeth this truth by many arguments and reasons out of scriptures and doctors.[288]

{Page 545}   John purndy practised the same[289]

{999}   Article 4 of Thomas Arthur if I shuld suffer persecution for preaching the gosple of god yet there are 7000 moe that wold preach the gosple as I doe now[290]

{Page 1111}   Lambertes answer to the B[ishop]s article 21 whether that men prohibited of B[ishop]s to preache as suspecte of heresie ought to cease preachinge, answereth that they ought to preache and confirmeth the same by arguments reasons and examples[291]

Mr Coverdale Bradford and many other lerned men and godlie preachers contynued preachinge in Queene Maries daies untill they were imprisoned, she and the B[ishop]s forbade them

{1979}   Edmund Allen his answere to sir John Baker[292]

To conclude if an Eldershipp tyrannise the mynister or people, the party injured ought to appeale to the Synode from a Synode to a provinciall counsaile and soe to a generall

---

[285] P. 435, Article 14 reads, 'That it is lawful for any man, either deacon or priest to preach the word of God, without the authority or licence of the Apostolicke sea or any other of his Catholickes.'

[286] This is 'the 14 article of J. Wickliffe': 'They which leave of preaching and hearing of the word of God for feare of excommunication of men, are alreadye excommunicate, and in the day of judgement shalbe counted the betrayers of Christ', p. 451.

[287] Tey is here quoting verbatim the text found on p. 655.

[288] The examination of William Thorpe, penned with his own hand, begins on p. 528 and is aptly cited on p. 532.

[289] John Purvey on p. 545 argued that 'al good Christians' were 'to teach and preach the Gospell to their neighbours'.

[290] 'He said, Good people, if I should suffer persecution for the preaching of the Gospel of God, yet there is 7000. more that would preach the Gospell of God, as I do now', p. 999.

[291] Tey has observed the following passage on p. 1111: 'In the xxi where you do aske, whether I do beleve that men prohibited of bishops to preach, as suspect of heresy, ought to cease from preaching and teaching, untill they have purged themselves of suspition, afore an higher Judge?' Lambert's answer is found on p. 1112: 'when men be wrongfully suspect or infamed of heresy, and so prohibited by Bishops for to preach the worde of God, that they ought for no mens commaundement to leave or stop. . .'.

[292] On p. 1979 there is an account of 'The talke or reasoning betwene Sir John Baker, Colins his chaplaine and Edmund Allen', in which Baker asks Allen 'who gave thee authority to preache and interprete? Art thou a priest? art thou admitted thereunto? Let me see thy licence', and Allen responds, 'I am persuaded that God hath geven me this autority as he hath geven to al other christians.' Foxe has added a marginal note that reads, 'In tyme of publicke corruption and in want of true teachers, it is not forbidden to any man to teach.'

The answer made by another godlie to the same poynte.[293]

1.   Two thinges especiallie are to be considered in the silencing of mynisters at this day: thone whether they who doe prohibite the preachinge have lawfull authority by the worde soe to doe.

2.   Secondlie whether the thinges urged upon the ministers are such as they may with good conscience suffer for and soe runne into the daunger of Suspension.

Concerning the first, though their place and callinge and authority be not that which yt ought to be by the worde, yet forasmuch as both that Jurisdiction and government which they exercise is warrantised by the lawes of this Realme, and the High Comission especially is agreed upon by Acte of Parliament and is not onlie from her ma[jes]ty, I wold therfore affirme (as I thinke) that neither the Authority of B[ishop]s is Antichristian <as> nor yet the same meerlie from the civill magistrate (affirmed in the 4 and 5 Articles before) especially that which they exercise by vertue of the high Commission if we looke into the righte use thereof. And hereupon I thinke yt may be answered, that forasmuch as our entrance hath bene by them, and is yet contynued of all that daily enter and that where just causes be of silencing man alone, I meane such as exercise the Church discipline may inhibite and utterly expell the mynisterie. I also thinke that the Church stability doth not stand nor depend upon man as is [fo. 34r] affirmed 2. Article before though a man kepe silence at the B[ishop]s prohibition, for if a mynister of Geneva shuld make a schisme in the Church there for administring with wafer bread, for that yt hath the similitude of the popish ceremony in their masse, I wold thinke the <Eld> Eldership there might proceed against him being obstinately opinatyve therein, even to the Censure of suspension, though otherwise yt mighte before be evident to the Church by his giftes that he were called of god; soe that there man above following the order of the worde of god mighte inhibite. And soe perhaps yt may be said of those who stand against the orders established in our Church in such ceremonies as are not of themselves evell but indifferent in their owne nature.

{3 Article}   Christ hath this authority soe committed to him that yet he doth exercise yt by men; who if they doe yt lawfully may both place and displace insomuch as he placeth none without men.

{6. 7. 8. 9. 10. Articles}   All these depend upon that which is said already, for if the B[ishop]s authority be any thinge in our Church and the causes likewise of their proceedinge such as I have mentioned, then must ministers take yt as the voice of god and his Authority, at the least wise if he be put out by the same hand he was put into his place and calling. No private man may preache, but such is the estate of those who are justlie disauthorized by the Church though before they were lawfully Authorised.

---

[293] This is surely Edmund Chapman speaking. Particularly important, and typical of Chapman's constructive moderation, are the points that 'forasmuch as disciplyne is not the essentiall note of a Church . . . And we have none other disciplyne then this which is this exercised.' Somewhat to the contrary, Calvinists of the second generation, and notably Theodore Beza, had taught that discipline, the third mark of the church, along with doctrine and sacraments, *was* essential. This was the foundation of the presbyterianism taught and practised by Andrew Melville in Scotland and, so far as they could, by Cartwright and Field in England. Probably few of Chapman's colleagues would have allowed episcopal government to be a legitimate form of discipline.

{11. 12} That of the Apostles (I take yt) is impertynente, forasmuch as they were not called by men if you saie that in the proportion it agreeth thus farre, that as mynisters have a callinge from god, so farre they ought to follow the Apostles. I thinke yt may safelye be denied, for that even that callinge which they have from god, they dare not assay to put in practise till the Church doth approve. And for Timothie and the rest, that prohibition was none other then we may be letted by Atheistes Papists or such like at this daye.

Thexamples alledged, if it be said that they respecte Antichristian B[ishop]s in deed, enemies to Christ in the fundamentall poyntes of salvation (when as we have not to doe with such) may perhaps also seeme impertynent. And I thinke that those generall speeches of theirs must be ranged within the listes of the due order of disciplyne. Now forasmuch as disciplyne is not the essentiall note of a Church, but yt may be the true church of god where yt is not rightly administered (though in deed a maymed Church sicke and languishinge) And we have none other disciplyne then this which is thus exercised. It remayneth that we laboure to enjoy our places, and followe on in the course of the mynisterie by such lawfull good meanes as we may and with bearinge soe much as with a good conscience we may beare, or els (if yt be lawfull) we must erecte disciplyne which we desire that we may proceed by the orders thereof appoynted and layde out by the worde of God.

Peruse and pardon

{26. meeting. foll. 5.}

I place this letter here bicause the comming of doctor Uxenbridge to dedham was moved unto the brethren in their meetinges, whether yt were convenient for to receyve him, being withstood by the Church of dedham, and at length yelded unto, and therupon doctor Chapman wrote his lettre to mr Stubs,[294] which here followeth

Grace and peace etc. The case of our Tutors enterteynement[295] being the second tyme proposed to our auncyents of dedham, a consent was geven with these Condicions, that if offence did rise of it, some publike knowledge mighte be geven out of the cause of his comminge viz for conference sake to wynne him, and if in reasonable tyme there appeared noe fruite of the paynes and meanes used for his good, you wold be as readie to remove him as now yow are to place him with us: A house very commodious is procured he shall have his choise of two rowmes, in thone wherof his bed may be placed, in thother his meate dressed, for which rowmes and for the use of some other necessaries, his lynen and bedding excepted I have promised ii s. a weeke: Let us be certified speedely of your and his determination that wood and such thinges necessary at his direction may be provided for in tyme. Salute mr doctor Uxenbridge in my name: The lord make him capable of that good

[294] John Stubbs, the author of the notorious *Gaping Gulph,* was Thomas Cartwright's brother-in-law, Cartwright having married his sister Alice. Stubbs's own wife, Anne, was a Brownist, and in August 1590 Cartwright wrote her a very long letter, in effect a treatise, trying to dissuade her from her separatism. (*Cartwrightiana, ed.* Albert Peel and Leland H. Carlson, Elizabethan Nonconformist Texts, I (London, 1951), 58–75.) It appears that while the conference with Oxenbridge was 'by the appointment of the Counsell', with a formal commission to proceed, it had actually been arranged by Stubbs, who was in 1584 a minor government functionary with some influence.

[295] The only joke Edmund Chapman is known to have made.

is entended to him ward by yow and yours to his eternall comforte in the lord Jesus.
Thus with all our most hartie commendacions to yow and mrs Stubs I end.
Aug[ust] 17. 1584
yours at commandement in the lorde
Edmund Chapman

[fo. 34v]

A note of the conferences which was betwene some godlie mynisters and D.
Uxenbridge the Papist being come to Dedham to that end by the appointment of the
Counsell[296]
{26 and 27 meeting. foll. 5.6.}

D. Uxenbridge wold not dispute till he saw their Commission from the lordes of the
Counsell that they had authority soe to doe. The ministers desired to begynne the
Accon with praier, but he denied to joigne with us in praier bicause he protested he
was not of our profession and soe the brethren kneeling downe to that worke, he
stood up and praied to himself.
Mr. Doctor Cricke was the first that disputed with him: And before the disputation
he desired to know of D. Uxenbridge his faith and opynion of the holie scriptures,
that they might have a ground of disputation for he wold rather have him beleeve,
then dispute of faith by reasons, which is one of the *parta inferni*
Therfore Mr Doctor Cricke desyred that they mighte come to this poynt what was
canonicall scripture: And gave this defynition of it: The Canonicall scripture of
thold Testament is that which of it self is sufficiente to confirme every point of
doctrine that was necessary for thold church to believe
Pap   I denie this defynition it is false: The Penteteuke may be sufficient *omnis*
definitio periculosa. I will pause on yt. Canonicall is that which is set downe as a
Canon or rule by the Church. I will bring a prooff out of Pet[er] who saith all scripture of thold Testament is regular wherof the Church sets a rule, and soe of the new
Church.[297]
Cr   This varieth from all lerned men. Jerom is against it, this definition might
serve for Esope fables[298] if the Church shuld agree of it. I will gather an argument of
your defynition. whatsoever the Church shall set downe is Canonicall, but they have
set downe Esope fables to be receyved into the Church: ergo it is Canonicall:
Pap   That is an impossible condition and yt cannot be the Church shuld soe farre
erre in a matter of faith nor it was nor never shalbe proved.
Cr.   Tutching the bookes of the Canonicall scriptures I reason thus: Only 22.

---

[296] The subject of the initial disputation between Crick and Oxenbridge was whether scripture or the
church enjoyed prime authority. In 1564, the thesis debated before Queen Elizabeth on her state visit
to Cambridge, asserted by Matthew Hutton against Andrew Perne, had been '*maior est scripturae*
quam ecclesiae authoritas'. See Patrick Collinson, *Elizabethan essays* (London, 1994), pp. 191–2.

[297] 2 Peter i. 21: 'For the prophesie came not in olde time by the will of man: but holy men of God spake
as they were mooved by the holy Ghost.'

[298] Reminiscent of John Field's remark that one might as well subscribe to Aesop's fables as to the
prayer book. See above, p. xci.

bookes had authority emong the Jewes to confirme doctrine for that Church ergo: 22 are only Canonicall[299]

Pap   how longe hath this bene: there were many bookes divine that were not Canonicall:

Crick   Then they were devine bookes of thold Testament

Pa   They were soe

Cr.   Then they were Canonicall for if they were divine they were of god.

Pa.   There are two causes of making the scriptures Canonicall, God first and then the Church.

Cr.   There can none make any thing Canonicall but godes worde, and none can make it soe but god.

Pa.   It is not Canonicall till the Church have set downe a rule

Cr.   If <it> this be true, then the authority of the Church is above godes

Cr.   There are but 22. bookes bicause the Jewes bible left to us have no more, els they have left to us an imperfect old Testa[ment] in hebrew, but they have not left an imperfect old Testa[ment] in hebrew, ergo ther be but 22. bookes

Pa.   They have left the Machabes in hebrew as Jerom saieth, And daniell was not *in hebraica lingua* but *in hebraicis literis*

Cr.   Thold Testa[ment] which the Church of the Christians hath receyved from thold Church of the Jewes conteyneth no more but 22. bookes therfore there be noe more Canonicall.

Pa.   The proposition is doubtfull bicause we know that the bookes from the first were divine but we know not when they were receyved to be Canonicall.

Cr.   Only those bookes had authority to confirme matters of doctrine, that were in the body of <thold> the Jewes bible or old Testament, but only 22. were in the body of the Jewes Bible, ergo

Pa.   I answere by a distinction of authoritie, one was an authority commonly knowen. 2 an authority they had in themselves though it appeared not to others. Ther is two senses of the body of the Jewes old Testament, some were Canonicall, and some after [fo. 35r] revealed by divine men which yet in some sense may be called in the body of the Jewes Testament

Cr.   In what tyme was this?

Pa   Betwene Christes tyme and Esras tyme.

Cr.   Are any bookes comparable to the 22.   Pap: None are comparable to the scriptures.

Cr.   Whatsover bookes the Churche mighte lacke without losse of that knowledge she shuld have for salvation, all those are out of the Canon: But all bookes but the 22. were such as the church of the Jewes had no losse by in knowledge of her salvation, therfore all besides the 22. be out of the Canon:

Pa.   The minor is false.

---

[299] There were different ways of numbering the books of the Old Testament but Josephus, Epiphanius and Jerome all gave the number of canonical books as 22. See Roger Beckwith, *The Old Testament Canon of the New Testament Church and its Background in Early Judaism* (London, 1985), pp. 235–73. Behind this debate lies the question of the status of the apocryphal scriptures, which were included in the Anglican lectionary, but which many puritans refused to acknowledge as 'scripture'. Crick in this debate affords such books no more credence than he would give to the Golden Legend (see p. 100).

Cr.   If those 22. doe conteyne that which is aboundantlie sufficient for the Church of the Jewes then she mighte want all besides, but those 22 did conteyne all was abundantlie sufficient, ergo she mighte want all besides:

Pa.   I denie the minor.

Cr.   If those bookes did not conteyne all that was abundantlie sufficient, then those bookes that supplie that want are more excellente, and to be preferred in that poynte before other bookes:

Pa.   It followeth not: for though they be not more excellent yet they are as sufficient as the rest

Cr.   There were excellent and famous thinges done by Christ and given out in doctrine by him and yet he saw not good to burden the Church with them, therefore your church doth ill to burden the Church of god with lesse famous thinges as the booke of Machabees and the rest. doe ye thinke ther is any more excellent spirite in the bookes of Tobith and Judeth then ther is in your *legenda Aurea*: is not that booke true.

Pa.   I compare noe booke with the holie scriptures.

Cr.   Let us proceed to another question: do yow not saie that the Church can not erre in matters of faith: Pap. yes:

Cr.   What are groundes for this point, is it not 13. 14 and 15 chapters of John wher he promiseth to send the comforter to lead them into all truth: and 16. math. hell gates shall not prevaile etc.[300]

Pa.   These be not thonlie groundes for every truth hath many groundes but these be the chiefest:

Cr.   what meane yow by Church.   Pa   do yow thinke the Church can erre:

Cr.   I saie the Church doth erre.   Pa.   Then I can geve yow no defynition of it:

Cr.   will yow draw me to your Church if yt erre? yow may not sticke to yt: geve me a definition of a Church that cannot erre:

Pa.   If yow will tell me what yow meane by this *Ecclesia est columna veritatis* I will:

Cr.   will yow hold that to be the Church as it is there commended   Pa.   yea

Cr.   Then geve a defynition of the Church?

Pa.   It is a collection of people gathered by the ministery of the Apostles and by their disciples as 10. ch. Hebrews:

Cr.   what meane you by matters of faith?   Pa.   I meane such thinges as be set downe in godes worde   Cr.   Then yt encludeth manners   Pa.   yea

Cr.   Then your meaning is, whatsoever is sett downe in the word of god ether tutching doctrine or manners that the Church cannot erre in: Pa.   yea and I ground my self upon christs wordes and promise that he wold be with them, and lead them into all truthe   Cr.   To whom did Christ speake these wordes.

Pa.   To the 12 Apostles

Cr.   did he speake yt to them severally considered in themselves or to the 12 altogether

Pa.   He promised it to the bodie of them and not to all for Judas was exempted, it was to the whole Church, to the 12 personallie and in them to all the Churche.

---

[300] Matthew xvi. 18–19, the great commission to Peter, was (and is) the foundation of the claim of the Roman Church to authority, even infallibility, in matters of faith.

Cr.   whether was that promise made to the 11 and their successors generallie or severally

Pa.   As yt happened it was to the 11.

Cr.   It was not a matter casuall but in truthe. If yt was spoken to every mynister in them, the promise must be to the successor as it was to the predecessor, but to the predecessor the promise was made without the determination of the Church, ergo so it must be to the successor.

Pa.   The promises to the Church are without condition, but to every particuler members with condicion if yow suffer with Christ yow shall reigne with him [fo. 35v]

Cr.   Christ praied for all, therfor all the Church may erre:

Pa.   I distinguish of the Church: ther is a Church of god predestinate, and a church militante which standes of good and badd, the church militant may erre but not the predestinate

Cr.   Peter being of the predestinate church did erre in that he refused to eate of meates as 10 actes the difference of meates being taken away.[301]

Pa.   he respected a speciall revelation:

Cr.   he could not erre if that be true that they shuld be lead into all trueth.

Pa.   he was not deceyved

Cr.   whosoever persuades himself that to be unlawfull which is lawfull is deceyved, but Peter did soe, ergo he was deceyved. he was spoken to in a vision or figure which was that as before he might not eate these thinges, now he might: and bicause there is a proportion of the figure and that was signified by it, he meaneth thou maiest joigne with the gentiles and have society with them therfore rise and eate. Peter 2 gal[atians][302] was blamed and therfore he might erre.

Pa.   he erred not

Cr.   whosoever is ignorant in any thing may erre in that thinge, but Peter was ignorant ergo.

Pa.   he was not ignorant

Cr.   whosoever is voyde of any thinge shuld be knowen is ignorant, but peter was soe, ergo

Pa.   he was not

Cr.   I prove it. Peter shuld have obeyed god at thie first commaundement <therfore he was> and have eaten therfore he was voyde of that he shuld have knowen, so was moses in that he disputed with god. So did John erre in worshipping the Aungell Revel[ation] 19.10[303]

Pa.   I wold have some auncient enterpreter to prove this.

Cr.   will yow have a better witnes then the Aungell: ether John failed or the Aungell found faulte with a thing was not to be found fault withall.

Pa.   Lyra saith that he thought it was *filius hominis* and it was not.

---

[301] Acts x. 14: 'But Peter sayd, Not so, Lord: for I have never eaten any thing that is polluted or uncleane.' Peter was out of order in so saying.

[302] Galatians ii. 11: 'And when Peter was come to Antiocha, I [Paul] withstood him to his face: for he was to be blamed.' The whole chapter concerns Paul's contention with Peter's judaizing tendencies, which Crick exploits to undermine Peter's supposed infallibility.

[303] When St John the Divine fell before the feet of an angel to worship him, he was told 'see thou do it not: I am thy felow servant, and one of thy brethren . . . Worship God.' So 'John' also could err.

Cr.   But Christ did not now appeare to them in that forme, he did yt afterward as 20 John,[304] therfore how answere yow that?

Pa.   he gave him civill honor?

Cr.   That is not true, for he gave him that honor that god chalengeth only to himself.

Cr.   The whole Church may be ignorant in a matter of faith.

Pa.   There is two kindes of ignoraunces: one disputes ther is no Resurrection, and bringes in arguments of Philosophie: Another kind of ignorance is thus, when a man holdes the same opynion, and saieth nothing, he meddleth not with it.

Cr.   It is a matter of faith and truth to knowe which bookes be Canonicall: the Church 400 yeares almost after the comming of Christ did acknowledge onlie 22. bookes to be Canonicall therfore ether the Church was ignorant in a matter of faith, or els to blame not to receyve more.

Pa.   The Church receyved more.

Cr.   The Counsell of Laodicea[305] hath only 22. bookes.

Pa.   The Counsell of Carthage[306] hath more.

Cr.   Could the one Counsell be lead by the spirite and not thother in soe shorte a tyme:

Pa.   The Counsell of Carthage was lead soe to thinke that thother bookes were Canonicall by these 3. thinges first by the doctrine in them conteyned. 2 by the tradition of the elders. 3 by thexposicion of fathers.

Cr.   all these are against them, for the doctrine in them is erronious, and the tradition <and> of the elders and exposition of fathers is against them for wheras it is said in Ecclesiasticus that it was the true Samuell[307] was raised up Jerom saieth it is *nefas* so to saie or beleve

Cr.   Christ saieth whersoever ther is two or three gathered in my name I am amongst them, therfor by your saying two or three so gathered cannot erre, for christ being amongst them leades them not into error.

Pa.   Some saie the Apocrypha bookes be Canonicall, some that they be not Canonicall but divine bookes made by holie men and some that they be frivolous and vayne and full of errors, which of these hold yow.

Cr.   Yow have heard myne opynion of them before, and soe with some debate further about yt, they concluded their conference

---

[304] John xx records the resurrection appearances of Jesus to his disciples. The rather abstruse point is whether these appearances were clearly distinguishable from the angel whom 'John' mistakenly worshipped in Revelation xix.

[305] According to some probably corrupt texts, the very shadowy Council of Laodicea (fourth century and not among the commonly accepted ecumenical councils) approved a list of canonical scriptures which excluded the Apocrypha and Revelation.

[306] There were in fact many Councils held at Carthage between 251 and 525. These were councils of the African Church and were not ecumenical.

[307] This concerns the encounter of Saul with the witch of Endor who conjured up the ghost of Samuel (1 Samuel xxviii). The apocryphal book of Ecclesiasticus held that it was indeed Samuel who spoke to Saul. 'After his sleepe also he told of the kings death, and from the earth lift he up his voyce, and prophesied that the wickednesse of the people should perish' (Ecclesiasticus xlvi. 20). But readers of margins of the Geneva Bible were told: 'It was Satan, who to blind his eyes tooke upon him the forme of Samuel.' This story was much discussed in the sixteenth century among students of witchcraft. Cf. the question whether the ghost of Hamlet's father was really a ghost.

[fo. 36r]

The nexte that disputed with him was Mr Stoughton

St.   *Sola fides iustificat*[308]

Pa.   It is daungerous to geve Assertions and except I had Counsels here and doctors I cannot discend to particularities, but I beleve as the Catholike Church beleveth, and I will tell yow what I thinke of Justification if I can fynd the text 5. gal[atians] 6 that faith working by love justifieth.

St.   Then yow hold that yow are justified by faith joigned with charity?

Pa.   I will goe no further then the texte. I dare descend no further into particularities knowing what a great daunger chaunge in wordes bringes in divinity.

St.   Whether do yow thinke he meaneth the ceremonies of the Jewes or of the gentiles?

Pa.   I said faith doth it by charity the fire hath two qualities heate and lighte and they be both together, so faith and charitie be together

St.   It is not the lighte that comfortes but the heate

Pa.   The comon acte of faith and love is to justify as the comon acte of the fire is to comforte

St.   But the proper acte of faith is to beleve, and the proper acte of Charity is to love. In the 7. luke faith only saveth beleve only and thou shalt be saved.[309]

Pa.   Charity is greater then faith if a man may compare yt.

St.   Abacuc saieth *Justus ex fide vivit*[310] and I reason hence thus: that wherby a man lyveth before god is yt, that onlie justifieth, but a man lyveth by faith only: ergo faith onlie justifieth.   Pa.   I deny the minor.

That which purifieth a mans harte onlie justifieth, but faith onlie purifieth the harte. Act 15[311] ergo faith onlie justifieth: Pap.   when it is said 5 gal[atians] *fides operans per charitatem* he sheweth what manner of faith it is that justifieth:

St.   Abraham beleved and was justified:

Pa.   Abrahams obedyence justified him: and he fled to the place in James. 2. ch[apter]. 24.[312]

St.   Then a man may be justified by one worke onlie if that be true which no papist will holde

Pa.   Yes a man may have salvation for geving of one cupp of water.

St.   he shall have a reward.   Pa   whie that is salvation:

St.   You will not take the word soe in other places. Let it passe but I demaund of yow what the Object of faith is, whether it be *intellectus*, *memoria* or *voluntas*.

Pa.   It is *intellectus*.

St.   Then the Objecte <is> of love is will: Pa.   he said will must worke with it

---

308 Thomas Stoughton goes straight for the jugular with Oxenbridge, asserting that only faith justifies. Oxenbridge is not entirely sure of his biblical ground but is quite correct in validating his catholic doctrine that the only justifying faith is *fides formata* by citing Galatians v. 6: 'faith which worketh by love'.

309 Luke vii. 50: Jesus to the woman who anointed his feet: 'Thy faith hath saved thee.'

310 Habakkuk ii. 4: 'the just shall live by his faith'.

311 Peter speaking in the Council of Jerusalem, Acts xv. 9: 'after that by faith hee had purified their hearts'.

312 James ii. 24: 'Ye see then how that of works a man is justified, and not of faith only.' This text, and the whole tenor of James's epistle, faced protestants with a task akin to that of squaring the circle.

St.   There is a proper subjecte of faith and of hope and of Charity, and every one hath his proper workinge

Pa.   The proper subjecte of faith is the soule

St.   Nay it is the power of the soule: but our question is whether we be justified by faith alone or love <ag> alone, or by both together, but I saie noe other vertue or quality justifieth but faith onlie:

Pa.   *Sola*, of his owne nature is *Generalis exclusiva particula*, and therfore use not the word onlie since the scripture useth it not.

St.   The scripture doth use it 7. luke

Pa.   There is difference betwene these *Sola fides iustificat* and *tantum crede*:

St.   There is none.   Pa.   Is ther noe difference of these, the kinge makes me riche, and the king onlie makes me riche, for this word onlie shuts out god that he justifieth not.

St.   Yow saie that onlie, in this sentence *sola fides iustificat* exclude, but in the 5. marke 36 wher it is said only beleve,[313] it encludes charity, yea of itself if the circumstances leade not to yt:

Pa.   he answered that faith did worke by charity

St.   If faith onlie obteyne for another any benefite then much more for my self: If christ looke onlie on faith in bestowing a temporall benefite, then faith shall obteyne a greater blessing for my self: If Christ Jesus be readie and willing to bestow temporall benefites with Crede onlie on others, he is much more readie to bestow eternall benefites on me for my faithe as 3. Rom[ans] 28.[314]

Pa.   I say as before faith and charity justify.

St.   They which are of age and baptised are reputed righteous: But they which doe beleve onlie are baptised, therfore they that do beleve onlie are reputed righteous.

Pa.   I denie the minor.   St.   I prove it by the example of the Eunuche 8 actes[315]

And soe this disputation ended for this tyme

[fo. 36v]

The third person of the mynisters that conferred with D. Uxenbridge was Mr Dowe

The question disputed of was this: whether Peter was head of the church that he was of[316]

---

[313] Mark v. 36: 'Be not afraid: onely beleeve.'

[314] Romans iii. 28: 'Therefore we conclude, that a man is justified by faith without the workes of the Law.'

[315] The story of the Ethiopian eunuch, who was baptized upon declaring his faith in Jesus Christ the Son of God, in Acts viii.

[316] This tiresomely scholastic argument concerns the duality of the church, visible and invisible, and whether Peter can have been head of both. Oxenbridge makes an interesting concession, perhaps indicative of his ambivalent posture as a church papist, that Peter would have had authority over a christian Nero only as a son of the church (*tanquam filius Ecclesiae*). This means that Peter could have excommunicated the emperor (as Ambrose excommunicated Theodosius) but had no power to depose him.

Do.   whosoever is head of the Church is head of the Catholike Church but Peter is not head of the Catholike church, therfor he is not head of the Church.

Pa.   I denie the Minor proposition

Do.   whosoever is head of the universall is head of the invisible:

Pa.   I denie yt. I distinguish that to be invisible that is not seene, nor seene to the governors and universall is visible.

Do.   The universall consists of *infinitis singularibus* but *infinita singularia* be *invisibilia.*

Pa.   I take *visibilia* to be *per intellectum*

Do.   But Peter was not visible *intellectu* but *oculo*

Pa.   He was visible both *intellectu* and *oculo.*

Do.   The Church was visible as appeareth at Peters sermon some being converted and yet it was invisible that were to be converted.

Pa.   These were both visible.

Do.   Is a Church that is in a particuler place only universall

Pa.   It is universall in some sence.

Do.   *Credo ecclesiam Catholicam*: must be of a Church not seene bicause faith is *eorum que non videntur*

Pa.   Petrus was *caput* visible *intellectu* and *aspectu*

Do.   What was Peter head of the Church *visibile intellectu* and *aspectu.*

Pa.   He was visible *per partes* and invisible for as christ is an invisible head so his church is invisible that a proportion mighte be betwene them.

Do.   Christ was head both of the visible and invisible Church being both god and man but Peter being but a man could not be head of the universall churche.

Pa.   he was head of the universall:

Do.   There cannot be a visible head of an invisible Church except he were both god and man.

Pa.   *Quae intelliguntur, non videntur.*

Do.   If Peter were heade then he was head of the Emperour:

Pa.   There was no Emperour of the Church then

Do.   But if their had bene any Emperor then baptised he had bene head over him:

Pa.   Not as he was an Emperor but *tanquam filius Ecclesiae*

Do.   Then he had not universall authority

Pa.   The baptising of Nero shuld not have hindred his authority

Do.   had he then universall universall [sic] authority

Pa.   I have answered before and so being wearie of this argument he desired to end the conference for this tyme

There was another conference betwene Mr Doctor Cricke and the Papist[317]

Cr.   Whatsoever is not of faith is synne.   Pa.   here is an Amphibology[318] for by faith is ment conscience

---

[317] When Crick returns to the fray, the subject is still faith, whether the faith that justifies is or is not *fides formata*. Oxenbridge's attempt to blind with science, quoting St Thomas Aquinas, is effective, since protestants too would concede that works justify in the perception of others.

[318] Ambiguity.

Cr.   without faith it is impossible to please god, then without love a man may
please him and have faith without love and therfor love is not the forme of faith:
Pa.   As the sould is forme of the bodie so love of faith.   Cr.   the soule is the
forme of man and not of the body
Pa.   Thomas Aquinas *Deus justificat effective, fides justificat apprehensive* and
opera justificat declarative
Cr.   If *charitas* be *forma fidei* then which is *materia* for *forma* is *materia forme*
they be not separated.
Pa.   I counte yt a defynition.
Cr.   It is a habite and therfore hath no forme:
Pa.   habites have matter
Cr.   Is it *forma mortua* or *vivae fidei*:
Pa.   It cometh to a dead faith and being joigned to yt makes it quicke
Cr.   Then it makes a divelish faith lyvelie
Pa.   Charity is a most heavenly thinge, and a dead faith is a divelish thinge and
these two cannot be joigned together.
Cr.   all develish faith must be joigned to love or some divelish faith to love to
quicken it: but *mortua fides est nulla fides quod non existit non est, fides mortua non
existit, ergo non est.*
Pa.   It is called dead not that it is dead but that yt wants the life of Charity

[fo. 37r]

[Cr.] *fides mortua* hath yt a forme?   Pa.   yes.   Cr.   what is the forme of yt:
Pa.   *Suum esse*
Cr.   *forma est quod dat esse*, what give *esse* to it,   Pa.   *Suum esse*
Cr.   Then *suum esse* hath *esse*:   Pa.   when charity cometh to it, yt is the
forme of yt.
Cr.   Charity is the forme of a lively faith then not of a dead faith for *unia et
mortua fides sunt privantiae* and cannot have *unam formam.* as *mors* is *privatio
vitae* soe *mortua fides* is *privatio vivae fidei*
Pa.   Faith and love be wrought together at the same instant therfore as yow saie a
dead faith and love arise both together
Cr.   *forma fidei mortuae* is <eh> *carentia charitate* say yow, but I say Charity is
the forme of a lyvelie faith, then faith is alyve before charity cometh.
And so ended the conference betwene these lerned men and the Papist: other conferences they had by way of persuasions with him which I noted not.

To <my> our beloved brethren mr doctor Chapman, doctor Cricke mr lewis and the
rest.[319]
Peace be upon us and mercy and upon the Israell of God.
Whereas (beloved brethren) at the tyme of the laste Parliament, order was taken by

---

[319] This letter would seem to indicate that recent events had contrived to reduce the membership of the
Braintree conference to a mere five men. In 1584–5 it could boast eleven members, headed by Robert
Wright and George Gifford (Bancroft, *Daungerous positions*, p. 75). Richard Parker later deposed
that it had included Ezekiel Culverwell, Richard Rogers, Gifford 'and others' (*ibid.*, p. 84). Why,
then, is Gifford not one of the signatories here? There is no simple answer to that question but for his
movements at this time see *BR*, p. 211 below.

consent of many of our godlie brethren and fellow labourers assembled at London, that all the mynisters which favoured and soughte the reformation of our church shuld sorte themselves together to have their meetinges to conferre about the matters of the Church: besides suche exercises as shuld most make for their profitinge every way: It was further advised that none shuld assemble above the number of tenn, and therfore they which exceeded that number shuld sorte themselves with others of their brethren next adjoiginge where defecte was: According hereunto: we your brethren, whose names are underwritten, have had our meetinges so oft as our troubles would give us leave: but find in regard of the smalnes of our number, and distance of place, that we stand in need of further ayde of some to be adjoyned unto us. whereupon understanding that God hath blessed you with store we are constrayned to make suite unto yow that yow wold of your abundaunce supply our want: and namely, considering that our beloved brother mr Newman is one who may be profitable to us, and in place most fytt both in respecte of yow and us, our earnest desire is, that yow wold yeld this benefite unto us, which we shall receive as a pledge of your love with thankfulnes and soe remayne in unfeyned love indebted to yow. The Lord our god and mercifull father multiply his graces upon us, that according to the manifold wants of his Church, and the times wherein we may live we may be enabled unto that high and <del>mighty</del> weightie service he hath called us unto. June. 7. Anno 1587.

yours in the truth.[320]

Richard Rogers   Ezekell Culverwell
Roger Carr   John Hockill
Giles Whitinge

An answer to the former letter.[321]

To our verie lovinge brethren mr Rogers mr Culverwell and the rest dd

Grace mercie and peace from god our father and form our lord Jesus Christ. As we may be broughte under some suspicion with yow (our verie loving brethren) in that your former letters have bene hetherto passed over with silence: soe we likewise hope your spirituall love to be such as yt will not suffer yow to conceyve that either yourselves or your request have bene layd aside without our regard, (for who are we that we shuld willinglie neglecte yow or the least of our brethren) but will rather thinke in your godlie wisdoms, that we mighte suppose silence in this case to be the best answere to yntymate our meaninges, being very lothe to have returned yow our deniall to any parte of your request: yet since understanding that you rested not soe satisfied, we caused lettres to be written, which notwithstanding we find by some occasions hitherto retayned in the handes of the writer. Now for your brotherlie demaund. Although we have heard that yt hath not seemed convenient unto diverse of good understandinge for one man to be of two meetinges,[322] yet the

---

[320] See *BR* for all five signatories.

[321] Dedham's excuse for replying to Braintree only six months after hearing from them is not entirely convincing.

[322] This was presumably one of the decisions sent down from London. It seems to have been abortive, since the Dedham minutes suggest that Henry Sandes continued to adhere to both Dedham and his Suffolk conference.

consideration of your selves your earnest desire with our care in common for the Church of Christ moving us much: we willinglie graunted (if he wold undertake bothe) that mr Newman shuld be knitt unto yow, soe as yt made noe disjoygning from us: but he havinge first and soe longe tyme fastened himself unto this society (from the which he seeketh not to be loosed) we dare not now put to our fingers to untie the knott. we reverence our faithfull brethren at London with their gratyous advises, and hartelie praise god for that good which the Church receyveth from them [fo. 37v] yet being best privy in our conference, what inconvenience we see likely to ensue by a separation: we praie and besech you lovinglie to respecte us, although in our consultacion we find not motives sufficient to persuade us to remove mr Newman. There hath bene some like motion made for others on Suffolke side,[323] but we cannot be induced to departe with any, who having joigned themselves are willing still to cleave unto us. Thus hoping that you will well accepte our good meaning in yelding yow that which we may, although we cannot wholie accomplish your request, we commend yow, all your Labors with the whole Israell of God unto the riches of his grace, who is in all Churches to be blessed for ever.

December 5 1587

your lovinge brethren in Christ

Edmund Chapman   Richard Crick
William Teye   Tho[mas] farrur
Robert Lewis   Richard Parker

Here followeth the formes of Subscription which was yelded by the mynisters in diverse shires, and places in this land
And first the Subscription of the mynisters of london
Apud Lambeth 6. December 1583 *Anno Regni* Elizab[eth] 26.[324]

At which daie and place the persons underwritten appeared before the most reverend father <John> in god John by the providence of god Lord Archbishop of Canterbury. John Bishop of London. John Bishop of Sarum. John Bishop of Rochester. Gabriell goodman Deane of Westminster, and being required to subscribe to

---

[323] Henry Sandes is meant, and perhaps Richard Crick.

[324] Richard Parker is mistaken. These are not 'the mynisters of london' but the eight Sussex ministers who were among the first to be seen by Whitgift in the early days of the subscription struggle, the reason being that the archbishop was exercising his metropolitan jurisdiction during the vacancy of the see of Chichester. (Collinson, *EPM,* pp. 249–51.) See 'a Briefe and true reporte of the proceedinges againste some of the ministers and prechers, of the diocese of Chichester for refusinge to subscribe to certaine articles', *Seconde parte,* I, 209–20, and many significant details to be found only in the full MS, DWL, MS Morrice, Old Loose Papers, 119–28. There is another copy of this paper in Northamptonshire Record Office, MS F.(M).P.63. The Sussex ministers were handled with kid gloves by Whitgift, Aylmer, Bishop John Piers of Salisbury, Bishop John Young of Rochester and Gabriel Goodman, dean of Westminster. This Whitgift instantly regretted complaining that it had been given out at court that the Sussex ministers had subscribed only 'with protestation', which provoked this declaration: 'I mean to perform this that I have taken in hand to the uttermost.' Bishop Young detected a hardening of attitude on the part of the Sussex ministers after they had met with Field's London conference. 'If I were as you, I would not care with how few such I were acquainted.' The signatures to this document correspond exactly to the subscriptions appearing on membrane 1 of LPL, *Carte Antique et Miscellene* XIII/60, and under the same date, 6 December 1583. This appears to have been a subscription roll kept at Lambeth for all clergy waiting on the archbishop and used, in effect, as a kind of 'visitors' book. The editors are grateful to Dr David Crankshaw for discussion on this point and for elucidating the likely nature of the document.

the booke of common praier set forth and allowed by the lawes and statutes of this Realme, they alledged that there were certayne Rubrikes in the said booke wherin there was conteyned some ambiguities or doubtes which moved them to require of the said most reverend father and the rest afore named the Interpretation of the said Rubrikes, which being made and geven accordinglie, the said most reverend and the rest declared and signified unto them, that tutching the Rubrikes, which they thought doubtfull, and named unto the said fathers their subscription was not required to any other sence then such as was not against the word of god, and agreable to the substance of religion now professed in this Church of England, and by law established, and according to the Analogy of faith and that their subscription is not to be extended to any thinge not expressed in the saide booke yet they desired to have their doubts severally answered that they might be satisfied particularly before they subscribed: the doubtes follow.

The Rubrickes that they named and made doubte of, was that in the later end of the preface set before the Catechisme in the Communion booke in these wordes. And that noe man shall thinke that any detriment shall come to children by deferring of their confirmation he shall know for truth that it is certeyne by gods worde that children being baptised have all thinges necessary for their Salvation and be undoubtedly saved: upon which wordes they moved this doubte, whether by these wordes the booke confirmed this opinion that the Sacrament of Baptisme did of it self conferre *grace tanquam ex opere operato* that is that whosoever is baptised must of necessity be saved *ex opere operato* though otherwise an hipocrite or Infidell. whereunto it was answered that the booke had noe such meaning, and that by these wordes it onlie dissuaded from the opinion which the papistes had of their Confirmacion called Bishoppinge which they beleve to be necessary to salvation, and do think that Children are not perfectlie baptised untill they be also bishopped, and therfore they make confirmation a Sacrament and bring their children thereunto being infantes wheras this Church of England hath no such opinion thereof but doth use yt to this end speciallie that children may know what their godfathers promised for them in their baptisme and also lerne to performe the same, and likewise that it may be knowen whether the god fathers have performed their promise in seeing those children enstructed as the booke requireth and therfore that Rubricke to conteyne nothing in it contrary to the word of god to the substaunce of religion now professed in this Church of England and by law established, or to the Analogy of faith: with which answer they were satisfied.

The second doubte was of this Rubricke in the forme of baptisme Then the Priest shall make a Crosse in the childs forehead and whether therby the crossing of the child were made an addition to the Sacrament as a part thereof and as though Baptisme were imperfecte without it wherunto it was answered that the booke had noe such meaninge and that the crossing of the child was only a ceremony signifi-cant and a profitable circumstance according to the wordes expressed in the booke, with which answer they were also contente.

[fo. 38r]

The third doubte was of these wordes in the booke of ordring deacons and priests etc Receyve the holie ghost etc whether therby was ment that the B[ishop] had authority to give the holie ghost etc. It was answered that the B[ishop] did not therby take upon him to geve the holie ghost, but onlie instrumentaliter as the mynister geveth Baptisme, when he saieth I baptise thee in the name of the father etc. wherby he doth not take upon him to be author or gever of baptisme but the mynister thereof onlie as John the Bap[tis]t did, for Christ onlie is the gever of the holie ghost and of Baptisme, John and others are onlie the mynisters of the Sacraments and of the ceremony. The wordes are Christes wordes used in the admitting of the Apostles to the mynistery and therfore used by us in the like action, to signify that god by our ministery and imposicion of handes as by his Instruments doth geve his holie spirite to all such as are rightlie called to the mynistery. with which answere they were likewise satisfied.

The last doubte was of baptising by women whereunto it was answered that the booke did not name women when it spake of private baptisme and that ther subscription was not required to any thing that was not <expressed> expressed in the booke: these resolucions and interpretations of these doubtes were mynistered to them by these John Canterb[ury] John London. John Sarum and Gabriell goodman wherupon we did voluntarelie and without any protestacion subscribe to the three Articles set downe for all preachers and ministers to subscribe unto:

Their names that subscribed

william hopkins	Tho[mas] Underdowne	John Bingham
Samuell Norden	John German	Thomas <Elye> Helye[325]
Anthony Hobson	Richard Wheateacker	

A forme of Subscription to the 3. fornamed Articles

To the first concerning her ma[jes]ties soveraigne Authority according to the 37. Article in the booke of Articles which is of Civill magistrates we most willinglie subscribe

To the 2. of the booke of Articles as far as by Parliament hath bene thought meete to be required, that is such onlie of them as concerne doctrine of faith and of the Sacraments taken them in that sense that is best as yt is meete for us to doe[326] and as the booke of the harmony of confessions have done in the Articles inserted in the Apologye of the Church of England we likewise most willinglie subscribe

---

[325] William Hopkins(on) was vicar of Salehurst (1572–97); Samuel Norden rector of Hamsey (1582–1605, deprived); Anthony Hobson vicar of Lyminster (1566–1605); Thomas Underdowne rector of St John sub castro, Lewes (1582–92); John German vicar of Burpham (occurs 1584); Richard Wheateacker (Whitaker) vicar of Amberley (c. 1577–85); John Bingham incumbent or preacher of West Hoathly (occurs 1583–4); and Thomas Helye (Healy) vicar of Warbleton and later also of Wartling (c. 1583–1605; 1602–5, deprived). See Roger B. Manning, *Religion and society in Elizabethan Sussex* (Leicester, 1969), pp. 200–1 and *passim* for the further careers of Helye, Norden and Underdowne.

[326] The wording of the 1571 Act 'for Conservation of Order and Uniformity in the Church' (13 Eliz. I, cap. 12), which gave statutory force to the articles of religion (the thirty-nine articles) provided for subscription 'to all the Articles of Religion which only concern the confession of the true Christian faith and the doctrine of the sacraments'. 'Which only' could be construed as a general comment on the articles in their entirety, or as limiting subscription to the more properly doctrinal of the articles. J. E. Neale argued that parliament, at the end of a complex and contentious political process, intended the second of these readings: *Elizabeth I and her parliaments, 1559–1581* (London, 1953), pp. 204–7. This has been doubted by G. R. Elton, *The parliament of England 1559–1581* (Cambridge, 1986), pp. 212–14, but there is no doubt that puritans, as in this document, consistently construed the Act in that sense.

For thother Articles in yt the booke of common praier and of Consecration, we most <humbly> humbly crave to be respected till such tyme as we may be satisfied according to the statute in this behalf in such points as yet seeme to us to be contrary to the word of god, and to the judgment both of other Churches professing the Gosple with us and of the best writers of our tyme: notwithstanding which points we promised as we have done heretofore to tender the peace of our Church and for these matters to make noe separation from it

Doubtes moved by the mynisters of Norwich and of places thereabout wherein they desired to be resolved[327]

Wheras in doubtes that may arise concerning any thinge in the Communion booke the preface annexed to the same booke not onlie geveth all men free libertie but willeth them to demaund the resolucion of such doubtes of the Bishop of the diocesse we therfor whose names are subscribed (not in deprivation [*recte* 'depravation'] of the booke or any thinge therein but for acquitinge of our consciences being now urged to subscribe therunto) humbly crave of your Lord the resolucion of these thinges followinge.

1. First for the Collecte upon the daie of the Nativity of Christ, we doubte how the same Collecte can be said seven daies together that Christ was borne every one of those daies <without> without untruth. the like may be said of the preface upon whit sonday at the Communion.

2. Secondlie we doubte how the porcions of scripture taken out of the booke of the Prophets, Acts of the Apostles and Apocalipse may be called Epistles without untruethe

3. Thirdlie for the Gosple appointed on the 20. sunday after Trinity we doubte how that which the text saieth; and is to be gathered by the Circumstaunce that Christ spake to the Pharises, may trulie be said that he spake to his disciples

[fo. 38v]

4. Fourthlie we doubte how the crosse in baptisme may be called a token of our warfare for Christ (the baptisme being in token therof in respecte of our dutie to god) without derogatinge from the Sacrament of Baptisme or els being a needles superfluity without <ed> edifyinge

Fiftlie in the preface before the Confirmation of children, we doubte how those wordes viz That it is certayne by gods worde that children being baptised have all thinges necessary for their Salvation and be undoubtedly saved, can trulie be verified by the word of god.

---

[327] Nine of these ministers: Woods, Morgan, Oates, Rannow, Sharpe, Lynacre, Mallis (or Mellis), Burdsell and Greene are found among the twenty 'Ministers of Norfolk' who petitioned the privy council in 1584 (*Seconde parte*, I, 223–5). The names of John More and 'Robert' Robarts (if this is a mistake for Thomas Roberts, as it seems to be), which head these 'Doubts', are absent from the petition, perhaps signficantly, since these were the most prominent of the Norfolk godly divines (see above, pp. xlv–vi) and their names lead the list of sixty-two ministers in Norfolk 'not resolved to subscribe' (*Seconde parte*, I, 244). Samuel Greenaway, curate of Tibbenham in 1584, was not a nonentity. He was More's officer in the Norwich parish of St Andrew's who organized unauthorized fasts, and by More's influence became minister of Westhall, a living in the gift of the Knyvetts, with whom he fell out, leading to his deprivation. (Collinson, 'PCM', pp. 313, 340, 658, 1263.)

As for other matters depending in controversie betwene the writers viz. of Baptisme by women, as is to be gathered by the wordes of the booke and the ratification of that Baptisme by the ministers hertofore, with the demaundes in publike Baptisme ether to the Infante or godfathers and thother doubtes in Confirmation, if yt please your L[ord] to resolve us of them, yt will be a great staie to our consciences. If otherwise us [sic] to our publike answere in writinge, we are to waite and hope for fuller Resolution from him that hath taken in hand to answer them. wherin untill we be resolved in our consciences by the worde of god, we dare not (as fayne we wold) soe freelie subscribe to all thinges conteyned in the booke, as we have bene and alwaies wilbe readie to subscribe and sweare to the first article concerninge her Majesties authoritye.

John More	Richard foster	John Burdsell
Robert Robarts	John bernarde	John Greene
Richard woods	Nicholas Aylande	Edward Reade
Samuell oates	Edward sharpe	John harrison
John Morgan	Tho[mas] Aldred	Richard Gibson
Vincent goodwin	Samuell Greneway	John Rawlins
Leonard Rannow	Robert lynacre	Thomas Searlbye
	Thomas mallis	

A forme of Subscription which mr more offred unto the Bishop of Norwich under his owne hand unto Bishop Freake[328]

I doe acknowledge and confesse that all the Articles of religion which onlie concerne the confession of the true christian faith and the doctrine of the Sacramentes authorised by Acte of Parliamente the 13. of her ma[jes]ties Reigne to be good, godlie, consonante and agreable to the word of god, all which I have hetherto most willinglie taught and professed, and mynde (god willinge) contynuallie to doe the same. And as for thother Articles comprised in the said booke tutchinge ceremonies, the discipline and governement of the Church and other orders now established, I doe acknowledge confesse and am verely persuaded in conscience their corruptions and imperfections not to be soe greate, as that for the same any man ought or may refuse to come to the Church, heare sermons and be pertakers of the Sacramentes. And further I do judge in my conscience and find by daily experience, that the unnecessary heatinge of such questions now in controversie in preaching or other publike Assemblies to breed disquiett in the Church of god and to bring mislikinge of the state now prochinge, are wisely to be

---

[328] This form of limited subscription dated from 1578, when John More offered it to Bishop Freke in the name of the other Norwich ministers. A copy, identical to this, was filed by Lord Burghley (HMC *Salisbury*, II, 228–9), following representations to the privy council. When on 3 May 1578 Henry Bird, a lay preacher of Norwich and ecclesiastical commissioner for the diocese, urged the leading gentry patrons of the Norfolk puritans, Nathaniel Bacon and William Heydon, to 'sollicit the cause of the Church' in London, it was to be on the basis of More's offer. Folger Shakespeare Library, MS Bacon I. T. 10.

foreseene, restreyned and avoyded, which I mynd and promise for mine owne parte (god willinge) carefullie to consider and performe. As farther for the takinge away of all offence, or the least suspition of mislikinge, not in my private prayers onlie hertelie but also in my publike exerci [fo. 39r] ses unfeignedlie together with thother states and callinges used namely to commend to god the righte reverend Father in god Edmund Bishopp of this diocesse, beseching God of his infynite goodnes for his Christ and Churche his cause, that as he hath committed unto him a greate charge and therfore will require agayne a great accompte at his hande, soe he will endue him with his speciall graces, and a mightie porcion of his holie spirite to performe the dutie of his place and to walke in singlenes of harte before him to the comforte of his Churche, and the confusion of Antichrist and his kingdome.

By me John More

The forme of Subscription by the mynisters in Leycestershire[329]

1.   The booke of Articles Tutching sound doctrine of faith and good workes we doe allow and embrace and detest all heresies condemned by the said Article speciallie Papistry and Anabaptistrye

2.   The booke of common praier setting forth the true religion comprehended in the same Articles we have hitherto receyved and used and none other certeine Ceremonies conteyned in the Rubricke of the same booke and certeine thinges supposed to be in the booke as baptising by women, question seeminge to be moved to Infants etc we desire to be reformed, and have exhibited our Judgments therin brieflie to the right reverend father in God our good B[ishop] who hath godlie and mildlie returned his answer therin, wherby we are more willinglie moved to this Subscription, and doe promise still to receive the same booke and none other, to administer the holie Sacramentes, and to use the praiers therein conteyned, and to maynteyne peace in the Churche of Christ.

3.   For the booke of ordring Bishops, mynisters and deacons and consequentlie the 36 Articles in the booke of Articles we have set downe our judgments to our B[ishop] and receyved his Answer, by which he certifieth us that the \<booke\> booke alloweth not three distincte orders in the mynistery, but that all are in the mynisterie of the word and Sacramentes Pares, and that the distinction is in government politicall to avoyde division, and to mainteyne peace, according to the which we subscribe. onlie protestinge, (which protestaction we humbly desire to be favourablie accepted) that if it shall hereafter appeare upon mature deliberation that any parte of the booke doth conteyne any thinge contrarie to godes worde, we mynd

---

[329] This statement, which exists nowhere else, and which certainly dates from 1584, is of considerable importance, especially for the give and take on both sides which it suggests. Note especially the remarkable confirmation which the signatories claim to have received from Bishop Thomas Cooper ('our good B[ishop]') that the Ordinal did not allow three distinct orders in the ministry, the distinction between bishops, priests and deacons being merely political. See Collinson, *EPM*, pp. 264–5: 'If one wants a proof-text for the argument that Elizabethan puritanism is not to be equated with presbyterianism, this, surely, is it.'

not by this our subscription to approve yt: and yet promise soe to deale as the peace
of the Church by us shall not be troubled

Doctor Chippendall[330]   Mr Ireton
Mr Sparke   Mr Higgins
Mr Boothe
Mr Blyth
and 300. more one Mr Jounson[331] onlie excepted

There is a forme of Subscription offered by the mynisters of Essex, you shall fynd it
in the 18 page before going

The letters which I have here written from one godlie mynister to another, these
subscriptions, and the rest of the writinges following I inserted them together in this
booke because they were conferred of in our meetinges, as I have noted on their
heades the meetinges wherin these thinges were moved, and the page wher yow
shall fynd them.
This booke I fynished in Kettringham being the work of one moneth space beside
myne ordenary exercises, ended I say the 10th of July. 1604.
Richard Parker. Laus Deo[332]

[fo. 39v]
blank

[fo. 40r]

I make no question ether of the Articles of Religion or of her ma[jes]ties authority

{Certaine pointes wherin R. Some. D[octor] of Divinity[333] is desirous to be resolved
before he yeld a generall subscription to my Lord of Cant[erbury's] Articles}

Certaine Chapters are prescribed in the Church wherin are grosse errors

{This chapter is presented to be read oct[ober] 10. at morning praier}
In the 2 verse of the 9. ch[apter] Judeth is commended the fact of Simeon which
killed the Sichemites, this is a manifest untruth, my reason is Jacob condemneth this
facte of Simeon and levi Gen[esis]: cap. 34 v. 30 and being on his death bed curseth

---

[330] The 'forme of subscription' is signed by a number of leading Leicestershire clergy, in the name of
virtually the entire ministry of the county. John Ireton, rector of Kegworth, had written to Anthony
Gilby of Ashby-de-la-Zouche in 1578, deploring the suppression of the prophesyings, 'the
Universities of the pore Ministers'. He attended an extended meeting of Field's London conference
in 1583, and with John Knewstub was on a short list of godly divines favoured by that faction for the
mastership of St John's College, Cambridge, in 1595. See Collinson, 'PCM', pp. 304, 379 b and c,
1016. Thomas Sparke, a quintessentially moderate puritan, was archdeacon of Stow (until 1582),
prebendary of Lincoln and rector of Bletchley, Buckinghamshire. With Walter Travers, he took part
in a conference with some bishops at Lambeth in December 1584, held before the earl of Leicester
and other magnates. See Collinson, EPM, pp. 269–70. In 1604 he would be one of the representatives
at the Hampton Court Conference, after which he very publicly conformed.
[331] Probably Jefferie Johnson, town preacher of Leicester, described by Bishop Cooper as 'a somewhat
rash man and so much as he dare inclin'd to novelties'. See Collinson, 'PCM', p. 190.
[332] See BR, pp. 243–4 below.

(Footnote 333 appears on page 115)

their wrathe against the Sichemites Gen[esis] 49. 5. 7. If any shall replye that almightie god (as Judith saieth) did give a sworde to Simeon to take vengeaunce of the Sichemites and that therfore Simeons fact was lawfull, my answer ys, that I deny that almightie god did arme him: if it be said that god may be accompted author of Simeons facte though not of Simeons synne: I answer that my speech is of Simeons synne and not of anie stroke that almightie god did beare in that action, for if this were a good argument, almightie god had some stroke in Simeons action therfore Simeons facte was good in respect of Simeon by the like reason we may justify the sale of Joseph by the patriarches and the betraying of Christ by Judas, bycause almightie god had some stroke in those accions, but every lerned man knoweth that in one and the self same action god is just and man may be unjust, *Idem opus sed non eadem causa.* August[ine] Epist: 48 ad vincentius.[334]

{This chap[ter] is prescribed to be read 11 of October at Morninge prayer.}
In the 12 verse of the 5. chapter of Toby, the Aungell Raphaell being required by Toby to shewe of what tribe he was, answered that he is of the kinred of Azarias and Ananias the great etc this is a manifest untruth for the elect Angels are of no tribe.

{This chap[ter] is prescribed to be read 17 November at Eveninge prayer}
In the 20 verse of the 46 chapter of Ecclesiasticus, it is written in the commendacion of Samuell that he prophecied after his death and told of kinge Saules death in which wordes ther is great untruth:[335] my reasons are, Samuell died about two yeares before this accident fell oute, if it had bene the true Samuell as in deed it was the dyvell, these absurdities wold follow first that it is in satans hande to commaund and remove by sorcery the soules of the deceased out of godes kingdome; secondlie that it is in satans hande to raise bodies out of the earth which apperteyneth to god alone. Thirdlie that almightie god alloweth askinge counsell of the deade which thinge is flatly forbydden by his ma[jes]ty Deut[eronomy] 18. 11.[336] {this place is mistaken in this copy} Esay 8. 19.[337] lastly if it were Samuell that appeared to Saule, he must appeare ether unwillinglie, or willinglie, to say that he appeared

---

333 Robert Some, a client of the earl of Leicester, whose chaplain he was, spent his whole career in Cambridge (he was also rector of Girton), and succeeded Andrew Perne as master of Peterhouse in 1589, a preferment he must have owed to Whitgift. In the 1590s, he was prominent among the Calvinist heads of houses who opposed the anti-Calvinism of Peter Baro and William Barrett, the events which provoked the Lambeth articles. See Peter Lake, *Moderate puritans and the Elizabethan church.* Some was one of the most senior academics and clerics to register his doubts about subscription. They are the most exhaustive and measured of any on record. Another version of 'Faults in the Book of Common Prayer' attributed to Some, is calendared in *Seconde parte,* I, 125–6. There is another version of Some's 'certaine points' in BL, Stowe MS 159, fos. 128–9. Some may appear in the Dedham record because he was the tutor and mentor of Thomas Stoughton. See *BR,* pp. 251–5 below.

334 Augustine, *Epistle ad Vincentium, Patrologia Latina,* ed. J. P. Migne (Turnhout, 1865), XXXIII, cols. 321–47.

335 See above, p. 102, n. 307.

336 Deuteronomy xviii. 11–14 forbids all kinds of sorcery. The relevant passage is found in verses 10–11, 'Let none be found among you . . . that asketh counsel at the dead.'

337 The marginal note suggesting the passage is in error is itself in error. The reference to Isaiah viii.19 is apt: 'And when they shal say unto you, Enquire at them that have a spirit of divination, and at the soothsayers, which whisper and murmure, Should not a people enquire at their God? from the living to the dead?'

unwillinglie, is to make him consent unto witchcrafte, if it be said the almightie god might aswell raise up samuell, as he did make moyses and Elias to appeare in Christes transfiguration, my answer is, first we must rest in godes written will and not dispute of his power. Secondlie the apparaunce of moses and Elias was not by sorcery but by a speciall dispensation of almightie god of which dispensation no generall rule must be made by us, if it be said that it is likely not to be the dyvell but Samuell bycause it fell out afterward to Saull according to the speech, my answer is that it is an ancyent practise of sathan somtymes to speak truth that he may joigne credyt in fowler matters, so did the pythoness Act 16. 16[338]

[fo. 40v]
If it be said that the mynister that is pressed by the booke of common prayer to read these lessons may tell the people that these are untruthes, my answer ys that it is not safe to doe soe in regard ether of the Papist or protestant, for the Papist which counteth these bookes Canonicall will give out very bitterly that our mynisters can fynd errors in the Canonicall scriptures, and the protestant if he be lerned may justly thinke much that such stuff is broched in godes Church, if he be ignorant it is the next way to seduce him, if it be said the mynister may omitt these lessons, I confesse that I like that course well, and if it be safest to omitte them, why shuld we be pressed to geve generall allowaunce to that booke which doth prescribe the reading of them.
{Decr: 4 sest concilii Trid:}[339]

In the orderinge of mynisters the Busshopp useth these wordes, take the holie ghost:

It is not lawfull for him to do thus, for christ when he used them did geve manyfest prooff of his godhead: Aug lib 15 de Trinit. cap. 26[340]

objection
Christ used these wordes (Receive the holy ghost) John 20. 22 therfore the B[ishops] may do the like in ordeyninge of mynisters.
The argument is verie weake, my reasons are first it was in our savior Christes handes to give to his Apostles at a sodaine the giftes of the holie ghost, if he had not, how shuld his Apostles who were never brought up in the scholes of lerninge be furnished for preachinge and disputacion as they were, but it is not in the B[ishop]s handes to do the like. Secondlie the B[ishops] have no commaundement to use the wordes Receive etc in the orderinge of mynisters nor promisse of blessinge at gods? handes in using them, I confesse it, god geves sufficient giftes to such as are called by his Ma[jes]ty and that the B[ishop] may laie his handes upon such as are already furnyshed when they are presented unto him, but the question is whether god geveth the holie ghost by this meanes, that is to say when these wordes Receive etc are uttred by the B[ishop] that the giftes of the holie ghost are not then given it is

[338] The reference is to St Paul's encounter in Philippi with 'a certaine maid having a spirit of divination'.
[339] *Canons and Decrees of the Council of Trent*, translated by H. J. Schroeder (Rockford, Illinois, 1978), pp. 17–18. The reference is to the 'decree concerning the canonical scriptures' which asserted that the apocryphal books were received as sound and canonical.
[340] Augustine, *De Trinitate*, book 15: *Patrologia Latina*, ed. J. P. Migne (Turnhout, 1865), XLII, col. 1079.

manifest, for many ignorant mynisters nether were nor are better furnished for all that speech of the B[ishop] so that to speake the best of these wordes, it must needes be graunted they be idlely uttred.

If it be said that the B[ishop] doth not undertake to give the holie ghost *virtualiter* but *instrumentaliter* bicause by praier they conceyve the holie ghost to such as are admitted to them, my answer is that I will not say that the popish B[ishop]s give out the like but I wold gladlie know whether these wordes Receive the holie ghost be a prayer and if they be a praier, to what braunch of praier they are to be referred. If any shall aske me whether I take them to be mynisters which are ordeyned according to the booke of ordinacion, I confesse that I doe, for otherwise I shuld doubte of myne owne admission.

Interrogatories are mynistered to Infantes in Baptisme[341]
{Aug[ustine]. Epist 23 ad Bonifacium}[342]
That they ought not to be mynistered to Infantes, my reasons are, first Infantes have not faith, that they have not faith it is manifest, for they have not understandinge of godes word which is the ground of faithe. Rom[ans] 10. 17.[343] yea Aug[ustine] saieth they have not *effectum fidei*. Secondlie the infant being asked whether he will be baptised cannot answer. Thirdlie the godfathers and godmothers desiring to be baptised do but trifle, for they have no such meaninge. If anie shuld gather of this that I mislike the Baptisme of Infantes, he deserveth rather a Censure then Confuter. If it be alledged out of Aug[ustine]. 23 Epist ad Bonifacium that the Infant which hath not *fidei effectum* may be said to have faith *propter fidei Sacramentum* that is to say by reason of Baptisme which Aug[ustine] calleth the Sacrament of faithe and therfor the Interro[gatories]: may be mynistered to Infantes my answer is as followeth, first, if the Sacrament of faith is faith how can the Infant be said to have faith which is not yet baptised and is therfore asked before Baptisme whether he beleve that he may afterward receyve baptisme, Secondly the Infant is not asked whether he hath the Sacrament of faith but whether he beleveth. lastly the Infant when he thus asked hath nether faith nor the Sacrament of faith for how shuld he have that which as yet he receyved not. [fo. 41r] Musculus saieth that this custome of mynistringe Interr: to Infantes is so absurd that it cannot be defended. Muscul[us]. de Baptis[344]

The mynistringe of Interr[ogatories]: to infantes did then begynn when those questions which were used in the Baptisme of such as were of yeares were drawne to the baptisme of infantes ether by the negligence or superstition of former tymes

341 Puritans who shared Some's doubts about this procedure could find themselves in trouble when they insisted on 'do you' (i.e. addressing the godparents, whom they also insisted should be the natural parents) rather than 'dost thou' (addressing the infant). See 'A note of those thinges the mynisters in Suff[olk] offred', pp. 120–2 below.

342 Augustine, *Epistle ad Bonifacium: Patrologia Latina*, ed. J. P. Migne (Turnhout, 1865), XXXIII, cols. 359–64. The relevant passage reads, *'Ac per hoc cum respondetur parvulus credere, qui fidei nondum habet affectum, respondetur fidem habere propter fidei sacramentum, et convertere se ad Deum propter conversionis sacramentum quia et ipsa responsio ad celebrationem pertinet sacramenti.'*

343 'Then faith is by hearing and hearing by the worde of God.'

344 See *Common places of Christian religion, gathered by Wolfgangus Musculus* . . . (London, 1563), fos. 291v–2r.

The syne of the crosse ought not to be used in Baptisme[345]

My reasons are, first the papistes do put such holines in it that they thinke the water of Baptisme without the signe of the crosse not to be sanctifyed. Secondly it hath bene abused by most abhominable superstition. if it be said that Churches and Church landes have bene likewise abused the reason is not like for we have both need of landes and Churches soe have we not of the signe of the crosse, and of the brasen serpent which was made and erected by godes commaundement and wherof ther was singuler use was for the abuse therof beaten in peeces yt is very equall that the signe of the crosse which hath not light in godes booke to shew yt by, nor thexamples of thapostles to rest upon after so notable abuse shuld not be lodged in the holie sacrament. Thirdlie it is daungerous to use allegoricall significations (and sithens that of the signe of the crosse) for it makes the popish sort to like better of the allegoricall signification for their Ceremonies, If it be said that the signe of the crosse is a preaching unto us of Christes death, I answer that the papistes may say as much for their Rood and Images which they call lay mens bookes. Lastlie it is a spice of Imagery which ought to have no place in the Sacrament. this word (Image) comprehendeth all representacions of mans devise brought into the Church in steed of Teachers if it be said that the signe of the crosse is apostolicall, and that though no mention is of it in godes booke it is conveyed to us by tradition from thapostles, my answer is, that if we admitt that we give great advauntage to the popish sorte under the cloke of tradition to thrust upon us a great deale of trumpery.

Allowaunce is given to such as be no mynisters to baptise in time of necessity, as they call it.[346]
{Epipha. *lib* 1. *contra hereses*}[347]
{Terte *de prescripte advers: heret:*}[348]
Before I set downe the wordes of the booke I must needes confesse that no lerned man (the Papistes excepted) thinkes it lawfull for eny, ether man or woman to admynister the Sacramentes but for the mynister alone. the reasons are, first it is a singuler honor in godes Church and therfore without lawfull callinge it may not be adventured on. Heb[rews] 5. 4.[349] Secondly the self same parties are authorised by Christe to baptise which are authorised to preache Math[ew] 28. 19.[350] Lastly the

---

[345] This was one of the principal shibboleths of all puritans. But the objections to it are here very robustly stated by someone in Some's position.

[346] The practice of midwives baptizing 'in time of necessity' was a major embarrassment to the reformed Church of England. James I took particular exception to it at the Hampton Court Conference. However, nothing was done about the practice in the Canons of 1604, while Canon 69 required ministers not to defer christening if the child were in danger of death. See *The Anglican Canons 1529–1947,* ed. Gerald Bray (Church of England Record Society, VI, 1998), 359. Some makes it clear that he would not have been happy with a canon which underwrote the assumption of the preface to the service of confirmation that 'children being baptised have all thinges necessarie for salvation and be undoubtedly saved'.

[347] See *The Panarion of Epiphanius of Salamis Book I,* trans. Frank Williams (Nag Hammadi Studies 35 Leiden, 1987).

[348] Tertullian, *Liber de praescriptionibus adversus haereticos: Patrologia Latina,* ed. J. P. Migne (Turnhout, 1844), II, col. 56.

[349] 'And no man taketh this honour unto him self, but he that is called of God, as was Aaron.'

[350] 'Go therefore, and teache all nacions, baptizing them in the Name of the Father, and the Sonne, and the holie Gost.'

admynistration of baptisme by women is a braunch of Marcions heresies and is condemned by Epiphanius and Tertullian.

These wordes are set downe in the booke of common praier (that is the pastors and Curates of all warne the people that without great cause they baptise not children at home in their houses: If it be said that these wordes give nether leave nor allowance to anie ether private men or women to baptise and that the meaning of the booke is to give direction to some mynister to baptise in the case in a private house, my answer is that the construction is manifestlie overthrowne by that which is written in thend of private baptisme in these wordes, viz: if they which do bringe the Infantes to the Church do make an uncerteine answer to the prestes questions and say that they cannot tell what they thought, did, or said in that great feare or trouble of mynd (as oftentimes it chaunceth) then let the priest baptise etc. If anie mynister did baptise an infant in that case, is it ether credible or likelie that he knew not what he did or sayde. If any shall replie that the B[ishop]s of England mislike and condemne midwyves baptisme and that it is verie equall, my answer that the wordes in private baptisme do beare no such force and the subscription [fo. 41v] is required of us not to the former Judgment of the B[ishop]s but to the wordes and meaninge of the booke

In the later end of the preface of confirmacion these wordes are written, and that no man shall thinke that any detriment shall come to children by deferring of their confirmacion he shall knowe for truth that it is certeyne by godes word that children being baptised have all thinges necessarie for salvation and be undoubtedly saved.

The popish sort teach that such as are baptised are but half christians before they be confirmed by the Bishopp. It is a grosse error, and is condemned as I take it by one parte of the sentence above alledged which parte of the sentence I do allow, that which I mislike is conteyned in these wordes viz it is certeyne by godes worde that Children being baptised <have all thinges necessarie for their salvation and> be undoubtedly saved. my reasons are, first no evidence can be shewed for this in godes booke for many which have bene circumcised and baptised have died out of godes favor: secondlie it strengthneth this popish argument viz Infantes being baptised are cleere (by reason of baptisme) of originall synne and they never committed actuall synne therfore they are undoubtedly saved. lastlie it favors this popish opynion viz that Sacramentes do take away synne and do conferre grace *ex opere operato*, for which absurdity they of Rhemes alledge Act[s] 22. 17:[351] John 3. 5.[352]

I confesse we ought to hope well of Infantes that are baptised bicause they are borne of Christian parentes and are within the compasse of godes covenant and by baptisme are incorporate into the visible Church, but to affirme peremperely that it is certeyne by godes worde that they are undoubtedly saved cannote be proved (as I take yt) by any sound divinity.

In the gospell upon sonday after Christmas daie which is taken out of the 1 Math ther is an error

---

351 The correct reference should be to verse 16: 'Now therefore why tariest thou? Arise and be baptised, and washe away thy sinnes, in calling on the Name of the Lord.'
352 'Jesus answered, Verely, verely, I say unto thee, except that a man be borne of water and of the Spirit, he can not enter into the kingdome of God.'

The wordes are these, when his mother Marie was maryed to Joseph etc but the text is thus when his mother Marie was betrothed or espoused to Joseph, if any shall tell me that this is a small fault, I doe not thinke soe, my reason is, ther are two degrees of Matrimony, *spousatia* and *Nuptia*, if for (betrothed) it were lawfull to translate (Maryed), the severall and distinct pointes of Matrimony shuld be confounded, which is against all both logique and <del>dyvinity</del> divinitye. Deut[eronomy] 20. 7. Math[ew]. 1. 18.

In the prefaces of the gospels upon the second sonday after Easter and upon the xxth sonday after Trinity ther is a manifest untruth taken verbatim out of the mass booke

These wordes are set downe in the preface, Christ Jesus said to his disciples wheras it is manifest by circumstance of the texte (John 10. Mathe 22. 15. 21. 45) that christ spake directly to the Pharises: If any replie that Christes disciples were then present and that therefore Christ may be said to have spoken to his disciples, my answer is that by the like reason we may say, that the dutifull subjecte is spoken unto very roughly by the Magistrate, because he is in place when traitors for their desertes are taken up verie sharplye.

The severall pointes above written, if ther were no more, are sufficient I truste, ether to procure a redresse, or to stay a generall subscription, I confesse very willinglie and frely, that it were best in my poore judgment to reforme such pointes as are amisse and to committe this godlie labor to skilfull men, for sure I am this good wold come of yt, first it wold please almightie god: Secondlie the lerned mynisters shuld be linked together more strongly against the Papistes [fo. 42r] Thirdly the mynisters and good subjectes wherof many are now at weeping crosse shuld be greatly cheared to enter into the holy mynistery, fourthly the Popishe and gracelesse sorte shuld more easely be wonne to religion or destroyed, lastlie the very gall of the Papist and ungodly man shuld be broken.

If ane shall tell me that excellent men were the publishers of the booke of common prayer and that it wold be some disgrace to our Church to alter yt, my answer is, first, though worthy men are to be accepted of, yet their oversight specially in Religion matters are not to be honored by subscriptyon. Secondly the reformation of the service booke can be no disgrace to us for men have their second thoughte wiser then their first and the popish sect in the late tyme of Pius the first did reforme our ladies psalter. to conclude, if the amendment of the book were inconvenient it must be soe in regard ether of the protestant or papist. It cannot be inconvenient in regard of the protestant, for a very great number do pray verie hartely to god for it, if it vexe the obstinate papist we are not to passe, for they whose capteynes deny that we have ether Church Sacramentes mynisters or Queene in England are not greatly to be regarded of us god preserve her excellent ma[jes]ty and confound her enemyes as he did Sisera, abimelech and Athalia.[353] Amen

A note of those thinges the mynisters in Suff[olk] offred[354]

---

[353] For the violent deaths of Sisera, Abimelech and Athalia, see Judges v. 26, Judges ix. 53 and 2 Kings xi. 16.

[354] There is another copy of this statement with only verbal differences, 'Their doubts and offer to the Bishop', in DWL, MS Morrice 1. 529–31, calendared, *Seconde parte*, I, 242.

We humblie crave of your Lord that the benefite of the law yelding us to repaire for resolucion if we shall doubt in any thinge may be graunted unto us, and bicause we wold not be tedious to your honor, we have set downe a fewe speciall pointes amongst diverse not to deprave the booke or any thinge therin conteyned but for the quietinge of our consciences hopinge if we may be resolved to these fewe to be the sooner persuaded to the reste

As for her Ma[jes]ties authority we have often sworne to yt and are now ready and at all other times frely to subscribe unto it and acknowledge yt.

1. First we are desirous seying the mynistery of the word and Sacraments belong unto a publike function by what authority of the word the administration of Baptisme may be permitted unto private persons which seemeth to be the meaninge of the booke

2. Secondly seying the Papistes do openlie teach that the crosse is to be worshipped with the same worshipp that is due unto Christe, and have a speciall sevice accordingly appointed to the honor therof called Officium Sacrae Crucis joigning practise with the doctryne, they do in playne wordes ascribe that to the crosse which belongeth unto Christe, and seyng ther is example in the scripture of abolishinge that which god himself commaunded to be erected when it was abused to Idolatrye, we are desirous to knowe by what authority of holie scriptures we may warrant our subscription to the Crosse being thus abused, and having the begynninge from forged and counterfecte writinges as the gospell of Nicodemus and the epistles of one Martialis being one of the 70 disciples as Chemnisius plainly proveth, not one commaundement being found in all the scriptures to use yt, nether one promise for the blessinge of yt.

3. Thirdly upon the questions in Baptisme we are desirous to be resolved whether our subscription be required to their meaninge, who do thinke that the answers made by the witnesses do concerne the witnesses themselves of which judgment the most reverend father the archbishop of Canturb[ury] in [fo. 42v] his booke extant declareth himself to be, or theirs who thinke they do concerne the Infantes only bycause they do thinke the infantes have faith and repentaunce of which mind are others unto whose conference some mynisters have bene referred tutching this matter. Concerning the later opynion if our subscription be required to that, then we crave resolucion what scripture will warrant every one that is brought to Baptisme . . . [part of the argument has been inadvertently omitted by the copyist at this point] . . . together mortification, to unfold every article of our belieff distinctly apart by it self. If the justification of thother opynion be required of us then we are desirous to knowe whether we shuld joigne with the most reverend father affirminge that the answer of the witnesses doth declare what they will endevour to performe to the Infantes, and that the meaning of these wordes (I do beleve) is nothing els but that I will doe myne endevor <del>to perform to the Infantes</del> that this child may beleve, ether els with other Lerned men, whose conference likewise some mynisters have used in this cause holding opinion that it conteyneth what the witnesses themselves do beleve into the which faith they desire to have the child baptised, and with this resolucion we desire to knowe (seyinge in the Church all thinges ought to be done to edifying and therfore a straunge tongue is banished to enterteyne our owne) why we shuld be bound to such wordes as our owne cuntreymen cannot understande, nether in truth do they declare and expresse the meaninge of our mynde, for these wordes

(I do beleve) do not in our english tongue signify I will do myne endevor that another may beleve, and likewise these wordes wilt thou be baptised doe not signify in our tongue wilt thou have another baptised.

4.   Fourthly we desire to be resolved seying we preach that the way is straite that leadeth to liffe and fewe ther be that find yt how we may safely say of every one that is buryed as the booke doth enjoigne us that we are in sure and certeyne hope of his Resurrection unto everlasting liffe without destroying that by our example which we built with our doctrine especially seing we have not wanted examples of some dying which have given sentence of themselves unto condemnation, some smitten with sodeyne death imediatly after the filthines of adultery committed.

5.   Fiftly we are desirous to know by what authority of the word we may justify the omitting to reade in the church some scriptures Canonicall and yet we entertayne in that place the readinge of scripture not Canonicall

6.   Last of all tutching the booke of ordring B[ishop]s and mynisters bicause we have it not, nether could we at this time come by it, therfore we crave that time may be given us to peruse it and afterward to geve an answer to it.

Also concerning the book of articles in such sort as the statute requireth consent unto them namely so farre as they belonge unto matters of faithe and the doctryne of the Sacramentes we see no cause why we shuld not subscribe unto yt[355]

Nicholas bounde	Thomas agast
William Harvy	Daniel Denise
Roger Nuttall	William Bennes
Roger Jeffrey	Georg webb
John Smithe	John English
John forth	Richard Kinge
William Rushbrooke	Robert Cottesforde
Lawraunce whittacres	
Thomas morse	
William browne	
John Cowper	
William flemming	
Robert Swete	
John Smith	

---

[355] Suffolk ministers: Nicholas Bounde (Bound), rector of Norton (see *BR*, pp. 188–9 below); William Harvey, unplaced; Roger Nuttall, minister of Westhorpe; Roger Jeffrey, unplaced; John Smith, unplaced; John Forth, unplaced; William Rushbrooke, rector of Hoxne; Laurence Whitacres, minister at Braiseworth, or Laurence Whitacres, rector of Bradfield; Thomas Morse, rector of Hinderclay (see *BR*, pp. 231–3 below); William Browne, rector of Culford; John Cowper, unplaced; William Fleming, rector of Endgate, Beccles; Robert Swete, vicar of Weybread St Andrew; John Smith, unplaced; Thomas Agast, unplaced; Daniel Denise, unplaced; William Bennes, unplaced; George Webb, unplaced; John English, rector of Boulge; Richard King, rector of Creeting St Peter; Robert Cottesford, vicar of Creeting St Mary and possibly rector of Beccles. It is likely that a good number of those ministers whom it is not possible to locate were in parishes in east Suffolk, many of which were impropriate, served by curates, and poorly documented. Most of these twenty-one names are duplicated in the list of sixty ministers in the archdeaconries of Suffolk and Sudbury 'that be suspended for not subscribeinge'. *Seconde parte*, I, 242–3.

[fo. 43r]

Mr Paget[356]

1. That her ma[jes]tie under god hath or ought to have the soveraignty or rule over all manner persons borne within her Realme domynions and cuntreys of what estate ether ecclesiasticall or temporall soever they be and that none other foreyne power, prelate, state, or potentate hath or ought to have any Jurisdiccion power superiority, prehemynence or authority ecclesiasticall or spirituall within her ma[jes]ties Realmes domynions or cuntreyes

2. That the book of common prayer and orderinge of B[ishop]s priestes and deacons conteyneth in yt nothinge contrary to the word of god and that the same may be lawfully used and that he himself will use the forme in the said booke prescribed in publike prayers and admynistration of the Sacramentes and none other.

3. That he alloweth the book of Articles of religion agreed upon by the Archb[ishop] and B[ishop]s of both provinces and the whole clergy of the Convocation holden at London in the yeare of our lord god 1562 and set forth by her Ma[jes]ties authority and that he beleveth all the articles therin conteyneth to be agreable to the worde of god

Mr Pagetes answer

The first article I do acknowledge to be most juste, I thanke god for her government, and I besech him longe to contynue yt accordinge to the same.
To the second I am sory that I cannot consente, I do reverence the booke bycause ther are many good thinges conteyned in it partly because it is established by her ma[jes]ties lawes, and for that it was set downe by those good fathers which excelled in godlines and zeale, but I cannot subscribe unto yt partly for the corruption of the scriptures in the gospels upon the second sonday after Easter and the xxty after Trinity, partly for the contrariety of the Apocryphall bookes (which are appointed to be reade) to the Canonicall scriptures, and some other thinges (which for brevity I do omitte, yet for obedyence to her Ma[jes]tie and love of the peace of

---

356 Eusebius Paget, a Northamptonshire minister deprived of his rectory of Old in 1574, became a 'posting apostle' in the Midlands before securing the Cornish rectory of Kilkhampton, through the good offices of Sir Francis Hastings, exercised through the patron, Sir Richard Grenville, where he later suffered a second deprivation. Paget was one of the most militant and high-profile of all Elizabethan puritans, and he has left a paper trail in several archives. See Collinson, *EPM*, pp. 143, 193, 276–7, 370–1; *Letters of Sir Francis Hastings, 1574–1609*, ed. C. Cross (Somerset Record Society, LXIX 1969), 25–7. Sir Walter Mildmay's papers contain a broadsheet endorsed by Mildmay 'Mr Pagett'. This is his answer exhibited to the high commission on 11 January 1584 (1585?), subscribed (his usual style) 'By me Lame Eusebius Pagitt minister'. It is followed by a statement evidently prepared by Paget's counsel: 'The general question is, whether the said highe Comissioners maie for or upon the premisses depryve the said mynister.' Northamptonshire Record Office, MS F.(M).P. 55a, 55b.

the Church, I do promise in publike prayer to use the booke and none other and humblie I sue not to be urged to all thinges in yt.

To the 3 I do subscribe according to the statute set forth in that behalf.

[fo. 43v]

A note of mr Somes tutching the book and of the mynisters in Suff[olk] and of mr Paget.

[fo. 44r]

{It was offred them the 20. of march 1585}

{29. meeting. foll. 7}

A profession freely made[357] and approved by the voyces and handes of us whose names are underwritten, that with one firme consent and harty affection we will (god enabling us) joigne together for the observation and mayntenaunce of all christian order aswell in our owne persons and families, as also in the whole body of the towne, and for the banishing of the contrary disorder so farre as shalbe shewed us by god his <worde> worde to be required at our handes so longe as god shall geve us liffe in this world, and namely in these particuler and principall poyntes followinge.

1.   Imprimis forasmuch as the lordes honor and glorye ought of all his true servauntes and professors to be chiefly tendred, and most zealously advaunced, our faithfull promise is not onlye in our owne persons to frequent with all care and joyfulnes the holie exercises of pure religion on the Sabboth daies in our owne Church and there to hold out quietly and reverently to thend of all the holy actions there of preaching, prayer, singing of psalmes and blessinge, but also with the like care and conscyence to use all good meanes in procuringe all in our families, and in all families in the towne to doe the same.

2.   Item wheras by order a longe tyme receyved we have had the communion mynistred once every monethe, for the more thankfull celebration of our redemption by the deathe of Christ, and encrease of our faithe in him and love one of us towarde another; we do not only desire to have the same so to be contynued, but also promise reverently to joigne in the same with the rest of our brethren, and to trayne, persuade, and move all others in the same our Congregation to do likewise.[358]

3.   Item wheras we understand to our just grieffe, that some evell disposed persons in this Congregation have bene bold dyverse waies to abuse the Sabbathe daye, by travaylinge abrode, by sellinge or buyinge their commodities in shoppes or streetes,

---

[357] But see below n. 361.

[358] Dedham, for a rural parish, was somewhat exceptional in celebrating the communion monthly, although this became almost standard practice in London. See Arnold Hunt, 'The Lord's Supper in early modern England', *Past & Present,* CLXI (November 1998), 39–83.

by comminge very late to the Churche, by behavinge themselves there unreverently in gasinge, talking, or sleepinge, by slipping out before thend of the whole action, by mispending the rest of the daye in vayne and unlawfull games and practises, or by drinkinge in the taverne or such like places, we promise to use all good meanes required of us to correcte and reforme these and all other such like abuses, and to labor with common consent that all in the towne shall come to the Church in due tyme, behave themselves ther dulye to thend, and that the rest of the daye be spent in holye and religious manner.[359]

4.   Item forasmuch as the lordes worshipp shuld be deere unto us at all tymes and the benefites of his <worde> worde pretious (whensoever it shalbe his good pleasure to <have> geve us the use of it) we promise not only to make conscyence in resorting to the same exercises on the lecture daies, but also to bringe with us soe many of our servauntes as are best able to understande the doctryne ther to be propounded[360] and further to persuade and procure by all good meanes that all the rest of the Congregation may endevour to doe the same.

5.   And bycause the poorer and weaker sorte have need of some good encouragement to joigne herin with us, we willingly promise to invite and enterteyne some of them at our tables every sabboth daye the rather that by this meanes we may gayne the better opportunitye to admonishe and exhort them to these and such like good workes and holy duties of Christianitye.

6.   Item wheras it is not onely required of us to heare and professe god his worde but also to reforme all our waies according to the pure rule therin it is further promised of every of us to deale justly and truly with all men in our affayres, especially with our owne brethren and fellow professors of this Congregation, being so farre from withholding any mans right and dutye from him, at the tyme when it is by our promise, or otherwise by a good conscyence to be yelded and paide, as that ther shall appeare in us a readynes of mynde, accordinge to our state, callinge and habilitye to helpe pleasure and comforte one another, and if at any tyme we shall faile herein, or in other such duties, that we will patiently and gladly yeld ourselves to be advertised or admonished by our brethren or mynisters therof, and also readely to reforme the same, without urginge any officer or others to use any further extremitye by lawe or publike authority for the constreiginge of us thereunto.

7.   And wheras the true mynisters of god his worde by reason of their callinges are most of all other subject to the malice of evell men, and that their just creditt availeth gretlye for the upholdinge of all good order and governmente, we promise not onlye for our selves and all oures to use them reverently, lovingly and

---

[359] *Pace* Kenneth Parker *(The English sabbath)*, this was the hallmark of what is most properly called sabbatarianism. Building on the doctrinal premise that the Sabbath was a whole natural day of twenty-four hours (see the debate between Sandes and Crick, pp. 53–70 above), sabbatarians insisted that the entire day be spent 'in holye and religious manner'. That excluded all secular recreation. The issue in the early seventeenth century centred on the royal 'Book of Sports', the importance of which in provoking emigration to New England and even the civil war can hardly be overestimated.

[360] Historians are divided over how far the doctrine preached in the sermons and lectures typical of the godly wing of the Elizabethan church were accessible to 'most people'. This is rare evidence that the godly themselves appreciated that not all illiterate people would necessarily benefit.

comfortably, but also to bende our selves to the uttermost of our power to defend and maynteyne the credytte both of their mynistery and persons against all such as shall wilfullye spitefullye practise to deface, hurte, or abuse them.

8.   And wheras the ignorant and rude persons take great encouragement by open knowne and publike offences committed as whordome dronkennes, robbery and such like especially being winked at or lightly proceeded againste, we promise for the preventing of all such publike offences and better repressinge of them, and also <the> for preservinge of all sortes of people in good order not only to oversee and regard carefullye all families and persons in the towne by visiting their houses and places of abode once in every quarter and by having a watchfull eie over them at all other tymes: but also fynding any suche intolerable disorder and enormity committed to joigne with one consent in a zeale for god his glorye, and love towardes the persons without all partialitye to proceed against all such offendors, even to thexecutinge of the full extremitye of lawes, if they cannot be persuaded humblye to submitt themselves in the publike confession of their follye, and acceptinge willinglye of some lesser and smaller correction judged necessary to be measured unto them for the terror of others.

9.   And wheras commonly it falleth out in so great a congregation that some wilfull, froward and factious persons are founde that for worldly and fleshly respectes, will devide and single themselves from the rest of the Congregation in thexercises of religion worde or Sacramentes, or in care of the good government of the towne and maynteynance of the good estate therof in every respecte, we promise to use all wise and lovinge meanes to reconcile <the> and trayne them to joigne comfortably and charitably with us and our mynisters: and if they shall shewe themselves still folishe, wilfull and obstynate in rejecting these good meanes, that <then> then we will after due admonition geven them testify our dislikinge of them by all such meanes as religion peace and love shall require and warrant

[fo. 45r]

10.   And bicause the practise and due observation of these pointes set downe requireth some good advise and deepe consideration to be used joyntlye together one of us with another, we promise religiously and comfortablye to meete once every monthe in such places as shalbe thought best for the hearinge, debatinge and ordringe of all <such> causes that shall fall out in our owne Congregation being such as we may deale withall by god his worde and the good lawes of this Realme, and havinge agreed of any order to be undertaken by us or any of us, that we will carefully and gladlye endever our selves afterward to the executinge and prosequutinge of the same to the best of our power.

11.   Fynally wheras not only for the discharge of our owne duties, comforte of our conscyences, and the better provokinge of our selves mutually to these and all good workes, but also for the better encouragement of our lovinge and faithfull mynisters we have willinglye joigned in this protestacion: we promise (god his mighty spirite enabling us) to hold out joyfully in the observation of these and all other good orders, tendring to godes glorye, the cherishing of peace emonge ourselves and procuring the good estate of this Congregation. and if hereafter all or the most of us (which god kepe us from by his good spirite) we shuld soe farre turne backwarde as

to slacke and faile in the same, then do we acknowledge our <~~selves~~> selves to be unworthy of their mynisterye and justlye to be forsaken and geven over of them, as they that in effect by soe doinge <~~shall~~> shall professe a desyre to be ridde of them, and to reject their doctryne and message.[361]

W. Buttor[362]
Ed. Sherman[363]
H. Sherman[364]
Pierce Buttor[365]
R. Clarke[366]
Tho. Allen[367]

[361] The whole tenor of this document (compared with the Swallowfield articles, see above, p. lvii, n. 165) suggests that it was clerical in its composition (Edmund Chapman and Richard Parker) and put in front of the 'ancients' of the town, rather than generated by them. However, the strongly reiterated promises do suggest that this document should be read as a covenant, reminiscent of those to be found in early New England towns.

[362] William Butter, clothier of Dedham, made his will on 13 May 1593, leaving most of his lands to his eldest son Pearce, his sole executor, who was granted probate on 19 November 1594. Monetary bequests totalled about £160, including remembrances of 20s each to Edmund Chapman and Henry Wilcock and £6 13s 4d to the poor of Dedham: Emmison, *Essex gentry wills*, pp. 277–9.

[363] Edmund Sherman, clothier of Dedham, made his will on 31 July 1599, leaving £100 and a substantial amount of property to his second wife, Anne, for life and thereafter to his son Edmund. Monetary bequests to his other ten children totalled £500. 'My brother' Henry Sherman and Simon Fenn 'my kinsman' were directed to sell a certain property for the discharging of these legacies. A tenement occupied by his sister was to be given after her death to the governors of Dedham School to be used as a dwelling house for 'a schoolmaster to teach children to read and write, who shall freely teach one poor child which shall be appointed from time to time by Edmund and his heirs for ever'. His 'loving friends' Edmund Chapman and Robert Lewis 'my brother-in-law' were appointed overseers with 20s each for their pains. Robert Lewis and Henry Sherman both witnessed the will. A codicil dated 20 December 1600 contains a further bequest to Edmund Chapman: £5 a year for five years 'if he continue so long at Dedham at 25s. a quarter'. Anne, his sole executrix, was granted probate on 30 April 1601. Emmison, *Essex gentry wills*, pp. 307–8.

[364] Henry Sherman 'the elder of Colchester' made his will on 20 January 1590, requesting burial in Dedham church and leaving £6 to Edmund Chapman and 40s to Richard Parker. £20 went to the poor of Dedham 'to be a continual stock for the poor to the world's end', at the discretion of the governors of Dedham School. Monetary bequests to his family totalled almost £300 whilst his personal effects included a silver-gilt goblet, silver spoons, tapestries, swords and 'my armour'. One of the witnesses, 'Oliver Pygge the elder', was perhaps father of the preacher. Sherman's sons Henry and Edmund were appointed executors and were granted probate on 25 July 1590. Emmison, *Essex gentry wills*, pp. 308–9.

[365] Pearce Butter, clothier of Colchester, made his will on [blank] August 1599. Monetary bequests totalled an impressive £720 as well as extensive property including 'Brook House'. His 'good friend' Edmund Chapman was to receive £5 a year for six years out of the lands in Thorrington left to his son John, as well as a lump sum of £13 6s 8d. £3 went to the poor of Dedham, a further £10 for the poor 'towards the augmentation of the town stock', and 40s to the poor of St James Colchester. There was a token bequest of 40s to 'my sister Sarah Northie widow'. His 'loving friend' Henry Sherman 'the elder', earlier mentioned as his 'cousin', was appointed joint executor along with his son William. Sherman was left £6 13s 4d for his pains. Edmund Chapman was appointed one of his overseers. William Butter was granted probate on 5 December 1600. Emmison, *Essex gentry wills*, pp. 279–81.

[366] Probably the 'Richard Clerk the younger of Dedham' mentioned in the will of Michael Upcher in 1575 and the Richard 'Clarke' who witnessed the will of William Ravens of Dedham in 1580: Emmison, *Essex gentry wills*, pp. 304, 314.

[367] With William Nevard, Allen was serving as churchwarden of Dedham in 1583: on 2 November both were called into consistory for failing to present Richard Parker at the episcopal visitation for not wearing the surplice: LMA DL/C/300, pp. 382–3. On 4 February 1584 Allen deposed that he and William Butter had been directed by Aylmer to signify to Stanhope that Parker's appearance before him should be respited until Parker had made answer to the archdeacon of Colchester concerning Whitgift's articles. The case was accordingly adjourned pending a new monition: *ibid.*, p. 734.

R. upcher[368]
J. upcher[369]
St. upcher[370]

[fo. 45v]

the protestacion that our People yelded unto willinglye

[fo. 46r]

Orders agreed upon the ixth of August by mr doctor Chapman, mr parker and the Auncientes of the Congregation of dedham to be diligently observed and kepte of all persons whatsoever dwellinge within the said Towne.

1.   Imprimis for the right use of the lordes daie, to be spent in holie exercises publikely and at home, in readinge and examyninge of their servauntes, all travaylinge to Fayres, markettes, mariage dynners, and dynners abroade, or in the towne lefte of.

2.   Item that all governors of household, carefully endevour themselves, to frequent their owne Churches before the begynninge of divine service, accompanied orderlie, and soberly with their servauntes, and whole family, as many as may be spared at home for necessary uses of Children etc.

3.   Item that they cause their youth to present themselves at the times appointed to be examyned in the pointes of their Catechisme.

4.   Item that the lordes supper be celebrated every first sondaie of every moneth.

5.   Item that maryed persons or housholders resort to the Church at sixe of the clocke in the morninge upon wednesday Thursday and saturday before the communion to be examyned accordinge to the divisions, and the youth the Saturday in the afternoone.[371]

6.   Item that every communion ther be a collection for the poore by one of the Churchwardens after the cuppe be delyvered,[372] and that they directe the Communicantes wher to sytte orderly and comly in their places.

---

[368] Perhaps Richard Upcher, son and heir of the Dedham clothier Michael Upcher, who died in 1575: Emmison, *Essex gentry wills*, pp. 314–15. See also *BR*, p. 243. At the time these orders were drawn up, Upcher was apparently no more than twenty years of age, young for an 'ancient'! Still in his twenties, he was active in establishing the truth about Richard Parker's philandering. Dr Pennie believes that Upcher had been an admirer of the vicar who was shocked to find that his idol had feet of clay.

[369] Not certainly identified.

[370] Stephen Upcher of Dedham, clothier, made a brief will on 20 September 1594, leaving the bulk of his estate to his son Stephen. This included 'certain marsh grounds' in Brightlingsea leased from Sir Thomas Heneage. To each of his four daughters he left £24, and 3s 4d to the poor of Dedham. He named Ralph King, rector of Little Bromley, and Richard Upcher (?his brother) as his executors in the event that Stephen refused executorship. John Upcher was one of the witnesses. 'Stephen Upcher the son' was granted probate on 15 October 1594. Emmison, *Essex gentry wills*, p. 316.

[371] The essence of 'the discipline' so far as the laity were concerned, a practice maintained in the Church of Scotland for centuries and known as 'eldering', but poorly documented in puritan England. Who was to do the examining, in the absence of 'lay ruling elders'? The 'ancients' (and elders in effect), or the ministers, who would have had their work cut out? (But see p. 138 below.) This is the only reference we have to the (geographical) 'divisions' of the town.

(Footnote 372 appears on facing page)

7.   Item that the Tuesdaie next followinge the communion mr doctor Chapman and mr Parker and the auncientes of the towne do meete at some convenient place ther to conferre of matters concerninge the good government of the towne. <to establish>

8.   Item that so many as shalbe admitted to the Communion promise and professe to live charitablie with all their neighbors, and if any occasion of displeasure arise, that they refraiginge from all discord, or revenging by wordes, actions or suites will firste make the mynister and two other godlie and indifferent neighbors acquaynted wth the state of their causes before they proceed further by lawe or compleint out of the towne.[373]

9.   Item that so many as be of habilitie invite to their howses one couple of such of their poore neighbors as have submitted themselves to the good orders of the Churche, and walke christianly and honestlie in their callinges, and others of lesse hability any one such person providinge no more for them then ordenary and so longe as they shall thankfullie accepte of the same.

10.   Item that all the housholders frequent the two lectures read every weeke with some of their servauntes, at the leaste as many as may be spared in regard of their trades and callinges.

[fo. 46v]

11.   Item that all the yonge children of the towne be taught to reade Englishe, and that the moity of that is given at the Communion be employed for the teaching of such poore mens children as shalbe judged unable to beare yt themselves, and a convenient place to be appointed for the teacher of them.

12.   Item that all masters and governors promise to receyve no prentises but such as can reade englishe.

13.   Item that none be suffred to remayne in the towne not havinge any callinge, that is not beinge a housholder, nor retayned of any.

14.   Item that every quarter mr doctor Chapman; mr Parker or one of them, with two or three of the auncientes of the towne, alwaies accompanied with one of the Constables, do visitt the poore, and chiefly the suspected places, that understandinge the miserable estate of those that wante and the naughtie disposition of disordered persons, they may provide for them accordinglie.

15.   Item that if anie be knowne to have knowne one another carnally before the celebratinge of their mariage, that none accompanie them to the Church, nor from the Church, nor dine with them that day, and that the Pastor at the baptisinge of the children of any such as be knowne to have committed such filthines before the

---

[372] This may be the only evidence we have (from anywhere) that the collections at communions were made by the churchwardens, virtually as part of the sacramental action. The practice raises an important question. Was this how Dedham raised its entire public funds for poor relief? Or were these collections supplementary to a poor rate? (See p. 138 below.) However, note the eleventh of these orders. A 'moiety' is a half, so that half the money collected at communions was used to support the 'petty' or English school.

[373] The Dedham orders share with the aspirations of other communities the desire to avoid not only public discord but litigation between neighbours.

celebratinge of their mariage do publikely note and declare out the fault to all the congregation to the humblinge of the parties and terrifyinge of others from the like filthie profaninge of mariage.[374]

[fo. 47r]

To the kings excellent majestie. 1604[375]
The humble peticion of 22 preachers[376] in London and the Suburbes therof
Vouchsafe most gratious Soveraigne a favourable and pitifull eare unto the humble peticion of manie your distressed subjectes, preachers of the gospell now called uppon in your Ma[jes]ties name to <appeare> approve by subscription and practise 5. severall bookes with certen Ceremoneyes therein prescribed. yf anie thing were commaunded us by your Ma[jes]tie which we might doe without offence to the highest Ma[jes]tie there is not a man amongst us that would not willinglie obaye the same thoughe it ware to the losse of all he hath yea of his verie lyfe; but being perswaded that the sayd Cerimonies and manie things else in thos bookes are repugnant to the word of God, we most humblie beseache your highnes to spare our Consciences in the same especiallie seing hetherto neyther our exceptions (a viewe whereof we have to shewe) have bene answered nor on sufficient reason gyven (according to your Ma[jes]ties proclamation) to prove the lawfulnes of the things imposed (we have hard and do beleeve) that your Ma[jes]tie have often sayed, that yf anie can shew the things required to be unlawfull: your highnes will not have anie urged, and except we be able by the evidence of holie scripture to prove the same we will redilye yeld to conformytye required, in the meane tyme it maye please your Ma[jes]tie in your Princlye wisdome to consyder that howsoever these things have

---

[374] One of the commonest offences presented in the church courts was cohabitation before (church) marriage, usually indicated by the birth of the first child in less than nine months after the marriage. Since betrothal before witnesses constituted the marriage in popular perception, there was an element here of culture clash, although the churchwardens, lay members of the community that they were, were bound by their office to support the law of the church in their presentments, while these orders suggest that marriage discipline was internalized in Dedham. (See Ingram, *Church courts, sex and marriage in England*.)

[375] The renewed enforcement of subscription in 1604, under the canons of that year, part of the backlash which followed the substantial failure of the Hampton Court Conference, was a replay of 1584 with rather more blood on the carpet, since many more ministers – some eighty – were deprived of their livings, more than at any other time between the 1560s and 1640s. See Kenneth Fincham and Peter Lake, 'The ecclesiastical policy of King James I', *Journal of British Studies*, XXIV (1985), 169–207, and Kenneth Fincham, ed., *The early Stuart church, 1603–1642* (Basingstoke, 1993), pp. 25–7, 75–6. These studies correct the arithmetic and much else in S. B. Babbage, *Puritanism and Richard Bancroft* (London, 1962). The destination and tone of this petition reveals very clearly what is known to modern historians: that the role of the monarch in the subscription crisis of 1604–5 was very different from that of Queen Elizabeth in 1584. James I was in the driving seat, and this petition is tailored to his known convictions and prejudices. See B. W. Quintrell, 'The royal hunt and the puritans, 1604–5', *JEH*, XXXI (1980), 41–58. There remains the question how a copy of this petition should have come to Richard Parker, now at Ketteringham, Norfolk. Evidently he was still on the mailing list of the revived conference movement.

[376] There is a similar list of names in Richard Rogers's diary: Knappen, *Two puritan diaries*, p. 31: 'In London, Mr Stephen Egerton, Mr Wooten, that learned minister, Mr C. Jackson, Mr Horne, Mr Smith, Mr Evans'. For many of these men, see Paul Seaver, *The puritan lectureships* (Stanford, 1970), pp. 223–6.

not heretofore bene by authoritie removed yet have they had quiett possession in thes Churches under the gospell since the first abolishinge of poperie that our late gratious Queene of happie memorie att the humble sute of the Commons in the Parliament signified her expresse will and pleasure yet upon record that no Preachers or ministers should be impeached <judged> indighted or otherwise molested or troubled for the rightes and Ceremonies in question that the common judgment of almost all the paynefull resiant ministers of the land is against them that they have bene longe distressed in manie places and generallie <distressed> distasted with the people of better note as hath appeared both in manie parliamentes of former tymes and also in this last p[arliament] in regard whereof we humbly beseache your highnes to take this burthen from our Consciences. And vouchsafe the contynewance of our mynisters att the least untill the ignorant and scandall ministers be removed non residentes reformed and all the Churche of this kingdome be provided of able godly and resident preachers: That poperie and Athisme gett not heedd amonge us to the ruyn of this famous Churche and Common welthe: and this we hope your Ma[jes]tie will not deney us the rather because we be the servantes of your god. Preachers of that fayth whereof your highnes is both <professor> professor and defender. We have alwayes sincearely favoured and to our power furthered your Just and lawfull Clayme to this kingdome, we are adversaryes to them that are adversaryes to your soule and bodie supremicie Crownes and kingdomes, we have bene brought up and taken degrees in the universities, we are manie of us become graye headed in the service of god and of this Church having preached the gospell som of us 10. yeares som 20. yeares, som 30 yeares som more and dyverse of us in this Cyttie adventured or <lyes> lyves by preachinge in the tyme of the late infection, neyther are we so fewe as is pretended [fo. 47v] to saye nothing of our bretheren which yeld with muche greefe and sorrow of hart, we have wyves and Children kinsfolkes and frends depending on us who are all undone yf we be displaced, God forbyd that it ever shold be sayd or written in succeding ages that in the dayes of so religious and learned a king so manie learned and paynefull pastors and preachers were cast out as unsavorie salt and that for refusing suche a subscription as in no age of the Churche was ever urged and is more then the Lawe of the land requireth, and for not using suche Cerimonies as are profitable to no prince nor subject and to speake the least have bene and contynew to be polluted with Idolatrye and in the meane tyme so manie dumbe ministers so manie scandalus ministers and non residentes the shame and bane of the Churche of god kept in, that so manie learned godly and manie of them aged men ware exposed to suche reproche and miserie as nether the dumb and scandalus ministers with thes of late nor monkes fryers and nunns in former tymes have bene. Oh that your Ma[jes]tie did knowe the reproche that is alredie fallen upon us yea upon the gohspell which we have preached: the insulting of the Papistes and prophaine persons the discurragement of younge studientes, the pittifull cryes of manie thousands most faythfull subjectes throughe out the land cheifely in your highnes Chamber and famious Cyttie of London. Yf your Ma[jes]tie did but heare and see thes wonderfull effectes your royall and compassionate hart (we are perswaded) could not be able to endure the same. But your Ma[jes]ties is an Angell of god to deserne more then is meete for us to speake, therfor forbareing to proceed further herein wee humblie cast our selves at your Ma[jes]ties feete for the continewance of our mynistrie to the

glorie of god and the salvation of his people through Jesus Christ whome we daylie
beseach to blesse your Ma[jes]tie and prosperitye for ever.

Rich[ard] Garder[377]	Anthony Erbery[378]	And[rew] Castelton[379]
Steven Egerton[380]	Lewis Hewes[381]	Josiah horne[382]
Tho[mas] Barbor[383]	Jo. Wethenam[384]	davyd Hopkins[385]
Tho[mas] Wilkocks[386]	W. Chiball[387]	Geo. Moore[388]
James Bamford[389]	Rob Smythe[390]	W. Bradshaw[391]
Anthony Wotten[392]	Sam horne[393]	Hue Gadgrine[394]
Evan Thomas[395]	Ed Snapp[396]	
Henry Jacob[397]	W. Laxton[398]	

[377] Richard Gardiner (Gardner), rector of Whitechapel, Middlesex 1570–1617(d.), was a moderate leader of the London godly throughout his long ministry who seldom fell foul of the ecclesiastical authorities during Elizabeth's reign: George Hennessy, *Novum repertorium ecclesiasticum parochiale Londinense* (London, 1908), p. 457; Collinson, *EPM*, pp. 320, 411–12. On 5 March 1605, however, he was called into consistory to certify of his conformity in using the prayer book, particularly with regard to kneeling at communion. The case was twice prorogued and drops out of sight after 7 June: LMA DL/C/617, pp. 562, 713, 786. It was revived on 24 November 1606 when he was again accused of receiving communion standing and administering to standing communicants: LMA DL/C/304, p. 742. No more is heard of the matter.

[378] Apparently unknown to the Oxbridge records, Erbery was active in the months following James's accession. In October 1603 he was one of four 'travellers to the Court' with a petition from the ministers of Chichester diocese, and on 15 May 1604 he introduced a bill into parliament accusing Richard Bancroft of treason: S. B. Babbage, *Puritanism and Richard Bancroft* (London, 1962), pp. 192–3, 239.

[379] Castleton, rector of St Martin Pomeroy [Ironmonger Lane], 1577–1617 (d.), appears to have hovered on the fringes of the conference movement. Towards the end of his ministry he went blind. He was called into consistory on 18 and 22 January 1605 for failing to provide a 'settled minister', and on 25 June the court noted a list of clergy who had preached on his behalf: LMA DL/C/617, pp. 231, 237, 277. He was presumably, therefore, suspected of harbouring unlicensed nonconformists.

[380] One of the foremost preachers of late Elizabethan London, and in a very real sense John Field's successor as the lynch-pin of organized opposition to the ecclesiastical establishment, Egerton was minister of Blackfriars from c. 1585 until his death in 1622. Yet after the events of 1604–5, when he was briefly suspended by Bishop Richard Vaughan, he seems to have maintained a self-imposed silence. See the entry by Brett Usher in *Oxford DNB*.

[381] Hughes, a prominent exorcist, was probably the man of these names who was briefly rector of St Helen, Bishopsgate c.1600–c.1603: Hennessy, *Novum repertorium*, p. 210. For his further career, see G. W. Cole, 'Lewis Hughes, the militant minister of the Bermudas and his printed works', *Proceedings of the American Antiquarian Society* (n. s., XXXVII, 1929); Michael MacDonald, ed., *Witchcraft and hysteria in Elizabethan London* (London/New York, 1991), pp. xvii, lvii. The editors are grateful to Dr Thomas Freeman for drawing the latter works to their attention.

[382] Horne (d. 1626) was born in Luton, Bedfordshire, and graduated BA from Trinity College, Cambridge, in early 1597. He was ordained deacon and priest at Witham, Essex, on 25 and 26 January 1598 by John Sterne, suffragan bishop of Colchester, and is thereafter credited with the vicarage of Orwell, Cambridgeshire, from 1599 and the rectory of Winwick, Lancashire, from 1616: *Alum. Cantab.*, II, 408; GL MS 9535/2, fo. 81v.

[383] A prominent preacher and lecturer in London from his arrival in the capital in c. 1574 until his death in c. 1604, Barbor (Barber) was vicar of Stoke Newington, Middlesex, between 1575 and 1580 but thereafter seems to have lived in the London parish of St Botolph Bishopsgate. He was one of the witnesses whose evidence in star chamber in 1591 helped to bring down the portcullis on the conference movement. See the entry by Brett Usher in *Oxford DNB*.

[384] Not identified. The likeliest possibility is that this entry enshrines a copyist's mistranscription of the signature of *Thomas Whetenhall*, whose *A Discourse of the Abuses now in Question in the Churches of Christ* (London, 1607) prompted Bancroft to authorize a raid on Whetenhall's house 'and the Lodging of Josyas Nichols' immediately upon its publication: see Babbage, *Puritanism and Richard Bancroft*, p. 145.

[385] Not identified.

(Footnotes 386–394 on facing page)

[fo. 48r]

The use of the Ceremonies unlawfull[399]

1. Whatsoever meere ecclesiasticall action appropriated to gods worshipp is not warranted eyther expreslie or by necessarie consequence in some place of holie scripture the same is contrarie to gods worde and simplie unlawfull but etc ergo

[386] Co-author with John Field of *An admonition to the parliament* (1572). (See above, pp. xxv–vi.) Having fallen out with Field, an embarrassing episode fully exploited by Bancroft in *Daungerous positions,* he became a prolific author in the vein of practical divinity and developed excellent social contacts. See the entry by Patrick Collinson in *Oxford DNB.*

[387] William Chibald was rector of St Nicholas Cole Abbey 1604–41 (d.): Hennessy, *Novum repertorium,* p. 345. In consistory on 16 January 1605 ('Chibull'), he was ordered to conform to the prayer book ceremonies, having failed to use the surplice or the cross in baptism: LMA DL/C/617, p. 161.

[388] Not identified.

[389] See *Oxford DNB.*

[390] Rector of St Nicholas Acon from 1600, Robert Smythe was summoned into consistory on 12 January 1605, following Bancroft's final episcopal visitation in 1604, for failing to observe the prayer book on the grounds he was 'not persuaded' of the lawfulness of all the ceremonies enjoined. He stated, in mitigation, that he duly prayed for the king and the royal family, always giving them their full titles. It is then noted that on 22 February he was 'deprived by my L.': Hennessy, *Novum repertorium,* p. 144; LMA DL/C/617, p. 132. It seems bizarre that he was immediately licensed (25 February) to serve the cure of Holy Trinity Minories: see Hennessy, *Novum repertorium,* p. 429.

[391] William Bradshaw announced his secession from the Elizabethan presbyterian tradition in his *English Puritanisme containening [sic] the maine opinions of the rigidest sort of those that are called Puritanes in the Realme of England* (1605). He is placed in context by Peter Lake, 'William Bradshaw, Antichrist and the community of the godly', *JEH,* XXXVI (1985), 570–89. He is presumably the Mr Bradshaw, preacher 'in Mr Redishe's house' in the parish of 'Christs' [Christ Church Newgate St], who was summoned into consistory on 22 January 1605 because he preached privately and was unlicensed. It was noted that he was 'in the country and so hath been this 3 weeks': LMA DL/C/617, p. 239.

[392] A noted preacher and former chaplain to Robert Devereux, 2nd earl of Essex. See *Oxford DNB.*

[393] Perhaps the man of these names from Hertfordshire who graduated BA from Queen's College, Oxford, in 1593 and proceeded MA in 1596; 'perhaps' minister of Impington, Cambridgeshire, 1629–31: *Alum. Oxon.,* II, 408. He was perhaps the 'Mr Horne curate of St Magnus' who was in consistory on 16 January 1605 for failing to use the surplice or the cross in baptism, being 'not persuaded' of their lawfulness, and suspended 22 February following: LMA DL/C/617, p. 179.

[394] Not identified.

[395] Probably Richard Rogers's 'Mr Evans' (see p. 130, n. 376 above) but not certainly identified. For 'Mr [ ] Evans of Cloke lane in London', see Babbage, *Puritanism and Richard Bancroft,* p. 189.

[396] Edmund Snape: see *Oxford DNB.*

[397] Jacob, the 'semi-separatist' leader, would later gather in Southwark a congregation which was ancestral to English congregationalism. He did not, however, deny that the Church of England was a true church. 'Mr Jacob curate of St Alban Wood St' was in consistory on 18 January 1605 and again on 23 February and 13 April as 'a minister living without cure'. It was noted that he was 'bound in the Commission court' to appear at a day's notice: LMA DL/C/617, pp. 195, 371, 609.

[398] Not identified.

[399] Although undated, this and the papers that follow relate to the circumstances of 1604–5. This is established by the reference to Richard Hooker and to a sermon preached at Paul's Cross in 1603 (see below p. 134).

prop[osition] prob[atum] deut[eronomy] 4. 2.[400] Esay 8. 20.[401] prov[erbs] 30. 6.[402] revelation 22. 18.[403] mathew 15. 13[404] *a fortiori* ex gal[atians] 3. 15[405]

2.   All Accons appropriated to gods worship ordayned by men are forbydden in the 2. Comande

The use of everye Cerimoney is such. [er]go.

3.   All outward formes and likenesses in gods worship ordayned by men to signifie and edifie withall and to stir up mens mynds unto god the same are forbidden in the 2 comandment etc. our cerimonies are suche. [er]go:

In the tract of Ceremonies: and Hooker (lib. 5. pag. 158)[406] condempneth all Cerimonies as vayne, which are not significant and addeth that Cer[emonies] destitute of signification, are no better then the idle gestures of a man whose mother wyttes are not maisters of that they doe er[go]: and the b[ishop] of Carleile[407] at Paules Crosse, Mat: 24.[408] 1603 confirmed and defended this use of them by the example of the Jewes setting up a new alter er[go] Joss. 22.[409]

4.   If Images in Churches etc. but ergo

The propro[sal?] proved, because the cer[emonies] are as Images etc

The Assump[tion]: proved Hbac 2. 18.[410] Jer[ermiah] 10. 8. 13.[411]

5.   All reliques and monumentes of idolatrie cheefelie in gods servis are unlawfull ergo etc.

---

[400] 'Ye shall put nothing unto the worde which I commande you, neither shall ye take ought ther from, that ye may kepe the commandements of the Lord your God which I commande you.'

[401] Isaiah viii. 20: 'To the Law, and to the testimonie, if they speak not according to this word; it is because there is no light in them.'

[402] 'Put nothing unto his words, lest he reproove thee, and thou be found a lyar.'

[403] 'If any man shall adde unto these things, God shal adde unto him the plagues, that are written in this booke.'

[404] 'But hee answered and said, Every plant which mine heavenly Father hath not planted shalbe rooted up.'

[405] 'Though it be but a mans covenant, when it is confirmed, yet no man doeth abrogate it, or addeth any thing thereto.'

[406] This is a remarkable reference. The first four books of Richard Hooker's *Lawes of ecclesiasticall politie* were published in 1593, the fifth in 1597. See *Of the lawes of ecclesiasticall politie: The fift booke* (1597) in *Richard Hooker: Of the laws of ecclesiastical polity*, ed. W. Speed Hill, Folger Library edition of the works of Richard Hooker, II (Cambridge, Mass., 1977).

[407] Henry Robinson (1598–1616), a conscientious, evangelical bishop, had been the closest friend and ally in Oxford of John Reynolds when he was provost of Queen's College, where Reynolds took up residence after retiring from the presidency of Corpus Christi College. Reynolds was the most senior and prominent of the puritan spokesmen at the Hampton Court Conference, where Robinson also appeared, on the episcopal side. But both Robinson and Anthony Rudd, bishop of St Davids, were in reality fellow travellers, the London minister Stephen Egerton advising the Northamptonshire puritans in November 1603 that Robinson was on their side. (BL, MS Sloane 271, fo. 23v.) Robinson published nothing, and no other record of this Paul's Cross sermon survives. See also Kenneth Fincham, *Prelate as pastor* (Oxford, 1991), pp. 86, 88n, 253.

[408] Matthew xxiv.

[409] Joshua xxii.

[410] Habakkuk ii. 18: 'What profiteth the image? for the maker thereof hath made it an image, and a teacher of lyes, though he that made it, trust therein, when he maketh dumb idoles.'

[411] The reference is to Jeremiah x. 8–13 beginning: 'But altogether they dote, and are foolish: for the stocke is a doctrine of vanitie.' and continuing in verse 10, 'But the Lord is the God of trueth: he is the living God, and an everlasting King: at his angre the earth shal tremble, and the nations can not abide his wrath.'

The propro[sition]: proved Exod[us]: 34. 13[412] deut[eronomy] 12. 3. 4.[413] Esa[y]: 30. 22.[414] Judg[es]: 23 etc[415]

6.   True worshipp[er]s must wor[ship] in speritt and truth etc. yf Christ here doe prescribe a manner of wor[ship] directlie contrarie to the wor[ship] of the Samaritans etc but etc ergo etc.

7.   Christ hath freed us from all Ceremonies etc for they be burthens those which ware appointed by god himselfe were burthens Actes 15. 10. 28.[416]

Considerations to staye from sudden yelding etc

1. It semeth to be a betraying of the cause of sinceritye, for which we have stood so long, and so a distroying of the thinge we have builded.

2. It will be a disgrace to those godlie learned, who have lyved, suffered, died etc.

3. It wilbe a prejudice to the posteritie etc.

4. <It> The urgers of them will not staye there etc.

5. It will greatlie greeve, and perhapps prejudice other reformed Churches viz that of Scotland.

6. We must be faythfull even in the least things etc.

7. mens inconstancie herein will greatlie lesson the authoritie, reverence, estimation etc. of theire ministrie etc.

8. It will harden papistes Athistes etc cause dyverse runn into scisme

9. It will quenche or checke the sperytt and graces in them who shall by a kinde of wresting and unwillingnes yeld etc. And alienate theire mindes from the bretheren by lyttell and lyttell.

10. It wilbe a justifying of all the unconscionable and unmercifull proceeding etc.

11. It will cause the bretheren to fall more heavelie upon them which stand out.

12. A discouragment to the knightes and Burgesses etc.

[fo. 48v]

Yf the B[ishop] proceed against anie it must be eyther as they are B[ishops] or highe Comissioners[417]

---

[412] 'But yee shall overthrow their altars, and breake their images in pieces, and cut downe their groves.'
[413] 'Also yee shall overthrow their altars, and breake downe their pillars, and burne their groves with fire: and yee shall hewe downe the graven images of their gods, and abolish their names out of that place. Ye shall not so do unto the Lord your God.'
[414] 'And ye shall pollute the covering of the images of silver, and the rich ornament of thine images of gold, and cast them away as a menstruous cloth, and thou shalt say unto it, Get thee hence.'
[415] There are only twenty-one chapters in the Book of Judges.
[416] 'Now therefore, why tempt yee God, to lay a yoke on the disciples necks, which neither our fathers, nor wee were able to beare?. . . For it seemed good to the holy Ghost, and to us, to lay no more burthen upon you, then these necessary things.'
[417] The argument of this paper is complex and technical. At issue is whether, under the terms of the Henrician and Elizabethan Acts of Supremacy, the bishops retain any jurisdiction of their own. The argument is that only the court of high commission, empowered according to the statutes and by the Great Seal, has any legitimate jurisdiction, and is to be obeyed. However, it could be (and has been) argued that when, after the passage of the Act of Supremacy, and with the lapse of the office of vicegerent for spiritual affairs (held only by Thomas Cromwell), the bishops, in that they continued to conduct visitations, were in effect also commissioners for the crown, the supreme head. See Margaret Bowker, 'The supremacy and the episcopate: the struggle for control, 1534–1540', *Historical Journal*, XVIII (1975), 227–43.

As B[ishops] they have no authoritie to proceed against anie subjecte for to send out prosses to cite men: to sytte in Judgment is a principall part of the Jurisdiction ecclesiasticall, This being by a statute of 1. Eliz Cap 1.[418] annexed to the Croune as a speciall prerogatyve royall. Now the statute of 35. Henr: Capt. 16[419] doth leave to the B[ishop]. suche privileges onlie as are not prejudiciall or derogatorye to the prerogatyve royall or the Lawes and statutes of this realm. And uppon this ground did the parliament 1. Edw. 6.[420] enact that all proces ecclesiasticall shold be in the kings name as are the process of the kings Court in the common Lawe.

{ob} What authoritie then is left to the B[ishops]

{Answ} *Quae ad admonicionem non quae ad jurisdictionem spectant*, as to make ministers to institute etc.

Wherefore if anie be cited, they maye <~~appeare~~> appeare to avoyd accon of slander: but they are in open place to protest syth all Jurisdiccion is in the kinges and that by theire oath to the Supremacie, they are bound to acknowledge none authoritie but that which is directed from his Ma[jes]tie: that therefore they doe not appeare as of duetie, neyther acknowledg the B[ishop's] Jurisdiction and authoritie in ecclesiasticall Causes, unles he hath sufficient warrant from his Ma[jes]tie under the broade Seale according to the statute of 1. Eliz[abeth]

The highe Commission is established 1. Eliz[abeth] and they must proceede eyther upon the statute or the Canons

1. Tuouching [sic] the statute yt ratifieth neyther the booke of Common prayer latelie erected , nor the former that was used all the Q[ueen's] tyme: But onelie the book of Edw[ard] 6. with 2. alterations specified in the statute, whereas that which hath bene heretofore used hath manie more alterations and therefore they cannot proceede against anie for the neglect of eyther of thes bookes, by vertue of that statute.[421] This statute doth not inflict anie speciall penaltie for omission or refusall of the vestmentes or ornamentes of the ministerye. and therefore no man can be touched in his lyvinge for the surplice by that Statute. And there is not anie other that doth comaunde it, onelie they maye be punished for contempt of the proclamation by imprisonment and no otherwise. As for the Canons yf they be confirmed,[422] and so the highe Commission execute the penalty of them. it wilbe a verie doubtfull pointe whether they can stretche so far as to put a Subject from his freehold. And if men put it to triall uppon the Common Lawe, it will seeme a verie hard case, for

---

[418] The Act of Supremacy of 1559.

[419] 'A Bill for thexamination of Canon Lawes by xxxiv personnes to be named by the Kinges Majestie' was a dead letter.

[420] 1 Edward 6, Cap 6 is a wrong reference which has no relevance.

[421] The legal-casuistical argument that the prayer book to which conformity and subscription were urged was not the book legislated in the Elizabeth Act of Uniformity may have originated with catholic exiles, but was exploited by puritan lawyers and parliamentarians, notably Robert Beale and James Morice, especially in the parliament of 1589. See 'Certain motions for a conference on religion, 25 February': 'The question shuld have bene whether we have any booke established . . . Seeing the statute requireth a Booke of Common Prayer with the three additions only, and not otherwise differing from the booke of 5 and 6 Edward 6 . . . whether the prelates have by the law of England any autoritie to alter the Booke at all.' Hartley, *Proceedings in the parliaments of Elizabeth I*, II, 445. See also Collinson, *EPM*, p. 399.

[422] This serves to date this document to 1605, soon after Convocation had approved the new canons, and while it was still uncertain whether they would receive parliamentary endorsement. (They did not.)

admytt that the convocation maie (for breache of Churche orders) disposses a minister of his Frehold why not anie other subject? and so by consequent, the wholl bodie of the Realme maie (if they transgres the Churche Lawes) be put out of there Lands and livings, and be enthraled to the Clergie as in tyme of papistrie which gapp will not easely be opened, sith it is graunted that thecclesiasticall lawes do properlie tend onlie to a spirituall chastisment

Conclutions upon the premisses

1. No B[ishop] except he have an highe Com[mission] can with anie coullor of law proceed against a minister.

2. The highe Com[mission] cannot inflict anie warrantable penaltie for omission of Surples or the bookes of common prayer now extant and in use by vertue of the statute

3. Yf anie be by the B[ishop] or Com[mission] deprived, he maie not withstanding keepe possession of his lyving untill <del>he maye</del> by the Common Lawe it be tryed whether the B. acte can deprive him of his frehold

The Manner how to keepe Possession

Let him provide that some one eyther wife, or Children, Servaunt or frend be alwayes in the Churche; and in the house night and daye, so none other can be inducted, yf anie offer to thrust or pull him or his out of the Churche, lett him not much contend, but being thrust out let him goe to the Justices, and deposing before them that he was thrust out of the possession againe. Yf the b[ishop] shall sequester his lyving, the lawe hath a direct course to dissolve the sequestracion.

[fo. 49r]

Good orders[423] to be observed in a reformed godlie church proved and collected out of godes worde[424] and authorised by the lawes

{The. 4. commandment.}

{Exo[dus] 19. 10. 11. Eccl[esiastes] 4. 17 Psal[m] 5. 3. Deut[eronomy] 31. 12 Josue 24. 15 Mat[thew] 13. 14 Mar[k] 4. 15 Act 7. 11}

1. Imprimis for the right use of the lordes daie: religiously to spend it in holie exercises publikely and at home vz preparing themselves by godly and heavenly meditations at home in the morninge, to call their houshold together to prayer, and having prayed the governors of houshold accompanyed with their whole family (excepting such as about necessary busynesses, as tending of children etc of neces-sity must abide at home) to resort to their owne church before the begynning of divine service and there to contynue reverently and soberly the whole tyme of exer-cise: then the Congregation dissolved to geve themselves to reade or to conferre with theire servauntes and Children, and examyne what they have learned out of the

---

[423] This is evidently another recension of the Dedham Orders (see above, pp. 128–30). It differs in several details, for example, in providing for quarterly rather than monthly communions.

[424] It would be tedious to reproduce the texts of all these biblical references, fifty in all. The interested reader is invited to pursue them in the Bible. Most are accurately cited and apropos.

worde read or sermon, and so diligently to resorte to the Eveninge service causinge their servauntes and children to be ready to answere to the Catechisme[425]

{Neh[emiah] 13. 15 16. 17. 18. Jer[emiah] 17. 24}

2.   Item that they carefully provide for their businesses that they maie not have any occasion (as nere as possibly they may) themselves or their servauntes to travaill upon the lordes daye ether to faires, mariage dynners or such like.

{Act 16. 15 vers 33. 34 Mar[k] 10. 13 1 Pet[er] 3. 21}

3.   Item when ther is anie to be baptised the father to come to the mynister the day before baptisme to conferre with the mynister in the principall pointes of baptisme, also at the time of baptisinge the childe the father to stand with thother suerties to answer for his childe.[426]

{Deut[eronomy] 23. 2 1 Cor[inthians] 7. 14 Exo[dus] 20. 6}

4.   Item if ther shall happen any child to be base borne such a child not ot be receyved to the holye Sacrament of baptisme, before the parentes at the least one of them shewe token of repentaunce to the contentation of the Congregation, or els some godlie kinsfolke of such a childe will promise before god and his holie Congregation to see and provide that the child be brought up in the feare of god and his true Religion.

{Act[s] 2. 42 20. 7. 2 chro[nicles] 19. 6 1 Cor[inthians] 11. 28 Numb[ers] 9. 6.}

5.   Item that once in a quarter the holie Communion be mynistered and warninge beinge given a convenient tyme before, every governor of houshold with such of their family as shall receyve to resort to their mynister to the Church at times conveniently appointed for the same, to assiste the mynister in the godlie examynation and due preparinge of them and theirs to the Communion, so that such as are meete and worthie may be receyved and the unworthie may be deferred with the consent of their owne masters.[427]

{1 Cor[inthians] 10. 17 6. 1. 2. Neh[emiah] 8. 10}

6.   That at every communion ther be a collection made for the poore by one of the Collectors, of such as willinglie and cherfully will geve of their owne benevolence, and such benevolence to be bestowed according to the discretion of the mynister, Collectors and 2 of the Hedboroughes[428] [fo. 49v]

{2 Chro[nicles] 30. 8. 9. 2 Kings 23. 3. Neh[emiah] 9. 38 Math[ew] 5. 9. 23. 24. 8. 15. 16. 17. 1 Cor[inthians] 1. 2. 3. 4.}

7.   Item that so many as shall communicate promise and professe to live godly and

---

[425] The outsider to the sabbatarian debate might wonder how the whole day was to be spent in 'holie exercises'. This spells it out, particularly laying down how to use the time between the morning and evening services.

[426] Puritans were insistent that the natural father of a child must act as godfather, or at least be one of the sureties.

[427] This answers a question raised earlier (see above, p. 128). Governors of households were to assist the minister in the examination and preparation of those due to receive communion.

[428] Again, a little more light is shed on a question raised earlier (see above, p. 129). The money collected at communions was 'for the poore', and the 'Collectors' for the poor (later under the terms of the Poor Law to be styled 'Overseers') were involved in distributing it.

charitably with all their neighbors, and if anie occasion of displeasure arise that they refraygne from all discord and revenge by wordes, gestures, actions or suites, and endevor themselves to be reconciled one to another: if that cannot prevaill to request a neighbor or two to unite them in frindshipp agayne, and if they prevaill not to desire the mynister with other of the godly neighbors to make peace betwene them and so all good meanes to be used before any compleynt, presentment or lawe be attempted out of the towne.

{Neh[emiah] 8. 1. 2. 3. Act[s] 5. 42.
8.   Item that all the housholders accompanyed with as many of their servauntes as conveniently they may frequent diligently the thursday Lecture[429]

{Math[ew] 3. Act[s] 9. 4. 5. Eph[esians] 5. 26.}
9.   Item that ther be no child baptised, no couples maryed but upon the Lordes daie or Lecture daye.

{Math[ew] 1. 19 1 Cor[inthians] 7. 39 Heb[rews] 13. 4}
10.   Item if anie be knowne to have knowne one another carnally before the celebration of their mariage, then none to accompany them to the Church nor from the Church nor dyne with them the day of Mariage, and that the pastor at the mariage or baptisinge of such a child begotten before mariage use some godly meanes with the parties to bringe them to repentaunce, to the satisfyinge of the godly offended by their fornication, to the humbling of themselves, and terrifying of others from the like filthie profaninge of the honorable estate of mariage.

{Deut[eronomy] 6. 7. 11: 19 Gen[esis] 18. 19 Psal[m] 119. 164 Dan[iel] 6. 10. 11.}
11.   Item that every Mr or parent use morninge and eveninge to praye together with their family that they examyne their servauntes and children in the principles of religion and that they geve themselves to reading and conference so that they may readely with understanding answer being asked in the Church concerninge sich principall pointes.[430]

{Rom[ans] 12. 13. Heb[rews] 13. 2 Toby 2. 2. Eccl[esiastes] 11. 29. 12. 1. 2. 4. 5. 6.}
12.   Item forasmuch as hospitality is commaunded by god and commended by men it shalbe good for every one of hability to invite to dynner on the lordes daie one, two or more of the godly poore neighbers encouraging them to walke honestly and religiously in their callinges

{Eph[esians] 6. 4. Proverbs 22. 6.}
13.   Item that all endevor themselves to learne to reade and write[431] and therfore all

---

[429] This appears to contradict the evidence of David Waine in consistory that Chapman preached on 'Tuesdays and Fridays': see above, p. lxxvi. The clerk of the court, taking down oral testimony at speed, may of course have misrendered it.

[430] This is rare and, for Dedham, unique evidence that the evening service (in all probability this refers to the evening) incorporated an element of catechizing, or a catechetical sermon, in which not only children but their parents were required to answer the points raised.

[431] Only here is an aspiration expressed that all children should learn to write. Historians of literacy believe that writing was taught as a separate skill and that many children who left school for employment were able to read but never learned to write.

maisters and parentes to call upon their servauntes to learne to reade and to set their
children to schole

{1 Sam[uel] 7. 16 Act[s] 5. 42 1 Thess[alonians] 4. 11 2 Thess[alonians] 3. 6. 10.
11. 12. 13. 14.}
14.   Item that once in a monthe the mynister, Constables and collectors and one or
two of the Hedboroughes goe to the howses and visite the poore, and note the disordered idle persons that understanding the necessitie of the poore, and the evell
disposition of the idle and disordered provision may be made for them accordingly
in tyme

[fo. 50r]

{Psal[m] 101 1 Th[essalonians] 2. 7. Eph[esians] 4. 28}
15.   Item that none be suffred to come into the Towne to inhabite but such as be
of honest and godly behavyor, and those that receive them in will provide that they
may not charge the towne, that none contynue except they be of some good and
honest trade or callinge to earne their livinge bye, nor any that are single persons,
not retayned as servauntes according to the statute.

{Proverb[s] 11. 14}
16.   Item that once in a monthe the mynister Constables collectors and other
hedboroughes of this towne meete together at some convenient place to conferre
and consult of matters concerning the good government of the Towne.

[fo. 50v]

The xiii th of January 1582. I was enjoigned to observe the booke of common praier
in all respectes, and to read the Queens Injunctions and weare the Surplice and to
certify the doinge of it the first Courte in Candlemas terme, or els to appeare personally before the Commissioners: but I appeared and yet through favour escaped their
handes and yelded not unto them, I praise god.[432]

The lawiers will counsell a man suspended to appeale to another Judge but it is but a
delay and further charge for remedy a mynister shall find none, being men of like
place and like affection.
The B[ishop] may excommunicate and suspend for not observing orders and he may
excommunicate us not only if we appeare not, but if we appeare and yeld not to their
orders they may excommunicate us for our obstinacy,
There be two kindes of suspension, one *ab officio* another *a beneficio* and the first
kind encludes both suspending from executing his function and from his lyvinge.
If we deale in our office of mynistery after suspension we be by their law irregular.
The Lord kepe me and all good men out of their handes and delyver us from their
Tyranny. Amen. Amen.

---

[432] 'The xiii th of January 1582': in new style therefore '1583', but the diocesan records indicate that
      Parker here refers to the events of late 1583 and early 1584: see *BR*, pp. 242, 244, n. 9 below.

[fo. 51r]

{55 meeting foll. 11. This answereth to the Question moved by Mr Doctor Cricke whether Churchwardens in our tyme be to be used. 75. meeting. foll. 13}[433]

What course in the best for a good mynister in thenglishe Churche, (where the right discipline is not in use) to take, when as publike offenders being unrepentaunt are not proceeded against to the cuttinge of them of, either from the Churche by the ecclesiasticall officers or altogether from libertye or liffe by the Civill Magistrate

Answere: {Proverb[s] 29. 24 Apocal[ypse] 2. 20}
That such a minister oughte not to be silente, slacke or carelesse in such a case of impunity, for that were to incurre parte of the faulte reproved but to use all good and lawfull meanes for the correctinge of such parties, and removinge of such offences: which are: of two sortes 1. Some common with other Christians 2. Others properly incident to his owne callinge of the mynistery.

{Esrah 9. 2. 3. 4. Esrah 10. 1. 2. 3. Psal[m] 119. 136 2 Cor[inthians] 12. 21}
1.   Of the first sorte are private prayers to the Archshephearde and Lorde of the folde, and of discipline with fastinge. Psalm 119. 136. 2. Cor. 12. 21.

{Gal[atians] 6. 1 1 Cor[inthians] 4. 14 2 Thess[alonians] 3. 15 1 Cor[inthians] 4. 21}
2.   Reprehensions, or admonitions if any place be lefte for yt, and oportunity ofred, not with the spirite of meeknes as Gal. 6. 1. or of love as 1. Cor. 4. 14 but of sharpnes and of the rodde as 1. Cor. 4. 21.

{1 Timoth[y] 6. 5 Gal[atians] 6. 20 1 Timoth[y] 5. 6}
3.   Withdrawinge from him the common tokens of love, as chearfull salutacions, countenaunces, gestures, society, and familiarity and such other duties of christian love, as pertayne to those of the houshold of faithe. gal. 6. 10 as to one dead being alyve and cutte of in deed, though not yet soe farre proceeded against in order of dicipline.

{Hebr[ews] 10. 24. 25}
4.   Mutuall provocation of others in the congregation to doe the like. Hebr. 10. 24. 25.[434]

---

[433] Richard Parker has put together his question asked at **55M**, 'what course a minister shuld take when disorders be risen up in a Church, and be publikelie reproved, and the chiefe of the parish, and the officers delt withall whom it specially concernes to reforme them, and yet nothing is done', to Crick's question at **75M**, 'tutching Churchwardens whether they and their offices were lawfull'. The arguments and places which follow are in search of an alternative system of discipline given the unreformed state of the church, in effect a replacement for a polity of churchwardens and their presentments to the church courts. Once again the interested reader is invited to pursue the various scriptural references in the Bible.

[434] On the advocacy of strict social shunning of the 'ungodly' and 'carnal', a matter with huge (anti)social implications, see Patrick Collinson, 'Wars of religion', Chapter 5 of *The birthpangs of protestant England;* Patrick Collinson, 'The cohabitation of the faithful with the unfaithful', in *From persecution to toleration: the Glorious Revolution and religion in England,* ed. O. P. Grell *et al.* (Oxford, 1991); Peter Lake, '"A Charitable Christian Hatred": the godly and their enemies in the 1630s', in *The culture of English puritanism, 1560–1700,* ed. C. Durston and J. Eales (Basingstoke, 1996), pp. 145–83. Some of these themes are more extensively explored in Peter Lake with Michael Questier, *The Antichrist's lewd hat. Protestants, papists and players in post-reformation England* (New Haven and London, 2002).

{2 Cor[inthians] 13. 1}
5.   Procuringe of some worthy Preachers, to approve by doctryne the goodnes of
the cause, and course undertaken by the minister, and to exhorte accordinge to the
measure of his credite, and giftes, to a further proceedinge of the Congregation
against such rebellious, and desperate offenders, till he be reformed or utterlie
excluded the company of the faithfull; or cutte of by the Magistrate, that in the
mouthes of two or three witnesses, every worde may stande

{Cantic[les] 2. 15}
6.   And callinge for the ayde of the Magistrate to enforce, both the private
offendors, and the negligent backwarde professors of the congregation, to their
christian duties in this behalffe

[fo. 51v]

{Gal[atians] 5. 12   2 Cor[inthians] 13. 2   2 Cor[inthians] 10. 5}
2.   Of the seconde sorte are publike prayers, conceyved especially for the
redressinge and removinge of such offences, and the worde of exhortation,
charginge and denouncinge in the most earnest manner, and such other spirituall
armor as is mentioned 2. Cor. 10. 5.   wherby the most stubborne and desperate
rebels may be subdued and leade away captives to Christe

{Esay 8. 11. 12   Math[ew] 7. 6   Tit[us] 3. 10. 11.   2 Chro[nicles] 26. 18   1
Cor[inthians] 5. 5   Hebr[ews] 12. 15   Apocal[ypse] 2. 2}
Barringe of them from the Communion,[435] with their Patrons and <favourers>
favourers, after the fore mentioned meanes have bene used with patience, love,
zeale and constancy, that soe they may be enforced to redresse and reformation, or
at least, an example of just severity and indignation against such may be lifted up, to
the terror of like evell disposed persons in other Churches, and to posterity.

{2 Reg[es] 3. 39   Revel[ation] 2. 5   1 Cor[inthians] 16. 22   2 Thess[alonians] 1. 8}
All which meanes beinge used <if they never repente> in prudence, zeale and love,
if they never repente, what remayneth but with patyence to wayte, till the lorde
himselfe come forthe clothed with Justice, to take vengeaunce on those that will not
obey the Gosple of our lorde Jesus Christe.

Finis.

---

[435] This effective excommunication stretched the prayer book rubric which allowed the minister to repel
notorious evil livers. In Essex it was an issue which caused serious trouble at East Hanningfield,
where William Seridge dechurched half his parish, and at Hatfield Peveral, where Thomas Carew
sent packing church papists whom Bishop Aylmer had hoped to 'win'. See Collinson, *EPM*, pp.
349–50; *Seconde parte*, II, 28–35.

[fo. 52r]

1. That private men joigning with their neighbours may deale for order ecclesiasticall in admonishinge and barringe from the Sacramentes, for wante of authority or other in the same place[436]

2. That our Churches consiste not of meere private men

To cutte of all other braunches or questions dependinge or incidente to our question, I entende to prove these two Propositions, implyinge the strengthe of that is in question.
In the first Proposition private men must be taken for such as are not only authorised to deale in ecclesiasticall affaires by the auncient and primityve order, nor by the government receyved in our Churche.

{1a *Ratio*} The Apostles were private men, their Apostolicall functions consistinge in prayer and preachinge sett aparte: yet dealte they commendably in the matters of almes and provision for the poore: Act[s] 6. 2. And soe in callinge, chosinge, and appointinge of mynisters and in the Censures of the Churche, for wante of other order established: moved with zeale, and care of their brethren not by election: Therfore if others moved with the like zeale for God his glory and love of their brethren, shuld undertake the same in a Church; utterlye voide of all publike order for governmente, whie shuld we doubte, but that the lorde will approve of the same?

{Rom[ans] 12. 3. 7 1 Pet[er] 4. 15 1 Sam[uel] 13. 9. 10. 12. 2 Chro[nicles] 26. 18 Abraham Gen[esis] 14. 7 Melchisedech Gen[esis] 14. 18 Job 1. 5 et 42. 8 cap. 29. 7. 14. 15. 16. Psal[m] 106. 30}
They in soe doinge, cannot justlie be accompted as rashe and busy bodies, presumers, intruders, nor ἀλλοτριοε πίσηοποι nor in the state with Saull: nor uzziah,[437] seeing they intermeddle not in thinges assigned and committed by order and authority unto others: but only undertake thinges most necessarye to be done; and which they standinge still, shuld utterly be lefte undone: seeinge they are not moved thereunto of curiosity, pride, ambition, vainglory, or other synister affection, but of meere zeale for God his glorye, and mutuall love, vertues, stronge, pure, and after a sorte infynite, and therfore thinges done of such causes, though not justifiable by any lawe, nay swervinge from the ordenary and common lawe, have bene well accepted of, and reputed with God as worthie and righteous actes.[438] Psalm 106. 30

By this Commission and warrante luther and others preached and the lorde blessed them.

---

436 The title of this essay on private men using discipline 'in the defect of others that shuld doe it' is provided by the endorsement on fo. 54v, p. 147 below. This 'lerned man' understood 'private man' as anyone not holding public office. This included the Apostles and extended to all Christians exercising themselves in what, by another definition, might be held to be public affairs.

437 More properly Uzzah, who put his hand to the Ark of the Covenant to stay it. 'And the Lord was very wroth with Uzzah, and God smote him in the same place for his fault, and there hee died by the Arke of God.' See 2 Samuel vi. 6–7.

438 This answers the common condemnation of puritans as 'busy controllers'.

{Objection Heb[rews] 5. 4[439] Answere}

If yt be objected, that they take upon them honor uncalled. Heb 5. 4. passing by the
place noted, as that which is not properly to be applied but to the callinge of
mynisters, I answere, that the lorde hath in effecte, thoughe not in ordenary and
open manner, authorised them soe farre to deale in such a case, in the absence and
wante of others, for wherfore els hath God endewed them with speciall welth,
hability, libertye, wisdome, experyence and the honor of old age, creditte and reverence, but to use yt for his glory, and the good of their brethren, in removinge evell
from Israell that

[fo. 52v]
{Psal[m] 125. 5}
she may be in peace to serve her God freely and at large.

{Exod[us] 20. 12 Levit[icus] 19. 32 1 Pet[er] 5. 5 Levit[icus] 24. 11. 12.}

If they must be honored as fathers and magistrates. Exod. 20. 12. Levit. 19. 32
whie ought they not to execute their authoritie, for which their honor is allowed
them: Then will yt be objected, they may and ought aswell take upon them to deal
in civill matters for the punishinge and committinge of a felon or murderer: and
whie not in the like case: viz in a free citie or towne, for wante of others appointed by
common and established order, as the people of Israell apprehended a blasphemer
and committed him to warde, without the boundes of their callinge, nothinge as yet
being in the lawe in that case for magistrates are but private men, when they goe
beyonde that commission of lawe wherby their dealinges are limited, as a Justice of
peace dealing in marinall or martiall affaires is but a private man, without speciall
commission from higher authoritie.

{Aunciente use}

whereunto may be added common use and custome in this our state in all parishes
wherin the Auncientes, have taken upon them to call and admonishe a notorious
offender and the whole body of the towne have yelded and submitted themselves
unto yt as that which was in force of lawe, noe lawe controllinge yt.

{2a Ratio Math[ew] 18. 16. 17.}[440]

Our savior geveth such private men authoritie to deal in hearinge, admonishinge,
rebukinge and excommunicatinge Math. 18. 17. for if we will walke in the playne
kinges highe way and rest in that sence which the place, and naturall signification of
wordes doe yelde, we must understande by those two or three, diverse auncient men
of good credite, as moste meete to heare, admonishe and persuade: and by the whole
churche, the body of a congregation, which for the most parte consisteth of private
men.

{3a Ratio 1 Cor[inthians] 5. 7 2 Thess[alonians] 3. 14 Hebr[ews] 12. 15. 16}

Accordinge to this rule and canon of Christ Jesus proceeded and practised the

---

[439] 'And no man taketh this honour unto himselfe, but he that is called of God, as was Aaron.'

[440] 'But if hee heare thee not, take yet with thee one or two, that by the mouth of two or three witnesses
     every word may be confirmed. And if hee will not vouchsafe to heare them, tell it unto the Church:
     and if hee refuse to heare the Church also, let him bee unto thee as an heathen man, and a Publicane.'

Apostles, laying the charge of good government, of separatinge the badde from the good, of purginge the leaven 1. Cor. 5. 7. of excludinge from common societie 2. Thess. 3. 14. of not suffringe any bitter roote to spring up, wherby many mighte be defiled. Hebr. 12. 15. 16. upon the whole congregation, that is to say upon such as were meete to deale in yt, for their wisdome, experience, sexe, states, creditt and acceptation, (and not upon such only as were specially picked out and chosen) if yt can be proved, that any such order of church elders, besides the mynisters, were then in those churches at those tymes established, as we wold have them in our Churches.

{1 Cor[inthians] 6. 1}[441]
The Apostle licenced the private Christians and professors in Corinthe to heare, judge and determyne of matters civill, risinge in their Churche and why not aswell in matters ecclesiasticall, being not of such difficulty nor daunger, for the peace of the Churche:
And the reasons being common, as stronge to warrant thone as thother, for we may conclude, that bycause the saynctes, thoughe private [fo. 53r]
{1 Cor[inthians] 6. 2. 3.} men, shall judge the world and angels, that therfore it were absurde, and injurious to barre them from judging and determyninge lower matters in the Congregation.

{5a Ratio Act[s] 6. 2}
Good widowes moved with the common duty of love, may attende upon impotente and diseased persons, without any publike, ordenary, or speciall callinge: Good men may performe the parte of deacons to the poore, thoughe uncalled of men, rather then they shuld perishe corporally: soe good Auncientes in a Churche, may deale for the curinge of spirituall diseases, rather then they shuld perishe spirituallye: Soe I conclude that private men in our sence, may call exhorte, admonishe and rebuke openly, and procede soe farre further, as may stande with the peace of the Churche, and the common lawe of the state and common welthe

The seconde Proposition
This is not denied, but of those that deny the whole Government of our churche, callinge of mynisters, with the whole authoritie and religion of our holie exercises, for if our Collectors, Sides men (as they are termed) and Churchwardens, be but private men, usurpers and intermeddlers in other mens offices and charges, havinge the callinge and authoritie that our church approveth, why shuld we not hold the like of the mynisters, who have noe better callinge, nor more authoritie, then they have receyved in this Church and of this Churche.

{1a Ratio a comparatis Jerem[iah] 23. 21}[442]
Then may we reason thus, the state of our governement ecclesiasticall how weake

---

[441] 'Dare any of you, having businesse against another bee judged under the unjust, and not under the Saints? Doe yee not know, that the Saints shall judge the worlde? If the worlde then shall be iudged by you, are yee unworthie to judge the smallest matters? Know yee not that wee shall judge the Angels? how much more things that pertaine to this life?'
[442] 'I have not sent these Prophets, saith the Lord, yet they ran: I have not spoken to them, and yet they prophesied.'

and imperfecte soever, discerneth of mynisters from Intruders, hirelinges, and such as runne before they be sente: much more shall yt be of force to put a difference betweene our Churche officers, and meere private men in deed, and be soe much more sufficient to authorise them then thother: by how much more there is lesse weighte in the matters they deale withall, then in those that the mynisters undertake.

Agayne for that our Church officers have more of the primityve order then our Mynisters: the mynisters being wholie imposed, and obtruded to the Churches by the Patron and Bushopp: and the Officers being firste chosen by the mynisters and people at home, then afterwarde also allowed, and approved by such as are appointed by authority, and soe solempnly by other entred into thexecution of their office.

And of this authorisement of mynisters and Church officers in our english congregations, we shall conceyve the better, if we discerne betweene the defecte of the substaunce in a government and circumstances or accidentall poyntes, thone resemblinge the liffe of a thinge, and thother but the outwarde face and coloure of the same.

[fo. 53v]

An example whereof may be taken, as an Introduction into this cause in the civill state, wherein accordinge to the auncyent speeche, a badd Magistrate is to be preferred to none at all, or to such as are private men altogether soe as none but Anabaptistes or such like will rejecte or excepte against such a Magistrate as entred disorderly and corruptly, or against such as are deputed by him or under him: Such a Majesty resteth in Magistracy, that the least parte of the truth or substaunce thereof draweth reverence to yt, from the common multitude and commaundeth obedyence at all their handes.

The like judgemente being holden of the ecclesiasticall government, we may reason thus.

Our english Church rejecteth not all governmente, maynteineth not a confusion, permitteth not every man to deale with the Worde and governmente that will, without order and difference: Our englishe Church requireth examination, approbation, ordination or admission of suche as are to deale in mynistery and governement: It committeth the care, judgment and charge of these thinges not to children, enemies, heretikes, or men of suspected doctrine, or flagitious liffe, nor to the rude and ignorante multitude, but to the lerned auncyente fathers and such as they shall depute, though not in such places, nor to such persons as we would have, or were to be wished in deed in some places: Therfore the thinges done by them, about this mynistery and governemente in our Churches, are not to be utterly rejected as voide and of noe valewe, and accepted noe more, then if they were done by private men, and devoyde of all authoritie.[443]

---

[443] 'Our english Church . . . all authoritie': the pragmatic argument, such as one might expect Edmund Chapman to deploy, that while the constitution and discipline of the Church of England was far from what it ought to be, yet it was not as if it had no constitution and discipline.

{1 Sam[uel] 2. 17 1 Sam[uel] 2. 17. 24 Act[s] 23. 5}

The mynistery and governmente in the daies of the kinges of Israell was not pure, but stayned, shaken and disordred in respecte of the Higher and inferyoure priestes of those that were already called and to be called in their manner of entraunce in, or of execution, especially at the appearaunce and full revelation of our Savyoure, when all thinges were at the worste: yet reade we not that the godly and purest worshippers renounced or rejected their mynistery, government, assemblies or holie exercises or were for soe doing approved of: yea our savyor and his followers presented themselves in the temple, used their mynistery, submitted themselves to the authority of their governmente, not commaundinge thinges simplye unlawfull or lawfull, nor discommaundinge thinges necessarie to be done.

{1 Chro[nicles] 6. 31. 32 1 Chro[nicles] 23. 27 Nehem[iah] 12. 45}

It will availe much for the holdinge of a sounde judgmente concerninge ecclesiasticall persons and actions in our Churche, to recorde with our selves thold state of the churche governmente in, and after Samuell his tyme, wherein diverse ecclesiasticall matters were translated from the Priestes (being negligent in their charge committed to them) to the people as 1. 2. kinges 12. 8. 9. and all thinges not <expressly> prescribed <especially> expresslye in the Lawe, were caried and ordered by the authority of the civill Magistrate as Nehem[iah] 12. 45. 1 Chron[icles] 6. 31. 32 1 Chro[nicles] 23. 27.
Finis

[fo. 54r]

blank

[fo. 54v]
[endorsement]
A lerned mans judgment what course a mynister shuld take with disordered persons and whether Auncientes in a Congregation may not use discipline in the defect of others that shuld doe it.

[fo. 55r]

{66. meeting. foll. 12}

I renue unto you, my most Reverend brethren, my sute,[444] for the obteyning of one to preach at my entrance into the Pastoral charge, which being proposed was shortly repelled and comming foorth was nipt in the head. It was sayd by divers that a request were to be made by meselfe unto some particular man: and by one that though it were imposed upon him, yet he woulde not do it, seinge the Church dealt as shee did, who in another cause of myne lykewise then debated, uttred this speech, that forasmuch as she caried herselfe as having all *in scrinio pectoris sui*, he would geve her no counsel if she sought it. The sentence I followed, but prevayled not, it

---

[444] Richard Crick's holograph letter to the conference. For some comments on this very important letter, see above, p. c.

seeming unto him, whome I would have intreated a matter to be agreed upon by
you. Which maketh me to returne againe a petitioner unto you all, and the seconde
tyme to knock at your gate craving to be lett in, and that my face may not be turned
away. If it be in your judgments to be graunted, I beseech you graunte it, that I may
appoynt a tyme for the purpose: if you thinke it not to be yeelded unto, let me knowe
it, that I may turne eyther to the right hand or to the left to see whether I may
obteyne so much favour of some good brother els where. I would have made this
sute unto you by woord of mouth, but that I feared least hearing the lyke boysterous
woordes, which I could not well lyke of, I should also chaunce to speake some that
should not greatly please, being become now at the length as jealous for the Honor
of the Church as any of you are for your owne, or for his whome she hath most
worthely throwne out. I wish with all my hart that the speeches had bene spared, as
they which will minister matter of triumph unto him over me, who since his departure, hath by his accoustemed way, sought my defacement. For I am certified by a
faithfull brother of our companie that he hath reported (for the upholding of his
credite and the trampling upon myne, according unto his threat, that yf I taried in
Barfold, I should live in as much disgrace as ever I had credite) that Mr Doctor
Chapman and I are fallen out about his cause. Nay let him triumph over me and
spare not, but he hath matter of crowing over the Church geven unto him by this
meanes, for if, that he might might [sic] maintaine his owne against my credite he
durst saye that of us, whoe have beene coupled in so strong a bond of amitie, as that
I trust tenn such swordes as he shall never hewe in sunder: will he not be bould to
saye that such a one, a principall man also of my peace, is at flatt defiance with the
whole Church for his sake to uphold his owne with the overthrow of her honor? If it
should come to the knowledg of the Church, I see well enough what would followe
upon it. They which were the principall in his casting out, would be at the same
poynt, as that standing in need of counsell they would professe themselves willing
to fetch it from as far beyond London as London is hence; rather then from you,
though you would begg to be of Counsel with them. For they are men, subject unto
infirmities as well as we, and they persuade themselves that their cause is able to
abyde the heate of the greatest fier, and the stroke of the heaviest hammer. wherin
they are of the same judgment with meselfe, who request all of you, who have
conceyved so hard an opinion of her for proceeding against him, without conferring
together to wryte downe the faults wherwith she is to be charged in the graund
action, which if I wash not out with such water, as that ther wilbe left scarce the
steppe of any letter after it, I will first of all publickly crave pardon of the whole
people, whome verie many tymes before we saw his eyes, and not once or twise
since his coming among us, when all thinges were yet intier and safe, I taught to
have libertie to do so much as they have done generally in the cause of his
removing: and then upon my knee will I both submitt meselfe unto him, as a great
trespasser, for suffring him to be unjustly throwne out, and become a most humble
suter for his restoring unto his former place, or if he will not that, for making him a
sufficient recompence for the injurie done. The other that were at the first somewhat
earnest for him, and in a litle tyme grewe so cold as that they would not have layd so
strong an hand upon him for his staying, as would have rent a paper cote: might be
occasioned to make a new broyle. which yet I feare not, because so far as I can
perceyve they lyke better of his departure, then ever they did of his being with them:

or if they do not, one woorde of my mouth would make them to do it quickly, as having favor with them all (some one perhaps excepted) and being able to lay open his nakednes in such sort, as they, which beare him any good will, would turne their faces backward that they might not behold it, which as hether towardes I have refrayned meselfe from; so I wish by his evill dealing I might not be forced to do, neither heere nor where he is. But this shall never come either to his or their eares. Amen. but I knowe as great cause to doubt it, as you do to be out of doubt. Howsoever it is, I wish for my part that I had beene deafe when they were uttred. for then I should have beene freed from my present feare, which maketh me, though with greefe, willingly to absent my selfe at this tyme from your meeting, whose faces I have seene as if I had seene the face of God, whose backes I have beholden with far greater joye, then ever I have done almost the eyes of any other companie. Thus most humbly praying my good God to guide you in your holie consultations, with his blessed spirite of Counsel and wisdome, to discerne those thinges which differ; and to see the right way which you are to walk in; and in lyke manner commending me selfe unto you all and everie one of you, looking for a kinde answer unto my request, to my comfort; I take my leave. from Bergholt the 30th daye
your loving brother to command
R. C.

[fo. 55v]
blank

[fo. 56r]
blank

[fo. 56v]

To my most Reverend brethren Mr Doctor Chapman, Mr Farrour, Mr Newman and the rest at Mr Teyes geeve these.[445]

---

445 The rest of fo. 56v is blank. On fo. 57r there follows *Propositiones ministrorum Scotiae Serenissimo Regi oblatae*, and on fo. 57v a document headed *Scriptum Archiepiscopi Sanctae Andrae in Scotis responsorum quorundam pastorum ad scriptum in Ecclesia Scotiae*, which continues to the top of fo. 58v, where the manuscript ends with the epigraph *Propositiones ministrorum Scotiae*. For reasons of space and complexity, and because a study of the East Anglian clergy during the 1580s is hardly the place to enter into a discussion of the history of the Church of Scotland, the editors have decided to omit these final items in Richard Parker's file of papers. Another copy of these documents survives as BL Additional MS 32092, fos. 73–5, to which the interested reader is referred, but it is obviously instructive that Parker, living in obscurity in Norfolk, should have had access to such material, indicative of close relations between Scottish and English presbyterians.

For an authoritative overview of Anglo-Scots relations during this period (which includes references to the Dedham material), see Gordon Donaldson, 'The attitude of Whitgift and Bancroft to the Scottish church', *Transactions of the Royal Historical Society*, 4th series, XXIV (1942), 95–115; reprinted in Donaldson, *Scottish Church History* (Edinburgh, 1985), pp. 164–77. See also Collinson, *EPM*, pp. 234–5, 275–7.

The Combination Lecture at Bury St Edmunds
(Chicago University Library Codex MS 109)

Editorial conventions

1. This transcript retains the original spelling, punctuation and capitalization, although all standard abbreviations have been silently extended and modern usage – j for i, u for v, v for u and th for the thorn – has been used. Other abbreviations have been expanded between square brackets.

2. Where parts of the text are missing, the same has been indicated through the use of < >.

3. Where the meaning of damaged or missing text can reasonably be inferred from the context the same has been supplied *in italics* and in < >.

4. Emendations made by Rogers which are still legible have been placed in < > and with a line through the text.

5. Marginal notes have been enclosed within curly brackets thus { }.

6. Numbers within square brackets [1] indicate footnote references inserted by Thomas Rogers within the text of the letter to the Bishop of Norwich and the points to which he responds.

[fo. 1r]

Th'information[1]

We have <*had by your*> L[ord's]. direction an exercise continued upon the <*Mon*>daie at Burie ever since your L[ord's]. comming to the diocesse,[2] whereunto <*at*> the beginning [1] we receaved all the Preachers about us that would <*wil*>lingly yeeld theire labors thereunto. But in continuance, time finding some disconvenience therein partly [2] because the giftes of some were too weake for the place and partly because some were too farre-of, we made separation of them as we might.

Th'answere

Beginninges commonlie are ominous. Such as theie be, such are these <*con*>clusions, good or bad. Theie which sit doune to theire meate with-ou<*t*> grace do seldome rise-againe with giving of thankes. The Grecians had theire χαίρειν or Εὐκρατζειν; the Latins theire *Salutem*, and sometyme from

---

[1] By the information, Thomas Rogers means the letter written and signed by ten ministers of the combination lecture, dated 1 April 1590, to Edmund Scambler, bishop of Norwich explaining why they have excluded Rogers from their membership. Rogers thus provides not only the text of the letter against him, but his detailed response to this letter.

[2] Scambler, bishop of Norwich, was translated to Norwich from Peterborough in 1585.

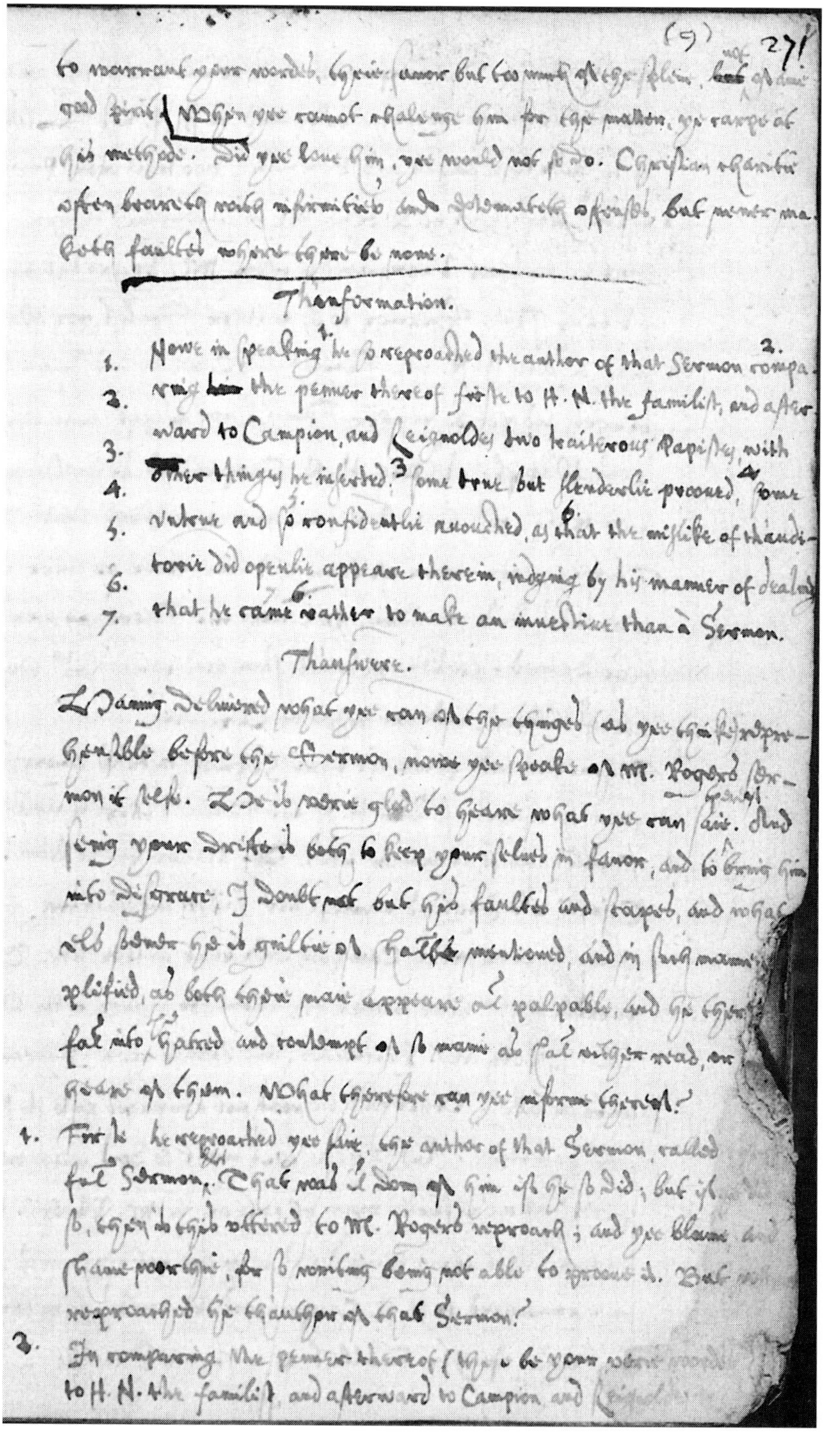

Plate 5 Folio 9 *recto* from Chicago Codex 109 (see pp. 163–4). *Photograph by kind permission of the Special Collections Research Center, University of Chicago.*

th'abundance of theire good wil *Saluterrimam*; Greate persons use theire Greetinges and comon < > Commendacions; S. Pauls manner was to write when he did χάρις ὑμιν και ειρήνὴ Grace be with you and peace etc.[3] There < *is* > grace aswell to be set afore wrightinge as to be said afore < >. I cannot thinke your proceeding and conclusion will be good <*when I* > see your exordium[4] so abrupt.

1. The Mondaie exercise at Burie[5] (if yee meane the < > of the same) was begunne I grante, by the direction of < > Norwich at his first comming unto the Bishoprick: yet not <*re*>caved as yee write, by all the Preachers about you, that would <*willing*> ly yeeld theire labors thereunto. Yee knowe their be moe < > about you and those (for anie deniall by them unto < > unto them < > made) willing to yeeld theier lab<*or*> < > propagation of the Gospel which never < >. [fo. 1v] into the nomber of the ministers of the worde upon the Mondaie at Burie, neither shal theie, if some of you maie let. Yee fancie not all your brethren, neither do all like you. This division I lament, and as we all maie, so theie on daie will rue which are the breeders and nourishers of the same.

2. Time that trieth all thinges hath showen howe for your partes the Burie exercise was not so deliberatelie begunne as it ought. For disconveniences, as yee write, did in deed arise: and therefore not a separation (as yee write) was made, but a set and certaine number of Preachers with free voices, and choise were appointed, successivelie, and in theire knowen courses to preach. Which was donn not < > for those causes by you alleaged < >, but for other purposes and respectes, hetherto unrevealed till this verie hower. Th'ende was neither on th'one side to disgrace, or debase, or discourage some that had bestowed paines and donn theire best endevours to benefit the Church; nor on th'other to puff-up < > others with a vaine persuasion of better giftes, but partlie to remove certaine disorders crept in among you (for till a choise companie was appointed, some preached often, yee knowe, some sildome, some not at all; beside, as the principall Senior praesent at the boorde[6] was affected either to himselfe ward, or to anie man els, even so he preached often or rarelie; moreover who so with moste voices was appointed, he might not refuse, unlesse his reasons were allowed by the major parte: lastly, no man ever knewe his turne, nor anie (whatsoever his businesse were, and the matter he had to handle never so waightie) had more than 7 daies at the moste, and some-time not 4 to provide for the place) partlie [fo. 2r] againe for th'enlarging of your freedome, who began to be enthralled by the former course. For spake anie man to your mindes, he was liked much, and his mouth used often: but did he once, or were he but suspected to crosse you in your fancies, he might not speake at all. For who might preach till he was nominated, and approved too by your table of consultacion? And when should he be nominated who varied, or were surmised in judgment to dissent from you in anie thing? That was fore-seene which is nowe come to passe. Yee might afore suspend, and put of a man at your plesure, and he might well be grieved, but had no remedie: but nowe when a certaine nomber out of

---

3   For example: Romans i. 7; 1 Corinthians i. 3; Galatians i. 3; Colossians i. 2.
4   The introductory part of a discourse or treatise.
5   See 'Lectures by combination' in Collinson, *Godly People,* pp. 476–80.
6   A reference to John Knewstub, rector of the neighbouring parish of Cockfield. See *BR*, pp. 220–3.

manie were appointed, and everie man knewe his daie, he would keep it and speak his conscience too, and though yee were offended thereat yet could none of you, nor all of you put him from his course. This some of yoe knewe full well; and therefore were driven unto dishonest shiftes, when yee could not orderlie proceed against that brother of whome yoe complaine, who was the onlie auctor that of manie, certaine should be chosen to preach, and that < > theis causes, and would not desiste till he had brought < > passe.

Th'information

For this yeare or two the exercise hath bine maintaine <*princi*>pallie [2] by those to whome your L[ord] hath nowe [1] subscribed <*M.* > Rogers [3] being also one of the companie.

Th'answere

1. This subscription was farre fetcht and about; and not < > for th'allowance of some nominated unto his Lordship, as, < > discountenancing of some unnamed. If yee see not your < > [fo. 2v] follie is the greater. Yoe have fine devises to get subscriptions.

2. But this is untrue that theie to whome his L[ord] hath nowe subscribed have bine the maintainers of th'exercise a yeere or two. It is well knowen some of them have not bine so long in the contrie; and some till nowe were never of th'exercise; and some never preached in theire oune course, but in the roome of other men.[7]

3. This is ambiguouslie set-donne, it carrieth two senses. If yoe meane that M. Rogers is one of the companie to whome his L[ord] hath nowe subscribed, it is untrue, and crosseth that which afterward in your complaint in theis wordes yee saie, Here-upon it was etc that your L[ord] was sued unto to ratifie a companie out of which M. Rogers was secluded. He is none of your companie. If yee meane that M. Rogers hath bine one of the companie for this yeare or two, though it be true, yet is it not the whole truth. For he hath taken great paines among you, not a yeare or two, but almost the tyme of a prenteship,[8] and is well rewarded in th'ende at your handes for all his labors.

Th'information

We have handled ordinarilie in our Mondaie exercise the epistle to the Romanes, and came in processe of time a little before the last feaste of the Nativitie unto the 12 chap.

Th'answere

It seemeth that both the writer hereof was some Novice of 2 <yeeres standing> or

---

7   Robert Lewis and John Warde had only arrived in 1589. See *BR*, pp. 224, 267.
8   The Statute of Artificers laid down a minimum term of seven years for apprenticeships. Although Rogers came to Horringer in the winter of 1581, this would place his participation in the combination lecture from about 1584, further evidence that participation in the exercise was not open to all ministers who simply wished to take part.

three yeeres standing at Burie,[9] and that your selves also have not all advisedlie pondred this <del>complaint</del> <Information>, who (except some fower or five of you) do knowe ful well that not a part of [fo. 3r] th'epistle unto the Romanes, but the two epistles of S. Paull unto the Thessalonians also have fully and wholie bine expounded since th'erecting of the exercise by the Bishop.

Th'information

Nowe in this 12 chap. there is a scripture a vers. 3 *ad* 9[10] upon which all those that write of discipline do confirme certaine particularities of Church officers.

Th'answere

Your wordes be verie peremptorie. Take heed yee saie not more in a line, than yee are able to approve in your life time. Yee have not all writers of discipline on your side. All antiquitie is against you in your positions. <del>And</del> Theie of the newe writers which favor you moste averre not that of Church-officers which of our Eng. faction from hence is delivered: and your selves also be distracted in th'interpretation of the place.

Theis wordes be too weake to sustaine so magneficall a building. If theie faile, yee fall. Theie do faile you, nowe yee storme.

Th'information

When this place came in order to be handled there [1] <*was a* > generall care had of all the companie that the truth should be delivered from that Scripture, but yet [2] so as <*no con*>tention should be raised concerning discipline among us.

Th'answere

1. Here is care upon care, generall and speciall, generall < > the companie, speciall that the truth of God should be delivered < > that Scripture, and that no contention should be raised concer<*ning*> discipline among you. [fo. 3v] I blame you neither for your care that the truth of God should be delivered from that Scripture, nor for your care that no contention be raised concerning discipline. God continue and encrease that care in all our mindes. But I like not that yee tearme your speculations about discipline, the truth: I like not againe that yee are so carefull as truth, yea as the truth of God to deliver them unto the people, which are not grounded upon those verses, nor yet in verie deed upon anie other places of holie Scripture.

---

9   Miles Mosse is clearly implied at this point. He moved from Norwich to Bury St Edmunds in late summer or autumn 1586.
10 The passage reads: 'For I say through the grace that is given unto me, to everie one that is among you, that no man presume to understand above that which is mete to understand, but that he understand according to sobrietie, as God hathe dealt to everie man the measure of faith. For as we have many members in one bodie, and all members have not one office, So we being many are one bodie in Christ, and everie one, one anothers members. Seing then that we have giftes that are divers, according to the grace that is given unto us, whether we have prophecie, let us prophecie according to the proportion of faith: Or an office, let us waite on the office: or he that teacheth, on teaching: Or he that exhorteth, on exhortation: he that distributeth, let him do it with simplicitie: he that ruleth, with diligence: he that sheweth mercie, with cherefulnes. Let love be without dissimulation. Abhorre that which is evil, and cleave unto that which is good.'

2. I like not lastlie that your care of avoidinge contention stretcheth no farder than your selves. Yee foresawe belike that yee should have adversaries. Your care was therefore that no contention should be raised concerning discipline among your selves. For a kingdome divided yee knowe cannot \<stande\> continue long. I would yee were as carefull for the generall peace and quietnes of the whole Church as yee are studious to continue a faction \<among\> by your selves.

The information

And therefore whereas there were some of our yonger men [1] to whom it fell by course to handle that Scripture (men of good giftes but not the fittest, as we thought, to handle that matter) we[2] by our common consent did take this order, that theie [3] should for this time omit theire course, and the handling of those verses should be [4] committed to the auncientest and discreetest of our companie.

Th'answere

In these fewe lines are manie untruthes.

1. Yee saie firste howe that Scripture above mentioned, fell by course to be handled by some of your younger men (so do yee tearme them). Which yee knowe is untrue. It fell ordelie unto them which did handle that Scripture. [fo. 4r]
2. Yee write next how those younger men were t'omit theire course for that time and that by a common consent of you all. That is againe untrue. There was no such order taken by anie common consent.

3. Thirdlie, yee signifie howe those yonger men should for this time omit theire course: which was not so, neither could be. The yonger men whome yee meane (for other yee could not meane) were M. Ward of Livermare,[11] Birde[12] and Greaves;[13] theie could omit no course of theire oune, because theie had no place among th'ordinarie preachers at Burie, till the laste \<sinisterlie extorted\> subscription from the Bishop of Norwich.[14] Els what needed his L[ord's] subscription, if theie were allowed before and that by them who were betrusted with the managing of that exercise?

4. Finalie, yee deliver howe the handling of those verses should be committed to the ancientest and discreetest of your companie, which is another untruth. There were no Committies chosen. For everie man spake in course and in his oune course too as

---

[11] See *BR*, pp. 266–7.
[12] It is not clear who this Birde was. Described as a young man and one who had no place among 'th'ordinarie preachers at Burie, till the last subscription from the Bishop of Norwich', would appear to rule out Samuel Bird of Cambridge and Ipswich as well as one Roger Bird who held the living of Wenhaston from 1565. Perhaps he is to be identified with one John Byrde who in 1603 was described as a 'bachelor of arte, preacher, heretofore scismatically affected', who held the rectory of Irsteade in Norfolk. See NRO VIS 3/3, fo. 100v.
[13] See *BR*, p. 215.
[14] This is interesting evidence of the control by the older members of the combination lecture over the participation of the younger ministers.

if fell unto him. Your care was not so greate as yee would beare the Bishop in hande.

Th'information

Theie were handled therefore [1] by M. Allen,[15] M. Knewstub,[16] <M.> Holt[17] and M. Whitfeild[18] and so [2] handled, as that no question <arose> among the people concerninge discipline: a speciall part o <f their> speech tending to this issue, viz to beate doune those which <   > wante of the discipline that theie desired, did condemne <the> Church of England, and would separate themselves from <us>.[19]

Th'answere

1. The ancientest therefore, by these wordes annexed to the premise <were> not onlie the ancientest, but the discreetest also of your companie <as> M. Allen, M. Knewstub, M. Holt and M. Whitfield.
The truth <where> of (as of other thinges in this letre) we whose names are <subscribed> are readie to justifie (John Knewstub, Reginald Whitfield, G <ualter Alen> [fo. 4v] (as for M. Holt he will rub his lip[20] when he heareth this, he would much more were his hande here unto)
But wil theie who are so readie to justifie themselves, of all in your companie, to be the discreetest, justifie also that this texte was committed unto them of truste to be handled, as men, of all other in the companie, moste willing, best able and everie waie fittest to handle the same according to your mindes? I knowe the men so well that theie wil not. And though theie were not so discreete (though of your companie perhaps the discreetest) in subscribing unto this both godlesse and witlesse information, theie will be better advised before theie affirme all herein to be true.

2. Theie handled theis verses, I grante: but that theie so handled them as that no question arose among the people concerning discipline, howe can yee saie? Are all the people of one minde? And are the people, thinke yee, so ignorant that theie perceave not unto what side the discreetest among you do incline? do all the people favor that part?
Assure your selves so manie of theire auditors, as in the matter of discipline

15 See *BR*, p. 184.
16 See *BR*, pp. 220–3.
17 See *BR*, p. 217.
18 See *BR*, pp. 267–8.
19 Clearly these were anti-separatist sermons in the vein of George Gifford's *A plaine declaration that our Brownists be full Donatists. Also a replie to master Greenwood, touching read prayer* (London, 1590). For an account of the Brownist movement in the vicinity of Bury St Edmunds, see Craig, *Reformation, politics and polemics*, pp. 103–9.
20 Akin to biting one's lip, indicating feelings of shame or embarrassment. Cf. M. P. Tilley, *A dictionary of proverbs in England in the sixteenth and seventeenth centuries* (Ann Arbor, 1950), p. 385: 'You licked not your lips since you lied last' or the line from *The Taming of the Shrew*, ii, 1, 250: 'Thou canst not frown, thou canst not look askance, nor bite the lip.' It is noticeable that Holt's signature was not on this letter to Edmund Scambler.

dissented from them, were theire adversaries, and moved questions enough about discipline, and those verses too, as yee thinke, the grounde of your devises.[21]

3. And though the wisest of your companie be no Brownistes, whome in theire Sermons theie labored to beate doune, yet I would theie were aswell affected to the praesent government of our Church as theie should be.
It is to be feared, albeit theie approve our Church, which the Brownistes do condemne; there is but too much affinitie other wise in divers pointes between them and the Brownistes.

[fo. 5r]

Th'information

At the [1] handling of the moste especiall matters M. Rogers himselfe was present, [2] and gave his consent and approbation to that which had bine spoken, [3] publiquelie in the hearing of us all, [4] and afterward privatelie to some of the ministers, as [5] also when he came to the place he professed that that which had bine spoken was delivered discreetly and to good purpose; withall [6] signifieng in verie earnest manner that he would not deale to the contrarie.

Th'answere

Hetherto your exordium for the more easie insinuating your selves into his L[ord's] bosome: Nowe followeth your narration, indeed your privie accusation, and that you are t'object against M. Rogers and his Sermon.

1. Yee saie therefore howe At the handling of the moste especiall matters M. Rogers himselfe was present. I answere, were the moste especiall matters handled by M. Holt and Whitfield, then surelie M. Rogers heard them. For he was at theire Sermons. But were theie handled by M. Alen and Knewstubs then againe he heard <them> not the moste especiall matters. For when theie preached he was not in the contrie.

2. Yee saie againe, M. Rogers gave his consent and approbation to that <which> had bine spoken. I answere, he gave no consent and approb <ation at> all to Mr. Alens and Knewstubs sermons. For he heard th <em not.> He useth not to justifie the thinges which he never heard nor < > he leaveth that to your selves.

3. Yee saie thirdlie, Publiquelie in the hearing of us all, he gave consent and appro-bation to that which had bine spoken. I answere firste <as a> fore it is untrue. He approved not the thinges he heard not < > he gave no consent, nor approbation to all which he heard. < > keth no other men to witnesse of his disliking some thinges < > [5v] selves, the moste I meane and beste of you whose handes are to this complaint against him. He well remembreth that in your hearing he publiquelie before you all testified his dislike of that interpretation, which M. Holt <following therein I knowe

---

[21] This is crucial evidence of the different views of the auditory in Bury on the matter of ecclesiastical governance, a point to which Rogers will return. See below, pp. 166–7, 169–70, 172–3.

whom> gave concerning prophecieng mentioned in the 6 verse.[22] And I am sure M. Knewstubs <even> at that verie instant, misliked that interpretation also aswel as he. He disliked also divers thinges tuching the doctor and his office <as namelie that he was onlie to teach, and neither to entreat, nor to applie his doctrine, nor to administer the sacrament.> which M. Whitfield delivered. And this not secretlie but openlie, nor faintlie, but so confidentlie did he finde fault withall, that M. Knewstubs saide in plaine wordes (though I muste saie smilinglie)[23] that he was in an error for so saing.

Mo thinges also he would have mentioned that liked him not, had the time served, which yee knowe is but verie short,[24] betweene the Sermon and the dinner at Michels.

He marveleth yee dare saie he publiquelie in all your hearinges gave his consent and approved all that was by them delivered, when contrariwise he publiquelie, and in your hearing founde fault with these thinges delivered by them.

4. Fourthlie yee saie, Privatelie also to some of the ministers he gave his consent, etc. I answere as afore, it is untrue. Had he not talked with one minister, he had not spoken privatelie with anie minister at all about the former Sermons; and that one minister was M. Lewes,[25] before whome he so approved that which had bine uttered, as M. Lewes saide expreslie howe M. Rogers the next Mondaie would marre all: and therefore surmised that he misliked somewhat.
Indeed he told M. Lewes that he would not deale against M. Whitfield, neither did he. For had M. Whitfields discourse of discipline never bine uttered M. [6r] Rogers had in purpose to saie that he did, and that against him, whose steps M. Whitfield in some thinges did moste praeciselie folowe.

5. Fiftlie also, when he came to the place he professed that that which had bine spoken was delivered discreetly and to good purpose, saie yee. I answere, he judged manie thinges to be discreetelie spoken, and to good purpose, not all. For both M. Holt uttered manie thinges for the better provision and ordering of the poore; and M. Whitfield much against the Brownistes for the credite of our Church, which were to verie good purpose and he approved them from his hart.

6. He signified sixtlie, yee saie, in verie earnest manner that he would not deale to the contrarie. I answere, The truth is he came not to controll them which before him had spoken, but to confute another whose Sermon was long afore in printe. His eie

---

22 Verse 6 reads, 'Seing then that we have giftes that are divers, according to the grace that is given unto us, whether we have prophecie, let us prophecie according to the proportion of faith.' The interpretation given in [Laurence Chaderton], *A fruitful sermon, upon the 3. 4. 5. 6. 7. and 8. verses of the 12 Chapter of the Epistle of S. Paule to the Romaines* (London, 1584), was that 'this speciall lawe concerneth onely such as be publique personnes in the Church', p. 57.

23 The difference between Knewstub's smile and Mosse's grin is noticeable. See below, p. 169. Part of this difference was perhaps generational. Rogers appears prepared to accept the criticism of the older Knewstub but not of the younger Mosse. This is also further evidence of the type of discussion that might take place after the sermon was delivered.

24 Evidence that the formal opportunity for any discussion following the sermon was not long, though presumably informal discussion might take place over dinner at 'Michels'.

25 See *BR*, pp. 223–5.

was neither upon them, nor theire doctrine. Before theie did preach, the substance of
M. Rogers sermon was collected; and had theie not preached, or had theie preached
otherwise than theie did (if the text had not bine too farre over past) yet was <M.
Rogers> he purposed to have uttered that which he did.[26]

Th'information

The next Mondaie came M. Rogers tooke [1] the place of ex <ercise and> we
expected that according to [2] our continual custome he sh<ould have> gon on with
the 9 verse, Let love be with-out di<ssimula>tion etc.[27] But he (as one that [4] had
quite forgotten the <state of the> the contrie, the [5] dangers of these times, [6] and
his speech used < > before) beginneth back-againe [3] at the 3. verse of the
ch<apter> and readeth them on unto the 9 verse.

Th'answere

1. What meane yee by M. Rogers taking the place of exercise the <next> Mondaie?
That he intruded himselfe into another mans roome? That <he> spake afore his time?
If that be the sense of your words, the < > [6v] greate which herebie yee offer him.
Yee knowe, he came not thereunto but orderlie and so lawfullie, as had he not then
preached, he had bine justly to be censured for his negligence. And his observing his
oune course, as none of you more carefulie ever did (for alwaies it was a religion to
him so to do) and immediatlie by order, as the next in his knowen place succeeding
those discreete, even the discreetest of your companie, doth speake plainlie, howe
that information is false, that those discreetest men were the Committees to entreate
of those verses. For theie were no more committed unto them than unto him, but that
theie fell into theire handes to be handled, before theie did into his.

2. But a fault was in him, as yee thinke, that he did not, as yee expected, and
according to your continuall custome, go on with the 9 verse, Let love be without
dissimulation etc. He did not indeed go on with the 9 verse, because he might not;
he might not, for then had he not discharged his dutie to God ward and his Church.
For manie thinges, upon the 6. 7. and 8 verses were necessarilie to be delivered,
before not uttered, which had he concealed, he might have pleased you right well,
but should have displeased God; to whome we are to give a rekoning aswel for
concealing that which he enjoineth us to speake, as for uttering that which ought not
to be spoken.
Neither did he abide upon those verses with-out good example. For neither was he
the firste that after others hath spoken of on and the same place of Scripture; neither
is it your continuall custome that everie daie a newe texte should be taken.

3. It is an untruth that he began back-againe (so yee write) at the 3. verse of the chap
and read them on unto the 9. verse. For, as it is notoriouslie knowen, he began at the
6. verse, and read unto the 9. which were the verie wordes that M. Holt, and

---

[26] Evidence that Rogers had planned his attack on Chaderton's sermon for some time and which helps
to explain how he was able to get his sermon published so quickly. The epistle dedicatory of *A
sermon upon the 6. 7. and 8 verses of the 12 chapter of S. Paul's Epistle unto the Romanes made to
the confutation of another sermon* was dated 13 April 1590.

[27] See above n. 10.

Whitfield had entreated of, and not those also whereof M. Alen and Knewstubs did speake [7r]

4. But he (as one that had quite forgotten the state of the contrie) beginneth (yee saie) back-againe at the thirde verse of the chap etc. Knowe yee what yee write? Doth his beginning back-againe (as yee phrase it) at the 3 verse, argue that he had quite forgotten the state of the contrie? Not his beginning back againe (me thinkes yee saie) but his uttering the thinges he did upon those verses doth plainlie showe howe he had quite forgotten the state of the contrie.

I would yee had no more forgot, and over-shot also yourselves in writing thus much, than he did forget himselfe, and the state of the contrie in uttering that which he did by occasion of those verses. He knewe ful wel what he saide, and the state of the contrie (which yee saie he had quite forgotten) was so fresh in his memorie, as he could not for his contries good but speake that which he did. Were yee such subjectes as yee should be, and loved the state of the contrie (as yee praetend) his wordes had never bine so ill taken of you, nor himselfe by you and your meanes, brought into obloquie for speaking and onlie for speaking his conscience freelie against the perturbers of the whole State, and so of the quiet state of the contrie wher<in> we live.

He spake nothing which is not allowed by the State, if that w<hich is> approved by the laufull auctoretie of the land, is allowed by <the> state. Wretched is the state of that contrie which cannot b<rooke> the same. Suffolk can brooke it wel enough. Yee offer wrong unto the contrie in insinuating the contrarie with your oune handes, and that unto his Lordship: and much unthankfull y< > unto that contrie wherein, and wherebie yee live. The magistrate here be right godlie; the ministers, dutifull; the people loiall, the < >tils, conformable; the yeomen, tractable unto all good causes < > [7v] of the major parte) theie love the Gospell, honor theire Prince, obeie her lawes, <like> approve her proceedings, He doth not forget <himself> the state of the contrie that unto and before such a people speaketh for the State against th'enimies thereof.

5. Neither was he forgetfull of theis dangerous times.[28] That which yee thinke should have made him silent, even the dangers of these times, moved him to speake. He told you so much immediatlie after his Sermon but it woulde not enter into you. When the ship is in danger the Mariners, if ever, are to looke unto theire tacling, and bestirre them; when th'enimies are at hande it is time to set beacons on fire and to crie Alarme. The ship of our welfare, even our Church and contrie, was, howesoever it nowe is through God his goodnes, in danger of wreck and submersion < > and should we sit still and suffer them to perish? Th'athenian oath was *Pugnabo pro patria et solus et cum aliis*, I will fight to deliver my contrie from danger both alone and with others.[29] M. Rogers hath taken th'athenian oathe, He will fight for his

---

[28] Most immediately a reference to the open war with Spain but also a reference to the furore caused by the publication of the Marprelate tracts and the hunt for its press. See W. Pierce, *An historical introduction to the Marprelate Tracts* (London, 1908).

[29] A reference to the oath of the Athenian ephebes. See *A selection of Greek historical inscriptions, vol. II from 403 to 323 BC*, ed. M. N. Tod (Oxford, reprint, 1950), pp. 303–7 and *From the end of the*

contrie (whereof he is a cittizen) and for the Church too both alone and with others, theie shall not miscarie if he maie helpe.

As Hilarie saide unto Constantius th'emperor, so do I unto you, It is no lesse dangerous to be still silent, than alwais speaking.[30] The daies are dangerous, it is no reason of modestie, but a signe of diffidence hence-forward to be silent.
The times are dangerous. It is true. But who the creators of those dangers? I knowe no danger <to be feared> in this land to be feared, but from disloiall subjectes, who are not to be feared of anie, but to be resisted by all. <Theie which are not to feare even princes tyrannizing, shall theie dread inferiors opposing themselves against a godlie prince?> [8r] <To ende therefore> In mine opinion therefore yee are faultie two manner of waies, firste in finding fault with M. Rogers for speaking, and for speaking too that which he did; Next in that yee are silent in theis dangerous times, when everie one that hath a tongue should speake, and everie one that hath an eare should heare wh<*at*> the Spirit saith against <our common divines> factious <heds> spirits.

6. Lastlie, it is untrue that he <*varied*> either forgot or varied from his former speech, whether yee meane his publique before you all, or his private <speech> unto M. Lewes.

Th'information

So [1] soone as he had red them, he leaveth [2] the texte and after [3] good approbation given to <them> that which had bine delivered, pulleth out of his bosome a Sermon, written long ago upon that place of the Romanes entituled [4] a frutefull Sermon upon the 12 of the Romanes[31] the author [5] whereof (not to speake of the Sermon) it [sic] thought to be a godlie and learned man. This Sermon M. Rogers tooke upon him [6] to confute, cleane [7] leaving his texte, and so spending his time contrarie [8] to all good order.

Th'answere

Unto sleight objections short answeres; and unto false assertions with-out proofe, bare denials maie suffice.

1. Untrue. He red not so manie by three verses, as yee have set doune.

2. This together with that afterward in this section, He cleane left < > besides that it is a false information, it is an idle repetition.

3. He approved theire wordes as afore is set doune. If he sp<*oke* > ter of them than

---

Peloponnesian War to the battle of Ipsus, ed. and translated by Phillip Harding (Cambridge, 1985), pp. 133–5. I owe these references to the kindness of Dr David Mirhady. It is notable that Rogers comes out as an affirmer of citizenship (rather than subjection) as the status of any loyal Englishman. See Patrick Collinson, 'The Monarchical Republic of Queen Elizabeth', in *The Tudor monarchy*, ed. John Guy (London, 1997), pp. 110–34; and 'The Elizabethan exclusion crisis and the Elizabethan polity', *Proceedings of the British Academy*, LXXXIV (1994).

[30] See Lionel Wickham, *Hilary of Poitiers, conflicts of conscience and law in the fourth-century church* (Liverpool, 1997), pp. 104–7.

[31] A reference to [Laurence Chaderton], *A fruitful sermon* (London, 1584).

theie deserved, theie have no cause to comp<*lain*> but he just cause to aske God forgivenes and so doth, I doubt <*not*> from the bottom of his harte.

4. Untrue. There is no Sermon so entituled.[32]

5. Who the author of that Fr. Sermon was he knoweth not therefore th'auctor of the same maie be a godlie and learned man. But this M. Rogers well knoweth that <~~both~~> manie both godlie <*and*> [fo. 8v] learned men, in doctrine and manners have erred; and all godlie and learned men, without Gods speciall grace and mercie, maie fall; and this man by manie thinges in his Sermon, which he tearmed both godlie and frutefull, hath showen himselfe neither learned nor godlie.

6. <~~That~~> A Sermon indeed M. Rogers tooke upon him to confute. Yet in so doing he neither left his texte, nor declined from good order. From on and the same herbe both the Bee sucketh-out honie for the comfort and the Spider poison for the destruction of man:[33] and from on and the same wordes of Scripture some gather truth for the benefit, others false-hood to the greate hurte of the Churche. Th'one sorte are to be strengthened, th'other to be beaten doune by the worde of God. And therefore by one place of Scripture, as occasion is offered, some aedifie th'ignorant, and some againe confute th'adversaries abusing the same unto the dishonor of God. (*Non solin vera docenda sed at falsa reprehendenda, ne errent simplices*) saith Luther wrighting upon the second chap[ter] of the Prophet Hosea,[34] Not onlie true thinges are to be taught, but false thinges also to be reproved, that the simple maie not be seduced.

8. Shall haeretikes, schismatikes, and other evill men abuse the Scriptures of God, and shall not Gods ministers discover unto them, and the Church theire follies, and make theire errors knowen, for the better warning unto <*the*> good meaning people? And doing so, do theie therebie leave, yea quite leave the texte, and that against all order, yea against all good order? Manie learned and worthie preachers have I heard over-throwing of that as erroneous, which adversaries have delevered as truth, from theire textes: yet never till nowe heard I of anie for so doing, charged to have quite left his texte contrarie to all good order. Yee have neither texte of Scripture, nor other good auctorities [fo. 9r] to warrant your wordes, theie savor but too much of the splene, not of anie good spirit.

When yee cannot chalenge him for the matter, ye carpe at his methode. Did yee love hime, yee would not so do. Christian charitie often beareth with infirmities and extermateth offenses but never maketh faultes where there be none.

Th'information

Nowe in speaking [1] he so reproached the author of that Sermon comparing [2] <*him*> the penner thereof firste to H.N. the familist,[35] and afterward to Campion,

---

[32] Rogers is being a pedant. For the full title, see above n. 22.

[33] 'Where the Bee sucks honey the spider sucks poison.' See Tilley, *A dictionary of proverbs in England in the sixteenth and seventeenth centuries*, p. 38.

[34] Martin Luther, *Praelectiones in prophetas minores* (1524) in *D. Martin Luthers Werke* (Weimar, 1895, reprint 1966), XIII, 6–13. This passage quoted by Rogers does not appear in this edition.

[35] A reference to Hendrik Niclaes, the Dutch mystical writer. See Christopher Marsh, *The Family of Love in English society, 1550–1630* (Cambridge, 1994), pp. 1, 17–27.

and Reignoldes, two traiterous Papistes,[36] with other thinges he inserted, [3] some true but slenderlie prooved, [4] some untrue and so [5] confidentlie avouched as that [6] the mislike of th'auditorie did openlie appeare therein, judging by his manner of dealing that he came [7] rather to make an invective than a Sermon.

Th'answere

Having delivered what yee can of the thinges (as yee thinke) reprehensible before the Sermon, nowe yee speake of M. Rogers sermon it selfe. He is verie glad to heare what yee can saie thereof. And seing your drifte is both to keep your selves in favor, and to bring him into disgrace, I doubt not but his faultes and scapes, and what els soever he is guiltie of shall be mentioned, and in such manner <exem>plified, as both theie maie appeare all palpable, and he ther <   > fall into the hatred and contempt of so manie as shall either read or <   > heare of them. What therefore can yee informe thereof?

1. Firste he reproached yee saie, the author of that Sermon called the <fruit> full Sermon etc. That was ill donn of him if he so did; but if he did <not> so, then is this uttered to M. Rogers reproach; and yee blame and shame worthie, for so writing being not able to proove it. But wh<erefore> reproached he th'author of that Sermon?
2. In comparing the penner thereof (these be your verie wordes to H.N. the familist, and afterward to Campion, and Reignoldes, two <traite> [fo. 9v] rous Papistes. The comparison was odious indeed, and to the penners greate reproach, were he compared to H.N. the Familist, as a Familiste, and to Campion and Reignoldes, two traiterous Papistes, as a traiterous Papist, if he deserved not to be so compared to them.

But he was not so compared to them. M. Rogers taketh the penner of that Frut Sermon to be neither Familist nor Papist; and yet maie be like both H.N. the Familist, and Campion and Reignoldes in some thinges, and yet be neither Familist, nor Papist, much lesse a traiterous Papist. As both H.N. Campion and Reignoldes might holde some truth, which he holdeth, and yet be no Protestants. The ancient Fathers, even everie of them, had some errror or other which the grosse haeretikes did maintaine, yet were the Fathers no haeretikes: and the damned haeretikes reteined some good thinges which the godlie Christians beleeved, and yet were no Christians.

Th'author and penner of that Sermon inserted among some good, some ill thinges; so doth H.N. the Familist, therein were H.N. the Familist and that author like. The author againe delivereth howe the Church of England wanteth her Pastors and Teachers; so doth Campion;[37] herein were Campion and that author like. Th'author thirdlie saith howe women are allowed to baptize in the Church of England; so doth

---

36 For Edmund Campion and William Reynolds, see A. O. Meyer, *England and the catholic church under Queen Elizabeth I* (London, 1915); P. McGrath, *Papists and puritans under Elizabeth I* (London, 1967), chapter 8.
37 See Edmund Campion, *Rationes decem* (London, 1581). Cf. P. Milward, *Religious controversies of the Elizabethan age* (Lincoln and London, 1977), pp. 54–9.

W. Raignoldes;[38] and herein were Raignoldes and that author like. Otherwise he was not compared unto H.N. Campion, nor Raignoldes. And I hope this might be donn with-out anie reproach at all inflicted upon th'author by M. Rogers. He is justly charged with theis thinges, and therefore not reproached; nor otherwise compared to H.N. Campion, and Raignoldes than thus, and therefore made neither Familist, Papist, nor Traitor. [fo. 10r] But for his mingling some noysome wordes and saienges among good thinges, besides that he was compared to H.N. the Familist, he was likened to R.H.[39] Penrie,[40] and such like; and for saieng howe the Church of England at this praesent wanteth her Pastors and Teachers, besides that he was compared to Campion, he was likened both to R.H. againe, that contentious Schismatique, an<d> to Miles Monopodios[41] that quarreling Soldior. It is worthie th'observation that yee saie he was reproached in that he was compared to H.N. the Familist, and to Campion, the traiterous Papist, and yet saie not howe he was reproached in being likened for the same thinges both unto R.H. Penrie, and Miles Monopodios. Yee sawe belike he was justlie, without anie reproach at all, compared to R.H. Penrie, and Miles Monopodios: but the reproach belike was for that he was likened herein to H.N. and Campion. Wherebie it should seeme that let a man in some thinges, though never so justlie, be likened unto anie either of the Familie, or traiterous Papist, he is reproached forsooth: but be he likened for the same thinges unto others either good men, or not so bad as Familistes, and traiterous Papistes, and it is unto <them> him no reproach at all. But the truth is M. Rogers did not reproach him in <likening him unto R.H. P> comparing him with H.N. and Campion and Reignoldes, because he did reproach him in likening him unto R.H. Penrie and Monopodios.

3. The next thing and the last (which is all that yee can saie tuching <the Ser>mon of M. Rogers, and had yee not theis two thinges, yee had no < > against him to object) is, that he inserted other pointes, some true <but> slenderlie proved, and some untrue but confidentlie avouched. Nowe <if> this be true, then surelie was his either weakenes, or negligence < > in proving the thinges which were true so slenderlie, and his boldness as greate in avouching other thinges as true that were false, so confidentlie. I have taken you with a greate manie untruthes alreadie; and there < > I suspect that yee have written even in this more than yee <can >. [fo. 10v] justifie, and complained of him with-out just cause. Which suspicion is the more encreased because I see no instances alleaged either of the true so slenderlie proved, or of the untrue pointes so confidentlie avouched.

And tuching his slender proving of some true thinges, surelie he was in fault if more substantialie he could have proved them, and yet would not through wilfull negligence: but if he did his good wil to prove that truth which he <did> maintained, and

---

38 See William Rainolds, *A refutation of sundry reprehensions, cavils, and false sleightes by which M. Whitaker laboureth to deface the late English translation and catholike annotations of the new Testament* (Paris, 1583).
39 Robert Harrison, *The writings of Robert Harrison and Robert Browne*, ed. A. Peel and L. H. Carlson, Elizabethan Nonconformist Texts II (London, 1953).
40 John Penry. See *The notebook of John Penry 1593*, ed. A. Peel (Camden Society, 3rd series, LXVII, 1944). Collinson, *EPM*, pp. 391–5.
41 Anthony Gilby's *A pleasant dialogue, betweene a souldior of Barwicke, and an English chaplaine* (London, 1581).

did also prove it (even as yee also his verie adversaries do heere confesse) then was not he in fault for proving, though but slenderlie, yet proving the truth which he had in hande, but in much fault are yee in complaining of him as an offender even for doing his dutie according to his giftes at the praesent tyme. More substantiall proofes yee maie expect from other men more substantialie seene in theis controversies. It sufficeth him to have affirmed the truth, and proved it, though but slenderlie.

And yet maie it be, that were yee affected towardes him and his doinges as <sometyme> acarst yee have bine, yee would write otherwise, and thinke that well: which yee nowe saie was but slenderlie proved. I am affraide yee write thes more of envie, than of judgement.

4. A greater fault cannot be in a minister of the worde, than to be a publisher of untruth. Yee charge M. Rogers with this fault. If yee be men of truth, showe him those untruthes. He taketh heaven and earth to witnesse he spake his verie conscience, and knoweth no untruth that he delivered.

Yee tuch the credite of his ministerie and empeach his doctrine; either convince him of untruthes, or acknoledg yee have abused him and his doctrine by this calumnious information.

5. And theis faultes of his (which in deed are none at all) are not extermated in charitie, but enlarged by art, and bombasted to thuttermost [fo. 11r] So and So, greate stitches and large cuts to make them seeme greate. For in speaking He So reproached the author etc., saie yee with other pointes he inserted some true but slenderlie proved, some untrue and So confidentlie avouched, as that the mislike of the auditorie did openlie appeare.

The sorer th'accusation, the greater the shame is of thaccused, if it be true: but the greater the credite, if it be false. To make a sore accusation yee are come in with he So reproached the author etc. and So confidentlie avouched untruthes etc., and yet was it neither so nor so. For he was so far from So reproaching th'author, that he reproached him in no sorte, and from avouching untruthes So confidentlie, that yee cannot alleage and prove anie untruth that he confidentlie avouched, no that he did avouch. And therefore it cannot be true that the mislike of Th'auditorie did appeare and that Openlie.

6. Afore yee tainted the whole contrie as not affected to the doctrine delivered by M. Rogers. For he quite forgetting the state of the contrie uttered that which he did. Here yee saie Th'auditorie (consisting of right worshipfull persons of the contrie and other good Christians)[42] did testifie theire misliking and that Openlie. Afore yee saide howe the penner of the Fr. Sermon was reproached by M. Rogers: heere I am sure yee reproach not on me but manie of great worship and auctoritie in the contrie, besides a great companie of other religious Christians of sondrie callinges, whose wis<dom>, gravitie, and carriadg of them selves is such, as theie would not,

---

[42] Further important evidence concerning the nature of the audience in Bury St Edmunds, both lay and clerical, as well as the conventions that governed the behaviour of the congregation when listening to sermons. It is noticeable that Rogers does not actually deny that some of the audience may have voiced their disapproval when he preached.

aud*<ibly and>* openlie, to the viewe on of another; I am out of doubt manifest the*<ir mis>*liking of anie doctrine delivered out of the pulpit by anie publique and approved *<prea>*cher of the worde, and that in the verie time of his preaching.

Theie know *<there>* is no Preacher but if he abuse his place, and utter anie thing e*<rrone>*ous, or otherwise scandalous, he maie be called unto an accompt for *<the>* same, and be condignelie punished. Theie knowe againe that such persons as shall, as yee write, testifie theire mislike and that openlie to the *<dis>*gracing of the preacher, and contempt of his doctrine, maie be *<called>* unto an accompt and be openlie punished for theire Open contempt. *<I do>* [fo. 11v] a wonder howe yee dare suggest theis thinges unto his Lordship. Can yee not be content to disgrace the Preacher and his doctrine but yee muste also with slanders abuse the auditorie?

7. But it seemeth yee have some grownde of your wordes when yee write howe it was the judgment of the auditorie that he came rather to make an invective than a Sermon. It maie be the judgement of some of you; the judgment of the auditorie it was never. By your oune happelie yee judg other mens affections.

If yee judg of his Sermon, not as of a Sermon, but as of an Invective, he much lamenteth that so wise men, as yee would seeme to be, are of no better judgment.

Howesoever yee entitle the same an Invective not a Sermon, he hath by that Invective discharged a good part of his dutie to the Church of England and done more good, the times considered, than by manie Sermons. It hath taken better affect in the auditories minde it shoulde seeme than yee could wish, yee so enveigh against it.

Theie which by Invectives deprave a setled state, muste by Invectives be oppugned.

Th'information

Of this course [1] he was lovinglie and gentlie admonished by the ministers generalie for his strange and unusuall manner of dealing. Since [2] which time he hath wholie absented himselfe from our companie, as if we had donne him injurie. [3] And yet his default was such as that the people of all sortes did espie it and since that time have witnessed theire mislike in sondrie places. So that since that daie there is no commoner speech among the people than of M. Rogers his sermon.

Th'answere

Yee have enformed his Lordship what yee can to make him growe into a dislike of that Sermon and of M. Rogers for uttering thereof. Nowe *<follows>* are we to heare τὰ ἐπομηνα, or what thinges fell out after the same. [fo. 12r] And here yee tell three thinges, firste what was donn to him by the ministers; next howe hee tooke the same; thirdlie what the judgment, and speech of the people was tuching that Sermon.

1. Nowe the ministers (so yee write your selves) what do theie? Forsooth generalie theie admonish him. Where-of? Of this course, and for his strange and unusuall manner of dealing. In what sorte? Lovinglie and gentlie.

I perceave your purpose is to omit nothing which maie procure either favor to your-selves, or envie unto him against whome yee write. Yet seeing yee hunte so greedilie after th'applause, it had bine for you by laudable and direct meanes to have procured the same, not by leasinges as yee have donn. For yee knowe it is not true that of the ministers (as yee call yourselves) he was admonished either generalie; or of this course; or in such sorte as yee have set doune.

Generalie he was not. For albeit there was a consent of some ministers (as there is unto this your Information): yet was there not a generall consent. For some ministers, and theie of your companie too allowed his Sermon, and commended the same which others did mislike; as some do utterlie condemne this your privie wrighting against him which others be so readie to justifie. Never call that a generall admonition which is given by three or fower, or a fewe mo ministers in a cor<*ner*>. I have noted the like in some other thinges both in private and oth<*er*> wise. If a fewe of you agree upon a thing, it is by and by given <*out*> that such is the Judgment of the ministers or the ministers of Suff<*olk*> or those be the desires of all those faithfull ministers that desire reformation: When manie both in the contrie, and as faithfull everie w<*ay*> never gave consent unto these devises, yea never so much as heard of them.

Of this course he was not admonished. For he taketh even all yea everie of you (of the ancienter sorte) to witnesse, w<*hether*>. [fo. 12v] th'admonition (as yee call it) which yee gave him concerned either his reproaching of thauthor of that Fr. Sermon by comparing him with H.N. etc. or anie untruth by him so confidentlie avouched; or the testified misliking of thauditorie. He knoweth none of you wil saie it; and if anie should, his oune conscience, and the rest of the companie will accuse him of untruth. Howe can yee saie then he was admonished of this course?

Indeed yee spake of his resuming the same texte handled by M. Holt and Whitfield (which yee call here his strange and unusuall manner of dealing); and that he should firste have communecated his purpose with you before he had so uttered his minde; and of other such thinges of small regard: but of this course, nowe laste mentioned, not one worde. Yea so farre were yee from admonishing him of anie either reproachfull speeches, or assertions savoring of untruthes, that being urged by him twice, or thrice to deliver what yee had observed from his mouth swarving from the Canonicall Scripture, it was answered, that he could not be charged with anie such thing. And that answere M. Knestubs gave.

Nowe had yee admonished him of this course (as yee did not): yet ought yee not upon that one admonition, nor yet two of your oune (unlesse he remaned perverse in a cause manifestlie wiked and scandalous to the Church) to have proceeded so farre as yee did in complaining of him unto auctoritie; much lesse for a cause so honest of it selfe, so necessarie for the whole Church, against all order of discipline, and rules of godlines, to deale against him in this sorte, never heard, unattainted, but once, yea never in truth offending, and if he once did, wherein he did slide or slip anie manner of waie, readie to be reformed, and to renounce as openlie, as he did publiquelie deliver his minde, if by Gods worde yee can convince him.

He deserved no admonition at all; howe can yee [fo. 13r] justifie this your accusation? He never was admonished of anie reproachful speeches and untruthes; howe can yee saie he was admonished of this course? He never but once, nor so much as once offended you by his preaching; and shall he be accused unto authoritie, and that afore he be admonished? Wil yee do that yee maie do, yea more than yee can justifie either before God or man, before yee have made it apparent even to the world that your adversarie is praefract, and will neither be persuaded by reason, nor moved by argumentes. I will tell you, did he favor your plats (as he doth utterlie dislike them) theis proceedings of yours would alienate his minde. If this course ye take against a fellowe Elder, the sworde not yet being in your handes, howe <s̶h̶o̶u̶l̶d̶ h̶e̶ b̶e̶ t̶r̶o̶u̶n̶c̶e̶d̶> would yee course him were yee of auctoritie? Your hot pursuings of him thus secretlie and indirectlie nowe, tell howe he should be then persecuted.

Neither lovingly nor gentlie did yee admonish him. M. Mosses[43] grinning at him in moste disdainfull manner before moste of you, and objecting so often unto him the Cambridg boies, maie tell you howe lovinglie and gentlie he was admonished. Successe Marten, and all yee Martinistes from charging our Bishops with hard using of the ministers:[44] Bend your selves henceforward against the Brother-hood. Yee cannot from all the Bishops proceedings theis 32 yeeres, all circumstances waied, produce an example of so in <ju>rious dealing against theire inferiors, as this of the Brethren against a fellow <min>ister. <line heavily erased – blotted out> theire roughnes is mildnes in comparison of theis mens gentle dealing. If the Bishops be severe, the lawes require it at theire handes; theis men are more than severe, and yet with-out commission.

2. Nowe upon that admonition what doth M. Rogers? Since that time he hath wholie absented himselfe from our companie, yee saie, as if wee had donn him injurie. Whether yee have donn him injurie or no, let others judg: I thinke your consciences tell you that yee have donn him [fo. 13v] wrong. And whether he hath since his preaching wholie absented himselfe from your companie, both M. Bownde[45] and Lewes can saie. Theie will testifie, I am sure, that this is false; and theire oune mouthes will condemn as untrue, which with theire handes theie saie theie are readie to justifie. For he was not onlie at theire Sermons immediatlie succeeding his, but in your companie also at Michels after the Sermons, and kept his place too according to the custome.[46] Marrie since, observing that he can do you no good and that yee set your selves in a course against him, and the cause he maintaineth <w̶h̶i̶c̶h̶ y̶e̶e̶ m̶e̶a̶n̶e̶ t̶o̶ k̶e̶e̶p̶> he hath refrained from your companie, and so wil refraine, til yee be reformed, and yet wil shunne no paines to do you good, as other-wise his brethren, neighbours, and fellowe ministers.

3. And for the people. His default was such (thus do yee write) as that the people of all sortes did espie it, and since that time have witnessed theire mislike in sondrie places. A lamentable event if it be true. But by the people of all sortes, if yee meane good and bad, all did espie his faultes and his greate default, and have also witnessed theire mislike in sondrie places, I muste needes saie your boldnes is exceeding greate that thus dare write unto his Lordship. There was never yet good man (that ever he could heare, some of you excepted) that spied such default as yee speake of, much lesse hath witnessed his mislike in anie, and therefore not in sondrie places. The speeches of mutinous heds are not to be regarded of him, but to be suppressed by others.

---

[43] See *BR*, pp. 233–4.
[44] Martin Marprelate. See W. Pierce, *An Historical introduction to the Marprelate Tracts.*
[45] See *BR*, pp. 188–9.
[46] Evidence that at dinner the ministers sat in order, possibly of seniority.

Againe by the people of all sortes, if yee meane of all callinges, it is againe untrue, and a soare attainting of divers worshipfull Justices, gentlemen, and others, who would not I am sure for anie thing be spotted with the leaste suspicion of that yee write, much lesse of depraving his Sermon in sondrie places.

If yee meane all that heard him did both espie his greate default, and also witness theire mislike in sondrie places, as yee write yee wot not what, and that which yee [fo. 14r] cannot proove, so for his parte he can against you bring good proofe of much good donn therebie in some of his auditorie, who comming to the Sermon of your verie judgment departed from the same of another minde, and have witnessed theire good approbation thereof in sondrie places. The good which he did upon some of the auditorie whome he knoweth right well, is an argument that he spake to the good liking of others, whome he knoweth not: who have aswell witnessed theire liking as others did theire mislike in sondrie places.

And this he can saie that whosoever els have in sondrie places testified either liking or mislike thereof, by this wrighting yourselves have opened your mislike, and that with your oune handes. And though yee have so donn (which I am sorie to see) yet forasmuch as it is not misliked, but allowed by the lawfull auctoritie of our Church, he waieth not a strawe what yee or others of like note do either thinke or report thereof.

Th'information

Whereupon [1] (as it was [2] reported crediblie to us) M. Rogers threatened before hand that [3] the next time that it came to his course to preach in the place againe, he would answere all those that spake against him, as insinuating [4] that he would deale in the matter againe. Nowe there [6] was no man which heard him be<*fore*> and sawe the issue [5] of that Sermon, but would have bine grie<*ved*> that there [7] was a worse to come, as fearing [8] from it some greate trouble like to growe in the contrie.

Th'answere

1. Here folowe other accidents. For yee saie, whereupon M. Rogers threatened.

2. Howe knowe yee that? It was reported crediblie to us that M. [fo. 14v] Rogers threatened. Yee knowe not so much therefore of yourselves, yee write it but upon the report of others. Do you beleeve al reportes? Theie which so do shall never wante sorowe.

He denieth this, he threatened not. Whie? it was reported crediblie to us that he did threaten. But what were theire names? Howe manie also were theie for nomber, that reported this? Were theire names knowen yee would be founde to credulous in crediting them who in this cause deserve no credite, as being his adversaries. And were theire nomber knowen, yee should appeare too injurious not onlie in receaving theire accusation, but also upon that in joyning against him in a complaint after this manner. Against an Elder {1 Tim. 5,19} receive none accusation, but under two or three witnesses, saith S. Paul: but yee have receaved an accusation, and accused also an Elder and raised al theis broiles upon thinformation, the privie information of one man, if the truth were knowen.[47] Yea were the truth knowen, I thinke that he neither

---

47   A reference to Robert Lewis. See above, p. 159.

did report this onto anie of you which afterward saie yee wil justifie the truth hereof, but unto another of your companie, thauthor of these jarres.[48] < scored out>

3. But be it he threatened? What did he threaten? Namelie that the nexte time that it came to his course to preach in the place againe, he would answere all those that spake against him. Is this to threaten, to saie before hande that the next time that it came to his course to preach in the place againe, he would answere all those that spake against him, is this to threaten? To saie he will injure no man in life, lymbe, or otherwise, yet will defend himselfe so well as he can against all his adversaries, call yee this to threaten? To saie, He wil maintaine the doctrine by him delivered and answer [fo. 15r] all those that spake against him, is this to threaten? If this be to threaten, then did he, and doth, and wil threaten. For he hath delivered nothing which he will not defende by Gods assistance, against all his adversaries.

4. Neither would he have yee to surmise that he doth insinuate such a thing. For he doth plainlie give you t'understand that the credite of his doctrine , which is not his but Gods, to th'uttermost of his power, he wil maintaine. This writing of yours is to weake to make him give grounde. Yee have some-what astonished him by your sinister dealing against him under-hand: yee shall never vanquish him in the cause.

The fault which hetherto ye have founde was his manner of handling thinges: nowe yee openlie dislike, and are not affraide to testifie it also under your handes, howe it is even the verie matter he uttered which yee do mislike as insinuating, yee saie, that hee would deale in the same matter againe. Theie which dissemble had need to have good memories. It bursteth-out which I have long suspected.
Yet marvell I much that yee which hetherto would not charge him with the matter, but with his manner of speech, do nowe chalenge him in this writing to my L[ord] of Norwich even for the matter he delivered. Th<ink> yee to finde my Lord more favorable towardes you than M. Rogers < > that he wil not suffer anie doctrine by him delivered to be defaced a<nd> his Lordship wil? The wordes uttered were M. Rogers, the cause ha<nd>led was his Lordships, yea the Princes. Theie all maintaine one and the same cause: the manner of defending it by them is divers. That which yee write against him, yee write against them. He is but weake, theie are mightie adversaries. Take heed what yee do.

5. Judg not of matters by the praesent eventes. Ill causes in mans eies have sometyme good event; and good matters il successe. Errors often [fo.15v] have manie favorers, and the truth fewe frendes: yet shall theie be abhorred and the truth prevaile.

I write not this as though th'issue of M. Rogers sermon was not good. For it had that good issue, as he unfainedlie doth, but sufficientlie shall never praise God for the same. The thoughtes of manie hartes are therebie discovered. He hath a greate part of his desires, and more maie have here-after for all this. The seed muste have a time to roote and fructefie after it is sowen. Even yee which nowe are his adversaries in this matter, maie be his frendes, and approove as much as yee have nowe condemned. As wonderfull matters have fallen out ere this. And he hath argumentes

---

[48] The implied reference to Miles Mosse is unmistakable.

not a fewe that yee write theis thinges more of affection to please some, than of judgment; and that divers of you by this information do both condemne that in your judgementes yee do approve, and approve that which in your judgmentes yee condemne.

6. Yee signifie againe as if all th'auditorie were offended at the Sermon. I muste answere yee againe, it is a greate reproach of so holie, and by manie titles so worthie an audience. Measure not th'auditorie by th'affections of some. Theie would be offended with you, if theie knewe what yee have written. Thinke not all faultie, because some are factious.

7. Againe, yee reproach not th'auditorie onlie <so much as> but the Sermon <itselfe> besides which yee cannot by theis wordes but counte to be bad, when by a praejudice yee condemne the nexte to come as worse. I perceave yee so accompt of Sermons, which otherwhile yee magnifie even unto the cloudes, as theie serve your humors. Theie which please you, and agree to your mindes, are good; but theie which crosse you, are forth-with bad Sermons.[49] It is not your speech but Gods worde that muste either justifie or condemne us all. A Sermon is neither good, because yee do justifie; nor Bad, because yee condemne it. Proove this to be so as yee tearme it by [fo. 16r] Gods word, and then shal I thinke you to be good men.

8. But your last wordes here, in two respectes, be worthie th'observation. First that anie threatning of M. Rogers, a poore man of small accounte, and on whose doctrine in his former Sermon in some thinges (as yee deeme) is onsounde, his proofes slender, and his cause bad, should daunte you, so manie, of such note, so wel backt, having a righteous cause, and the truth on your side. Yet do yee plainlie confesse if his former hath not, yet the verie rumor of his next Sermon hath made you, and others of th'auditorie affraide. And surelie had yee not thus written, your verie actions, and practesing by sinister and indirect meanes both to seclude, and keep him from his course of preaching, doth plainlie <publish> proclaime that he hath freighted you, and that his next comming to Burie would quite have over-throwen the buildinges, when his former Sermon did so shake the foundacion of <your> the new devised government. I never knewe good men, as yee counte your selves, in a good cause so fearefull.

Next, it is to be observed that yee feared greate troble was like to growe in the contrie by that Sermon. This is nowe the second time that in this information yee have had relation to the Contrie. Afore yee delivered, that had he remembered the state of the Contrie, he would never have preached that which he did: here yee saie that had he preached againe <it> was feared that greate troble was like to have growen in the contrie therebie < > If his Sermon was to confirme, as yee suppose his former Sermon < > to answere his adversaries that spake against him; and his former Sermon was, as it is, sufficientlie by all good auctorities, approved, what troble w<as> likelie to growe in the contrie by the same? If he spake for the State that nowe is as he did, and his doinges by the laufull auctoritie of our Church is

49 Cf. Richard Bancroft's 'platform of a precisian's sermon' in *Tracts ascribed to Richard Bancroft*, ed. A. Peel (Cambridge, 1953), pp. 71–3.

orderlie allowed, is it possible that the Contrie, even the Contrie and Countie of Suffolk, would be trobled, and greatlie trobled about a Sermon spoken to so good purpose, and so lawfulie approve<*d*> [fo. 16v] Are yee so privie to the hartes of some that yee <knowe> can deliver afore hand that troble even greate troble would growe in the Contrie, if he should either speake to that purpose as afore, or confirme that which afore he spake? Be it farre fro mine hart to conceave so of Suffolk, and Suffolk men. For my part thinke yee what yee liste, I cannot thinke so ill of them, naie I cannot but conceave well of them, whome I knowe are as wel affected to her majestie, the true religion, and her godlie proceedinges, as anie people within her dominions: and if in Suffolk all thinges be not so well as were to be wished, the reason is, not because the doctrine delivered and maintained by M. Rogers is published, but for that it is not made knowen and more preached in the Contrie. The not preaching thereof, or the preaching the contrarie, trobleth <and greatlie trobleth> the contrie, and the whole land greatelie.

Th'information

Hereupon [1] it was (viz. for peace [3] sake, and to avoide [4] a threatened danger) that your L[ord] was sued unto to ratifie a companie out [2] of which M. Rogers was secluded, as not doubting [6] but this might be donn in that regard without abuse of your Lordship the rather [5] because your L[ord] heretofore gave autoritie to some of us to dispose of that exercise.

Th'answere

1. This is your conclusion, and sutable surelie to the premises. It should seeme his Lordship is offended greatelie with some bodie. Yee labor therefore in theis wordes t'assuage his displeasure, and to purchase his wonted favor.
2. Th'offense his Lordship hath conceaved is for that he was made to ratifie à à [sic] companie out of which M. Rogers was secluded: not for ratifieng a companie (even a certaine companie of preachers for the better ordering of the [fo. 17r] Burie exercise) but for that he was drawn by a <subtile practise> Pharisaicall practese contrarie to his meaning to seclude M. Rogers. He knewe whome he was to ratifie, theire names were afore praesented in a paper: but whome he was therebie to seclude, he knewe not, for that was concealed. Neither knewe he that he was to ratifie a companie to th'end M. Rogers might by his authoritie be secluded, who would not (thei knewe full wel) neither could be secluded from his place but by his authoritie, or by some hier power.
And surelie howesoever his Lordship is offended (as he hath good cause) yet M. Rogers is so farre from grieving himself thereat, that he is much comforted, firste because not laufulie, but indirectlie; nor by the justice of his governors, but through the malice of his aequals, he was secluded. Next for that he was secluded also for so good a cause, even for speaking his conscience freelie for the praesent government of the Church, against the open depravers, perturbers, and adversaries of the same. But he cannot but be much grieved to see both his Lordship and others so notoriouslie abused; and a cause of such importance by his putting-doune in theis partes (after a sorte) to be over-thrown.

3. But yee give reasons of this action. Which had theie bine uttered at the firste

plainlie together with your purpose (by his L[ord's] approbation) to seclude M. Rogers, it had bine seasonablie donn, and to your comm<*en*>dacion, but alleaged nowe as theie be, do plainlie showe that he was then secluded with-out reason. Yet have yee reasons for your actions, yee deserve the more favor. What then were the causes?

The first was yee saie, a regard of peace. As if there could be no peace if he continued his course. Which tendeth much to his reproach, who is wel knowen by nature to be a peaceable man, and as farre from a contending spirit as anie of you all that set your handes against him. *Tam sum misericors judices quam vos, tam mitis quam qui lenissimus*, saith Tullie, so maie he saie of himselfe. {Orat pro P. Sylla} I am as ful of compasion as yee, my <*judges*> [fo. 17v] as gentle, as the mildest, <~~of you all~~> and as litle delight in contention as who doth leaste.[50]

If he were vehement and earnest the times, the cause he handled, the verie dangers imminent whereunto we are all like to fall except theie be speedilie praevented, urged him there-unto. Having saide, and delivered his conscience, he hath donn. He neither entred into theis controversies afore, neither wil againe but upon urging necessitie.

He loveth peace but so it be godlie; and hateth contention from his harte, if it be wiked. There is a wiked peace and there is a godlie contention. Peace is not so to be regarded, that godlines be over-throwen; nor contention so to be abhorred, that the truth by silence or negligence be betraied.

When manie oppose themselves against a just cause, some are to defend it. Theie are not contentious that defend, but theie contentious that oppugne the same.

Looke wel about your selves, and examine your oune consciences, whether he in uttering that he did, and standing in the maintenance of that, which in his verie conscience he knoweth is the truth, or yee which professedlie withstand him and his doctrine are the troblers of the Church.

Assure your selves it wil one daie be knowen whose doctrine moste tended unto the Churches peace. In the meane space as men are guided by the holie Spirit, so let them judge.

4. The secund cause was t'avoide a threatened danger, as yee saie. Men wil do much t'avoide dangers, especialie if theie be threatened. He that is threatened is warned: and he that being warned afore hand wil take no warning, if he fall into dangers maie thanke himselfe. I cannot blame you, if being threatened, yee seeke to save your selves. [fo. 18r] Howe yee were threatened hath bine afore declared. All the threatening yee had was even by your oune confession that the nexte time it came to his course to preach in that place again he would answere all those that spake against him. Should yee be grieved to heare him answere his adversaries? Or be yee his adversaries that yee are so grieved?

And yet what need yee feare, being his adversaries, if that which either he delivereth be unsounde; or which yee maintaine, be the truth? Let them feare that resiste the truth. And though yee hold contrarie opinions unto him, and unsufferable, yet is

---

[50] Cicero, *Pro Sulla*, section 87 in *Cicero, the speeches*, translated by L. Lord (Cambridge, Mass., 1964), pp. 346–7.

there no danger to be feared, unlesse yee openlie contend to the disquieting of the Church.

Will yee therefore be with-out feare of danger? Be quiet. Keep both your mouthes from speaking, and your handes from writing that yee cannot justifie, and yee maie live long enough, the Lord be thanked, with-out dread of danger. These therefore be good wordes, but a frivolous <reason> cause of M. Rogers seclusion.

Yee would alleage somewhat t'excuse <yourselves> the matter, but yee knowe not what.

5. A thirde and last cause hereof is, for that his Lordship heretofore gave autoritie to some of you to dispose of that exercise. His Lordship no dou<*bt*> might, as he did, give autoritie unto some of you to dispose thereof, and < > might yee not do that yee did. For yee might not by his autoritie seclu<*de*> anie men once appointed to the place without good cause. Yee had no juste cause to seclude him. And therefore did it not by his L[ord's] auctoritie.

<And> But had yee cause, and just reason too of secluding him: yet might it not be donn by everie man of the companie, but either by all those appointed by his L[ord] to that ende which were in nomber sixe (of which number both by your oune choose, I meane the chiefest and moste ancient < > among you, and also by a speciall letre directed unto him from h<*is L[ord]*> [fo. 18v] M. Rogers was one) or by fower of them. Nowe he was not secluded by five, nor by fower <of them>, nor yet in verie deed by anie one of them, nor so much as by anie two of the whole companie, but by one man, and that to th'utter disliking of divers of them, as themselves have testified whiche nowe to gratifie that one man, are content not onlie t'approve his action, but to discredite themselves also by theire handie writing.

Therefore as this is no true cause: so is it an untrue information.

6. Saie not therefore this is no abuse of his Lordship, but plainlie confesse that he was abused by that manner of dealing. And besides confesse that yee have synned against his Lordship; and against your brother; and against the auditorie that heard him; and against the contrie where-in yee live; and against the Prince by whom yee live well; and against the truth, and against God himselfe <by this your writing> and so heaped syn upon synn by this youre information. I am not deceaved in my conjecture. As yee began, so yee ende. Yee neither wished his L[ord] wel in the beginning, neither bid him in th'ende Fare well.

Th'informers

The truth of this, we whose names are heere subscribed,[51] are readie to justefie.

Burie St Edmunds   1 Aprilis

John Knewstub

Reginald Whitfield

Gualter Alen

Thomas Seffray

John Warde

Nicolas Bownde

---

[51] For all ten signatories, see *BR*.

[fo. 19r]
Rychard Grandidge
Robert Lewis
Leonard Greaves
Lawrence Whittaker

Th'answerer

1. M. Rogers is more sorie to read this than anie thing els. He saith yee can not before God, or man, justifie that yee have above set donne. He therefore chalengeth you for manie grosse untruthes, and slanderous suggestions.
And for his Sermon he is readie for anie thing yet objected to justifie it, and everie part of it against you all, or anie of you, in anie place, or by anie good <meanes> course which for the best quietnes of the Church, maie in wisdome be appointed.

2. Not al of you are able to justifie that which yee have nowe written; nor anie of you, some thinges. Some of you never heard that Sermon of his, will theie condemne that which theie never heard?
Will yee whose names are here subscribed justifie the truth hereof? If yee meane yee will justifie that which hereof is true, yee saie wel: but manie, and the moste thinges here be either untruthes, reproaches or slanders, will yee justifie them? Can yee?
This readines to justifie ye wot not, nor care not what, bewraie<s> much malice; and mindes which waigh not what theie write, so theie maie discredite them or that which theie fancie not.

3. The firste of Aprill, when this was written, was the firste daie of the generall Assises at Burie St Edmundes, A° 1590. The firste of Aprill, it seemeth, the honorable Judges with the rest of the Gentlemen, and Commons of the contrie were < > not so occupied at Burie St Edmundes in one kind, for the go<od of some > [fo. 19v] but at the same verie time and toune yee were as much busied in another kinde for the hurt of some. Theie met openlie, yee secretlie and classically. The fructes of theire assembling is notablie knowen to the greate good of the contrie: and this letre (brought to <light> my sight by Gods providence, contrarie to your expectation) testifieth in part th'end of your meeting at Burie St Edmundes 1° Aprilis.

4. I observe your nomber, and I marke your names also.
For nomber yee are tenn. And so yee are tenn to on, and tenn against on. This yee marke also, and conceale it not from your favorers. I have heard some of you glorie in your nomber; and have founde that of the people some that cannot reprove M. Rogers for his doctrine: do yet mislike him onlie for that in theis causes he is alone. It is theire simplicitie that theie judge no better; and it is your follie to glorie of your nomber. I would it were onlie the comon peoples fault, and not the fault also of other men of more eminencie both, in the Church and contrie, to be carried awaie with the greater part, and go with the nomber not waighing the cause thoroughlie, and in judgment.
And yet, though yee are nowe tenn to on, M. Rogers is not alone. He hath his favorers, and moe coadjutors than yee thinke, or than yee would he had. He is not single, nor singled from all, nor yet singular. If some in theire places showe not

themselves as theie should, the more to blame them theire silence, negligence, or
< > ought not to praejudice the common cause of our Church.

Were he destitute of all frendes and favorers it might dismaie him < > he had not a
juste cause, and the truth on his side: but standing in and for the truth, he could not
be dismaide though he were alone. For greate is the truth, and together with her
pertakers, be theie fewe <or> manie, shal still praevale.

5. Your names signifie who, as your nomber howe [fo. 20r] yee are. John Knewstub,
Reginald Whitfield, Gualter Alen etc. yoe are al well knowen, so are your giftes.
This enterprise wil make you better knowen.

I lament for the Churches sake that John Knewstub, Reginald Whitfield, Gualter
Alen and the rest of your are so overshot.

Y<our> credites, John Knewstub, Reginald Whitfield etc. cannot so further good
causes: but bad matters, such as by this writing yee have undertaken, will both
diminish your oune credites and hinder the good proceedinges of the Gospell, which
is a thing moste rufull, but yet the fructes of faction.

I see John Knewstub, Reginald Whitfield, Gualter Alen, Thomas Seffray etc., I
looke for Miles Mosse, and I cannot spie his name either firste or last. Wil not he
justifie the truth hereof, as yee will, because his hande is not heere? Will he that was
the firste and foremost in this action against Thomas Rogers, be neither the firste
nor last, nor at all in this writing? Hath hee left you quite that yee have not his hand?
But I am answered me thinkes againe and againe. We have his hande; for this was
his handie werke, saith one. Though <del>we have not</del> his hande be not, yet <we have>
his hed is heere, saith another, <del>the cause is secret saith a thirde, he was our</del>
<del>secretarie</del> and we have his hart <is with us> and this sufficeth.

Finis

[Rogers's last sentences at first read: 'Though we have not his hande, yet we have
his hed saith another. The cause is secret, saith a thirde, he was our secretarie and
his hart is with us, and this sufficeth.']

D. Bernard epis 2[52]
quid me pudeat scribere, quod illos non puduit facere? Si pudeat audire, quod
impudenter egerunt; non pudeat emendare, quod libenter non audiunt.

[fo. 20v]

> Articles drawn (according to the verie thoughte of the classical Brethren,
> (the Informers above mentioned) for the wel managing of theire Moondaie
> exercise at Burie, and such like els-where in Marcate townes, on
> Mercate-daies.[53]

1. Be verie warie and circumspect whom bee catalogued in the rowle of the
ordinarie Preachers; For therein consisteth the life or death of the exercise, for a
great part.

---

[52] Bernard of Clairvaux, Epistola II 'ad Fulconem puerum qui postea fuit Lingonensis Archidiaconus',
    Patrologia Latina, ed. J. P. Migne (Turnhout, 1865, reprint 1966), CLXXXII, col. 84.
[53] Satirical articles in the vein of Martin Marprelate.

2. A choice being made, let a special care be had that peace be kept, and continued among our selves, and that there be no oppositions one against another (howsoever wee oppose ourselves against publique order in our ministerie and assemblies)

3. There wil unavoidablie be distractions, unlesse we be al of one minde, and of one judgement.

4. Take heed that none be of our number which is ignorant of the praesent State of the contrie of Suffolk for th'ecclesiastical government; or affecteth not the opposition that therein is made by us, and our Brethren, against publique lawes; or favoreth and regardeth the ecclesiastical government established by Q. Elizabeth and the State.

5. It is our minde, and wil, that (as wee maie, keeping ourselves with out danger) the people our followers especialie, be advertised that the State of Suffolk in particular; and the State of the Church of England in general, are divers, and opposite at this day, so as what the Church, and States of the Church of England do approove, and like of, the States of Suffolk (wee meane our selves, and our maintainers in the contrie) cannot brooke, and contrariwise. For example

6. The Church and States of England approove the praesent Ecclesiastical government nowe in use, under the Queenes majestie, by Archbishops, Bishops etc. < > States, that is the classical ministers, and theire disciples which are not a < > [fo. 21r] Suffolk do not so.

7. In Suffolk (to such a State have we brought the contrie) the number is not smal (especialie of ministers, more than in anie contrie in <*this*> land, that would pull the raines of goverment from the nowe and alwais received eclesiastical; and put them into the handes of certaine newelie devised consistorial and laical Elders and States-men in everie parish: the Church and State of England is against such an upstart State, and Statesmen in what contrie soever.

8. The judgement of the Church of England tuching doctrine and discipline is knowen by the bookes of Common Praier by lawe established, the booke of the 39 articles of religion, by act of Parliament also confirmed, and agreeably unto them, by the labors of D. Whitegift (nowe Archb. of Canterburie) against T.C.[54] (whom some cal turbulent T.C.); of D. Bridges against the learned discourse[55] (though manie thinke it but a vane discourse); of D. Sutcliffe,[56] Some,[57] Hooker[58] Tooker[59] and the like.

9. The judgment of the true church of England indeed (for wee are of their minde, which thinke and write that if God have anie church or people in the land and

---

[54] John Whitgift, *An answere to a certen Libel intituled, An admonition to the Parliament* (London, 1572); John Whitgift, *The Defense of the Aunswere to the Admonition, against the Replie of T. C.* (London, 1574). See Milward, *Religious controversies*, pp. 30–2.

[55] John Bridges, *A Defence of the Government Established in the Church of Englande for ecclesiastical matters, contayning an aunswere unto a Treatise called, The Learned Discourse of Eccl. Government* ... (London, 1587).

[56] Matthew Sutcliffe, *A Treatise of Ecclesiasticall Discipline* (London, 1590).

[57] Robert Some, *A Godly Treatise containing and deciding certaine questions, touching the ministerie, sacraments and church* (London, 1588).

[58] Richard Hooker, *Of the lawes of ecclesiasticall politie* (London, 1593); *The fift booke* (London, 1597). The references to Hooker and Tooker were clearly added by Rogers at a later date.

[59] William Tooker, *Of the Fabrique of the Church and Church-mens livings* (London, 1604).

contrie the title (Puritane) is given them:[60] and the auctor of that worthie, frutful and godlie Sermon on Rom. 12 (which wee do subscribe unto) saith The Church of England (which is ourselves and our companies) abhorreth and loatheth the callinges of Archb. Bishops, Deanes etc.) tuching pointes of State and Churche policie is expressed in the bookes and wrightinges <professedlie penned and printed against those foresaid bookes and persons, chiefelie in the wrightinges> principalie of T.C.[61] J. Penrie;[62] Udal,[63] Demon of dis.,[64] Eccles dis.,[65] counterpoyson[66] and (to omit manie mor of like nature) the bynamed, viz the Fructful Sermon, the godlie sermon upon certaine verses Rom. 12. (al which wee do highlie commend though the Queens majestie by her Lawes and Proclamations yea and the whole state of this common weale (as tending unto civil broiles and dissention) do condemne them utterlie.

10. If it therefore happen (which God forbid) that anie of this Mercate exercise do publiquelie speake either on the behalfe, and for the contineance of <the> established orders and officers in the Church of England; or in m<agni>fication either of the 39 Art. of religion in the forementioned booke contained; or of the booke of Common Praier, commonlie tearmed the Communion booke; or of the bookes of the most reverend Father<s D.> Whitegift; D. Bridges, D. Sutcliffe etc.

Or against the treatises, and discourses (by some called and esteemed no b<etter> [fo. 21v] than Libels against the good estate of the Church of England) explaining fullie our desires, whether it be against the Admonition unto the Parliament,[67] the Supplications unto the Parliament;[68] the learned dis.,[69] Eccles dis.[70] Demon of dis.[71] The counterpoys.[72] Miles Monop,[73] the Fruct Sermon[74] or such like, to one and the same ende penned, printed and throughout the realme among al States dispersed:

---

60 The well-read Rogers is quoting, sardonically, from the puritan tract *A dialogue concerning the strife of our Church* (London, 1584), p. 49.

61 Thomas Cartwright. See *Cartwrightiana*, ed. L. H. Carlson and A. Peel (Elizabethan Nonconformist Texts, I, London, 1951); A. F. Scott Pearson, *Thomas Cartwright and Elizabethan Puritanism* (Cambridge, 1925).

62 See above n. 40.

63 John Udall, author of *The State of the Church of Englande laide open in a conference betweene Diotrephes a Byshop, Tertullus a Papist* (London, 1588) and other treatises. See Collinson, *EPM*, pp. 377–8, 387–8, 391.

64 John Udall, *A demonstration of the trueth of that discipline which Christe hath prescribed for the government of his church* ([East Molesey], 1588).

65 Walter Travers, *Ecclesiasticae Disciplinae et Anglicanae Ecclesiae ab illa aberrationis, plena e verbo Dei, et dilucida explicatio* (La Rochelle, 1574).

66 Dudley Fenner, *A counter-poyson, modestly written for the time, to make aunswere to* (London, 1584).

67 John Field and Thomas Wilcox, *An admonition to the parliament* (1572).

68 *A lamentable complaint of the commonalty, by way of supplication to Parliament, for a learned ministery* (London, 1585).

69 William Fulke, *A briefe and plaine declaration, concerning the desires of all those faithfull Ministers, that have and do seeke for the Discipline and reformation of the Church of Englande: which may serve for a just Apologie, against the false accusations and slanders of their adversaries* (London, 1584). Fulke's text was published by John Field, who gave it the running title of 'The Learned Discourse of Ecclesiastical Government'. See Milward, *Religious controversies*, p. 79.

70 See above n. 65.

71 See above n. 64.

72 See above n. 66.

73 See above n. 41.

74 See above n. 22.

Vowe wee, and promise and, as anie is allowed to speake in this verie Mercate exercise, let him promise likewise and vowe, never to have peace with such a person, til hee hath altered his minde, and rentired himselfe in a League with us, against the present State of Englands Church, the rites, orders, officers and protectors of them whosoever.

11. Let our proceedings against M. Rogers of Horninger in this contrie ever be in minde, whom (for none other cause but onlie for going with the State of the realme and not going with us of the newe < > State of Suffolk; and for open displaieng and confuting the said Fruct sermon <which was> made for a grea< > past, agreeablie to our mindes and for such a State as wee wish < >ome, and would have other contries to be in) we have made an example both to those of his minde, following his steps, what theie maie expect at our handes; and to our successors, with what endlesse and perfect hatred theie are to be pursued, that shal dare to thwart, and crosse us, or our Brethren wheresoever in our political courses and discourses about Discipline; and troble the sweete peace among us, and therebie hinder us from that State and Soveraigntie in the contrie and countie of Suff. which wee manie yeares have sought for, but nowe by his meanes and such like, are farther of <than ever> there from than ever.

12. Wee had not our wills of him, in no respecte, but the more wee stird the more loth some wee prooved, wee must needes confuse to the States of the land and states too, < > States indeed without usurpation of the contrie (the more is our griefe). If ever yet we obtaine power answerable to our wils, let him looke not to finde us unto him, as the Bishops are to us. Manie thinke theis to be over-severe, hee should saie so upon just cause. And take an ende of our Articles and Remembrances upon our former Information <and that to the Bishop of Norwich>

BIOGRAPHICAL REGISTER

Biographical Register

In 1905, R. G. Usher observed that 'the number of names and persons occurring in the book, their comparative obscurity and often recurrence, have led me to place in alphabetical order in the Introduction such biographical notes as would traditionally have appeared in footnotes' (p. vi). The present editors, with considerably more evidence at their disposal than Usher believed existed, have followed suit in the following Biographical Register. It includes all those involved in the activities of the two conferences of Dedham and Braintree, either as fully-fledged members or as signatories to documents which the Dedham conference prepared and circulated, as well as notices of the more important of the Suffolk ministers mentioned in Chicago MS 109. The intention is that these entries may be read 'complete', as one would read entries in any biographical dictionary, without constant reference to footnotes of the 'see above' variety. If this has involved a certain amount of repetition of material deriving from the main texts and from their footnotes, it seems a small price to pay for saving the interested reader from constantly having to move backwards and forwards between the biographies and the body of the book. For the same reason, direct quotations from the Dedham minute book are cited by means of 'internal' reference – that is, by following them with an emboldened, bracketed reference to the meeting(s) from which they are taken (i.e., **27M**; **35, 36 MM**).

Allen, Walter (Gualter)
Andrewes, Bartimaeus
Beamont, Stephen
Bound, John
Bound, Nicholas
Byrde, William
Carr, Roger
Catelyn, Ranulph
Chapman, Edmund
Cocke, William
Crick, Richard
Culverwell, Ezekiel
Dent, Arthur
Dowe, Richard
Farrar, Thomas
Gale, Arthur
Gifford, George
Grandidge, Richard

Greaves, Leonard
Hawden, Ralph
Holt, Robert
Huckle, John
Knevet, Thomas
Knewstub, John
Lewis, Robert
Lowe, Thomas
Monke, Robert
Morrice, Thomas
Morse, Anthony
Mors, Thomas
Mosse, Miles
Negus, William
Newman, Laurence
Northey, George
Parker, Richard
Rogers, Richard

Salmon, Edmund
Sandes, Henry
Searle, Robert
Seffray, Thomas
Stoughton, Thomas
Tey, William
Tilney, John
Tuke, George
Tunstall, William
Tye/Tie, Thomas
Upcher, Thomas
Walthar, John
Warde, John
Whitfield, Reginald
Whiting, Giles
Whittaker, Lawrence
Wright, Robert

ALLEN, WALTER (GUALTER) (d. 1602)

Rector of Erwarton, Suffolk, 1575–86 (resig.); rector of Rushbrooke, Suffolk, 1586–97 (resig.); rector of Stanton All Saints, Suffolk, 1597–1602 (d.)

Allen matriculated pensioner at St John's College, Cambridge, at Michaelmas 1560, but moved to Christ's, whence he graduated BA in 1563 and proceeded MA in 1566.[1] Fellow of Christ's from 1564 to Christmas 1573, he served as college preacher (1570–3), dean (1570 and 1572) and senior proctor (1572–3). He was one of the eighteen Masters of Arts who petitioned Sir William Cecil for the restoration of Thomas Cartwright as Lady Margaret Professor in July 1570 and one of the twenty-five who renewed the plea in August 1570. He proceeded BD in 1577.[2] Rector of Erwarton from 1575, he nevertheless appears to have been living in Rushbrooke, seat of Sir Robert Jermyn, where he may have been serving as preacher, by the early 1580s. His daughter Fayth was buried there on 8 June 1583 and a son Thomas was baptized on 9 August 1584.[3] He succeeded Clement Paman as rector of Rushbrooke in June 1586.[4] Another son, Richard, baptized on 13 December 1586, was buried on 4 February 1589, and a daughter Dorothy was baptized on 27 July 1588.[5]

Throughout these years, Allen appears to have been, with John Knewstub, one of the leaders of the godly clergy in west Suffolk. By 1590 Thomas Rogers could speak of Knewstub, Allen and Reginald Whitfield as men who were 'al well knowen'[6] and numerous references attest to Allen's participation in the conference movement throughout the 1580s. When in May 1582 Oliver Pigge wrote to John Field about the possibility of holding a synod in Cambridge, he reported that 'M Allen liketh well of the matter'.[7] Allen and Knewstub represented Suffolk at the Cambridge synod of 1587 and Allen was also involved in the national meetings held in London during parliamentary sessions in the late 1580s.[8]

In 1597 Allen became rector of Stanton All Saints, his successor at Rushbrooke being Robert Lewis. An inventory of his goods dated 10 September 1602 describes him as 'preacher of the word of God', itemizing among much household stuff 'six small mapes and five small pycktures'. His books were valued at £20 and his goods *in toto* came to £143 14s 4d.[9]

1. *Alum. Cantab.*, I, 20.
2. Peile, *Biographical register*, I, 76.
3. *Rushbrooke parish registers*, ed. S. H. A. Hervey (Suffolk Green Books VI, 1903), 2, 52–3.
4. NRO DN/REG/ 14, fo. 137v.
5. *Rushbrooke parish registers*, pp. 2, 53.
6. See above, p. 177.
7. Bancroft, *Daungerous positions*, p. 45.
8. PRO Star Chamber 5A 49/34.
9. NRO Inv 18/328.

ANDREWES, BARTIMAEUS (1551–1616)

Curate of Rochford, Essex, 1574; vicar of Braintree, Essex, 1576–7 (resig.); vicar of Great Wenham (Wenham Combust), Suffolk, 1578–85 (resig.); town preacher of Great Yarmouth, Suffolk, 1585–1616 (d.)

Andrewes matriculated sizar from Jesus College, Cambridge, at Michaelmas 1570.[1] When ordained by Bishop Edwin Sandys of London on 6 July 1574, he stated that he was 'of Braintree', had been born in Bocking, Essex, was now aged 23, and had recently been scholar of St John's College, Cambridge.[2] Later that month he was listed as curate of Rochford, at Sandys's second episcopal visitation, which suggests dependence on

Robert 2nd Lord Rich. Indeed, on 13 July 1576, at Rich's petition, he was granted letters patent for the vicarage of Braintree by the Lord Keeper, Sir Nicholas Bacon, but resigned the living within weeks, perhaps in order to return to Cambridge.[3] He was ordained priest at Ely on 21 December 1576, and when granted a preaching licence in 1577 was stated to be BA.[4] He was presented to the crown living of Great Wenham in 1578 at the petition of William Spring of Lavenham, the sureties against his payments for first fruits including the London goldsmith Gabriel Newman, friend of many godly clergy.[5]

Andrewes was a popular preacher, whose *Certaine verie worthie, godly profitable sermons upon the fifth chapter of the Songe of Solomon* were published in 1583. But his gifts were held by a fellow member of the Dedham conference to have consisted 'rather in exhortation than in doctryne' (**Extra M**, 17 February 1585). He made few interventions in the business of the conference but was twice chosen to speak and twice acted as moderator, on the second occasion when the conference met at his own house (**4, 11, 14, 17MM**). By the twenty-first meeting, Andrewes disclosed his intention to move from Wenham to Great Yarmouth, explaining his reasons (most notably an inadequate stipend, irregularly paid) on 1 February 1585 (**27M**).[6] The conference members proceeded to liaise between Andrewes and 'the people' of Wenham, and on 17 February 1585 an extraordinary meeting was held in Dedham at the house of Edmund Sherman, at the request of the bailiffs of Yarmouth, one of whom was present. At over a thousand words, the record for this debate is the longest for any item of business in the history of the Conference. Opinion went against Andrewes, but he departed for Yarmouth nonetheless, the conference resigning itself to his departure, and, in effect, to its lack of jurisdiction in such a matter.

At Yarmouth, Andrewes exhorted one of the largest parochial congregations in England – and that from a pulpit, perhaps especially erected for him, that was over ten feet tall. The dedication of his *Verie short and pithie catechisme: for all that will come prepared to the supper of the Lord* (1586) suggests that his arrival was considered a considerable event, both for himself and for the town. Although there are details of his appointment and its conditions in the Assembly Book of the borough (1579–98),[7] surprisingly little is known about his tenure of this prominent position, which he held until his death.

He was survived by three sons, Bartimaeus (rector of Magdalen Laver, Essex, from 1619 until his death in 1631), John and Samuel, and by two daughters, Abigail and Sarah, all of whom were left shares in their father's house in Great Yarmouth. There was also property in two other Suffolk parishes, including East Bergholt.[8]

1. *Alum. Cantab.*, I, 29.
2. GL MS 9535/1, fo. 151v.
3. BL, Lansdowne MS 443, fo. 238r; Reg. Grindal, fos. 188r, 189r.
4. *Alum. Cantab.*, I, 29; LMA DL/C/333, fo. 76v. The licence emphasized his preaching at Fordham: he had presumably been invited there by the rector, Thomas Upcher.
5. BL, Lansdowne MS 443, fo. 257r; PRO E334/9, fo. 150r.
6. The Great Yarmouth authorities had offered him twice as much.
7. NRO C 19/4 (1579–98).
8. PRO PCC PROB 11/127 (49 Cope), fo. 383r.

BEAMONT (BEMANT, BEAMOND), STEPHEN (c. 1554–1616)

Rector of Easthorpe, Essex, 1579–1609 (resig.)

Son of William Beamont of Cambridge, Stephen Beamont attended school at King's College, Cambridge, for six years before being admitted pensioner at Gonville and Caius on 14 April 1572. He matriculated in 1573, graduating BA in early 1576, and was ordained deacon at Ely in 1578.[1] Instituted rector of Easthorpe (BA) on 22 May 1579 at the presentation of Richard Atkins of London,[2] he compounded on 5 June.[3] He was licensed on 28 January 1580 to marry Katherine Pudney, spinster,[4] and ordained priest by John Aylmer, bishop of London, on 30 March that year (BA; rector of Easthorpe; aged 26).[5]

Beamont's nonconformist activities had come to the attention of the authorities by the summer of 1583. At the episcopal visitation on 11 July he was recorded as an unlicensed preacher who was to be inhibited after Bartholomewtide unless licensed by then.[6] Thereafter matters moved swiftly. On 29 July he was indicted at Chelmsford assizes, charged with failing since entering the benefice to use the surplice at any time, with ignoring the Book of Common Prayer and with 'seditiously' celebrating 'other services'. His churchwardens[7] – stated to have been appointed 'by the election of the said Stephen' – were indicted because they had 'incited and abetted him' although knowing him to be of 'evil conversation' and using 'an unauthorized rite'. Although he was released on bail on this and three further occasions, the case dragged on until he and the churchwardens were officially discharged on 19 July 1585.[8] Meanwhile he had in late 1584 subscribed both to the form of limited subscription agreed by the Dedham conference and to 'Certain requests' submitted to Archdeacon Withers.[9]

Beamont contrived to survive for a further twenty-four years, despite constant demands for his conformity. Present at the visitation of 1586 as rector and preacher at Easthorpe, he was ordered to produce his preaching licence at a later date and to certify that he had worn the surplice and observed the ceremonies.[10] Thereafter he was one of the many suspended for refusing the surplice and had a day set for his deprivation.[11] At the visitation of 1589 he was 'expressly monished not to preach but when he readeth divine prayer and weare the surples'.[12] In 1592 he was listed merely as *concionator notus*.[13]

Excused from the visitation of 1598,[14] Beamont is recorded as one of the 'diligent and sufficient' clergy of Essex in 1604.[15] James I's drive for ritual conformity that year appears to have re-inforced his nonconformist convictions. On 27 March 1605, following Bancroft's last episcopal visitation (July 1604), he was summoned into consistory for the surplice but the case was three times prorogued on the grounds that he was 'sick of the stone'.[16] He finally appeared on 7 June, desiring 'further tyme' for conference with Bishop Richard Vaughan or with his appointees and confessing that he had performed nothing which he had been 'enjoyned to performe'. He was ordered to use the surplice and the ceremonies and so certify at the forthcoming visitation.[17] On 7 November he was again in consistory, having pleaded before the episcopal visitors that he still desired to confer with Vaughan, who had directed him to confer with Archdeacon (Thomas) Withers or with Dr (Richard) Corbet as to his conformity. From this point his case was consistently prorogued (seven times in all) for the rest of Vaughan's brief episcopate.[18] Vaughan's sympathy towards moderate puritan aspirations was probably at the root of it.

Under Vaughan's successor, Thomas Ravis, Beamont was again put under pressure. Called into consistory 19 May 1608 to show his preaching licence and to certify of the surplice, he stated he had a preaching licence granted by Bancroft 'and likewise hath worn the surples'. He was nevertheless enjoined to use the ceremonies of the church 'as he was bound'.[19]

Beamont resigned within months, very probably to forestall deprivation by the High Commission.[20] He made his will, as of Abberton, Essex, on 1 September 1616. Primarily an equitable disposal of properties in Easthorpe, Copford, Messing and Little and Great Birch to his wife and executrix, Katherine, and his sons Gamaliel and Benjamin, it was proved in the consistory court of London on 6 September 1616.[21]

1. *Alum. Cantab.*, I, 119; Venn, *Biographical History*, p. 69.
2. Reg. Grindal, fo. 196r. Atkins had acquired the manor and advowson from the poet and translator Arthur Golding: Louis Thorn Golding, *An Elizabethan puritan* (New York, 1937), pp. 75, 77, 93–4, 109, 133.
3. Sureties John Cottesford of St Peter Cheap, goldsmith, and Robert Fermor of St Faith, mercer: E334/9, fo. 174r.
4. LMA DL/C/333, fo. 191r.
5. GL MS 9535/2, fo. 12r.
6. GL MS 9537/5, fos. 3r, 63r. A later hand has added the ukase that he must not be so admitted (*Ac non sit admissus*).
7. Thomas Pudney, husbandman, and Richard Cranefeld, ploughwright. Pudney was presumably either his father- or brother-in-law.
8. ERO, Essex Assize File I, 35/25/T[rinity], nos. 31, 32. Summarized in J. S. Cockburn, ed., *Calendar of assize records: Essex indictments Elizabeth I* (HMSO, 1978), nos. 1407, 1450, 1501, 1552, 1600.
9. See above, pp. 82, 87.
10. GL MS 9537/6, fo. 142v.
11. *Seconde parte*, II, 163, 261.
12. GL MS 9537/7, fo. 46r. Ordered to certify on 2 October.
13. GL MS 9537/8, fo. 55r.
14. GL MS 9537/9, fo. 101r.
15. 'A Viewe', p. 4.
16. LMA DL/C/618, p. 413; /617, pp. 672, 741.
17. *Ibid.*, p. 783.
18. *Ibid.*, pp. 900, 941; LMA DL/C/304, pp. 335, 347, 638, 661, 674, 685.
19. LMA DL/C/307, p. 489.
20. Gamaliel Beamont, MA, his son and successor, was instituted on 11 November 1609: Reg. Bancroft, fo. 143r. Ezekiel Culverwell and William Negus had both been deprived in March 1609.
21. LMA DL/C/360, fos. 269v–71r. There were also minor bequests to his daughters Susan, Marie and Martha.

BO(U)ND(E), JOHN (c. 1544–1617)

Rector of Great Horkesley, Essex, 1580–1617 (d.)

Son of John Bound of Aylsham, Norfolk, Bound attended school there for six years before matriculating sizar from St John's College, Cambridge, at Michaelmas 1569. Aged seventeen, he migrated to Caius as pensioner on 26 October 1571, graduating BA in 1573 and proceeding MA in 1576.[1] He was ordained deacon by John Aylmer, bishop of London, on 21 December 1580 (MA; lately of St John's; now of Colchester; born Norwich diocese; aged 28 or so).[2] Instituted rector of Great Horkesley on 23 December 1580 at the presentation of Sir Thomas Lucas,[3] he compounded for the benefice on 6 February 1581.[4]

Listed present at the episcopal visitation of 1583,[5] Bound is not known to have resisted Archbishop Whitgift's articles during the following months but subscribed the form of limited subscription agreed by the Dedham conference in late 1584.[6] Present at the visitation of 1586, he was stated to be unlicensed to preach.[7] He was, however, listed as a preacher in 1589 and in 1592 as *concionator notus*[8] but does not seem to have been formally granted a diocesan preaching licence until 23 September 1595.[9]

In November 1589 Bound promised Richard Parker that he would act as one his compurgators following the suit brought against Parker by John Martin, but in the event failed to put in an appearance.[10] He was licensed on 17 January 1590 to marry Mary Ball, spinster, daughter of John Ball, yeoman of Little Horkesley.[11] At Bancroft's primary visitation in 1598 he stated that he always wore the surplice and 'will use all Conformitie touchinge the ceremonies of the Churche'.[12] Listed as one of the 'diligent and sufficient' clergy of Essex in 1604,[13] Bound is not known to have been arraigned for any nonconformist activities thereafter. His successor was instituted, following his death, on 20 January 1618.[14]

1. *Alum. Cantab.*, I, 176; Venn, *Biographical history*, p. 68. Not rector of Little Thorpe, Norfolk, 1602–27, as stated in both authorities.
2. GL MS 9535/2, fo. 14v.
3. Reg. Grindal, fo. 200r.
4. PRO E334/9, fo. 221v.
5. GL MS 9537/5, fo. 64v.
6. See above, p. 87.
7. GL MS 9537/6, fo. 143r.
8. GL MSS 9537/7, fo. 47r; /8, fo. 55v.
9. LMA DL/C/336, fo. 26v.
10. LMA DL/C/616, p. 205.
11. LMA DL/C/334, fo. 319r.
12. GL MS 9537/9, fo. 101v.
13. 'A Viewe', p. 4.
14. Reg. Bancroft, fo. 234v.

BOUND(E) (BOWND(E)), NICHOLAS (d. 1613)

Rector of Norton, Suffolk, 1585–1611; rector of St Andrew Norwich, 1611–13 (d.)

The son of Robert Bound, physician to the Duke of Norfolk, Bound matriculated sizar from Peterhouse, Cambridge, at Michaelmas 1568, and proceeded BA in early 1572. He was elected fellow that year, proceeding MA in 1575. He was incorporated at Oxford in 1577, and was ordained deacon and priest at Ely on 2 June 1580.[1] He was instituted to Norton, where the patron was the godly Suffolk magistrate Robert Ashfield of Stowlangtoft, on 3 November 1585.[2] He appears, however, to have been resident in Norton from 1581 as his five children, Hannah, Nathaniel, Abigail, Priscilla and Susan were born and baptized there between January 1582 and August 1591.

Bound possessed important connexions among the godly. Following the death of his first wife, he married the widow of John More, the 'Apostle of Norwich', who had died in 1592. Bound edited his *Three godly and fruitfull sermons* in 1594 and, in dedicating More's *A table from the beginning of the world to this day* (Cambridge, 1593), said that the work had come into his hands 'by a certaine hereditarie right'.[3] Bound's mother married as her second husband Richard Greenham, and his sister married John Dod.[4] His links with the godly magistrates of Suffolk and Norfolk were equally strong. We find him writing to Bassingbourne Gawdy in Norfolk on 20 July 1582, reminding Gawdy of his verbal promise made in Sir Robert Jermyn's house to repay a debt contracted by Sir Edward Clere, Bound having laid out money for Clere's son's education in Cambridge.[5] Bound dedicated his *An epistle of comfort for the afflicted*, dated 26 August 1594, to Jermyn and his patron Robert Ashfield, who God had 'so neerely joyned . . . in situation of the country, in office and calling, in frendship, in kindred, and yet neerest in profession and religion', apologizing that his work was unworthy of those 'who have deserved so well of a long time of thr [sic] commonwealth and church in our countrey, especially my selfe in many respectes am much bound unto you both'.[6]

Created DD at Cambridge in 1594, Bound is best known for *The doctrine of the Sabbath* (1595), which was dedicated to Robert earl of Essex, with his coat of arms, suggesting that Bound was one of his chaplains. This work began life as a series of sermons on the Ten Commandments preached in the Bury exercise. Bound wrote that he had been 'solicited to publish my Sermons upon the tenne Commandements by certaine of my godly brethren auditors of the same'[7] and elsewhere in the work likened the meetings of the godly to 'so many firebrands layde together'. 'Though every man hath some grace of Gods spirit in himselfe, yet is it greatly increased by conference.'[8] Bound maintained that all christians were commanded to rest on the seventh day of the week as much as the Jews were on the Mosaic sabbath and that the entire day ought to be devoted to acts of worship and godly service. He launched a strong attack on the games and sports that profaned the day and the work reflected and no doubt stimulated the growth of sabbatarianism among the godly in England. In *The holy exercise of fasting* (1604), Bound distinguished between public and private fasting but ruled that private fasts need not be confined to the family of one house but could include persons 'out of divers households gathered together upon their owne private motion; yet orderly and in the feare of God.'[9] If this suggested a step in the direction of a gathered church, Bound's dedication of the work to John Jegon, bishop of Norwich, which assured him 'how readie we are, and shall be, to yeild obedience to all your lordship's godly proceedings', blessing God 'not only for your comming among us, but much more for your continuance with us, and over us',[10] suggests the opposite.

In the 1603 survey of the diocese of Norwich, Bound was described as a doctor of divinity and preacher and 'of honeste life and conversation', with the words 'scismatically affected' following his name struck through.[11] He moved to Norwich in 1611, becoming rector of St Andrew (John More's parish), but died two years later and was buried in his church on 26 December 1613.

1. *Alum. Cantab.*, I. 176. It is unlikely that he was ever vicar of Fulbeck, Lincs., as here stated.
2. NRO DN REG/14/, fo. 128r. He compounded for the benefice on 28 September following: PRO E334/10, fo. 104r.
3. John More, *A table from the beginning of the world to this day* (Cambridge, 1593), Epistle dedicatory.
4. Collinson, *Religion of protestants*, p. 141, n.3.
5. BL, Add MS 27960, fo. 16.
6. Nicholas Bound, *An epistle of comfort for the afflicted* (London, 1594), Epistle dedicatory.
7. Nicholas Bound, *The doctrine of the Sabbath* (London, 1595), Preface.
8. *Ibid.*, p. 219.
9. Nicholas Bound, *The holy exercise of fasting* (Cambridge, 1604), homilies seven and eight.
10. *Ibid.,* epistle dedicatory.
11. NRO DN VIS 3/3, fo. 91r.

BYRD(E) (BIRD(E)), WILLIAM (d. 1599)

Rector of Boxford, Suffolk, 1563–99 (d.)

One of the original signatories of the Dedham conference, a fact long obscured by R. G. Usher's omission of his name, he was perhaps the William Bird who matriculated at Christ's College, Cambridge, in 1552 and may have graduated BA from St John's in 1556.[1] If so, he was one of the oldest members of the conference. Was he also the William Bird 'driven out' of Dedham with his wife during Mary's reign?[2]

At Boxford, Bird succeeded his namesake (and relative?), William Byrde, rector since 1553.[3] On the arrival in the parish of his son-in-law, Henry Sandes, as preacher and lecturer, Bird was perhaps content to play second fiddle. By 1585 he may even have begun to exhibit symptoms of senility. When the conference met at his house in Boxford on 4 October that year, Sandes took his father-in-law's place as speaker, excusing him because of 'sundrie busines that he had' (**36M**). The following month, Sandes proposed that Bird 'geve over his place to a third man, being aged' (**37M**). Nothing was concluded, but Bird was appointed speaker for the next meeting, to be held at Langham on 6 December (**38M**). This sounds cruel, for Langham is a long way from Boxford, and it was winter. In the event, Bird arrived late and Richard Dowe took his place. Bird was appointed speaker for the next meeting to be held at Stratford St Mary, but whether he came up to scratch is not recorded (**39M**). Yet when the conference met in Sandes's house in Boxford in May 1589, its penultimate meeting, Bird was able to function as moderator (**79M**).

The parochial history of Boxford after this date is obscure. 'Mr Chambers' – presumably Thomas Chambers, a friend of John Knewstub and a future rector of Assington, Suffolk – is mentioned in wills of 1596 and 1597 as 'minister' of Boxford.[4] Yet William Bird remained rector of Boxford until his death, surviving his wife by a year.[5] Joseph Bird, who may or may not have been a relation of William Bird, and/or Samuel Bird, sometime schoolmaster of Cockfield and minister of St Peter, Ipswich, became rector in 1600.[6]

1.   *Alum. Cantab.,* I, 156; Peile, *Biographical register,* I, 49.
2.   See above, p. lxiii.
3.   *Boxford churchwardens' accounts 1530–1566,* ed. Peter Northeast (Suffolk Record Society, XXIII, 1982), 106. It is possible that these two William Birds were one and the same, but an incumbency beginning in 1553 would not square with what seem to be the facts of a brief university career, and would necessarily imply that he had conformed under Mary.
4.   SRO Bury St Edmunds, WI/54/47; WI/56/76; will of Thomas Lovell, PRO PCC PROB 11/116 (85 Wingfield).
5.   *Topographer and Geneaologist,* ed. J. G. Nichols, I (London, 1846), 162.
6.   NRO, DN/REG/14, fo. 285r.

CARR, ROGER (?1543–1611)

Rector of [Little] Rayne, Essex, 1573–1611 (d.)

Carr matriculated sizar from Pembroke College, Cambridge, at Michaelmas 1566, graduating BA in early 1570.[1] He was instituted to Rayne on 23 January 1573 at the presentation of Henry Capell of Rayne Hall[2] and ordained priest by Edwin Sandys, bishop of London, on 6 January 1574 (BA; aged 30; born 'Runthmell', York diocese).[3] By this time he was certainly married.[4]

Granted a diocesan preaching licence on 28 November 1581,[5] Carr became a member of the Braintree conference, probably at its inception a few months later. In July 1583 he passed unscathed through John Aylmer's third episcopal visitation, presenting his preaching licence as required.[6] Early in 1584, however, he was one of the twenty-seven Essex ministers who petitioned against Archbishop Whitgift's drive for conformity by means of subscription to his three articles.[7] Present as a licensed preacher at the episcopal visitation of 1586, he was subsequently suspended.[8]

On 8 March 1587 a bill was introduced into parliament, well into its stormy final session, for the restoration of Carr, George Gifford, Ralph Hawden, John Huckle, William Tunstall and Giles Whiting. It looks very much like a specific appeal from the Braintree conference and was possibly designed to reinforce Sir John Higham's motion that same day for the 'amendment of some things whereunto ministers are required to be sworn' – a direct attack on Whitgift's most recent disciplinary proceedings.[9] Tunstall and Whiting were subsequently deprived of their benefices but Carr survived, remaining a member at Braintree probably until it ceased to meet. With Culverwell, Huckle, Rogers and Whiting he wrote to the Dedham conference on 7 June 1587, asking for the secondment of Laurence Newman.[10]

He was admonished to wear the surplice at the 1589 episcopal visitation and again told to certify that he was using it in that of 1592.[11] He is not known to have been cited thereafter for nonconformist practices and was probably one of those who after 1604, when James I insisted on the reintroduction of Whitgift's three articles as his yardstick of conformity within the church, reluctantly conformed. He was, however, listed amongst the 'diligent and sufficient' clergy of Essex in 1604.[12] His successor at Rayne was instituted on 20 January 1612, following his death.[13] He appears to have died intestate.

Three published works assigned to 'R.C.' were formally attributed to Carr, earning him an entry in *DNB*.[14]

1. *Alum. Cantab.*, I, 296. A younger brother, William, followed him to Pembroke and was rector of Twinstead, Essex, 1581–1615 (d.): *ibid.*
2. Reg. Grindal, fo. 169v. Often found as 'Little' Rayne in contemporary records to distinguish it from contiguous 'Great Rayne', by this time universally known as Braintree.
3. GL MS 9525/1, fo. 152r. Presumably Rothwell, in the West Riding.
4. His daughter Joan was married at Rayne in 1593. Eight younger children are recorded as baptized there between 1575 and 1594: ERO D/P 126/1. Of these, Gamaliel (b. 1587) succeeded his uncle William as rector of Twinstead.
5. LMA DL/C/333, fo. 270r.
6. GL MS 9537/5, fos. 2v, 55v.
7. *Seconde parte*, I, 225.
8. GL MS 9537/6, fo. 138r; *Seconde parte*, II, 164, 260.
9. *Seconde parte*, II, 258–9; for Higham's bill, see J. E. Neale, *Elizabeth I and her Parliament, 1584–1601* (1957), p. 162.
10. See above, p. 107.
11. GL MS 9537/7, fo. 37r; /8, fo. 36r.
12. 'A Viewe', p. 4.
13. Reg. Bancroft, fo. 164v.
14. See the entry by Brett Usher in *Oxford DNB*. *The defence of the soul against the strongest assaults of Satan* (1578) appears to be no longer extant (not in STC). *A Godly learned and fruitfull Sermon* (1584) on the fourteenth chapter of St John was dedicated to Sir William Pelham by one John Jorden, who claimed to have no personal knowledge of the author. The copy which survives in Lambeth Palace Library (shelfmark 1574. H.14; STC 21483) has a manuscript attribution on the flyleaf to 'D. Squire' – presumably Dr Adam Squire, archdeacon of Middlesex. *A godlie Form of Household Government* (1598) is now known to have been by Robert Cleaver (STC 5382).

CATELYN, RANULPH (1554–1613)

Rector of Great Wenham, Suffolk, 1585–1613 (d.)

Ranulph Catelyn was the son of Richard Catelyn, serjeant-at-law and gentleman of London. The family seems to have originated in Norfolk since Ranulph was apparently educated at Wymondham, where an elder contemporary was Richard Dowe. His elder brother Richard Catelyn matriculated at Gonville and Caius College, Cambridge, in 1561, went on to Lincoln's Inn without graduating and became lord of the manor of Woolverstone, Suffolk. Ranulph Catelyn matriculated pensioner at Caius from 1572, aged eighteen, five months after Richard Dowe had become a fellow-commoner there, and it seems reasonable to assume that a lifelong friendship developed between them. Catelyn became a fellow-commoner in 1575, proceeding BA in early 1577 and MA in 1580.[1] It is not known when and where he was ordained, and his whereabouts between 1580 and 1585 are unknown. But in 1585 he succeeded Bartimaeus Andrewes as rector of Great Wenham, on the presentation of Thomas Wyles of Great Wenham, who had the living in his gift *pro hac vice*, by grant from Thomas Cavendish of Trimley, Suffolk.[2] It sounds as if, following the resignation of Andrewes to the dissatisfaction of his flock, the 'people' of Wenham had been allowed their own free choice by a sympathetic patron.

Within four months of his induction at Wenham, Catelyn was proposed for membership of the conference and was formally admitted on 7 March 1586 (**40, 41MM**). Although within six months he had acted as both speaker and moderator (**46, 48MM**), there is evidence from the minutes of Catelyn's pastoral inexperience. When the conference met at his rectory in August 1587 (**59M**), he asked for prayers 'for his Church and people', which may indicate trouble. When the conference next met at Wenham, in October 1588 (**72M**), Catelyn needed advice on how to deal with two parishioners who were 'in hatred one against thother for wordes defamatory'. Could he admit them to communion? And how should he handle 'some froward poore men that were every way disordered'? And what was to be done when his people were given notice of a communion and told to present themselves for examination, but refused?

Catelyn was socially one of the better connected members of the Dedham conference, and he may have been part of a godly kinship network. In one of the most remarkable of all puritan wills, 'Mr Catelyn a student in the universitie of Cambridge' was left £10 by the wealthy widow Elizabeth Walter, daughter of John More, the most prominent of the godly magistrates of Ipswich and connected with William Cardinal, founder of the Dedham lectureship, who left a total of almost £1400 to godly causes.[3] This was after Catelyn's time, and the beneficiary may have been Robert Catlyn, subsequently a very radical vicar of All Saints Northampton,[4] although unknown to the university records. Almost nothing is known about Catelyn's incumbency at Wenham outside the record of the Dedham conference, except that in a visitation held in 1606 it was reported that the parish had not acquired the canons of 1604, and that Catelyn never wore the surplice, 'for that they never had any untill a weke before their examination'.[5] However, he was not disturbed, and remained rector of Wenham until 1613. Venn makes Catelyn rector of Naughton, Suffolk (n.d.) and of Holbrooke, Suffolk, in 1586. But it is unlikely that he was a pluralist, and Thomas Stoughton was at Naughton from the mid-1580s.

1. *Alum. Cantab.*, I, 308; Venn, *Biographical history*, p. 71.
2. NRO, DN/REG/14, fo. 129v.
3. PRO, PCC PROB 11/73 (15 Leicester); Collinson, 'PCM', p. 865.
4. HMC, *Various Collections, iii. Tresham Papers*, pp. 121–2.
5. NRO, DN/VIS/4/2/2.

CHAPMAN alias BARKER, EDMUND (c. 1538–1602)

Canon of Norwich, 1570–?6 (?resig.); lecturer of Dedham, Essex, 1577–1602 (d.)

Perhaps from the family of these names long established in Sibton, Suffolk,[1] Chapman matriculated sizar from Gonville Hall, Cambridge, in November 1554. He graduated BA from Trinity in 1559, becoming a fellow in 1560 and proceeding MA in 1562. He was University Preacher in 1567, proceeding BD in 1569.[2]

He was ordained deacon at Norwich 8 June 1566 ('Chapman *alias* Barker').[3] At the petition of John Whitgift, Master of Trinity, he received letters patent on 16 March 1570 from the Lord Keeper, Sir Nicholas Bacon, as canon of the first prebend in Norwich cathedral, and was installed on 24 March.[4] It is one of the ironies of Elizabethan churchmanship that, having successfully promoted Chapman to a prebendal stall, Whitgift immediately emerged as Thomas Cartwright's strongest opponent and Chapman as one of Cartwright's most prominent supporters. Later in 1570 Chapman and other members of the Norwich chapter – Thomas Fowle, George Gardiner and John Walker (later archdeacon of Essex) – entered the cathedral and destroyed the organ.[5]

As town preacher at Bedford in 1572, Chapman was suspended by Thomas Cooper, bishop of Lincoln, for contentious sermonizing. An oblique reference to his recent 'displacement' in a letter of Archbishop Matthew Parker, dated 15 November 1573,[6] led earlier writers to assume that he must have been deprived of his prebend and as the Norwich chapter records make no mention of the installation of a successor, this assumption has been perpetuated in the modern edition of Le Neve's *Fasti*.[7] In fact, on

12 April 1574, George Gardiner, by now dean of Norwich, asked Bishop Parkhurst to 'trauell' with Chapman 'that he may stay upon his prebend and [receive] some other helpe in Norwich' – presumably one of the city's livings.[8] Likewise, the local godly seem to have been concerned lest he should depart for want of a reasonable income. On 28 June 1574 William Heydon wrote to Nathaniel Bacon: 'Be not forgetfull of Mr Chapman, who wilbe a good helpe for the liften up of Christe, if wee *by your good meanes* may injoye him'.[9] He was still in residence in Norwich on 3 January 1575 when Parkhurst noted with displeasure that during the Christmas season he and others had 'enveighed against the mannor of the singing' in the cathedral 'indiscreetly and contrary to Her majesties godly proceedings and my liking'. His name also occurs on a list of those who had not observed order hitherto but, probably in late 1573 or else in 1574, had 'promysed a conformitie requiring a respette of tyme'.[10]

The balance of probabilities, therefore, is that Chapman finally resigned his prebend because it did not provide an adequate income or else, after the arrival of Edmund Freke as bishop in November 1575, following Parkhurst's death, recognized that the writing was on the wall.[11] He seems thereafter to have severed all connexion with Norwich but maintained some influence in and around Bedford for at least a further decade.[12]

In 1577 John Aylmer, bishop of London, informed Lord Burghley that Chapman, William Charke, John Field and Thomas Wilcox were currently preaching 'God knows what' in private households.[13] Chapman gravitated to the Stour valley, where his brother-in-law, William Cardinal of Great Bromley, Recorder of Colchester and an MP in the parliament of 1572,[14] created a lectureship for him at Dedham.[15] Although no preacher was listed there during Aylmer's primary visitation of London diocese in July 1577, Chapman was granted Aylmer's licence to preach throughout Essex on 2 November following, as of Dedham.[16] The foundation of the Dedham lectureship can thus be dated to the autumn of 1577. It is probably no coincidence that Chapman was incorporated BD, and then proceeded DD, at Oxford on 7 and 10 July 1578.[17] Robert, earl of Leicester, was Chancellor of Oxford and whilst Chapman's elevation was not necessarily his personal seal of approval for the Dedham lectureship it was undoubtedly intended to send out a very strong signal to Aylmer – of whose elevation Leicester had probably disapproved – that Chapman could expect his backing in a crisis.

Although Chapman was not listed as preacher at Dedham in the episcopal visitation of 1580,[18] Aylmer wrote to inform him on 12 January 1581 that he had suspended Timothy Fitzallen, vicar of Dedham since 1578, and invited him to act as *locum* during Fitzallen's 'inhibition', threatening his suspension if he failed to comply. Presumably Chapman did so.[19]

In October 1582 Chapman was organizer-in-chief of the Dedham conference and remained its presiding intellect until it ceased to meet in June 1589. It first met on 3 December 1582 at Crick's house in East Bergholt, when Chapman acted as moderator and was chosen speaker for the next meeting at his house in Dedham (**1, 2MM**). On 4 February 1583 Chapman asked the conference's advice 'tutching the publishing' of a short catechism, the brethren having 'perused and allowed' its doctrine (**3M**). His only accredited work, it appeared anonymously the same year as *A catechisme with a prayer annexed, meete for all christian families*, the prayer being followed by the initials 'E.C'. It enshrines the proposition that true faith in God is implanted 'by no other means but by the preaching of his holy word' (sig. A6v).

Excused from Aylmer's visitation in July 1583, Chapman was summoned to appear in consistory as a matter of routine before Bartholomewtide,[20] but his appearance is not recorded in the concurrent act book of office. He and the other Dedham members seem to have distanced themselves from – indeed, may have been partly shielded by – the storm which blew up in October over Aylmer's suspension of Colchester's town preacher, George Northey, whilst Chapman himself seems to have been in no way implicated in Richard Parker's troubles over the surplice at this time.

The Dedham papers have disappointingly little to tell about the subscription crisis of 1583–4. There is no hint that Chapman was suspended for not subscribing and by August 1584 he was even proposing that a 'reconciliation' be offered to the bishops; he found that the brethren were against him (**21M**). After the collapse of Whitgift's campaign in the ensuing weeks Chapman appears to have been undisturbed until after the episcopal visitation of 1586. Although merely listed present by the visitors on 22 July he was one of those suspended for the surplice in that visitation 'and since'.[21] But once again there is no hint of this in the minutes – this despite the fact that he was appointed one of the commissioners for Lexden deanery appointed to oversee the newly-introduced clerical exercises, first held in Colchester on 16 September.[22]

On 5 February 1588 Parker asked what he might do 'for supplie of his place', being now suspended again by Aylmer (**65M**). Since there was no meeting in the first week of March it would seem that Chapman had taken it upon himself to go to London and plead with Aylmer personally on Parker's behalf. He was certainly present on 9 March in Aylmer's chapel at Fulham when the bishop announced his intention of carrying out the ordination of Thomas Ryther. With his chaplain, Nicholas Smith, vicar of Fulham, Aylmer proceeded with all the formalities as far as the laying on of hands and then requested Chapman to assist. Chapman refused. When ordered to do so Chapman again refused, saying that he would go no further than remember Ryther in his prayers. Aylmer and Smith thereupon completed the ordination. Aylmer immediately 'sat judicially', demanding to know Chapman's reasons for refusal. He replied that, his own business being finished and prayers over, he had been on the point of departure and that Ryther was personally unknown to him. Aylmer thereupon read out Ryther's letters of commendation and asked him why, for his manifest contumacy, Chapman should not be coerced with the usual ecclesiastical penalties. Chapman offering no reason, the bishop formally pronounced him contumacious and suspended him from all his functions and from preaching.[23]

It was a mean cat-and-mouse tactic and it surely explains the first entry in the next Dedham meeting on 31 March, when William Tey asked the brethren to consider whether the bishops 'were anie longer to be tolerated or noe' (**66M**). Since, however, Chapman agreed at the same meeting to preach at Crick's 'election' to the 'pastoral charge' at East Bergholt, his suspension cannot have lasted long. Alternatively – and there are many alternatives in the Dedham records – he ignored it.

The eightieth and last meeting of the conference took place on the eve of Aylmer's most decisive visitation yet, that of July 1589. Chapman, however, did not come under any kind of threat[24] and was not subsequently called into consistory. Indeed, despite his earlier iconoclasm, Chapman's eirenic superintendency at Dedham belies the claim of its contemporary opponents that the movement was led only by irresponsible hotheads. He frequently urged restraint and moderation on less temperate colleagues and was not one of those leaders examined or prosecuted between 1589 and 1592 for their clandestine activities.

At Aylmer's last visitation in September 1592 he was merely listed present as doctor and licensed preacher. He was excused attendance from Bancroft's primary visitation (1598) but this does not seem to argue declining health: in the last months of his life he was still lecturing twice a week, on Tuesdays and Fridays.[25] In William Cardinal's will (January 1596) he received substantial property in Great Bromley as long as he remained lecturer. By his own, dated 12 May 1601, he bequeathed half his goods and all his property in Dedham and nearby Ardleigh to his wife, Susan, their son Paul (now just fourteen) to inherit after Susan's death. Bequests to his second son, John, included a property in Bread Street, London. His daughter Susan was to receive £200 at marriage or majority but his daughter Chrispian is mentioned only in the codicil. There were minor bequests to his brother Nicholas and his sons Thomas and Edmund. No member of the Dedham conference was remembered.[26]

Chapman died on 7 November 1602, aged sixty-four. Two of the three executors appointed renounced executorship and letters of administration were therefore issued to the third, Simon Fenn, clothier of Dedham, on 10 February 1603.[27] Chapman's gravestone and funeral monument in Dedham survive and have been described in print.[28]

1. See John Moore, 'Sibton Church', *Proceedings of the Suffolk Institute of archaeology and natural history*, VIII (1892–4), 60–4. This article mentions two men named Edmund Chapman *alias* Barker, to one of whom there is a memorial inscription.

2. *Alum. Cantab.*, I, 321. The identification with the Marian exile from Hastings who was living in Aarau with a wife and child in 1558 must be discounted: C. H. Garrett, *The Marian exiles* (Cambridge, 1938), p. 79. It was probably this man who was ordained deacon by Nicholas Bullingham at Lambeth, on behalf of Matthew Parker, archbishop of Canterbury, on 10 March 1560: *Reg. Parker*, I, 342 ('Edmundus Barker'). He is probably identifiable with *Edward* Barker, appointed a Six Preacher at Canterbury that year, who died in 1570 as rector of Westbere, near Canterbury: Strype, *Parker*, I, 144; II, 25; Derek Ingram Hill, *The Six Preachers of Canterbury cathedral* (Ramsgate, 1982), p. 31. In that case there was a third clerical Edmund Chapman active at the beginning of Elizabeth's reign: rector of Marsham, Norfolk (1559–76) and erroneously identified by the Venns with the present subject.

3. NRO, ORR/1b, fo. 42r.

4. BL, Lansdowne MS 443, fo. 182v. *Fasti*, Ely, Norwich, Westminster and Worcester, p. 51.

5. PRO SP12/73/171; *Parkhurst*, p. 41.

6. *Parker Correspondence*, p. 450.

7. *Fasti*, Ely, Norwich, Westminster and Worcester, p. 51.

8. *Parkhurst*, p. 239.

9. BL, Add MS 41,140, fo. 7r; our italics.

10. *Parkhurst*, pp. 221, 254.

11. Collinson, *EPM*, p. 223.

12. He had the ear of Lord Keeper Bacon. On 19 December 1572 Thomas Wells received letters patent for the vicarage of Milton 'Harney' (?Ernest), Bedfordshire, on the petition of Bedford's town preacher (*concionator ville Bedford*); on 20 April and 24 July 1573 John Kytchener and William Gulson received letters patent respectively for the rectories of Gravenhurst, Bedfordshire, and Thrapston, Northamptonshire, both at the petition of 'Mr Chapman *concionator*': BL, Lansdowne MS 443, fos. 207r, 208v, 210v. As late as 2 August 1585 he solicited the Dedham members for a suitable candidate for 'the pastors place in Bedforde' (**33M**).

13. Collinson, *EPM*, p. 202.

14. Hasler, *House of commons*, I, 536–7.

15. By mid-1578 at the latest Chapman had married Susan Cardinal. The marriage took place neither in Dedham nor in Great Bromley but on 9 April 1579 the Dedham parish registers record that 'Mr Chapman buryed a child of his'. Paul, son of Dr Chapman, was baptized in Dedham on 20 March 1582 and a second son, Ezechiell, on 3 December 1583. Paul was buried on 19 October 1586 and Ezechiell on 1 June 1587. A second Paul, who was to survive his father, was baptized on 10 January 1587. The baptisms of a second surviving son, John, and of two daughters, Susan and Chrispian (sic), are not found in the Dedham registers. Richard Wane, 'clerke', who oversaw the transcription of the old paper registers on to parchment at the end of the century, noted amongst the baptism records that from January 1588 until September 1590 there was 'nothing to be found'. The baptisms of John and Chrispian probably fall into this period. Susan, the elder daughter, was presumably baptized elsewhere during the early 1580s. There are similar gaps (1587–9) in the marriage records and (January 1588 – October 1590) in the burial records: ERO D/P 26/1.

16. GL MS 9537/4, fo. 32r; LMA DL/C/333, fo. 90r.

17. *Alum. Oxon.*, I, 261.

18. GL MS 9537/4, fo. 95v.

19. LMA DL/C/333, fo. 242r; see above, pp. lxxi–ii, for the full details.

20. GL MS 9537/5, fo. 63v.

21. GL MS 9537/6, fo. 142v; *Seconde parte*, II, 261.

22. GL MS 9537/6, fos. 145v, 178r. The other commissioners included Archdeacon Withers and Laurence Newman.
23. LMA DL/C/334, fo. 211r.
24. GL MS 9537/7, fo. 46r.
25. GL MSS 9537/8, fo. 55r; /9, fo. 100v; LMA DL/C/303, fo. 550r: entry concerning Meredith Powell, vicar of Dedham, dated 29 March 1602. This may be a clerical error. See above, p. lxxvi.
26. Registered will, PRO PCC PROB11/101 (16 Bolein).
27. *Ibid.*
28. G. H. Rendall, 'Dedham tombstones', *Transactions of the Essex archaeological society,* new series XVIII (1928), 245–53.

COCK(E)(COOKE), WILLIAM (d. 1619)

Perpetual curate of St Giles, Colchester, c. 1585–1619 (d.)

A non-graduate, Cocke served in Colchester successively as sequestrator of St Nicholas (c. 1577–80) and sequestrator of St James (1580–c. 85) before becoming perpetual curate of St Giles, a donative in the gift of John Lucas.[1]

At the episcopal visitation of 1583 he was inhibited from preaching in his own cure until properly licensed. Almost immediately granted a diocesan licence,[2] he was thereafter accepted by the local godly, putting his signature to the form of limited subscription drawn up by the Dedham conference in late 1584 and to 'Certain requests' submitted to Archdeacon George Withers.[3] At the episcopal visitation of 1586 he was nevertheless ordered to attend the newly inaugurated clerical exercises. He was at the same time admonished to wear the surplice once one had been provided, and shortly afterwards was under threat of deprivation for failing to do so.[4] He survived further monitions on the question of the surplice at the visitation of 1589 and in that of 1592 was described as *concionator notus.*[5]

Cocke was listed amongst the 'diligent and sufficient' clergy of Essex in 1604.[6] A brass tablet on the south wall of the nave of St Giles church records that he was buried in 1619, having been pastor there for thirty-four years, and his wife Anna in 1625.[7]

1. GL MS 9537/10, fo. 39v; GL MS 9537/4, fos. 31r, 93r; LMA DL/C/333, fo. 195v; GL MS 9537/5, fo. 58v.
2. GL MS 9537/5, fos. 3r, 58v; licence not found in vicar general's books but rehearsed in the visitation call book of 1598: GL MS 9537/9, fo. 104v.
3. See above, pp. 82, 87.
4. GL MS 9537/6, fo. 139v; *Seconde parte*, II, 164, 261.
5. GL MS 9537/7, fo. 40v; /8, fo. 51v.
6. 'A Viewe', p. 6.
7. Davids, *Annals*, p. 114.

CRICK, RICHARD (d. 1591)

Minor canon and lecturer, Norwich Cathedral, 1571–c. 1579; preacher at East Bergholt, Suffolk, c. 1580–91 (d.)

Richard Crick was the son of Nicholas Crick, a tailor of Hadleigh, who survived him. He married Hannah Beamond, sister of Julian Beamond, a substantial Hadleigh clothier, who brought to the marriage a house in Hadleigh.[1] With Edmund Chapman, Crick was one of the heavyweights of the conference. Like Chapman, he was a beneficiary of the wealthy clothier and gentleman, William Cardinal, and with Chapman, in the same year, and probably thanks to the sympathetic interest of the earl of Leicester as chancellor of the University, became a DD of Oxford. He had matriculated from Magdalen in 1562, had taken his BA in 1566 and his MA in 1570, and was a fellow of the college from

1564 to 1571.[2] He left Oxford to become a chaplain to Bishop John Parkhurst of Norwich and a minor canon of the cathedral, joining a staff which included his future colleagues in the Dedham conference, Chapman, who was a canon, and Richard Dowe, another minor canon. His prime function would have been one of preaching, but he was also one of the ecclesiastical commissioners for the diocese.[3]

There was soon evidence of Crick's militant nonconformity. In July 1573, in the aftermath of the furore over *An admonition to the parliament* (1572), he preached a sermon at Paul's Cross in London in support of the admonitionists, 'saying that they sought a godly reformation and a perfection in the government of the churche', things reported to Archbishop Parker to have been 'sediciously uttered'.[4] Crick slipped Parker's noose and returned to Norwich, hoping to resume his cathedral lectures, but Parkhurst suspended him, pending advice from Parker.[5] Parkhurst was finding that his efforts to bring in new hot protestant blood to reform a typically conservative cathedral chapter had blown up in his face. Already, in the summer of 1570, before Crick's arrival on the scene, four of the new men had taken it upon themselves to demolish the organ and to commit other unspecified 'outrages', which had provoked letters of severe rebuke from the queen to Parkhurst and from Leicester to Parker.[6] In December 1573, Parkhurst commended his chancellor for 'restraining' Crick's 'rashe attempt' (whatever that was), and laid down a standard establishment, middle-way line. 'Spare no person, aswell such as being to foreward nede a sharpe bitte and reyne to restreyne ther haste, and such also as being to slowe do wilfully and stubbornely, like resty jades drawe backward, and therfore deserve sharpe sporing.'[7] Crick was presumably a prominent participant in the Norwich prophesyings set up during the vacancy of the see following the death of Parkhurst, a 'presbyterian' model for what was later done at Dedham.[8]

With the arrival of Parkhurst's successor, Bishop Edmund Freke, Crick and his friends were in trouble and were suspended. In September 1576 Crick was one of six Norwich preachers petitioning Lord Burghley for relief,[9] and two years later was one of seven signing a limited submission.[10] Not long after this Crick, in spite of his troubles now Dr Crick, with Dr Chapman and Richard Dowe, left Norwich for the Stour valley in what looks like a planned migration. In 1580, the Ipswich magistrates corresponded with Crick about the appointment of a preacher, the earliest evidence we have that he had moved into their vicinity.[11]

Crick settled at East Bergholt, on the Suffolk bank of the Stour. Chapman's brother-in-law and the founder of the Dedham lectureship, William Cardinal, owned two of the four East Bergholt manors, and other Cardinals had substantial interests in the parish.[12] So we can safely assume that Cardinal was behind Crick's placement. At the time of his death, Crick described himself, and was so described by those who made the inventory of his goods, as 'pastor of the Churche of God in (or, according to the inventory, 'of') Eastbergholt'.[13] He probably claimed this title only after the displacement of his Dedham conference colleague, John Tilney. The 1585 will of the East Bergholt glover John Backhouse, witnessed by William Cardinal, made a bequest to 'Mr doctor Cricke of Eastbergholt', and money for the poor to be distributed 'at the discretion of Mr doctor Crick', but does not accord him any status in the parish.[14] There is no evidence that either Crick or Tilney was ever in possession of the rectory of East Bergholt, although in the year of Crick's death the crown did present Dr William Jones, a founding fellow of Emmanuel College, Cambridge, and a man of impeccably moderate puritan convictions, who served the parish for forty-five years.[15]

When the conference met at East Bergholt, it was at 'Hog Lane', which eighteenth-century maps and an enclosure award identify as a public highway leading in a north-easterly direction from the nucleus of the village towards Manningtree, with two farms both called Hog Lane.[16] No doubt Hog Lane was where Crick lived, in what his inventory suggests was a substantial house (and, for the purposes of secret meetings, a 'safe house'), with a study containing £20-worth of books.[17] However tempting it may be to locate some kind of separatist congregation at Hog Lane, and in 1606 there was evidence of separatism in the parish,[18] the Dedham ministers were not separatists, and Tilney and Crick both probably ministered in the parish church, having received some kind of calling from 'the people' (*scil.* William Cardinal?). In January 1584, Crick was listed among Suffolk ministers suspended for not subscribing to Whitgift's articles,[19] but although there are no surviving records of the archdeaconry of Sudbury which would record any steps taken to deal with him, it is likely that he enjoyed effective immunity from ecclesiastical discipline. Crick had chosen his place of exile from Norwich well.

The first meeting of the conference was held at East Bergholt (**1M**) (but Hog Lane was mentioned for the first time only in September 1583 (**10M**)), with Crick the speaker and Chapman the moderator; the second at Chapman's house at Dedham, Chapman the speaker, Crick the moderator (**2M**). Crick took the leading role in the debates about the Sabbath which dominated early meetings of the conference, and which have left behind so much paper, all that survives of his prowess in divinity.

In November 1584 (**24M**), Crick asked the conference 'how he shuld deale with some obstynate contemners of his doctryne', and in the following year he repeatedly raised the issue of 'some disordered persons' (**30M**), who had disturbed him in his ministry (**28M**) and 'wold not heare nor come to the Communion' (**29M**). Crick was told to use his pastoral gifts to 'draw them forwarde and to wynne them', and, if that failed, and as a last resort, to excommunicate them, although some thought he should 'rather desire the chieff and forwardest in the Congregation to deale with them', and if that didn't work, to bring them before a magistrate for punishment as 'raylors' (**32M**). It is interesting that no-one suggested that the churchwardens should be asked to present the offenders to the archdeacon's court. East Bergholt continued to be a disorderly place, and in March 1587, Crick had to complain about the 'outrage' of a 'skimmington'[20] conducted while he was absent at Hadleigh, to the detriment of his 'credit' (**54M**). Separatism among the most 'forward' may also have been a problem. In March 1586 Crick wanted to know whether he might pray in public for 'those that single themselves from the Church', as 'men diseased' (**41M**).

When Bartimaeus Andrewes declared his intention to abandon his parish of Great Wenham for the post of town preacher at Yarmouth, Crick was the most outspoken critic of the move, insisting on the inseparability of the bond joining a pastor to his people (**Extra M**, 17 February 1585). Crick's 'congregationalist' convictions would soon affect him personally and directly. When, in 1587, 'the church' of East Bergholt decided to dispense with the services of John Tilney and to choose Crick in his place, the conference avoided open discussion of the matters between Crick and Tilney, or Tilney and the church, referred the issue to six senior members (**59, 61MM**), but was initially reluctant to accept Crick's 'calling to be Pastor of Barfold', 'in dislike of the people's course in rejecting and receyving their Pastors without counsell of others' (**65M**); although it was agreed at the next meeting that Chapman, who made himself the go-between in Crick's dealings with the conference, should preach at Crick's 'election' to the charge (**66M**). Perhaps some of the conference members had taken the side of Tilney, who in March 1586 had asked, pointedly, 'how he might deale to kepe one out that went secretlie to supplant him' (**41M**). Two months later, the conference met in East Bergholt, not at Hog Lane but at Tilney's house (**44M**). At this point, Crick was evidently on the verge of transferring his allegiance to the Suffolk conference with which Henry Sandes enjoyed cross-membership (**53M**). He was by now no longer on speaking terms with his brethren of the conference. In a letter which he was obliged to write since he could not confront them face to face (there had been 'boysterous woordes', perhaps on both sides), he pulled rank on Tilney, referred to his 'evill dealing', and took responsibility for the fact that he had been 'moste worthely throwne out'. Crick declared that he was as 'jealous' for the honour of what was now his church as any of them were for their own, and that in future his church would seek advice from as far beyond London as London was from East Bergholt, rather than from Dedham, 'though ye would beg to be of counsel with them'.[21]

Crick's last recorded intervention in proceedings, and in history, was when, in January 1589, he put the formal question whether churchwardens and their offices were lawful (**75M**). Now what lay behind that? Through these elusive entries, the murky religious politics of East Bergholt are seen, as in a glass, darkly. Crick died in 1591, leaving three sons, Joseph, Samuel and John, and two daughters, Hannah and Marie, all minors.[22]

1. Will of Richard Crick, probated 14 January 1592, NRO, 199 Andrewes (MF 69); Muskett, *Suffolk manorial families*, II, 323. So 'the ungodlie sermon' made by 'mr Beaman of hadleigh, defacing the man of Antwerpe' (**11M**), which Crick was deputed to investigate, had perhaps been preached by a relation. On his death in 1580, Julian Beamond left £20 to Crick, £5 to Edmund Chapman and a copy of Foxe's *Actes and monuments* to the church of Hadleigh. See Craig, *Reformation, politics and polemics*, p. 174, n.96.
2. *Alum. Oxon.*, I, 349.
3. *Parkhurst*, p. 130.
4. London, Inner Temple Library, MS Petyt 538, vol. 47, fol. 476.
5. *Parkhurst*, p. 215.
6. PRO, SP 12/73/68; Magdalene College, Cambridge, Pepysian Library, MS 'Papers of State', II, 633–40. 7.
7. *Parkhurst*, p. 217.
8. Collinson, *EPM*, pp. 213–14.
9. Copies of the petition in *Seconde parte*, I, 143–6; BL, Add MS 48101, fos. 132–4 (where it is described as a 'supplication of Norwich ministers to Parliament').
10. Copies in *Seconde parte*, I, 146; BL, Add MS 48023; PRO SP 12/126/4,5, and in the Dedham papers (see above, p. 87).
11. SRO Ipswich, Ipswich Chamberlain's Accts., no. 18 (1580).
12. W. A. Copinger, *Manors of Suffolk*, vi (Manchester, 1910), 18, 21; T. F. Paterson, *East Bergholt in Suffolk* (Cambridge, 1923), pp. 118–21, 168; will of William Cardinal, PRO, PCC PROB 11/92 (97 Lewyn); 1574 will of Richard Cardinal, clothier of East Bergholt, mentioning his brother Adam Cardinal, also of East Bergholt: SRO Ipswich, IC/AA2/25/2–35.
13. NRO, 199 Andrewes (MF 69); NRO, DN/INV/913 (MF/RO/483/2).
14. SRO Ipswich, IC/AA2/30/358.
15. Paterson, *East Bergholt in Suffolk*, p. 78; Sarah Bendall, Christopher Brooke and Patrick Collinson, *A history of Emmanuel College, Cambridge* (Woodbridge, 1999), p. 44.
16. SRO Ipswich, V 5/5/3.1; Ipswich Public Library, Local Pamphlets, East Bergholt Enclosure Award, 942.64, p. 4.
17. NRO, DN/INV/913. But in April 1585, the conference met 'at Barford at Hoglane at Mr Cockrels'.
18. NRO, DN/VIS/ 4/2/2, 'Estbarfolde'.
19. *Seconde parte*, I, 243.
20. See above, p. 36.
21. See above pp. 147–9.
22. NRO, will of Richard Crick, 199 Andrewes (MF 69).

CULVERWELL, EZEKIEL (c. 1554–1631)

Preacher at Felsted, Essex, c. 1587–92; rector of Great Stambridge, Essex, 1592–1609 (depr.)

Second son of Nicholas Culverwell of St Martin Vintry (d. 1569), London merchant and member of the Haberdashers' Company, and his wife Elizabeth (d. 1589), Ezekiel

Culverwell graduated BA at Oxford 1573, proceeding MA in June 1577.[1] His college is not known to the records but in view of his father's endowment of a 'preachership' in divinity there in his will, it was undoubtedly Magdalen. Thus, like John Field, he was probably a disciple of Magdalen's president, Laurence Humphrey. Incorporated MA at Cambridge in 1578,[2] he was involved in clerical 'exercises' there organized by his brother-in-law, Laurence Chaderton, who had married his sister Cecilia.[3] According to his own account, he was ordained deacon and priest at Lincoln in 1585, by which time he was probably married.[4] Nothing is known of his first wife.

Culverwell arrived in Essex as household chaplain at Leighs Priory, principal seat of Robert 3rd Lord Rich, probably in late 1586 or early 1587, in the aftermath of John Aylmer's episcopal visitation of 1586. Establishing a strong friendship with Richard Rogers, lecturer of Wethersfield, he joined the Braintree conference of ministers, earning Rogers's admiration for re-energizing it.[5] His nonconformity soon came to Aylmer's attention and as 'preacher of Felsted' he was amongst those recorded as suspended 'in his last visitation and since for the surplice'.[6] With Carr, Huckle, Rogers and Whiting he wrote to the Dedham conference on 7 June 1587, asking for the second-ment of Laurence Newman.[7]

At the visitation of July 1589 Culverwell was present and ordered to administer the sacraments according to the Book of Common Prayer.[8] Having failed to certify that he had done so in early October, he found himself faced at the end of the same month with a comprehensive series of twenty-one articles, probably drawn up by Thomas Rust, vicar of Felsted, in which his nonconformist practices were comprehensively scrutinized. The court hearings were admirably handled by Edward Stanhope, Aylmer's vicar general, who refused to turn the case into a witch-hunt and in mid-November ostensibly achieved a reconciliation between Culverwell and Rust.[9]

Culverwell was still listed preacher of Felsted at the visitation of 1592 and ordered to catechize instead of delivering afternoon sermons.[10] On 23 December that year he was instituted rector of Great Stambridge at the presentation of Robert Lawson, doubtless after some promise of partial conformity.[11] In 1598 he married as his second wife Winifred (nee Hildersham), widow of Edward Barefoot.[12] He was present at the 1598 visitation as rector and a preacher licensed by Aylmer in 1585 (sic).[13] Following the death in 1603 of Arthur Dent, Culverwell saw his *The Ruine of Rome* through the press, adding a dedicatory epistle to Lord Rich.[14] In April 1605 he solemnized the marriage of Mary Forth of Great Stambridge to John Winthrop, future Governor of Massachusetts.[15]

Put under pressure following the promulgation of the constitutions and canons of 1604, Culverwell refused to pay clerical dues that year on the grounds that he would rather give up his living than 'compromise himself to the canons of the church'.[16] He was called into consistory on 22 March 1605, following Richard Bancroft's last visita-tion in 1604, being 'not persuaded that it is expedient' to use the prescribed ceremonies. He failed to attend because of illness: William Negus, also summoned that day, pledged that he would appear by the last day of term.[17] He duly did so on 13 May 1605 and was ordered to attend the High Commission.[18] No further monition is recorded.

Culverwell was summoned into the consistory court on 7 November 1605 for failing to appear at Richard Vaughan's primary visitation that summer but the case was there-after prorogued, on no fewer than seven occasions, throughout Vaughan's short episco-pate.[19] Again cited on 7 November 1607 for absence from the primary visitation of Thomas Ravis, having been excused *per literas*, he only appeared on 10 December. He confessed he had not used the surplice or the sign of the cross; admitted some standing, some sitting to communion; and had used the prayer book but 'not in all points'. Asked if he would conform, he refused 'and as he hathe laboured so he will looke to satisfy his conscience'.[20]

There is no further reference in the consistory court records until 22 March 1609 when the vicar general recorded that intimations dated 20 March were to be dispatched to the patrons of Great Stambridge, Leigh, Little Leighs and Vange, void by the deprivations of Ezekiel Culverwell, William Negus, William Buckley and Camille Rusticens respectively. 'All 4 the same 20th of Marche depriued by the highe Commission[er]s'.[21] All four were back in consistory on 4 and 21 May following to explain their contempt in failing to conform to rites and ceremonies; all were then dismissed pending a new monition.[22]

Culverwell apparently spent the rest of his life in London, where he became part of a godly network which included John Burgess, John Dod, Richard Sibbes, Richard Stock and James Ussher, as well as his nephew William Gouge. He published *A treatise of faith* (1623) and other tracts.[23] His will, dated 5 July 1630, was proved 9 May 1631 in the commissary court of London.[24] He was buried in the parish of St Antholin on 14 April 1631.[25]

1. *Alum. Oxon.*, I, 362.
2. *Alum. Cantab.*, I, 432.
3. Samuel Clarke, *A general martyrologie* (1677), part 2, p. 133. See Collinson, *EPM*, p. 126.
4. LMA DL/C/616, p. 97.
5. Knappen, *Two puritan diaries*, pp. 53–63.
6. *Seconde parte*, II, 260.
7. See above, p. 107.
8. GL MS 9537/7, fo. 33v.
9. LMA DL/C/616, pp. 6, 97, 160.
10. GL MS 9537/8, fo. 65v.
11. Reg. Grindal, fo. 270r.
12. *London marriage allegations* (London, 1887), I, 256. It is possible that Winifred was sister of Arthur Hildersham.
13. GL MS 9537/9, fo. 128r. There is no record of a diocesan preaching licence in the vicar general's books.
14. His reference to his 'near conjunction' with his 'late brother' (sig. 1v) later led to the erroneous assumption that Dent had married a daughter of Nicholas Culverwell. It remains possible, however, that the first Mrs Culverwell was Dent's sister.
15. Winthrop later wrote that it was Culverwell who had converted him to true religion, and the two men continued to correspond long after Mary Winthrop's death. Two of the only three surviving letters of Culverwell (the latter dated 1618) were preserved by Winthrop himself: *Winthrop papers*, I, 234–5.
16. PRO SP14/10A/48; dated 2 December 1604.
17. LMA DL/C/618, p. 260.
18. LMA DL/C/617, p. 682.
19. *Ibid.*, p. 899; LMA DL/C/304, pp. 311, 351, 637, 662, 672, 686, 698.
20. LMA DL/C/306, pp. 11, 64.
21. LMA DL/C/339, fo. 57r. Successor instituted by his deprivation 27 March 1609: Reg. Bancroft, fo. 129r.
22. LMA DL/C/308, pp. 3, 38–9.
23. For which see David Como, 'Puritans, predestination and the construction of orthodoxy in early seventeenth-century England' in Peter Lake and Michael Questier, eds., *Conformity and orthodoxy in the English church, c.1560–1660* (Woodbridge, 2000), pp. 64–87.
24. GL MS 9171/26, fos. 147v–8r. Principal legacies were to his daughter Sarah Barefoot (£100), she to be sole executrix, and to her son Benedict (£200). In the event of Benedict's death before majority, £100 was to be bestowed on the Feofees for Impropriations, the other £100 to Sarah for her sole use. Minor bequests included £10 to 'Margaret Cheuers for her self and her son, Ezekiel' and one third of all his Latin books to Ezekiel 'Chevers', very probably his godson and subsequently the most celebrated of all New England's godly schoolmasters.
25. J. L. Chester and G. J. Armytage, eds., *The parish registers of St Antholin, Budge Row, London . . . and of St John Baptist on Walbrook*, Harleian Soc., VIII (1883), 65.

DENT(E), ARTHUR (c. 1553–1603)

Curate of Danbury, Essex, 1577–80; rector of South Shoebury, Essex, 1580–1603 (d.)

Born in Melton Mowbray, Leicestershire, son of William Dent, Arthur Dent matriculated pensioner from Christ's College, Cambridge, in November 1571, graduating BA in early 1576 and proceeding MA in 1579. He was ordained deacon at Peterborough on 29 March 1577 and priest by John Aylmer, bishop of London, on 16 May 1577 (BA; of Christ's; born Melton; aged 24).[1] Appointed curate by George Withers, rector of Danbury and archdeacon of Colchester, he was listed present at the episcopal visitation on 13 July 1577.[2] He was cited before the archdeacon of Essex[3] on 11 December that year for refusing to church women who wore 'kerchiefs', on the grounds that the practice was 'superstitious', and on 28 May 1578 for conducting an irregular marriage.[4] He received a diocesan preaching licence ('Denton', MA) on 10 October 1579.[5] Present at Aylmer's second episcopal visitation on 11 July 1580,[6] Dent was instituted rector of South Shoebury on 17 December 1580 at the presentation of Robert 2nd Lord Rich, compounding for the benefice on 19 December.[7]

When Rich and Aylmer clashed during the following months over quasi-congregational meetings at Rochford Hall, orchestrated by Robert Wright, Dent appears to have been unsympathetic to his patron's proceedings. He was one of several local clergy who deposed that preachers had been 'openly examined and rebuked for their sermons in a great audience in the Hall'.[8] Thus from the beginning the evidence for Dent's involvement in the politico-religious agitation of the 1580s is ambivalent. His reputation as one of the most successful religious authors of his time was, however, established by the publication in 1583 of *A sermon of repentance*, preached at Leigh, Essex, on 7 March 1582, which was reprinted almost forty times up to 1642.[9] During Aylmer's visitation of 1583 he was described as preacher at Leigh as well as rector of South Shoebury, and although producing his preaching licence was ordered to attend Aylmer personally.[10] He was not further troubled, yet in March 1584 he was one of seven Essex preachers, including George Gifford, whom Aylmer interviewed about Whitgift's demand for unqualified subscription to his new articles. He was given a fortnight to deliberate, and was subsequently one of the twenty-seven Essex ministers who petitioned the privy council for protection.[11] On 1 July 1584 he was again before the archdeacon of Essex on charges of ritual nonconformity and for refusing the surplice.[12] Although it was later stated that he had been 'sondrie times troubled' for omitting the cross and the surplice,[13] he nevertheless appears to have escaped prosecution during the episcopal visitation of 1586,[14] probably because he had been appointed one of six clerical commissioners to oversee exercises for the instruction of the less able clergy in Rochford deanery.[15] Not until 1589 did his persistent failure to wear the surplice receive attention at an episcopal visitation but again that charge, and the lesser one of omitting weekday services, appear to have been dropped after a routine period of excommunication. In 1592 he was merely listed present as a licensed preacher.[16]

Altogether, once Whitgift had been forced to moderate his original demand for unqualified subscription, Dent was not singled out, like Gifford, as one of the ringleaders against whom further measures were to be taken. Yet a ringleader in some sense Dent certainly was, playing a major role in the discussions about the Book of Discipline (1585–7).[17] He is not known, however, to have been subsequently presented for nonconformist practices. At Bancroft's primary visitation in 1598 he was merely listed present as a licensed preacher.[18]

His third published work, *The Plaine-Mans Path-Way to Heaven* (1601) – 'wherein every man may clearly see whether he shall be saved or damned' – was dedicated to Julius Caesar and reached a twenty-fifth edition by 1640, thus becoming one of the most frequently reprinted English books of its time; a forty-first edition appeared as late as 1831.[19] *The Ruine of Rome: or An Exposition upon the whole Revelation* was with the printer when Dent succumbed to fever, dying within three days. His will, dated 7 January 1603, is thus a brief document which left everything to his wife, Margery, 'for the education of all my children'.[20] Ezekiel Culverwell, one of its witnesses, saw *Ruine of Rome* through the press, adding a dedicatory epistle to Robert, 3rd Lord Rich.[21] It appeared only days before Elizabeth's death in 1603.[22]

Two short studies are: Maurice Hussey, 'Arthur Dent, rector of South Shoebury (1553–1603)', *Essex Review*, LVII (1948), 196–201; and Elizabeth K. Hudson, 'The "Plaine Mans" pastor: Arthur Dent and the cultivation of popular piety in early seventeenth-century England', *Albion*, XXV (1993), 23–36.

1. *Alum. Cantab.*, II, 33; Peile, *Biographical register*, I, 119; GL MS 9535/1, fo. 154r.
2. GL MS 9537/4, fo. 44v.
3. Although archdeacon of Colchester, Withers was officially subject as rector of Danbury to the jurisdiction of the archdeacon of Essex.
4. Both cases are given *verbatim* in William H. Hale, *Precedents and proceedings in criminal causes . . . extracted from the act-books of ecclesiastical courts in the diocese of London . . .* (London, 1847), pp. 167, 169.
5. LMA DL/C/333, fo. 179v.
6. GL MS 9537/4, fo. 104v.
7. PRO E334/9, fo. 219r. His sureties were the godly goldsmith Robert Aske, and John Dente, salter, of St Bartholomew the Less, his father's brother. John Dente's widow later married Sir Julius Caesar, to whom Arthur was to dedicate *Plain man's pathway* in 1601 (see below).
8. BL, Lansdowne MS 109, fo. 7v.
9. Ian Green, *Print and protestantism in early modern England* (Oxford, 2000), p. 612.
10. GL MS 9537/5, fos. 4r, 79r, 80v.
11. LMA DL/C/334, fo.19r; *Seconde parte*, I, 225.
12. ERO D/AEA 12, fo. 129v.
13. *Seconde parte*, II, 164.
14. He was merely noted present as rector and preacher at South Shoebury: GL MS 9537/6, fo. 150r. Not listed amongst those Essex ministers suspended at the visitation 'and since' for the surplice: *Seconde parte*, II, 261.
15. GL MS 9537/6, fo. 178v.
16. GL MSS 9537/7, fo. 76r; /8, fo. 25r.
17. See above, p. 86.
18. GL MS 9537/9, fo. 128r.
19. It influenced both John Bunyan and Richard Baxter, who recast it in 1674 as *The poor man's family book*, abandoning Dent's homely dialogue for connected prose.
20. LMA DL/C/359, fo. 389r. Nothing is known of his children: no parish records survive for South Shoebury before 1704.
21. His reference to his 'near conjunction' with his 'late brother' led to the erroneous assumption that Margery Dent was Culverwell's sister. It nevertheless remains possible that the first Mrs Culverwell (d. c. 1597), otherwise unidentifiable, was Dent's sister.
22. It reached a tenth edition by 1656 and seems to have found favour with the evangelical movement, being reprinted five more times between 1798 and 1841. Seven posthumous works bearing Dent's name were in print by the end of 1614, some perhaps spurious attempts by unscrupulous printers to profit from his popularity. For the four most successful see Green, *Print and protestantism*, p. 613.

DOW(E), RICHARD (d. 1608)

Minor canon of Norwich cathedral, c. 1573–c. 1580; ?vicar of Emneth, Norfolk, c. 1576; vicar of Stratford St Mary, Suffolk, 1588–1608 (d.)

Richard Dowe, son of Henry Dow of Attleborough, Norfolk, attended Wymondharn school and matriculated a sizar of Corpus Christi College, Cambridge, at Michaelmas 1566. He proceeded BA in early 1570 and MA in 1573, having been admitted fellow-commoner at Gonville and Caius in June 1572. He was ordained priest at Norwich in

December 1572 and became a minor canon of Norwich cathedral. One of these names occurs as vicar of Emneth, Norfolk, in 1576: so far a conventional Norfolk clerical career.[1] But with the arrival in the diocese of Bishop Edmund Freke in 1576, Dowe was suspended, was one of the Norwich ministers who petitioned Lord Burghley for relief,[2] and two years later made a limited submission to the bishop.[3] Not long after this, Dowe migrated to the Stour valley, apparently as part of a concerted plan involving his Norwich colleagues, Dr Edmund Chapman and Dr Richard Crick. His presence at Stratford St Mary can be documented from December 1580, when he witnessed a Stratford will.[4] In November 1581 his daughter Dameris was baptized in Stratford church. Ten more children of Richard and Susan Dowe were to follow her to the font, the last in July 1605, three years before Dowe's death in 1608: Daniel, Mary, Elizabeth, Susan, Barionah, Ami, Raboshry, Bathsibrye, Sarah and Abigail.[5] Susan Dowe was still living in Stratford in 1610, when a local innkeeper left her a small legacy.[6]

Already in 1581 Dowe is identified in the baptismal register as 'minister', but for some years he remained unbeneficed. At the first meeting of the Dedham conference, of which he was a founding member, the question arose as to his 'placing', whether at East Bergholt (where Richard Crick had already settled) or at Stratford (**1M**). At the second meeting it was resolved that he 'shuld accepte of his callinge at Stratforde' (**2M**), where the third meeting was held in February 1583, presumably in Dowe's house (**3M**). In May 1583, the conference thought it 'inconvenient' ('verie' deleted) that an 'ordinary lecture' provided by Dowe at neighbouring Higham should become a fixture (why? 'For diverse causes' was struck out) (**6M**). In July 1584, Dowe had to ask the conference what to do, 'one having gott the presentation' to the living of Stratford, normally in the gift of the crown (**20M**). He was advised to seek legal counsel, and to get the parish to join with him. In January 1584 (or 1585?) Dowe was included as vicar of Stratford in a list of Suffolk ministers suspended for not subscribing to Archbishop Whitgift's articles.[7] But he was not yet vicar, and it was only in 1587/8 that Dowe's position was regularized as vicar, following the death of the previous incumbent, John Christian.[8] That religious life in Stratford was not all conducted according to law is suggested by Dowe's interesting question in May 1584 'whether it were convenient a woman shuld pray having a better gift than her husband', a question deemed at the next meeting 'not necessary to be handled' (**18, 19MM**). In the diocesan visitation of 1597, Dowe was presented for not wearing the surplice for the past year, and for not making the annual perambulation of the parish. 'He usewally keepeth a day of preaching, viz. the Weddensdaye.'[9]

As one of the Norwich three, Dowe appears to have been third in the pecking order of a society ostensibly composed of equals. He was speaker at the third meeting (**3M**) and moderator of the fourth (**4M**). He took the lead in recommending prayer and fasting in the build-up to the parliament of 1584–5 (**26M**), and he was a very active participant in the affairs of the conference throughout its history.

1. *Alum. Cantab.*, II, 58; Venn, *Biographical history*, p. 70; Francis Blomefield and C. Parkin, *An essay towards a topographical history of the county of Norfolk*, VIII (London, 1808), 409.
2. Copies of the petition in *Seconde parte*, I, 143–6; BL, Add MS 481101, fos. 132–4 (where it is described as a 'supplication of Norwich ministers to Parliament').
3. Copies in *Seconde parte*, I, 146; BL, Add MS 48023; PRO, SP 12/126/45, and in the Dedham papers (see above, pp. 000–00).
4. SRO Ipswich, IC/AA2/28/183.
5. SRO Ipswich, parish registers of Stratford St Mary (microform reference, but barely readable on microform, J 559/39).
6. SRO Ipswich, R43/127.
7. *Seconde parte*, I, 242.
8. NRO, DN/REG/14, fo. 159v.
9. *Redman's visitation*, p. 154.

FARRAR alias OXFORD, THOMAS (c. 1538–1608)

Rector of Shimpling, Norfolk, 1563–72 (resig.); vicar of Boxted, Essex, 1572–3 (resig.); rector of Langham, Essex, 1573–1607 (resig.)[1]

Born in Bury St Edmunds, Suffolk, Farrar matriculated sizar from Christ's College, Cambridge, in November 1555 ('Oxford'), graduating BA in early 1559 ('Oxforth'). He became a fellow of Corpus Christi, proceeding MA from Corpus in 1562.[2] Meanwhile he had been ordained acolyte and subdeacon ('Oxforde'), as of Norwich diocese, by Edmund Bonner, bishop of London, on 11 March 1559 (title: Corpus Christi College, Cambridge, *'ubi est socius perpetuus'*). He was ordained deacon ('Oxford') by Edmund Grindal, bishop of London, on 14 January 1560 (BA of Corpus; born Bury, Suffolk; aged 22) and priest on 25 January 1560, at a massive ceremony in which Grindal ordained thirty-five deacons, including Percival Wiburn and John Aylmer, and thirty priests, including James Calfhill and John Foxe.[3]

Rector of Shimpling, Norfolk, 1563–72,[4] he was collated vicar of Boxted by Bishop Edwin Sandys of London on 18 December 1572 ('Farrar *alias* Oxford'), quickly relinquishing it for the much more valuable rectory of Langham, to which he was instituted on the crown's presentation, in the right of the duchy of Lancaster ('Ferrar *alias* Oxford'), on 29 January 1573.[5] He compounded for the benefice ('Farrar *alias* Oxford') on 4 July 1573.[6] His early years at Langham appear to have been untroubled.[7]

It is difficult to resist the conclusion that behind Farrar's change of name in the 1560s there lay a deep desire to shake off his 'Marian' past. Although a founder member of the Dedham conference, signing next after Chapman and Crick, Farrar appears to have maintained a very low profile. In March 1583 he was chosen one of four speakers for the following meeting (**4M**). He was host for the first time in June 1583 (**7M**).[8] He first propounded a question later the same month: what was he to do about a 'wicked man' who had come to Langham apparently with the bishop's authority (**8M**)? This note of anxious timidity set the tone for most of his contributions over the next five years.

At the episcopal visitation of 1583 he was one of the many Essex preachers who claimed to have a licence but failed to exhibit it, and accordingly he was to deliver it into the consistory court before Bartholomewtide.[9] He must have done so to Stanhope's satisfaction for no more is heard of the matter. The experience appears, however, to have unnerved him. One of four speakers at a fast in February 1584, he was urged by the conference 'to renewe his exercise of prechinge in his owne congregation' (**15M**). Moderator the following month, he contributed 10s to the relief of Henry Wilcock in April and acted as speaker in July (**16, 17, 20MM**). In August he was worried what to do about a bastard child who had been secretly left in his church, and he was also one of those delegated to urge Thomas Lowe to resume his attendance at the meetings (**21M**). In September he and Chapman were chosen to negotiate about Andrewes's departure from Wenham (**22M**). In January 1585 he was one of those chosen to confer with Dr Oxenbridge, and later in the same meeting he propounded another of his anxious questions: should he take part in a commission convened to examine witnesses in a dispute between 'a bad mynister and his people' (**26M**)? Although again delegated to confer with the congregation of Wenham, he remained notably silent during the discussions surrounding Andrewes's departure (**27M, Extra M**, 17 February 1585). As one who had exchanged under-funded Boxted for better-endowed Langham he may have felt that discretion was the better part of disputation. In September he was advised not to baptize the child of a couple who were not his parishioners (**35M**).

Following Aylmer's episcopal visitation in July 1586, Farrar was one of the many who came under threat for the surplice.[10] On 14 November, in what appears (for him) to have been a bold initiative, he went to Fulham for a personal confrontation with the bishop, armed with a letter (but from whom it is not apparent) asking Aylmer's 'favour' on his behalf. He was treated to a fair specimen of Aylmerian invective and was told that he and all others like him who would not obey the queen's commands would be deprived within three months. Aylmer counted such behaviour as no better than rebellion and 'deadly sin', and had frequently preached as much before the queen herself.[11]

Farrar returned to Langham in some perplexity. On 5 December he signified to the brethren that he had come to his third admonition to conform but got little sympathy. He was reminded that the whole matter had been discussed at 'Mr Birdes house',[12] where it had been resolved that no-one should yield to the surplice 'bicause they sought to haue us yeld unto all the ceremonies'. Farrar contrived to remain in place but there is no record of any further proceedings in consistory. Later at the same meeting Farrar moved that 'his brother of Holbrooke' be admitted to the conference, a proposition which (perhaps in compensation for his slap in the face over yielding to Aylmer) was allowed (**51M**). Nothing ever came of it, however: in March 1587 he was forced to report that 'he found noe readines' in his brother 'bicause he wold not be tied to a place' (**54M**).[13]

Aylmer had not finished with Farrar: in April 1587 Farrar required advice as to 'his appearinge before the B: yt was said he shuld haue letters of Commendacon and so goe to the meetinge of the brethren in London and haue their aduise' (**55M**). In May he pointed out that he was about to be suspended 'or if he went not to be excommunicate'. It was 'thought best' that he 'tarie at home, and abide thexcommunication for soe he shuld gaine some longer tyme, and he might be absoluted by a Proctor: but some doubted whether by the worde he might be absolved by a Proctor' (**56M**).

In August 1587 Farrar was one of those chosen to 'determine' Tilney's case and was appointed speaker for the following meeting (**59M**). In December he was one of the six signatories to the letter refusing Newman's secondment to Braintree.[14]

For the rest of the conference's existence Farrar's name occurs only as host, moderator or speaker (**62, 65, 74MM**). In July 1589 Farrar freely admitted to Aylmer's episcopal visitors that he did not wear the surplice and was duly ordered to do so and to certify.[15] On 5 November Laurence Lyde, vicar of Ardleigh, appeared in court with a letter from Farrar explaining that he was unable to attend. Agreeing to a new monition for 24 November, the judge warned Lyde that if Farrar failed to appear on that occasion he would be deprived forthwith.[16]

Farrar accordingly turned up on the appointed day and the usual cat-and-mouse tactics ensued. He once more admitted that he did not wear the surplice. Because he had apparently tried to excuse himself to Aylmer personally on the grounds that 'the conscience of the people were weake' the judge was armed with a personal mandate from the bishop. Farrar was ordered, before 6 February next, to have conference with Archdeacon Withers 'at least 3 or 4 times' on the subject of the surplice and his canonical duties; and to teach his parishioners 'the true use of the surplice and ceremonies' of the Church of England 'whereby they may be drawn to his like of his ministry using those things, & so to wear the surplice upon some Sunday' before that time. Otherwise he was to appear on 6 February and face the consequences of his disobedience.[17]

As so often, nothing further is heard of this indictment. At Aylmer's final visitation in the summer of 1592 he was once again present as a licensed preacher and ordered to appear on a later date to certify that he wore the surplice.[18]

He was ordered at Bancroft's primary visitation in September 1598 to show his preaching licence before leaving court.[19] Listed amongst the 'diligent and sufficient' clergy of Essex in 1604,[20] he was on 26 March 1605, following Bancroft's final visitation of 1604, summoned because he did not use the surplice 'everie daie appoynted'. He stated that he now used it 'continually' and that the churchwardens could certify as much.[21] He resigned Langham in early 1607 in favour of his son John.[22]

Farrar made his will, as 'cleric' of Langham, on 14 November 1607. It was proved at Colchester (Consistory Court of London) on 18 March 1608.[23]

1. He has often been confused with a younger Thomas Farrar, who graduated BA from Peterhouse, Cambridge, in early 1584 and was rector of St James Colchester 1591–1610: *Alum. Cantab.*, II, 123. There is nothing to prove that the two men were closely related.
2. Peile, *Biographical register*, I, 62; *Alum. Cantab.*, III, 292 ('Oxford').
3. GL MS 9535/1, fos. 79v, 83v, 86v.
4. *Alum. Cantab.*, III, 292.
5. Reg. Grindal, fos. 169r, 169v. Presentation record not found in surviving records of duchy of Lancaster: PRO DL42/100.
6. PRO E334/8, fo. 337r. His successor at Boxted was Thomas Morse.
7. Duly present at the three episcopal visitations of 1574, 1577 and 1580, he is found in the consistory court records only when granted a diocesan preaching licence ('*praesertim* Langham') on 23 June: GL MSS 9537/3, fo. 80r; 9537/4, fos. 32r, 96r; LMA DL/C/333, fo. 79v. No act books of office survive for the visitations of 1577 and 1580.
8. The conference met at his house on a further six occasions: **18, 25, 38, 50, 63, 75MM**. He was chosen moderator for the next meeting on four occasions: **23, 30, 38, 42MM**.
9. GL MS 9537/5, fos. 3v, 64v.
10. *Seconde parte*, II, 164, 261.
11. *Ibid.*, II, 193.
12. Presumably the forty-eighth meeting, but there is no reference to the matter in the minute book itself.
13. But see above, p. 34, n.12.
14. See above, pp. 107–8.
15. GL MS 9537/7, fo. 47v.
16. LMA DL/C/616, p. 127.
17. LMA DL/C/616, p. 186.
18. GL MS 9537/8, fo. 56r.
19. GL MS 9537/9, fo. 101v.
20. 'A Viewe', p. 4.
21. LMA DL/C/618, p. 421. This may indicate that the new constitutions and canons of 1604 propelled Farrar, now nearing 70, into abandoning ritual nonconformity.
22. John Farrer received letters of presentation for the benefice from the chancellor of the duchy of Lancaster on 23 June 1607 and was instituted as his successor on 10 September: PRO DL 42/100, fo. 32r; Reg. Bancroft, fo. 107r.
23. LMA DL/C/359, fos. 364v–6v. An exhaustive document, occupying almost four-and-a-half sides of a registrar's transcript, and leaving no detail to chance. Its godly preamble pondered 'the frailty and uncertainty of our life and that all flesh is grass and glory of it as the flower of the field . . .'. To be buried in the chancel of Langham between his two wives 'buried there before, being assured to receive the same my body in far better condition an immortal body and glorified at the day of the general resurrection, though now it be but vile and wormsmeat and shall be turned into dust'. Properties in Langham were bequeathed to sons Thomas and Anthony (evidently clothiers), and to son-in-law Thomas Warner, provision being made in each case for his third wife, Christian, during her lifetime. Two unmarried daughters were to receive £30 each at 22 or marriage. There were lesser bequests to three other daughters and a step-daughter. Thomas was directed to pay Farrar's brother George of Holbrook an annuity of 16s for as long as he lived. £4 was bequeathed to the poor of Langham 'to buy a piece of meadow or other ground' for their use and benefit 'for ever'. There were bequests of 10s to 'Mr Dr [Richard] Dove' and to Robert Lewis, 'my brother-in-law'; 5s to 'Mr Sage of Dedham' and 'Mr Rogers'. Altogether, monetary bequests amounted to at least £170. John Farrar was appointed sole executor, inheriting the residue of the estate.

GALE, ARTHUR (d. 1622/3)

Schoolmaster of Dedham, Essex, 1589–97; rector of Semer, Suffolk, 1598–1622/3 (d.)

Gale matriculated pensioner from Christ's College, Cambridge, at Lent 1578, along with Nicholas Culverwell, youngest brother of Ezekiel, and John Udall. He graduated BA in early 1582, proceeding MA in 1585.[1] He appears to have been the son of Edward Gale of Hadleigh. His sister Sarah married Julian Beamond of Hadleigh, whose brother-in-law was Richard Crick, which helps to explain the link with Crick.[2] He may have been related to the Edwardston clothier Thomas Gale who, in his will of 1585, 'for that I have receyved manye spirituall benefittes to the singuler comforte of my soule by the preachinge of certeine godlie preachers', left 'benevolences' to five of them, including Henry Sandes, William Bird and John Knewstub.[3] Gale joined the Dedham conference on 27 June 1586 and, with Edmund Salmon, agreed to be bound by its orders on 8 August (**45, 46MM**).

Thomas Stoughton excepted, Gale may have been the only trainee minister to have been admitted to membership of the conference. After playing very little part in its business, although in August 1587 he was chosen as speaker (**59M**), two meetings were held at Dr Crick's house in East Bergholt 'for Mr Gale' (**60, 72MM**), whatever that may have meant. Since Gale delivered to the conference Crick's angry letter about his election to the pastorate of East Bergholt, it appears likely that he was receiving his training in Crick's household (**66M**).

In 1588 Gale obtained a schoolmaster's licence for the diocese (or province?) of Canterbury, which may suggest that he was teaching in one of the neighbouring Canterbury peculiars, Bocking or Hadleigh.[4] In December 1588 the schoolmaster of Dedham, William Bentley, was appointed schoolmaster of Colchester. Bentley had never been a member of the conference, although, judging by the favourable references sent to Colchester by the likes of William Whitaker, Laurence Chaderton and John Knewstub, he was well thought of among the godly.[5] According to another referee, George Northey, town preacher of Colchester, there had been talk of 'some disagreement' between Bentley and 'some' in Dedham, but 'even Paul and Barnabas did disagree'.[6] In March 1589, Gale succeeded Bentley as Dedham's schoolmaster and asked the conference for their prayers (**77M**).

Gale appeared at Aylmer's episcopal visitation on 24 July 1589, stated that he had been licensed by the archbishop of Canterbury's vicar general without subscribing to the articles, duly subscribed, and on the following day received a licence to teach in Dedham and elsewhere throughout the diocese.[7] He was again listed as present at Aylmer's last visitation, in 1592.[8] Gale probably remained at Dedham until 1597, but in February 1598 he was ordained priest in Norwich by John Sterne, suffragan bishop of Colchester.[9] He became rector of Semer, Suffolk,[10] in the same year and died there in 1623, leaving substantial property to his five sons, Edward, Nathaniel, Bezalell, Arthur and John.[11]

1. Peile, *Biographical register*, I, 144–6; *Alum. Cantab.*, II, 188.
2. Julian Beamond's will was witnessed by Arthur Gale in 1586. See J. J. Muskett, *Suffolk manorial families*, 2, 323; PRO PCC PROB 11/70 (1 Spencer).
3. Proved both in the Prerogative Court of Canterbury (dated 2 November 1585) and in the court of the archdeacon of Sudbury (dated 2 November 1586): PRO PCC PROB11/73 (5 Leicester); SRO Bury St Edmunds, R2/41/125.
4. Peile, *Biographical register,* I, 145.
5. For the testimonials, see ERO (Colchester), Morant MS D/Y 2/4, pp. 97, 113, 131, 135, 143, 149–50, 173, 193, discussed in Collinson, 'PCM', pp. 598–606.
6. ERO (Colchester), Morant MS D/Y 2/4, p. 193.
7. GL MS 9537/7, fo. 46r; LMA DL/C/334, fo. 276v.
8. GL MS 9537/8, fo. 55r.
9. *Alum. Cantab.*, II, 188.
10. Bullen, *Catalogue*, p. 21.
11. PRO, PCC PROB 11/ 141 (29 Swann).

GIFFORD, GEORGE (1548–1600)

Undermaster at Brentwood School, Essex, c. 1574–81; curate of All Saints with St Peter Maldon, Essex, ?early 1581–2; vicar of All Saints with St Peter Maldon, 1582–4 (depr.); restored as town preacher of Maldon, ?late 1584–1600 (d.)

Gifford was the son of Boniface Gifford of Dry Drayton, Cambridgeshire,[1] evidently a member of the household of John Hutton of Dry Drayton, MP for Cambridgeshire between 1563 and 1572.[2] That he was student at Hart Hall, Oxford, for several years before 1568, as stated in older authorities, seems unlikely but cannot be absolutely refuted. He graduated BA from Christ's College, Cambridge, in early 1570, proceeding MA in 1573.[3]

Evidently eschewing an academic life, Gifford married Agnes (Anne) Lennard, of Taunton, Somerset, at St Mary Woolnoth, London, on 21 April 1572.[4] In 1573 he published the first of many books, an English translation of William Fulke's *Praelectiones*.

Undermaster at Brentwood School no earlier than autumn 1574, and living at nearby Mountnessing,[5] he was presumably recommended for this teaching post by William Fulke, rector of contiguous Great Warley from 1571. Although a layman, he participated in prophesyings at Brentwood, with the sanction of John Walker, archdeacon of Essex.[6] He and Anne were nevertheless summoned before Walker's official on 25 November 1575 for failing to receive communion at Mountnessing.[7] Both were ordered to certify that they had received there on 12 January 1576 but failed to do so.[8]

Ordained deacon and priest by John Aylmer, bishop of London, on 15 December 1578 (MA of Mountnessing; aged 30) Gifford was granted licence to preach throughout the diocese the same day.[9] Since he is nowhere mentioned as a curate in the episcopal visitation of 1580, he presumably continued at Brentwood as schoolmaster/chaplain.

Yet within months Gifford gravitated to the borough of Maldon and a curacy under Fabian Withers, vicar of the combined parishes of All Saints and St Peter. During the incumbency of Robert Williams (1566–73) and then of Withers, elder brother of George Withers, archdeacon of Colchester, a godly magistracy and a godly ministry had combined to make Maldon a centre of advanced protestantism[10] and, as in Colchester, there was mounting confrontation between the godly clergy and the bishop of London during the 1580s.

That confrontation may be said to have dated from Aylmer's decision in 1581 to investigate parochial affairs. For unknown reasons Gifford soon found himself under restraint pending an investigation by appointees of the ecclesiastical commissioners. The chamberlains' accounts for that year mention disbursements (23 October) for the 'diet' of the bailiffs, justices 'and other her majesty's commissioners sitting about the examination of certain persons by virtue of a Commission directed from the bishop of London touching Master Gifford and Master Withers'.[11] The commissioners exonerated Gifford and Aylmer accordingly restored him to his preaching. On 16 December Aylmer directed letters of sequestration for the vicarage to '[ ] cleric' and to two parishioners, William Vernon and William Bantoft: Fabian Withers, *vicarius pretendens*, had not appeared on 12 November to answer articles as directed and had been pronounced contumacious and excommunicated. The vicarage was declared sequestered because of his negligence and contumacy.[12]

Gifford is first found officially listed as curate at an archidiaconal visitation on 27 April 1582. Within days Withers had resigned the vicarage. Since new letters of sequestration were issued on 30 May 1582 as a result, it was probably to Gifford that they were dispatched.[13] Then on 30 August 1582 Aylmer instituted him to the vicarages of All Saints with St Peter, stated to be void by Withers's free (*liberam et spontaneam*) resignation, at the presentation of Richard Francke. Orders to induct him were dispatched the same day to Archdeacon Walker and a new diocesan preaching licence was issued to him as incumbent.[14]

It was probably precisely at this time, under Aylmer's very nose, that Gifford became a founder member of the Braintree conference. Although excused from the episcopal visitation in July 1583 until Bartholomewtide,[15] he was summoned into consistory on 7 October to answer a variety of charges.[16] On 16 October Gifford appeared before Aylmer himself at Fulham and was ordered to administer the sacraments *sub poena iuris*. He was ordered to certify on 14 November but from that point his case was consistently prorogued until Easter 1584.[17]

The reason, no doubt, was that by 20 October Aylmer had decided to use Archbishop Whitgift's newly devised articles to move against the Essex radicals[18] and Gifford was undoubtedly one of his prime targets. On 5 March 1584 he was one of three Essex clergy called for examination (*aliquandum colloquium*) by Aylmer, who at first asked, then admonished, and finally ordered Gifford to assent to them (*rogavit, monuit et iussit*). Gifford kept his head, merely craving time to consider his position. At the end of the interview Aylmer allowed him until 20 March to make assent before Archdeacon Walker: thereafter he faced certain suspension.[19]

Twenty-seven ministers of southern Essex quickly solicited the privy council for protection. Their petition was almost certainly organized by the Braintree conference.[20] On 6 May, however, it was stated that Gifford himself was suspended from office by excommunication.[21]

Another petition, signed by fifty-two Maldonians and addressed to Aylmer, pleaded for his restoration, pointing out that Aylmer's own commissioners had 'not long time since' acquitted Gifford on all charges of sedition and irregularity.[22] A copy reached Lord Burghley, who intervened with Whitgift on Gifford's behalf. On 29 May the archbishop replied that he had consulted Aylmer, was convinced that Gifford was 'a ringleader of the rest' and intended to call him before the High Commission: 'his deserts may be such as will deserve deprivation'.[23]

Gifford was duly deprived in June or July but no details of the proceedings survive. Meanwhile, on 4 May, the Dedham conference had 'thought good' that 'a generall meeting of lerned brethren' should be convened 'about the cause of subscriptions' (**18M**). It was agreed that it should take place (in London) on the first day of Hilary term, on the eve of the 1584 parliament, and Chapman and Gifford headed the list of ten Essex delegates chosen.[24] On 1 February 1585 the Dedham members further agreed that Knewstub (for Suffolk) and Gifford and Robert Wright (for Essex) should be 'moued to deale for the church' (**27M**).

All this is solid evidence that, despite his deprivation, Gifford continued to be one of the prime movers amongst the Essex godly. Meanwhile his former patron, Richard Francke, was staging a small coup of his own, almost certainly with Gifford's connivance. On 18 January 1585, at Francke's presentation, Aylmer instituted Mark Wiersdale to the combined vicarages of All Saints and St Peter, merely stated to be *iam vacantem*.[25]

Wiersdale, evidently a rather unstable hothead, was a non-graduate of 28 who seems to have picked up in Brentwood where Gifford had left off. Despite several serious clashes with authority there as curate of South Weald, he had contrived to surmount them.[26] His institution to Maldon did nothing to deter him from his dangerously maverick methods of proceeding. In April 1585 he offered to lay a wager with another local clergyman that the queen was not entitled to be styled Queen of France and Ireland. This incident led to his indictment at Chelmsford midsummer Assizes[27] but not before he had been summoned before Archdeacon Walker on 25 May for this and yet more liturgical irregularities.[28] On 4 September letters of sequestration were issued to Thomas Keeler and Thomas Preston, churchwardens of All Saints, and to John Pagett and Brice Smith, churchwarden of St Peter, because Wiersdale had left the cure unserved and absented himself from the vicarage.[29]

Wiersdale's self-removal was evidently the direct result of his indictment for denying the queen's titles and his efforts to repair the damage by seeking the protection of Sir Francis Walsingham. On 24 November he appeared in consistory, claiming that he had obtained the queen's pardon for those matters in which he was said to have transgressed, and promising henceforth to be resident in his benefice if its sequestration were to be revoked. Sir Edward Stanhope decreed that, having received letters from Walsingham, letters of relaxation would be issued 'under seal' upon his receipt of the queen's pardon. Meanwhile Wiersdale was naturally ordered to observe all the established laws of the realm.[30] Walsingham seems to have had some difficulty in securing the pardon, for he appealed to Stanhope again in similar terms some weeks later, and Stanhope made an almost identical order on 11 March 1586.[31]

Gifford's precise role in these proceedings is unknown, but it would appear that Aylmer had, under pressure, sanctioned his continuing in Maldon as official preacher either in late 1584 or early 1585. Yet he is next found, along with John Knewstub and Dudley Fenner, as chaplain to the earl of Leicester at the beginning of the campaign in the Low Countries in December 1585.[32]

He had evidently returned by 20 July 1586 when, at the episcopal visitation, Wiersdale was listed present as vicar and Gifford as preacher.[33] But the hard-won compromises of the past few months were suddenly in tatters, not impossibly because of the very rude reception Aylmer received at the hands of the townsmen on his arrival, an episode which he vividly described to Lord Burghley.[34] Gifford was again suspended for refusing the surplice while, in what appears to have been an act of bravado rather than common sense, Wiersdale immediately 'resigned his pastorall charge' to Gifford. Aylmer refused to re-admit him, although he was officially presented by Richard Francke, but 'hath sett an other there'. Wiersdale, being now suspended, 'ys gone to Cambridge to live there a while'.[35] He never returned to Essex.[36]

It would seem that this discouraging – indeed, foolhardy – train of events prompted Gifford to return to the Low Countries. He may even have been present at the battle of Zutphen on 22 September 1586, when Sir Philip Sidney was fatally wounded. Sidney sent for him on 30 September and Gifford appears to have remained in constant attendance until his death on 17 October, subsequently writing *The manner of Sir Philip Sidney's death* which, though containing striking personal details, was written more to edify the reader than to provide an accurate historical account. Two (evidently corrupt) transcriptions of the original remained in manuscript until 1973, when a collation of them was printed as an appendix to Sidney's minor prose works.[37] With a fellow-minister, 'Mr Fountain', Gifford was left £20 in the codicil to Sidney's will.[38]

On 8 March 1587 Gifford was one of the six members of the Braintree meeting – the others were Carr, Hawden, Huckle, Tunstall and Whiting – who petitioned parliament for restoration.[39] The two latter were to be deprived of their benefices, whilst Gifford is not recorded in the archdeacon of Essex's visitations of April 1587 or April 1588.[40] Nor did he sign the Braintree meeting's letter asking for Newman's secondment on 7 June 1587,[41] and on 16 August that year he was one of those preachers banned by name from the London pulpits.[42]

There can be no doubt, however, of his continuing presence in Maldon or of his continuing prominence in provincial and national synods. In 1587 he acquired a property in Maldon's third parish, St Mary, a peculiar of the dean and chapter of Westminster, and perhaps transferred his preaching activities there for a while. During this period affairs in Maldon certainly descended into a state of acrimonious confusion since, following Wiersdale's resignation, Bishop Aylmer claimed the benefice *per lapsum* and on 23 May 1587 collated the non-graduate Robert Palmer, a pluralist.[43] The town broke up into contending factions, although it seems that Palmer and Gifford did not become personal enemies.[44]

Gifford was officially listed as town preacher once more by April 1589 and at the episcopal visitation of July that year he was present and not further summoned into consistory.[45]

Although battles continued to rage in Maldon,[46] the demise of the conference movement appears to have put an end to any serious pursuit of Gifford by Aylmer and Whitgift. Whilst his name was frequently mentioned during the star chamber trials of 1590–1, Gifford himself was never summoned. Part of the reason, no doubt, was his increasing eminence as a protestant polemicist and in particular his vigorous and sustained denunciations of separatism: in 1591 he preached at Paul's Cross a stirring call for protestant unity, lest the papists triumph, emphasizing obedience to the godly magistrate.[47] The evidence of the dedications to his many tracts and volumes of sermons suggests, moreover, that he could rely on the patronage of Lord Burghley and Robert Devereux, earl of Essex.[48]

Gifford was present at Aylmer's last episcopal visitation on 7 September 1592 when he and Palmer were ordered into consistory; the sequel is unknown.[49] He was merely listed present as a licensed preacher at the episcopal visitation of 1598.[50] He made his will on 8 May 1600 as 'preacher of God's word in Mauldon'. The Consistory Court of London granted probate on the following 31 May.[51]

1. J. J. Howard and J. L. Chester, eds., *The visitation of London*, I (Harleian Soc., 1880), 314.
2. Kinsman of Matthew Hutton, later archbishop of York: Hasler, *House of commons*, II, 359–60. Gifford later dedicated a sermon to John Hutton as one who 'long time have professed the glorious Gospell of Jesus Christ' with the observation that 'I was brought up under you, my parents receiving benefites dailye from you': George Gifford, *A Sermon on the Parable of the Sower* (1582), sig. A2v.
3. *Alum. Oxon.*, II, 563; *Alum. Cantab.*, II, 213; Peile, *Biographical register*, I, 98.
4. J. M. S. Brooke and A. W. C. Hallen, eds., *The registers of . . . S. Mary Woolnoth and S. Mary Woolchurch Haw . . . London 1538–1760* (Harleian Soc., 1880), p. 127.
5. The township of Brentwood, technically a hamlet within the parish of South Weald, had begun to outstrip the ancient parish because of its strategic position on the main road from London to Chelmsford. The school was founded in 1558 by Sir Anthony Browne of Weald Hall, Chief Justice of the Common Pleas, and his wife Dorothy (*nee* Huddlestone).
6. In July 1576, when Walker defended the prophesyings in his archdeaconry (see above, p. xxxvii), he reported that one of the moderators 'of late' had been William Fulke. As for lay participation, Walker admitted that one Gifford 'a schoolmaster' had been 'suffered to speak sometimes when such ministers as were appointed to speak did fail, partlie for necessity . . . and partlie for that he is an universitie man and well exercised in the Latin tongue and in the scriptures, & therefore doth well teach': LPL MS 2003, fo. 12r.
7. Gifford admitted that he had not received communion at Mountnessing for a year but had done so instead 'at my Lord Rich's', presumably the parish church of Little Leighs. He was further accused, during 'a provisie in the pulpett', of telling his auditory to do 'as some ministers teache and not as thaie doe'. He admitted the charge but claimed he 'spake it not to the slander of anie ministers': ERO D/AEA 9, fo. 13v. Walker's defence in 1576 of his participation in the prophesyings is thus a good example of the way in which the godly would close ranks in a crisis.
8. The matter was held over until 8 February but again they failed to appear. On 14 March it was noted that they were excommunicated for failing to certify. The case then drops out of sight: ERO D/AEA 9, fos. 30v, 39r, 47r.
9. GL MS 9535/2, fo. 4r–v; LMA DL/C/333, fo. 130r.
10. Petchey, *A prospect of Maldon*, pp. 199–200.
11. Leonard Hughes, *Guide to and history of All Saints' church, Maldon* (privately printed, 1909): appendix (by Andrew Clark), p. xvi.
12. LMA DL/C/333, fos. 271v, 272r–v.

13. ERO D/AEV 2, fo. 73v; LMA DL/C/333, fo. 287r; the name of the recipient has been left blank in this registered copy.

14. GL MS 9531/13, fo. 206r; ERO D/AEM 4, fo. 13v; LMA DL/C/333, fo. 298r.

15. GL 9537/5, fos. 4r, 83v. Marginal note: 'regard thacte sped at Chelmsford & the letter that Mr Hutchinson hath'.

16. He said no service on Wednesdays and Fridays, 'neither upon Sundays as order requireth'; had ordered a servant and a 'poor man' to go haymaking on St Peter's day; did not observe the prayer book or wear the surplice at communion. Ordered to observe the book and to certify. The haymaking charge was apparently dropped, all relevant matter being struck through. But Derek Helden, rector of Little Stambridge, and John Huckle, another member of the Braintree conference, were charged with preaching often in Maldon without licence. The churchwardens of St Peter's were summoned for not presenting that a play had been performed in the church. When they claimed that they had presented it to Mr King, the commissary, Gifford asserted the truth of their statement: LMA DL/C/300, pp. 222–4.

17. *Ibid.*, pp. 287, 403 (continued until 23 November), 443 (continued until 'Hillary'), 654 (continued until Easter). He was listed present as vicar at the archdeaconry visitation of 11 February 1584: ERO D/AEV 2, fo. 98r.

18. See under George Northey in *BR*, p. 240.

19. DL/C/334, fo. 18r.

20. *Seconde parte*, I, 225.

21. LMA DL/C/301, p. 166.

22. BL, Lansdowne MS 68/48.

23. BL, Lansdowne MS 42, fo. 105r: endorsed 'with the petition on his behalf' but that now survives as *ibid.*, MS 68/48.

24. See above, pp. 90–1.

25. Reg. Grindal, fo. 216r.

26. Wiersdale matriculated sizar from Trinity College, Cambridge, at Easter 1576: *Alum. Cantab.*, IV, 401; ordained deacon by Aylmer on 21 December 1582 as of Trinity College, Cambridge; born East Deeping, Lincs., he was now aged 26: GL MS 9535/2, fo. 20r. As curate of South Weald he was on 19 March 1583 suspended by Archdeacon Walker because he was 'no preacher' and a nonconformist: ERO D/AEV2, fo. 83v. Present at the episcopal visitation on 16 July 1583, he was described as preacher at South Weald and curate of Brentwood. He had broken every rule in the book, preaching there and elsewhere, although only a deacon and unlicensed, and never assisting at communion. He was accordingly inhibited from preaching until admitted priest: GL MS 9537/5, fos. 5v, 103r. There is no evidence that he was ever ordained priest in London diocese but, after conference with Aylmer, he was admitted to serve as curate of Brentwood or elsewhere on 26 August 1583: LMA DL/C/333, fo. 346v. On 15 May 1584 he confessed in the archidiaconal court that he neither wore the surplice nor administered communion 'according to the booke for brevitie of tyme', delivering the cup 'from one to another' without using the prescribed words. On 22 July he further admitted that he never used the sign of the cross in baptism or the ring in marriage (because none had ever been offered him), did not catechize and still had not worn the surplice: ERO D/AEA12, fos. 106v, 118r.

27. J. S. Cockburn, ed., *Calendar of assize records: Essex indictments Elizabeth I* (HMSO, 1978), no. 1597: verdict unknown. Depositions concerning the matter survive as PRO SP12/178/27 and are discussed in F. G. Emmison, *Elizabethan life: disorder* (Chelmsford, 1970), pp. 53–4.

28. To the former catalogue of errors it was added that he failed to say weekday services, did not use the surplice, did not pray for the queen according to the injunctions and refused to church women after childbirth. He was ordered to confess his guilt during divine service and to certify: ERO D/AEA 12, fo. 265v.

29. LMA DL/C/334, fo. 61v.

30. LMA DL/C/301, p. 488.

31. *Ibid.*, p. 533.

32. Fenner, Gifford and Knewstub were jointly given £30 'at Middelburg' on 14 December 1585. Leicester was at Middelburg only between 11 and 17 December: Simon Adams, ed., *Household accounts and disbursement books of Robert Dudley, earl of Leicester, 1558–1561, 1584–1586* (Camden Society, 5th series, VI, 1995), 368.

33. GL MS 9537/6, fos. 75v, 151r.

34. BL, Lansdowne MS 50/40.

35. *Seconde parte*, II, 164, 260. Sequestration was granted on 10 August 1586 to Robert Weston, MA, curate there, Christopher Lyving and Brice Smith, churchwardens, because the combined benefices were now vacant by Wiersdale's resignation: LMA DL/C/334, fo. 109r. Robert Weston is not otherwise known to the diocesan or the Maldon records.

36. Subsequently minister of Gaddesby, Leics, 1588–90 and rector of Costock, Notts., 1595–1639 (d.): *Alum. Cantab.*, IV, 401.

37. Katherine Duncan-Jones and Jan van Dorsten, eds., *Miscellaneous prose of Sir Philip Sidney* (Oxford, 1973), pp. 161–72. Duncan-Jones and van Dorsten had no inkling of Gifford's existing connexion with Leicester nor his long-standing ties with the Rich family, expressing surprise that Gifford should have been 'summoned' in this manner but quite reasonably pointing out that there is no subsequent reference to the matter, or to Sidney, in any of Gifford's later works, nor any hint that he became *persona grata* with Sidney's family as a result. The tentative conclusion was that Gifford's role was smaller than his account suggests and that there is 'a strong possibility' that the narrative was 'basically a piece of pious myth-making' (p. 162). Myths, however, are not created by leaving material in manuscript. Why, then, did this successful author never publish a narrative which would undoubtedly have been a runaway bestseller? The answer is surely that it was in the first place a very private document; that on Gifford's return home he was approached by Lady Rich – Sidney's 'Stella' – to supply her with a *memento mori*; and that Gifford duly responded in pious vein, delighted to be able to report that at the end Sidney had made his peace with God on the subject of their relationship.

    Gifford keeps himself out of the narrative until the night before Sidney died. From there it is virtually a running dialogue between the two of them as the life ebbed out of him. In the early hours of 17 October there was much earnest discussion because Sidney feared that his prayers to God were going unheeded. He added: 'I had this night a trouble in my mind: for searching myself, methought I had not a full and sure hold in Christ. After I had continued in this perplexity a while, observe how strangely God did deliver me – for indeed it was a strange deliverance that I had! There came to my remembrance a vanity wherein I had taken delight, whereof I had not rid myself. It was my Lady Rich. But I rid myself of it, and presently my joy and comfort returned': *ibid.*, p. 169. When, on her own deathbed, Lady Rich called for Lord Rich, from whom she had subsequently been divorced, repudiating her second marriage and begging his forgiveness, was she remembering Gifford's account of Sidney over twenty years earlier and staging a vivid re-enactment?

38. Duncan-Jones and van Dorsten, eds., *Miscellaneous prose of Sir Philip Sidney*, p. 222.

39. *Seconde parte*, II, 258–9.

40. ERO D/AEV 2, fos. 175v, 197v.

41. See above, pp. 106–7.

42. *Seconde parte*, II, 231–2.

43. Reg. Grindal, fo. 232r. Palmer resigned the vicarage of Great Waltham on appointment but Aylmer was tactless enough to collate him to that of Great Wakering (another centre of advanced protestantism) on 28 June following: *ibid.*, fo. 232v.

44. Petchey, *A prospect of Maldon*, pp. 202, 210–15.

45. ERO D/AEV2, fo. 205v; GL MS 9537/7, fo. 65v.

46. Petchey, *A prospect of Maldon*, pp. 215–21.

47. See Leland H. Carlson, ed., *The writings of John Greenwood 1587–1590* (1962); *The writings of John Greenwood and Henry Barrow 1591–1593* (1970).

48. For a brief survey of some of these volumes see the entry in *New DNB* by Brett Usher. For a detailed discussion, see Dewey D. Wallace Jr, 'George Gifford, puritan propaganda and popular religion in Elizabethan England', *Sixteenth-Century Journal*, IX (1978), 27–49.

49. GL MS 9537/8, fo. 32v.

50. GL MS 9537/9, fo. 119r.

51. It consists mainly of modest bequests, including property in Maldon, to sons John, Daniel, Samuel, Jeremy, George and William; daughters Mary and Martha; and 'the child whereof my wife now goeth'. 'Good friends' remembered include Ralph Hawden of Langford, who would shortly succeed Robert Palmer as vicar of All Saints with St Peter. His wife ('Agnes') was appointed sole executrix: LMA DL/C/359, fo. 210r.

GRANDIDGE, RICHARD (d. 1619)

Rector of Bradfield St Clare, Suffolk, 1579–1619 (d.)

Grandidge matriculated sizar from St John's College, Cambridge, at Michaelmas 1567, graduated BA in early 1572 and was ordained priest at Ely, 17 April 1579.[1] Presented to Bradfield St Clare that year by Sir Robert Jermyn, he remained there for the rest of his life.[2] In 1580, he was one of ten preachers remembered in the will of Frances Jermyn, Sir

Robert's sister, with a Tremellius Bible 'fayer bound.'[3] His name appears on the lists of Suffolk ministers suspended for not subscribing and 'not resolved to subscribe' to Archbishop Whitgift's three articles in 1584.[4] He reported in 1603 that he held no other benefice, that the parish had only sixty-four communicants and that there were no recusants.[5] In the same year he was included on a diocesan list of 'bachelor of arte, preachers, heretofore scismatically affected'.[6] He made his will on 9 November 1619, leaving small bequests to his sons John and Isacke and to his daughters Anna, Rebecca and Judith and their children. Mr John Yates or any other godly preacher was to receive ten shillings for a funeral sermon.[7] Grandidge was buried on 9 December 1619.[8]

1. *Alum. Cantab.*, II, 247.
2. Bullen, 'Catalogue', p. 319.
3. SRO Bury St Edmunds, IC 500/1/40/30.
4. *Seconde Parte*, I, 242.
5. 'The condition', p. 2.
6. NRO DN VIS 3/3, fo. 100v.
7. NRO NCC 1621 55 Hudd.
8. NRO Inv 31/32.

GREAVES, LEONARD (d. 1615)

Vicar of Thurston, Suffolk, 1589–?; rector of Sprowston, Norfolk, ?–1615 (d.)

In the Chicago MS, Thomas Rogers describes Greaves as 'a yonger man' who gave way to the more senior men of the Bury exercise when it came to his turn to preach.[1] Licensed to preach on 18 March 1581, he was instituted to the vicarage of Thurston on 23 July 1589.[2] Still there in 1603, he was included ('Graves') in a list of 'ministers, preachers, noe graduates, scismatically affected heretofore.'[3] That year he reported that there were 170 communicants in the parish, that it was a crown living worth £6 13s 4d, and that Robert Bright of London was the present patron.[4] Nothing more is known of Greaves until the end of his life, when he drew up his will in Sprowston on 11 October 1615. He possessed lands in 'Heveningland' – Heveningham, Suffolk, or Hevingham, Norfolk? – had seven children and made bequests of £4 each to the poor of Sprowston, Bassingbourne, Cambridgeshire – his birthplace? – and Thurston. The will's most notable feature is the link it establishes with Zachary Catlin, who had married his daughter Marie. Probate was granted on 21 October 1615.[5] The total value of his goods and chattels was assessed at £189 2s 7d.[6]

1. See above, p. 156.
2. *Registrum Vagum*, p. 207.
3. NRO DN VIS 3/3, fo. 104r. It is impossible, therefore, that he was the Cambridge graduate of this name who was vicar of Oundle from 1583 and proceeded BD in 1595: *Alum. Cantab.*, II, 248.
4. 'The condition', p. 7.
5. NRO 181 Angell.
6. NRO Inv 27B/93.

HAW(K)DEN (HAWDYN), RALPH (c. 1555–1619)[1]

Curate or preacher at Langford, Fryerning and Margaretting, all Essex, intermittently from 1583 to 1600; vicar of All Saints and St Peter Maldon, Essex, 1600–19 (d.)

Hawden matriculated sizar from Christ's College, Cambridge, in December 1572, graduating BA in early 1577 and proceeding MA in 1580.[2] His ordination record has not been found but he seems to have abandoned Cambridge for a roving ministry: he was granted licence to serve any cure in the archdeaconries of Essex and Colchester on 6 November 1581.[3]

At the episcopal visitation of 1583 Hawden was on 15 July listed as curate of Langford. Failing to appear, and noted *concionator in aliis ecclesiis*, he was suspended for preaching 'abroade' without licence.[4] He was one of the twenty-seven ministers of southern Essex who petitioned against subscription to Whitgift's three articles early in 1584.[5] Later that year he signed the form of limited subscription drawn up by the Dedham conference and 'Certain requests' made to Archdeacon George Withers. He was also chosen for the 'generall conference' arranged to take place on the eve of the 1584 parliament.[6]

On 23 October 1585 he was examined by Aylmer in the presence of Anthony Barners, patron of the living, who had presented him to the rectory of Fryerning. Aylmer found him sufficiently qualified in Latin and the scriptures but when asked if he would accept not only the thirty-nine articles but also Whitgift's newly issued three, Hawden stated that he well knew of the latter (*bene cognovisse*) but was unwilling to consent to them. Aylmer therefore refused to institute him.[7]

On 3 March 1586, as of Margaretting, he was indicted at Chelmsford assizes for baptizing a child in Chelmsford church without using the sign of the cross. The indictment was removed to Queen's Bench by writ of *a certiorari* and he was not finally discharged until 24 July 1587.[8] On 7 May 1586 he nevertheless received a diocesan preaching licence at the commendation of Archdeacon Withers, with the assistance of members of the bishop's household (*per famulos Domini Episcopi apud Fulham*).[9] On 26 July 1586 he was present at the episcopal visitation as preacher of Fryerning and was subsequently suspended for failing to use the surplice or make the sign of the cross in baptism.[10] On 8 March 1587, with George Gifford, John Huckle, William Tunstall and Giles Whiting, Hawden made supplication to parliament for restoration.[11] In Hawden's case the immediate sequel is unknown but he is not listed in the visitation book of 1589. By 1592, however, he is found once more as preacher of Langford: the episcopal visitors inhibited him until he received a new licence under Aylmer's seal. He is not listed there in 1598.[12]

Hawden was appointed an overseer of George Gifford's will in May 1600 – once again 'of Langford' and one of his 'good friends' – with specific instructions as to the disposal of his library.[13] On 5 September 1600 he was instituted vicar of All Saints with St Peter Maldon at the presentation of Richard Francke.[14] He made his will on 28 October 1619; it received probate (Consistory Court of London) on 10 November following.[15]

1. Disastrously confused with Ralph Hough, vicar of Rayleigh (1594–1609 (d.)), by Jay Pascal Anglin, who accordingly misled W. J. Petchey: Anglin, 'The court of the archdeacon of Essex 1571–1609', Ph.D thesis, University of California (1965), p. 436; Petchey, *A prospect of Maldon, passim.*
2. *Alum. Cantab.*, II, 333; Peile, *Biographical register*, I, 124.
3. LMA DL/C/333, fo. 267r.
4. GL MS 9537/5, fos. 4v, 91v.
5. *Seconde parte*, I, 225.
6. See above, pp. 82, 87, 90–1.
7. LMA DL/C/334, fo. 65r.
8. J. S. Cockburn, ed., *Calendar of assize records: Essex indictments Elizabeth I* (HMSO, 1978), nos 1640, 1645, 1749, 1818.
9. LMA DL/C/334, fo. 91v.
10. GL MS 9537/6, fo. 152r; *Seconde parte*, II, 164, 260.
11. *Seconde parte*, II, 258–9.
12. GL MSS 9537/8, fo. 28v; /9, fo. 115r.
13. LMA DL/C/359, fos. 210v–11r.
14. Reg. Bancroft, fo. 19v.
15. LMA DL/C/360, fos. 384v–5r. Property in Latchingdon and Lawling went to his younger son James. Property in Bradwell-iuxta-Mare was to be sold and the profits to be divided between

daughters Elizabeth, Isobel and Joan at twenty-one or marriage. There were smaller bequests to his (?married) daughters Sarah and Mary and the residue was left to his wife Johan, she to be executrix. His overseers were his eldest son John and sons-in-law Henry Bachelor and Edward Emersham.

HOLT, ROBERT (d. 1613)

Rector of Ingham, Suffolk, 1571–1613 (d.)

'M. Holt' is several times mentioned in the early pages of the Chicago manuscript as an active member of the Bury exercise and one who appears to have been on familiar or even friendly terms with Thomas Rogers.[1] It is significant, for example, that Holt did not sign the letter of complaint from the other members to Bishop Scambler.[2]

One John Holt was incumbent of Bradfield Combust, Suffolk, some five miles south-east of Bury,[3] but the member of the Bury exercise is more likely to have been Robert Holt, rector of Ingham, a parish less than four miles to the north. This man matriculated sizar from St John's College, Cambridge, in 1561, graduating BA in early 1565 and proceeding MA in 1568. He was ordained a deacon at Ely on 29 July 1565.[4] Instituted to Ingham in 1571,[5] Holt held the living until his death. In 1603 he reported that the parish had fifty communicants, with no recusants or separatists. Sir Nicholas Bacon was the patron.[6] In the diocesan survey carried out that same year, Holt is one of those (including Thomas Rogers) who were listed as 'masters of arte, preachers of honest life and conversation'. His living was worth £12 16s 0½d annually.[7]

Holt's will corroborates the image of a learned protestant conformist. He drew it up on 2 March 1613, trusting through God's

> immensurable mercie in the meritt of Christe Jesus to be an Inheritour of the kingdome of heaven. And my bodie being duste and ashes I betaketo the earthe in certaine hope of eternall lyfe desyring to be buryed in the chauncell of Ingham by my firste good wyef. And to have the grave stone layd on me whiche I have longe kept and is in my litle barne whiche put me in mynde of my mortallitie.

He possessed a number of properties in the area and made very specific bequests. His son-in-law, Thomas Goddard, was to receive 'Gualter on the smalle Prophette' and his best 'wallnuttree chaire'. He left his son Jeremy all his books, 'wishinge him to bestowe somme of the Englishe bookes on his systers, suche as are fittest for them'. Probate was granted on 19 April 1613.[8]

1. See above, pp. 157, 158–9.
2. See above, pp. 175–6.
3. Bullen, 'Catalogue', p. 306.
4. *Alum. Cantab.*, II, 400.
5. *Registrum Vagum*, p. 191, where his name is mistakenly given as John Holte.
6. 'The condition', p. 13.
7. NRO DN VIS 3/3, fo. 95r.
8. NRO 3 Cooney.

HUCKLE, JOHN (c. 1553–1625)

Preacher at Good Easter, Essex, c. 1582–4; curate of Aythorpe Roding, Essex, ?1584–8; curate of Hatfield Broak Oak, Essex, <1589>; lecturer of Hatfield Broadoak, c. 1600–25 (d.)

Nothing is known of Huckle's origins or early career except that he graduated BA from Christ's College, Cambridge, in early 1574.[1] He is first found in the London records at the episcopal visitation of 1583 as preacher at Good Easter, where Robert, 3rd Lord Rich was laying claim to ordinary jurisdiction over against the bishop. Absent on 9 July, he presented himself at Chelmsford on 18 July and claimed that he was licensed to preach by Archbishop Grindal 'but never spake personally with him'; that he had been ordered by the bishop of Lincoln (Thomas Cooper) 'about ii or iij yeres agoe' and left Lincoln diocese without letters dimissory. He admitted preaching at Chelmsford, Roxwell, Maldon, Stebbing, Chignal St Mary and St James, and at 'divers other places' in London diocese by virtue of Grindal's licence, but had never administered the sacraments, even in Good Easter 'where he readeth'. When asked if he was prepared to do so, he asked for 'respite for that he is not yet resolute'. In the upshot he was ordered to enter into bonds not to preach anywhere in the diocese and to attend Aylmer personally on 25 July following at Much Hadham, bringing with him his Letters of Orders and his preaching licence.[2]

With Derek Helden, Huckle was summoned into consistory on 7 October 1583 for preaching 'often' in All Saints Maldon without licence, presumably at the invitation of the vicar, George Gifford.[3] No more is heard of the matter but these initial clashes were soon superseded by Archbishop Whitgift's demand for clerical subscription in early 1584. Huckle – either still suspended or else suspended a second time – was one of twenty-seven Essex ministers who petitioned the privy council in protest at the archbishop's proceedings.[4] The privy council, perhaps at the instigation of Lord Rich, took up his case, soliciting Aylmer for his immediate restoration. Aylmer replied on 28 April that he 'dare not' restore Huckle 'who hath shewed himselfe a daungerous man, not only himselfe denyinge Athanasius creede, but bringeinge two other preachers into the same error of Arrianisme, which opinion he held againste me in diverse conferences'. Ignoring the issue of subscription, he merely stated that he could not in conscience set Huckle at liberty until he had 'better and longer experience of him'. The council – Burghley, Knollys, Warwick, Walsingham, Charles Howard and Henry Sidney – reacted swiftly, replying on 4 May that they had examined Huckle themselves, found him free of any taint of Arianism, 'clear and sound in religion', and saw no reason why he should not exercise his ministry.[5] Aylmer probably refused to give way since on 7 May he took the precaution of informing Burghley personally that he had made 'humble' answer to the council's letter, reiterating that at visitation he had found Huckle 'a very busy disordered man, an enemy of the peace of the church, an impugner of the book, a gatherer of night conventicles, and of late a busy disputer against Athanasius creed', and last of all 'an obstinate denier to subscribe'. Thus he 'dare not but with great triall readmit him to preach, being but a simple scholar and therefore easily carried into errors'. He trusted that both Burghley and the council would permit him to use his discretion 'in the ordering of further offenders unknown to your LL. and much complained of to me . . . divers years past'.[6]

Meanwhile Huckle had become a member of the Braintree conference and seems to have continued to be associated with it for the rest of its existence. He was one of those chosen for the 'generall' conference arranged to take place on the eve of the 1584 parliament.[7]

He migrated to Aythorpe Roding, where he continued to hold night 'conventicles'.[8] At the episcopal visitation of 1586, described as curate there, he was indicted for refusing to baptize an illegitimate child which had subsequently died. In the aftermath he was suspended for refusing the surplice.[9] With Roger Carr, George Gifford, Ralph Hawden, William Tunstall and Giles Whiting, he petitioned parliament for restoration on 8 March 1587.[10] Despite the almost immediate deprivation of Tunstall and Whiting from their benefices, the Braintree conference continued to meet, and with Carr, Culverwell, Rogers and Whiting, Huckle wrote to the Dedham conference on 7 June 1587 requesting the secondment of Laurence Newman.[11]

Huckle is not mentioned again in the diocesan records until the episcopal visitation of 1592, when he is found as preacher of Hatfield Broad Oak: still refusing to subscribe, he was inhibited until prepared to do so.[12] Although he is not found in the episcopal visitation book of 1598 he was by 1600 firmly established in Hatfield Broad Oak in a lectureship financed by the Barringtons, the most important godly family in Lord Rich's orbit. Here, Huckle's wife won 'a great name . . . for skill . . . in training up young Gentlewomen'.[13] Licensed to preach without subscription in 1605,[14] he was called into consistory on 16 May 1608 when James Tompsett, vicar of Hatfield Broad Oak, appeared on his behalf and deposed that Huckle was now a 'diseased man so much troubled with the palsy & the colick that he is not able to appear'. He was ordered nevertheless to administer in a surplice according to the canons.[15]

Huckle survived to marry a second wife, Anne Hopkins, widow, at St Anne Blackfriars, London, on 23 October 1615.[16] He remained at Hatfield Broad Oak until his death.[17] He made his will on 18 April 1620, adding a codicil on 21 April 1625. Probate was granted (PCC) on 13 May following.[18]

1. *Alum. Cantab.*, II, 423; Peile, *Biographical register*, I, 113.
2. GL MS 9537/5, fos. 2r, 47r, 109v.
3. LMA DL/C/300, p. 222.
4. *Seconde parte*, I, 225.
5. *Ibid.*, II, 245–6.
6. BL, Lansdowne MS 42/42.
7. See above, pp. 90–1.
8. Collinson, *EPM*, p. 379. The aged rector, Laurence Clayton, had been instituted as long ago as 1548 at the presentation of William Parr, marquess of Northampton: GL MS 9531/12, fo. 169v. It is not clear who was presently patron of the living (and thus, perhaps, also of Huckle) since in 1587 Clayton's successor was collated by Aylmer *per lapsum*: Reg. Grindal, fo. 236v.
9. GL MS 9537/6, fo. 40v; *Seconde parte*, II, 164, 260.
10. *Seconde parte*, II, 258. For the likely context, see above, p. 190.
11. See above, p. 107.
12. GL MS 9537/8, fo. 70v.
13. Nicholas Guy, *Pieties Pillar: or, a sermon preached at the funerall of Mistresse Elizabeth Gouge* (1626), p. 39. One of Mrs Huckle's charges was Elizabeth Coys. It was probably Ezekiel and Winifred Culverwell (*nee* Hildersham) who in 1604 selected her from the Huckle establishment as a suitable wife for Ezekiel's nephew, William Gouge.
14. LMA DL/C/338, fos. 303v, 217v.
15. LMA DL/C/307, p. 417.
16. GL MS 4509/1 [unpaginated]. Presumably the ceremony was performed by William Gouge, the minister there.
17. Arthur Searle, ed., *Barrington family letters 1628–1632* (Camden Society, 4th series, XXVIII, 1983), 13.
18. PRO PCC PROB11/145 (54 Clerke). Following an extraordinarily individual preamble, he directed that his freeholds in Peldon be sold to best advantage by his executors, with the assistance of his 'good friend' Richard Hildersham of Hatfield (steward of the Barrington estates) and distributed amongst his family. Bequests to the four unmarried daughters of his late sister, Agnes Bingham, totalled £220. His wife was left £100 'in full discharge of an obligation where I stand bound to pay her such a sum' and her three unmarried daughters by her first marriage, Gersham, Bethia and Pheby, 20s each. One of his executors, Edward Rowse of Moreton, glover, received £10 and his wife, Elizabeth (?his daughter by his first marriage), lands in Stevenage, Herts. In the codicil he added an annuity to his wife of £5 out of a lease from an (unnamed) Oxford college. Altogether monetary bequests totalled at least £360.

KNEVET(T), THOMAS (d. 1626)

Rector of Milend [St Michael Mile End] (Colchester), Essex, 1585–1626 (d.)

Knevett, of unknown parentage, graduated BA from Jesus College, Cambridge, in 1578, proceeding MA in 1581 and commencing BD in 1595.[1] He was possibly the 'Mr

Knevet' listed as schoolmaster of Feering (about seven miles southwest of Colchester) in July 1580.[2]

No ordination record has been found and Knevett is nowhere listed in Essex during the episcopal visitation of 1583. Although he was not one of the twenty-seven ministers of southern Essex who appealed against subscription in early 1584, he nevertheless signed the limited form of subscription drawn up later that year by the Dedham conference.[3] He was instituted rector of Milend (MA) by John Aylmer, bishop of London, on 13 March 1585 at the presentation of Sir Thomas Lucas.[4] Present as rector and preacher there at the episcopal visitation of July 1586, he was subsequently suspended 'for preching in his owne charge without a lycense'.[5] On 4 October 1588 he was ordered to present a theological exercise to Archdeacon George Withers.[6] At the episcopal visitation of 1589 he was present, but ordered to certify in October that he wore the surplice and observed the Book of Common Prayer.[7] During that of 1592 he was listed as *concionator notus*.[8]

Present at Bancroft's primary visitation of 1598, he was ordered to 'attend to be approved' – perhaps, since he was now BD, as a commissioner for the clerical exercises rather than for his conformity.[9] Listed as one of the 'diligent and sufficient' clergy of Essex 1604,[10] he is not known to have been arraigned subsequently for any nonconformist practices. His successor was instituted on 22 September 1626 and his (unnamed) widow granted letters of administration on 17 October following.[11]

1. *Alum. Cantab.*, III, 5.
2. GL MS 9537/4, fo. 98r.
3. See above, p. 87.
4. Reg. Grindal, fo. 217v.
5. GL MS 9537/6, fos. 53v, 140r; further listed as 'rector' and preacher of the donative curacy of St Giles but inhibited from preaching until licensed: *ibid.*, fos. 52r, 139v. *Seconde parte*, II, 164, 261.
6. ERO D/ACV 1, fo. 71r. There is nothing necessarily sinister in this monition: it seems possible that Withers had taken on the task of supervising those studies which in 1595 resulted in the award of a BD degree.
7. GL MS 9537/7, fo. 41v.
8. GL MS 9537/8, fo. 52r.
9. GL MS 9537/9, fo. 105v.
10. 'A viewe', p. 6.
11. LMA DL/C/342, fo. 234v.

KNEWSTUB, JOHN (1544–1624)

Rector of Cockfield, Suffolk, 1579–1624 (d.)

Knewstub was undoubtedly the most influential and powerful of the godly ministers who participated in the Bury combination lectures. His godly connexions stretched well beyond the *pays* of west Suffolk. Born in Kirkby Stephen, Westmorland in 1544, he matriculated pensioner of St John's College, Cambridge, at Michaelmas 1561, graduating BA in early 1565. He proceeded MA in 1568 and BD in 1576. A fellow of St John's from 1567, he was appointed university preacher in 1570.[1] During his Cambridge years, Knewstub was not only a strong supporter of Thomas Cartwright[2] but also a member of a group that included Laurence Chaderton, Ezekiel Culverwell, Lancelot Andrewes and John Carter, who met regularly for spiritual edification. This seems to have proved seminal for his later involvement in combination lectures and conferences in East Anglia.[3]

He was instituted rector of Cockfield, Suffolk, on 13 August 1579.[4] The patron of the living was Sir William Spring and the parish of Rushbrooke, only four miles to the north, was the seat of Sir Robert Jermyn. It is telling that he dedicated *An aunsweare unto certaine assertions tending to maintaine the Churche of Rome* (1579) 'to those gentlemen in Suffolke whom the true worshipping of God hath made right worshipfull'.[5]

Knewstub established his public reputation in the late 1570s, most notably with his popular lectures on the twentieth chapter of Exodus, first published in 1577.[6] Two years later, his famous confutation of the Family of Love appeared, as did his attack on the church of Rome and a printed version of his Good Friday sermon preached at Paul's Cross in 1576.[7] These works demonstrate that he was a client of the Dudleys. The *confutation* was dedicated to 'his very good Lord and Maister Ambrose, Earl of Warwick', and his Lectures on Exodus to Anne countess of Warwick, as 'some remembraunce of my thankefulnesse and dutie toward any of that honourable house of Warwick, to the which I am (in the Lord) so many wayes indebted'.[8]

Unmarried (a fact which impressed his colleague Richard Rogers, who spoke of 'his contentation in a sole life'),[9] Knewstub's energy, personality and presbyterian leanings made him the virtual superintendent of the moderate puritan tradition within west Suffolk. In 1577 an agreement was negotiated between the magistrates and townsmen of Bury St Edmunds whereby the nomination of the clergy serving Bury's two parish churches was committed to John Still, archdeacon of Sudbury, and to Knewstub.[10] In a similar initiative the parishioners of nearby Lawshall agreed to give £10 to support a preacher 'so as he might have bene such a one as Mr Knewstubb and other good men would have allowed'.[11] And in January 1581, Knewstub was given a roving commission by the privy council to advise the bishops of London, Winchester, Lincoln, Salisbury and Worcester on the best means of combatting the Familist heresy.[12] During these years there are numerous references to his preaching activities in Suffolk, Essex and Cambridgeshire, and he was the recipient of many bequests to be found in the wills of the godly.[13]

Thanks to Bancroft's detective work, we know that Knewstub corresponded closely with John Field in London and that he played host to 'an assembly of three-score Ministers, appointed out of Essex, Cambridge-shiere, and Norfolke, to meete the eighth of May, 1582. at Cockefield, (Maister Knewstubs towne) there to conferre of the common booke'.[14] Despite his standing, he was not immune from the increasing pressures for strict conformity to the prayer book and in the troubled summer of 1583 Oliver Pigge wrote to Walsingham from Bury gaol with the report that, as well as himself, 'sondrie other godlie and learned preachers' had been 'indighted at this last assises, of which number Mr John Knewstub is sayd to be one.'[15]

The godly network sustained him: he, Dudley Fenner and George Gifford all accompanied the earl of Leicester as his chaplains during the campaigns in the Low Countries in 1585–6.[16] Knewstub preached the sermon on St George's day 1586 at Utrecht, when Leicester deported himself 'with such decorum and Princely behaviour'.[17] By the middle of 1586, John Stubbs reported to Lord Willoughby that 'Mr Newstubbe is safely returned, and desires me to put you earnestly in mind for providing and procuring a preacher for Berghen op Zoom.'[18] In September 1587, Knewstub and Walter Allen represented Suffolk in the synod held in Cambridge.[19] Following the death in 1595 of William Whitaker, Master of St John's College, Cambridge, Knewstub was one of several compromise candidates suggested by the fellows as his successor.[20]

Sixty years of age when King James convened the Hampton Court conference in 1604, Knewstub was one of the four leading nonconformist ministers – the others were Laurence Chaderton, John Reynolds and Thomas Sparke – summoned to attend at James's personal behest. Their very moderate stance famously irritated James, who concluded that their objections to episcopal government were trivial, and accordingly enraged their less moderate colleagues and followers.[21] Thus the case for any serious revision of the Elizabethan settlement of 1559 was lost for ever. Knewstub's thoughts on the matter are not on record.

Doubtless he came under immediate pressure to conform. In 1605 his friend and colleague William Bedell wrote to Samuel Ward, entreating him 'to provide for Mr Knewstub yf you may any young man that would be his Curate and teach in his parish that would weare the surplice.'[22] Although Knewstub appears to have managed to avoid any serious punishment for his persistent nonconformity, he was still presented in the episcopal vistation of Norwich in 1611 because he neither wore the surplice nor used the sign of the cross in baptism.[23]

Knewstub survived in Cockfield for a further thirteen years, and wrote his will on 20 May 1624, declaring that he was of perfect memory and in good health. He bequeathed his soul to Almighy God,

> onlie good and blessed forever, from whome as I have once receaved the mercies of creation and redemption so have I beene followed hetherto, with the fruites of those favoures to a just clayme of a faithfull creator and redeemer on the behalfe of his divine Majesty towardes mee and to a most true profession on my behalfe of that which hee (by his Prophet) affirmeth, that all his shall saie and sweare to wytt, That in the Lord they have righteousnes and strengthe, soe as the whole seede of Israell shalbee justified and glorie in the Lord.

He had previously established two exhibitions at St John's for the scholars of Kirkby Stephen and Cockfield, 'to witnes to all the world my thankfull acknowledgment of all those mercies which I mett withall in that right worshipfull and most worthie societie'. He had no wife or children and his bequests to fellow ministers speak tellingly of the depth of friendship which he had established over forty years. His 'auncient good friend Mr Henry Sandes of Groton, clarke', was left £5. Humphrey Munnings of Brettenham, 'Mr Chambers' of Assington, 'Mr Peachie' of Great Waldingfield and 'Mr Chamberlin, minister of Hunston' each received 40s. His 'reverend good friend Mr [Ezekiel] Culverwell of London' was left a piece of gold worth 22s. Eleven shillings each went to 'Mr Beadle of Horningsheathe', 'Mr Hall of Walsham in the willowes', 'Mr Edgar of Hawstead', 'Mr James Wollfenden of little Weltham', 'Mr Harrison of Sudbury', 'Mr Stansby of little Waldingfield', 'Mr Morgan of Bildeston' and 'Mr Willson of Sudbury'. The will also makes clear that he was on good terms with John Winthrop of Groton and with the chorographer Robert Ryece of Preston. Knewstub died on 29 May 1624, and he was buried in Cockfield churchyard. His will was proved (PCC) on 15 June 1624.[24]

1. *Alum. Cantab.*, III, 28.
2. H. C. Porter, *Reformation and reaction in Tudor Cambridge* (Cambridge, 1958), p. 190.
3. Samuel Clarke, *Lives of sundry eminent persons in the later age* (London, 1683), p. 2.
4. NRO DN/REG/14, fo. 38v.
5. John Knewstub, *An aunsweare unto certaine ascertions . . .* (London, 1574), epistle dedicatory.
6. John Knewstub, *The lectures of John Knewstub upon the twentieth chapter of Exodus . . .* (London, 1577). Other editions appeared in 1578, 1579 and 1584.
7. John Knewstub, *A confutation of . . . the Familie of Love* (London, 1579); *A sermon preached at Paules Crosse . . .* (Lonodon, 1579).
8. Epistle dedicatory.
9. Knappen., *Two puritan diaries*, p. 59.
10. BL, Egerton MS 1693, fo. 98r.
11. BL, Add MS 38492, no. 63, fo. 107.
12. *APC*, XII, 317.
13. For example, he was one of ten preachers bequeathed Tremellius bibles 'fayer bound' in the will of Frances Jermyn, sister of Sir Robert, in 1580: SRO Bury St Edmunds IC/500/1/40/30.
14. Bancroft, *Daungerous positions*, pp. 44, 120–2.
15. PRO SP 12/161/33.
16. Adams, ed., *Household accounts . . . of Robert Dudley, earl of Leicester*, p. 368.

17. J. Bruce ed., *Correspondence of Robert Dudley, Earl of Leycester* (Camden Society, 1st series, XXVII, 1844), p. 238.
18. HMC, *Ancaster*, p. 25.
19. BL, Harley MS 7029, pp. 127–8.
20. BL, Lansdowne MS 79, fo. 156r.
21. See, for example, [Henry Jacob] *A Christian and modest offer of a most indifferent conference, or disputation* (London, 1606), sig. D3r.
22. Bodl., Tanner MS 75, fos. 126, 129, 130v.
23. NRO DN VIS 4/3 [unfoliated].
24. PRO PROB 11/143, fo. 429r.

LEWIS, ROBERT (c. 1550–1618)

Rector of Markshall, Essex, 1573–82 (resig.); vicar of St Peter Colchester, Essex, 1579–89 (resig.); preacher at Bury St Edmunds, Suffolk, 1589–98; rector of Rushbrooke, Suffolk, 1598–1618 (d.)

Born in Colchester, son of John Lewis (d. by 1569 as of Lydd, Kent), Lewis went to school there and was admitted pensioner at Gonville and Caius College, Cambridge, on 6 February 1569, aged eighteen. He graduated BA from St John's in early 1572, proceeding MA from Caius in 1575. Meanwhile he had been ordained priest at Rochester on 17 February 1573.[1]

Instituted rector of Markshall on 20 February 1573 at the presentation of Edward Deraugh, Lewis compounded for the benefice on 5 May following.[2] Nothing is known of his tenure there beyond the fact that he was recorded present at the episcopal visitations of 1574, 1577 and 1580.[3] He resigned Markshall by 30 August 1582.[4]

Meanwhile he had been collated vicar of St Peter Colchester by Archbishop Edmund Grindal, *pleno iure*, on 3 December 1579.[5] On 4 March 1581 the vicarage was sequestered because Lewis had failed to compound for his first fruits.[6] Since its value was pitched at a rough-and-ready £10 per annum, the threshold below which first fruits for vicarages were not payable, it seems likely that he was subsequently excused.[7]

One of the most active members of the Dedham conference, Lewis is recorded as chosen for, or acting as, host, speaker or moderator on an impressive eighteen occasions.[8] His prominence reflects his status as the senior beneficed clergyman in Colchester but underlying the many references to him is the naked truth that he and George Northey, common preacher, were openly vying for the support of the Colchester godly in the public arena. This accounts for the fact that on 4 February 1583, at his first recorded intervention, he propounded whether the people should leave their pastor 'when he teacheth to goe to heare others ordenrely' (**3M**).

In May 1583 he and Dowe were appointed to deal with Richard Jones, rector there, about the Manningtree plays (**6M**). During the following weeks he attempted to deal, without success, in the matter of Periman (**7M**). In June he was advised to cease expounding upon Genesis since Northey was now doing so in his public lectures (**8M**).

On 11 July, by which time he was also serving the cure at St Runwald, he claimed before Aylmer's episcopal visitors to have a diocesan preaching licence but did not hand it in; he was ordered to do so that afternoon.[9] He and Tey were appointed on 5 August 1583 to confer with lawyers about the legality of their meetings (**9M**). In early October he was called back into consistory on the charge that he had not worn the surplice because none was available. The churchwardens were accordingly ordered to provide one.[10]

In April 1584 Lewis contributed 10s for Henry Wilcock (**17M**). He informed the brethren on 3 August 1584 that Whitgift was offering 'Articles to some and an othe', desiring to know what should be done; it was agreed that 'we shuld heare something by the brethren to whom the othe was offred' (**21M**). In the event – though the minutes never allude to the fact – both Lewis and Richard Parker were suspended for not subscribing at this time.[11]

In October Lewis moved a question of 'filthines' and confession which was not debated (**23M**). In January 1585 he was one of six members delegated to confer with Dr Oxenbridge (**26M**). Involved in the great debate over Andrewes's departure from Wenham, he and Newman conveyed Andrewes's final apologies for his absence in March (**Extra M**, 17 February 1585; **28M**). His request on 5 April for a ruling as to what to do about those who deserted him on the Sabbath when Northey preached was prudently deferred, but on that occasion he also conveyed the message from Tey, following the death of his brother Thomas, which elucidates so many of the more obscure references which follow (**29M**).

Lewis continued to press for some kind of arbitration between himself and Northey, and in August 1585, probably with extreme reluctance, Chapman, Crick and Tey agreed to 'deale' with Northey and the bailiffs (**33M**). In October he conveyed another letter from Tey, still struggling to reconcile his duties at Peldon with his new responsibilities at Layer Hall (**36M**).

By February 1586 Lewis was facing a new threat: the attempt of Mrs Katherine Audley, true patron of St Peter Colchester, 'for his removinge out of his place' (**40M**). Her attempts were in some way parried but they may in the long term have decided Lewis to resign the benefice since there can be little doubt that she was indeed the true patron and Lewis's collation by Grindal technically illegal.

Once again present before Aylmer's visitors on 22 July 1586, Lewis was listed as preacher, vicar of St Peter and curate of St Runwald.[12] He was one of the many who were subsequently suspended for refusal to wear the surplice and threatened with deprivation.[13] For the moment, however, he seems to have been more concerned that his parishioners preferred Northey's sermons to his own. In March 1587 he proposed that 'a pastor should have his own people' and Chapman, Crick and Tey were again delegated to speak to Northey (**54M**). Chapman and Crick reported back in April that they had 'moved Mr Northie for Mr Lewis his people, and he said, he wold not deal in yt'. Lewis craved further negotiations but the matter was 'not consulted of' (**55M**).

On 12 June 1587 Lewis asked advice about how to deal with the fact that he was currently excommunicated (**57M**). In August, with Newman, he was chosen to attend a 'generall meeting' in Cambridge and was one of six members delegated to attempt to heal the rifts between Crick, Tilney and the congregation at East Bergholt (**59M**). On 5 February 1588 he asked 'what he might do for his matter soe often propounded to them whether he might not receive another calling being offred him, deferred' (**65M**). On 2 June he propounded whether he might wear the surplice rather than forsake his ministry: it was 'generally' thought he should not yield and a full answer was deferred 'till we heard from our brethren' (**68M**).

Lewis took formal leave of the conference on 13 January 1589, being 'called' to Bury St Edmunds (**75M**).[14] There he served until 1598 as one of two preachers in the parish of St Mary who between them shared an annual stipend of £80.[15] In 1598 he was presented by Sir Robert Jermyn to the rectory of Rushbrooke. In 1603, during John Jegon's primary visitation of Norwich diocese, he was included in a list of preachers and masters of arts 'heretofore scismatically affected'.[16] He seems to have been allowed nevertheless to go his own way. At the 1611 visitation it was recorded that 'Mr Lewes doth not weare the surplise at all neyther dothe he weare the capp or typpett'. The parish possessed no 'regester booke to regester the straunge preachers'.[17]

Lewis made his will as 'minister of the word of God and parson of Rushbrooke' on 9 January 1616 [sic] and was buried at Rushbrooke on 10 March 1618.[18] The will received probate (PCC) on 23 April 1618.[19]

His wife Mary, daughter of Nicholas Clere, alderman of Colchester, made her own will on 12 October 1620. It contains a huge number of bequests to family and friends, in particular the children of her brother Nicholas Clere and her sisters Anna Sherman, Jane Thurston, 'Read' and Elizabeth Weston. Her principal bequest, however, was £100 to the Master 'and Seniors' of St John's College, Cambridge, to be 'put to the best use for the said college that the said Master and seniors and Mr Beadle, preacher of the word of God in Horningsheath . . . Suffolk, and my executor . . . shall devise and think fit of'.[20]

1. *Alum. Cantab.*, III, 81; Venn, *Biographical history*, p. 64; ERO (Colchester), Morant MS D/Y 2/10, p. 33.
2. Reg. Grindal, fo. 170v; PRO E334/8, fo. 331r.
3. GL MSS 9537/3, fo. 83v; /4, fos. 33v, 98r.
4. Reg. Grindal, fo. 206r.
5. LPL, Register of Edmund Grindal, part 2, fo. 532v.
6. LMA DL/C/333, fo. 249v. There is no record in the relevant composition books, PRO E334/9 and 10, that he ever compounded.
7. The legend that he was the Robert Lewis imprisoned in Newgate for nonconformity in November 1581 derives from Davids, *Annals*, p. 113, was perpetuated in Usher, 1905, p. xlii, and is thus enshrined in Venn, *Alum. Cantab.*, III, 81. The Newgate prisoner is in fact stated to be a husbandman of 'Hascame' (?Harescombe), Gloucestershire: PRO SP12/150/74.
8. **2, 4, 13, 17, 18, 26, 27, 28, 30, 33, 40, 48, 49, 53, 58, 61, 68, 72MM**.
9. GL MS 9537/5, fos. 3r, 60r. No preaching licence has been located in the vicar general's books, either before this date or afterwards.
10. LMA DL/C/300, p. 184.
11. *Seconde parte*, II, 164.
12. GL MS 9537/6, fo. 140v.
13. *Seconde parte*, II, 164, 261.
14. He wrote to the Colchester bailiffs from Bury on 18 February 1589 in an attempt to solve a local dispute: ERO (Colchester), Morant MS D/Y 2/8, p. 189.
15. Accounts of guildhall feoffees: SRO Bury St Edmunds HD 1150/1.
16. NRO DN VIS 3/3, fo. 98r.
17. NRO DN VIS 4/3, [unfoliated] fo. [ ].
18. *Alum. Cantab.*, III, 81.
19. PRO PCC PROB 11/131 (28 Mead). Requested burial at St Mary's Bury St Edmunds as near as possible to the body of 'my dear and faithful brother Mr George Estey as conveniently may be'. Personal bequests to his loving brethren James Wallis, minister of 'Stow Lanthorne', Suffolk; Mr Ward, parson of 'Livermeere'; Mr Bedell and Mr Helye, preachers at Bury; and Mr Wolfenden, parson of 'Little Weltham'. The residue to his 'true and faithful wife Marie Lewis', daughter of Nicholas Clere, late alderman of Colchester, she to be sole executrix. His 'loving brethren in law', Thomas Haselwoode and Thomas Thurstone, aldermen of Colchester, to be overseers.
20. PRO PCC PROB 11/136 (109 Soame). The legacy to St John's is rehearsed in ERO (Colchester) Morant MS D/Y 2/10, p. 33. The money was used to set up a closed scholarship at the college: see G. H. Martin, *The history of Colchester Royal Grammar School* (Colchester, 1947), pp. 37–8.

LOWE, THOMAS (c. 1553–1615)

Curate of Little Dunmow, Essex, 1577–?9; vicar of Gosfield, Essex, 1579–80 (resig.); curate of St Leonard Colchester, Essex, ?1580–2; rector of St Leonard Colchester, 1582–1615 (d.); rector of St Mary Magdalen Hospital, Colchester, by July 1586 (probably until death)

Nothing is known of Lowe before he graduated BA from Clare College, Cambridge, in early 1576. He was ordained deacon at Ely on 21 December following.[1] He may have briefly gravitated to Chapel-en-le-Frith, Derbyshire, but was doubtless the curate of Little Dunmow listed present at John Aylmer's primary visitation of London on 6 July 1577.[2] He was ordained priest by Aylmer on 6 October 1577 (BA of Clare; aged 24 or so).[3]

Although instituted vicar of Gosfield (BA) on 28 July 1579 at the nomination of William Dean, *armiger*, and his wife Anne Lady Maltravers to the patron, Edward 17th earl of Oxford, Lowe's title was evidently deemed to be ineffective, no residence clause being inserted in his letters of institution – a circumstance probably discovered when he presented them at Aylmer's second visitation on 6 July 1580. He was therefore re-instituted, and the error rectified, on 18 August 1580. Yet on 14 November letters of sequestration were issued to the churchwardens following his resignation.[4]

Since Gosfield's revenues were slim, Lowe may have considered himself just as well off as a curate in Colchester. Perhaps also the godly had marked him out as successor to Thomas Upcher at St Leonard, for on 8 April 1582, as curate there, he received letters of sequestration because the benefice was now vacant.[5] On 9 May he was instituted rector of St Leonard, a crown living in the hands of the Lord Chancellor, following Upcher's resignation.[6]

Lowe was listed present, as rector of St Leonard and a preacher licensed by the bishop of London, at Aylmer's third episcopal visitation on 11 July 1583, but was ordered to bring in his licence in the afternoon.[7] In fact he had none, and it was probably at this time that Aylmer gave him personal permission to preach without formal licence.[8]

Although an original signatory of the Dedham meeting, Lowe is not actually mentioned in the minutes until 2 September 1583, as one of four speakers at a fast at East Bergholt (**10M**). Yet during the meeting of 5 August 1583 – that immediately following the visitation – someone observed that 'our meetinges were knowen and thretned' (**9M**). Was this Lowe, running scared after his recent encounter and subsequent accommodation with Aylmer? It might account for the fact that he is thereafter virtually lost to sight. Although speaker at his own house in Colchester on 1 December 1583 (**13M**), he is not listed as contributing to the relief of Wilcock in April 1584 (**17M**). Later that year he subscribed the limited form of subscription drawn up by the Dedham conference[9] but by 3 August 1584 'it was thought good' that he be 'ernestly delt withall' to rejoin the meeting 'with diligence and cherfulnes'. William Tey was delegated to confer with him to find out why he had absented himself from the conference and, if he 'prevailed not', to enlist the help of Farrar and then Chapman and Parker (**21M**). No more is heard of Lowe in the Dedham minutes and thereafter he was relegated by the brethren to the status of non-person.

Present at Aylmer's episcopal visitation on 22 July 1586, Lowe was stated to have been admitted a preacher by Aylmer *privatim* on '15 July 1586'. By this point, too, he had also been nominated 'rector', and appointed preacher, of St Mary Magdalen's Hospital in Colchester but was admonished 'not to meddle' with the profits of the 'parsonage and hospital'.[10]

It was a sufficient peg for the Dedham brethren by which to hang him. Far from being 'painful' or 'sufficient' in the version of the survey of Essex clergy finalized in the wake of the visitation of 1586, Lowe is merely listed as double-beneficed in Colchester.[11] In 1589, however, he was one of the Colchester clergy whom Aylmer's visitors trusted to oversee the exercises of the less able clergy.[12] He was never again involved in any nonconformist activity and whereas his surviving colleagues were all described as 'diligent and sufficient' in 1604, he was merely written off as double-beneficed.[13]

Lowe made his will on 15 August 1615 and died within hours, since on 23 August a successor was instituted to St Leonard. The will was probated (Consistory Court of London) on 4 September 1615, letters of administration being issued to Benjamin Jones since Thomas Lowe, cleric, his son and executor, was then in Ireland. Thomas Lowe was subsequently granted probate as executor on 10 November.[14]

1. *Alum. Cantab.*, III, 110.
2. GL MS 9537/4, fo. 20v.
3. GL MS 9535/1, fo. 157r.
4. Reg. Grindal, fos. 196r, 199r; GL MS 9537/4, fo. 89v; LMA DL/C/333, fo. 234r.
5. LMA DL/C/333, fo. 282v.
6. *Ibid.*, fo. 205r.
7. GL MS 9537/5, fos. 3r, 59r.
8. In 1586 it was stated that he had been licensed by Aylmer *privatim* on 16 July 1586: GL MS 9537/6, fo. 140r. It seems likely that this is an error for 1583.
9. See above, p. 87.
10. GL MS 9537/6, fos. 53r, 140r: at St Mary Magdalen he is listed as 'Robert', an error oddly uncorrected by the visitors. He is also listed as 'Robert' in Archdeacon George Withers's first surviving call book of visitation on 19 September 1587 but the name is here corrected to 'Thomas': ERO D/AEV 1, fo. 34r. The history of St Mary Magdalen's Hospital is a matter for conjecture between 1548 and 1610. Since it had acquired parochial status in the thirteenth century it did not come under threat at the time of the dissolution and by letters patent of 1558 the advowson was granted to the bishop of London: *CPR 1557–8*, p. 400. These appear to have been ineffective since on 28 May 1562 the Lord Keeper issued letters patent for the appointment of Benjamin Clere at the petition of the archdeacon of Colchester: BL, Lansdowne MS 443, fo. 117v; *CPR 1560–3*, p. 415. No formal record of institution, however, survives in Grindal's register. On 31 January 1577 Bishop Edwin Sandys's vicar general dispatched an intimation to the unnamed patron 'or donor' (*seu donatori*) of St Mary Magdalen, demanding that he make presentation without delay following Clere's resignation: LMA DL/C/333, fo. 59r. Thereafter the cure is regularly listed vacant until Lowe's appearance in 1586 but no letters of sequestration, nor any formal instrument of institution or collation for Lowe, are recorded. Aylmer perhaps availed himself of the existence of the 1558 letters patent to make a personal appointment but it is hard to see why in those circumstances he should have forbidden Lowe the use of the profits both of the parsonage and of the hospital. See also *VCH Essex, IX*, p. 327.
11. *Seconde parte*, II, 162.
12. LMA DL/C/616, p. 40.
13. 'A Viewe', p. 12.
14. Reg. Bancroft, fo. 207v; LMA DL/C/360, fos. 221r–v. Lowe requested burial in St Leonard churchyard as near as possible to his first wife. Bequests to his second, Priscilla, included a lump sum of £240. His son and executor, Thomas, received £100, all his plate and his books. There were minor bequests to his daughter and son-in-law, Anne and Daniel Stevens, and £20 to their children equally divided. He left £5 to the poor of St Leonard but does not mention St Mary Magdalen Hospital. In a codicil he committed the will for safekeeping to Benjamin Jones, pending Thomas's return from Ireland.

MONKE, ROBERT (d. 1601)

Rector of Woodham Ferrers, Essex, 1561–1601; rector of Wakes Colne, Essex, 1565–1601 (d.)

Monke matriculated pensioner from Queens' College, Cambridge, at Easter 1544. Scholar from 1543 to 1548, he graduated BA early in 1547 and was fellow of Queens' 1560–2.[1] Meanwhile he had been ordained deacon and priest at Lambeth by Nicholas Bullingham, bishop of Lincoln (BA), on 10 March 1560.[2] He was instituted rector of Woodham Ferrers on 19 July 1560 (BA) at the presentation of Sir Walter Mildmay; and rector of Wakes Colne on 7 November 1565 (BA) at the presentation of Robert Christmas, acting as executor of John earl of Oxford.[3]

Although evidently a convinced protestant from an early date and (to judge from his university record) possibly an untraced Marian exile, Monke is not known to have engaged in any overt nonconformist activities after the accession of Elizabeth. From 1565 he was resident at Wakes Colne, five miles north-west of Colchester, maintaining a curate at Woodham Ferrers, about twenty miles to the south.[4] He was listed merely as double-beneficed in the Essex survey of the ministry in 1586[5] and his appearance as chief signatory in 1584 to 'Certain requests' to Archdeacon Withers[6] was presumably a flagrant emotional appeal: he was undoubtedly the archdeaconry of Colchester's oldest surviving protestant incumbent. He also signed the Dedham conference's form of limited subscription that year.[7] He was still listed present as preacher at both his benefices at the episcopal visitation of 1592.[8]

At Bancroft's primary visitation in 1598 Monke was stated to be an octogenarian and excused attendance because of age.[9] His successor at Wakes Colne was instituted by his death on 8 December 1601.[10] Letters of administration were granted for his estate on 11 December 1601 to his widow, Margaret, and his son, Timothy, cleric.[11]

1. *Alum. Cantab.*, III, 199.
2. *Reg. Parker*, p. 343.
3. Reg. Grindal, fos. 115v, 137v.
4. Roger Norden, his curate there in 1574, was ordered to wear the surplice *sub poena iuris*: GL MS 9537/3, fo. 105v.
5. *Seconde parte*, II, 161.
6. See above, p. 82.
7. See above, p. 87.
8. GL MS 9537/8, fos. 21r, 54r.
9. GL MS 9537/9, fos. 100r, 125r.
10. Reg. Bancroft, fo. 31v.
11. LMA DL/C/338, fo. 35r.

MORRIS (MOR(R)ICE), THOMAS (d. 1602)

Rector of Chipping Ongar, Essex, 1576–8 (resig.); rector of Layer Marney, Essex, 1577–1602 (d.)

Although possibly brother of James Morice, Attorney of the Court of Wards and Liveries,[1] Thomas apparently received no university education and is first found in the records when instituted rector of Chipping Ongar on 18 August 1576 at James Morice's presentation.[2] Inducted on 3 October, he was excused from attending John Aylmer's primary episcopal visitation in July 1577.[3]

The Morices were related to the Tukes of Layer Marney and Thomas married Margaret, sister of George Tuke (d. 1572).[4] He was granted letters patent by the Lord Keeper, Sir Nicholas Bacon, for the rectory of Layer Marney on 25 November 1577 at the petition of Sir Henry Cocke, ward of the living's patron Peter Tuke, a minor (son of George), and was instituted two days later.[5] Doubtless for that reason he installed a curate at Chipping Ongar in December 1577 – Richard Vaughan, future bishop of London, who was instituted as his successor on 22 April 1578.[6]

Present at Aylmer's second episcopal visitation on 7 July 1580, he was granted a preaching licence for the whole diocese on 12 February 1582.[7] Morice passed unscathed through the visitation of 1583, when he was listed ill, and through that of 1586 and its aftermath.[8] His sole contribution to the Dedham records was his signature to the form of limited subscription drawn up in 1584.[9] He was again present before Aylmer's visitors in July 1589 but was not subsequently called into consistory.[10] He was present at the episcopal visitation of 1592 as a licensed preacher and as a preacher licensed by Aylmer '1591' at that of 1598.[11] Meanwhile he had been licensed on 18 October 1597 to marry Margaret, widow of John Lukyn, vicar of Asheldam.[12]

There can be no doubt that Morice's sympathies lay broadly with colleagues who were more actively involved with the Dedham conference and his apparent conformity in these critical years is probably more apparent than real. The patronage of the Tuke family and of James Morice was probably enough to ensure that he remained undisturbed.

Following Bancroft's second visitation in 1601 he was called into consistory on 29

March 1602 – evidently after a serious clash with his churchwardens – because he did not use the cross or wear the surplice at baptism, or indeed at any other time if it could be avoided, 'for the last tyme he wore it he cast it from him in scorne'. The churchwardens also reported that he had kept a pregnant servant in his house and then 'married her to his man': she remained in his employ and 'to their knowledge she never did any penaunce'. They further deposed that his own daughter became pregnant in his house by one 'John Stoneham, as they supposed'. They were sure the couple never did open penance and were now married and still living in Morice's house.[13] It is unclear what directives were given by the judge but these allegations were made as Morice lay dying. He made his will on 1 February 1602 and probate was granted (Consistory Court of London) on 1 April following.[14]

1. James Morice (d. 1596) bequeathed to Isaac Morice 'my nephew and godson goods in the custody of my brother, his father': Emmison, *Wills of Essex gentry & yeomen*, pp. 10–11. Thomas's eldest son was called Isaac (see n.14 below).
2. Reg. Grindal, fo. 188v.
3. ERO D/AEM 4, fo. 6v; GL MS 9537/4, fo. 54r.
4. See legacy to Morrice and his wife Margaret, her 'aunt and uncle', in the will of Elizabeth Tuke of Layer Marney, daughter of George Tuke, dated 25 July 1593: Emmison, *Wills of Essex gentry & yeomen*, pp. 75–6.
5. BL, Lansdowne MS 443, fo. 243r; Reg. Grindal, fo. 191v.
6. Reg. Grindal, fo. 193r.
7. GL MS 95374/4, fo. 97v; LMA DL/C/333, fo. 276r.
8. GL MS 9537/5, fo. 65r; /6, fo. 143r.
9. See above, p. 87.
10. GL MS 9537/7, fo. 47v.
11. GL MS 9537/8, fo. 56r; GL MS 9537/9, fo. 101v.
12. LMA DL/C/337, fo. 2r.
13. LMA DL/C/303, p. 560.
14. LMA DL/C/359, fos. 264v–6r. During an elaborate Calvinist confession of faith he requested burial in the chancel of Layer Marney, as near as possible to his 'former' wife's grave, ending with the hope that through Christ's death and passion, 'in whose name and in whose spirit I am washed, sanctified and justified', he was 'made meet to be a citizen of the heavenly Jerusalem, with all the holy Angels and saints of God, there to laud and magnify his most holy name for ever, world without end'. He bequeathed 6s 8d to some 'godly learned minister' for a funeral sermon and a copy of Calvin's *Institutes* in English 'with silver clasps on the cover thereof', which had belonged to his sister, Margaret Tuke, to his 'wellbeloved nephew' Brian Tuke, who had given it him on condition that he should bequeath it back if Tuke outlived him. There were further bequests of books to daughters Elizabeth Goodwin and Anne Janson, wife of Lancelot Janson, vicar of Heybridge, Essex, and £10 each to his daughters Jane, Thomazyn and Margaret Morrice. To his second wife, Margaret, he left a total of £80.

His four sons were Isaac, William, Thomas and Humphrey. Isaac, 'mercer of London', was left £10 on condition he did nothing to vex or molest his stepmother, Margaret, and 'use her in all kindness as he hath done heretofore' or claim further goods from William, appointed executor. After further family bequests he appointed Brian Tuke overseer, with 20s for his pains, and directed that 13s 4d be paid to his friend John Lucas, rector of Layer Bretton. Tuke and Lucas were the witnesses and it was presumably they who added a noncupative codicil: 'in his last sickeness' Morrice had doubted whether his assets would amount to as much as the £80 left to Margaret and the £80 left jointly to his children, desiring that Margaret should have £80 'full out' and the residue divided between his children.

MORSE, ANTHONY (c. 1560–1603/4)

Rector of Hinderclay, Suffolk, 1597–1603 (d.)

Morse was the only clerical member of a family which, for its prominence, benefactions and piety, may have been accorded some kind of primacy amongst the godly of the Stour valley.[1] Fourth and youngest son of Edward Morse (d. 1557), clothier of Stratford St

Mary, Suffolk, and his wife Julian (?*nee* Forth), he matriculated pensioner from Christ's College, Cambridge, in June 1575, graduating BA in 1579 and proceeding MA in 1582.[2] One of the original signatories of the Dedham conference, he was evidently ordained by the time that it first convened, but seems to have been content to live in Stratford St Mary in the house of his mother and eldest brother Edward. This state of dependency and his reluctance to give it up runs like a diapason through his career. In the will of his brother-in-law, John Roger of Fobbing, Essex, yeoman (October 1584) – husband of his late sister Lydia – Morse received 20s and was given custody of his son John to 'bring him up in the fear of God and learning', with £5 over and above the reasonable costs of his keeping and board. Yet in a codicil Roger stated that young John was to remain at Chelmsford (at the grammar school?) until Lady Day next and that Anthony was to have the keeping of him 'if he do keep house by himself, if not that Mr Richard Dreamer should keep him until Anthony should keep house by himself'.[3]

Active throughout the entire life of the conference, 'Mr Morse' is first recorded as speaker in March 1583 and was appointed moderator for the following meeting (**4M**). He fulfilled one or other of these functions on a further nine occasions.[4] In June 1583 he was delegated with Chapman and Stoughton to solicit opinions from 'godly men in Cambridge' concerning the Sabbath (**8M**). In October he and Dowe were delegated to procure articles against an unsatisfactory minister at Higham, Suffolk (**11M**). In April 1584 he contributed 10s for the relief of Henry Wilcock (**17M**). Next month it was agreed that he should accept a calling in Sir Dru Drury's house, with certain (unspecified) conditions (**18M**).

When on 1 February 1585 the conference met at the Morse household in Stratford, it was immediately 'moved' that Edward Morse '(being a good man and we assembled in his house)' might be admitted 'for that tyme'. The brethren agreed – how, in the circumstances, could they have refused? – provided 'it might not be made an example hereafter for others to doe the like'. At the same meeting Morse asked whether he might go to 'a private place' where Oliver Pigge was now serving;[5] the question was deferred (**27M**). At the extraordinary meeting of 17 February 1585 it was, however, decided he should stay at home because this proposed posting 'was but private as his mother's house was'. In October 1585 he was delegated to supply Tey's place at Peldon while Tey sorted out his dead brother's affairs (**36M**). Two months later he asked for 'better assurance than the brethrens charge' for preaching at Peldon, 'lest he come into some trouble'. Once again the matter was deferred (**38M**). In January 1586, however, it was agreed that 'as good assurance as might be' should be procured – presumably from Archdeacon Withers. Later that day Chapman moved that because he 'had bene now a long tyme tried for his hability to teache', Morse should now accept the 'place to teach godes people now offred'. The brethren agreed, but Morse himself craved time to consider (**39M**). In February he was again urged to consider the offer – which proves to have been the benefice of Belsted, Suffolk – and to give an answer (**40M**).

No more is heard of the matter, or of Morse, until January 1587 when the conference again met in Stratford St Mary. On this occasion he asked if he might preach at Mr Forth's at Butley, 'being requested to exercise his guifte'. It was agreed, provided he thereafter 'proceed further, to accepte of a callinge there or els where' (**52M**). In February he asked if he should request Bishop Scambler's allowance 'for his peace' in Butley: 'it was thought best he shuld' (**53M**). In March, however, he reported that Scambler would give no allowance to preach without presentation to a place, so he could not go there (**54M**).

He went – or was dispatched – nonetheless. In June he asked whether he should continue at Butley without authority: it was agreed that it was not safe unless 'he meant to take yt as his charge'. Someone ventured the opinion that although the living was small he might well take it and supply 'the want' himself – good evidence that he was regarded by his colleagues as a man of independent means (**57M**). Once again, however, he resisted this attempt to tie him down since in October he was given leave to go to Butley 'for a tyme' until Forth could secure a permanent preacher (**61M**). Thereafter he is mentioned in the minutes only as host or speaker.

As far as we know, Morse remained unbeneficed throughout the life of the Dedham conference and for several years afterwards. He compounded as rector of Hinderclay on 26 February 1597.[6] His will, dated 4 August 1603, received probate (PCC) on 20 September 1604 (sic).[7]

1. See the Introduction, p. lx, above.
2. Peile, *Biographical register*, I, 131. Peile knew nothing of his family background or future career. The Venns tentatively and erroneously identified him with Anthony Morse of Uggeshall and Wrentham (d. 1609): *Alum. Cantab.*, III, 216.
3. Roger also bequeathed 20s and 10s respectively to his brothers-in-law Edward and Nathaniel Morse and made bequests to the children of his late brother-in-law William Morse: Emmison, *Essex wills: the archdeaconry courts 1583–92* (Chelmsford, 1989), no. 1.
4. Chosen speaker for **22, 44, 58, 71MM** (in the event apparently absent), **72, 76MM**; chosen moderator for **26, 36, 51, 65MM** (at his house at Stratford). For the possibility that the 'Mr Morse' mentioned in **4M** was *Thomas* Morse, see below p. 232.
5. Unidentified: obviously not Sir Dru Drury's, where Morse had already succeeded Pigge during the previous months.
6. Thomas Hayes of St Mary Aldermanbury, draper, and Roger Gwyn of St Stephen Walbrook, grocer, stood surety: PRO E334/12, fo. 73r.
7. All his copyhold lands in Stoke Nayland, Suffolk, and his lands in Boxted, Essex, were left to his wife Elizabeth for her lifetime; afterwards to his nephew Azaell, his brother Edward's son, on condition Azaell pay £20 between them to the surviving children of Anthony's brother Nathaniel. There were bequests to the three sons of his brother William, to the poor students of Cambridge (£4) and to the poor of Stratford and of Hinderclay (40s each). His 'cousin [John?] Bounde' and 'my loving cousin his wife', each received a ring and Mr Dowe, 'preacher of the word of God at Stratford', 20s. Books of stated value went to Mr Smythe of Rickinghall, 'Mr Ravens' [schoolmaster of Dedham?], Mr Wallys, Mr Hall, Mr Chamberlain of Hunston and Mr Redritch of Butley. His wife Elizabeth received the residue of his estate and was appointed sole executrix, his 'brother' Henry Farr to be supervisor: PRO PCC PROB 11/104 (77 Harte).

MORS(E), THOMAS (c. 1548–97)

Vicar of Boxted, Essex, 1573–8 (resig.); rector of Hinderclay, Suffolk, 1583–?95 (?resig.); rector of Foxearth, Essex, 1595–7 (d.)

Although born in Dedham, Thomas Morse does not appear to have been related to the Morses of Stratford. A non-graduate,[1] he was collated vicar of Boxted on 17 December 1573 by Edwin Sandys, bishop of London.[2] He was probably, therefore, the Thomas Morse who had married Margaret King at Boxted on 26 May 1573.[3] Ordained priest by Sandys on 9 April 1574 (born Dedham; aged 26 or more), he was present at Sandys's second episcopal visitation in July 1574.[4] Called into consistory on 8 November 1576 and ordered to wear the surplice – only five other Essex clerics are known to have been so summoned during Sandys's episcopate – he refused on the grounds that he would offend his parishioners and so 'hinder his ministrie'. He was accordingly suspended until he could be induced to do so (*quoad induci posset*) and warned not to preach or conduct divine service. On condition he conform, he was restored on 9 February 1577, by special mandate from Sandys, to ministration in his own parish *et non alibi*.[5]

Present at John Aylmer's primary visitation in July that year, Morse was subsequently summoned to a personal interview with Aylmer at Fulham and on 7 October summarily suspended from office pending further conference.[6] He resigned Boxted by 10 March 1579 and yet is undoubtedly the Thomas Morse, cleric, who was granted a diocesan preaching licence on 26 May following.[7] He is nowhere listed in London diocese during Aylmer's second episcopal visitation in 1580. Subsequent events suggest that he may have continued to live privately in Boxted and engaged in a 'roving ministry'.

Although not a signatory to the Dedham conference, Morse seems to have been closely involved with it during its early months. In the first place it was evidently necessary to specify that it was *Anthony* Morse who was originally 'chosen for the Assembly'.[8] Secondly, on 4 March 1583 – the only occasion when the conference met at Boxted – 'Mr morse' was the speaker (**4M**). It was as a result of this meeting, moreover, that the conference wrote to Thomas Cartwright on 19 April, and Thomas Morse was one of those who signed the letter.[9] This is the only time that his full name is found amongst the Dedham papers and he was the only signatory who was not originally 'chosen for the assembly'.

Was he also the 'Mr Morse' who at that same meeting was chosen moderator for the following month? If so, he is unlikely to have been present, since the fifth meeting took place on 8 April 1583, the same day that Morse was instituted rector of Hinderclay at the presentation of Sir Nicholas Bacon.[10]

He is almost certainly, therefore, the 'Thom. Mors' who was in 1584 amongst the Suffolk clergy suspended for refusing subscription.[11] He returned to Boxted the following year, where as 'mynyster, of Hinderclaye' he married Margery Boggas on 24 November 1585.[12] Two sons of Thomas Morse, Jeremy and James, were buried at Hinderclay on 11 August 1588 and 16 November 1590.[13]

He returned permanently to Essex during the episcopate of Richard Fletcher and on 12 August 1595 was instituted rector of Foxearth.[14] He appeared the same day before Edward Stanhope in consistory. In an entry unique in the London records at this time it is rehearsed in minute detail that Morse must subscribe not only the thirty-nine articles but also the three *articulis sinodalibus pro uniformitate ceremonie ecclesie Anglicane*. He was further ordered to appear before Stanhope or his deputy in Braintree church on 20 September (that is, during Fletcher's episcopal visitation) to show his letters of orders and letters dimissory. He was then enjoined, according to his subscription and oath of canonical obedience, always to use the prayer book at Foxearth; to wear the surplice; to administer sacraments to himself kneeling and to none that did not kneel; to use the sign of the cross in baptism and a ring in marriage; and to observe the book strictly in churching women and burying the dead. He was finally ordered to bring in on 20 September the churchwardens' certificate that he had performed all things according to law: he would then be required on oath to state that it was a true certificate.[15] Following this baptism of fire he was granted a diocesan preaching licence on 13 September.[16]

Morse made a hasty will, without religious preamble, on 10 November 1596. It received probate (PCC) on 8 April 1597.[17] His successor at Foxearth had been instituted on 7 March.[18]

Why three successive bishops of London should have placed such merciless emphasis on Morse's ritual conformity is something of a mystery.

1. *Alum. Cantab.*, III, 217, confuses him with *Robert* Mors, who matriculated pensioner from Christ's College, Cambridge, in June 1566. Robert Mors's later career was unknown to Peile: *Biographical register*, I, 93.
2. Reg. Grindal, fo. 173r.
3. ERO D/P 155/1.
4. GL MS 9535/1, fo. 152v; GL MS 9537/3, fo. 80r.
5. LMA DL/C/333, fos. 54r, 59v; LMA DL/C/9, p. 457.
6. GL MS 9537/4, fo. 32r; LMA DL/C/333, fo. 88v.
7. Reg. Grindal, fo. 195v; LMA DL/C/333, fo. 163r.
8. See above, p. 4.
9. See above, pp. 72–3.

10. NRO DN/Reg/14/20, fo. 90r.
11. *Seconde parte*, I, 242–3.
12. ERO D/P 155/1 [unpaginated].
13. London, Society of Genealogists, Hinderclay Bishops' Transcripts.
14. Bishops' certificates to the exchequer, PRO E331/London/7, m. 1. Fletcher's institutions are missing from the episcopal register; bishops' certificates do not state cause of vacancy or patron.
15. LMA DL/C/336, fos. 14r–v.
16. *Ibid.*, fo. 19v.
17. PRO PCC PROB 11/89 (26 Cobham). He left £20 each to nine surviving children: John, Samuel, Daniel, Joseph, Jeremy, James, Nathaniel, Philip and Sarah. His second wife, Margaret, mother of five of the children, received the residue of his estate and was appointed sole executrix, provided she enter into bonds for the performance of the will in the event of her remarriage. If she refused to enter into bonds the executorship was to pass to John, who was in that case to pay her a lump sum of £80. If she remained unmarried, Morse desired that she should will £5 each to his four children by his first wife: these were obviously John, Samuel and Daniel but whether the fourth was Joseph or Sarah is not apparent.
18. LPL, Register of Whitgift, volume II, fo. 282r.

MOSSE, MILES (1558–1615)

Vicar of St Stephen, Norwich, 1585–6 (resig.); preacher of St James, Bury St Edmunds, Suffolk, 1586–97; rector of Combes, Suffolk, 1597–1615 (d.)

Mosse was born in the parish of Chevington, Suffolk, in 1558, son of Miles Mosse, a yeoman. He studied at the grammar school in Bury St Edmunds for six years[1] and was admitted a pensioner of Gonville and Caius College, Cambridge, on 14 April 1575. He graduated BA in early 1579 and commenced MA in 1582.[2] In February 1583, he was fined 3s 4d for breaking the head of master Thexton during the performing of a satire composed and produced by Thomas Mudd at Pembroke Hall, possibly attesting to a hot temper. Mudd was imprisoned for three days in the town's gaol for words spoken about the mayor.[3] Mosse was ordained priest on 7 October 1583 (Lincoln diocese) and was licensed to preach on 8 April 1584.[4] In 1585 he was appointed vicar of St Stephen Norwich, where he came to know John earl of Mar, one of the Scottish presbyterian lords in temporary exile in England, who was for a time 'an Auditor of my Ministery'.[5] In 1586 he moved from Norwich to Bury St Edmunds where he served as preacher of the parish of St James, receiving the handsome stipend of £40 per annum.[6] He proceeded to the degree of BD in 1589 and DD in 1595. In 1597, he accepted the rectory of Combes, one of the wealthier livings in the archdeaconry of Sudbury, to which he was instituted on 27 May and where he remained until his death.[7] In 1603, described as a 'doctor of divinity, preacher and of honest life and conversation', he reported that Combes had 250 communicants, that 'he hath no other Lyvinge besides and preacheth twise everye Sabboeth'.[8] He was buried in the parish church on 13 September 1615.

Mosse made a modest name for himself as a preacher and author. In 1613, he preached at Paul's Cross in London on 'justifying and saving faith distinguished from the faith of the Devils'. The published version of his sermon was dedicated to the Lord Chief Justice Edward Coke and contained passages full of high praise for Queen Elizabeth's religious policies.[9] He seems to have been the organizing force behind the remarkable bestseller entitled *A garden of spirituall flowers*, first published in 1609, consisting of posthumous treatises of practical divinity by Richard Rogers, Richard Greenham and William Perkins, with brief contributions from Mosse and one George Webb.[10] He is best known for his lectures on usury published in 1595 under the title, *The Arraignment and Conviction of Usurie*, which began life as a series of six sermons delivered at the Monday exercise in Bury between March and July 1594.[11]

Mosse possessed impeccable godly credentials yet remained on harmonious terms with the episcopal authorities. He must have known John More, the 'Apostle of Norwich', and in Bury was on close terms with men such as John Knewstub, Nicholas Bound, Walter Allen and Reginald Whitfield as well as with the Master of Emmanuel, Laurence Chaderton. It was in the context of the Bury exercise that he quarrelled most famously with Thomas Rogers, and he may have led the effort to exclude Rogers from the exercise as a punishment for his public attack on the presbyterian principles expounded by Laurence Chaderton in his anonymously published tract, *A fruitfull sermon*. When Mosse republished the popular catechism by John More and Edward Dering with a short preface dedicated to the Bishop of Norwich, in which he complained that 'men will speak before they have learned' and that 'manie ministers of the word write much but preach little', Rogers, stung and suspicious, took these as an attack on his own considerable efforts as a writer. Rogers responded at length in *Miles Christianus or a just apologie of all necessarie writings and writers specialie of them which by their labored writings take paines to build up the Church of Christ*, the opening lines of which wished Mosse 'more soundnes of judgement, more substance of learning with more wisdome and discretion in all his actions'.

His most lasting achievement was the erection in 1595 of the parish library of St James in Bury St Edmunds. He persuaded the neighbouring clergy, gentlemen and townsmen to donate books to the library, and some of these donations are still recorded in the hand-written bookplates pasted into the volumes. Mosse himself donated a number of volumes, among others commentaries by Aretius, Bullinger's *Decades* and the works of John of Damascus. By 1599, the library possessed more than two hundred volumes, primarily theological works.[12] A faded inventory of his goods survives which provides further evidence of some of the books owned by this learned cleric.[13]

1. *Biographical list of boys educated at King Edward VI Free Grammar School, Bury St Edmunds 1550–1900*, ed. S. H. A. Hervey (Suffolk Green Books, 13, 1908).
2. *Alum. Cantab.*, III, 220; Venn, *Biographical history*, p. 81.
3. A. Nelson ed., *Records of Early English Drama, Cambridge* (Toronto, 1989), p. 308.
4. *Registrum Vagum*, p. 191.
5. *Scotlands welcome* (London, 1603), sig A2.
6. Craig, *Reformation, politics and polemics*, p. 112n.
7. *Registrum Vagum*, p. 191.
8. 'The condition', p. 22.
9. Miles Mosse, *Justifiying and Saving Faith distinguished from the faith of the Devils In a Sermon preached at Paul's Crosse in London, May 9, 1613* (Cambridge, 1614).
10. *A garden of Spirituall Flowers Planted by Ri Ro, Wil Per, Ri Gree, M. M. and Geo Web* (1609).
11. Miles Mosse, *The Arraignment and Conviction of Usurie* (London, 1595).
12. Craig, *Reformation, politics and polemics*, pp. 116–21.
13. NRO INV 27B/98.

NEGUS, WILLIAM (c. 1559–1616)

Assistant town preacher, Ipswich, Suffolk, 1584–5; rector of Leigh, Essex, 1585–1609 (depr.)

Negus possibly hailed from the extensive clan of this name in and around Bedford, and was perhaps related to the obscure Marian exile Richard 'Nagors', who subscribed the 'new discipline' in Frankfurt in April 1557.[1] He matriculated sizar from Trinity College, Cambridge, at Easter 1573, graduating BA in early 1578.[2] Nothing is known of his subsequent whereabouts until he surfaces as assistant town preacher in Ipswich, with whose authorities he made a 'covenant' for a year in early 1584.[3]

Negus first appears as a member of the Dedham conference on 1 June 1584 when he was offered advice 'tutchinge his estate and dealinge with his people' (**19M**). Thus differences had already arisen between Negus and Robert Norton, town preacher of Ipswich since 1577, probably because Negus had voiced objections to Norton's holding the rectory of Aldeburgh, Suffolk, with his preachership. The situation deteriorated rapidly. On 1 July Negus was advised to 'tarry with his parish if the godlie desired it and wold mainteyne him' (**20M**), but by the end of September he had been suspended by the bishop of Norwich, Edmund Freke. He alleged to the conference that Freke had 'pro-ceeded with him against law' and therefore thought he might preach again. He was told to seek the advice of 'wise and discreet lawyers . . . and if it be not against law then to proceed' (**23M**). The Ipswich authorities now appear to have taken matters into the own hands: Negus's one-year contract was not to be renewed, for on 16 November they appointed Robert Wright as assistant preacher for one year from Michaelmas 1585 at a salary of £50.[4]

Negus remained under suspension for at least sixteen weeks, on 1 February 1585 asking for the brethren's prayers since he was about to go to London 'for his restoring to liberty in his callinge'. He was successful, and was back within the fortnight (**27 and Extra MM**). Since he is unlikely to have gone to London to confront the bishop of Norwich he had perhaps engaged the sympathy of the privy council.

Affairs in Ipswich had, however, gone from bad to worse during his absence. On 1 February, while Negus was spending the day with his brethren at Stratford St Mary, the town court had noted that 'libels and seditions' had been recently scattered abroad against the 'governors and preachers'. The bailiffs (joint mayors) ordered that the remarkable sum of £40 be awarded to any parishioner 'finding such libels, or opening them, or disclosing the actor, maker, spreader or consenter of or to such libels'. At the same meeting the court was forced to make up the balance of Norton's wages from the treasury, direct contributions from the townsmen 'failing in the collection', and there can be little doubt that one of the causes of this major disaffection was economic. In 1582 Norton's salary had been raised from £50 to £73 6s. 8d – an astounding amount, even for a wealthy borough – and thus, if Negus was being paid £50, the townsmen were paying in excess of £120 a year for a preaching ministry. Of this sum about three-fifths was paid out of the treasury and the remainder from their direct contributions.[5] It is not surprising that they should have baulked at lavishing such generous sums on men so readily disposed to quarrel, especially since Negus had now been officially suspended for over four months.

Thus on 17 February Negus once again tackled the Dedham brethren on the subject of his departure, 'the most part of his parish standing against him and haveing covenanted with him to be there one year, yet brake their covenant and did even thrust him out'. He further admitted that he now had 'a good callinge offred him to the congregation of Lee'.[6] Although Negus did not say so in so many words, this 'callinge' was a straight, old-fashioned offer of a well-endowed benefice from an influential patron, Robert 3rd Lord Rich. The conference urged patience and delegated Chapman and Crick to mediate with the Ipswich bailiffs. In such circumstances it seems almost impertinent that Negus should at the same meeting have agreed with William Tey that Bartimaeus Andrewes should not leave Wenham because of the 'neere conjunction' between a pastor and his people (**Extra M**, 17 February 1585).

Such efforts as Chapman and Crick made to secure harmony in Ipswich came to nothing. The borough had split into contending factions and on 1 March the borough court took the bull by the horns. The 'difference' between Norton and Negus had 'spread in the Great Court into parties, and some foul words were spoken'. Therefore a committee was appointed to confer with both men to 'conclude for the departure or continuance of them, or either of them'.[7] Chapman and Crick nevertheless remained surprisingly sanguine: on 8 March, when Negus appeared to be havering between remaining at Ipswich and accepting Leigh, the conference thought it 'meet', if he were allowed 'convenient tymes to exercise his ministery and a good callinge to them, not conditionall nor subiecte to soe much reading of service', that he should remain in Ipswich 'bicause of the want of pastors, and for feare, lest if he went noe pastors shuld be gotten afterwarde' (28M). Thus it would appear that the conference was unaware at this point that Robert Wright had already signed a contract to succeed Negus at Michaelmas.

Why did Negus, who must have known the truth, not enlighten them? It would seem that he was being less than honest and indeed, behind their backs, he was on 31 March 1585 instituted to Leigh at Rich's presentation by John Aylmer, bishop of London.[8] He had the good grace to attend on 3 May, informing the brethren that he had accepted Leigh and 'if they liked it to allow of him, if not to admonish him, thanking god for the benefits of the meeting, acknowledging he had failed in many thinges, and craved their prayers to god for him' (30M). Without further comment he passes out of the Dedham minutes.

Although never cited in the Essex archdeaconry court for nonconformity, Negus spent the rest of his life parrying the visitations of five successive bishops of London. On 23 July 1586 he was inhibited from preaching because only licensed in Suffolk, and was ordered to a personal interview with Aylmer. He was suspended as a result.[9] The circumstances of his restoration are unknown, but he never abandoned the path of ritual nonconformity. He was later stated to have been licensed to preach by Aylmer in '1588'.[10] He was under threat again during the 1589 visitation and was ordered to certify that he had worn the surplice by 3 October.[11] Present as a licensed preacher at Aylmer's last visitation in 1592 and Bancroft's first in 1598, he does not seem to have been troubled for the surplice on either occasion.[12]

But in 1604, with Whitgift's three articles incorporated within the new constitutions and canons, he was probably suspended by Bancroft since he stated in court on 22 March 1605 that he remained unsatisfied about 'the lawfulness and expediency' of the ceremonies and wished to be 'better informe[d] . . . in theis or any other his doubtes'.[13] On the following 13 May he was one of five southern Essex clergy, including Ezekiel Culverwell, summoned before the high commissioners because they had not certified that they observed the ceremonies.[14] No more is heard of the matter, probably because the new bishop of London, Richard Vaughan, put an end to all Bancroft's disciplinary cases pending his own primary visitation. Although, like many others, his case remained technically before the vicar general as late as June 1606,[15] Negus escaped further summons until after Vaughan's death in March 1607.

Following Thomas Ravis's primary visitation in 1607, Negus was summoned to a personal interview with him 'to be showed the waye wherein he is to walk for that he desyred to be showed the waye before he enter into conformitie'; he was to certify in consistory on 7 November that he had done so and also provided a conformable curate to read public prayers. He seems not to have appeared and was again summoned before Ravis. On 10 December Ezekiel Culverwell submitted a letter from Negus stating that he was 'sick of an ague & not hable to appear . . . desyring his Lo: that he shall not impute it unto any . . . contempte but only to the weaknes of his body'.[16]

There is no further reference to Negus in the consistory court records until 22 March 1609, when the vicar general recorded that intimations dated 20 March were to be dispatched to the patrons of Great Stambridge, Leigh, Little Leighs and Vange, void by the deprivations of Culverwell, Negus, William Buckley and Camille Rusticens respectively: 'All 4 the same 20th of Marche deprived by the highe Commission[er]s'.[17] They were back in consistory on 4 and 21 May following, to explain their contempt in failing to conform to the ceremonies, but were dismissed pending a new monition.[18] Negus's successor, John Simmes, was instituted following his deprivation on 3 August 1609.[19]

Negus lived on in Leigh and was buried there on 8 January 1616. His original will, dated 16 August 1615, survives at the Essex Record Office.[20] In 1619 Jonathan Negus (1592–1632) brought out his father's only known work, *Man's Active Obedience, or the Power of Godliness*, with a dedication to Sir Thomas Smith (1558?–1625) and prefaces by John Simmes and Stephen Egerton. Since the dedication alludes to Smith's 'good affection and respect' for William Negus and the 'liberal allowance' granted for some years to Jonathan, it is likely that Smith, cousin by marriage of Ezekiel Culverwell, subsidized Jonathan's education at Eton and Cambridge.[21]

1. C. H. Garrett, *The Marian exiles* (Cambridge, 1938), no. 296.
2. *Alum. Cantab.*, III, 240.
3. W. H. Richardson, *The Annals of Ipswich . . . by Nathaniel Bacon, 1654* (Ipswich, 1884), pp. 314, 342. It seems that this covenant involved his taking on responsibility for one of the Ipswich parishes as a salaried minister but it is not clear which. Like other town preachers, 'he may have had a connection with St. Mary-le-Tower': Diarmaid MacCulloch and John Blatchly, 'Pastoral provision in the parishes of Tudor Ipswich', *The Sixteenth-Century Journal*, XXII (1991), 457–74 (at p. 471n.).
4. Richardson, *Annals*, p. 341.
5. Richardson, *Annals*, pp. 314, 330, 333, 341.
6. Leigh: a thriving fishing-port at the head of the Thames estuary, now known as Leigh-on-Sea.
7. Richardson, *Annals*, p. 342.
8. Reg. Grindal, fo. 217v. Not the least surprising aspect of this episode is that, Rich and Aylmer having been daggers drawn since the Rochford Hall affair of 1579–80, the bishop did not apparently attempt to block Negus's promotion or attempt to insist on his subscription to Whitgift's three articles: further proof, perhaps, that Aylmer only invoked them on rare occasions after the collapse in late 1584 of Whitgift's national campaign to enforce them.
9. GL MS 9537/6, fos. 71r, 149r. The meeting took place at Witham, and Negus sent an account of it to John Field: 'The cause of my suspension was only this. Beinge convented before the B. at Wittham, and there by him demaunded whether I had worne the surplice since my coming to Lee. My answere was that as I had not worne yt, so I had never refused yt, for there was none offered, nor any in the parish to be worne. He further asked me if I would weare yt if it were provided. My answere was, I desired his favoure that I mighte proceede in my ministery untill such time as there were a surplice made, and that he knewe I refused to weare yt. He, not satisfied with this answere, urged mee to saye I would weare yt, or I would not. But I, standinge to my former answere, and desiringe that it mighte be accepted, he conclused thus, seing yow will not promise to weare yt, we will suspend yow till yow will.
    Whatsoever the godly brethren shall agree upon concerning a supplication for the libertie of us, the ministers suspended, to be put upp at this present parlament, I willingely, as if I were present, do assent thereunto. By me, William Negus.'
    Aylmer's demands were not as draconian as Negus claimed. His narrative is filed with a petition from twenty-eight inhabitants of Leigh, expressing their 'great greife . . . that we are deprived of our spiritual comforte'. They understood, however, that his liberty might be 'redeemed . . . by wearinge the surplice at some times, and that you shall not be urged any further'. Thus, though they regretted the necessity, they begged him not to desert them for 'such a trifle': *Seconde parte*, I, 274–5; see also II, 164, 262.
10. GL MS 9537/9, fo. 127r.
11. GL MS 9537/7, fo. 74v.
12. GL MS 9537/8, fo. 23v; GL MS 9537/9, fo. 127r.
13. LMA DL/C/618, p. 250.
14. LMA DL/C/607, fo. 683r.
15. LMA DL/C/304, pp. 328, 349, 638, 662, 674, 685.
16. LMA DL/C/306, pp. 10, 63.
17. LMA DL/C/339, fo. 57r.
18. LMA DL/C/308, pp. 3, 38–9.
19. Reg. Bancroft, fo. 137r.
20. ERO D/ABW 27/225. £3 6s 8d was left to the poor of Leigh, his remaining assets to his family. Reversion of a lease to his eldest son, Samuel, and the bulk of his evidently extensive library – including 'written notes apperteyning to my studdies & scholarly exercises' – went to his third, Jonathan, then a Cambridge undergraduate. There were lesser bequests to daughter Mary and second son Joseph, appointed executor in the absence of Samuel, 'now at sea'. John Simmes,

Negus's successor as rector of Leigh, was to be overseer and receive his copy of Foxe's *Book of Martyrs* 'as a pledge of my love and brotherlie affection towards him'.

21. Nicholas Tyacke, *The fortunes of English puritanism, 1603–1640* (Dr Williams's Library lecture, 1990), p. 9.

NEWMAN, LAURENCE (c. 1546–1600)

Vicar of (Great) Coggeshall, Essex, 1576–1600 (d.)

Newman matriculated sizar from Queens' College, Cambridge, at Lent 1565, as of Essex, graduating BA in early 1568. He was ordained deacon at Ely on 21 December that year, aged 22. He proceeded MA in 1571, remaining a fellow of Queens' until 1572.[1]

Instituted vicar of Coggeshall on 10 February 1576 (MA) at the presentation of Robert 2nd Lord Rich,[2] Newman came under suspicion for nonconformist practices almost at once, probably for allowing irregular preaching at Coggeshall.[3] He nevertheless contrived to share his pulpit officially with William Dyke until at least the summer of 1583,[4] meanwhile receiving a diocesan preaching licence on 26 July 1578.[5]

On 11 July 1583 Newman was ordered to a personal interview with Aylmer at Much Hadham for failing to produce his preaching licence before the episcopal visitors, but appears to have come away unscathed.[6] He was nevertheless one of the twenty-seven Essex clergy who petitioned against Whitgift's articles in early 1584[7] and must have been suspended for his refusal to subscribe them in May or June.[8] It was precisely at this time that he joined the Dedham conference, the second member to be admitted after its inception.[9] He is first mentioned on 1 June, when he was delegated to go to London to consult with Field and the rest about a 'generall meeting'. He asked if he might get a 'standing supply for his place' (**19M**).[10] On 7 September the conference met at Newman's house in Coggeshall,[11] when he and Tilney asked whether they might preach although suspended. They were advised not to do so, 'considering the state of the tyme' but Newman further asked if he might go to Whitgift and 'yeld to that subscription is offred to the xxxvij article': he received no encouragement (**22M**). Next month he suggested that 'he and his people' might go to Aylmer for his 'liberty', Whitgift being willing that he should be restored 'if the Bishopp wold'; it was 'not delt in' (**23M**).

At this point Newman either defied his colleagues or else they reluctantly allowed him to exercise his own conscience in the matter. In a memorandum unique in the London records it is recorded that on Saturday 28 November 1584, 'Mr archdeacon Coton'[12] accompanied Newman to the vicar general's office, where Newman 'delivered a note in writing whereunto he had subscribed and whereof he said my L. of London had accepted; in presence of Mr Coton testifying that my L. had accepted that his subscription & thereupon released him of his suspension; & that my L. had sent that note to be kept in the office:/By me Wm Coton'.[13]

On 3 May 1585 he wanted to know how far a minister might 'safelie' read from the Book of Common Prayer (**30M**). Two months later he and Sandes were delegated to seek the judgment of brethren in Cambridge as to the prayer book, separatism and the authority of bishops, but had to report back that these questions had not been debated (**32, 33MM**).

On 8 November 1585 Newman asked the brethren's allowance for a short catechism that he had compiled but 'there was nothing concluded for it' (**37M**). It was never published. By January 1586 he was wondering 'how farre a minister might goe to the hazarding of his ministry for the surplice' (**39M**). On 22 July 1586 he was present at Aylmer's fourth visitation and was one of those suspended then or subsequently for the surplice:[14] this despite the fact that he was at the same time appointed one of the commissioners for Lexden deanery to oversee the newly introduced clerical exercises, which were to be inaugurated at Colchester on 16 September.[15]

On 2 January 1587 Newman reported that the Braintree conference had asked him to join them permanently but stated that he would not do without the brethren's permission, preferring to continue at Dedham. He also raised the question 'what course the ministers suspended for the surplice, and like to be suspended shuld take' (**52M**). On 8 August following, Newman and Lewis were delegated to attend another 'generall meeting' at Cambridge and were also involved in the matter of Tilney's leaving East Bergholt. Newman also finally abandoned thoughts of joining the Braintree conference, preferring the company he presently kept (**59M**).[16] In the circumstances it is perhaps strange that he appears to have contributed little to Dedham's last twenty meetings. Since it is clear from his earlier activities that he was a rising star within the conference movement, it may be that his decision to offer Aylmer a form of subscription in late 1584 had swiftly led to his 'demotion'. The Dedham conference's final act, however, was to elect him speaker for the eighty-first meeting, destined never to take place (**80M**).

At Aylmer's penultimate episcopal visitation on 24 July 1589 Newman was admonished to preach only when he read service wearing the surplice. He was ordered to certify at Chelmsford on 2 October but no more is heard of the matter.[17] He was absent from the visitation of 1592 but listed present at that of 1598.[18] He seems to have died intestate, and was buried at Coggeshall on 18 March 1600.

1. *Alum. Cantab.*, III, 241.
2. Reg. Grindal, fo. 186r. He compounded for the benefice on 12 February 1576, with sureties Robert Jegon and Thomas Gray, both of Coggeshall, clothiers: PRO E334/9, fo. 71v.
3. The vicar general promoted a case at instance against him and Oliver Pigge, listed for hearing on 23 January 1577 but postponed *ex gratia sua* until the next court day (29 January), after which no more is heard of it: LMA DL/C/9, pp. 427, 445.
4. Newman was present at the episcopal visitation of 1577 with '[ ]Dixe', preacher; at that of 1580 with 'Mr Dixe', preacher; at that of 1583 with 'William Dickes', preacher: GL MSS 9537/4, fos. 33r, 997v; 9537/5, fo. 62v. Dyke was involved in the irregular, 'quasi-congregational' activities at Lord Rich's seat, Rochford Hall, between 1579 and 1581. Lord Rich's bastard uncle, Richard, Robert Wright and Dyke were as a result imprisoned by the High Commission, headed by Aylmer, on 7 November 1581. Aylmer described Dyke as 'a verie disordered man, & a violent innovator': BL, Lansdowne MS 33, fo. 50r. For these and his later activities at St Albans, see Collinson, *EPM*, pp. 321, 373–4, 405, 440, 446, 456.
5. LMA DL/C/333, fo. 120v.
6. GL MS 9537/5, fo. 62v.
7. *Seconde parte*, II, 225–6. 'William Dike' is the first signatory, Newman the third. No member of the Dedham conference as then constituted put his name to this petition, which is essentially a checklist of nonconformists in central and southern Essex, and probably the work of the Braintree conference. The two exceptions are Thomas Upcher and John 'Witton', probably John Wilton, rector of Aldham.
8. Restored on 28 November (see below), he was later stated to have been suspended 'allmost halfe a yeare' for not subscribing: *Seconde parte*, II, 163.
9. Since his signature follows that of Sandes and precedes those of Tilney and Negus he must have been admitted on or before 6 April 1584, when Tilney is first mentioned (**17M**).
10. If this was a precautionary measure pending his (now inevitable) suspension, why did the conference suppose that anyone nominated by Newman would subsequently be allowed by Aylmer to officiate in his place? Perhaps, therefore, he was planning to spend some weeks in London: he is not mentioned as participating in the twentieth and twenty-first meetings.
11. He was chosen host, speaker or moderator on a further seventeen occasions: **23, 24, 26, 29, 32, 40, 43, 46, 50, 51, 58, 59, 67, 68, 70, 76, 80MM**.
12. William Cotton, archdeacon of Lewes, prebendary of Sneating in St Paul's and a chaplain of Aylmer's; subsequently bishop of Exeter (1598–1621) (d.).
13. LMA DL/C/301, p. 397.
14. GL MS 9537/6, fo. 142r; *Seconde parte*, II, 261.
15. GL MS 9537/6, fos. 145v, 178r. The other commissioners included Archdeacon Withers and Edmund Chapman.

16. For the Braintree conference's official letter asking for his secondment and Dedham's tardy reply, see above pp. 106–8.
17. GL MS 9537/7, fo. 45v.
18. GL MS 9537/8, fo. 54v; /9, fo. 100r.

NORTHEY, GEORGE (c. 1550–93)

Common preacher of Colchester, Essex, 1580–93 (d.)

Member of an extensive Colchester family, Northey matriculated pensioner from Clare College, Cambridge, at Easter 1563, graduating BA early in 1567 and proceeding MA in 1570. He was ordained deacon and priest ('Northen') at Ely on 1 December 1580.[1] Within days he was appointed as Colchester's common preacher, in succession to Nicholas Challoner, at Challoner's entreaty on his deathbed, with a salary of £40 per annum.[2] He married Challoner's widow Sarah (*nee* Clere) shortly afterwards.[3]

In the episcopal visitation call book for July 1583, Northey was described as preacher at St Botolph and noted absent.[4] Although there is no reference to his subsequent suspension in the act book of office it must have taken place at the end of September or during the first days of October. It unleashed a furious battle of wills between the Colchester authorities, the town's influential patrons and the bishop of London. The correspondence which ensued gives us our first intimation of John Whitgift's intention to introduce a new form of subscription in the shape of his three articles.[5]

On 8 October the bailiffs of Colchester applied to Sir Thomas Heneage, claiming that if Northey were silenced the whole town would be 'in greate distresse' since there would be only one preaching minister left in the borough.[6] They also fired off a letter to Bishop Aylmer and received (or arranged for) a letter to themselves from eleven prominent inhabitants, urging them to take all steps to secure Northey's restoration.[7] Aylmer replied to Heneage on 10 October, mentioning the new articles and on that basis refusing to restore Northey. Heneage wrote to the bailiffs protesting that he had done everything possible on Northey's behalf and hoping that he would not forsake his profession because he found 'a Warte in the Chirche'.[8]

The bailiffs had other strings to their bow. Not only did they reapply to Heneage on 14 October, declining to have a preacher they did not know forced upon them: they also dispatched an 'officer' of theirs, John Harman, with letters (dated 20 October) to be handed personally to Aylmer and to Sir Francis Walsingham. Aylmer remained adamant, telling Harman flatly that Whitgift's articles meant that he was powerless to act further in the matter. Harman, however, scurried back to Heneage and secured his approval of the application to Walsingham, promising to solicit him at the earliest opportunity.[9]

Nothing came of this manoeuvre. Walsingham appears to have kept a low profile and on 22 October Aylmer, perhaps encouraged by a lack of positive response from the privy council on Northey's behalf, once more informed the bailiffs that he was not prepared to restore him without subscription. He suggested 'Mr Stearne' – John Sterne, future suffragan bishop of Colchester – as an acceptable alternative to Northey, and pointed out that there were 'other good preachers' to be had, such as Thomas Upcher. Heneage followed this up on 24 October, stating that he had again tackled Aylmer but that if Northey was not prepared to subscribe it was 'without my power' to obtain their suit.[10]

Still the bailiffs persevered. They attempted to engage the sympathy of the earl of Leicester,[11] on 12 December further soliciting the earl of Warwick, to whom Northey was 'not unknown'.[12] On 2 March 1584 they again applied to Walsingham, believing that other preachers had been restored, and at about the same time to their former common preacher, William Cole, now President of Corpus Christi College, Oxford, and an old friend of Aylmer's. Cole duly solicited Aylmer but found him inflexible, heavily recommending on 1 June that Northey subscribe the articles.[13] The collapse of Whitgift's campaign for full subscription in the following weeks finally secured Northey's restoration but neither the diocesan nor the borough records reveal the precise circumstances.

Northey was present as preacher of St Botolph at the episcopal visitation of 1586. He was stated to have been admitted preacher *per verbum* by Aylmer but was ordered to administer the sacraments before Michaelmas and to certify that he had done so.[14] He was subsequently suspended again and heads the list of the 'sufficient, painfull and carefull prechers and ministers' molested in Essex.[15]

At the 1589 visitation Northey was present as preacher in the parish of St James and again ordered to certify that he had administered the sacraments.[16] In 1592, still of St James, he was merely listed present ('Noordye') as *concionator notus*.[17]

Given his 'roving brief' as Colchester's senior godly pastor, Northey's relations with his fellow clergymen were not always harmonious. The bailiffs told Heneage in October 1583 that they suspected his suspension 'was upon some purpose wrought by some of the unlarned ministers hys enemies'.[18] Many of Robert Lewis's comments in the Dedham minutes reveal a running battle between them, Northey's public sermons drawing away many of Lewis's parishioners from his regular services. It is striking also that the privy council, so quick to protect others who refused subscription in 1583–4, does not appear to have acted decisively on his behalf and that the Dedham minutes never once allude to his year-long suspension.[19] There is also a curiously oblique letter from the bailiffs to Arch-deacon Withers, dated 19 May 1585, denying 'contencion' in the town and insisting that there was 'good agrement' between Northey and the Colchester ministers and peace and quiet in the town, and that nothing should be done to 'provoke the contrarie'.[20]

Northey made his will as 'Master of Arts and preacher of the Word of God in Colchester' on 10 July 1593. It received probate in the archdeaconry court of Colchester (no date given).[21] Northey died in the parish of St James on 23 July 1593 and was buried there the next day. The Latin epitaph inscribed in the parish register, mentioning that he was of small stature, was transcribed by T. W. Davids.[22]

1. *Alum. Cantab.*, III, 267.
2. ERO (Colchester), Borough of Colchester Assembly Book, 1576–99 [unfoliated], under 22 December 1580; Morant MS D/Y 2/6, p. 83; Byford, 'Price of protestantism', p. 312.
3. *Ibid.*, pp. 316, 353.
4. GL MS 9537/4, fos. 92v–3v; *Alum. Cantab.*, III, 267; GL MS 9537/5, fos. 3r, 58v.
5. Collinson, *EPM*, pp. 246, 256–7; for a full analysis of the surviving correspondence see Byford, 'Price of protestantism', pp. 327–41.
6. ERO (Colchester), Morant MS D/Y 2/6, p. 81.
7. *Ibid.*, pp. 83, 135.
8. ERO (Colchester) Morant MS D/Y 2/4, p. 153; D/Y 2/6, p. 84.
9. *Ibid.*, pp. 85, 89, 95.
10. *Ibid.*, pp. 91–2, 99.
11. The draft of their petition to Leicester survives as ERO (Colchester) Morant MS D/Y 2/4, p. 121.
12. *Ibid.*, D/Y 2/6, p. 105.
13. *Ibid.*, D/Y 2/6, pp. 87, 107.
14. GL MS 9537/6, fo. 139v.
15. *Seconde parte*, II, 163, 261.
16. GL MS 9537/7, fo. 41r.
17. GL MS 9537/8, fo. 51v.
18. ERO (Colchester), Morant MS D/Y 2/6, p. 85; Byford, 'Price of protestantism', p. 323.
19. Northey signed neither the Dedham conference's form of limited subscription nor 'Certain requests' to Archdeacon George Withers (above, pp. 82, 87). In 1588 he admitted that there had been disagreement between himself and 'some in Dedham': ERO (Colchester) Morant MS D/Y 2/4, p. 193.
20. *Ibid.*, D/Y 2/4, p. 117; Byford, 'Price of protestantism', p. 325.

21. F. G. Emmison, ed., *Essex Wills: the Archdeaconry Courts 1591–1597* (Chelmsford, 1991), no. 814. His liquid assets perhaps amounted to £400. There were bequests to Sarah's daughters, Mary and Anne Challenor, of £50 each at age twenty or marriage, and bequests to their own children Thomas, Nathaniel and Sarah. Residual legatees were the children of his brothers-in-law Robert Byrde and John Clere. There were no bequests to any fellow clergy.
22. Davids, *Annals*, pp. 106–7.

PARKER, RICHARD (c. 1552–1611)

Vicar of Dedham, Essex, 1582–90 (resig.); vicar of Ketteringham, Norfolk, 1601–11 (d.)

Despite considerable confusion in the records, it seems clear that Parker was the man of these names who matriculated sizar from St John's College, Cambridge, at Easter 1574, graduating BA in early 1578 and proceeding MA in 1581.[1] He was ordained deacon by John Aylmer, bishop of London, some time between 18 August and 6 September 1577 (scholar of St John's; aged 25)[2] and priest on 29 September 1579 (BA of St John's; born Baldock, Hertfordshire).[3] Following the resignation of Timothy Fitzallen, he received letters of presentation to Dedham from Sir Ralph Sadler, chancellor of the duchy of Lancaster, on 27 June 1582.[4] He was instituted on 30 June, compounding for the benefice on 5 July.[5]

Although an original signatory of the Dedham conference and subsequently its (official?) secretary, Parker does not record his own presence at any meeting until May 1583, when he asked advice for preventing the conventicles of Periman (**6M**). He was present at the episcopal visitation on 11 July 1583 as vicar and preacher.[6] In the aftermath of the visitation Robert West, called into consistory for failing to receive communion, retorted that he had not done so since Fitzallen's departure because Parker would not 'kepe the order of the quene's book'. He denied certain 'stubborn wordes' but admitted saying that 'if Mr Archdeacon Withers might rule the Quene should be obeyed'. For good measure he added that when Withers sent word to Dedham to observe the Book of Common Prayer, Parker had said that he would do so 'for their sake that sent the worde but otherwise I could find now to spend the tyme better'; and that he had never worn the surplice since his 'cominge thither'. Parker and the churchwardens were accordingly ordered into consistory to answer articles.[7]

The case rumbled on, the churchwardens (William Nevard and Thomas Allen) deposing on 2 November that they had not presented Parker for his refusal to wear the surplice before the episcopal visitors because they had previously done so in the archidiaconal court and had believed that to be sufficient. There were further charges of unruly behaviour against West, who on 4 December pleaded that he could not bring a certificate that he had received communion because Parker still refused to accept him. The case was adjourned until Hilary term 1584.[8] By his own account, Parker was on 13 January ordered to observe the prayer book and wear the surplice and to certify 'in Candlemas terme' or else appear before the Commissioners. 'Through favour' – he does not say whose – he 'escaped their handes and yelded not unto them'.[9] West being excommunicated for his failure to appear on 16 January, the case was adjourned twice more before the end of the month.[10]

On 4 February Thomas Allen appeared in consistory on Parker's behalf and explained that he and William Butter had received letters from Aylmer signifying that the case be 'respited' until Parker had made answer in the archidiaconal court concerning Archbishop Whitgift's new articles. It was accordingly adjourned indefinitely, pending a new monition.[11] Whilst there is no official record of the fact, Parker was subsequently suspended by Aylmer for refusing the articles.[12]

His name does not occur again in the minutes until 6 April 1584, when he gave 5s, the least of all contributions, for Henry Wilcock (**17M**). He was moderator for the first time in August and delegated to speak with Thomas Lowe about his absence from the meetings. He also suggested a fast, a motion 'deferred to the next meeting save one' (**21M**). Thereafter he is mentioned only as host or moderator until the aftermath of the episcopal visitation on 22 July 1586. He was present on that occasion as vicar and preacher, licensed (*ut dicitur*) by Aylmer and ordered to bring his licence into consistory.[13] In the event he was one of those suspended for refusing the surplice and had 'a day set' for his deprivation.[14]

Chosen host for August 1586 and speaker for September (**45, 46MM**), he asked a serious question for the first time only on 6 February 1587, concerning disorders in the church (**53M**). He raised his question again at the next three meetings and then in September, but on every occasion the matter was deferred (**55, 56, 57, 60MM**). In August he supported Chapman's motion for 'the good of the Church' (**59M**).

On 5 February 1588 he asked what he might do for a supply of his place, being suspended by Aylmer (**65M**). Since, on 17 February, in an abject letter to William Tey, Parker spoke of 'this lewd woman who is the ground of my troubles',[15] it is undoubtedly an oblique reference to the case of Marion Barker, an adulteress whom Parker had refused to admit to communion even though she had done penance in church. In late 1587, via the archdeaconry court, she had brought a suit against him before the High Commission.[16]

The Barker affair subsided and by January 1589 Parker was preoccupied with other pastoral concerns within his parish (**75M**). At the episcopal visitation in July he was detected for not wearing the surplice and ordered not to read service or administer the sacraments unless he did so.[17] He was not called into consistory thereafter but instead left to the discretion of the archdeacon's official. In February 1590 the churchwardens were forced to report that the new surplice had been appropriated and burnt by Parker and his wife: there had also been a violent altercation in the church with Richard Upcher, who had been obliged to present Parker's nonconformity to the official of Archdeacon Withers.[18]

Nothing at all is known of Parker's wife but to judge from the scandal which now engulfed him he had married within the very recent past: it seems implicit in the accusations of sexual misconduct which began to come to light in late 1589 that he had remained a lonely young bachelor until his final months in Dedham. The story of his disgrace has already been told above since it belongs to the mainstream of Dedham's extraordinary history and doubtless contributed to the failure of nerve which seems to have overtaken the conference members during the last months of its existence.[19]

The case was initiated in consistory on 5 November 1589 and was to continue into the summer of 1590. Thereafter Parker could hardly have continued at Dedham. He resigned the vicarage on or before 14 September 1590, when Henry Wilcock received letters of presentation as his successor.[20] Summoned to London that winter to give evidence about the conference movement, Parker evidently told everything he knew, revealing not only the names of the Dedham members but also the existence of the Braintree conference.[21]

Parker's whereabouts thereafter are unknown until, on 9 June 1601, he was instituted to the vicarage of Ketteringham at the presentation of Thomas Thetford.[22] Apparently he had been ministering there for some months before this since the parish register contains a note: 'Anno 1600. Here begyneth the names of the persons registered by me Richard Parker'.[23]

During John Jegon's primary visitation of Norwich diocese in 1603 Parker was listed among the 'mynisters, preachers no graduates (sic) of honest life and conversation'. His vicarage was stated to be worth only £6 per annum.[24] Since it was sparsely populated, his parochial duties must have been light, and it is perhaps to that fact above all that we owe the survival of the Dedham papers. Parker also continued to acquire and to file, particularly during the seismic years 1603–5, a number of documents concerning ecclesiastical affairs. Given the comparative obscurity in which he was now living, this circumstance argues that John Field's death in 1588 had not destroyed the 'propaganda machine' with which his name is so closely associated, and that relevant material continued to be widely copied and circulated throughout the godly network.[25] Parker also found time from September 1606 to transcribe part of the surviving parish register and in 1608 described in some detail the reconstruction of the church after the fall of its steeple on 20 July that year.[26] He was buried at Ketteringham on 30 June 1611.[27]

1. *Alum. Cantab.*, III, 307.
2. GL MS 9535/1, fo. 154v: date and place of a series of four ordinations omitted.
3. GL MS 9535/2, fo. 9r.
4. PRO DL 42/100, fo. 10v.
5. Reg. Grindal, fo. 205v; PRO E334/10, fo. 16v; sureties were William Renchcrofte, innholder, and Thomas Wilson, grocer, both of St Benet Gracechurch, London.
6. GL MS 9537/5, fo. 63r. No formal preaching licence has been traced.
7. LMA DL/C/300, p. 313.
8. *Ibid.*, pp. 382–3, 505.
9. See above, p. 140. Although Parker has clearly written 'xiii th of January 1582' (that is, new style 1583), the sequence of events makes it clear that this must be an error for '1583' (that is, new style 1584).
10. LMA DL/C/300, pp. 651, 657, 674, 728.
11. *Ibid.*, p. 734.
12. *Seconde parte*, II, 164.
13. GL MS 9537/6, fo. 142v.
14. *Seconde parte*, II, 164, 261. In May 1587 the archdeaconry court duly took cognizance of Parker's failure to wear the surplice (ERO D/ACA 14, fos. 144r, 154r) but, as was its frequent practice, quietly shelved the matter until again chivvied into action during the episcopal visitation of 1589.
15. See above, p. 77.
16. ERO D/ACA 14, fos. 77v, 154r, 233v; D/ACA 17, fo. 16r.
17. GL MS 9537/7, fo. 46r. The detection before Aylmer's visitors was inevitable once Stephen Ellinot, churchwarden, had been forced to admit before the archdeaconry court in April 1589 that the parish still lacked a surplice. On 30 May, however, Parker was released by the court on his assertion that Aylmer had given him leave to 'use his conscience in that respecte' until the July visitation: ERO D/ACA 17, fos. 155v, 191r.
18. ERO D/ACA 17, fos. 293v, 295r.
19. See above, pp. lxxiii–iv.
20. PRO DL 42/100, fo. 16r.
21. Collinson, *EPM*, p. 408. For the possibility that his full co-operation was the price he paid for being allowed to resign rather than undergo deprivation, see above, p. lxxiv, n.243.
22. NRO DN/REG 14/20, fo. 300r.
23. NRO PAR Ketteringham, microfiche 8, p. 14.
24. NRO DN/VIS/3/3, fo. 103r.
25. The letter book of Robert Smarte of Preston Capes, Northamptonshire, provides similar evidence of godly 'networking': see Collinson, *EPM*, p. 435.
26. NRO PAR Ketteringham, microfiche 8, p. 3.
27. *Ibid.*, p. 74.

ROGERS, RICHARD (1551–1618)

Curate of Radwinter, Essex, 1574; lecturer of Wethersfield, Essex, c. 1577/8–1618 (d.)

Rogers, one of the most influential godly writers of his time, was born in Chelmsford, Essex, son of John Rogers, carpenter, and his wife Agnes (*nee* Carter), and was baptized on 29 June 1551.[1] He matriculated sizar from Christ's College, Cambridge, in November

1566, graduating BA early in 1571 and proceeding MA from Gonville and Caius in 1574.[2] He was ordained priest by Edwin Sandys, bishop of London, on 21 December 1571 (BA: scholar of Christ's; born Chelmsford; aged '24').[3]

He was present as curate of Radwinter at Sandys's second episcopal visitation on 19 July 1574, serving under William Harrison, author of the *Description of England*.[4] His tombstone states that he served at Wethersfield for 'fourtie one yeares and upwards', which suggests a date for his arrival prior to April 1577.[5] Yet tombstones are not invariably reliable and Rogers is not found listed there or elsewhere in the diocese during John Aylmer's primary visitation in July 1577. Perhaps, then, his tenure as lecturer in Wethersfield began in late 1577 or early 1578. He was certainly present as schoolmaster and preacher at the episcopal visitation of July 1580.[6]

Probably a founder member of the Braintree conference,[7] Rogers was ordered as a result of the episcopal visitation of July 1583 to produce the preaching licence which he claimed to have from the archbishop of Canterbury's vicar general for Aylmer's personal inspection.[8] In early 1584 he was one of the twenty-seven Essex ministers who petitioned against Archbishop Whitgift's three articles.[9] In the event he was suspended for refusing them, but Aylmer restored him after thirty weeks, after the intercession of Sir Robert Wroth, and according to his own testimony he remained unmolested for the rest of Whitgift's life.[10] In fact, following the visitation of 1586, he was again summoned to a personal interview with Aylmer but probably escaped a further period of suspension.[11] By early 1587, from which point his fragmentary diary survives, he had formed a strong friendship with Ezekiel Culverwell, whose arrival in Essex as chaplain to Robert 3rd Lord Rich and preacher at Felsted appears to have energized the Braintree conference.[12]

At the visitation of 1589 Rogers came under more severe scrutiny. He was ordered to administer the sacraments according the Book of Common Prayer, to use the surplice and to certify that he had done so on 1 October.[13] On 25 November he frankly admitted in court that he had not administered communion since his last presentment but was granted a further respite until Easter 1590 because he was able to produce a letter from Ambrose earl of Warwick (most conveniently dated 24 November) observing that Rogers was his chaplain and that he 'hath some occasions as need shall serve to use him'.[14]

Despite his own asseverations, it is clear that Rogers remained under periodic pressure for another fifteen years. At Aylmer's last visitation in 1592 he was described as unlicensed to preach and ordered to catechize[15] and at Bancroft's first visitation in 1598, still unlicensed, he was ordered to appear before the High Commissioners (*Commissionariis Regiis*).[16] He was called into consistory on 3 May 1605, following Bancroft's last visitation in 1604, to attend Bishop Richard Vaughan 'to be resolved of his doubts touching his conformity in the ceremonies'.[17] The case was prorogued and Vaughan was disinclined to continue it. On 10 May, three days before Rogers's scheduled reappearance, Josias Clark, *armiger*, affirmed that since his citation 'it pleased my L: Bishopp of London to giue order that Mr Rogers should staye his appearance in this Court' until Vaughan 'should specially send for him himself'. He added that the order had been signified to Rogers by a letter written 'by one Mr Watner servant to the L. Knowles'.[18] Evidently Archbishop Bancroft was disposed to pursue the matter but after October 1605, following further intercession by Knowles, he left Rogers in peace. Rogers acknowledged Knowles's good offices in his diary and described Vaughan as one who had 'permitted all the godly ministers to live peaceably and to enjoy liberty in their calling.'[19] Rogers was further shielded by Knowles during the episcopate of Vaughan's much less sympathetic successor, Thomas Ravis (1607–9).[20]

Rogers had by now become one of the founder-members of a godly clan whose influence on the future of English Calvinism and the history of New England is beyond parallel.[21] In 1602 he published one of the most celebrated of all works of practical divinity, his *Seven treatises*, which was reprinted six times over the next thirty years. He died on 21 April 1618 and was buried at Wethersfield, having made a lengthy will on 15 April. He left most of his property to his second wife, Susan, by whom he appears to have had no children, and to his sons Daniel and Ezekiel by his first wife (whose name was Barbara), the latter receiving all his Latin, Greek and Hebrew books. Minor bequests included a copy of the *Seven treatises* to his 'cousin [John] Rogers of Dedham', lecturer in succession to Edmund Chapman. His three executors were Susan, his 'beloved cousin' John Wright, esquire, of Romford, Essex, and his son-in-law Francis Longe. Probate was granted to Longe (Consistory Court of London) on 30 April 1618.[22]

1. Knappen, *Two puritan diaries*, p. 19.
2. *Alum. Cantab.*, III, 479; Peile, *Biographical register*, I, 97–8.
3. GL MS 9535/1, fo. 151r. As Knappen observed (p. 19, n. 5), his stated age of 24 conflicts both with his baptismal record and the evidence of his tombstone, which gives his age at death as 68. Yet if the two latter are correct he was below canonical age at ordination. There seems to be no way out of this conundrum.
4. GL MS 9537/3, fo. 72r.
5. For the tombstone, see Knappen, *Two puritan diaries*, p. 22, n. 11.
6. GL MS 9537/4, fo. 91r. Presumably on the basis of the tombstone, the entry in the old *DNB* hazarded 'about 1577', whilst Knappen (*Two puritan diaries*, p. 20) suggested 'a year or two' after his proceeding MA in 1574. This was wisely to ignore Peile, who inexplicably gives '1572', a date refuted by the Radwinter evidence. Although perhaps no more than a typographical error, '1572' was unfortunately enshrined in *Alum. Cantab.* and has therefore inevitably been repeated by many later writers.
7. For the disturbances which resulted when Edmund Chapman preached at Wethersfield in late 1582, at what may have been its inauguration, see Collinson, *EPM*, p. 220.
8. GL MS 9537/5, fo. 57r.
9. *Seconde parte*, I, 225.
10. Knappen, *Two puritan diaries*, p. 29.
11. GL MS 9537/6, fo. 139r; *Seconde parte*, II, 163, 261.
12. Knappen, *Two puritan diaries*, pp. 53–63.
13. GL MS 9537/7, fo. 38v.
14. LMA DL/C/616, p. 108. Rogers never once mentions Warwick in his diary. This manoeuvre surely demonstrates how the godly network could spring into action at a moment's notice to provide a convenient safety-net for a threatened member.
15. GL MS 9537/8, fo. 37r.
16. GL MS 9537/9, fo. 96v. This entry confirms Knappen's surmise that the Rogers mentioned by Samuel Ward as under threat at this time was indeed Richard: Knappen, *Two puritan diaries*, p. 126.
17. LMA DL/C/317, p. 673.
18. *Ibid.*, p. 679.
19. Knappen, *Two puritan diaries*, pp. 31–2.
20. On 24 November 1607 he was ordered to certify that he had attended Ravis concerning his conformity, having been admonished not to preach in any other church but Wethersfield. 'Mr Cluit towld me Thos Poll it is my L: pleasure his cause shold be continued until thende of hillarie Terme & then my L: Knowles steward towld me his L: had (?)exonerated him untill midsomer': LMA DL/C/306, p. 38.
21. For the ramifications of this godly connexion, see Sarah Bendall, Christopher Brooke and Patrick Collinson, *A history of Emmanuel College, Cambridge* (Woodbridge, 1999), pp. 188–91.
22. LMA DL/C/360, fos. 314r–16r. For Rogers' family connexions see Knappen, *Two puritan diaries*, pp. 22–5.

SALMON, EDMUND (Flor. 1573–1604)

Rector of Erwarton, Suffolk, 1586–?

Edmund Salmon matriculated as a pensioner from Jesus College, Cambridge, at Easter 1573, and proceeded BA in early 1577.[1] He may have begun his clerical career as an assistant to John Knewstub at Cockfield, Suffolk, since on 21 July 1580 he and Knewstub witnessed the will of Margaret Hilles of that parish.[2] He must have been much involved in arrangements for the extraordinary conference held at Cockfield in May 1582. By 1583, he was living in the neighbouring village of Bradfield Combust, where a son, John, was buried on 27 May and another son baptized on 2 June.[3] He was perhaps still at Bradfield (but not beneficed?) when in January 1584 he was suspended for not subscribing to Whitgift's articles.[4] On 5 May 1586, he was instituted vicar of Erwarton, which Walter Allen had resigned on being presented by Sir Robert Jermyn to the rectory of his own parish church, Rushbrooke. Salmon was presented to Erwarton by Sir Philip Parker: a good example of Suffolk 'ministry and magistracy' in action.[5]

Promptly, on 30 May 1586, Henry Sandes proposed 'Mr Salmon, pastor of Erwerton' for membership of the Dedham conference (**44M**), and he was admitted on 8 August (**46M**). He was the speaker in October, when the conference met at William Bird's house in Boxford (**48M**). Subsequently, Salmon seems to have played a minor role in the conference, although he could be relied upon to pose pastoral teasers. On 10 July 1587, when the conference met in Salmon's own rectory, he asked what he should do with the sum of £1 which had been gathered at a fast in aid of the French church (in London?), and this was clearly considered to be a silly question (**59M**). A year later, Salmon needed to be advised 'how he might know a witche', a question which revealed a variety of opinions on that subject, and whether boys of sixteen years of age might put on their hats in church (**67M**). At the very last meeting of the conference he asked whether he could baptize a child born to a vagrant Irish woman. He was told that he could not (**80M**).

In the diocesan visitation of 1597, Salmon was presented for not having worn the surplice for three years and for not having read the Injunctions.[6] Punishment was reserved, but it appears that he was not disturbed and was still rector in 1603.[7] Salmon bows out of history as one of the Suffolk ministers to whom Nicholas Chaplin of Chelsworth left pairs of gloves in 1604.[8]

1. *Alum. Cantab.*, IV, 3.
2. SRO Bury St Edmunds, R2 ICC 500/2/38.
3. SRO Bury St Edmunds, Bradfield Combust parish registers.
4. *Seconde parte*, I, 243.
5. NRO, DN/REG/14, fos. 136v, 137v.
6. *Redman's Visitation*, p. 152.
7. Bullen, *Catalogue*, p. 21.
8. Muskett, *Suffolk manorial families*, III, 82.

SANDES, HENRY (1549–1626)

Vicar of Preston, Suffolk, 1578–c. 1582; preacher at Boxford, Suffolk, c. 1582– c. 1624

Henry Sandes, who was born in 1549 and died in 1626,[1] and whose name was always thus spelt, must nevertheless have sprung from the extended Sandys lineage of north-west England, which gave the Elizabethan church Archbishop Edwin Sandys, since in August 1585 he asked the Dedham conference to advise 'the brethren' in Lancashire how they might strengthen the powers of the ecclesiastical commission in that county (**34M**); and in August 1587 he requested the conference to make representations to a sympathetic assize judge, riding the Lancashire circuit, to punish someone who had libelled against Richard Midgeley, vicar of Rochdale (**59M**). But to his Dedham brethren, Lancashire was a far-away country of which they knew little ('it was thought unmeete to deale in it the persons being soe far of'). The fact that Sandes matriculated from St John's College, Cambridge (at Michaelmas 1569),[2] also suggests a northern origin and perhaps an initial intention to follow another profession (law?), since he took no degree. St John's at this time was as good a place as any to 'get religion'. One is reminded of what happened to another intended law student, the Lancastrian Laurence Chaderton, after his arrival in Cambridge.[3]

On 13 November 1578, Sandes was instituted vicar of the Suffolk parish of Preston, presented by the author of the *Breviary of Suffolk,* Robert Ryece.[4] Sandes's funerary monument in Boxford church records that he had preached there for forty years, which might suggest that he had moved from Preston to Boxford in 1586. But Sandes retired from Boxford to Groton no later than 1624, and he was certainly already at Boxford when he joined the Dedham conference as a founder member in October 1582.[5] So let us place him in Boxford no later than 1582. Of the founder members, Sandes was one of the heavyweights, balancing the troika displaced from Norwich. Sandes was 'preacher of Boxford', not rector, and he married the daughter of the rector and fellow conference member, William Birde, although in generational and intellectual terms which are not very accessible to us he clearly outranked his father-in-law.

There was no endowed lectureship at Boxford such as William Cardinal had established at Dedham. So who footed the bill for Sandes's ancillary ministry? One suspects private means. But one of his most faithful supporters was Adam Winthrop of nearby Groton, the father of John Winthrop, first governor of Massachusetts, and brother-in-law of John Still, a future bishop but in the days of the conference a sympathetic archdeacon of Sudbury. Indeed, it was probably Winthrop who brought Sandes to Boxford. Winthrop paid Sandes a modest annual stipend of £1, later increased to £2. But he was not so much a patron as a close friend, who shared Sandes's intellectual and religious interests. His diary records Sandes's grave illness in 1596, and the fact that he was the victim of a robbery in 1597. When Sandes retired in old age, it was to Winthrop's Groton and in his will he asked to be buried 'on the other side of the Chancell dore over against the place where Mr Addam Winthropp lieth buried'.[6]

Sandes, an immensely acceptable figure among the Suffolk godly, was showered with benefactions. Johanne Barflet, a Boxford widow, left him 40s, Thomas Goymer, a Boxford ashburner, 10s, Thomas Gale, a clothier of Edwardston, 40s, Edward Appleton of Edwardston £5, Elizabeth Barret, widow, of Aveley, £10, while Nicholas Chaplin of Chelsworth favoured him with a pair of white gloves. His fellow preachers were no less generous. The bequest of Sandes's lifelong friend, John Knewstub (a fellow north-countryman and rector of the neighbouring parish of Cockfield for forty-five years) was £5, heading the list of his remembrances to fellow ministers; while Thomas Lovell, minister of Great Waldingfield, remembered Sandes with 10s, appointing Knewstub and Sandes as overseers of his will.[7]

Sandes energized a little godly commonwealth in Boxford. In 1596 a Free Grammar School was erected by public subscription (Johane Barflet was one of the subscribers) on land given by Adam Winthrop, and Sandes, with Knewstub and Winthrop, was among the first governors.[8] In 1608 the 'chief inhabitants' held a town meeting and drew up a social charter comparable to the orders 'agreed upon' by the vicar and 'auncients of the Congregation of Dedham', and to the articles adopted at a town meeting of the 'chieffe inhabitants' of the Berkshire/Wiltshire parish of Swallowfield in 1596.[9] As Sandes became older, his preaching ministry at Boxford was supplemented by a combination lecture maintained on a Thursday by neighbouring ministers. In 1620 Adam Winthrop recorded all fifty-two Thursday lectures made by a total of twenty-five preachers.[10]

Sandes was one of the most proactive members of the Dedham conference, particularly in the long drawn out debate over the sabbath in which he engaged with Richard Crick. Although he later fitted the pattern of the moderate establishment puritan, rarely if ever troubled by the ecclesiastical authorities (like Knewstub), in the pages of the conference minutes Sandes appears as a radical presbyterian, as well as an extreme sabbatarian. In January 1584, with the ministers confronted by Whitgift's articles, it was Sandes and another radical, William Tey of Peldon, who were deputed to review the prayer book and to note what things in it could be used with a good conscience, and what not (**14M**). In the same month Sandes was listed as 'Preacher of the Word of God' among those Suffolk ministers suspended for refusing to subscribe.[11] In June 1585, Sandes moved that a plan should be made 'for the helpinge forward of discipline the next Parliament' (**31M**). In June 1588, he asked the conference to consider 'whether the course of the B[ishops] were such and of such moment, that they were not to be thought of as brethren, and soe to be delt withall in our publike and in our private speeches and praiers'. The debate which followed was inconclusive and one suspects that Edmund Chapman ensured that it should be so (**68M**).

It may be that Sandes's hard line was the position taken up by the other conference of which he was also a member, referred to in the minutes as 'another company' (**57M**), meeting in Suffolk, which perhaps lacked the moderating influence of Chapman at Dedham. Sandes was uncertain where he would stand in conscience if the two conferences were to disagree in their judgments. The internal politics of this seems to have been that the Suffolk conference was disposed to subscribe to the Book of Discipline, whereas at Dedham 'to geve our handes tutchinge our judgment in matters was not thought saffe in any respecte' (**56M**).

1. Sandes's funerary monument in Boxford church, the text printed by Francis Peck, *Desiderata curiosa* (London, 1732–5), VI, 22: 'He lyved 77 Years, and dyed the 9 of Novemb[er] 1626'.
2. *Alum. Cantab.*, IV, 19.
3. Bendall, Brooke and Collinson, *A history of Emmanuel College, Cambridge*, p. 32.
4. NRO, DN/REG/14, fo. 31r.
5. John Knewstub's will, made 22 May 1624, speaks of 'my auncient good friend Mr Henry Sandes of Groton'; PRO, PCC PROB 11/143 (53 Byrde).
6. *Winthrop papers*, almost *passim*; Francis J. Bremer, 'The heritage of John Winthrop: religion along the Stour Valley, 1548–1630', *The New England Quarterly*, LXX (1997), 515–47; will of Henry Sandes, NRO, NCC Mittings, fo. 296.
7. SRO Bury St Edmunds, WI/54/47, WI/56/76, R2/41/125 (and PRO, PCC PROB 11/73 (5 Leicester)); Muskett, *Suffolk manorial families*, I, 324, 279, III, 82; PRO, PCC PROB 11/73 (5 Leicester); PROB 11/143 (53 Byrde); PROB 11/116 (85 Wingfield).
8. Bremer, 'The heritage of John Winthrop', pp. 534–5; SRO Bury St Edmunds, WI/54/47.
9. Bremer, 'The heritage of John Winthrop', pp. 537–8; Steve Hindle, 'Hierarchy and community in the Elizabethan parish: the Swallowfield Articles of 1596', *Historical Journal*, XLII (1999), 835–51.
10. Bremer, 'The heritage of John Winthrop', pp. 532–3.
11. *Seconde parte*, I, 243.

SEARLE, ROBERT (d. 1610)

Rector of Lexden, Essex, 1576–1610 (d.)

Searle, a non-graduate, was ordained by Edmund Guest, bishop of Salisbury, on 3 March 1573[1] and instituted rector of Lexden on 30 May 1576 at the presentation of Thomas 3rd earl of Sussex.[2] He was present at Aylmer's primary visitation of London on 10 July 1577 and was granted a diocesan preaching licence on 19 July following.[3]

Searle was presumably related to Robert Searle, grocer of St Nicholas parish, whom Foxe records as an expert harp-player[4] and as fleeing Colchester at the age of thirty-eight with his wife and children after Mary's accession. He spent his time 'in woods and Groves abroade in Essex' until he sickened and died at Easthorpe.[5]

Kinship with a local martyr would certainly explain why, despite his lack of a university education, the younger Robert was prominent amongst the Colchester godly. He was present at the episcopal visitations of 1580 and 1583, on the latter occasion failing to bring in his preaching licence: he was to exhibit it in the afternoon but apparently failed to do so.[6] In late 1584 he was one of the local clergy who signed the form of limited subscription preserved in the Dedham papers and a signatory to 'Certain requests' submitted to Archdeacon Withers.[7]

Following the episcopal visitation of 1586 Searle was called before Aylmer and had 'a daie set' for deprivation for refusing the surplice.[8] He survived, only to be ordered in that of 1589 to certify on 2 October how often he had worn the surplice on the Sabbath.[9] Nothing more is recorded of any nonconformist activities[10] but Searle was listed as one of the 'diligent and sufficient' clergy of Essex in 1604.[11] He was called into consistory on 12 September 1606 for failing to repair his parsonage house.[12]

Searle was probably three times married: his (?)second wife Anna (nee Lorance) was buried at Lexden on 1 October 1597 after ten years of marriage.[13] In his undated will he left to his (?)third, Anne, all the household stuff she had brought him at marriage but none of his own, since without his consent she had appropriated household goods and plate, 'I know not what', and bestowed it on her daughter and son-in-law at the time of their marriage. He nevertheless left her £100, to be paid at the rate of 40s a year 'if she live to receive it', provided that she 'challenge no thirds' out of his lands. His eldest son, Samuel, received the freehold which Searle had bought for £30 from his father, unless his father wished to buy it back. Thomas Allen, his son-in-law,[14] received £40 out of the £50 already in his hands, the other £10 going to Searle's daughter Elizabeth, Thomas's wife. Searle's second son, Thomas, received all his houses and copyhold lands and his books.

If none of his children had issue he established a trust, the property to be administered by the rector of Lexden 'for the time being', he to pay 20s a year to Searle's next of kin 'if they so demand', 5s a year to the poor of Lexden, and 40s a year to a schoolmaster to teach four poor boys English and writing in Lexden 'till they be fit to go to be prentices'. The condition was that the incumbent rector be a preacher of the gospel and 'shall use it diligently'; 'otherwise I will the whole & due rent to be given by the said parson to the several preaching ministers in the town of Colchester equally divided'.

Thomas Allen and Samuel and Thomas Searle were made joint executors provided they performed their duties amicably and without going to law, taking the advice of John 'Walfur', Searle's father-in-law, his 'brother' Mr Halsnett and four other named friends; to each of these he left 'a good pair of gloves in token of my last kindness and farewell'. The whole was 'written with my own hands not without passionate grief [and] sorrow for some things therein inserted'. Probate was granted (Consistory Court of London) on 29 March 1610.[15]

1. ERO D/ACA 14, fo. 281r.
2. Reg. Grindal, fos. 187v–8r. He compounded for the benefice on 15 June 1576, with sureties Robert Bell of St Laurence Pountney, clothworker, and John Gynes of St Peter Cornhill, haberdasher: PRO E334/9, fo. 82v.
3. GL MS 9537/4, fo. 31r; LMA DL/C/333, fo. 78r.
4. Perhaps an oblique reference to the fact that at this time 'scripture songs' were sung in Essex, even at weddings, by musicians protesting against Mary's proceedings.
5. Foxe, *A & M* (1563), p. 1678. This account is one of many short narratives under the heading 'The persecuted in Essex' never republished in later editions. The editors are indebted to Dr Thomas Freeman for providing a transcript.
6. GL MS 9537/4, fo. 92v; /5, fos. 3r, 59r.
7. See above, pp. 82, 87.
8. GL MS 9537/6, fo. 104v; *Seconde parte*, II, 164.
9. GL MS 9537/7, fo. 41r.

10. At the episcopal visitations of 1592 and 1598 he was simply noted as present and a preacher licensed by Aylmer: GL MS 9537/8, fo. 52r; /9, fo. 105r.
11. The living was stated to worth £66 13s 4d: 'A Viewe', p. 6.
12. LMA DL/C/305, fo. 181r.
13. Davids, *Annals*, p. 113.
14. Probably the man of these names mentioned in the minute book: see above, p. 127.
15. LMA DL/C/360, fos. 23r–4v.

SEFFRAY (SEFFEREY, SEFFARIE), THOMAS (d. 1631)

Vicar of Depden, Suffolk, 1589–1605 (depr.); 'clerk of Stradishall' in 1631

Seffray's name has been frequently misrendered as 'Jeffray'. Was he therefore the Thomas 'Jeffraye' recorded as matriculating sizar from Clare College, Cambridge, at Michaelmas 1572, graduating BA in early 1575 and ordained priest at Norwich on 30 November 1579?[1] Thomas 'Seffery' was certainly vicar of Depden from 1589.[2] He reported in 1603 that there were two hundred communicants in his parish and that there were no recusants or separatists. The patron of the living was John Jermyn esquire.[3] Seffray was deprived in 1605 for nonconformity.[4] At the root of the matter, perhaps, was his objection to kneeling at communion. Thomas Rogers (a hostile witness), speaks in his *Two dialogues . . . concerning kneeling* (1608) of Seffray's 'chusing rather . . . to abide the censure of authority' and of having forgone 'a sweete and competent living', rather than 'to condemne his vanities'.[5]

Seffray appears to have remained in the vicinity of Bury St Edmunds for the rest of his life. When he drew up his will on 8 October 1631 ('Sefferey'), he described himself as 'clerk of Stradishall'. His good and loving wife, Margaret, received £100 on condition that she give over her thirdes and the dower due unto her out of his messuages, landes and tenements. She was left all his household stuff except what remained in his house in Bury, and had choice of his 'greate Bible' and of four English books. His son Thomas received the rest of his books. His other sons, Josias, Dennys and Samuel, and daughters, Sarah, Lydia, Ann, Elizabeth, Phebe, Prescilla, Martha and Rebecka (were some of these daughters-in-law?) received various monetary sums. No mention was made of his former incumbency in Depden.[6] An inventory of his goods drawn up on 28 October 1631 provides clear evidence that he 'commuted' regularly between Bury and Stradishall. In Bury there were eighty small books in his study and in Stradishall a bed, some plates, a chamber pot, his apparel, forty-five books and a surprising amount of ready money (£444).[7]

1. *Alum. Cantab.*, II, 466.
2. Bullen, 'Catalogue', p. 313.
3. 'The condition', p. 31.
4. NRO DCN REG 15, book 21, fo. 18v: John Playford is here stated to have been instituted to Depden following the deprivation of Thomas 'Seffarie'.
5. Thomas Rogers, *Two dialogues or conferences* (London, 1608), epistle dedicatory.
6. NRO 218 Purgall.
7. NRO Inv 37/190.

STOUGHTON (STOCKDEN, STOC(K)TON), THOMAS (?d. 1622)

Rector of Naughton, Suffolk, 1586–93(?) (?resig./depr.); curate of Great Burstead [Billericay], Essex, 1594–1600; rector of Coggeshall, Essex, 1600–6 (depr.)

According to his own testimony, Stoughton was 'bred and borne' in Sandwich, Kent.[1] He matriculated pensioner from Trinity College, Cambridge, at Michaelmas 1573, graduating BA from Queens' in early 1577 ('Stockden'). He became a fellow of Queens' in

1579, proceeding MA in 1580.[2] He was probably a pupil and protégé of Robert Some (fellow of Queens' 1562–89).[3]

Stoughton was living on the Essex/Suffolk border by October 1582 when he became a founder member of the conference. At the first meeting he asked if 'fornication make affinity', a question deferred and not subsequently resurrected (**1M**). Since in March 1583 the place chosen for the following meeting was East Bergholt 'at Mr Stoctons' (**4M**), he was perhaps undergoing clerical training there at the hands of Dowe, Crick or Tilney. In June 1583 he was delegated with Chapman and Morse to confer with 'some godly men' in Cambridge about the Sabbath (**8M**). Next month he was moderator (**9M**) and in September one of four speakers at a fast in East Bergholt (**10M**).[4] He is not mentioned again until August 1584, when it is recorded that he and Dowe had dealt with certain Suffolk gentlemen about 'ill mynisters' (**21M**). In September he was moderator at Coggeshall, was nominated to speak at next month's fast and asked if he 'might safelie in conscience preach being requested thereunto he being yet no minister'; the matter was 'not delt in' (**22M**). In January 1585 he was amongst those appointed to confer with Dr Oxenbridge (**26M**). At the extraordinary meeting of 17 February 1585 he cast his vote against Andrewes's departure from Wenham, arguing that a preacher should not resign his calling for the lower function of teacher.

Since on 5 April 1585 Stoughton was delegated to supply Tey's place at Peldon until further notice, following the death of Thomas Tey (**29M**), he was clearly ordained some time between September 1584, when he was still 'no minister', and late March 1585. No ordination record, however, has come to light.

In June 1585 he was appointed speaker for the next meeting at Bergholt 'at Mr Tylney's' (**31M**). In August he was concerned about arcane irregularities in the prayer book (**33M**). In September he asked advice about accepting a living: the brethren urged him to accept 'if his affection stood unto the people and that he might have a lawfull callinge to them, and quietly passe through the Bs handes' (**35M**). On 4 October he was permitted to 'send letters agayne to Kent about his livinge', his originals having 'perished by the way' (**36M**). No more is heard either of this Kent living or of Stoughton until March 1586, when he was chosen moderator for the April meeting (**41M**).

When in June 1586 Crick asked if Stoughton should accept the living of 'Nawton', it was agreed that he should (**45M**). On 14 July 1586 he was duly instituted by Edmund Scambler, bishop of Norwich, to the rectory of Naughton, Suffolk, on the presentation of John More of Ipswich, a leading godly merchant and magistrate and business partner of William Cardinal.[5] In 1588 More's daughter, the wealthy widow Elizabeth Walter, left Stoughton £5 in her will.[6]

Since Naughton is only about eight miles north of East Bergholt, Stoughton was able to continue to attend meetings regularly but never acted as host in his new parish and seems to have retained his domicile in East Bergholt.[7] By April 1587 he had clashed with his parishioners and also, perhaps, with his new patron. Crick asked whether Stoughton should leave Naughton, 'having bene at soe great charge and like to be at more, and none wold beare any part with him, and yet having tried his right, yt was feared he shuld not be at quiet'. It was agreed that Mr More should be consulted 'and if he wold not defend his righte and beare his charge, then to leave it'. Some members thought it 'hard to leave the people and make Mr More to begynne suite a fresh agayne' (**55M**). This judgment may have given Stoughton pause for thought since, despite his further problems, the conference never again discussed the possibility of his resignation.

In October 1587 Stoughton and Crick were embroiled in the dispute between Tilney and the congregation of East Bergholt (**61M**). In February 1588 he asked whether he might refuse communion to his 'froward' churchwarden and so 'hazard his peace', but the question was deferred (**65M**). In December he wanted advice about a case of fornication in his parish (**74M**). In April 1589 his motion 'tutching his benefice' was debated at length but the result goes unrecorded (**78M**).

Stoughton's career after the demise of the conference is clear in outline but baffling in detail. He evidently married as soon as he was in receipt of a regular income from Naughton, remaining incumbent until at least January 1593.[8] He was listed on 9 April 1594 as curate of Great Burstead, Essex, under its vicar, Timothy Oakley, and was still serving Oakley's successor, William Pease, on 1 April 1600. On 23 September 1594 he told the archdeacon of Essex's official that he was admitted to preach (in London diocese) by John, bishop of Colchester, but was ordered to administer the sacraments and certify that he had done so by Christmas.[9]

He published *A generall treatise against poperie, and in defence of the religion by publike avthoritie professed in England and other churches reformed* (Cambridge, 1598), with a dedication to Robert 3rd Lord Rich, dated from 'Billerim' on 7 March.[10] Listed present as a licensed preacher at the visitation of 1598,[11] it was probably he rather than Pease who on 10 July 1599 made the remarkable entry in Great Burstead's register recording the burial of Elizabeth Watts, widow, 'sumetyme wyfe' of Thomas, 'blessed marter who suffered in the fyre at Chelmesford 1555'.[12]

Stoughton was instituted vicar of Coggeshall (MA) at Lord Rich's presentation, in succession to Laurence Newman, on 12 December 1600.[13] Charged in consistory on 29 May 1602 for failing to read public prayer, he was ordered to reappear on 2 July, when he confessed that he did not wear the surplice.[14] On 16 April 1605, reminded that he had been admonished to do so at Bancroft's last visitation, he was ordered to appear before Bishop Richard Vaughan and the commissioners on Friday next. He did so and, after a curious exchange, the case was continued.[15] Stoughton was deprived of Coggeshall by the High Commission before 4 April 1606, when Ralph Cudworth (father of the Hebraist) was instituted at Lord Rich's presentation.[16] He thus became the only Essex incumbent deprived for nonconformity during Vaughan's episcopate.[17] Yet in June 1606 it was reported that he 'doeth often expound the Word in his deske'.[18]

In 1610 he published *The dignitie of Gods children. Or an exposition of 1. Iohn 3.1.2.(3). Plentifully shewing the comfortable, happie and most blessed state of all Gods children, and also on the contrarie, the base, fearefull, and most wofull condition of all other that are not the children of God*, dedicating it to 'the nobility and gentry of Greate Britaine' and signing the epistle dedicatory from Great Totham, Essex – just south of Coggeshall – on 16 April.[19] By 1616, when he published *Two profitable treatises*, he had returned to his native Sandwich and was living at St Bartholomew's Hospital.[20] He was still there, living in poverty, at his death.[21]

1. *Two profitable treatises: I. Of Davids Love to the Word: II. Of Davids meditation on the Word of God* (London, 1616), sig. #.
2. The Venns (*Alum. Cantab.*, IV, 165, 172) confused his career with that of a contemporary ('Stockton') who graduated BA from St John's College, Cambridge, in 1577. The evidence of the minute book shows that it must have been this man, and not the future vicar of Coggeshall, who was ordained deacon and priest at Lincoln on 13 February 1582. The earlier confusion is perpetuated in Patrick Collinson, *The birthpangs of protestant England: religious and cultural change in the sixteenth and seventeenth centuries* (Basingstoke, 1988), p. ix, in a discussion of Stoughton's works.
3. At the end of his life he recalled being present at Hampton Court 'about some 43 yeares past' (c. 1579) when Some preached before Elizabeth: *The Christians Sacrifice: Much better then all the Legall Sacrifices of the Iewes; . . . with the Authors Postscript to his children, as it were his Last Will and Testament unto them* (London, 1622), epistle dedicatory to Robert 2nd earl of Warwick and his son and heir Robert Lord Rich, sig. b3v. The point of the reminiscence was to extol Robert 2nd Lord Rich for his 'humilitie to be as carefull (yea also painefully) to see all things in [the] pulpit to be fit for him, as if he had beene some inferour (sic) officer in the chappell to have looked unto such things'.

4. The meeting of 3 February 1584 took place at Hog Lane but Stoughton is not mentioned (**15M**) and is not amongst those recorded as giving money for Henry Wilcock in April (**17M**).
5. NRO, Reg/14/20, fo. 138v. He compounded for his first fruits the following week: PRO E334/10, fo. 128v.
6. PRO PCC, PROB11/73 (15 Leicester).
7. In November 1586 the next meeting was assigned to be at Hog Lane 'for Mr Stocton'. He was duly present, urging public prayers at a time of famine (**50M**). The evidence of subsequent meetings is that he continued to maintain a presence in East Bergholt. In January 1587 he was chosen moderator for the following month at Crick's house (**52M**) and in May 1587 was chosen moderator for the next meeting at Tilney's (**56M**). He was involved in Tilney's dispute with his parishioners in October (**61M**) and in October 1588 chosen speaker for the next meeting at East Bergholt (**72M**).
8. Thomas and John, sons of Thomas and Catherine Stoughton, were baptized there on 3 July 1588 and on 13 January 1593: 'Bishops Transcripts of Naughton, Suffolk, 1563–1812', transcribed by L. Haydon Whitehead: copy at Society of Genealogists. John (d. 1639) was a prominent London lecturer at St Mary Aldermanbury from 1631 until his death: *Alum. Cantab.*, IV, 171; Paul Seaver, *The puritan lectureships* (Stanford, 1970), pp. 50–1, 138, 257, 264, 324, 366.
9. ERO D/AEV 3, fos. 51r, 55r, 72r, 80v, 97v, 111v, 241v.
10. Billericay, a growing town which was technically a hamlet within the parish of Great Burstead, a living in Rich's gift, for which see pp. xxxiii–iv, above. The epistle dedicatory is a commonplace paean of praise to a godly patron, but the tortuous opening gambit suggests that the godly safety-net had 'rescued' Stoughton from Suffolk and perhaps secured him a chaplaincy in the Rich household:

    Right Honourable, your favour having beene such towards me, as that both either upon my commendation before I was by face known unto your Lordship, and especially my selfe sithens that time have thereby fared the better, I could not [but] in all dutie thinke of some way, whereby to shew my selfe in some measure thankfull for the same. . .: *A generall treatise against poperie*, sig. J3.

    At the end of his life he explained that he had been brought to Rich's attention 'by the commendatorie testimonie of that grave and religious gentleman Mr Iohn Butler of Toby Esquier, now also at rest with the Lord', *The Christians Sacrifice*, sig. a2. For John Butler of Thoby Priory, Essex, 'client gentleman' of Rich, MP for Maldon in 1586 and 1589, and father-in-law of Robert Wright, see Hasler, *House of commons*, I, 519–20.
11. GL MS 9537/9, fo. 131r. He was ordered to attend 'Mr [Samuel] Harsnett', at this time one of Bancroft's examining chaplains: Bancroft had authorized Harsnett to examine the credentials of all those holding preaching licences, and the majority, Stoughton included, emerged unscathed.
12. ERO D/P 139, unfoliated.
13. Reg. Bancroft, fo. 22v.
14. LMA DL/C/303, p. 847. No further directive or monition is added.
15. LMA DL/C/617, pp. 626, 645–7. On 18 April he made answer to a detection against him that, preaching at Billericay on Shrove Tuesday, he 'made a very factious sermon'. Praying for the king, he put in 'a straung addition . . . Lett us pray for Kings majestie James King of great Brittaine France & Ireland Defendor of the faiethe And over all persons & Causes supreame governor According to the word'. Stoughton could not 'now certaynly saye whether he did use that forme of prayer in those words . . . but he himself belevithe rather that he did then otherwise for . . . he did preach in Billeriky Chappell uppon shrov tewsdaye last & he doth oftentimes in his sermons use that form of words in his prayer for the Kings majestie. According to the word his reason is as he sayethe that he hath got a place [i.e. his vicarage of Coggeshall] whare there hath byn som Brownists that hathe made som question of the Kings supremacie. And before he hathe used this forme who is now examined uppo' showe that his majesties [?'title', omitted] is grounded uppon gods word & for no other cause he sayethe he did ever use the same.' His original signature – 'Thomas Stoughton' – is appended in the record.

    The second part of the detection was a deposition by William Pease, who claimed that after his sermon Stoughton told him that he had come 'to take leave of his people to whom he was so muche beholding and sayd farther that he never looked againe to preach in the place'. Pease urged him 'to yeald and to subscribe & lyve to doe good in the Churche' but 'still he towld Mr Pease he would never do it'. Amongst 'muche other speech' Pease argued that the lawfulness of the cross in baptism 'as it was now explaynd' must be apparent to any man of 'indifferent Judgment'. Stoughton retorted that 'it was now worse than ever it was'.

    Stoughton alleged that he and Pease had had no such conversation after his sermon 'to his now remembrance'. Rather, Pease had asked him to dinner on the Sunday before his sermon, which he had preached at Pease's 'earnest entreatie' made to him 'long before'. At dinner there had evidently been heated words about Stoughton's conformity – they are lost because of damage to the manuscript – but his final statement survives. He declared that he had said

> that he was never so much wedded to any opinion that he hadd but uppon better reason out of the word of god he could be content & would change his mynd. And that towchinge the Crosse he . . . sayethe that Mr Pease & he . . . had som speech which now he remembrethe not but he sayethe that he . . . sayd as he now remembreth that it was a thing made now by the Cannon more doubtfull then it was before. And otherwise then this he . . . sayethe he doth not remember nor believe this complaynt or detection whereon he is examined to be true in any part thereof.

16. Reg. Bancroft, fo. 92r.
17. Stoughton had evidently managed to reduce Coggeshall to a state of acrimonious confusion. It was probably this fact, rather than his ritual nonconformity, that was at the root of Vaughan's decision to proceed to extremes. Some of the evidence survives in a flurry of presentments before the archdeacon of Colchester, Thomas Withers, during 1604. Largely concerned with his failure to baptize children, or with their fathers' refusal to present their children for baptism, they substantiate Stoughton's assertion that Coggeshall remained a hotbed of separatism ('Brownism'): S. B. Babbage, *Puritanism and Richard Bancroft* (London, 1962), p. 154; quoting ERO D/ACA 27 and 30, *passim*.
18. ERO D/ACA 30, fo. 196r: quoted in Babbage, *Puritanism and Richard Bancroft*, p. 154.
19. *The dignitie of Gods children*, sigs. A2 and (a).
20. He dedicated it to the Mayor and Jurats, not only because he had been born and bred there but also 'because of the kindnesse that both heretofore, and also of late I haue receiued of you . . .' They were principally to be blessed for their 'christian respect' of him and also 'as the Lords gracious instrumants of my good'. After a lengthy exhortation that they should continue to ensure that the Lord's Day was properly observed and stamp out drunkenness, Stoughton signed off from his 'chamber in the Hospitall of St Bartholomewes by Sandwich' on 3 September 1616: *Two profitable treatises*, sigs. #, #v, A4v.
21. *The Christians Sacrifice*, sigs. a2r–B2r. The epistle dedicatory to Warwick and his son Rich reminds them that he had dedicated the *Treatise against poperie* to Warwick's father out of gratitude and admiration, and therefore 'I thought I might the more presume of your Honorable acceptance of these my paines, the rather because in respect of my manifold infirmities by age, they may be my last . . .'. Paragraphs of praise for the Rich line end with a plea that his 'poor treatise in my olde and poore state' might be acceptable 'in testimonie and thankfull minde' for favours received 'long since' from Robert 3rd Lord Rich. He was now 'ready to be dissolved, and to laye downe *my earthly Tabernacle . . . the time of my departing being at hand . . .*'. He signed this epistle from 'my poore lodging in the poor Hospitall called S. Bartholomewes by Sandwich in Kent' on 20 August 1622.

Following a text of some 251 pages, Stoughton appended *The Authors postscript to his Children as it were his Last Will and Testament unto them*, dated 22 August 1622. His principle bequest was his four published works, duly named in order of composition, with the apology that he could give none of them 'any portion of worldly riches'. What follows is an almost surreal deathbed meditation. God's mercies towards him had been 'more than to my own father. I have lived twice his age and twelve years more. Whereas he had but myself alone, God hath given me 12 children, whereof I have yet 7 living, besides the children of some of my children. Let none of them be grieved that I have left you nothing of my inheritance in Kent, neither of my lands since, that I purchased in Suffolk, as also in Essex, all being now gone, and the price thereof spent . . . I confess I have spent the more for the gracing of my ministrie, and the provoking of others to bounty, and by so gracing my Ministrie to win the more unto God. What other things have bin the meanes of my present povertie, as also of the base account that my selfe and ye are in by that meanes, though I need not be ashamed to relate, yet for other reasons I spare to speake. I might perhaps have left you somewhat if I had bin more frugall for the things of this life . . .' (*ibid.*, pp. 252–6).

TEY, WILLIAM (c. 1545–94)

Rector of Peldon, Essex, 1569–94 (d.); rector of Little Bentley, Essex, 1572 (resig.); rector of Rougham, Suffolk, 1573–83 (resig. or depr.?)

In social terms William Tey – as, despite Richard Parker's orthography, the name should properly be spelt – was the most distinguished member of the Dedham conference and it is against his formidable family background and protestant connexions that Tey's career has to be understood.[1] Third son of John Tey (1521–68) of Layer Hall and Aldham Hall, Essex, and his wife Constance (*nee* Robartes), Tey matriculated pensioner from Trinity College, Cambridge, at Michaelmas 1561, was made scholar in 1567 and graduated BA in early 1568. He proceeded MA in 1571.[2] He was ordained deacon on 2 May 1569 by Edmund Grindal, bishop of London (BA; scholar of Trinity, Cambridge; born Layer-de-la-Haye; aged 23).[3] He was instituted rector of Peldon, a living formerly in the family's own gift,[4] on 6 May 1569 at the presentation of his mother.[5] Instituted rector of Little Bentley on 25 May 1572 at the presentation of Edmund Pirton, he had resigned by the following 13 January,[6] probably because he had now been instituted rector of Rougham at the presentation of his uncle or first cousin, Robert Drury.[7] He had married by early 1575: he and his wife, Parnell, daughter of Henry Boade of Rayleigh, Essex, were both remembered in his mother's will that year.[8]

If it seems odd that this future puritan firebrand[9] should have consented to become a pluralist it was perhaps part of a wider strategem: by 1580 Tey had installed Oliver Pigge at Rougham as his *locum tenens*, apparently ceding him all or most of the tithes. This riled Robert Drury, his patron, who had the backing of Edmund Freke, bishop of Norwich. When Freke suspended Pigge in May 1581, Drury took the opportunity to withhold the tithes. The privy council sided with Pigge and when Freke refused to restore him they examined him themselves, subsequently informing Freke that the proceedings against him had resulted from malice. He was therefore restored, but in 1583 Drury brought an action against Tey for continuing to permit Pigge's liturgical irregularities, once again withholding the tithes. In July 1583 Pigge was imprisoned at Bury St Edmunds for altering the baptism service. His petition to the Bury justices for release survives because he dispatched a copy to Sir Francis Walsingham, with a covering letter complaining of the justices' severity in refusing him bail and requesting a further hearing before the privy council.[10] Pigge was thereafter released but it was apparently at this time that Tey relinquished the rectory of Rougham, perhaps under pressure from Robert Drury.

Meanwhile Tey had become a founder member of the Dedham conference but is not mentioned in the minutes until May 1583, when the radical temperament he would steadily exhibit over the next six years is well demonstrated by a challenging proposition concerning summoners' citations into ecclesiastical courts (**6M**). Although it was agreed that the matter should be discussed next month, it was silently dropped. On 11 July 1583 Tey was present at Aylmer's third episcopal visitation but, exhibiting no preaching licence, was ordered to a personal interview with the bishop before Bartholomewtide.[11] Speaker at his parsonage house in August, he was delegated with Robert Lewis to consult with 'some godlie lawier' as to the legality of their meetings (**9M**).

In January 1584 Tey and Sandes were appointed to review the prayer book as to what might be used 'with a good conscience and what not' (**14M**). In April he contributed 20s on behalf of Henry Wilcock and also delivered his 'judgment and reasons' concerning the prayer book (**17M**). He was chosen for the 'general conference' called to coincide with the 1584 parliament.[12] In June he suggested organizing petitions from parishioners on behalf of their 'deprived' pastors and evidently argued that it was legitimate for them to continue preaching, even if 'forbidden by the magistrate': he found that his colleagues were against him (**19M**). In July a bewildering proposition concerning 'Christs office' was thought good to be 'better weighed' and so deferred, never to be resurrected (**20M**). In August he was delegated to find out why Thomas Lowe had dropped out of the conference (**21M**) and in September was one of those who signed 'Certain requests' to Archdeacon Withers.[13]

In January 1585 Tey was indignant that the Essex proctors for the forthcoming convocation had been refused by Aylmer (**26M**).[14] Next month he argued tortuously in favour of Andrewes's departure from Wenham (**27M**) but at the extraordinary meeting which followed a fortnight later he reversed his opinion (**Extra M**, 17 February 1585).

Tey was absent on 5 April 1585: Robert Lewis conveyed a message that the brethren 'praie for godes blessing upon his busyness now left unto him by reason of his brothers deathe'. He asked that they should help him with 'a contynuall supplie in his place' at Peldon for the next four Sundays. Thomas Stoughton was asked to take on the duty and 'yielded unto it' (**29M**). The facts behind this entry are that, having apparently been divorced from his wife Eleanor in 1579,[15] Thomas Tey, *nuper de Layer, armiger*, had just died intestate. On 2 April 1585 William was granted letters of administration (*fratri n[atu]rale*).[16] Since the couple had no surviving children, William was regarded in law as his heir, a circumstance which was to have serious repercussions and is an important factor in understanding a number of entries in the Dedham minutes.

Tey is not heard of again until appointed speaker on 28 June for the following meeting on 2 August. Having now inherited the manor of Layer-de-la-Haye[17] he asked 'what course he might take to obteyne one for to read a Lecture at Layer on the Sabboth daie'. Evidently to his chagrin 'it was deferred' and he urged the matter again on 16 August and on 6 September, when the meeting took place at his parsonage house in Peldon. This time it was agreed that the brethren 'wold helpe him and come together in concourse as they shuld be requested to preache' (**32, 33, 34, 35MM**).[18]

On 4 October 1585, via a letter to Lewis, Tey again requested help in supplying his place at Peldon, asking that Anthony Morse accept the charge (**36M**). Morse did so but by December was requesting 'better assurance than the brethrens charge' for his preaching there. In January 1586 they agreed to obtain 'as good assurance as might be' for his doing so (**38, 39MM**). As speaker in May 1586, Tey was concerned about churchwardens' oaths at the forthcoming episcopal visitation and in June as to whether Aylmer might again urge subscription to Whitgift's articles (**44, 45MM**).

Tey was present before Aylmer and his visitors as rector and preacher of Peldon on 22 July 1586, subsequently appearing on the list of Essex incumbents suspended in the visitation 'and since' for the surplice.[19] His suspension is nowhere referred to in the minutes. In March 1587 he was one of those appointed to negotiate with George Northey over Lewis's continuing complaints. He also urged that the book of discipline be 'vewed' but the matter was deferred and then again when the conference met at his house in Peldon in April (**54, 55MM**).

On 8 May 1587, the very day that the conference was meeting at Boxford, a second set of letters of administration for Thomas Tey's estate was issued to William as next of kin.[20] His legal rights in the matter had undoubtedly been challenged by the former Mrs Eleanor Tey and by this means were presumably sustained. During the summer, with her second husband, Thomas Warren, she took matters into her own hands, leading a riotous mob through Peldon and forcibly repossessing Layer Hall. Fourteen of the thirty persons involved, including the Warrens themselves, were indicted at the next quarter sessions. Tey remained in possession.[21]

In June 1587 he again urged that the book of discipline be viewed but the matter was once more deferred (**57M**). It was further postponed because of his absence in August (**59M**). In March 1588, when the conference met at Layer Hall with Tey as speaker, he asked whether the bishops 'were anie longer to be tolerated or noe' (**66M**). This was probably his response to Aylmer's recent suspension of Edmund Chapman.

Tey appears to have taken very little part in the conference during its final months but on 2 June 1589 the eighty-first meeting, destined never to take place, was scheduled for Layer Hall with Tey as moderator (**80M**).

When Aylmer's episcopal visitors reached St Mary Colchester on 24 July 1589, Tey, like several of his colleagues at Dedham, fell under more serious scrutiny than at any time during the life of the conference. Incredibly, it now emerged that he had never sought a preaching licence from any recognized authority:[22] 'he is not otherwise licensed as he saieth to preach but that he is a minister'. He was then inhibited from 'all office' of his ministry until he conformed himself to 'the order of the Church of England'.[23] Matters moved swiftly. On 5 November he appeared in consistory as one of Richard Parker's compurgators and also because he had been ordered to certify that he had used the prayer book and surplice at Peldon or else face deprivation. He stated that his case was now before the High Commissioners, who had suspended him on the previous Friday pending his willingness to conform. The Official thus waived his rights in the matter, enjoining Tey to return on 14 November to certify that he had provided a 'sufficient person' to say prayers using the surplice, or else to see the revenues of Peldon sequestered for that purpose. He failed to appear and the living was duly sequestered.[24] The London court books then fall silent on the matter but he had extricated himself before Aylmer's last visitation in September 1592 when – still without a diocesan preaching licence – he was listed as *concionator notus* but ordered to certify by 4 December that he had used the surplice.[25]

Letters of sequestration issued to the churchwardens on 1 March 1594 were, because of Tey's death, subsequently revoked, and a new sequestration granted to Anthony Mannock and others on 7 May. Letters of administration for his estate had meanwhile been granted to his widow, Parnell, on 16 March 1594.[26] With Tey's death the cadet line of the Teys passed out of the ranks of Essex's landed families.[27]

1. The Tey family had settled near Colchester by the end of the thirteenth century, taking its name from the parish of Marks Tey. Walter de Tey was summoned to parliament in 1300. Settled at Marks Tey and at Brightwell Hall, Suffolk, succeeding generations of Teys also acquired the Essex manors of Bottingham Hall (in Copford), Peldon, Aldham (Hall) and (before 1400) Layer-de-la-Haye. By 1364 they had also become patrons of the parish of St Runwald, Colchester. Their prosperity appears to have reached its peak by the 1420s, when John Tey I was evidently in possession of all these estates and others besides. At his death they were divided between two sons, John Tey II and Robert Tey. The senior branch of the family inherited Marks Tey, Brightwell Hall, Bottingham Hall and Peldon; the cadet branch Layer-de-la-Haye and Aldham Hall. The grandson of John Tey II, Sir Thomas Tey (d. 1540), a Henrician courtier who was present at the Field of Cloth of Gold, left four daughters, and his patrimony was divided between them. The eldest, Margaret, inherited the Brightwell estate and married Sir John Jermyn. The order in which the other three were born is not clear but Frances inherited the manor of Peldon and married William Bonham, MP for Maldon in 1539 and subsequently a gentleman pensioner (d. 1547 or later). Mary married Sir Thomas Neville 'of Oldeholte in Essex' and Elizabeth Sir Marmaduke Neville (1506–45), fourth son of Richard 2nd Lord Latymer (1468–1530). Marmaduke's eldest brother, John 3rd Lord Latymer (d. 1543), was the second husband of Katherine Parr, soon to be Henry VIII's sixth queen. Eleanor Neville was the only surviving child of Sir Marmaduke and Elizabeth Tey.

Of the cadet branch, the grandson of Robert Tey, Thomas Tey II (1486/8–1543) was MP for Maldon in the reformation parliament of 1529, probably owing his place to the fifteenth earl of Oxford. By his wife Jane, sister of Sir Clement Harlestone, he had an only son, John Tey III (1521–68), who entered Jesus College, Cambridge, in 1537 as a fellow-commoner. He succeeded his father in the estates of Layer-de-la-Haye and Aldham on 20 April 1543 at the age of twenty-two, and married Constance, daughter and heiress of John Robartes. The couple reared seven children past infancy. Their eldest son was Thomas Tey III (d. 1585) and their third William, future rector of Peldon.

Thomas Tey III matriculated fellow-commoner from Trinity College, Cambridge, at Michaelmas 1559 and was probably the Cambridge student who in 1560 contributed verses on the restoration of Bucer and Fagius over the signature 'Thomas Teyzi'. Thus there can be little doubt that the Teys were deeply conscious of their family connexions and were firmly aligned with the humanist/protestant tradition associated with Queen Katherine Parr. Thomas succeeded to his father's estates at his death on 29 May 1568 and married Eleanor, daughter of Sir Marmaduke Neville and Elizabeth Tey, Katherine Parr's niece by marriage.

This account is based on the biographical notices and pedigrees in Morant, *Essex*, I, 197–8, 202, 411–13; in Walter C. Medcalfe, ed., *The visitations of Essex* (Harleian Soc., 1878–9), I,

109–10; II, 551; and in S. T. Bindoff, *The house of commons, 1509–1558* (3 vols., London, 1982), I. 463–4; III. 436–7.

2. *Alum. Cantab.*, IV, 216.

3. GL MS 9535/1, fo. 143r.

4. The Tey family had presented to the rectory from 1466 until 1523 but Frances Tey and her husband William Bonham sold the manor and advowson to the crown in April 1544 for £680: Bindoff, *House of commons, 1509–1558*, I, p. 464. A grant by the crown to William Petre and his wife that month was relinquished in December. In 1551 the crown granted them to Sir Thomas Darcy 1st Lord Darcy of Chiche: Newcourt, *Repertorium*, II, 466. Before William Tey's presentation a caveat for the benefice was entered by Henry Bonham who claimed the next presentation by right of a grant from William, his brother, and Frances, dated 15 August 1545 (sic): LMA DL/C/332, fo. 203v. William Tey compounded for Peldon on 7 May 1569, with sureties Richard Aburford of Colchester, *generosus*, and Thomas Cockerell of Fordham, yeoman: PRO E334/8, fo. 172v.

5. Reg. Grindal, fo. 150r. Constance had acquired a *pro hac vice* right of presentation from Edmund Pirton of Little Bentley, *armiger*, as executor of Robert Darcy of St Osyth, formerly granted a *pro hac vice* presentation by his brother, John 2nd Lord Darcy of Chiche. The typographical misrendering of this entry to '1596' in Newcourt's *Repertorium* (II, 466–7) has bedevilled most subsequent accounts of Tey's career.

6. Reg. Grindal, fos. 172r, 174r. Tey finally compounded for Little Bentley on 4 May 1574, three months after his successor's institution, with sureties Thomas Tey of Layer-de-la-Haye, *armiger*, and Richard Aburforth of Colchester, *generosus*: PRO E334/9, fo. 10v.

7. William's sister Elizabeth, elder daughter of Thomas Tey III, had married Robert Drury of Rougham: Medcalfe, ed., *Visitations of Essex*, I, 297. Tey compounded for the benefice on 31 January 1573, with sureties Thomas Cammocke of St Andrew Holborn and Thomas Geines of the Inner Temple, *generosi*: PRO E334/8, fo. 319r.

8. Thomas Tey III was made sole executor provided he gave bonds to William, to Edmund Pirton and to Thomas Penny (deprived of the prebend of Newington in St Paul's in 1570 for nonconformity) for the true performance of the will. Dated 15 January, proved 4 November 1575: Emmison, *Essex gentry wills*, p. 133.

9. For details of some of his frequent appearances in the archdeaconry court of Colchester, see Anthony W. Gough, 'The rectors of Peldon', *Transactions of the Essex Archaeological Society*, 3rd series, VII, 61–70 (at p. 64).

10. PRO SP12/158/79 and 80; 161/33. For Pigge see Brett Usher's entry in *New DNB*.

11. GL MS 9537/5, fos. 3r, 66r.

12. See above, pp. 90–91.

13. See above, p. 82.

14. No independent evidence on this matter survives in the diocesan records or in Aylmer's extant correspondence.

15. Sentence was given in the *negotium . . . separationis matrimonii* for Thomas Tey, *armiger*, and Eleanor his wife on 11 February 1579: LMA DL/C/10, p. 584. The London act books of instance do not, however, record what the sentence was in any *negotium*: presumably a separate series of sentence books has perished.

16. PRO PROB 6/3, fo. 139v [modern foliation].

17. Morant states that William had already purchased Aldham Hall from his brother and sister-in-law 'for himself and his heirs': Morant, *Essex*, I, 203.

18. Tey's importunity on the subject is explained by the fact that he had no control over the parochial affairs of Layer-de-la-Haye. A benefice appropriate to the priory of St Botolph, Colchester, it passed after the dissolution to the Audley family, who thereafter were entitled to the tithes, provided they appoint a perpetual curate with a stipend. Roger Goodwin was appointed in the 1570s and was still in place in 1595, when he was granted a preaching licence: GL MSS 9537/4, fos. 33r, 97r; /5, fo. 65r; /6, fo. 59r; /7, fo. 48r; /8, fo. 56v; LMA DL/C/336, fo. 36r.

19. GL MS 9537/6, fo. 143v; *Seconde parte*, II, 261.

20. PRO PROB 6/4, fo. 14r [modern foliation].

21. ERO Q/SR 100–105; F. G. Emmison, *Elizabethan life: disorder* (Chelmsford, 1970), p. 121.

22. Even more mysterious is the circumstance that Aylmer had let the matter pass: in 1583 Tey had been called to personal interview at Hadham *specifically because* he had shown no licence to the episcopal visitors: GL MS 9537/5, fo. 3v.

23. GL MS 9537/7, fo. 49r.

24. LMA DL/C/616, pp. 119, 126, 160: yet no letters of sequestration are recorded in the vicar general's book, nor any letters of revocation.

25. GL MS 9537/8, fo. 57r.

26. LMA DL/C/335, fos. 162v, 166r, 174v. Letters of administration for what remained of Thomas Tey's assets were granted to John Davies of Berechurch, Essex, yeoman and kinsman, because of William's death, 25 November 1595. PRO PROB 6/5, fo. 153r [modern foliation].

27. He had already ('about 1592') conveyed the manor of Aldham Hall to the crown, which re-granted it to Charles Cornwallis. Thomas Tey, presumably his son and successor, received licence to sell the lordship of Layer to Peter Bettenson on 12 September 1596: Morant, *Essex*, I, 203, 411–13. (But Morant wrongly assumed that this younger Thomas Tey must have been son and heir of William's dead (and childless) elder brother.) Nothing further can be said of the children of William and Parnell Tey since no parish registers for Layer-de-la-Haye or Peldon survive before the eighteenth century.

TILNEY, JOHN (flor. 1571–1605)

Unbeneficed 'pastor' of East Bergholt, Suffolk, c. 1582–c. 88; rector of Holton St Peter, Suffolk, 1589–1600; rector of Santon, Norfolk, 1602–?

John Tilney, a founder member of the Dedham conference, was admitted to Corpus Christi College, Cambridge, in 1571, making it more than likely that he was a Norfolk man. He proceeded BA in early 1577, MA (from Magdalene) in 1580, and was ordained priest at Norwich in January 1581.[1] In all probability he was part of the planned migration from Norwich to the Stour valley which led to the setting up of the conference. He settled in East Bergholt a little after Dr Richard Crick, and although neither he nor Crick was ever beneficed in the parish, Tilney served as pastor, initially with the support of 'the people' (the Cardinal family, primarily?), whereas Crick may have been accorded the status of 'doctor' within the presbyterian ministerial economy.

In January 1585 Tilney put a pastoral question to the conference: should he marry a young man of twenty-four to a woman over fifty (**26M**)? He was advised to deal with 'the chieff of the parish' (Cardinal?) to find out how far the matter had gone, and if possible to dissuade the parties from proceeding. In November 1585 Tilney sought advice about baptizing children whose parents had refused to communicate in the Lord's Supper (**37M**). East Bergholt's troubles again engaged the conference when it met in the parish in December 1586. Could Tilney marry a man 'who having ever resisted his mynistery, and countes him noe minister nor their church noe Churche', if he would not confess his fault. He got a complicated answer. It was 'daungerous' to refuse to marry the man, so better let 'the Congregation' forbid it, which would prevent the calling of the banns, and might 'drawe him . . . into the Church'. If the man was warned before the sermon that he could only be married in church if he made a confession, he would have the sermon time to consider his position (**51M**). But in the event the 'fellow' was denied his wedding, 'for his vile speeches against our Church', and got himself married in a private house 'by one Greenwood', perhaps an early appearance in the historical record of the separatist martyr John Greenwood (**54M**).

Tilney was one of the conference's hardliners. In January 1584 he stood suspended from his ministry for refusing to subscribe to Whitgift's articles.[2] In the following July, he asked the conference whether he should show up at the ecclesiastical court, having received his third summons. It was thought that he should not (**20M**). By September he and Lawrence Newman of Coggeshall were asking whether they could continue to preach and exercise their ministry in spite of being suspended. 'It was not thought good to presse soe farre considering the state of the tyme' (Chapman's voice?) (**22M**). At the next meeting, in October, Tilney again demanded reasons why he should not preach, in defiance of his suspension. Discussion was adjourned, and Tilney and Newman were asked to produce reasons why they should preach in spite of being silenced: which was where the matter rested (**23M**).

By the spring of 1586, there were warning signs that all was not well between Tilney and the majority party in East Bergholt. He asked 'howe he might deale to kepe one out that went secretlie about to supplant him', and was advised to 'stirre up the chieff of his parishe [Cardinal?] to use all meanes to prevent it'. It appears likely that this someone was none other than Richard Crick, who was present at the very meeting in which Tilney voiced his complaint, with Crick asking what to do about unnamed parishioners who 'did single themselves from the Church' (**41M**). By August 1587 it was clear that the congregation wanted to replace Tilney with Crick, and Tilney asked the conference to consider 'his matter of departure from Barfold'. The conference thought this should not be openly debated, and delegated the cause to six of its members, Chapman, Newman, Lewis, Dowe, Farrar and Sandes (**59M**). In September Tilney wanted to know whether he could warn 'the people' of his impending departure. 'Some thought it meet and some thought otherwise' (**60M**). A month later, the townsmen of East Bergholt presented their grievances against Tilney through Crick and Thomas Stoughton. Once again, the conference sought to limit its involvement (**61M**). But in June 1587 the conference had rather pointedly met at East Bergholt, not in Crick's house but in Tilney's (**57M**), and when in February 1588 Crick asked for advice 'tutching his calling to be pastor of Barfold', some members spoke critically of 'the peoples course in rejecting and receyving their Pastors without counsell of others' (presumably themselves), although the majority thought Crick fit to undertake the charge (**65M**). But there was some reluctance to preach at Crick's election, although Chapman did it (**66M**).

In a letter which Crick wrote when feelings were running too high for him to confront the conference face to face,[3] Tilney was described as a man whom the church 'hath most worthely throwne out'. If the congregation were to be found at fault in what it had done, Crick, who had taught them before Tilney's arrival, would 'crave pardon of the whole people', and would go down on his knees 'as a great trespasser, for suffring him to be unjustly throwne out', and to become a suitor for his restoration, or would make recompense. But Crick clearly thought such a scenario unlikely. Tilney, according to Crick, had few supporters, but such was his own influence with almost all of them that he could easily persuade even that minority of his 'nakednes', so that they would desert him. 'So far as I can perceyve they lyke better of his departure then ever they did of his being with them.' What was the nature of Tilney's 'evill dealing'? One notes, as so often in the affairs of men, that minutes are not designed to tell us the truth, the whole truth, and nothing but the truth.

And so Tilney disappeared from the Dedham scene. He soon resurfaced in a Suffolk parish, Holton St Peter, farther north, where he was rector from 1589 to 1600.[4] Bishop Redman's visitation of 1597 revealed that he had lost none of his old radical charisma. In addition to some of the usual nonconformist irregularities (not wearing the surplice, omitting parts of the service, not reading the injunctions, not going on perambulations, not churching women), the visitors were presented with a lively clip from one of Tilney's sermons. 'There are some ministers have greate plenty and forty men waytinge at theire table, and ride uppon their Cocke horses with their wooden daggards and smyte the godlye out of their places, but I hope the godlye shalbe placed agayne and those sett beside their Cockhorses.'[5] Here is a possible clue that Tilney's offence at East Bergholt had been the practice of what was called 'personal preaching', naming and shaming from the pulpit. On 20 January 1602, the mayor and burgesses of Thetford presented John Tilney to the living of Santon in Norfolk[6] which he may have combined with the living of St Mary in Thetford, for we last catch sight of him in a visitation book from 1604/5 as of St Mary's, for having 'since March 1601 reviled Mr Gallowes curate of that church calling him dombe dogge and used many other reprochfull wordes against him'. He failed to appear and was excommunicated. On 12 December 1605, Thomas Seaman appeared and appealed for Tilney who was absolved and restored.[7]

1. *Alum. Cantab.*, IV, 243.
2. *Seconde parte*, I, 242. On this list Tilney's name is garbled as 'Tylmen'. But since his parish is given as 'Bargholte' there is no doubt that this is our man.
3. See above, pp. 147–9.
4. *Alum. Cantab.*, IV, 243.
5. *Redman's visitation*, p. 129.
6. NRO DN REG 14, fo. 296v.
7. NRO DN VIS 4/1, unfoliated.

TUKE, GEORGE (c. 1557–?c. 1592)

Preacher at Great Birch, Essex, 1582–4/5 (?suspended)

Tuke was probably the illegitimate son of George Tuke of Layer Marney, Essex (d. 1572).[1] He graduated BA from Pembroke College, Cambridge, in 1581 and was ordained deacon by John Aylmer, bishop of London, on 21 December following (BA of Pembroke; born Layer Marney; aged about 24).[2] He was granted a diocesan preaching licence on 12 February 1582.[3]

He was evidently soon under suspicion for nonconformist practices. Arthur Wright of Stebbing, tailor, was called to Chelmsford quarter sessions on 1 February 1583 to give evidence about a sermon preached at Stebbing by Tuke, 'preacher at [Great] Birch'.[4]

As such Tuke appeared before Aylmer's episcopal visitors on 11 July 1583 without his preaching licence, and was ordered to produce it before Aylmer himself at Much Hadham a few days later.[5] By 5 August he had conveyed a message to the Dedham conference that no minister summoned to interview with Aylmer should present himself until specifically sent for (**9M**). The result of his own interview was an appearance in consistory at the beginning of October. He was charged with not receiving communion at Easter and of not administering it himself at Great Birch. He claimed some scruples on the subject but was nevertheless ordered to administer and certify that he had done so on 4 December.[6] On 23 November, apparently in response to a further summons, he admitted that he had not worn the surplice, was ordered to do so whenever he preached and yet at the same time forbidden to preach at all until he had subscribed Whitgift's new articles. Thus, with George Northey, he was the earliest casualty of Aylmer's drive to enforce the articles in London diocese. On 4 December the matter of his certification concerning administration of communion was adjourned until Hilary term.[7]

Tuke is not thereafter found in the London diocesan records but in May 1584 he was chosen as a delegate to the 'general conference' designed to coincide with the 1584 parliament.[8] He lingered under threat at Great Birch until October 1584, when the conference noted that Aylmer had again demanded that he observe the prayer book and administer the sacraments or else cease his preaching. He was willing to submit if the brethren would approve his action, but they would not commit themselves to unequivocal advice (**23M**). Presumably therefore he accepted their tacit judgment that submission was tantamount to betrayal, and gave up his post. He is not found listed at Great Birch in the first surviving archdeaconry visitation call book (1586–8).[9]

His movements thereafter are unaccounted for. He has been identified with the man of these names who was preacher at Chesterfield, Derbyshire, in 1595[10] but since he goes unmentioned in the will of his half-sister Elizabeth in 1593, it is just as likely that he had died.[11] No will or grant of administration, however, has been found amongst the London diocesan records.

1. His executors, James Morice and his wife's brother Peter Osborne, were to administer the lease of his manor of Brook Hall in Tolleshunt Knights, Essex, 'to see it occupied to the most advantage until George my son, son of Amy Easton otherwise called Carter, commonly called George Tuke, is 21, and the yearly profit to be employed towards his education and bringing up and the

residue delivered to him then'. He was to remain in Osborne's custody during his minority, if Osborne was willing: Emmison, *Essex gentry wills*, pp. 134–6.
2. *Alum. Cantab.*, IV, 271. GL MS 9535/2, fo. 17v.
3. 'Tooke'; no domicile or cure mentioned: LMA DL/C/333, fo. 277r.
4. ERO QS/R 84/54.
5. GL MS 9537/5, fos. 62r, 3r (confirmatory note, but date defective).
6. LMA DL/C/300, p. 186.
7. *Ibid.*, pp. 450, 517.
8. See above, pp. 90–91.
9. D/ACV 1, fos. 9v, 37r, 47v, 76r.
10. *Alum. Cantab.*, IV, 271. He cannot have been the preacher of St Germans, Cornwall, stated in the mid-1580s to have been suspended 'long since': *Seconde parte*, II, 262. Another man of these names, perhaps his son, is listed as curate of Stepney, Middlesex, in 1607: GL MS 9537/10, fo. 89r.
11. Emmison, *Wills of Essex gentry & yeomen*, pp. 275–6.

TUNSTALL, WILLIAM (c. 1558–1622)

Curate of Great Totham, Essex, c. 1583–4; vicar of Great Totham 1584–7 (depr.); vicar of Mayland, Essex, 1592–8 (resig.); again vicar of Great Totham 1598–1608 (resig.); rector of Goldhanger with chapelry of Little Totham, Essex, 1608–17 (resig.); canon of Canterbury 1613–22 (d.); vicar of Halstow, Kent, 1617–19 (resig.); vicar of Chislett, Kent, 1619–22 (d.); rector of Sturry, Kent, 1619–22 (d.)

Born in Durham, Tunstall matriculated pensioner from Christ's College, Cambridge, at Michaelmas 1576, aged 18. He graduated BA in early 1581, proceeding MA in 1584.[1] He is nowhere listed during the episcopal visitation of July 1583, but as curate of Great Totham was ordained priest by John Aylmer, bishop of London, on 21 December that year, stating his age as 25 or so.[2]

Instituted vicar of Great Totham on 15 February 1584 at the presentation of Nicholas Clerk,[3] he was probably already a member of the Braintree conference and his nonconformity soon came to the attention of the authorities. He was one of those who in September 1584 signed 'Certain requests' to Archdeacon Withers.[4] In October 1585 Tunstall and his patron were summoned into consistory on unspecified charges, both objecting that they had not been provided with a copy of the articles upon which they were to be examined.[5] The case appears to have been abandoned but it probably sealed Tunstall's fate. In July 1586 he was present at the episcopal visitation and suspended for not yielding to the surplice or using the cross in baptism. Within weeks his benefice was sequestered and a day set for his deprivation.[6] With George Gifford, Ralph Hawden, John Huckle and Giles Whiting he made supplication to parliament on 8 March 1587 for restoration.[7] By now, however, his case had been transferred to the High Commission and on 5 May he was deprived.[8] Perhaps for that reason he was not one of those who signed the Braintree conference's letter to Dedham on 7 June 1587.[9]

He remained in the vicinity, and by the summer of 1589 was preaching at Inworth, Essex, claiming before the episcopal visitors on 24 July that he was licensed to preach by the archdeacon of Leicester. They pointed out that, deprived by the High Commission, he was expressly inhibited from preaching within London diocese until again licensed by the bishop, archbishop or one of the universities. No more, however, is heard of a further summons into consistory.[10]

He was instituted vicar of Mayland on the presentation of William Wiseman on 12 May 1593.[11] He resigned on re-institution to Great Totham, at the presentation of William Aylett, on 4 July 1598.[12] On 25 September following, at Bancroft's primary visitation, he was ordered to attend the vicar general to obtain a preaching licence.[13]

On 2 January 1604 Tunstall received letters patent for the next Canterbury prebend in

King James's gift to fall vacant, and was accordingly instituted by Archbishop George Abbot as canon of the 5th prebend on 11 October 1613.[14] Meanwhile he had been instituted rector of Goldhanger on 10 May 1608, at the presentation of Sir John Sammes, resigning Great Totham before 18 December that year.[15] He resigned Goldhanger before 31 October 1617,[16] thereafter remaining beneficed in Kent. He was buried in Canterbury Cathedral 8 November 1622. His will was probated in the Consistory Court of Canterbury.[17]

1. *Alum. Cantab.*, IV, 272; Peile, *Biographical register*, p. 138.
2. GL MS 9535/2, fo. 23r.
3. LPL, Register of Whitgift, I, fo. 453r. Aylmer of London should have instituted but this would appear to be one of those cases of 'provincial business' which fell to Whitgift *'jure devoluto'*: see David M. Smith, *Guide to bishops' registers of England and Wales* (London, 1981), p. 21.
4. See above, p. 82.
5. LMA DL/C/301, pp. 456, 458–9, 463.
6. GL MS 9537/6, fo. 154v; *Seconde parte*, II, 164, 260.
7. *Seconde parte*, II, 258–9.
8. LMA DL/C/334, fo. 152v.
9. See above, p. 107.
10. GL MS 9537/7, fo. 47v.
11. Reg. Grindal, fo. 274v.
12. *Ibid.*, fo. 304v.
13. GL MS 9537/9, fo. 116r.
14. *Fasti*, Canterbury, Rochester and Winchester, p. 24.
15. Reg. Bancroft, fos. 116v, 125v.
16. *Ibid.*, fo. 231v.
17. *Alum. Cantab.*, IV, 272.

TYE (TIE), THOMAS

Layman?

That Thomas Tye was a layman is strongly suggested by circumstantial evidence. No man of these names is found as a clergymen in or around Colchester during the 1580s. He was also a man of independent means, able to find a substantial sum out of his own pocket when asked.

'Mr Tye' is not mentioned in the minutes until 4 November 1583 when he is recorded as speaker at Stratford St Mary (**12M**). On 13 January 1584 he was asked to provide money for Henry Wilcock 'and it shuld be repaid him the next meetinge' (**14M**). On 3 February 'mr.Tie' reported that the money was duly paid to Wilcock, 'he being released before out of prison' and it was agreed that a letter be written to Wilcock 'to repay it or to promise payment of yt' (**15M**). It emerges that Tye had handed over £6 15s 0d since on 6 April the brethren stumped up the sums which they had originally pledged themselves to find. Although Tye's own contribution was only 10s (as opposed to 20s by Chapman, Crick, Tey and Sandes), the remaining £6 5s 0d was apparently handed over to 'mr Tye that laid it out' and a further letter was to be sent to Wilcock to admonish him for not acknowledging receipt (**17M**). Except for the fact that on 1 June 1584 he was moderator when the conference met at Chattisham (**19M**), the minutes make no further reference to 'Mr Tye'.

All of the above assumes that Parker's orthography is consistent: the manuscript *appears* to make an invariable distinction between (Thomas) *Tye* and (William) *Tay(e)* and indeed as original signatories they spelled themselves respectively as 'Thomas Tye' and 'Willi[a]m Teye'.[1]

Altogether, despite Thomas's signing himself 'Tye' and Parker's flying in the face of local usage by using 'Tay(e)' rather than 'Tey(e)', there must be a strong possibility that these spellings are a convenient form of shorthand on Parker's part for distinguishing between the brothers Thomas and William Tey(e), the former of whom was lord of the manor of Layer-de-la-Haye. The hypothesis is strengthened, if not proven, by the fact that no more is heard of 'Mr Tye' after June 1584 and that William Tey reported the death of his brother on 5 April 1585 (**29M**).

Where it impinges on the narrative of the conference, the history of Thomas Tey is given, separate from that of Thomas 'Tye', in the entry on William Tey.

1. See above, pp. 4–5.

UPCHER, THOMAS (?c. 1536–?96)

Rector of Fordham, Essex, 1561–95 (?d.); rector of St Leonard Colchester, Essex, 1571–82 (resig.)

Upcher, a reformed freewiller and Marian exile,[1] was ordained deacon and priest by Edmund Grindal, bishop of London, on 25 April and 4 June 1560 (born Bocking, Essex; aged '24').[2] He was collated rector of Fordham by Grindal on 8 July 1561.[3]

One of those who helped to mould the protestant identity of early Elizabethan Colchester, Upcher served the cure of vacant St Leonard probably throughout the 1560s, with dispensation from Grindal to minister without the surplice.[4] He was eventually instituted to the living on 13 July 1571 at the crown's presentation, having been granted letters patent on 3 April at the petition of Thomas Watts, archdeacon of Middlesex, a fellow exile in Frankfurt. For reasons unknown he resigned it by 8 April 1582, his successor being Thomas Lowe.[5] During his incumbency the town was divided in its allegiance towards a drive for 'moral reformation', spearheaded by Upcher after the death in 1570 of Archdeacon James Calfhill, and culminating in a libelling campaign against him in 1574/5, from which he emerged victorious.[6]

His engagement thereafter with more radical activities is far from clear. His 'withdrawal' to Fordham in 1582 may have been a signal that, with George Northey in place as common preacher and Thomas Lowe installed as his successor at St Leonard, he was content to leave Colchester's further reformation to a younger generation of whose radicalism he did not necessarily approve. Indeed, when Aylmer suspended Northey in late 1583, he answered complaints that the town would be bereft of preaching with the observation that 'other good preachers' were readily available, such as 'Mr Upchur'.[7] Yet he was one of the twenty-seven Essex ministers who petitioned against Whitgift's three articles in early 1584,[8] signed the limited form of subscription agreed at Dedham thereafter, and subscribed his name to 'Certain requests' addressed to Archdeacon Withers in September 1584.[9] He nevertheless survived Aylmer's visitation of 1586 without suspension or threat of deprivation for the surplice or other ritual matters. He was untroubled at the visitation of 1589, and in that of 1592 merely listed present as rector of Fordham and as *concionator notus*.[10] He presumably remained there until death, probably in early 1596, but no probate record has been found.[11]

1. His early career is accurately summarized in J. W. Martin, *Religious radicals in Tudor England* (London, 1989), p. 70.
2. GL MS 9535/1, fos. 88v, 91v. Given his activities as a freewiller ten years earlier, his stated age can hardly be correct and is perhaps an error for '34'.
3. Reg. Grindal, fo. 121r.
4. Byford, 'Birth of a Protestant town', p. 39; Collinson, *Grindal*, pp. 114, 172–3.
5. Reg. Grindal, fo. 161v (institution omitted by Newcourt and thus by all subsequent accounts); BL, Lansdowne MS 443, fo. 193r; LMA DL/C/333, fo. 282v.
6. Byford, 'Birth of a Protestant town', pp. 44–5.
7. ERO (Colchester), Morant MS D/Y 2/6, pp. 91–2.

8. *Seconde parte*, I, 225.
9. See above, pp. 82, 87.
10. GL MS 9537/8, fo. 55v.
11. Fordham's next rector, Thomas Withers, was instituted by Archbishop Whitgift, *sede vacante*, by virtue of a lapse to the crown, on 15 January 1597: LPL, Register of Whitgift, II, fo. 281v.

WALTHAR, JOHN

? Rector of Widford, Essex, 1561–3 (depr.); rector of Aldham, Essex, 1563–99

The name of 'John Walthar' is found only in the Dedham papers as a signatory to the limited form of subscription agreed by the conference in 1584.[1] The likeliest guess is that this is a mistranscription of the signature of 'John Walphar' and that this man was therefore the non-graduate minister instituted rector of All Saints Colchester on 17 October 1571 ('Walford').[2] He had been ordained deacon (27 May 1561) and priest (25 July 1562) by Edmund Grindal, bishop of London ('Welfare').[3] As rector of All Saints, he was regularly present at episcopal visitations from 1574 onwards and was never arraigned for nonconformist practices. At that of July 1586 he was assigned to attend the newly inaugurated clerical exercises while at that of September 1607 the visitors noted that he was an old man. He had resigned the benefice by May 1609.[4] It seems probable that he was also the John 'Walfur' whom Robert Searle descibed as his father-in-law and appointed one of the overseers of his undated will in 1609/1610.[5]

It was only as sequestrator and then curate (c.1574–96) of another Colchester parish, the rectory of St Mary-at-the-Walls, that his nonconformity ever drew the fire of the authorities. At the episcopal visitation of July 1583 he was detected for omitting the epistles and gospels when he conducted divine service and for wearing the surplice 'very seldom'. Called into consistory in October that year, he was duly ordered to observe the Book of Common Prayer in all things.[6] This was presumably the prelude to his signing the form of limited subscription which was agreed in 1584.

1. See above, p. 87.
2. Reg. Grindal, fo. 162v.
3. GL MS 9535/1, fos. 102v, 108v.
4. GL MSS 9537/6, fos. 54r, 140v; /10, fo. 41r.
5. See above, p. 250.
6. GL MSS 9537/5, fo. 59v; LMA DL/C/300, fo. 184v.

WARDE, JOHN (d. 1631)

Rector of Great and Little Livermere, Suffolk, 1588/91–1631 (d.)

Not to be confused with the distinguished preacher briefly of Bury St Edmunds and more notably of Haverhill,[1] who was the father of the more famous son, Samuel, town preacher of Ipswich.[2] This John Warde was a younger and less distinguished man who seems to have matriculated as a sizar from Christ's College, Cambridge, at Easter 1579. He proceeded BA in early 1582 and MA in 1586.[3] Probably ordained priest in the diocese of Norwich, in December 1586, he was instituted to the two livings of Great and Little Livermere, the latter on 4 December 1588 and the former on 7 March 1591, with a dispensation for his plurality.[4] In 1603, he reported that there were eighty-nine communicants with no recusants or separatists. He said that 'he hath twoo Benefices booth Rectoryes, Great Lyvermeare and litel Lyvermeare distant the one from the other not past half a Myle, he is a Master of Art of xviii years continuance, he hath dispensation under the broade Seale. Lyvermeare magna valued in the Kings Booke at xv^{li} xvii^{s} xi^{d} and litel Lyvermeare at vi^{li} xii^{s} ix^{d}.' Edward Francis was the patron of little Livermere.[5]

Warde's will makes clear that he remained in the Livermeres until his death in early 1631.[6] He was on close terms with Robert Lewis, rector of Rushbrooke, who left his copy of 'Mytylene in two volumes' to 'his loving brother Mr Ward parson of Lyvermeere'.[7] The father of eight children, four sons and four daughters, he drew up an unremarkable will on 6 December 1630 which was granted probate on 4 February 1631.[8] An inventory of his goods survives.[9]

1. Craig, *Reformation, politics and polemics*, p. 112, n. 192.
2. Frank Grace, ' "Schismaticall and Factious Humours", Opposition in Ipswich to Laudian church government in the 1630s' in *Religious dissent in East Anglia, III*, ed. D. Chadd (Norwich, 1996), 97–119.
3. *Alum. Cantab.*, IV, 331.
4. *Registrum Vagum*, p. 200.
5. 'The condition', pp. 5–6.
6. NRO O.W. 234. Thus *Alum. Cantab.*, IV, 331 is in error to state that he moved on to Ampton, Ipswich and Dennington.
7. PRO PCC PROB 11/131 (28 Mead).
8. NRO O.W. 234.
9. NRO Inv 36/255.

WHITFIELD, REGINALD (d. 1608)

Vicar of Cherry Hinton, Cambridgeshire, 1573–80 (resig.); rector of Barrow, Suffolk, 1580–1608 (d.)

The little that is known about Reginald Whitfield does not accurately reflect his standing among the godly clergy of west Suffolk. His signature comes second in the list of those who wrote to Scambler about Thomas Rogers's behaviour in the Bury exercise, and with John Knewstub and Walter Allen, Whitfield was one of the more senior figures in the conference movement around Bury. He matriculated pensioner from Christ's College, Cambridge, at Michaelmas 1564.[1] He proceeded BA in early 1568 and MA from Peterhouse in 1571. Elected a fellow of Peterhouse in 1569, he retained his fellowship until 1580, serving as bursar in 1575–6. He was ordained a deacon in the diocese of Ely on 2 June 1570 and served as vicar of Cherry Hinton, Cambridgeshire, from 1573. He was presented to the living of Barrow, Suffolk, by the godly magistrate, Sir John Higham, and was instituted rector on 18 July 1580.[2] He was among those ministers of Suffolk suspended for not subscribing and 'not resolved to subscribe'.[3]

He nevertheless remained rector of Barrow until his death in 1608. In 1603, he was included on a diocesan list of 'Mrs of Artes, preachers, heretofore scismatically affected'[4] and reported that he served a parish of some 190 communicants, with no recusants and held no other living.[5]

His will was a singular document which sheds some light on his godly views and his library. He described himself as 'pastor of Barrow' and spoke of 'having bene a poore labourer there in the Lordes vineyeard a long tyme' and bequeathed his soul into the hands of God, 'my most mercifull and loving father in Jhesus Christe by whose precious death and bloud shed I hope only to be saved being made of God unto me wisdome righteousnes sanctification and redemption.' He left £10 to the poor in Barrow and divided his goods between his three daughters and two sons. Son John was bequeathed 'Mr Calvin upon Job', a 'great English Bible covered with leather', 'the booke of Martyrs which his Mother in lawe gave him' and 'Mr Bezaes groundes of Christian religion.' Sir John Higham, his 'loving Patron', was given 'Mr Gifford sermons upon the

revelation', while Lady Higham received 'Mr Allens Catechisme.' Other bequests of
Calvin's sermons on the Psalms, 'Mr Knewstubbes workes', 'Mr Estyes booke', 'Mr
Allens doctrine of the ghospell' and 'Mr Perkins workes' went to his daughters, and the
rest of his books 'in Greeke Latin and English' went to his son Thomas.[6] His will was
granted probate (PCC) on 18 August 1609.

1. *Alum. Cantab.*, IV, 393.
2. Bullen, 'Catalogue', p. 318.
3. *Seconde parte*, I, 242.
4. NRO DN VIS/3/3, fo. 98r.
5. 'The condition', p. 3.
6. PRO PCC PROB 11/114 (79 Dorset), fo. 174r.

WHITING, GILES (c. 1553–1627)

Curate of Ovington, Essex, c. 1579–82; rector of Panfield, Essex, 1582–7 (depr.); rector of Etton, Northants, 1587–1627 (d.)

Whiting matriculated sizar from Trinity College, Cambridge, at Michaelmas 1569, graduating BA in early 1574.[1] He was granted a preaching licence (BA) for Ovington or elsewhere in the diocese on 15 May 1579[2] and was present as curate of Ovington at the
episcopal visitation of July 1580.[3] Instituted rector of Panfield on 2 October 1582 at the
presentation of George Cotton, *armiger*,[4] he was probably a founder member of the
Braintree conference. Present at the episcopal visitation on 10 July 1583, he duly
presented his diocesan preaching licence and does not seem to have been examined for
nonconformist practices.[5] In early 1584, however, he was one of the twenty-seven Essex
ministers who petitioned against Whitgift's articles.[6] It was probably in the aftermath of
the subscription crisis that he was 'greatlie molested for matters of the booke', having
his benefice sequestered and 'a daie set for his deprivation'.[7]

He survived to face Aylmer at the episcopal visitation of 1586 and was summoned to
a personal interview with him the same afternoon.[8] He was soon suspended for the
surplice 'and hath a daie againe set him for his deprivation'.[9] With Carr, Gifford,
Hawden, Huckle and Tunstall he petitioned parliament for restoration on 8 March
1587.[10] He was, however, deprived of Panfield by the High Commission on 13 May
1587.[11]

For the moment he remained in the vicinity as a member of the Braintree conference:
on 7 June, he was one of the five signatories to the conference's letter asking for the
secondment of Laurence Newman.[12] Before the end of the year, however, he removed
permanently to the diocese of Peterborough and was instituted rector of Etton,
Northants, on 25 November 1587. In 1591 he published *Giles Whiting, his short questions and answers to be learned of the ignorant before they bee admitted to the Lord's
supper.*

He married Mary Carew of Essex: they had four sons and three daughters. Whiting
was buried at Etton on 20 June 1627. His will was granted probate in the Consistory
Court of Peterborough.[13]

1. *Alum. Cantab.*, IV, 394.
2. LMA DL/C/333, fo. 162v.
3. GL MS 9537/4, fo. 90r.
4. Reg. Grindal, fo. 206v. Mystery, however, surrounds his appointment. Both he and John Padgett
    compounded for the benefice on 4 October with the same two sureties, Simon Peryn, baker, and
    William Hide, *generosus*, both of the Savoy, London. A marginal note against Padgett's entry
    states 'Geo Cotton, *armiger*': PRO E334/10, fo. 22v.

5. GL MS 9537/5, fo. 55r.
6. *Seconde parte*, I, 225.
7. *Ibid.*, II, 163. There is no hint of these proceedings in the diocesan act books, and whilst those of the archdeacon of Middlesex are not extant it is more likely that the case was heard from the beginning before the High Commission.
8. GL MS 9537/6, fo. 136r.
9. *Seconde parte*, II, 163, 260.
10. *Seconde parte*, II, 258.
11. LMA DL/C/334, fo. 153v.
12. See above, p. 107.
13. H. I. Longden, *Northamptonshire and Rutland clergy. From 1500* (Northamptonshire Record Society, 15 vols., 1938–41), XV, 49.

WHITTAKER, LAWRENCE (d. 1622)

Rector of Bradfield St George, Suffolk, 1575–1622 (d.)

Whittaker matriculated pensioner from St John's College, Cambridge at Michaelmas 1567, graduating BA in early 1571.[1] He was instituted to the rectory of Bradfield St George, close to Bury St Edmunds, in 1575 remaining there until his death. In 1584 he was among the Suffolk ministers suspended for not subscribing to Archbishop Whitgift's articles 'and not resolved to subscribe'.[2] In 1603 he reported that there were no recusants or separatists in the parish, and that it contained 159 communicants.[3] The patron was Sir Robert Jermyn, and Whittaker was one of the ten preachers who in 1580 received a 'Tremelius bible fayer bound' in the will of Sir Robert's sister, Frances.[4] In 1611, he was presented during the episcopal visitation for failing to wear the surplice. He appeared and promised conformity.[5] He wrote an unremarkable will on 14 October 1622. Probate was granted (Consistory Court of Norwich) on 13 February 1623.[6]

1. *Alum. Cantab.*, IV, 384. A contemporary of these names held the living of Braiseworth, south of Eye, from 1573 until his death in 1600: *ibid.*
2. *Seconde parte*, I, 242. Whittaker of Braiseworth appears only on the list of those 'not resolved to subscribe'.
3. 'The condition', p. 3.
4. SRO Bury St Edmunds, IC 500/1/40/30.
5. NRO DN VIS 4/3, unfoliated.
6. NRO 186 Bradstritt.

WRIGHT, ROBERT (?1550–1624)

Unordained preacher in private households, c. 1576–9; household chaplain to Robert 2nd Lord Rich, Christmas 1579 to February 1581, and to Robert 3rd Lord Rich, late 1581; in prison November 1581 to September 1582; preacher at Fryerning, Essex, <July 1583 to October 1584>; assistant preacher and then town preacher of Ipswich, Suffolk, 1585–90; rector of Dennington, Suffolk, 1589/90–1624 (d.)

Son of John Wright of Wright's Bridge in the parish of Kelvedon Hatch, Essex,[1] Wright matriculated pensioner from Christ's College, Cambridge, in June 1565, graduating BA (first in the *ordo*) in 1569 and proceeding MA in 1572. He was probably sublector of the college (1573 and 1574) but never became a fellow.[2] In 1574 he quit Cambridge to follow Thomas Cartwright to Heidelberg. With three Christ's contemporaries, including Samuel Culverwell, brother of Ezekiel, he enrolled at the university on 31 January 1575.[3] After the death of the Elector Palatine Friedrich III in October 1576, Heidelberg's

Calvinist regime collapsed and it was probably at this juncture that he returned to England. Although unordained, he began a career of itinerant preaching in godly house-holds, including those of Lords St John of Bletso and Grey of Wilton, and of John Butler of Thoby Priory, Essex, later MP for Maldon.[4]

At Christmas 1579 he reached Rochford Hall, Essex, secondary seat of Robert 2nd Lord Rich. In what has been seen as an early exercise in congregationalism, Rich requested his household to accept Wright as their 'teacher' and 'perhaps esteemed hym as his Pastor'. Throughout 1580 Wright organized religious services, catechized the household and inveighed against the inadequacy of the local clergy. Local animosities were aroused.[5]

After Rich's unexpected death in February 1581, Wright went to the Low Countries, where he was ordained by 'Villiers, and other mynisters at Antwerpe'.[6] Returning to Rochford by the summer, he married John Butler's daughter, Jane: their first child was born in February 1582.[7] In September the third Lord Rich and his bastard uncle Richard visited John Aylmer, bishop of London, to solicit a preaching licence for their protégé. When Aylmer refused without assurances of Wright's conformity and knowledge of his orders, Richard Rich physically assaulted him.[8] This led directly to a trial before the High Commissioners on 7 November 1581, as a result of which Wright, Richard Rich and the preacher William Dyke were imprisoned for their irregular activities and for maintaining that to celebrate Elizabeth's accession day as a 'holy day' was to make her an idol.[9] Presided over by Aylmer himself, it is the earliest trial before the now fully-fledged court of High Commission for which substantial documentary evidence survives. The case engaged the interest of Lord Burghley, who at the beginning of May 1582 sent Wright, now in the Gatehouse, a set of 'notes' (a digest of the depositions used against him at his trial), evidently with a strong hint that a satisfactory written rebuttal of them might expedite his release. Wright grasped the opportunity with alac-rity, vigorously defending himself against his opponents (including Aylmer) with a four-page 'answere to the note of matters proved against me by sworne Witnesses'.[10] In September 1582 Aylmer was evidently pressured by Burghley into agreeing to Wright's release in return for his 'good allowance' of English orders and the prayer book.[11] Since he had throughout his trial stoutly maintained that he had never denied the validity of the one or the basic tenets of the other, such 'allowance' will scarcely have taxed his conscience.

Wright was almost certainly a founder member, with George Gifford, of the Braintree conference, which probably first met in late 1582. On 15 July 1583, at Aylmer's epis-copal visitation, he was listed as preacher of Fryerning, Essex, claiming to hold a preaching licence from Archbishop Grindal.[12] Aylmer does not appear for the moment to have pursued him but on 6 October 1584 Wright was called into consistory for preaching at Fryerning without administering communion. He claimed that he was not admitted to do so and a later hand has added that 'he is alreadie inhibited by my L.'[13] Meanwhile, on the eve of the 1584 parliament he, John Huckle and Gifford had been selected for a 'general' conference, and in February 1585 he and Gifford were chosen as the Essex delegates to attend the 'national synod' which met in London during the last session of parliament.[14]

In the wake of the enduring quarrel between Robert Norton, town preacher of Ipswich, and his recently appointed assistant, William Negus, Wright covenanted with the Ipswich authorities on 16 November 1584 to succeed Negus from Michaelmas 1585 at the substantial salary of £50.[15] In the event, the breach between Norton and Negus led to the resignation of both men during 1585 and Wright seems to have taken sole charge of preaching duties on his arrival. On 9 March 1586 it was agreed that another preacher should be procured to assist him, but although the matter was duly referred to the next assembly nothing seems to have come of it.[16] In May that year the admission of Edmund Salmon of Erwarton to the Dedham meeting was 'staied' until it was ascertained whether Wright 'do labor to procure such a like meeting about him as wee' (**44M**). Since Salmon was admitted at Dedham in August (**46M**) it seems there never was an Ipswich conference.

Wright was formally elected town preacher on 8 September 1586 on a one-year contract, renewable 'from year to year during the pleasure of the Town and the said preacher'. He was at first allowed only a modest four marks for the expenses of removing his family to Ipswich, but on 26 September was granted a further £7 6s 8d.[17]

He remained one of the leaders of the conference movement, and in one of his more hare-brained outbursts Martin Marprelate drew attention to certain 'Martinists' in East Anglia. 'There is Moore, there is Alme [?Allen], there is Knewstub, there is Wright, with many others, all very seditious men'. It was a pity, chirruped Martin, that 'so many worshipfull and good nurtured knights and gentlemen, are carried away with them, and their waywardnes, as in those partes are seduced'.[18] Yet like Norton before him, Wright seems to have quarrelled with the town authorities over his acceptance of a benefice. Having succeeded William Fulke (buried 28 August 1589) as rector of the nearby crown living of Dennington, he left Ipswich abruptly in early 1590.

Surprisingly, no more is heard of radical activities for the rest of Wright's long life and it is possible that his gradual absorption into the ranks of the Suffolk squirearchy curbed his earlier radicalism. In 1621 he erected a memorial to William Fulke in Dennington in which he described himself as *sacrae theologiae professor*. His own memorial inscription states that he and Jane raised eight children past infancy and that he had 'spent his yonger daies in the Studie of Divinitie in sundry Universities, at home and in foraigne Contries'. Jane was buried on 23 October 1610 and he was interred beside her on 7 April 1624, in his seventy-fourth year. Memorial tablets to his second and fourth daughters, Elizabeth and Anne, both of whom predeceased him, survive at Dennington.[19]

A detailed genealogical table of his sons' descendants was compiled by the county historian of Leicestershire John Nichols. His second son Nathan (d. 1657), alderman of London, expanded his father's legacy to the parish into the Dennington Charity Estate and was the father of Sir Benjamin Wright, Bt, whose title became extinct in 1738. His fourth son, Ezekiel, later rector of Thurcaston, Leicestershire, was the father of Sir Nathan Wright, Lord Keeper of the Great Seal (1700–5).[20]

1. J. Burke, *Extinct baronetcies* (London, 1844), p. 586; John Nichols, *The history and antiquities of the county of Leicester* (4 vols., London, 1795–1815), III, 219.
2. Peile, *Biographical register*, I, 91; *Alum. Cantab.*, IV, 476.
3. A. F. Scott Pearson, *Thomas Cartwright and Elizabethan puritanism* (Cambridge, 1925), pp. 131–2.
4. BL, Lansdowne MS 109, fo. 7r.
5. *Ibid.*, fo. 7r–v; BL, Lansdowne MS 36, fo. 158r.
6. BL, Lansdowne MS 109, fo. 7v; the reference is to the influential Calvinist minister Pierre Loiseleur de Villiers. The expedition was perhaps deliberately financed by Lord Rich: 'Mr Wrighte' was left £20 in his will, probated on 7 June 1581: Emmison, *Essex gentry wills*, p. 13.
7. BL, Lansdowne MS 36, fo. 162r.
8. BL, Lansdowne MS 33, fo. 48r.
9. BL, Lansdowne MS 33, fo. 50r; for William Dyke, father of Daniel and Jermiah Dyke, and later spiritual mentor to Anne Lady Bacon, see the entry by Patrick Collinson in *Oxford DNB*.
10. BL, Lansdowne MS 36, fos. 159r–62r.
11. BL, Lansdowne MS 36, fo. 52r.
12. GL MS 9537/5, fo. 86v.
13. LMA DL/C/301, p. 272.
14. Bancroft, *Daungerous positions*, p. 75; see above **27M**.

15. Richardson, *Annals of Ipswich*, p. 341.
16. *Ibid.*, p. 346.
17. *Ibid.*, pp. 345, 347.
18. *The just censure and reproofe of Martin Junior* [1589], sig. Aiv.
19. [Anon.], 'Monumental inscriptions in Dennington Church', *Proceedings of the Suffolk Institute of Archaeology and Natural History*, VIII (1894), 77–9.
20. Nichols, *County of Leicester*, III, 219.

APPENDICES

Appendix 1
Dedham Grammar School

Dedham grammar school was founded by letters patent from the crown dated 14 May 1575, enrolled on membrane 17 of what is now filed as PRO C66/1136. It is calendared thus in *CPR (1572–75)* (London, HMSO, 1973).

3270) 14 *May* 1575. Grant that there shall be a free grammar school in [*m.17 contd.*] Dedham, co. Essex, to be called the free grammar school of Queen Elizabeth in Dedham. Appointment of Edward Walgrave of Lawford, co. Essex, Edward Waldegrave, his son and heir apparent, Robert Gurdon of Asshington [*recte* Assington], co. Suffolk, John Gurdon, his son and heir apparent, William Cardinale [sic] of Bromley Magna, John Worthe, vicar of Dedham, William Butter, Pierce Butter, his son, Ralph Sterlinge, Robert Sterlinge, Richard Sterlinge, Robert's son, John Browne the elder, John Browne, his son, Michael Upcher, Richard Upcher, his son, Henry Sherman the elder, Henry Sherman the younger, his son, Edmund Sherman, also Henry's son, Louis Sperhawke, Nathaniel Sperhawke, his son, John Upcher, Robert Luffkyn, John Wood and Richard Wood, his son, to be governors.

Incorporation of the governors. Whenever a governor shall die, the survivors may elect another inhabitant of the town in his place. Licence for the governors to hold certain lands (named) in Bradfeild [*recte* Bradfield] and Wrabnes [*recte* Wrabness], co. Essex, and such other lands as shall hereafter be conveyed to them, to the yearly value of £40, so that they be not held of the Crown in chief or by knight service. Power for the governors to make orders and rules for the government of the school, and to acquire lands without fine or fee for the Queen's licence in this behalf.

William Lyttlebury late of Dedham by his will desired that, for the instruction of the youth of the same town and of Ardley [*recte* Ardleigh], Great Bromley, co. Essex, and Stratford, co. Suffolk, and the relief of the poor of Dedham, a free grammar school should be founded in Dedham, for the maintenance of which he gave to the persons above-named (except Worthe) the said lands in Bradfield and Wrabnes. By Q.

Appendix 2
The Dedham Lectureship

Tradition asserts that William Cardinal of Great Bromley, Essex, and East Bergholt, Suffolk, founded the Dedham lectureship in order to create an influential, 'godly' base for his brother-in-law, Dr Edmund Chapman. Whilst there is no direct evidence that he actually *endowed* it, there must be a strong presumption that he laid the economic interstices without which it could not have existed. Perhaps, indeed, it was by guaranteeing Chapman a 'minimum wage' during his own lifetime that Cardinal was able to persuade the leading inhabitants of Dedham to support it in perpetuity by voluntary subscription. Thereafter it was maintained by quarterly collections among the inhabitants and administered by a local trust.[1]

Thus matters continued until 1704 when the incumbent lecturer, the distinguished biblical commentator William Burkitt, succeeded in placing it on an endowed footing. He enlisted the support of the archbishop of Canterbury, the bishop of London and other benefactors. With the proceeds he purchased the Lecture House and its grounds, leaving the property at his death as 'a habitation for all future Lecturers', and negotiating a trust which thereafter associated the lectureship with the grammar school.[2]

Examining the wills of Dedham and East Bergholt testators between 1560 and 1640, Alan Pennie has suggested that many of the 'legacies' – some of them substantial – which were made to Chapman and his successors were not legacies at all. Rather, they directly reflect the obligations of the testators with regard to the contributions they had agreed to make towards the maintenance of the lectureship. In 1596, for example, Thomas Glover left Chapman £10 in yearly instalments of fifty shillings, explaining that he did so 'in full consideracion of my stipende'. Bequests such as Robert Smith's in 1583 (£8 at the rate of four nobles a year) and Henry Sherman's in 1610 to Chapman's successor, John Rogers (£8 at forty shillings a year), 'appear to have been similar continuations of the testator's annual payment towards the maintenance of the lecturer for a period of four to six years'. It was far more usual, however, to bequeath him a lump sum. Forty-nine out of fifty-six testators did so, three leaving ten shillings, nineteen of them twenty shillings and the remainder sums ranging from forty shillings up to £10.[3]

Questions remain. Why should testators like Thomas Glover, Robert Smith and Henry Sherman have considered it necessary to continue financing the Dedham lectureship after they were dead and gone? Was it regarded as a moral obligation, or was it in the nature of a 'benevolence' – 'voluntary' yet at the same time *de rigeur*? Or perhaps (although no testator appears to have admitted the fact) these bequests are more in the nature of a curious protestant continuation of the pious catholic habit, which seems to have disappeared with considerable abruptness after Elizabeth's accession, of leaving money to the high altar 'for tithes negligently forgotten'?

---

[1] G. H. Rendall, *Dedham in history* (Colchester, 1937), p. 52.
[2] *Ibid.*, pp. 146–50.
[3] A. R. Pennie, 'The evolution of puritan mentality in an Essex cloth town: Dedham and the Stour valley, 1560–1640' (unpublished Ph.D thesis, University of Sheffield, 1991), pp. 108–10. For other bequests to Edmund Chapman, by William Butter (1593), Edmund Sherman (1599), Henry Sherman 'the elder' (1590) and Pearce Butter (1599), see above, p. 127, nn. 362–5.

Appendix 3
A Sermon Preached by Edmund Chapman

'A Sermon preached by Mr D Chapman at Dedhame in essex upon the fyrste to
the coryntheans the 3 chapter 7.8.9. verses therof'

The only sermon by Edmund Chapman known to survive consists of six-and-a-half
closely-packed manuscript pages, occupying folios 34r to 37r of Ellesmere MS (EL) 34
B 5 preserved at the Huntington Library, San Marino, California.[1] It ends in the middle
of folio 37r with the postscript 'Soli deo gloria amen yo[u]r lovyng frend in
christ/Rychard Parker', in the same hand which has written the rest. Since the writer is
unlikely to have been Parker himself,[2] we appear to be confronting a more-or-less accurate copy of a transcript which Parker originally made either from Chapman's papers or
from full sermon notes taken by him when he heard it delivered.[3]

For what reason, and by what route, did this sermon come into the possession of Sir
Thomas Egerton 1st Lord Ellesmere?[4] If it is indeed a copy, why does Parker's own original manuscript not survive among the papers preserved as Rylands MS 874? There are no
obvious answers to these questions. Forensic problems aside, the sermon is obviously of
intrinsic interest to historians of the Stour Valley but its content, perhaps laundered for
transcriptional purposes, is both problematic, limited in its implications and anodyne. The
verses from Paul's first letter to the Corinthians on which it is based are used to support
the central thrust of Chapman's principal theme: that godly congregations are duty-bound
to support their godly pastors – morally, legally, spiritually and financially. As it now
exists it is impossible to tell whether it reflects Chapman's eirenical disposition or
whether, on the contrary, it was polemically intended. The latter seems the more likely
reading. Although it is stated that the sermon was preached in Dedham, it is tempting to
link it with the induction of Richard Crick to the deeply divided church of East Bergholt in
1587. Alternatively, it directly addresses (for it certainly echoes) the principal concerns of
John Keltridge during his beleaguered year in Dedham in 1577–8.[5] In the latter case it may

---

[1] 'Alternative but less preferred' references to this manuscript are EL 6162, fos. 34–7 and EL 6168
(information kindly supplied by Mary L. Robertson, Curator of Manuscripts). In the top left-hand
margin of fo. 34r '2552' has been crossed through and '6168' substituted.

[2] The handwriting is close to Parker's own but also bears a marked resemblance to the contemporary
secretary hand used by the court officials of the diocese of London.

[3] As here preserved, it would appear to be far too short to be a transcript of a sermon which had been
fully set down on paper (by Chapman), and yet far too long to be a fair copy of notes taken down
aurally (by Parker). The best guess, perhaps, is that Chapman handed over to Parker the sermon notes
from which he extemporized at much greater length and that Parker used these as an *aide memoire*
when writing out his own notes and recollections of the sermon as actually delivered.

[4] Sir Thomas Egerton, Elizabeth's last Lord Keeper of the Great Seal (1596–1603), was retained by
James I. Created lord chancellor and first Lord Ellesmere in 1603 and first viscount Brackley in 1616,
he was succeeded as lord chancellor by Francis Bacon in March 1617. His papers provide the
historian with a startling variety of material.

[5] See above, pp. lxvi–lxxi. For example, Chapman uses Paul's admonitions to the squabbling
Corinthians to remind his auditory that they must 'beware . . . to regard one [minister] & deface an
other, and make their choice [that] such a one should be h[e]ard & regarded, but wee will stoppe oure
eares at that is delyveryed by an other . . .' (fo. 35r)

have been preached regularly by Chapman as a stick with which to beat Dedham's 'alter-native congregation' and accepted by Parker on his arrival in 1582 as a 'standard text' which he took the trouble to imbibe and memorize for himself.

Chapman's most arresting observations are reserved for his peroration. The office of minister 'is not a mat[t]er of ease & syttyng in his Chayre, & gevyng sentence & verdicts on their brethren, & syttyng in Commysion & sending out articles agaynst them' – a pretty brutal sideswipe at the local commissaries and archdeacons, even such godly examples as John Still and George Withers – 'But an office of paynes to this end . . . [that] we must lerne to ascrybe our conversyon to [Christ] . . . And so lett not us call our selves by the names or Lutheryans or Calvenysts as the philosophers skollers did, But by the name of Christ . . .'[6] That, to a rural congregation which consisted largely of middling-to-.prosperous clothiers, he should have mentioned 'scholastic philosophy', let alone Luther and Calvin in the same breath, surely argues a remarkable degree of sophis-tication in Dedham's leading parishioners.

---

6   Fo. 37r.

TOPICAL AND GENERAL INDEX

INDEX OF PERSONAL NAMES

Petre, Sir William: 259 n. 4
Piers, John, bishop of Rochester, Salisbury and
    archbishop of York: xlvii, 108
Pigge, Oliver: l, lxxxi, lxxxii, 12 n. 36, 19, 127 n.
    364, 184, 221, 230, 256; ?father: 127 n. 364
Piggott, Reginald: xvi
Pirton, Edmund: 256, 258 nn. 5 and 8
Playford, John: 251 n. 4
Poll, Thomas: 246 n. 20
Porter, Harry Culverwell: xiii
Powell, Meredith: lxxvi, 195 n. 25
Preston, Thomas: 211
Pudney, Thomas: 187 n. 7; Katherine: 186
Pullan (Pulleyne), John, archdeacon of
    Colchester: xxxv, lxvii n. 206
Purvey, John: 95

Rainoldes: see also Reynold(s)
Rainoldes, William: cxiii, 164–5
Ram, Robert: lxxviii
Rannow, Leonard: 112
Radcliffe, Thomas, 3rd earl of Sussex: 249
Ravens, Richard: lxxvi n. 250; William: 127 n.
    366, 231 n. 7
Ravis, Thomas, bishop of London: 186, 200, 236,
    245
Rawlins, John: 112
Reade, Edward: 112
Redishe, Mr: 133 n. 391
Redman, William, bishop of Norwich: 261
Redritch, Mr, of Butley: 231 n. 7
Renchcrofte: 244 n. 5
Reve, John, abbot of Bury St Edmunds: xliv
Reynold, John: lxiv n. 188
Reynoldes, John: 134 n. 407, 221
Reynoldes, Richard: lxiii
Reynoldes, William: see Rainoldes
Rice, Mr: 24 n. 7
Rich, Richard 1st Lord: xxxiv, xxxviii; bastard
    son, Richard ('Dick'): xxxviii, xl, 239 n. 4,
    270; son and heir, Robert 2nd Lord: xxxviii, xl,
    185, 202, 212 n. 7, 238, 239 n. 4, 253 n. 3,
    270; grandson, Robert 3rd Lord and 1st earl of
    Warwick: xxxix, xl, 18 n. 58, 35, 200, 203, 214
    n. 37, 218, 219, 235, 236, 237 n. 8, 239 n. 4,
    245, 253, 254 nn. 10 and 21, 270, 271 n. 6;
    granddaughter-in-law, Penelope (née
    Devereux; wife of 3rd Lord): xl, 214 n. 37;
    great-grandson, Robert 2nd earl of Warwick:
    253 n. 3, 254 n. 21; great-great-grandson,
    Robert Lord Rich (son of 2nd earl of
    Warwick): 252 n. 3, 254 n. 21
Ridley, Nicholas, bishop of Rochester and of
    London: xxxiv
Rivius, Joannes: cv
Robartes, John: 258 n. 1
Roberts, Thomas ('Robert'): xlv, xlvi, xlvii, xlviii,
    112
Robertson, Mary L.: xvi, 275 n. 1
Robinson, Henry, bishop of Carlisle: 134
Robson, Anthony: lxiv n. 188
Roger, John: lx, lxxxi, 230; son, John: 230

Rogers, John, lecturer of Dedham: lxxviii, 246,
    276; Richard: xiv, xv, xli n. 97, xlii, lxxxi,
    c–ci, cxiv, 40, 46 n. 147, 90, 106 n. 319,
    107–8, 130 n. 376, 190, 200, 207 n. 23, 218,
    221, 233, 244–6; father, John: 244; mother,
    Agnes (née Carter), 244; 1st wife, Barbara:
    246; 2nd wife, Susan: 246; sons, Daniel,
    Ezekiel: 246
Rogers, Thomas: civ–cxii, cxv–cxvi, 53 n. 188,
    151–80 passim, 215, 217, 234, 251, 267; wife,
    Bridget (née Wincol): cv
Rose, Thomas: lix
Rowse, Edward: 219 n. 18; wife, Elizabeth: 219 n.
    18
Rudd, Anthony, bishop of St Davids: 134 n. 407
Rushbrooke, William: 122
Rust, Thomas: 200
Rusticens, Camille: 201, 236
Ryece, Robert: 222, 248
Ryther, Thomas: 194

Sackville, Thomas: cv
Sadler, Sir Ralph: lxvi, lxxii, lxxiv, 242
Sage, Henry, vicar of Dedham: lxxvii, 207 n. 23
St John, Oliver, 3rd Lord St John of Bletso: 270
Salmon, Edmund: lxxv, lxxxviii, ci, 5, 31, 33, 34,
    35, 36, 39, 41, 42, 46, 208, 246–7, 271; son,
    John: 247
Sammes, Sir John: 264
Sandes, Henry: xxiii, lxii n. 178, lxxxiii, lxxxiv,
    lxxxvi, lxxxviii, lxxxix, xc, xcii, xcv, xcvi,
    xcvii, xcviii, ci, cxiii, 4, 5, 6, 9, 11, 12, 13, 14,
    15, 16, 17, 18, 20, 23, 24, 25, 26, 27, 28, 31,
    32, 33, 35, 37, 38, 40, 41, 43, 44, 45, 46,
    53–70, 83, 107 n. 322, 108 n. 323, 189–90,
    198, 208, 222, 239 n. 9, 247–9, 256, 261, 264
Sandys, Edwin, bishop of Worcester, London and
    archbishop of York: xxxvi–xxxvii, xxxviii,
    xxxix, lxv, lxvii, 76 n. 240, 184, 190, 205, 227
    n. 10, 231, 238, 245, 247
Scambler, Edmund, bishop of Peterborough and
    of Norwich: xxx, xlix, cv, cvii, cix, cx, cxi, 36
    n. 118, 151, 157 n. 20, 173–5, 217, 230, 252,
    267
Schilders, Richard: 86 n. 265
Scott Pearson, A.F.: xvi
Seaman, Thomas: 261
Searlbye, Thomas: 112
Searle, Robert: xli n. 97, 82, 87, 249–51, 266; 2nd
    (?) wife, Anna (née Lorance): 250; 3rd (?)
    wife, Anne: 250; sons, Samuel, Thomas: 250;
    daughter, Elizabeth (Allen): 250; (?) kinsman,
    Robert: 249; father-in-law, John 'Walfur': 266
Seckford, Thomas: liii, lv
Seffray, Thomas: cx, cxv, 175, 177, 251; wife,
    Margaret: 251; sons, Dennys, Josias, Samuel,
    Thomas: 251; daughters, Ann, Elizabeth,
    Lydia, Martha, Phebe, Prescilla, Rebecka,
    Sarah: 251
Seridge, William: 142 n. 435
Shakespeare, William: 28 n. 92
Sharpe, Edward: 112

INDEX OF PLACE-NAMES

INDEX OF SCRIPTURAL REFERENCES

INDEX OF CLASSICAL, PATRISTIC, MEDIEVAL AND REFORMED REFERENCES

PUBLICATIONS

1. VISITATION ARTICLES AND INJUNCTIONS OF THE EARLY STUART CHURCH. VOLUME I. Ed. Kenneth Fincham (1994)
2. THE SPECULUM OF ARCHBISHOP THOMAS SECKER: THE DIOCESE OF CANTERBURY 1758–1768. Ed. Jeremy Gregory (1995)
3. THE EARLY LETTERS OF BISHOP RICHARD HURD 1739–1762. Ed. Sarah Brewer (1995)
4. BRETHREN IN ADVERSITY: BISHOP GEORGE BELL, THE CHURCH OF ENGLAND AND THE CRISIS OF GERMAN PROTESTANTISM 1933–1939. Ed. Andrew Chandler (1997)
5. VISITATION ARTICLES AND INJUNCTIONS OF THE EARLY STUART CHURCH. VOLUME II. Ed. Kenneth Fincham (1998)
6. THE ANGLICAN CANONS 1529–1947. Ed. Gerald Bray (1998)
7. FROM CRANMER TO DAVIDSON. A CHURCH OF ENGLAND MISCELLANY. Ed. Stephen Taylor (1999)
8. TUDOR CHURCH REFORM. THE HENRICIAN CANONS OF 1534 AND THE *REFORMATIO LEGUM ECCLESIASTICARUM*. Ed. Gerald Bray (2000)
9. ALL SAINTS SISTERS OF THE POOR. AN ANGLICAN SISTERHOOD IN THE NINETEENTH CENTURY. Ed. Susan Mumm (2001)
10. CONFERENCES AND COMBINATION LECTURES IN THE ELIZABETHAN CHURCH. DEDHAM AND BURY ST EDMUNDS 1582–1590. Ed. Patrick Collinson, John Craig and Brett Usher (2003)

Forthcoming Publications

LETTERS OF THE MARIAN MARTYRS. Ed. Tom Freeman

THE PARKER CERTIFICATES. Ed. Ralph Houlbrooke and Helen Parish

THE BRITISH DELEGATION AND THE SYNOD OF DORT. Ed. Anthony Milton

THE UNPUBLISHED CORRESPONDENCE OF ARCHBISHOP LAUD. Ed. Kenneth Fincham

THE DIARY OF SAMUEL ROGERS, 1634–1638. Ed. Tom Webster and Ken Shipps

THE DIARY OF JOHN BARGRAVE, 1644–1645. Ed. Michael Brennan, Jas' Elsner and Judith Maltby

THE 1669 RETURN OF NONCONFORMIST CONVENTICLES. Ed. David Wykes

THE CORRESPONDENCE OF THEOPHILUS LINDSEY. Ed. G.M. Ditchfield

AN EVANGELICAL MISCELLANY. Ed. Mark Smith and Stephen Taylor

THE PAPERS OF THE ELLAND SOCIETY. Ed. John Walsh and Stephen Taylor

THE DIARY OF AN OXFORD PARSON: THE REVEREND JOHN HILL, VICE-PRINCIPAL OF ST EDMUND HALL, OXFORD, 1805–1808, 1820–1855. Ed. Grayson Carter

ANGLO-CATHOLIC COMMUNICANTS' GUILDS AND SOCIETIES IN THE LATE NINETEENTH CENTURY. Ed. Jeremy Morris

Suggestions for publications should be addressed to Dr Stephen Taylor, General Editor, Church of England Record Society, School of History, University of Reading, Whiteknights, Reading RG6 2AA.